Wireless All-in-One Desk Reference For Dummies®

Cheat Sheet

Wireless Networking Shopping List

Router
PC adapter
Laptop adapter
Access point
Media player
Print server

Popular Wireless Equipment Manufacturers

Company	*Specialties*	*Web Site*
D-Link	Networking	www.dlink.com
Garmin	GPS	www.garmin.com
Linksys	Networking	www.linksys.com
Motorola	Phones, networking	www.motorola.com
NetGear	Networking	www.netgear.com
Nokia	Phones	www.nokia.com

Range and Speed of Wireless Networking Technologies

Technology	*Range*	*Speed*	*Notes*
802.11a	150 feet	54 Mbps	Used mostly in offices
802.11b	300 feet	11 Mbps	Compatible with 802.11g
802.11g	300 feet	54 Mbps	Compatible with 802.1g

Commercial Wi-Fi Providers

Provider	*Web Address*
Boingo Wireless	www.boingo.com
Sprint PCS Wi-Fi Access	www.wifi.sprintpcs.com
T-Mobile	www.t-mobile.com/hotspot/
Verizon Wireless	www.verizonwireless.com
Wayport	www.wayport.com

Wireless All-in-One Desk Reference For Dummies®

Cheat Sheet

Wi-Fi Hotspot Directories

Directory	*Web Site*
HotSpot Haven	www.hotspothaven.com
JiWire	www.jiwire.com
NodeDB.com	www.nodedb.com
The Wi-Fi FreeSpot Directory	www.wififreespot.com
Wi-FiHotSpotList.com	www.wi-fihotspotlist.com
Web In-Flight	www.webinflight.com
WiFiMaps.com	www.wifimaps.com
Wi-Fi Marine	www.wifimarine.org
Wi-Fi Zone Finder	www.wi-fizone.org
Wireless Librarian	www.people.morrisville.edu/~drewwe/wireless/

Major U.S. Airports with Wi-Fi Access

Chicago O'Hare International. About 15 or so hotspots are spread across the airport, mostly in individual airlines' frequent-flyer lounges. T-Mobile, Telia HomeRun, and iPass are among the service providers.

Los Angeles International Airport. Boingo Wireless, iPass, and T-Mobile all offer Wi-Fi service. Boingo covers six terminals.

Dallas Ft. Worth International Airport. Boingo Wireless, T-Mobile, iPass, and Wayport provide coverage in various areas throughout the airport.

Atlanta Hartsfield International. T-Mobile and iPass provide most of the wireless access, which is located mainly in airline lounges.

Denver International Airport. iPass, T-Mobile, and AT&T Wireless are the mile-high Wi-Fi providers.

Wireless ALL-IN-ONE DESK REFERENCE FOR DUMMIES®

Wireless ALL-IN-ONE DESK REFERENCE FOR DUMMIES®

by Todd W. Carter

WILEY

Wiley Publishing, Inc.

Wireless All-In-One Desk Reference For Dummies®

Published by
Wiley Publishing, Inc.
111 River Street
Hoboken, NJ 07030-5774

Published by Wiley Publishing, Inc., Indianapolis, Indiana

Published simultaneously in Canada

For general information on our other products and services or to obtain technical support, please contact our Customer Care Department within the U.S. at 800-762-2974, outside the U.S. at 317-572-3993, or fax 317-572-4002.

Wiley also publishes its books in a variety of electronic formats. Some content that appears in print may not be available in electronic books.

Library of Congress Control Number: 2005921455

ISBN: 0-7645-7496-5

Manufactured in the United States of America

10 9 8 7 6 5 4 3 2 1

1O/SV/QS/QV/IN

WILEY

About the Author

When not transmitting Wi-Fi signals from his Cubs hat, Todd W. Carter likes to stare out the window, contemplate world travel he'll likely avoid because of pesky shoe inspections, and dream of selling 100,000 copies of this book. He's single, lives in west Michigan, and hopes this bio leads to a date with a female reader. (E-mail him at date@toddcarter.com.) Due to advances in the medical sciences, the 39-year-old Carter is postponing his midlife crisis until 2014. This and much, much more on his web site at www.toddcarter.com.

Dedication

To Michael, who bravely defends Twyckingham against all enemies, real or imagined.

Author's Acknowledgments

My agents, Neil Salkind and Lynn Hall, always had an encouraging word that somehow got me past another deadline and kept my keyboard clicking and clacking. Thanks. Thank you also to Dan DiNicolo for writing Books II and IV, Brian Underdahl for writing six of this book's chapters on various topics, and Darlene Underdahl for writing the Internet directory.

Publisher's Acknowledgments

We're proud of this book; please send us your comments through our online registration form located at www.dummies.com/register/.

Some of the people who helped bring this book to market include the following:

Acquisitions, Editorial, and Media Development

Contributors: Dan DiNicolo, Brian Underdahl, and Darlene Underdahl

Project Editor: Tonya Maddox Cupp

Acquisitions Editor: Tom Heine

Technical Editor: Justin Kamm

Editorial Manager: Robyn Siesky

Permissions Editor: Kimberly Ward Skeel

Media Development Supervisor: Richard Graves

Editorial Assistant: Adrienne Porter

Cartoons: Rich Tennant (www.the5thwave.com)

Special Help: Laura Moss

Production

Project Coordinator: Nancee Reeves

Layout and Graphics: Jonelle Burns, Andrea Dahl, Lauren Goddard, Stephanie D. Jumper, Melanee Prendergast, Heather Ryan, Jacque Roth, Mary Gillot Virgin

Special Art: Some photos courtesy Linksys

Proofreaders: Vickie Broyles, John Greenough, Leann Harney, Jessica Kramer, Carl William Pierce, Sossity Smith, Evelyn Still

Indexer: Anne Leach

Publishing and Editorial for Technology Dummies

Barry Prvett, Vice President and Publisher, Visual/Web Graphics

Richard Swadley, Vice President and Executive Group Publisher

Andy Cummings, Vice President and Publisher, Technology Dummies

Mary Bednarek, Executive Acquisitions Director, Technology Dummies

Mary C. Corder, Editorial Director, Technology Dummies

Publishing for Consumer Dummies

Diane Graves Steele, Vice President and Publisher

Joyce Pepple, Acquisitions Director

Composition Services

Gerry Fahey, Vice President of Production Services

Debbie Stailey, Director of Composition Services

Contents at a Glance

Introduction 1

Book I: Pulling the Plug 7

Chapter 1: Living Without Wires 9
Chapter 2: Choosing Internet Access...17

Book II: Planning Your Network.. 23

Chapter 1: Putting Together a Wireless Network 25
Chapter 2: Choosing Hardware Made Easy 35
Chapter 3: Setting Up Routers 47
Chapter 4: Setting Up Other Hardware 61
Chapter 5: Decoding DHCP...73
Chapter 6: Installing an Adapter on Your PC 85
Chapter 7: Adapter-ing..103
Chapter 8: Troubleshooting Network Hardware 127

Book III: Configuring Networks.. 143

Chapter 1: Exploring Windows XP Networking 145
Chapter 2: Managing Available Networks 149
Chapter 3: Creating Bridges 159
Chapter 4: Configuring Printers...165
Chapter 5: Confirming Your Network Works...171

Book IV: Security and Troubleshooting 181

Chapter 1: Using a Safety Net...183
Chapter 2: Managing User Accounts...205
Chapter 3: Solving Network Problems 221

Book V: On the Road 247

Chapter 1: Putting a Network in Your Lap(top)..249
Chapter 2: Connecting PDAs to Networks...261
Chapter 3: Synchronizing PDAs over a Network 273
Chapter 4: Picking a BlackBerry..287
Chapter 5: Finding Wi-Fi Hotspots...303
Chapter 6: Setting Up a VPN Connection 315
Chapter 7: Strapping on Microsoft SmartWatch..325

Book VI: Networking Technologies 339
Chapter 1: Roaming into Cell Phone Territory 341
Chapter 2: Choosing and Using Cordless Phones 351
Chapter 3: Gathering around the Family Radio Service 359
Chapter 4: Picking Peripherals 363
Chapter 5: Cutting Your Bluetooth 371

Book VII: Home Technology 395
Chapter 1: Your Entertainment Center 397
Chapter 2: Setting Up Gadgets 409
Chapter 3: Chatting with Motorola's IMfree 419
Chapter 4: Sharing Multimedia Files with Windows XP..............................437
Chapter 5: Using TiVo's Home Media Features 447
Chapter 6: Exploring Digital TV and Satellite Radio 461
Chapter 7: Forecasting the Weather from Your Patio 469
Chapter 8: Security in the Air via Motorola 483

Book VIII: Global Positioning Systems.........................493
Chapter 1: Getting Uncle Sam to Ante Up 495
Chapter 2: Finding Your Way in the World 507
Chapter 3: Exploring with the Rest of GPS 519

Glossary...529

Internet Directory 535

Index 591

Table of Contents

Introduction 1

About This Book 1
System Requirements 2
What You Don't Have to Read 3
How This Book Is Organized 3
Book I: Pulling the Plug 3
Book II: Planning Your Network 3
Book III: Configuring Networks 4
Book IV: Security and Troubleshooting 4
Book V: On the Road 4
Book VI: Networking Technologies 4
Book VII: Home Technology 5
Book VIII: Global Positioning Systems 5
Icons 5
Where to Go from Here 6

Book I: Pulling the Plug 7

Chapter 1: Living Without Wires 9

Bidding Adieu to Wired Life 9
A whole world of wireless possibilities 9
Cutting the cords 11
Keeping your options open 12
Connecting to the World on the Go 12
Connecting your PC on the go 13
Connecting for voice and messages 14
Addressing the Downside: You're Always On 14
Your wireless network is always on 14
Your wireless gadgets are probably open, too 15
Taking back control 15

Chapter 2: Choosing Internet Access 17

Using Satellite Service 18
StarBand 18
DirecWay 20
Maxing Out with WiMax 21
Wi to the max 21
Local Multipoint Distribution System (LMDS) 22

Book II: Planning Your Network 23

Chapter 1: Putting Together a Wireless Network 25

Figuring Out Your Hopes and Dreams 26
Reaching Clear Across the Household 27
Checking for Obstacles and Interference 28
Totaling Up the Damage 29
Creating a Hardware Shopping List 32

Chapter 2: Choosing Hardware Made Easy 35

Choosing the Wares Is Not Hard 35
- 802.11a 36
- 802.11b 37
- 802.11g 37
- Multi-standard devices 37

Starting with DSL or Cable Modem 38
Modem Options 40
Routing Through the Router 41
Pointing Toward Areas That Need Coverage 44

Chapter 3: Setting Up Routers 47

Some Assembly Required 47
Fiddling with the Innards 50
- A password of your own 53
- Just like clockwork 54
- Nothing but 'net 55
- Attack of the (MAC) clone 58
- What's in a name? 59

Chapter 4: Setting Up Other Hardware 61

Bridging Multiple Networks 61
Configuring Your Access Points 62
Serving Your Print Needs Wirelessly 64

Chapter 5: Decoding DHCP 73

Examining Your Address Options 73
- What DHCP server? 73
- Static versus dynamic 74

Putting Dynamic Addresses to Good Use 76
Heading off Trouble 78
Getting some Static 81

Chapter 6: Installing an Adapter on Your PC 85

Taking the Lid Off Your PC 85
Physically installing your adapter....................86
Who's driving? 89
Installing adapter utilities 94
Saving Some Time with USB Adapters 96
Plug away....................97
Driving Miss Lazy 99
Again, utilities 101

Chapter 7: Adapter-ing 103

Configuring Your Wireless Adapter 103
Starting at Zero....................103
Using your wireless adapter's utilities 116
Making Sure It Works 120
Wireless connection status....................120
Viewing available wireless networks 122
Traveling to utilityland 123
Estimating Your Range 124

Chapter 8: Troubleshooting Network Hardware 127

Shooting Down Hardware Trouble....................127
Fixing a router....................128
Fixing other access points 129
Working on adapter cards....................130
Taking a Wrench to the Software 133
Upgrading your hardware's firmware....................133
Updating network adapter drivers....................138
Upgrading adapter utilities 141

Book III: Configuring Networks 143

Chapter 1: Exploring Windows XP Networking.....................145

Installing Is Child's (Plug and) Play 145
My Network Places 146
Adding to the Start menu 146
Removing from the Start menu....................146
Mingling with Different Networks 147
Creating an Infrastructure Network....................147
Creating a Computer-to-Computer Network....................147
Enabling Internet sharing....................148

Chapter 2: Managing Available Networks 149

Finding Out What's Out There 150
Viewing Available Networks 152
Managing Preferred Networks 153
Adding a preferred network 154
Removing a preferred network 154
Viewing a network's properties 154
Reordering preferred networks 154
Using the Advanced Networking Options 155
Viewing an Available Network's Signal Strength 157

Chapter 3: Creating Bridges 159

Bridging with Windows XP 160
Creating a bridge 160
Adding a network to a bridge 162
Removing a network from a bridge 162
Deleting a bridge 163

Chapter 4: Configuring Printers 165

Learning to Share 165
Feeling Selfish and Turning Off Sharing 167
Adding a Network Printer 167
Changing the Default Printer 169

Chapter 5: Confirming Your Network Works 171

Flexing Your Signal Strength 171
Monitoring Your Network 173
Viewing your network's activity 173
Viewing a real-time networking graph 174
Changing the networking information you see 175
Stumbling Upon Network Stumbler 176
Downloading and installing NetStumbler 176
Using NetStumbler 177

Book IV: Security and Troubleshooting 181

Chapter 1: Using a Safety Net 183

Safety First, but Security Firstest 183
Hackers, Crackers, and Slackers 184
Plugging Your Security Holes 185
Making your SSID invisible 186
Tying down the MAC hatch 188

Introducing WEP, WPA, and Weep 189
Read 'em and WEP 190
Upgrading to WPA 195
Authenticating with 802.1x....................198
Fixing Holes Before You Leak....................199
Hardening your software....................200
(Un)plugging the hardware....................202

Chapter 2: Managing User Accounts 205

Deciding Who Plays Administrator....................205
What's the Access Level, Kenneth? 206
Creating User Accounts....................207
Deleting User Accounts 210
Changing User Accounts 212
Changing the name....................212
Creating a password....................214
Changing a password....................216
Removing a password....................216
Changing the picture....................217
Changing the account type 218
Disabling the Guest Account 219
Restoring the guest account....................220

Chapter 3: Solving Network Problems 221

Houston, We Have a Problem 221
1: Define the problem in a general sense 222
2: Isolate the problem 222
3: Define the problem as specifically as possible....................223
4: Test possible solutions one at a time 223
5: Fix the problem and document the solution 223
Starting with Windows XP....................223
Depending on Device Manager....................224
Working with wireless network connections....................227
Connecting to other devices....................234
Finding the Culprit among Hardware 235
Feeling router woes....................235
Dealing with modem blues....................236
Fielding problems with other hardware....................238
Getting Cozy with Network Tools 239
ipconfig....................239
ping....................242
tracert 244

Book V: On the Road 247

Chapter 1: Putting a Network in Your Lap(top) 249

Discovering Your Options for Wire-Free Access 249
- Choosing the slower but somewhat expensive option 250
- Choosing the faster but somewhat limited option 250
- Choosing the gimme-it-all option 251

Getting Carded...251
- Using a wireless cellular data card..252
- Using a wireless network card...253

Getting Out and About..254
- Finding Wi-Fi hotspots 255
- Power backup on the road 256
- Printing while on the road..258

Lounging at Home 260

Chapter 2: Connecting PDAs to Networks 261

Reaching into Your Pocket PC 262
- Manually configuring your network..263
- Using the Dell WLAN utility..265
- Using the Dell Site Monitor 266

Going Mano y Mano with Palm PDAs 267
- Configuring your Palm 267
- Confirming your settings...269
- Making the connection 270

Making a VPN Connection, Literally 270
- Configuring your Palm for VPN 271
- Connecting a la VPN with your Palm 272

Chapter 3: Synchronizing PDAs over a Network 273

Getting a Pocket PC to Coordinate 273
- Running with ActiveSync..274
- Syncing information from a Pocket PC 275

Synchronizing a Palm PDA..276
- Configuring HotSync on your PC...276
- Configuring HotSync on your Palm 277
- HotSyncing to your PC from your Palm...279

Giving It an AvantGo 279

Using AvantGo Wireless 284

Chapter 4: Picking a BlackBerry 287

Avoiding a Raspberry 287

Picking a Model, Any Model...288
- BlackBerry 7200, 7500, and 7700 Series...289
- BlackBerry 5790...290

Biting into the Main Features 290
Navigating 292
Turning it on and off 292
Sending and receiving e-mail 292
Making a phone call 296
Adding a contact to the address book....297
Browsing the Web....299
Checking Out the Sidekick II....300

Chapter 5: Finding Wi-Fi Hotspots 303

Getting Thee to a Directory....303
Paying for the Goods: Commercial Providers 305
Going Public....307
In airports....307
In hotels 308
In the (city) clouds....309
McWireless and others 310
Clenching Your Security Blanket....312

Chapter 6: Setting Up a VPN Connection 315

Setting Up a VPN Connection 315
Connecting to a Remote Computer Using VPN....319
Creating an Incoming VPN Connection 320

Chapter 7: Strapping on Microsoft SmartWatch 325

Picking and Choosing....325
Beaming the World 326
Flipping through the WristNet Channels....328
Calendar....328
Horoscopes 328
News....328
One-way Instant Messaging....329
Lottery results 329
Sports....329
Stocks....329
Weather....330
Adding Daily Diversions 330
Registering Your Watch....331
Getting Personal with MSN Direct Service....333
Installing the Outlook Software....336
Taking a Glance at This Feature 338

Book VI: Networking Technologies 339

Chapter 1: Roaming into Cell Phone Territory 341

Selecting a Plan 341
Choosing a Phone: Do I Really Need Those Fancy Things? 343
Size 344
Talk time 344
Cameras 344
Headsets 345
Games 345
Web enabled 346
Messaging 346
Staying Healthy 347
Putting Your Number on the Move 348

Chapter 2: Choosing and Using Cordless Phones 351

Cutting the Cords 351
Analog phones 352
Digital phones 353
Choosing Your Frequency 354
900 MHz 354
2.4 GHz 355
5.8 GHz 355
Featuring Cordless Phones 355
Avoiding Interference 357

Chapter 3: Gathering around the Family Radio Service 359

Calling All Radios 359
FMS according to the FCC 360
Keeping the family unit intact 360
Distancing Yourself with GMRS 361

Chapter 4: Picking Peripherals 363

Unplugging Your Desktop 363
Cordless Mice in Seattle 364
Microsoft mice 364
Logitech mice 366
Trackballs 368
Finding the Home Row: Keyboards 368
Microsoft wireless keyboards 368
Logitech wireless keyboards 368
Getting with the Game Controllers 369
Cordless RumblePad 369
Freedom 2.4 Cordless Joystick 370

Chapter 5: Cutting Your Bluetooth 371

Opening Wide 372
Getting to the nitty-gritty 372
Connecting to various and sundry devices 373
Exploring its insides 374
Styling and profiling 375
Using Peripherals 376
Making Your Devices Discoverable 378
Pairing Your Devices 379
Installing a USB Bluetooth Adapter 379
Moving Files between a PC and Mac 382
Moving from Tooth to Pocket (PC) 385
Moving within Earshot of Your Cell Phone 388
Setting up the headset 388
Sending a Photo to Your PC 389
Staying Safe with Bluetooth 392
Bluejacking 392
Bluesnarfing 393

Book VII: Home Technology 395

Chapter 1: Your Entertainment Center 397

Entertaining the Wireless Way 398
Playing some tunes 398
Did I really look like that? 399
Hollywood on a hard-drive platter 400
Looking at the Latest Gadgets 401
Netgear Wireless Digital Music Player 402
Linksys Wireless-B Music System 402
D-Link MediaLounge Wireless Media Player 403
Sound Blaster Wireless Music 403
Gateway Connected DVD Player 403
PRISMIQ MediaPlayer 403
Apple AirPort Express 404
Roku SoundBridge 405
Other media players 405
Combining the uncategorizable 406
Wi-Fi'ing to Your Car Stereo 406

Chapter 2: Setting Up Gadgets 409

Exploring Gadgets Galore 409
Adding a Media Server to Your Home 410
What is a media server? 410
Who makes media servers? 411

Moving Some of Everything with PRISMIQ MediaPlayer 412
Setting up the PRISMIQ MediaPlayer 412
Using the PRISMIQ MediaPlayer 414
Looking into Internet Video Cameras 416

Chapter 3: Chatting with Motorola's IMfree 419

Getting Ahold of Your Messager 419
Setting Yourself Up for Freedom 420
Installing software on your PC 420
Running the software 422
Powering up and registering 422
Setting up your PC 423
Creating an AIM screen name 425
Installing AOL's AIM software 428
Using IMfree 430
The keys to chatting 430
Getting a move on 431
Avoiding interference 431
Emoticoning and abbreviating 433

Chapter 4: Sharing Multimedia Files with Windows XP 437

Tuning In to Sights and Sounds 437
Taking a looksee at video 438
Sharing Your Files on a Network 438
Blocking Access to Files 440
Changing a shared folder to unshared 440
Hiding a folder from others 442
Assigning a Drive Letter to a Network Folder 442
Switching off automatic connections 443
Disconnecting from a mapped network drive 445
Browsing Your Network 446

Chapter 5: Using TiVo's Home Media Features 447

Turning on the TiVo 447
Making a Connection 449
Configuring your TiVo 450
Configuring TCP/IP settings 452
Switching to broadband access 453
Testing the connection 454
Troubleshooting the connection 455
Peer to Peer, Yes Sir! 457

Chapter 6: Exploring Digital TV and Satellite Radio 461
Wanting My HDTV 461
Understanding All Those Terms 462
Going Shopping for a High-Definition TV Set 463
Built-in tuner 464
HDTV ready 464
Blown Away by My Reception 464
Receiving HDTV over the air 464
Receiving HDTV via satellite TV 465
Receiving HDTV over cable TV 466
Grabbing for the Heavenly Sound 466
But Sirius-ly, folks 467
XM marks the spot 467

Chapter 7: Forecasting the Weather from Your Patio 469
Taking the Station Out of the Box 469
Installing and Using Weather Software 473
That's heavy 473
Getting graphic about it 475
Telling the web about your weather 478

Chapter 8: Security in the Air via Motorola 483
Digging Through the Goodies 483
Setting Yourself Up for Security Success 485
Setting up the hardware 485
Installing the software 486
Configuring the software 488
Arming the system 491

Book VIII: Global Positioning Systems 493

Chapter 1: Getting Uncle Sam to Ante Up 495
Knowing Where You Are 496
Achieving Missile Precision — Almost 497
How the military uses GPS 497
Civilians can find their way, too 498
Some other satellite navigation systems exist (almost) 499
Using GPS 500
Taking a hike 500
On the road again 500

On a bike ride 501
It's a bird, no, it really is a plane.....501
Just for fun 501
Exploring Your Options 502
Choosing a portable unit.....502
Driving around with a vehicle GPS unit.....502
Merging your laptop with GPS 503
Using GPS with a Pocket PC 504
Using a GPS-enabled cell phone 505
Saying Goodbye to AAA?.....505
Making a Connection with Your PC.....505
Upgrading software and maps 505
Downloading your life's movements.....506
Using your GPS with your laptop 506

Chapter 2: Finding Your Way in the World 507

Giving Some Latitude to Your Longitude 507
A Quick Course on Mapping.....508
A bit of simple geometry 508
Latitude.....509
Longitude.....509
Elevation 510
Coordinating Your Coordinates.....510
Explaining How GPS Works 511
Reading a GPS Display.....513
Finding Your Waypoints 515
Understanding how waypoints work.....516
Creating waypoints 516

Chapter 3: Exploring with the Rest of GPS 519

Seeking and Hiding with Geocaching.....519
Going for the cache.....519
Hiding the bounty.....521
Finding Your Ancestors 523
A very grave matter 523
Where is (old) home sweet home?.....526

Glossary 529

Internet Directory.....535

Index.....591

Introduction

Isn't it about time you cut the wires in your life? Of course, I think so. Otherwise, I wouldn't have spent months writing what you are about to read. And while I'm sitting here typing on a keyboard that's wired to my computer that's wired to the electrical outlet, you should follow what I say and not what I do.

This is what I say: Pull out those wires! Shop for personal electronics with an eye toward making all things wireless. A wireless keyboard works just as well as a wired one, so why not use it and free your desk from the constricting cord? (Yes, I'm a hypocrite, but ignore that for now. I do have a wireless mouse.)

Of course, like me, you find that your world still needs some wires. Last I checked, there isn't wireless electricity, unless you count batteries. Just as many consumers have foregone their landline phones for cellular phones, you can find dozens of ways to reduce the tangle of cords you call your home entertainment center or computer network. By using something called Bluetooth technology, you even can cut the wire between your headset and cell phone.

Let those wires go! Breathe deep. Exhale. Now toss out those wires! You can do it. Freedom is out there for the taking. I want you to reach your *full* wireless potential. Hopefully, this book moves you in that direction.

About This Book

Wireless All-In-One Desk Reference For Dummies is all about wireless technologies. I cover just about everything, from networking to digital TV broadcasting to cell phones.

If that sounds like a hodgepodge for one book, think again. I separate topics into mini books and further into chapters within each book.

With this book in hand, you can do all kinds of cool things:

- Choose the right wireless networking hardware.
- Install and configure a wireless network in your home or small office.

- Troubleshoot your networking hardware.
- Configure printers so you can use them across your network.
- Plug security leaks and keep them plugged.
- Connect your laptop computer to wireless networks while on the road, as well as keep it constantly supplied with power.
- Connect and synchronize Pocket PCs and Palm PDAs with wireless networks.
- Purchase, configure, and use a BlackBerry e-mail device.
- Use a Microsoft SmartWatch to catch the latest news and other information from your wrist.
- Choose and use cellular telephones.
- Use media servers to play your music and view photos on your home entertainment center.
- Set up your own weather station.
- Use GPS technology for things like finding your way home and locating cemeteries for genealogy research.

The first time I use a technical phrase in the book, I italicize it, so look out for that.

System Requirements

For the sections about wireless networking, I assume you are running Windows XP on your computer. Earlier versions of Windows don't let you connect to a wireless network with the ease of Windows XP, so I recommend upgrading to the latest version before setting up your network.

I don't cover Mac OS X or Linux in this book. It's not because they aren't wonderful operating systems conducive to wireless networking. Instead, whole books are devoted to both operating systems and wireless networking, so I focus on what most people are running these days. Whatever your view on monopolies, Windows XP still dominates the market.

Not everything in this book is about Windows XP. You find chapters on Pocket PCs and Palm PDAs, cell phones — and even an entire mini book on GPS. Obviously, you need some of that equipment to get the most from those chapters.

What You Don't Have to Read

Actually, you don't have to read anything if you don't want to. It's a free country. But I bet you didn't pay to not read this book. Assume you want to read everything that's precisely on topic and not a sentence more.

That's okay. You can skip two types of information without losing the big picture:

- ✦ Information marked by a Technical Stuff icon, which I discuss a little later in this introduction. This information appeals to your inner geek, but it's not absolutely necessary reading.
- ✦ Sidebars. These bits and bytes are off the beaten path. They're interesting (I hope!), but not essential.

Still, these two groups of information make up a small portion of the book. Reading them won't consume that much time. Plus, you will make me happy for having read them. (This book contains a hidden wireless transmitter that reports back to me what you have and have not read, so don't think I don't know.)

How This Book Is Organized

Wireless All-In-One Desk Reference For Dummies contains eight mini books, each of which focuses on a general wireless topic. I wrote in a way that lets you easily find the topic you want to read about, skipping the others for the time being. For example, one mini book focuses on wireless networking, while another contains information about cell phones and other wireless technologies. When feasible, I've kept an entire mini book about one topic, such as networking or GPS. This is what the eight mini books contain.

Book I: Pulling the Plug

I tell you about all the ways to cut your cords and live in a wireless world. Wireless technology has an advantage to its wired counterpart in that you can move anywhere and stay in touch. There's the rub: You're always in touch. Do you really want that? I also talk about some wireless Internet access technologies and how to choose one.

Book II: Planning Your Network

The nitty-gritty starts here, with talk of hardware such as routers and adapters. If and when you're ready to network wirelessly in your jammies, from the safety of your own den, you should take a crack at these chapters. Or at least take a peek. Already there and wrestling with some of your products? Hardware troubleshooting advice to the rescue.

Book III: Configuring Networks

I start with an explanation of Windows XP's wireless networking capabilities, including its almost effortless plug-and-play technology. Then I move into managing available wireless networks, which you find helpful both at home and away. Creating a bridge between a wired and wireless network is covered, as is printer configuration. Finally, I assist you in making sure your network is doing its thing.

Book IV: Security and Troubleshooting

This brief but power-packed mini book makes you aware of the dark side of wireless computing and lets you know what you can do to best protect yourself. You can begin by getting a grip on the accounts that are available on your home network, and those instructions are here. These troubleshooting ideas are another way I help you keep your system running smoothly.

Book V: On the Road

This book covers a wide variety of wireless technologies. It begins with using your laptop, including the installation of a wireless adapter card and managing your power so you don't run out of juice. Then I move into the connecting of your Pocket PC or Palm PDA to a wireless network, as well as synchronizing those devices with the network. One of the more popular wireless gizmos is the BlackBerry, which I discuss in this book. I also tackle the important issue of finding Wi-Fi hotspots by using directories and other resources.

While you're on the road, connecting via a virtual private network (VPN), communicating with your office is crucial, so I cover that topic in depth. Finally, not everything has to be serious: With a Microsoft SmartWatch, which I cover in this book, you can be ready with news, sports and, of course, the time.

Book VI: Networking Technologies

Starting with cell phones, this book discusses selecting a service plan and choosing a phone. It also talks about some other important issues, like health concerns and number portability. A second chapter talks about a similar topic: cordless phones. Which cordless phone technology should you choose? Another wireless technology, but one that gets less attention, is the Family Radio Service (FRS). With two or more FRS radios, you can stay in contact with people within a mile or so of each other while on vacation and elsewhere. This book also covers the burgeoning technology called Bluetooth, which is a short-range version of Wi-Fi technology. Finally, I go through some wireless peripherals you may want to include on your desk.

Book VII: Home Technology

This book is a lot of fun. In it, you discover the newest gadgets that bridge your computer with your home entertainment center — using a wireless network to transmit music, video, and photos from your PC. Then I walk through the setups for a couple devices. I also help you connect and use a device called IMfree, which lets you chat online without being tethered to your computer. This book also provides help moving multimedia files around using Windows XP, and then explores some of TiVo's wireless features. Finally, I talk about digital TV and satellite radio services before heading into a completely other area: setting up and using your own wireless weather station.

Book VIII: Global Positioning Systems

The global positioning system (GPS) is the U.S. government's gift to all of humankind. Read about the technology behind it and how you can use it, but first check out my list of things to consider when choosing a GPS unit. After that, I describe some common GPS terminology that helps you in your quest, whatever it may be. Finally, you discover a couple of ways to use GPS technology that go beyond simple navigation, including using it for something called geocaching.

Icons

I point out some issues or topics to you with the use of icons.

TIP

A tip is a helpful bit of information that hopefully helps you accomplish a specific task a little easier. By flagging tips with icons, you can quickly find nuggets of helpful information.

REMEMBER

Everyone needs a reminder now and then about something that's already been mentioned. That's where the Remember icon comes into play. Sometimes, the icon indicates something that's common sense or that you already know, but I point it out just in case.

WARNING!

Whoa, Betsy! You should know some important things, and I point out these with a Warning icon. Heed these or proceed at your own risk. I keep these to a minimum so that when you see one, you know it really is important.

TECHNICAL STUFF

Are you a geek? There's nothing wrong with that, as geeks now rule the world. If you see a Technical Stuff icon, it's likely the content is something you'll enjoy reading because of its technical bent. Geeks aren't dummies, but Dummies books are for geeks, too. Even if you're not a geek, it can't hurt to discover something new.

Where to Go from Here

Scissors ready? The next step is to begin cutting the wires that constrain your lifestyle. Instead, embrace radio waves and all things wireless! (Don't actually *embrace* them, as that effort is futile. They also can fry you; just look inside your microwave oven while it's running. But you know what I mean.) Lie upon the psychiatrist's sofa, as it were, and reject your old, constrained wired life. Free those demons.

See you in the wireless world!

Book I

Pulling the Plug

The 5th Wave By Rich Tennant

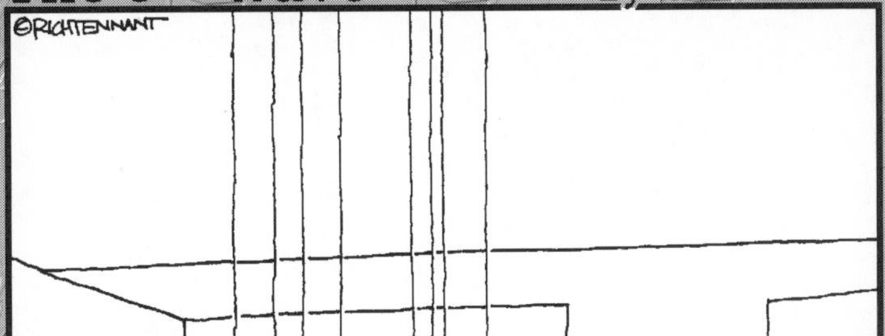

"Frankly, the idea of an entirely wireless future scares me to death."

Contents at a Glance

Chapter 1: Living Without Wires 9
Chapter 2: Choosing Internet Access 17

Chapter 1: Living Without Wires

In This Chapter

- **Goodbye, wired life**
- **Connecting to the world on the go**
- **Dealing with the downside**

In many ways, gadgets can be very handy. Just one little problem exists with most of your gadgets, however, and that's all of those darn wires that you need to run them. That's why it's so exciting that so many new gadgets come in wireless varieties. By getting rid of the wires, life is just so much more convenient. This chapter describes some of the basics of going wireless. As you see, the wireless life will have you wondering how you ever put up with that tangle of wires. But, as you also see, going wireless does have some downsides.

Bidding Adieu to Wired Life

When you think about it, wires can be a real hassle. They really limit your ability to move freely and to place things where you want them. A very good example of this? Your ordinary, everyday telephone. If you use a wired telephone, you have to sit at your desk or stand next to the wall phone to have a conversation. If the doorbell rings, you have to tell the person on the other end of the line to hold on while you go see who's at the door. If you're using a cordless phone, you can simply continue your conversation while you walk to the door.

A whole world of wireless possibilities

Now multiply the convenience provided by your cordless phone to include the whole multitude of gadgets that fill your home. Just imagine how these additional examples might apply to your situation:

- **You're stuck with a slow dial-up connection to the Internet.** You might find that a high-speed wireless connection, either through a satellite connection or a fixed wireless connection, enables you to finally have that broadband connection you've always dreamed of — even if a DSL or cable connection is not available in your area. With the broadband Internet connection you can enjoy all sorts of streaming content that simply isn't practical over a dial-up connection.

✦ **You're pretty much solo at your computer.** By adding a wireless network to your home, you can share files, printers, your Internet connection, music you've downloaded, and multiplayer games without the hassle of running wires. If you want to move a PC from one place to another, you can do it and not worry whether a handy network outlet is nearby. Why, you can even take your wireless laptop out into the backyard and surf the Internet in a lawn chair under your favorite tree.

✦ **You're stuck at home waiting on messages and phone calls.** With a wireless PDA, you are within reach of e-mail at your favorite coffee shop — you don't have to worry about missing that important message from a potential new client. You may even listen to an Internet radio station so you don't have to listen to the rants from a fanatical talk radio show host. Figure 1-1 shows an example of a text message using a Pocket PC. Book V talks more about PDAs.

Figure 1-1: My wireless Pocket PC can send and receive messages with the built-in messaging application.

✦ **You're sans cell phone.** It's hard to imagine another device that can help you keep in touch nearly as well as a cell phone. With it, you can quickly check to see what someone's scribbled notes on your shopping list really mean. Don't take a chance that what looks like *sour cream* in someone's poor handwriting is actually *whipping cream!*

✦ **You've experienced the wonders of trying to keep track of your whole family at the shopping mall or amusement park.** You're going to love the new *Family Radio Service (FRS)* two-way radios. Imagine how much more convenient it is getting everyone back to the car when all you need to do is call them on your radio.

✦ **You're sick of the wiry clutter at your desk.** Cutting the wires to your keyboard and mouse sounds like a sure way to kill your computer, but wireless peripherals are simply so much more convenient than their wired counterparts — especially if your desk is such a mess that you haven't seen the top of it in years.

- **You're a home-entertainment technology junkie.** For example, you can set up one computer to hold all of your music from your CDs or from Internet downloads, and then play that music on your home entertainment system without putting an ugly PC in the living room and without running another tangled mess of wires.
- **Your cup of tea is Howard Stern.** Wireless is the way to go now that he's moved to satellite radio. Plus, no commercials!
- **Your family vacations seem more like battles over who can or cannot read a map.** You're going to love how GPS technology can keep you from ever having to ask directions again. Figure 1-2 shows my GPS receiver as it determines my exact position.

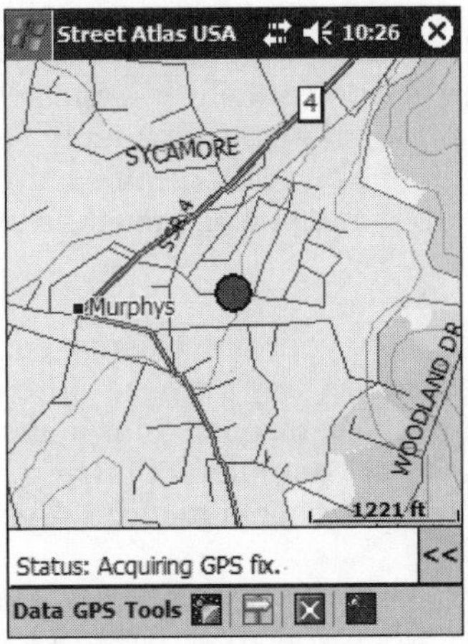

Figure 1-2: With a GPS receiver you never have to wonder where you are.

I guess if that list doesn't have you thinking about the possibilities for a wireless life, nothing will — but even this list only scratches the surface.

Cutting the cords

Now that you've seen some of the ways that you can go wireless, what's next? Actually, that depends. You probably have to do some shopping, either to replace existing wired equipment or to add wireless equipment. In either case, it helps to plan ahead because so many different types of wireless equipment exist and you want to make sure the things you buy work together. That's where this book helps.

Consider the example of the wireless home computer network. As you discover in Book III, home computer networks adhere to a couple different standards, and it's important to make sure that all the equipment you buy for your home computer network works with the same standard. As you discover in Book VII, the type of equipment you choose for your home computer network can have a great impact on how useful your network is in supplying entertainment options.

When buying wireless equipment, go for higher performance rather than lower price. That way you won't close off your future options because the equipment you bought can't handle the demands of the need to process more data.

Keeping your options open

Once you get the wireless bug, it can be awfully tempting to want to get rid of every cord. As tempting as that may be, just remember that you probably want to keep your options open. You might, for example, want to make sure that you have at least one wired phone in your home because cordless phones typically won't work if there is a power failure — unlike wired phones, which generally don't need a separate power supply. (Even though the handset on a cordless telephone runs off rechargeable batteries, the base station that it uses to connect to the phone line must be plugged into a power outlet to function.)

Remember, too, that just because some of your old, existing equipment is wired, doesn't mean that it no longer serves any purpose. Sure, you probably prefer the convenience of playing music through your home entertainment system, which is connected to your computer, but that won't do you much good if you want to listen to some old, vinyl records. (I've never seen a PC with a built-in turntable.)

Don't forget to stock up on batteries when you go wireless. Some wireless devices run through batteries at an amazing rate; consider buying a battery charger and rechargeable batteries for your devices. They help you save money in the long run. You may want to check out iGo (www.igo.com) to find just the battery you need.

Connecting to the World on the Go

Wireless devices really do open up a whole new world for you, and not just when you're at home, either. Sure, it's pretty obvious that a cell phone enables you to connect to the world when you're on the go, but other wireless devices offer plenty of on-the-go options, too.

Connecting your PC on the go

To successfully communicate with someone, you generally have to both be using the same language. It doesn't really matter what language that happens to be as long as you both understand it.

Likewise, computers need to use a common language to communicate. Modern wireless home networking equipment uses one of several standardized methods of communication that were developed to enable different brands of computers and networking equipment to successfully interact. You may have heard of these standards — especially if you've tried wading into the sometimes confusing world of wireless networking. These standards go by names like 802.11b, 802.11g, and 802.11a, but they also are known by the slightly less precise Wi-Fi label.

TECHNICAL STUFF

Even though the Wi-Fi label is applied to all three wireless networking standards doesn't mean those standards are identical. Of the three, 802.11b is the slowest but also the least expensive when you're buying hardware. 802.11g and 802.11a are rated for similar speeds (about five times as fast as 802.11b), but are incompatible with each other because they operate on different radio frequencies. 802.11b and 802.11g are generally compatible with each other, but can only communicate at the slower 802.11b speed. Just how fast are these different standards? That's impossible to say because your results vary greatly depending on dozens of factors (which you discover in Books II and III).

What does all of this have to do with connecting your PC on the go? I'm glad you asked. Wi-Fi isn't limited to use on home networks. Wi-Fi is also for wireless office networks and is becoming widely available other places, too. Want some Internet along with your coffee? Every Starbucks coffee shop now offers customers a Wi-Fi connection. (This type of connection is often called a *hotspot.*) If you'd rather have a Big Mac and fries while you surf, head on over to McDonald's — most of their stores have free Wi-Fi connections, too.

TIP

Head on over to the Wi-Fi-FreeSpot Directory (www.wififreespot.com) to find free high-speed Internet access hotspots.

Wi-Fi hotspots generally have a very limited range. In most cases you need to be within the building to get a reliable connection (and some hotspots are specifically designed to limit the range so that you can only connect if you're inside, where you are expected to be patronizing the store). Even those hotspots specifically set up to cover a broader area typically only spread their signal a few hundred feet from the hotspot's antenna, though, so Wi-Fi isn't a good option if you can't settle in one place close to the hotspot.

What can you do if you want a wireless Internet connection but aren't always within range of a Wi-Fi hotspot? One option is an AirCard from Sierra Wireless (www.sierrawireless.com). The AirCard comes in several models — each one designed for a specific type of service. Some models connect via the Sprint PCS Network, some with the AT&T Wireless Network, and some with other flavors of cellular service, too. Generally you should do your homework, choose the service plan that's right for you, and then buy the AirCard that works with that service. Sometimes cellular service providers even offer special pricing on the AirCard because they know that once you're hooked you're probably going to spend a lot of money on your monthly service plan.

Connecting for Voice and Messages

Even though most people think of computers when they think about connecting on the go, sometimes a PC is overkill. Sometimes all you need is simply the ability to send and receive text messages. A couple of different types of wireless devices easily handle this duty:

- ✦ Wireless PDAs, including some models of the Palm and the Pocket PC, can easily send and receive text messages.
- ✦ The BlackBerry is a wireless device specifically designed for text messaging. It has a small, but serviceable, keyboard for entering messages.
- ✦ Most cell phones now support *short messaging service (SMS)* so you can send and receive text messages.

You read more about connecting on the go in Book V.

Addressing the Downside: You're Always On

If the wireless world has one big problem, it's that always being connected means that people can contact you at any time. Sure, it's convenient to flip open your cell phone to quickly ask someone a question, but don't forget that it is just as convenient for someone to dial your cell phone number and interrupt whatever you're doing.

But once again, you shouldn't limit your concerns simply to the fact that anyone can call your cell phone at any time.

Your wireless network is always on

Wireless home networks are awfully convenient because you can simply fire up your PC anywhere within range and connect. This convenience has its dark side, too. As long as your wireless network is working, a neighbor or a stranger driving by can conveniently try to connect to your home network. Remember, the fact that your wireless network doesn't require someone to connect using a physical network cable means it's much easier for someone you don't want on your network to gain access.

You can, of course, apply some security measures to make it harder for people to break into your wireless home network. In fact, it's not only possible, but it's also essential that you enable your wireless network's security features if you don't want to run into serious problems. See Book IV for more information on this very important topic.

Your wireless gadgets are probably open, too

Imagine how difficult it would be to keep your automobile safe if the manufacturers were in the habit of delivering cars without locks because they felt that locks were too complicated for the average driver. In most major cities you'd probably be able to measure in minutes (or hours, at the most) the time before your car was stolen.

Unfortunately, the manufacturers of many wireless devices do something similar to building cars without locks. Rather than building in advanced security features (or, as is the case with wireless home networking gear — leaving the security features turned off by default), manufacturers often opt for dumbing down their products so they work as soon as you take them out of the box. Bluetooth-equipped cell phones present an easy target for snoopers for this reason. (See Book VI for more information on Bluetooth technology and the security risks that are involved.)

In reality, the manufacturers probably are correct; so few people bother to read the technical sections of their product manuals that enabling features that increase security would result in many calls for help from new users. Or, even worse from the manufacturer's perspective, it could result in products being returned to the stores because "it doesn't work."

You can go a long way toward protecting your wireless world by taking a few minutes to understand (and use) whatever security measures are offered by your wireless devices. Remember, the harder you make it for a thief or a snoop, the more likely he'll move on and find an easier target.

Taking back control

Yes, going wireless does make life more convenient, and often a lot more fun, too. Keeping things in perspective is important, as well as making sure that the convenience isn't overshadowed by letting the wireless devices control your life rather than the other way around. You do have the ultimate weapon if you're willing to use it, and that's the on/off switch.

Chapter 2: Choosing Internet Access

In This Chapter

- **Using satellites for Internet access**
- **Microwaving without food**
- **Maximizing access with WiMax**

You probably connect to the Internet using DSL or cable modem service, both of which deliver data over fat broadband pipes. (If you're going online via a dial-up connection, I hope you're considering switching to high-speed Internet broadband access before venturing much further into this book. Faster broadband access is really a prerequisite for connecting to the Internet nowadays if you don't want to spend your time in the front of your computer waiting for things to load.)

But what if you live in an area that doesn't have either DSL or cable modem broadband service? What's a computer user to do? (Thank goodness you at least have access to Dummies books!) If you live someplace where the local telecommunications providers haven't gotten around to offering broadband service, you can always turn to at least one other option.

In many cases this option is satellite Internet access. In some areas, you might be able to subscribe to something called *fixed wireless,* which means the company broadcasts a signal directly to your home (and you back to them). Both of these options can be expensive, but they are options.

In even fewer areas, entire cities or city centers are covered by Wi-Fi access, a topic I also talk about in Book V, Chapter 5.

REMEMBER

I cover another wireless Internet technology that uses the cellular telephone network elsewhere in the book. You can find information about *cellular-based packet data networks* in Book VI, Chapter 1. In addition, some cellular carriers are launching so-called *3G* (third-generation) networks that provide mobile data services. I cover this in Book VI, Chapter 1, too.

Using Satellite Service

Just like Dish Network and DirecTV deliver television programming directly to your home, satellite Internet providers provide you with broadband access that you can use to do anything you would do on the Internet over DSL and cable modem services.

Satellite service is great for folks who are off the beaten path (or don't even have a path nearby). The service also is an alternative if you simply dislike your current DSL or cable modem provider.

Beware some downsides:

- ✦ You need a clear view to the south, as that's where the satellite is orbiting — right over the equator.
- ✦ Bad weather can slow or cut off your Internet access, just like heavy rain and snow prove a pain in the rear end to satellite TV viewers.
- ✦ Trees that grow in your satellite path are not your friends. And as I learned the hard way, don't set up service in winter, when the trees have no leaves. As soon as spring comes, those leaves are growing back and obstructing your once-great clear view to the south.

StarBand

StarBand satellite service is available throughout the entire United States (yes, even Alaska and Hawaii), Puerto Rico, and the U.S. Virgin Islands. It's a two-way, always-on broadband service similar to DSL and cable modem service. It only works with PCs, so Mac users need to look to a service that supports Mac users.

Monthly service fees start at $49.99 with new equipment and $39.99 with used equipment. A one-time equipment fee includes the satellite dish and satellite modem. An installation fee also applies, as StarBand requires that a professional install the equipment.

The company promises download speeds of up to 500 kilobits per second (kbps) for the residential service. You can pay more and get higher download speeds with the Telecommuter service (up to 750 kbps) and Small Office service (up to 1 megabit per second). The Residential Starter Plan, which is the plan that costs $39.95 with used equipment, offers download speeds of up to 250 kbps.

Table 2-1 shows StarBand prices at the time I'm writing this book. (Actually, they're constantly updated, as I sneak into your home and update the prices in this book every other month. Sorry about the cookies. The milk was expired.)

Table 2-1 Prices for StarBand's Basic Residential Service

Suggested Equipment Pricing	*Monthly Fee for 1-Year Contract*	*Monthly Fee for 2-Year Contract*	*Monthly Fee for 3-Year Contract*
$699.99	N/A	N/A	$49.99
$499.99	$69.99	$69.99 1st year	$69.99 1st year
		$59.99 2nd year	$59.99 2nd year
			$49.99 3rd year
$199.99	$99.99 1st year	$99.99 1st year	$99.99 1st year
	$69.99 thereafter	$59.99 2nd year	$59.99 2nd year
			$49.99 3rd year

Also at the time I'm writing this, StarBand was introducing a new souped-up service called StarBand 481. It has a suggested price of $699.99 for the equipment and an $89.99 monthly charge for a one-year contract. For a three-year contract, the fee drops to $79.99 in the second year and $69.99 in the third year.

TIP

This newest service gives you a higher upload speed (100 kpbs if you use something called Turbo Mode), to which you can add a static address (so you can host a Web site, for example) for $4.99 a month. The download speed is the same as the other service: up to 500 kpbs. A higher upload speed is necessary for someone who, for example, uploads a lot of photos for eBay auction listings or transmits files to others.

Traveling with connections

Now you can take your Internet connection on the road! StarBand has a service that lets you mount a satellite antenna on your RV so you can stay connected no matter where you travel in the United States. Sounds too good to be true, but it's not — once you recover from the shock of learning that the equipment will cost you six grand.

The FCC requires a professional installer to mount the self-pointing satellite dish on your RV's roof. When you're ready to connect, fire up your PC (or your Mac) and the system takes several minutes to get everything going, including automatically pointing the satellite dish in the right direction. It costs anywhere from $75 to $90 a month, depending on the length of the contract. You've got to love America.

In many cases, you cannot make a virtual private network (VPN) connection over the StarBand residential services. (Book V, Chapter 6 talks about VPNs in depth.) Other applications don't "perform efficiently" over satellite Internet services, according to StarBand. These include *voice over IP (voIP)* applications and online games that require split-second reaction times (because of a latency period between the time you send a command and when it comes back to Earth from the satellite).

How does StarBand work? A 24" × 36" satellite dish antenna is mounted on or near your home and is aimed at StarBand's satellite located 22,300 miles above the equator. (Good thing you don't pay by the mile!) Two coaxial cables connect the satellite dish to the company's satellite modem, which in turn is connected to your computer via a USB or Ethernet connection. StarBand sends and receives over the antenna, moving information back and forth to the Internet. It does this through the StarBand hub facility, which also connects to the satellite.

It won't be long before we'll have all have our own broadcast stations, transmitting our images and words via satellite to an adoring worldwide audience.

DirecWay

DirecWay, which was formerly called DirecPC, offers a satellite Internet service very similar to StarBand's. For its home package, it advertises up to 500 kpbs for both upload and download speeds, but says the upload speed could be lower during peak periods.

Fair Use Policies

Both StarBand and DirecWay employ something they call *fair use policies.* In a nutshell, the policies may limit how much bandwidth you can consume in a given time period. They're designed to keep a small number of users from monopolizing the services.

StarBand "reserves the right, and will take necessary steps, to prevent improper or excessive consumption of bandwidth used to provide the service," according to its acceptable use policy. Further, it is "your responsibility to ensure that your activity does not impose an unusually large burden on the StarBand network or otherwise negatively affect the integrity of the system." I suppose "unusually large burden" is in the eye of the beholder — in this case, StarBand's.

As for DirecWay, it maintains a "running average" fair access policy. "Fair access establishes an equitable balance in Internet access across the DirecWay services by service plan for all DirecWay customers regardless of their frequency of use or volume of traffic." It adds, "To ensure this equity, you may experience some temporary throughput limitations." In other words, if you use too much bandwidth, they may temporarily cap how much you can use in the future.

The "up to" 500 kbps speed is a little misleading, however. If you continuously download 169 kbps, the company's fair access policy kicks in; see the accompanying sidebar. So if you plan to download a lot of MP3s and other large files, you need to look at the 169 number, not the up-to 500 kbps figure.

The service provider also limits to 22 the number of concurrent Internet connections. Unlikely a problem for simple Web surfing, but once you have a Web browser, e-mail program, music download software, and other Internet applications working all at the same time, the 22 connections begin to want for more.

DirecWay has two pricing plans:

- Up-Front Purchase Plan.
  - Equipment purchase price: $599.98.
  - Service fee, $59.99 per month.
  - Term commitment: 15 months.
  - Hardware warranty: 15 months.
- Promotional Plan.
  - Activation fee: $99.99.
  - Service fee: $99.99 per month.
  - Term commitment: 15 months.
  - Equipment warranty: 30 months.

Maxing Out with WiMax

The newest term in the wireless arena is *WiMax,* which stands for world interoperability for microwave access. It's a broadband wireless service that has the capability to provide service for people who get around.

One firm predicts that by 2009 more than 7 million subscribers worldwide will be using the fixed version of WiMax (not including mobile uses). What's so great about WiMax is that it's like having ubiquitous Wi-Fi access. Whether you're in your home, in your backyard, or in your car, you would have constant Internet access.

Wi to the max

WiMax has the possibility of providing fast Internet access throughout a metropolitan area (unlike local multipoint distribution system, which I describe next). Think about cell phones and how they continue to work as you move around. You don't have to turn off your cell phone when you leave your house and then turn it on again when you get in your car, so why should you have to do that with wireless Internet access? If WiMax makes the kind of splash that pundits predict, you won't need to do that.

Right now, with laptops dominating as the main way people connect wirelessly to the Internet — via Wi-Fi — you might wonder why you'd need omnipresent Internet access. But consider that just a few years down the road, before this book is hopefully into its second edition (buy a second copy, please!), personal digital assistants will become as useful as cell phones are now (and likely will include a cell phone as a feature).

WiMax will require new access adapters in desktop and laptop computers because it's incompatible with Wi-Fi technology. Some experts are predicting that WiMax will grow faster than Wi-Fi. For instance, Intel sees WiMax capabilities for mobile phones as early as 2006, with some notebook computers getting the technology that year. By 2008, Intel expects WiMax functionality on half the world's notebooks.

Local Multipoint Distribution System (LMDS)

Until WiMax really takes off, residential and business customers who want or need their Internet access delivered wirelessly have had to settle for something called *local multipoint distribution system (LMDS)*. LMDS is a line-of-sight technology, so you need a clear view from one antenna to the other. The technology works either by providing a broadband connection from one antenna to another, or from one antenna to many others. If you have this service locally, the company installs a microwave antenna on your house and points it toward its microwave antenna, located up to five miles away.

LMDS can achieve a speed of 500 MBps each way, so it's a powerful service. However, the line-of-site requirement and equipment costs don't make it a service likely to bust out of a niche.

Book II

Planning Your Network

The 5th Wave By Rich Tennant

Contents at a Glance

Chapter 1: Putting Together a Wireless Network 25
Chapter 2: Choosing Hardware Made Easy 35
Chapter 3: Setting Up Routers 47
Chapter 4: Setting Up Other Hardware 61
Chapter 5: Decoding DHCP 73
Chapter 6: Installing an Adapter on Your PC 85
Chapter 7: Adapter-ing 103
Chapter 8: Troubleshooting Network Hardware 127

Chapter 1: Putting Together a Wireless Network

In This Chapter

- **Determining your wireless network needs**
- **Figuring out your network's required range**
- **Sorting out interference issues**
- **Determining hardware costs**

Ask around and you find that from butchers to bakers to candlestick makers, more and more people are setting up networks in their homes. Some are doing it to share a high-speed Internet connection between two or more computers, while others are looking for a way to challenge family members to a round of the latest multi-player game. What makes things really interesting is that people are connecting their networks without actually connecting them at all. In a world without wires, to air is not only human, but also pretty darn cool.

Unless you're terribly fond of drilling holes and fishing cables through walls and floors, a wireless network is the way to go. It spares friends and family members the need to navigate over ugly blue Ethernet cables (running smack through your living room), while turning your whole house into a giant Internet-ready hotspot. With the proper gear in place, any suitably equipped PC, laptop, or PDA can connect to your wireless network from the kitchen or bathroom, and maybe even from the picnic table in the back yard.

While going wireless typically makes the job of installing a network much easier, wireless networks are not without issues of their own. Instead of formulating a battle plan for dealing with a mess of wires, you need to think about things like signal barriers (concrete walls) and potential sources of interference (cordless phones). Believe it or not, even your microwave oven can get in on the act and cook up an issue or two!

With that in mind, what you need is a plan. As luck would have it, this book is designed to help you through all the dirty details of planning for and then setting up a wireless network of your very own. Take some time to get your ducks in a row before you start, and your wireless network may just end up the envy of the neighborhood.

Who said air was just for breathing?

Figuring Out Your Hopes and Dreams

Seeing as you're thinking about setting up a home network, start giving some thought to what you hope to accomplish. Setting up a network for the fun of it is, ahem, *fun,* but you should have some practical goals in mind as well.

The decision to set up a network almost always has something to do with sharing. Don't worry; I'm not talking about sharing in the half-of-your-peanut-butter-and-jelly-sandwich kind of way. Moving away from food for a moment, I'm talking about sharing computer stuff. The kind where you take a resource and make it available to more than one user simultaneously. In fact, it doesn't even matter whether you're talking about a wired network or a wireless one.

Being able to share the following things are the most common reasons for setting up any type of network at home:

- **Internet access.** Sharing Internet access, and especially a high-speed connection, is probably the most common reason for setting up a home network. Cable or DSL connections have plenty of bandwidth, allowing more than one user to surf at the same time without issue.
- **Printers.** Buying a printer to attach to each PC in your home can get pricey in a hurry. Why buy four printers when all you really need is one? Once a printer is shared on your network, any user will be able to print their files without issue.
- **Files.** Back in the Pre-Cambrian period, people used to exchange files using flat plastic squares known as floppy disks. With a network, users can exchange or share files from any PC.
- **Games and programs.** If you're into gaming, a network allows you to enjoy multi-player games with friends and family members, not to mention other people on the Internet.

Of course, you may not be interested in sharing with anyone. The network may be for you and you alone. That works too, in a configuration I like to call "the network of one." When you implement the network of one, your goal is usually mobility or convenience. If you have a wireless network and a laptop, you have the freedom to plunk yourself down just about anywhere and surf away to your heart's content. No more need to worry about dragging 25 yards of cable following you around, either. Sweet.

Going wireless has additional benefits:

- **Mobility and convenience.** Laptops or PDAs equipped with a wireless network card provide access to your network and the Internet from any location within range. Tired of working at your desk? Head out to the deck with your laptop and work from there instead!
- **Reducing clutter.** With a traditional wired network, every computer is physically connected to the network. When you need to connect PCs at opposite ends of your home, you need to run the appropriate cables. Not so with wireless, where being disconnected is part of the deal.
- **Easy expansion.** Adding computers to a wired network means drilling more holes and running more cable. In contrast, computers can be added to a wireless network instantly by installing a wireless network adapter card — no fuss, no muss.

When all is said and done, the benefits of going wireless are hard to beat. That's not to say that potential issues don't exist. In particular, you need to think about the outer limits of your network and possible obstacles in your path.

Reaching Clear Across the Household

In a perfect world, the maximum distance your wireless network could span would never be an issue. In the real world, however, wireless networks are subject to range limitations. This has a great deal to do with the technical details of the radio frequencies involved, but I spare you the physics lesson for now. The biggest issue to be concerned with is whether your wireless network will work from one end of your house to the other if need be.

REMEMBER

As a general rule, the closer your PCs with wireless network adapters are to your wireless *router* or *access point* (the devices that act like wireless hubs), the better they perform. Wireless networks tend to have an effective indoor range of anywhere between 100 and 150 feet depending upon the wireless standard in use. Keep in mind that this represents the maximum distance between any single PC and an access point. If you need to span much longer distances, you probably need to add a wireless range extender to your network.

The biggest factor influencing your network's potential range is the wireless standard you choose to go with. Wireless networks fall into the Institute of Electronic and Electrical Engineers (IEEE) 802.11 standard. As such, you find wireless networking equipment designated as 802.11*something*. That something will be the letter a, b, or g.

You read more about the 802.11 wireless networking standards in Book II, Chapter 2. For now, it's enough to be familiar with the distance limitations associated with each, as outlined in Table 1-1.

Table 1-1 Comparing 802.11a, -b, and -g

	802.11a	*802.11b*	*802.11g*
Indoor Range	100 feet	150 feet	150 feet
Frequency	5 GHz	2.4 GHz	2.4 GHz

Using Table 1-1 as a reference, you could safely say that going with 802.11b would easily meet your distance requirements if you needed to span 120 feet, right? Unfortunately not. While the ranges associated with a wireless networking standard are standard, other factors require consideration. In some cases, a wireless PC using 802.11b has no trouble contacting an access point 170 feet away. At the same time, another device may be unable to connect from only 90 feet away. Asking "What gives?" right now would be a great question with excellent timing.

The answer, in a nutshell, is twofold. First, not all wireless networking equipment is created equal; some devices are more powerful, while others are better engineered. Second, I haven't really touched on the bane of wireless networks — the evil duo of obstacles and interference.

Checking for Obstacles and Interference

Take away potential obstacles and sources of interference and most wireless devices are capable of reaching distances of almost double what you can expect indoors. Unfortunately, any home is usually a smorgasbord of both obstacles and interference. You do better trying to work around these issues than through them. Your family probably wouldn't be happy to find exterior walls missing on account of your wireless network problems.

REMEMBER

When it comes to a wireless signal's range, the most common and problematic obstacles encountered include just about anything heavy and solid. For example, trying to send radio waves through a solid concrete wall is troublesome. Wood, on the other hand, is more porous and presents less of an issue. Your wireless network most often needs to contend with these obstacles:

- **Solid concrete and brick walls.** Anything that's very heavy and solid presents a hearty barrier to wireless network signals. Seeing as you can't usually knock them down (at least without a great deal of effort), you want to concentrate on working around them.
- **Steel anything.** Expect issues any time you position wireless networking equipment next to lots of metal. That means your furnace, steel beams, and so forth.
- **Believe it or not, windows.** No, not the operating system, but rather the ones that let sun in and keep the rain out. Glass does present a minor obstacle, but usually isn't a very big issue.

Once you're done figuring a way through the maze of obstacles, you need to sort sources of interference. Wireless networks are susceptible to electromagnetic interference like any electrical device, but particularly those that work in the same frequency range. For example, some of the common culprits follow:

- **Cordless phones.** In particular, 2.4-GHz cordless phones that work in the same frequency range as both 802.11b and 802.11g devices. If you plan to install a wireless network based on either of these standards, you might want to consider using a 900-MHz cordless phone model.
- **Microwave ovens.** It might seem surprising, but most microwaves work in the 2.4-GHz range as well. All this means is that you might run into connectivity issues if you're trying to surf and nuke at the same time. Keeping your laptop or PDA away from your running microwave should solve the issue.
- **Any other 2.4-GHz devices.** A host of consumer electronics devices ranging from wireless speakers to wireless cable TV transmitters use the 2.4-GHz frequency range. If you use these types of devices regularly, you can expect to run into interference issues.

Most wireless networking equipment is designed to contend with interference issues, so the end result is typically a short loss of connectivity or degraded signal. Eliminating these sources of interference is generally your best bet in gaining better network performance.

You now have the lowdown on the potential communication issues your wireless network is up against. Now I'd like to have a chat about your money.

Totaling Up the Damage

One trillion dollars! Okay, not really. (I had you for a second, though.) Actually, when it comes to setting up a wireless network, your timing couldn't be better.

Only a few short years ago you could easily have spent close to a thousand dollars on the hardware required to set up a simple wireless network in your home. Thankfully, mass production and economies of scale have brought the prices of wireless networking gear to a level that can meet just about anyone's budget.

It's hard to guess how much the equipment for your wireless network will cost. In the same way that you can purchase one new car for $12,000 while another costs $100,000, the same is true of wireless networking equipment. Some manufacturers offer bare-bones hardware with more limited features and a shorter warranty, while others offer you everything but the kitchen sink. This doesn't mean that you actually need every "extra." As you read through this book you get a better idea of the most important features to consider.

Wireless network equipment does have some common price ranges:

- **Wireless routers.** A *wireless router* is an all-in-one device that acts as a hub for your wireless PCs and a broadband router for your Internet connection, as shown in Figure 1-1. A wireless router typically sets you back anywhere from $30 to $120.

Figure 1-1: A wireless router.

- **Wireless access points.** If you already have a wired broadband router, you can use a wireless *access point* to act as a hub for your wireless PCs. Wireless access points typically cost about the same as a wireless router.
- **Wireless network adapters for desktop PC.** Adding wireless capabilities to a desktop PC involves installing a wireless *peripheral component interconnect (PCI)* adapter like the one shown in Figure 1-2. A PCI adapter is designed to connect to an unused PCI slot in your PC; you usually find at least one and often many more "empty" PCI slots on a computer's motherboard. PCI adapters typically cost in the ballpark of $35.
- **Wireless network adapter for laptops.** The most common setup for a laptop means installing a wireless PC card like that shown in Figure 1-3. These network adapters usually run you between $40 and $80. Alternatively, newer laptops support adding wireless capabilities by installing what is known as a *mini-PCI adapter,* a small internal circuit-board type card installed into a covered expansion bay on the bottom of a laptop. Prices of these vary greatly, from as low as $40 to as high as $200. If you're lucky, your laptop may already have one built in.

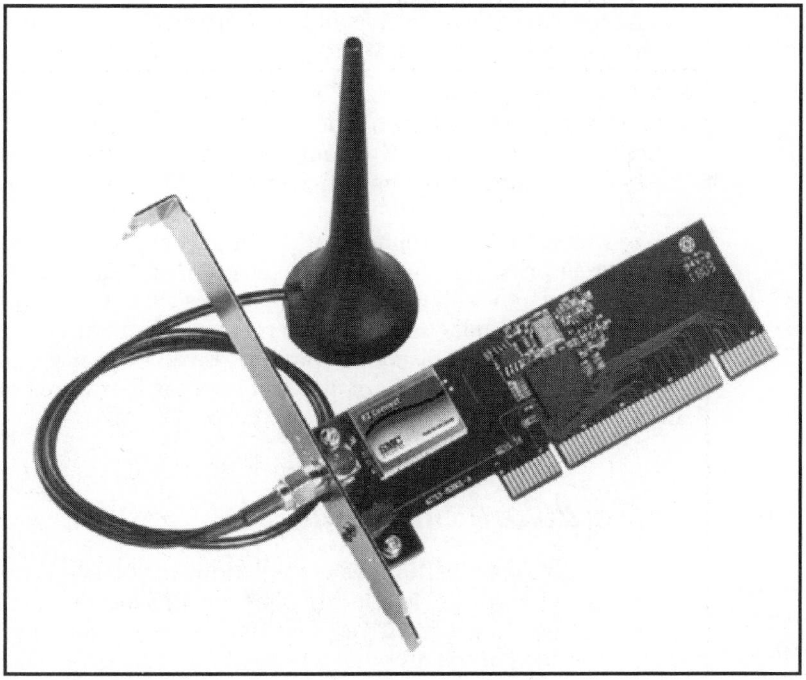

Figure 1-2: A wireless PCI adapter.

Figure 1-3: A wireless PC card.

- **USB wireless network adapters.** Another alternative for adding wireless networking to a desktop PC or laptop is to use a USB wireless network adapter. These devices plug into an available USB port on your PC and typically cost between $20 and $40.
- **Wireless range extenders.** These devices are only necessary if the distance your wireless network needs to span is greater than the capabilities of your wireless network adapter and access point allow. Expect to pay somewhere in the, um, range of $80 to $120 for these devices.

TIP

If you're willing to shop around a little, all the gear you need can certainly be had at a great price. Besides your local electronics retailer, be sure to check prices with different online stores and auctions sites. While you're at it, keep an eye open for manufacturer's mail-in rebates. Competition between wireless vendors is stiff and discounts via rebates can be pretty significant. You read more about the specifics of different wireless hardware devices in Book II, Chapter 2.

Creating a Hardware Shopping List

Now that you've got a better idea of the hardware you need and some of the potential issues involved, it's time to start creating a shopping list. You're not quite ready to complete it yet; save that for after Chapter 2, when you have a better idea of exactly what you need with respect to specifications and so forth.

For now, draw up a list of the devices you know you need:

- One wireless router or a wireless access point (if you want to continue using a router that you already have). I strongly suggest the wireless router, as it makes things less cluttered and easier to manage in the long run.
- One wireless network adapter for every computer that will be part of your wireless network. That usually means one PC card (or mini-PCI card) for laptops and either a PCI or USB wireless adapter for all desktop systems.

Do your best to resist the urge to run out and purchase your equipment right away. Remember that information is power. You get all the details you need to make the best decision very soon. If you just can't resist the urge to buy something immediately, head out and buy some carrots. Granted, they have nothing to do with wireless networking, but they *are* tasty *and* good for you.

Chapter 2: Choosing Hardware Made Easy

In This Chapter

- Selecting a wireless networking standard
- Working with a broadband modem
- Picking a wireless router
- Selecting hardware for better range

It's time to get down to the business of choosing your wireless hardware. I'm not going to endorse any particular manufacturer's equipment since "quality" has a lot to do with specific device models, their features, and your home environment. Instead, I concentrate on helping you through the various wireless networking standards and issues like choosing an appropriate broadband modem and wireless router. As an added bonus, I even disclose the secret codes that extend the range of your wireless devices!

Okay, you got me again. There are no secret codes. There *is* a trick, though. Leaving the details until the end of this chapter is my way of adding a little more suspense to an already riveting tale.

Choosing the Wares Is Not Hard

Once you've made the decision to go wireless, you need to decide which standard to follow. Back in the old days (about 4 years ago), all wireless networking equipment followed the same standard. Today, you need to decide whether you prefer the letter A, B, or G when choosing your wireless network cards or router.

REMEMBER

Wireless networking devices fall into the IEEE 802.11 standards. When you're out there comparing equipment, you see devices marked 802.11b, 802.11g, and 802.11a. Those little trailing letters are important, as they dictate not only the maximum speeds and distances possible, but also their level of interoperability.

For example, 802.11b equipment is compatible with 802.11g, but not 802.11a. Getting a great deal on an 802.11b network card does you no good if you've snagged an 802.11a wireless router. As such, you need to pay attention to the standards. If you want to keep things simple, stick with the same standard for all your equipment. Table 2-1 provides an overview of the major elements of each 802.11 standard.

Table 2-1 Comparing FRS and GMRS

	802.11a	*802.11b*	*802.11g*
Indoor Range	80–100 feet	150 feet	150 feet
Frequency	5 GHz	2.4 GHz	2.4 GHz
Speed	54 Mbps	11 Mbps	54 Mbps
Compatibility	802.11a networks only	802.11b and 802.11g networks	802.11b and 802.11g networks

It's also worth noting that all of your equipment doesn't need to come from the same vendor. An 802.11b wireless network adapter card from producer SMC works with an 802.11b wireless router from Linksys without issue. As long as you stick with compatible standards, you should never run into major interoperability issues.

The following sections outline each of the 802.11 standards in more detail.

802.11a

When it first arrived on the wireless scene, 802.11a was touted as the next BIG thing. Capable of running at speeds up to 54 Mbps, it far outpaced the maximum possible speeds associated with 802.11b networks. Furthermore, because 802.11a devices work in the 5-GHz frequency range, they weren't subject to the interference issues associated with 802.11b equipment.

Unfortunately, the higher speeds of 802.11a gear came with a cost — namely shorter range. Where 802.11b or -g networks support a range of around 150 feet, 802.11a networks can span just slightly more than half that distance. The 802.11a standard also lacks backwards compatibility with 802.11b, which at the time forced people to go with one standard or the other.

TIP

Today, 802.11a equipment is most commonly used on corporate networks. Home users would do well to avoid this standard, except in cases where interference in the 2.4-GHz range is a serious issue.

802.11b

Even though it's the slowest of the three standards, 802.11b was the first on the scene and remains the most widely deployed wireless networking standard. 802.11b equipment works in the 2.4-GHz frequency range and can span a maximum distance of up to 150 feet indoors. On the speed front, 802.11 tops out at 11 Mbps.

Because 802.11b devices work in the 2.4-GHz range, they're subject to interference issues from everything from cordless phones to wireless speakers. In most cases, these interference issues are intermittent, but in some cases they can bring your network to a standstill.

If you're looking for a way to implement your wireless network with the least expense possible, 802.11b is the way to go. 802.11b wireless routers and network adapter cards can usually be had for a song, although it largely depends on how good a singer you are.

802.11g

If it's a combination of speed and flexibility that you're after, the best wireless standard to follow is 802.11g. Not only is 802.11g equipment fast at 54 Mbps, but it's also fully *backwards compatible* with the 802.11b standard. That means that your 802.11g wireless network adapter can work on an 802.11b network, or that your 802.11g wireless router can support clients with 802.11b cards.

802.11g is a great choice for home networks at almost five times faster than 802.11b. However, because it also works in the same 2.4-GHz frequency range, it may be subject to interference issues with equipment like 2.4-GHz cordless phones. Like 802.11b, 802.11g equipment has a maximum indoor range of around 150 feet.

At the end of the day, 802.11g equipment offers you the best bang for your buck. Not only is it compatible with the vast majority of wireless networks, but it's also less expensive than the 802.11a alternative.

Multi-standard devices

Most of the wireless networking equipment that you come across support one of the 802.11a, -b, or -g standards. However, many vendors now offer models that incorporate all of the standards in a single device. For example, the SMC EZ-Stream wireless network adapter shown in Figure 2-1 is just one example of a device that supports 802.11a and -g (and by extension, 802.11b).

Figure 2-1: A wireless network adapter that supports 802.11a, -b, and -g.

As a general rule, wireless network adapter cards, routers, and access points that support all three 802.11 standards are more expensive. However, if you regularly need to move your laptop or PDA between networks that use different standards, the investment may be well worth it. At a minimum, it saves you the hassle of constantly switching network adapters.

Starting with DSL or Cable Modem

Sharing a high-speed Internet connection is usually the top reason people consider installing a network at home. In most cases, the service they want to share is cable or *digital subscriber line (DSL)* Internet. Both cable and DSL services are readily available in metropolitan areas, and increasingly in rural locations as well. It's hard to deny the benefits of going with a broadband (the fancy generic name for high-speed) connection, especially when compared to the relative snail's pace of dial-up.

While dial-up connections may be much slower, they tend to be available and accessible to everyone. All you need is a regular phone line, a traditional modem, and a dial-up account with an *Internet service provider (ISP)* to be ready to go. You can even share a dial-up Internet connection over a home network using techniques like the Windows XP Internet Connection Sharing feature. That's not to say that sharing a dial-up connection is either fast or fun, just that it's possible.

If your plan is to share an Internet connection, cable or DSL is the way to go. Whether the service is available in your area is another story completely. Chances are good that if you have cable TV service running to your house, cable Internet service is available. If your area doesn't have access to cable TV, then you can pretty much eliminate cable Internet as an option.

DSL service, on the other hand, works over your existing phone lines. Unfortunately, DSL service is subject to distance limitations and tends to be unavailable in rural areas. If you're in a larger city or town, however, chances are good that a local provider (or your telephone company) offers the service.

Of course, you may be lucky enough to live in an area where you have access to both cable and DSL Internet. Sweet! If this is the case, you can at least comparison shop to determine who offers the best deal. In most cases, the monthly rate offered by the provider includes both service fees and rental of a broadband modem similar to the one shown in Figure 2-2.

Figure 2-2: A broadband cable modem.

Now, here's where things get tricky. In some cases, the ISP lets you choose whether you want to rent the modem or purchase your own. In others, they don't give you a choice at all — you need to use their modem, end of story. Unfortunately, working with broadband modems isn't as simple as traditional modems. Different service providers follow different standards, so a broadband modem that works with one cable or DSL service may not work with another.

Of course, that makes it difficult for you to just pop out and purchase your own modem. Over the long term, you save a great deal of money by purchasing rather than renting if you have the option. However, this also depends on how long you plan to stay with the provider. A rental modem is simply returned if you cancel your service. A modem you own sits in your closet and gets dusty if you decide to switch. Do the math to figure out which option works best for you.

You can expect to pay anywhere between $50 and $200 for a broadband modem. The key is finding out from your ISP whether you're allowed to supply your own modem, and if so, what makes or models are supported. Once they supply you with a list, be sure to check some of the popular online auction sites for good deals on used models. With a little searching you can often pick up a modem that will work with your service for a fraction of its original price.

Modem Options

Cable and DSL modems tend to come in three different varieties. The first (and most common) is in a housing that makes it look much like a hub or a traditional external modem. They have one port that connects to the cable or DSL service, and then a second wired Ethernet port. The Ethernet port connects to your PC or a router on your network.

The second type of modem that you come across includes a USB port rather than an Ethernet port. These devices plug directly into an available USB port on your PC. While they get the job done, these modems are typically used with a single PC, although some newer broadband routers also provide built-in USB ports. (Book I, Chapter 2 tells you more about Ethernet and USB.)

The last model you may encounter are internal modems meant to be installed inside your PC. These types are generally least popular, because they're more work to connect and much easier to damage.

If your ISP is supplying the broadband cable modem and gives you a choice between an external and USB model, go external. Same deal if you plan to purchase your own modem. These models provide the greatest degree of flexibility and can connect to just about any broadband router, wireless or otherwise. Choosing a USB modem means greatly narrowing possible router alternatives.

Routing Through the Router

Once you have your broadband modem sorted, start thinking about a wireless router. In a nutshell, the *router's* job is to act as an access point for wireless client systems on your network, while at the same time functioning as the intermediary between your home network and the big, bad Internet.

Now, before getting too deep into all this router business, it's worth noting that you don't necessarily need a wireless router. If you already have a wired broadband router in your possession, you could add a plain old access point to your network, similar to the one shown in Figure 2-3. However, you're going to pay close to the same amount for a wireless router as you would for an access point. With that in mind, picking up the wireless router usually makes more sense. It does more stuff, and dealing with only one device helps reduce clutter.

Figure 2-3: A wireless access point.

When you're out shopping for a wireless router, take care to ensure that it's a router in your hands rather than an access point. Wireless routers and access points from the same vendor often look deceivingly similar.

Assuming that you're going to take my advice, it's worth knowing what a router actually does before you run out and buy one. It's also important to be familiar with different wireless router features to be sure that the model you select has everything you'll need.

So what exactly does a wireless router do? A little bit of everything, of course! The router part's primary job is to handle requests bound for the Internet on behalf of computers on your network. In other words, servers on the Internet think requests have originated from your router and know nothing of your home network. The wireless part acts as a hub for your wireless systems, allowing them to communicate with each other and ultimately access the Internet.

Beyond these critical functions, wireless routers typically include a whole range of standard and added-value features. Some of these key features are pretty much standard on any wireless router:

- **A firewall.** It's a safe bet that any router you pick up includes a built-in firewall to keep the bad guys out of your home network. However, not all firewalls are created equal. If possible, look for a model that includes a *stateful* firewall, as they offer a higher degree of protection.
- **A built-in DHCP server.** Another feature standard in pretty much all router models is a built-in DHCP server component that's responsible for allocating IP addresses to clients on your network. Book II, Chapter 5 has more on DHCP.
- **Web-based management.** Rather than require you to install a separate management program, routers are almost always configured via a web browser.

Going a step further, you may want to take a closer look at some of the cool bells and whistles included with certain wireless routers:

- **Integrated Ethernet ports.** If your home network will ultimately include both wired and wireless computers, look for a wireless router that offers a built-in four-port Ethernet switch. This saves you the trouble of needing to purchase a separate hub or switch for wired systems.

- **Built-in print server.** Newer wireless router models often include a built-in print server component that allows you to plug your printer into a USB port on the router. This easy and effective option makes your printer part of your wireless network.
- **Detachable antennae.** Just in case, look for a model that includes detachable antennae. Most wireless routers include antennae that attach to the unit using what are known as *reverse SMA plugs*. If you ever need to add a larger antenna to deal with distance issues, you can simply unscrew the old ones and plug in the new.
- **Sleek design.** It doesn't really matter what your wireless router looks like, but a sharp design is always cool and makes for a better conversation piece. You *do* want your friends to be impressed, don't you?

REMEMBER

Once you're done browsing through the cool section, be sure that the wireless router you choose includes support for each of the following:

- **MAC security.** Short for *Media Access Control.* Almost all wireless routers include this feature, which basically allows you to control exactly which wireless systems are allowed to connect to your network. MAC security takes advantage of the fact that every network adapter card has a MAC (hardware) address that uniquely identifies it.
- **WEP support.** Short for *Wired Equivalent Privacy,* this older wireless encryption protocol is supported by almost all wireless devices. I'd be surprised if you could find a wireless router that doesn't support WEP.
- **WPA support.** Short for *Wi-Fi Protected Access,* WPA is a newer and much more secure wireless encryption protocol. You may find support for WPA hit and miss, but you definitely want it. If you find a wireless router that lacks WPA support, you may be able to add it via a firmware upgrade.
- **Ability to upgrade firmware.** No excuses here — you definitely want a wireless router that supports firmware upgrades. A router's firmware is like its operating system. Upgrading firmware typically adds support for new features (like WPA), patches any security holes that may have been discovered, and ultimately helps protect your investment longer term. If support for firmware upgrades isn't listed on the router's packaging, check for details on the vendor's web site.

Before you lose sleep worrying about what wireless router to choose, let me put your mind at ease. Any new wireless router that you purchase is almost certain to include all of the features listed here, along with another million more. When in doubt, the back of the product package (or the vendor's web site) will surely provide the answers you seek. Go forth and route!

Pointing Toward Areas That Need Coverage

Remember those secret range-extending codes I mentioned? Right. They may not exist, but you can help extend the range of your wireless network. Sometimes the distance your wireless network needs to span is simply too great, or signals just can't reach a particular area of your house. If this happens to you, it's time to find a creative solution.

First and foremost, carefully consider where to locate your wireless router. You want it to be as close as possible to all of your wireless devices to minimize distance, obstructions, and interference issues. If necessary, try moving your wireless router to different locations in your home and then check your wireless signal strength on all PCs. (Book III, Chapter 5 tells you how.) There's really no better method that trial and error here, and no super-secret technique that I can bestow upon you.

Once you've found what appears to be the most suitable location for your wireless router, you may still encounter what are known as *dead spots.* Some areas in your home just can't gain access to your wireless network for any of a myriad of possible reasons. It might be that you never need wireless access from these locations and it isn't an issue. However, if you do, a couple of potential solutions exist:

- **Add a range extender.** A range extender is typically a small powered device that acts as a type of wireless repeater. It helps propagate wireless signals from between your wireless PC and router by giving them a boost along the way. Unfortunately, range extenders aren't cheap and typically cost between $60 and $120. However, adding them to your wireless network is typically as simple as plugging them in — no configuration required.
- **Play with your antennae.** No, not the ones on your TV, but rather those on your wireless router or network cards. The antennae on a wireless router can usually be adjusted to point in different directions, so try that first. If your wireless network adapter cards include external antennae, try giving them a whirl as well.
- **Add a bigger antenna.** In cases where the distances you want to span are simply beyond the reach of the wireless standard in use, adding or changing the antennae on your wireless gear often does the trick. Many

wireless devices include a small adjustable external antenna that can be screwed on or off. The antenna connectors (reverse SMA plugs) allow you to attach larger antennae if necessary, which in turn can extend your wireless network's range.

For example, adding a larger omnidirectional antenna like the one shown in Figure 2-4 to your wireless router can extend its range by an additional 50 percent. Along the same lines, you could add a directional antenna like the one shown in Figure 2-5 to extend your signal in a more focused manner. Whether you're looking for a way to get your wireless working in the back yard or a dead spot, a larger or more powerful antenna is often your best bet. Expect more powerful add-on antennae to set you back anywhere from $20 to $45.

As a general rule, hold off purchasing any device to extend your network's range until you're sure you need it. Most wireless networking equipment is pretty capable right out of the box. Placement of your wireless devices is generally the key, and a little time spent testing is time well spent.

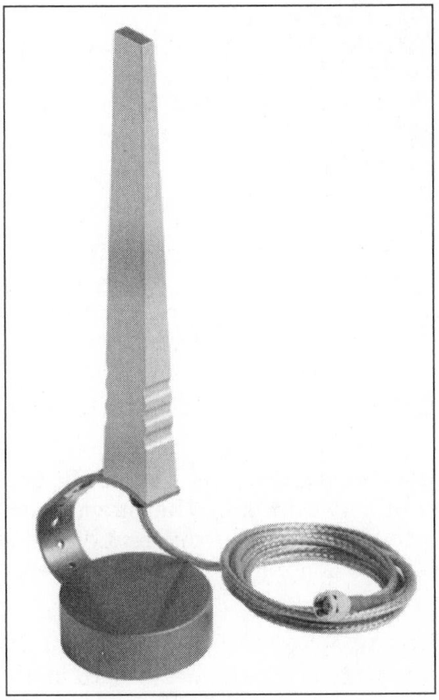

Figure 2-4: An omnidirectional antenna.

Figure 2-5: A directional antenna.

Chapter 3: Setting Up Routers

In This Chapter

- **Assembling your router**
- **Connecting the router to your network**
- **Configuring router settings**
- **Cloning your hardware address**

So you're sitting there staring at your wireless router's shiny new box. The packaging tells you it does everything short of cooking your dinner, and probably includes a whole slew of pretty pictures and diagrams. Ah, the excitement!

Before you get too worked up, you should note that most wireless routers require some assembly (no tools, thankfully), a little connecting, and at least minimal configuration. The good news is that none of the steps involved are particularly difficult. In fact, by the end of this chapter you'll probably be surprised at how easy it is getting a wireless router set up. You shouldn't actually tell anyone that, though. Your wireless setup will seem much more impressive if everyone thinks you're a networking super genius!

Some Assembly Required

Every time I purchase a new piece of computer hardware, I can't help feeling like it's my birthday. So the wrapping might not be as exciting (and I usually resist the urge to shake the box), but it's still like opening a present. Without further ado, go ahead release the hounds! In the absence of hounds, opening the router's box will suffice.

You should find these goodies inside the box:

- ✦ The wireless router
- ✦ Two detachable antennae, currently detached
- ✦ One 3-foot length of Ethernet cable
- ✦ A power supply cord for the router
- ✦ A user manual and a CD or floppy disk
- ✦ Other bits and pieces required for your model

Before you start connecting things, take a moment to confirm that everything that's supposed to be supplied with your wireless router has been. In most cases you find a listing of what you should have in the router's user manual. If anything is missing, you need to either pack everything up to exchange it or call the vendor to have them send you that part.

With all the necessary bits in hand, you're ready to start assembling your router, and connecting it to your modem:

1. **Attach the two supplied antennae to the back of the unit.**

   These usually just screw on to the SMA connectors at either end of the back of the device, as shown in Figure 3-1. Once attached, both antennae should be pointing sky high.

2. **Connect one end of the supplied Ethernet cable to the WAN port on the back of your router.**

   The port should be clearly marked and separate from any other Ethernet-type ports that your model includes. An example is shown in Figure 3-2.

Figure 3-1: Connecting antennae to a wireless router.

Figure 3-2: Connecting the Ethernet cable to your router's WAN port.

3. **Plug the other end into the back of your cable or DSL modem.**
4. **Connect the router's power cable and plug it into a wall outlet or power strip.**

   If your network includes wired computers as well, now's the time to connect them. Assuming that your wireless router includes built-in wired switch ports, connect Ethernet cables to the network card on each computer and then to an available port on the switch. Physically speaking, you're done. The network connections are complete!

In truth, you may only need to make one physical connection — the one between your wireless router and broadband modem. You can't just leave that Ethernet cable connected to your wireless router hanging, so make sure you plug the other end into the back of your cable or DSL modem. Most broadband modems include only a single Ethernet port (usually marked LAN, Network, or Ethernet), so finding the right one shouldn't be too hard. Once complete, your router and modem will be forever connected (cosmically, at least), as shown in Figure 3-3.

Figure 3-3: Connecting a wireless router to a broadband modem.

TIP

In the best-case scenario, your modem and wireless router are close to one another and the 3-foot cable included with your router is long enough. However, if these devices are farther than 3 feet apart, you need to get your hands on a longer Ethernet cable that spans the distance between the devices. You can pick up a new Ethernet cable at just about any computer retailer.

Once your router and broadband modem are connected, at least a couple of the LED lights on the front of your router should be lit. At an absolute minimum, the PWR (power) LED should be solid green. If your broadband modem is also powered up, then the Link or Act (Activity) light for the router's WAN port should be blinking (at least intermittently) as well.

Fiddling with the Innards

If you already have a wireless network adapter card correctly installed in your PC or laptop, you should see a message stating that a new wireless network has been found in the Windows XP taskbar. Once this message appears, select the option to connect to the new network. If you don't have a wireless network adapter card installed yet, you must get to that before you can configure your router. The installation of adapters is covered in Book II, Chapter 6, while adapter configuration is outlined in Book II, Chapter 7.

TIP

If you don't have any wireless network adapter cards installed yet and your wireless router includes built-in Ethernet switch ports, you can use a wired connection to connect to and configure the router.

With a network connection in place, it's time to get down to the business of router configuration. In almost all cases, you configure your router from a web browser. The steps listed here are the first on your router configuration adventure, with more steps to follow as the chapter progresses.

1. **To get at your router's management or configuration interface, you need its factory-configured IP address.**

   The easiest way to find this address is to check the user manual that shipped with the router, as it varies between devices and manufacturers. In most cases this address will be 192.168.*something*.1, but it could be different for your model.

2. **Fire up Internet Explorer or your favorite web browser and type the address in the format** http://192.168.2.1.

3. **After pressing the Enter key, you should be presented with your router's login screen, similar to the one shown in Figure 3-4.**

   You won't get far at your router's login screen without the required password. All wireless routers ship with a default administrative password used to access their management interface.

4. **Head back to the user manual supplied with your router to determine the password for your model.**

   TIP

   If you've purchased a used wireless router, the default password may have been changed. If the default password doesn't work, use a paperclip to hold down the Reset button on the back of the router according to the instructions in the router's user manual. This restores the router to its original factory settings, including its original password.

5. **Enter the password for your router and click the Login button.**

   You are presented with the router's configuration interface in all its glory, as shown in Figure 3-5. The screen shown is for an SMC wireless router, and you can expect the interface to be different for models from other vendors. You've completed the first step in configuring your router.

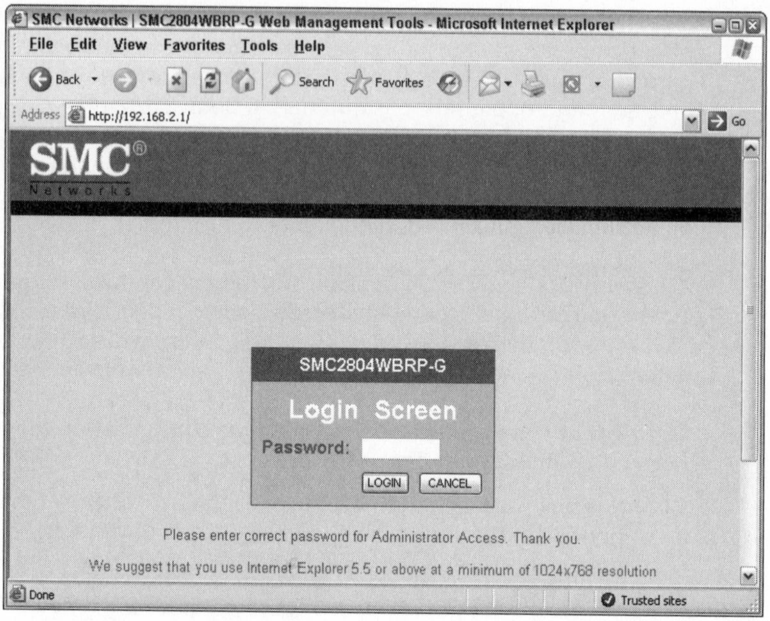

Figure 3-4: The login screen for a router's management interface.

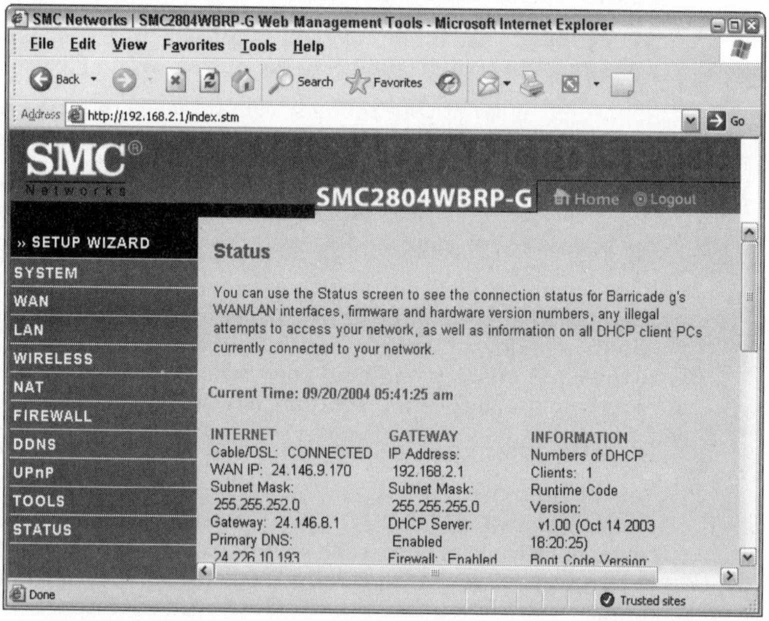

Figure 3-5: The management interface for an SMC wireless router.

Having successfully entered your router's management interface, it's time to get to the business of basic configuration tasks. These key elements need to be configured at this point:

- ✦ A new password
- ✦ The router's date, time, and time zone
- ✦ Settings for your Internet connection
- ✦ The router's MAC address (maybe)
- ✦ A name for your wireless network

I won't just leave you hanging; the following sections outline each of these areas in more detail.

A password of your own

WARNING!

After connecting to your router's management interface for the first time, you should make changing its default password a priority. Not only will configuring a personal password make it easier to remember, but it will also greatly improve the security of your wireless router. If you leave the password as it stands, any user within range can potentially connect to your router, log on to the management interface, and change settings at will — not a happy thought.

To change your router's password, look for a section in the management interface called Password, System, or similar. Changing the password should be as simple as entering the current password once and the new password twice, as shown in Figure 3-6.

TECHNICAL STUFF

Many models allow you to specify a *timeout value.* This number controls how long the management interface can sit idle before you are required to log on again. In other words, after this idle time has passed you are logged out automatically.

Remember that a good password is one that's easy for you to remember, but hard for others to guess. As a general rule, pick a password that's at least eight characters long and includes a combination of letters, numbers, and special symbols. For example, "MoTheR~81" would be a better or stronger password than "mother".

Of course, the more complex your password, the more likely you are to forget it when you need it. If you ever forget your router's password, keep in mind that you always have the option of using the Reset button on the back of your router to restore factory settings, including the original default password. However, pressing the Reset button also erases any other settings that you may have configured.

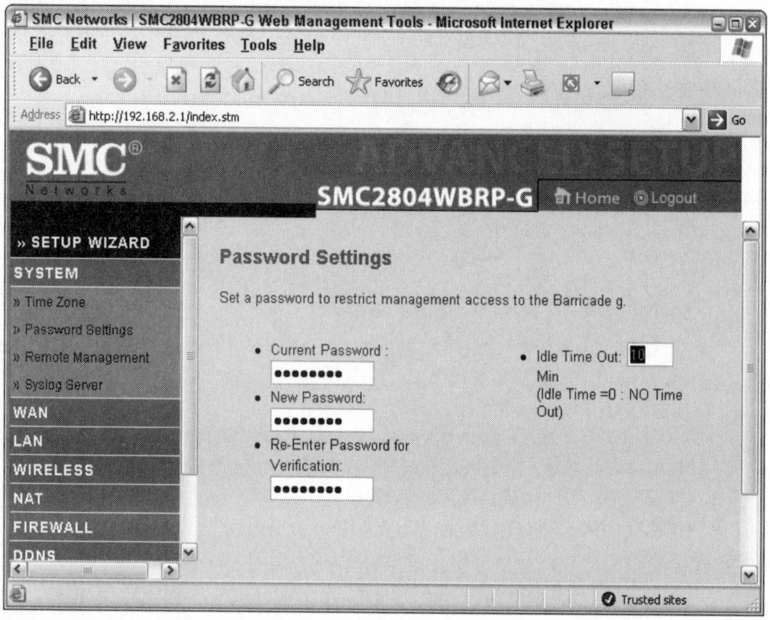

Figure 3-6: Changing the router's password.

Just like clockwork

While not as critical as changing its password, it's still a good idea to set your router's date, time, and time zone information correctly. This ensures that any information logged by the router has a correct time and date associated with it, which ends up being useful should you need to do any troubleshooting or investigative work down the line. Plus, what good is a clock that tells the wrong time?

Changing your router's date and time is usually accomplished from a section marked Time Zone or Settings. To help keep things accurate, all you usually need to do is specify your time zone and let the router do the rest. As shown in Figure 3-7, the router automatically contacts time servers on the Internet to ensure its clock is synchronized and correct. It's that easy!

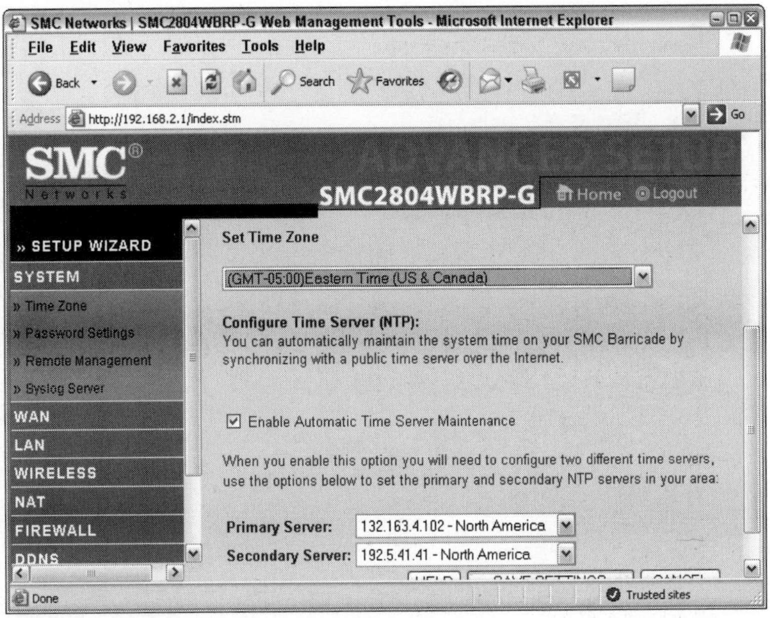

Figure 3-7: Changing the router's date and time settings.

Nothing but 'net

No more stalling. With your equipment configured and connected, it's time to get this fancy new wireless router of yours online. Actually, depending on how your ISP sets things up, you may already be online. Almost all routers are configured to automatically request an IP address from your service provider as soon as they're plugged in and connected to your modem. If you're lucky, your router has already obtained an address and is ready to rock.

The easiest way to check your current status is to head to the home page in your router's management interface. This is usually the Status section, which tells you whether you're currently connected or disconnected from the Internet, as shown in Figure 3-8. If you're connected, then you really have no worries, and there's no additional configuration required.

The automatic configuration I've described is most common if you're using a cable-based Internet connection. If you're connected via DSL, however, there's a good chance that your ISP uses a protocol called *Point-to-Point Protocol over Ethernet (PPPoE)* or the *Point-to-Point Tunneling Protocol (PPTP)* that requires you to provide a username and password in order to connect.

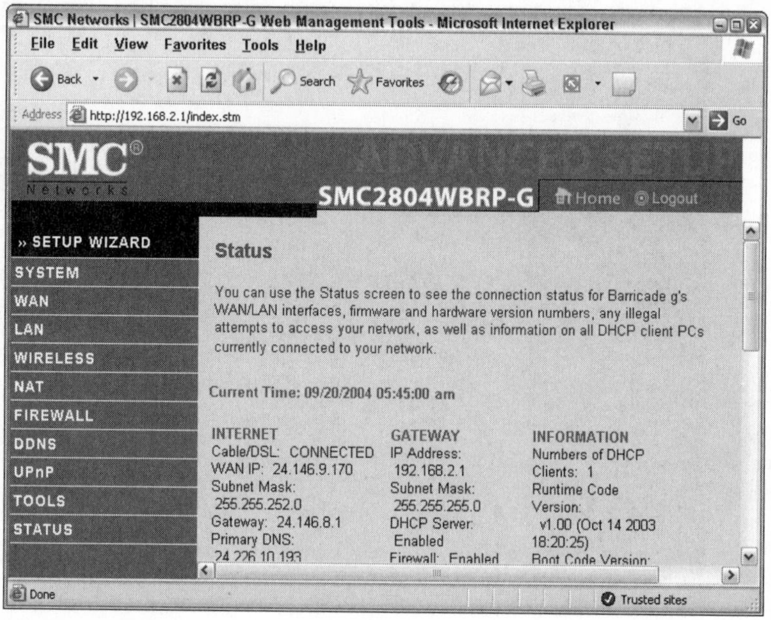

Figure 3-8: Your router should include a Status screen that outlines whether your Internet service is connected.

If you are using a DSL Internet connection, your ISP should have provided you with the username and password you need. With this information in hand, you can get down to the business of adding your logon information to the router's configuration such that it handles the connection process for you automatically.

To do this, look for a section named WAN or Internet in your router's management interface. Many wireless routers include a wizard-type, stepped procedure that allows you to specify your Internet connection type, as outlined in Figure 3-9.

After selecting the appropriate connection method (PPPoE in this case), you are prompted to supply your username and password. Enter the information provided by your ISP, as shown in Figure 3-10.

Once you've entered the appropriate user information and saved your settings, your router should connect to the Internet automatically and allow you to surf away from any computer on your wireless network. Enjoy!

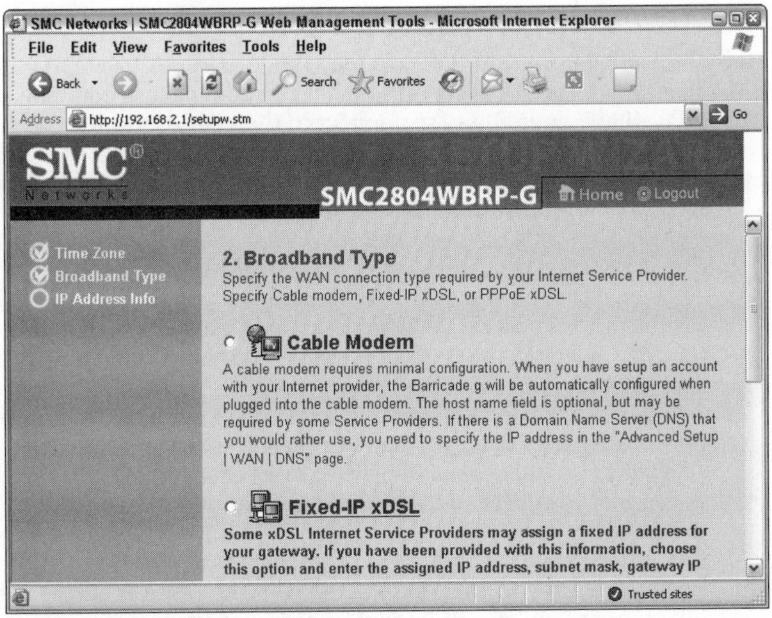

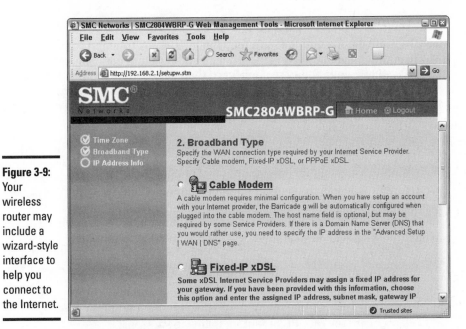

Figure 3-9: Your wireless router may include a wizard-style interface to help you connect to the Internet.

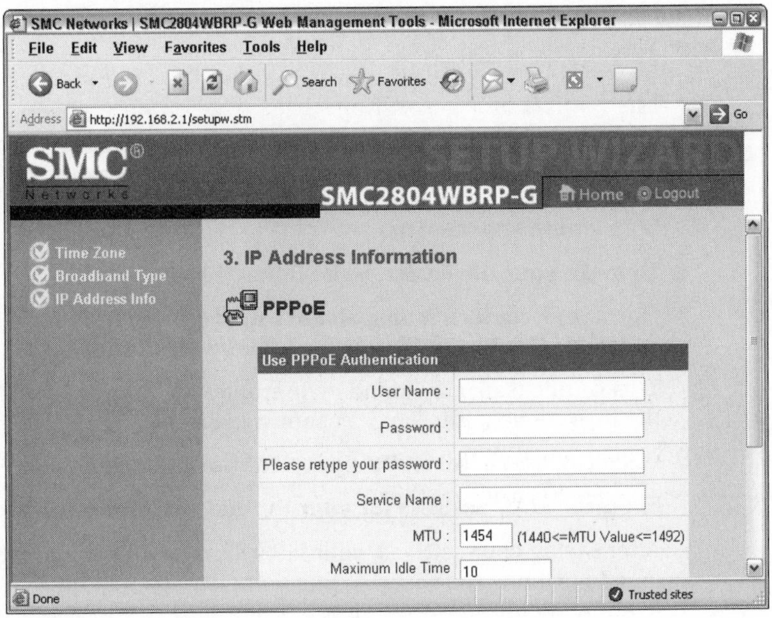

Figure 3-10: DSL Internet connections often require that you supply a username and password.

Attack of the (MAC) clone

Depending upon your ISP, you may run into issues trying to connect a router to your Internet service. Although it's becoming less common, many cable ISPs still tie your ability to connect to their service to the hardware (Media Access Control or MAC) address of your primary PC. In these cases, the ISP assumes that you're connecting the modem they supplied to an Ethernet network card on your PC or laptop.

This means the provider's servers are expecting any request for an IP address to come from your PC's MAC address. Once you throw a router into the mix, it's the one requesting the IP address, and it has a different MAC address than your PC. As such, the request for an IP address is often denied.

Thankfully, many routers include a way to circumvent this problem. Specifically, they use a technique called MAC address *cloning* to pretend to be your PC in the eyes of the ISP. Basically, all you need to do is find the MAC address of your PC and then configure the router to use that MAC address instead of its own.

To find the MAC address associated with the wired Ethernet network adapter card on your PC or laptop, follow these steps:

1. **Open a command prompt.**
2. **Type** ipconfig /all.
3. **Press Enter.**

   The entry you're looking for is found under a heading called Ethernet adapter Local Area Connection, and specifically a value called Physical address. It will look something like 00-01-02-03-04-05, and may include both letters and numbers.
4. **To make your life easier, write down this address.**
5. **Open your router's management interface and look for a setting called MAC Address Cloning or Change MAC Address.**

   This setting is usually found in or around the Internet or WAN section of the management interface, as shown in Figure 3-11.
6. **Once you find it, select the option to change or clone your MAC address.**
7. **Enter the MAC address for your PC that you found earlier.**

   After saving your settings, your ISP will treat your router just like your PC and be none the wiser. At this point, you should be able to obtain an IP address and surf away without issue.

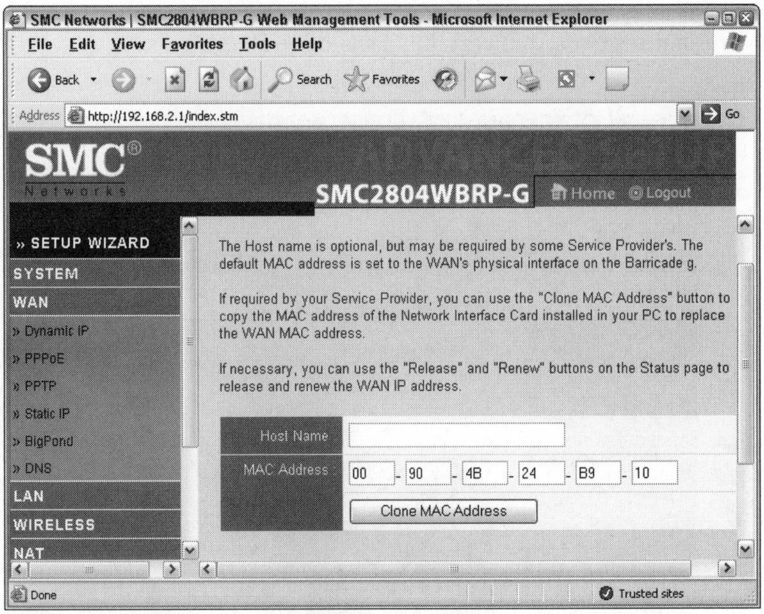

Figure 3-11: Many hardware routers allow you to change your MAC address.

If your particular router does not include a MAC address cloning feature, all is not lost. You may be able to add this functionality to your router by upgrading its firmware. I outline the ins and outs of upgrading your firmware in Book II, Chapter 8.

What's in a name?

Last but not least, it's important to give your new wireless network a name. In much the same way that a wireless router ships with a default password, it also ships with a default *Service Set Identifier (SSID).* The SSID represents the name of your network, and all devices on the wireless network must be configured with the same name.

All wireless equipment vendors use a slightly different default SSID. For example, SMC literally uses SMC as the SSID on its wireless routers. You should make a point of changing the SSID value to something unique for your network — maybe your name, the name of the family dog, or whatever tickles your fancy. Your wireless router broadcasts this name to the world, allowing wireless computers within range to find and connect to your wireless network.

You generally find the setting to change your router's SSID value in the Wireless section of its management interface, as shown in Figure 3-12.

Once your new SSID is configured, your wireless network finally has its unique name, and certainly feels more loved.

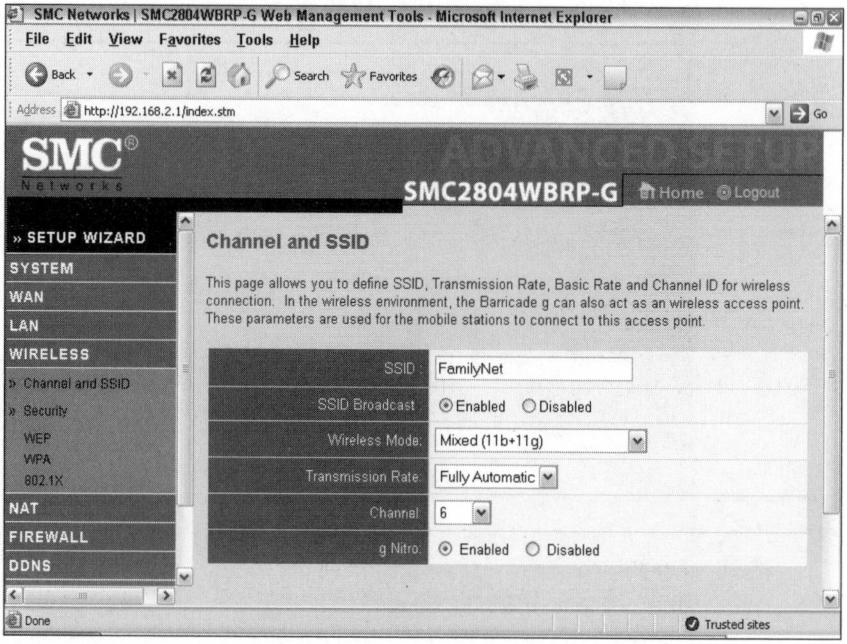

Figure 3-12: Change the SSID on your wireless router to give your network its own name.

Chapter 4: Setting Up Other Hardware

In This Chapter

- **Understanding network bridges**
- **Connecting and configuring access points**
- **Adding a wireless print server to your network**

If you like to keep things simple, chances are good that your wireless network consists of little more than a wireless router and a couple of client computers with wireless network adapters installed. However, a whole range of wireless equipment is out there, ready to meet just about any need imaginable.

I'm not going to try and impress you with tales of people adding coffee makers and toasters to their wireless networks, but I have to admit that it would make a good story. Instead, I'm going to concentrate on some of the more practical wireless networking devices that you're likely to come across and how they're set up. Just replace the toaster with a bridge, the coffee maker with an access point, and throw in a print server for good measure.

Can you feel the excitement?

Bridging Multiple Networks

In a world with places to go and valleys to cross, bridges help connect things. In the world of networking, a *bridge* is a device that connects different types of networks. In the old days, a bridge might interconnect two wired networks that were using different technologies, such as Ethernet and Token Ring. Today, the most common reason for bridging networks is to interconnect wired and wireless systems.

You may not have realized it, but if your wireless router includes integrated Ethernet switch ports, you already have a bridge! These ports allow you to connect wired computers to your network, which can then communicate with your wireless systems without issue. The router handles all of the bridging-related functions between the two networks automatically, allowing you to kick back, relax, and enjoy your integrated wireless and wired network.

In effect, any wireless hardware device (or even technique) that interconnects a wired and wireless network can be considered a bridge. For example, a wireless access point is technically a bridge, since it connects wireless clients to a wired network. Another example of a bridge is shown in Figure 4-1. This wireless Ethernet bridge from SMC connects to any device with a wired Ethernet network adapter, instantly turning it into a wireless system.

Figure 4-1: A wireless bridge.

Windows XP even includes a software feature, known as Network Bridge, to bridge different types of network connections. As networks evolve to include different technologies and connection methods, bridges help span the divide and add flexibility to existing wired and wireless networks. You read more about implementing hardware and software bridges in Book III, Chapter 3.

Configuring Your Access Points

The simplest way to configure a wireless network at home is to use a wireless router. A *wireless router* acts as the broadband router to share your high-speed DSL or cable Internet connection, as well as an *access point* (the wireless hub component) for the wireless client systems on your network.

However, in cases where you have an existing wired home network in place, you might opt to add a wireless access point to your network instead. In this setup, it's assumed that your existing broadband router will continue to be responsible for sharing your Internet connection and firewall-related functions, while the wireless access point will simply extend the network to allow wireless systems to connect.

Adding a wireless access point to an existing network in this way is typically very simple. All you need to do is use the cable supplied with the access point to connect its Ethernet port to an available port on a hub or switch on your network. The hub or switch might be a separate hardware device or be integrated into your wired broadband router.

Figure 4-2 illustrates the most common setup for a home network that includes both a wireless access point and a wired router.

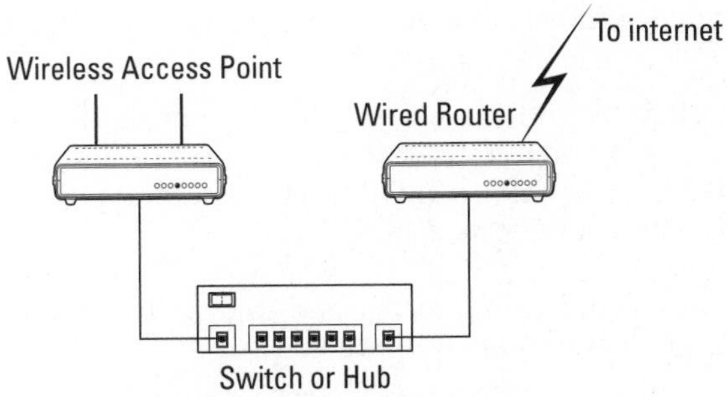

Figure 4-2: Typical network layout when a wireless access point is used.

Ultimately, configuring a wireless access point is very similar to configuring a wireless router. However, you need to consider a few key issues to avoid conflicts with other network devices, such as your existing router.

You must configure these main settings on the access point:

- **SSID and wireless settings.** Just like with a wireless router, your wireless access point needs to be configured with a *Service Set Identifier (SSID)* value that acts as the name by which wireless client computers and other hardware identify the wireless network. Additionally, most access points allow you to configure a variety of wireless settings, including the types of clients allowed to connect (802.11a, 802.11b, 802.11g, or some combination thereof), transmission rates, the channel over which communication should occur, and so forth.
- **New administrative password.** Much like a wireless router, wireless access points are typically configured via a web-based management interface that allows you to make changes to the device via a web

browser, rather than needing to use a separate piece of software. To secure your wireless access point, you should change the default password to a new unique value.

- **TCP/IP settings.** Depending on your access point's make and model, it may already have a default IP address configured. If this address is not in the same range as other devices on your network, or if it conflicts with an existing address, you must change it to a unique and correct value. For example, if all your other network devices use 192.168.1 as the first three values in their IP addresses, then the access point should as well. A conflict occurs when more than one device uses the same IP address, so the last number in every device's IP address should be different. If a conflict does exist, both devices have problems communicating over the network.
- **DHCP settings.** Most wireless access points include a built-in DHCP server component to allocate IP addresses to wireless clients. If your network already includes a DHCP server (your broadband router, for example), you should disable the feature on the access point to avoid conflicts.
- **Security settings.** A wireless access point includes a variety of settings to improve security on the wireless portion of your network. You should take full advantage of these capabilities to ensure that the wireless portion of your network remains secure.

You read more about configuring security-related settings on wireless routers or access points in Book IV, Chapter 1.

REMEMBER

While most home networks only have (and need) a single wireless access point, additional access points can be added and may be necessary to extend your wireless network's range or coverage. If you plan to add access points to your network, it's important that they be configured with the correct SSID name for your wireless network and have their own unique IP address assigned.

Serving Your Print Needs Wirelessly

A print server is another popular piece of equipment that makes a nice addition to any wireless network. In a nutshell, a *wireless print server* is a device to which you can connect an existing wired printer. Once connected to the wireless print server, the printer effectively becomes another wireless-enabled device on your network.

TIP

Why would you want to add wireless capabilities to your printer? That's a good question, and one with a few possible answers:

- **Being able to select a better or more convenient location for your printer.** Traditionally, printers are connected directly to a USB or parallel port on a nearby computer. When connected to a wireless print server, the printer can be located in any convenient location within range of the wireless network.
- **Eliminating the need to dedicate a PC to printer sharing.** Although Windows systems are capable of "sharing" a connected printer with other systems on your network, being able to use that printer requires the PC to be powered up. When connected to a wireless print server, you no longer need to leave a PC on just to make access to a connected printer possible.
- **Reducing printing bottlenecks on your network.** On a busy network with regular printing needs, a desktop PC that is also acting as a print server can become a bottleneck or choke point. Dedicating a wireless print server to the task helps free up resources on a desktop PC and eliminates printing-related performance issues.

If you do decide to add a wireless print server to your network, it's worth taking a closer look at the various models available and their capabilities. For example, some wireless print servers include the ability to connect more than one printer to the device, like the Linksys Wireless-G PrintServer shown in Figure 4-3. This model allows you to connect up to two printers simultaneously, via its USB and parallel ports.

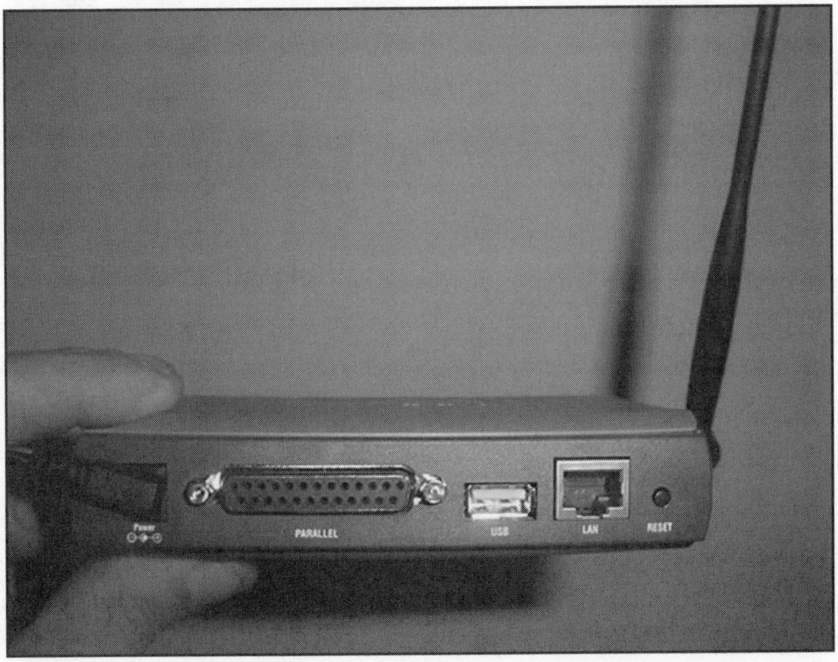

Figure 4-3: The Linksys Wireless-G PrintServer.

While a dedicated wireless print server is certainly an option, you may also want to consider a wireless router with a built-in print server component. For example, the SMC Barricade model shown in Figure 4-4 includes all of the features that you would expect to find in a wireless router, but also adds a built-in print server component that allows you to connect a USB printer. Once connected to your wireless router, the printer effectively becomes part of your wireless network. If you decide to go this route, the main issue to consider is that your printer must be located close to your router (within the USB cable length), which may or may not be convenient.

Adding a wireless print server to your network isn't terribly difficult, but typically involves a number of steps. These steps involve making physical connections, installing the print server software, and configuring the print server to use the correct driver(s) for your printer.

These steps are specific to a Linksys Wireless-G PrintServer, so be sure to follow the steps outlined in the setup guide provided with your model. Follow these steps to add a wireless print server to your network:

1. **Connect your printer to the appropriate port on a wireless print server.**

   For example, if your printer uses a USB connection, connect its USB cable to the USB port on the wireless print server.

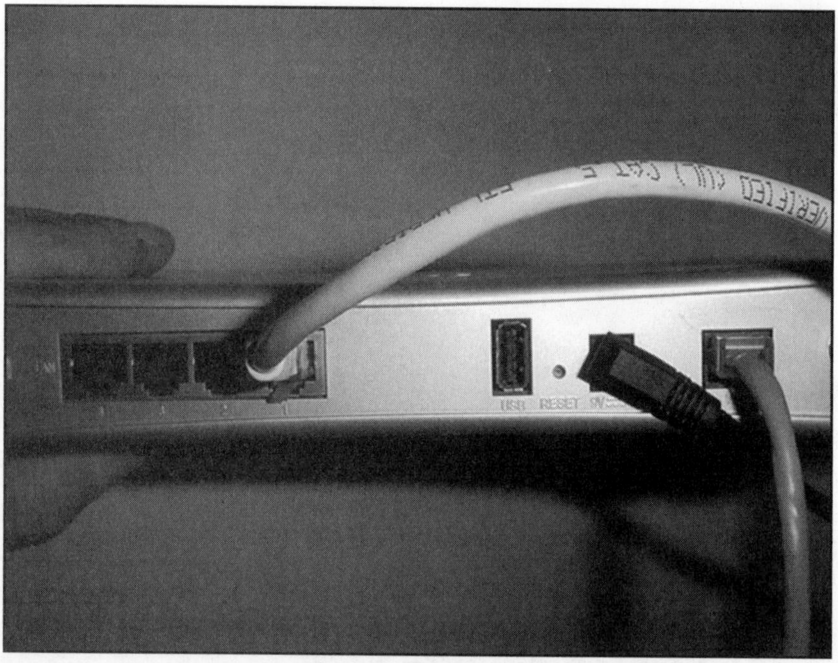

Figure 4-4: The USB port on this wireless router allows it to function as a wireless print server for a USB printer.

2. **Connect the Ethernet cable supplied with your print server to the LAN port on the print server and an Ethernet port on a hub, switch, or router on your network.**

   This is the connection that will be used to configure the wireless print server from your PC.

3. **Connect the power adapter to the wireless print server, and then to an electrical outlet.**

4. **Power on your printer.**

   With the printer and wireless print server physically connected and powered up, you can begin installing the software for the print server.

5. **Insert the CD included with the wireless print server into the CD-ROM drive of a computer on your wireless network.**

6. **If the Setup Wizard for the print server doesn't start automatically, run the SetupWizard.exe file on the CD.**

7. **When the Setup Wizard screen appears, click the Setup Wizard link shown in Figure 4-5.**

   At the Select PrintServer screen, your print server should be automatically detected and listed, as shown in Figure 4-6.

8. **On the Select PrintServer screen, click Next.**

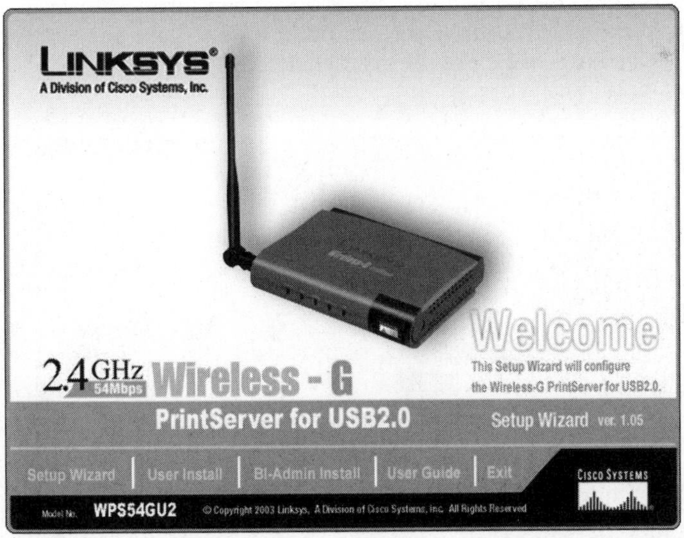

Figure 4-5: The Setup Wizard for a Linksys print server.

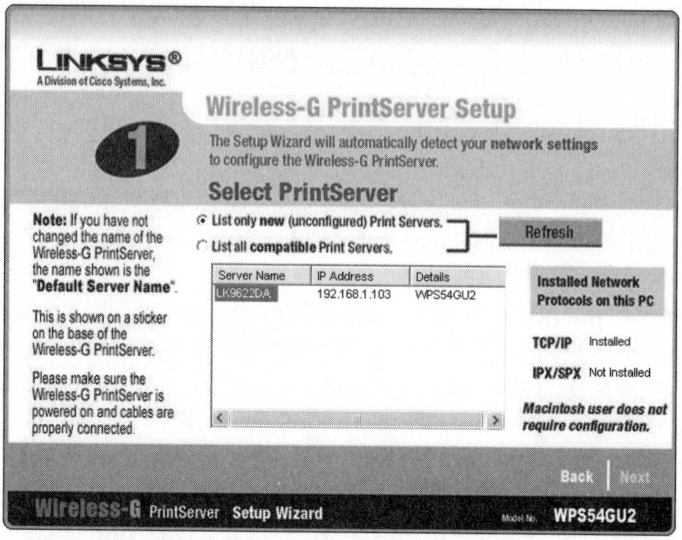

Figure 4-6: Automatically detecting the new print server.

9. **At the Password screen, enter the default password for the print server. Then click Enter.**

   In the case of the Linksys Wireless-G PrintServer used here, the default password is admin. Check the user manual supplied with your print server for the password used on other makes and models.

10. **At the Basic Settings screen, enter a new name for your print server (as shown in Figure 4-7) and click Next.**

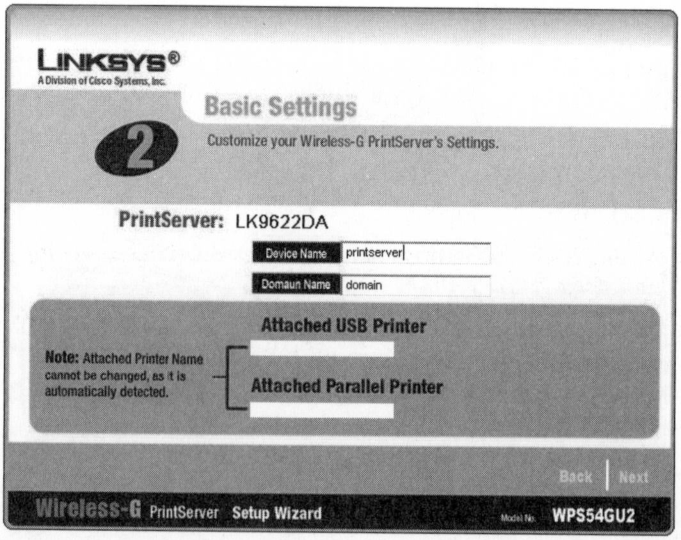

Figure 4-7: Configuring a new name for the print server.

11. At the IP Settings screen, do one of two things:

- **Select Set IP Configuration Manually to specify an IP address.**
- **Leave the default setting intact (Automatically Obtain an IP Address [DHCP]) to have the print server use DHCP to obtain an IP address, as shown in Figure 4-8.**

TIP

If you plan to manage the print server's settings from its built-in web-management capabilities, it makes a great deal of sense to manually configure an IP address.

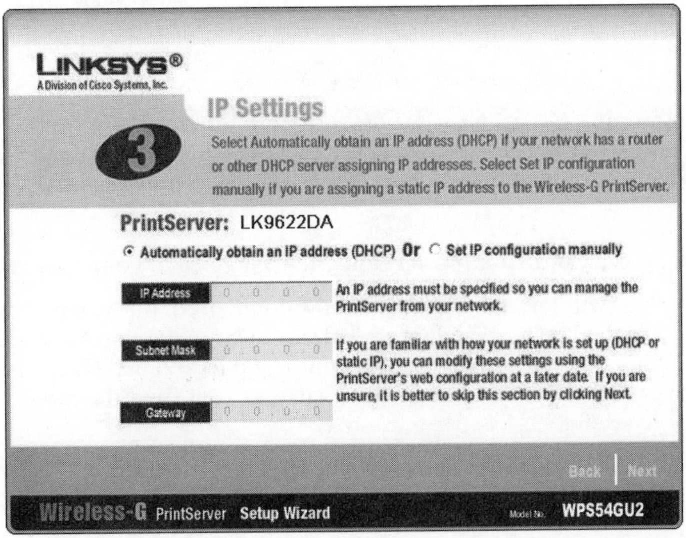
LINKSYS®
A Division of Cisco Systems, Inc.
IP Settings
3
Select Automatically obtain an IP address (DHCP) if your network has a router or other DHCP server assigning IP addresses. Select Set IP configuration manually if you are assigning a static IP address to the Wireless-G PrintServer.
PrintServer: LK9622DA
Automatically obtain an IP address (DHCP) Or Set IP configuration manually
IP Address
An IP address must be specified so you can manage the PrintServer from your network.
Subnet Mask
If you are familiar with how your network is set up (DHCP or static IP), you can modify these settings using the PrintServer's web configuration at a later date. If you are unsure, it is better to skip this section by clicking Next.
Gateway
Back
Next
Wireless-G PrintServer Setup Wizard
Model No. WPS54GU2

Figure 4-8: Configuring the IP address setting for the print server.

12. At the Set PrintServer's Password screen, enter the current password for the print server. Then enter a new password and confirm it.

If you're not sure of what the password is for your print server model, it should be listed in the device's user manual.

13. Click Next.

14. At the Wireless Settings screen, enter the SSID name for your network and click Next.

15. At the Wireless Security Settings screen, ensure that WEP security is disabled, as shown in Figure 4-9. Click Next.

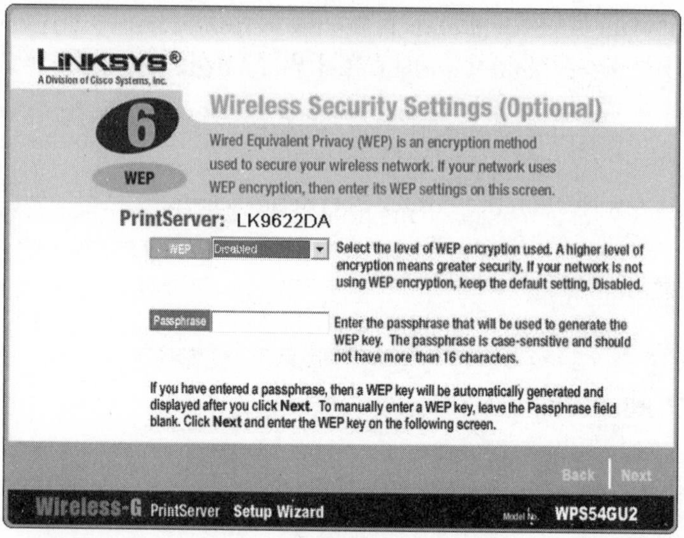

Figure 4-9: Ensuring that wireless security is disabled.

16. **At the Confirmation screen, click Yes to save your new settings.**

    Your wireless print server is now configured, but you still need to configure the Linksys PrintServer's driver. The remaining steps assume that your printer was previously connected to and installed on the PC from which you are working, which ensures that the printer's drivers will be accessible.

17. **At the Congratulations screen, click User Install.**

    This opens the Print Server Driver Setup screen.

18. **At the Welcome screen, click Next.**
19. **At the Choose Destination Location screen, click Next.**
20. **At the Select Program Folder screen, click Next.**
21. **At the Setup Complete screen, click Finish.**

    The Print Driver Setup program starts automatically.

    Although the Linksys PrintServer's driver is now installed, you still need to install the driver for your printer. Don't worry — you're almost there!

22. When the Information dialog box appears, ensure that your printer is connected to the wireless printer server and powered on. Then click OK.

At the Printer Port Setup screen, your printer should be detected automatically, as shown in Figure 4-10.

23. Click Next on the Printer Port Setup screen.

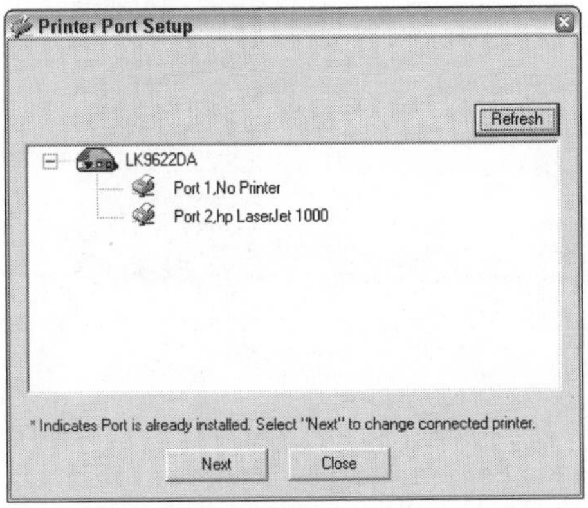

Figure 4-10: The printer connected to the print server is detected.

24. When the Add Port dialog box confirms that the print server port was added successfully, click OK.

25. When the Configure Printer Port screen appears, click the printer name that you want to associate with the printer port. Then click Connect.

26. At the Printer Port Setup screen, click Close.

Your wireless print server is now installed and configured, and the connected printer is ready to accept print jobs. Fire at will!

TIP

Once installed and configured, the advanced settings of most wireless print servers can be configured via a web browser. Use these steps to access this interface:

1. Open your favorite browser and enter the IP address of your wireless print server.

2. When prompted, type the password that you configured while installing the print server software.

This opens the print server's management interface, as shown in Figure 4-11.

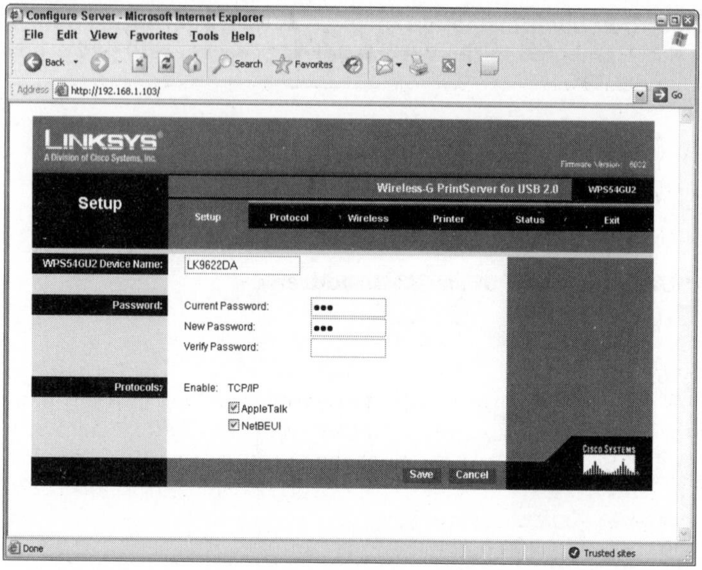

Figure 4-11: The management interface for the Linksys Wireless-G PrintServer.

In most cases, the management interface for a wireless print server includes the ability to add or change a variety of settings. The management interface for the Linksys Wireless-G PrintServer includes five main configurable areas:

- **Setup.** This section allows you to change the print server's name and administrative password and control which network protocols it communicates via.
- **Protocol.** This section configures network settings such as the print server's IP address, subnet mask, and default gateway. If other protocols are enabled (such as NetBEUI or AppleTalk), they are also configured from this section.
- **Wireless.** This section configures general wireless settings such as an SSID name and network type, as well as security settings such as encryption.
- **Printer.** This section configures various printer settings, port properties, and so on.
- **Status.** This section is for viewing configuration and protocol settings for the device, reviewing details of the print server's firmware, and upgrading the firmware if necessary.

Of course, the settings available for your particular wireless print server model may be slightly different, so check the user manual supplied with your model for details.

Chapter 5: Decoding DHCP

In This Chapter

- Understanding DHCP
- Using DHCP
- Deciding when to use static addresses

Every device on your wired or wireless network needs its own Internet Protocol (IP) address, just like every house in a neighborhood needs its own street address. You can let the machines handle this tedious task for you or, for reasons masochistic or otherwise, you can manually assign these addresses to network devices.

In this chapter I talk about the feature that automatically hands out addresses. It's called *Dynamic Host Configuration Protocol* or *DHCP*. You need to know at least a little about DHCP because it is enabled on your wireless router or access point by default, and you may want to use it on your network rather than configure IP address settings manually. I also discuss some situations where manually assigning a network device to a static address may be a better bet.

Examining Your Address Options

When it comes to assigning IP addresses and related settings to computers on your network, you do have choices. On the one hand, you can let a DHCP server do things for you, without the need to lift a hand. If you want complete control, however, you may opt to configure all required settings manually. The following sections outline what a DHCP server is and look closely at your addressing options.

What DHCP server?

If you take a closer look at the box that your wireless router or access point was packaged in, you're almost certain to see a built-in DHCP server. While it certainly sounds fancy, don't expect to find any extra hardware or another computer in the box. The DHCP server in question is a feature, not a thing, buried deep within the router's software.

In a nutshell, a *DHCP server* is responsible for assigning IP addresses and related setting to computers when requested. When a computer is configured to obtain its IP address automatically, it broadcasts a request over the network when it starts up, asking for an IP address. When a DHCP server (in this case, the feature built into your wireless router or access point) hears this request, it allocates IP address settings to the computer that made the request.

Most wireless routers and access points ship with their DHCP server feature enabled by default. That's good for you, especially if you want to keep things simple. When DHCP is up and running, you avoid the need to manually configure every computer on your network with its required IP address settings.

Static versus dynamic

Say your network includes a desktop computer, a laptop computer, a wireless router, and a wireless print server. All of these devices require their own IP address. An IP address for your network devices looks something like this: 192.168.1.105. The last digits differ for each computer and hardware device on the network. Without getting too technical, the first three groups of numbers identify the network in this case, where the last grouping represents a unique computer on the network.

You can assign IP addresses to your access points, computers, multimedia servers, and other networked gizmos one of two ways:

- **Manually assign each item a *static address.*** This means it always has the same IP address, even after you shut down everything and reboot. These permanent addresses can be messy when adding new devices to your network. Not only is it hard remembering which addresses have already been assigned, but accidentally assigning the same address to two computers creates a conflict that doesn't allow either device to communicate correctly.
- **Let the machines obtain their own addresses, dynamically.** Most routers and wireless access points have a built-in DHCP feature that automatically assigns a unique IP address to every device on a network. (See Figure 5-1.) This ensures that IP addresses don't conflict. Just like the Postal Service needs a distinct address for every household, your wireless network's components also must each have a different address.

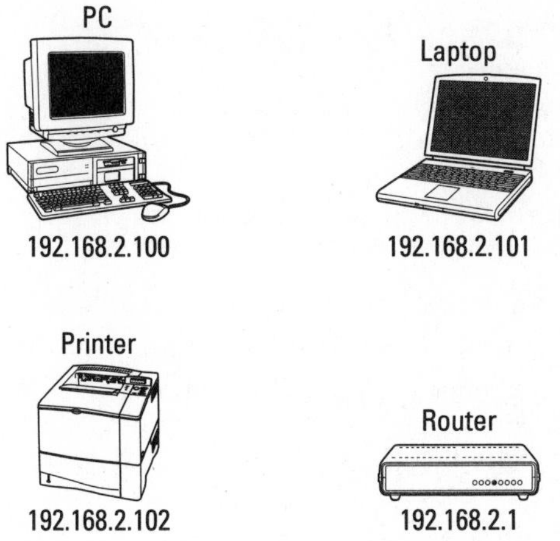

Figure 5-1: DHCP assigns each device its own IP address.

When each device on your network requests an IP address from the DHCP server (in your case, probably built into a wireless router), that server replies with at least the following information:

✦ **IP address.** This will usually look something like my earlier example of 192.168.1.105. Any number from 1 through 254 is okay for the last group of numbers. (By the way, in case you want to impress your friends, each group of numbers is called an *octet.*)

✦ **Subnet mask.** For the network you're creating, this number is usually 255.255.255.0. A *subnet mask* allows computers on a TCP/IP network to perform a calculation that determines which computers are on its own network, and which are on other networks (such as the Internet).

✦ **Default gateway.** This is the IP address of the gateway that leads to your broadband Internet connection. In the wireless network you're building in this chapter, your router acts as the default gateway. Its IP address is probably either 192.168.1.1 or 192.168.2.1.

IP addresses in the 192.168.x.x range are reserved for internal, private use. These addresses are not used nor are they valid on the public Internet. Millions of networks may use an IP address like 192.168.1.111 and never conflict with each other. Instead, they are only used for *intranets,* which are internal networks. Ultimately your router translates the private IP addresses used on your home network to the single public IP address assigned to you by your ISP.

Putting Dynamic Addresses to Good Use

How do you get DHCP up and running? Well, you usually don't need to do a thing — almost all routers and wireless access points have their DHCP component already enabled to make your life easier. In cases where you do need to do something, turning DHCP on or off is usually as simple as selecting the option to enable or disable it from the router's (or access point's) setup interface.

Your router or access point for DHCP settings usually have a section in the setup pages, although the name of this section often differs depending on the manufacturer. Some simply call it DHCP, while others may describe it as an IP Address Pool. An example from one router manufacturer, SMC, is shown in Figure 5-2.

Using the SMC wireless router example, here are the DHCP settings available:

- **DHCP server.** You enable or disable the server here. For the SMC model shown (and most brands for that matter), the default setting is enabled.
- **Lease time.** This indicates the length of time that a device on the network retains the IP address assigned to it by the DHCP server. In effect, the client computer "borrows" the IP address from the pool until the lease period ends, after which it can be allocated to another computer. No need to worry about losing addresses; your client computers periodically "renew" their leases without any input from you. You seldom need to change the default lease time outside of personal preference.
- **Start IP.** The first IP address in the pool can be assigned to client computers or other devices.
- **End IP.** The last IP address in the pool. As a general rule, you only need as many addresses in your pool as you have client computers or devices. In this example, 100 IP addresses are available to be leased (from 192.168.2.100 to 192.168.2.199), which is probably far too many. Instead of using 192.168.2.199 as the end address, 192.168.2.102 is a better choice for a network where 3 computers require dynamic addresses.
- **Domain name.** On larger networks, clients may require their DNS domain name be assigned by DHCP as well. For a small home network, you don't need to enter anything.

The DHCP component on your router or access point may include a few additional features or settings:

- **DHCP clients log.** This handy table lists devices that have been assigned an address, including information like their name, MAC (hardware) address, and the IP address they're leasing. An example is shown in Figure 5-3.
- **DNS server.** Up to three spaces are often provided for entering DNS server addresses. In most cases, you do not need to configure these addresses. However, if you find that you cannot reach web sites by name (such as www.google.com), you should enter the DNS server addresses provided by your ISP.
- **WINS server.** This setting is used to configure the IP address of a WINS server on the network. This setting is meant for larger networks since home networks typically don't use WINS. In other words, you can safely leave this setting blank.

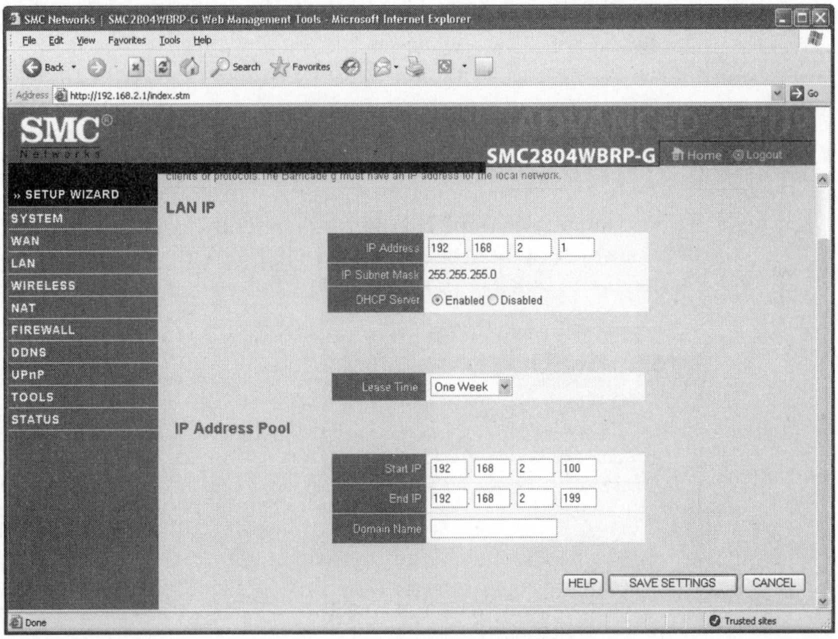

Figure 5-2: A router's DHCP configuration screen.

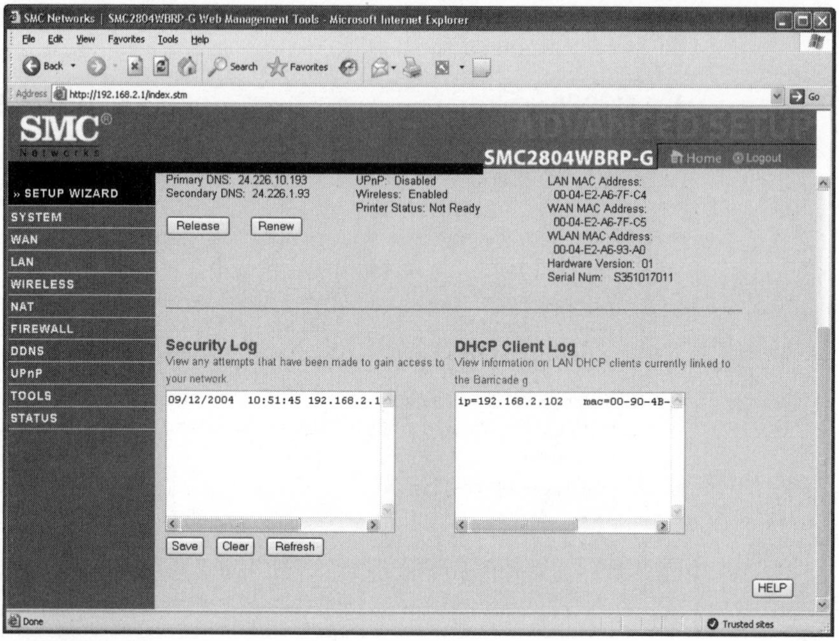

Figure 5-3: A list of the network clients assigned dynamic addresses.

Heading off Trouble

If you configured your DHCP server correctly as per the instructions in the previous section, you see a message in the Wireless Network Connection Status dialog box like that shown in Figure 5-4.

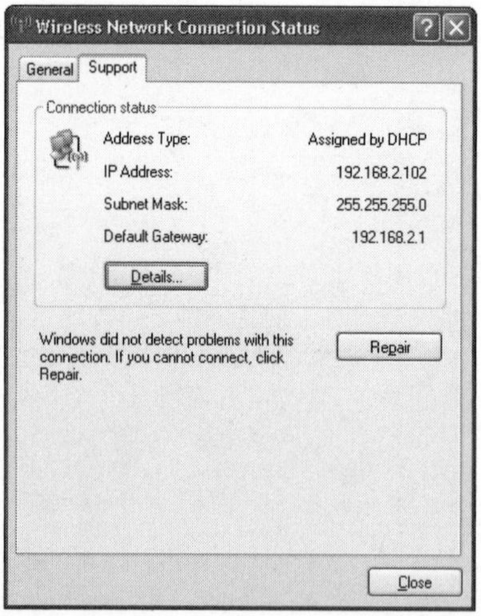

Figure 5-4: A client with an automatically assigned address.

However, if a network client is unable to obtain a dynamic address automatically from the DHCP server, the Wireless Network Connection Status dialog box looks more like the one shown in Figure 5-5.

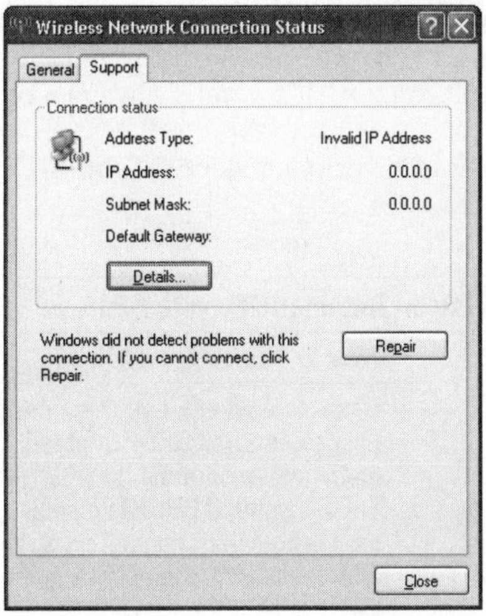

Figure 5-5: DHCP fails; "Invalid IP Address" displays instead.

After making some additional tries to obtain a dynamic address, a client that cannot reach the DHCP server may default to what Windows XP calls an *automatic private IP address,* shown in Figure 5-6.

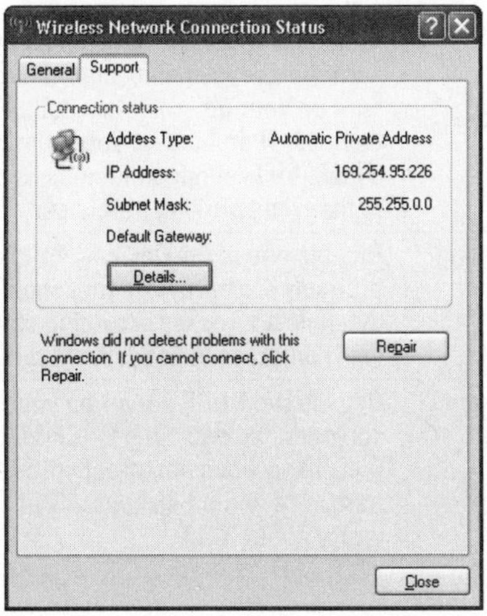

Figure 5-6: Unable to get a dynamic address, this PC falls back to a default address.

An automatic private address looks something like 169.254.x.x (each x representing a number) and means your network client — your desktop PC or laptop, for instance — is unable to communicate with the DHCP server.

Windows XP assigns itself an address in the 169.254.x.x range if it can't get an address automatically from the DHCP server. It's basically saying, "Hey, I asked for an address. You didn't give me one (or didn't hear me), so now I'm running my own show with 169.254.x.x." It's almost always a bad sign.

You may get that default address for various reasons. Table 5-1's troubleshooting tips may help.

Table 5-1: Pinpointing and Solving an Automatic Private Address

What May Be Happening	*How to Fix It*
DHCP is not enabled.	Determine whether your access point (probably your router) has DHCP enabled. You can see this on the setup screens for your router or other access point. If DHCP is disabled, enable it and then reboot your computers so they can get new addresses from the access point.
If your computers are defaulting to 169.254.x.x, it may be because your access point is too far away from your computers. If the signals don't stretch from the access point to your computers, the computers cannot communicate with the access point to request an IP address.	Move the access point or the computers so your network has strong signals. Then reboot your computers and see if you're getting a 192.168.x.x address rather than one in the 169.254.x.x range.
Gremlins abound.	If nothing seems to work, shut down everything. Turn the access point/router on and let it boot. Turn on your other access points or network devices. Then boot up your computers. This simple trick, although tedious, is often the solution to many networking problems.
You have more than one device acting as the DHCP server and handing out IP addresses.	Disable one of the devices. Your main router is probably the hardware that should be assigning dynamic addresses. Anything else that's assigning IP addresses needs to be turned off.
You're using Windows XP's Internet connection sharing (ICS) feature.	Disable the DHCP server on your access point. You cannot disable the DHCP function on ICS. (This likely does not affect you; if you're using the hardware setup I discuss in Book II, you needn't worry about ICS.)

Getting some Static

Sometimes static is better. Static addresses, that is. (Of course, you may think that everything I write is static. If you knew how dynamic I am, you wouldn't suggest that.)

You may sometimes want to assign IP addresses manually, rather than letting the DHCP server do all the work. With Windows XP, you can choose to assign your computer a static address so that its IP address is always the same.

Even after you reboot your access points and computers, any device assigned a static address keeps that address. The router or other multifunctional access point continues to assign dynamic addresses to other network devices that do not have a static address.

Why would you want to assign a static address?

- Turning off the DHCP server and assigning static addresses prevents unauthorized users from automatically getting an address if they connect to your wireless network. This may prove more inconvenient than its worthwhile, however.
- Assigning one or two network devices a static address may be necessary so they can be accessed from the Internet for game playing or other activities.
- In some cases (such as when using a print server) you always want the network device to have the same address.

If you're using a second access point (to increase your network's range, for instance), turn off its DHCP server. The router is already assigning dynamic addresses, so you don't want a second DHCP server mucking up things.

To assign a static address to your desktop computer, follow these steps:

1. **Right-click the Wireless Network Connection icon on your taskbar and select Open Network Connections.**
2. **In the Network Connections window, right-click the network connection you want to change.**

   A menu appears.
3. **Select Status from the menu.**

   The Wireless Network Connection Status dialog box appears.
4. **Click Properties.**

   The Wireless Network Connection Properties dialog box appears.

Strolling through addresses

You can easily determine the IP address assigned to your router or a multipurpose access point on your wireless network. Use a command-line command to check on the router's gateway address and other information. Knowing which address is assigned to your wireless router is useful if you need to troubleshoot problems like not being able to connect to the Internet. Just follow these steps:

1. Run a command prompt.

   You can find it under Start, All Programs, Accessories, Command Prompt. A Command Prompt window is a DOS-like command line environment from which you can enter commands on a Windows system.

2. Type **ipconfig /all** and press Enter.

   The listing shows the default gateway address, which is the same as your router's address. The listing also shows whether DHCP is enabled, as shown in the figure.

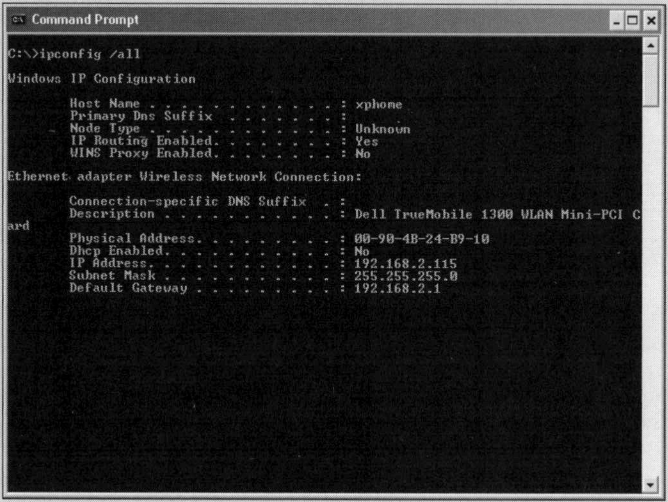

Command Prompt
C:\>ipconfig /all
Windows IP Configuration
Host Name . . . . : xphome
Primary Dns Suffix . . . . :
Node Type . . . . : Unknown
IP Routing Enabled. . . . . : Yes
WINS Proxy Enabled. . . . . : No
Ethernet adapter Wireless Network Connection:
Connection-specific DNS Suffix . :
Description . . . . : Dell TrueMobile 1300 WLAN Mini-PCI Card
Physical Address. . . . . : 00-90-4B-24-B9-10
Dhcp Enabled. . . . . : No
IP Address. . . . . : 192.168.2.115
Subnet Mask . . . . : 255.255.255.0
Default Gateway . . . . : 192.168.2.1

A listing of network settings.

5. **In the middle section, select Internet Protocol (TCP/IP) and click Properties, as shown in Figure 5-7.**

   The Internet Protocol (TCP/IP) Properties dialog box appears.

6. **Select Use the Following IP Address.**

   The static addresses areas lights up.

7. **Enter the IP address, subnet mask, and default gateway you want to use, as shown in Figure 5-8.**

   The IP address is similar to 192.168.1.115. The subnet mask is 255.255.255.0, which should fill in automatically. The default gateway is the IP address of your router.

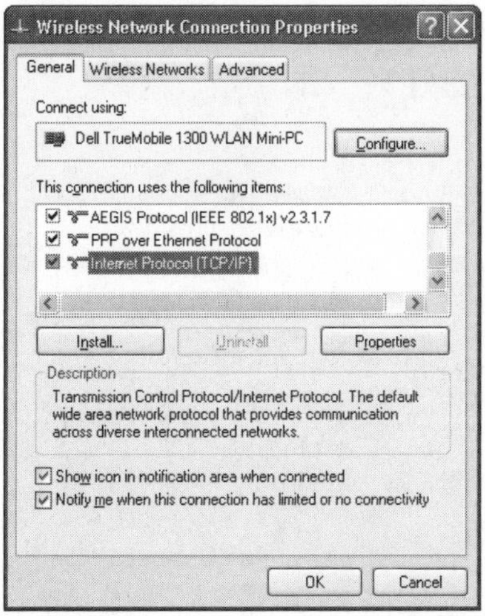

Figure 5-7: Select Properties for Internet Protocol.

TIP

Either see your router's instruction manual for the default address or see the box for a way to learn this default gateway address.

8. **Under Use the Following DNS Server Addresses, enter two DNS server addresses, which your ISP can provide.**
9. **Click OK.**

   The Wireless Network Connection Properties dialog box appears again.
10. **Click Close to finish.**

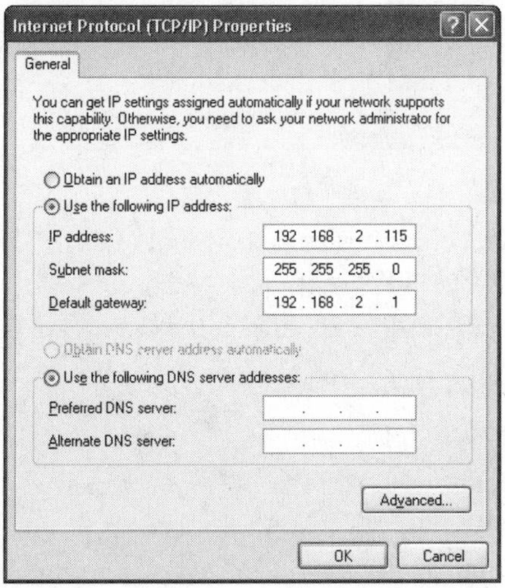

Figure 5-8: Enter information for creating a static address.

Chapter 6: Installing an Adapter on Your PC

In This Chapter

- Physically installing a PCI wireless network adapter card
- Installing adapter card utility programs
- Connecting a USB wireless network adapter
- Installing drivers and utilities for a USB wireless network adapter

The time has arrived — the time to finally install a wireless network adapter in your desktop computer. While you can't choose whether you will or won't install an adapter (you have to if you want the computer to connect to your wireless network), you do have some choice on the style front. Specifically, you have the right to choose whether you prefer the clean and crisp internal model or a sleek and sassy external hybrid. This is probably the first and only place that you ever see a wireless network adapter described as sassy. You read it here first (and, quite probably, last).

If you decide to go internal, you're looking at installing a PCI wireless network adapter card. This option involves popping the hood on your PC, but keeps the card cleanly tucked away at the back of your system. The second option is adding a USB wireless network adapter, the choice that makes installing as simple as plug, plug, and play. The only downside of going the USB route is that it adds yet another device to your desktop (albeit a small one).

Here's the good news: Installing a wireless network adapter really isn't all that tough. Whether you want to stay inside or keep it outside, I explain exactly what you need to know to get the job done in this chapter.

Taking the Lid Off Your PC

If you decide to install an internal PCI wireless network adapter card, be prepared to take that top off — your computer, of course. While the physical installation may be the frightening part, it takes a few steps to get your PCI adapter up and running.

Specifically, you must complete these three steps to get your wireless network adapter card working:

- Physically installing the network adapter in your PC.
- Installing the driver for the network adapter card.
- Installing the client software for your network adapter card (depending on what operating system you're using)

Each of these steps is looked at in more detail in the following sections.

Physically installing your adapter

Opening up your computer to install an internal wireless network adapter card can be scary, especially if you've never opened a computer case before. Inside you find all sorts of frightening cords, cables, and components that make you think you need an engineering degree to sort them out. The key is to take a deep breath and remain calm. You won't be on the inside for long, and the process is actually much easier than you might expect.

REMEMBER

Any internal wireless network adapter card is of the PCI variety. *PCI* is just the term used to describe the slot the card fits into, so don't worry about me getting all technical on you now. Your computer almost certainly includes one empty PCI slot for your adapter to fit into, if not a few.

The card installation itself is pretty straightforward, and I give you the step-by-step breakdown in a moment. In the meantime, it's worth noting that these adapters come in two main styles:

- A single PCI card that includes all of the necessary hardware as an integrated unit, as shown in Figure 6-1.
- An adapter-style card, into which you slide a PC card wireless network adapter, the same as those used for a laptop.

While the adapter-style cards were popular when wireless networking gear first started making its way into desktop computers, most of the cards you find marketed to home users today are of the all-in-one variety — one piece, plain and simple.

TIP

If you do purchase an adapter-style card for your PC, be sure that the kit you buy includes both the PCI adapter and the wireless PC card itself. If not, you could end up spending twice as much money if you need to purchase both separately.

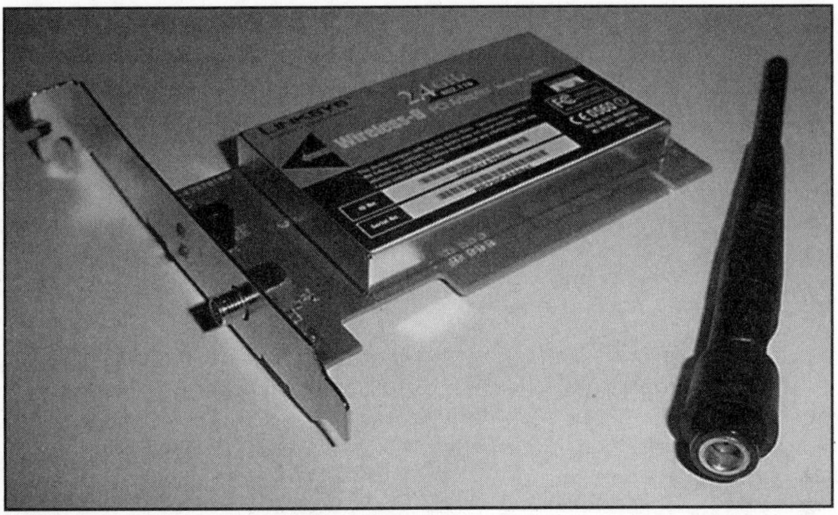

Figure 6-1: A PCI wireless network adapter card prior to installation.

Assuming that you have your wireless PCI adapter sitting open in front of you, it's time to get this show on the road! Follow the steps to install your new wireless PCI adapter in your PC:

WARNING!

1. **Turn off your PC and disconnect the power cable for additional safety.**
2. **With the power cable safely disconnected, remove your computer's cover.**

   It may be secured by hand screws or require a Phillips screwdriver to remove.
3. **With the cover removed, look for an available PCI slot.**

   The size of this slot should match the length of the pinned portion of your wireless network adapter card. Most PCs have anywhere from 2 to 6 PCI slots available. Figure 6-2 shows an empty PCI slot.
4. **Remove the small, metal cover plate blocking the front of the PCI slot, if one is present.**
5. **Slide your wireless network adapter card into the PCI slot.**

   Ensure that all of the pins on the card are touching the slot's. While you should need to apply pressure to the adapter card to get it seated in the slot firmly, you should not force the card into the slot. Figure 6-3 shows a wireless network adapter card installed in a PCI slot.

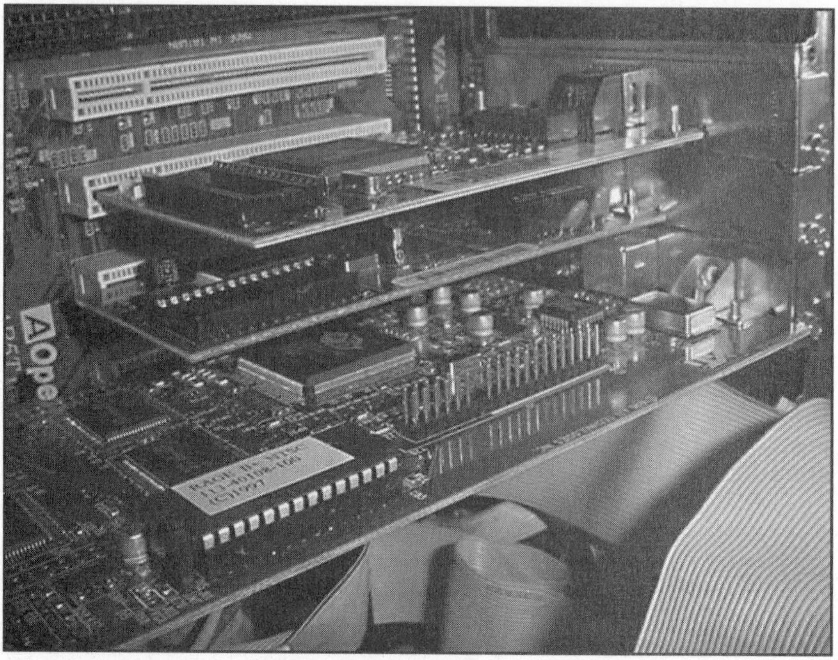

Figure 6-2: Your PC requires at least one free PCI slot to install the adapter.

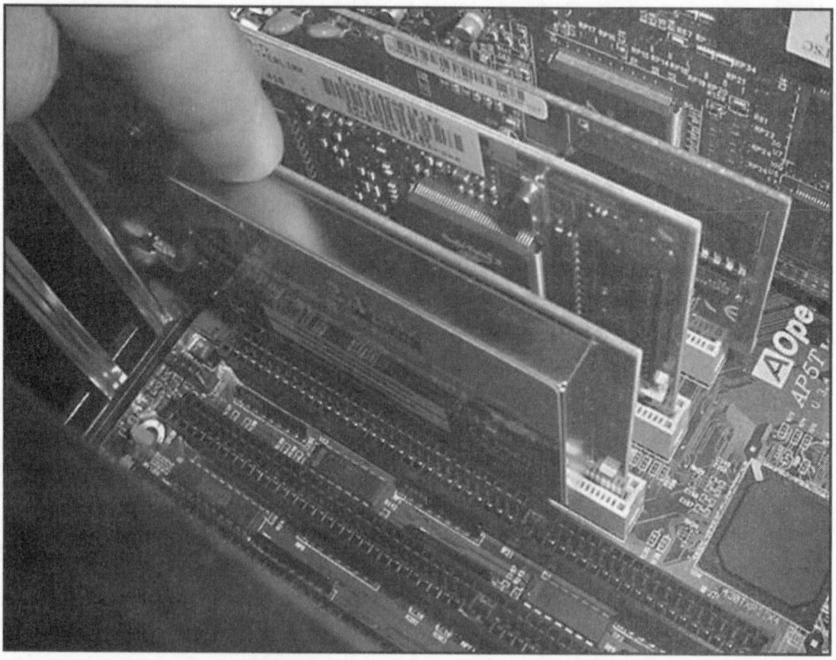

Figure 6-3: Install the adapter card by pressing it firmly into the PCI slot.

6. **With the adapter card firmly connected, replace the cover on your PC.**
7. **Screw the antenna supplied with the wireless network adapter card onto the antenna port on the card, as shown in Figure 6-4.**

   The antenna typically screws on horizontally, after which you can bend it via a hinge mechanism into a vertical position. Your PCI wireless network adapter card is installed!

REMEMBER

If you're installing a PCI wireless network adapter card on a computer running any operating system other than Windows XP, you typically need to install the adapter's software *first,* prior to physically installing the hardware. This can vary from manufacturer to manufacturer, so check the installation instructions provided with your model for complete details.

Who's driving?

Once your wireless network adapter card is physically installed, it's time to restart your PC and get down to the business of installing the drivers that allow Windows XP to make use of it.

Figure 6-4: Attaching the antenna to the wireless network adapter card.

In simple terms, a *driver* is the software component that acts as an intermediary between the operating system and a piece of hardware. It contains the specific instructions that the operating system needs to get the hardware functioning as it should. While Windows XP immediately recognizes any new hardware that you have installed, it typically can't communicate with that hardware until the proper driver is configured.

The driver for your wireless network adapter card should have been included with the hardware on an accompanying CD. If you don't have the CD for your adapter card, you can always download the necessary drivers from the manufacturer's web site. Once you find your adapter model on the site, look for a link to a section called Drivers or Downloads, and then download the necessary file to your hard drive.

At this point, I'm going to assume that your wireless network adapter card is physically installed and that you've restarted your computer. After you log on, Windows XP should display a balloon message in the taskbar saying that a new device has been found, as shown in Figure 6-5. In this case, the message that appears simply states that an Ethernet Controller has been found, rather than anything specific about your make or model.

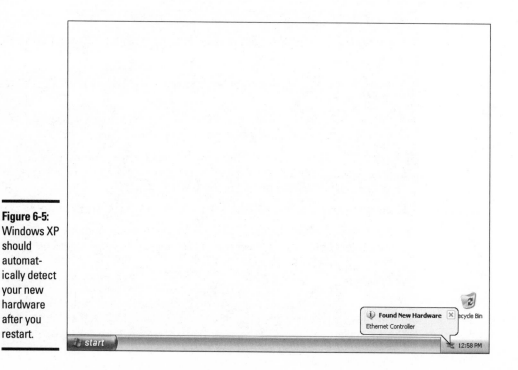

Figure 6-5: Windows XP should automatically detect your new hardware after you restart.

Clicking the balloon message that appears on the taskbar opens the Found New Hardware Wizard, as shown in Figure 6-6. This is the tool you use to walk through the process of installing the driver for your wireless network adapter card.

Found New Hardware Wizard
Welcome to the Found New Hardware Wizard
Windows will search for current and updated software by looking on your computer, on the hardware installation CD, or on the Windows Update Web site (with your permission).
Read our privacy policy
Can Windows connect to Windows Update to search for software?
Yes, this time only
Yes, now and every time I connect a device
No, not this time
Click Next to continue.
< Back
Next >
Cancel

Figure 6-6: The Found New Hardware Wizard opens automatically to help you install the proper drivers.

To complete the installation of the driver for your new hardware, follow these steps:

1. **At the Found New Hardware Wizard screen, select No, Not This Time. Click Next.**
2. **When prompted regarding what you would like the wizard to do, select Install from a List or a Specific Location. Click Next.**
3. **At the Please Choose Your Search and Installation Option screen, ensure that your CD-ROM drive is listed under Include This Location in the Search, as shown in Figure 6-7.**
4. **Insert the CD-ROM provided with your wireless network adapter card.**

   If you downloaded the driver files from the manufacturer's web site, be sure to enter the drive letter and folder where they are stored on your hard drive instead.
5. **Click Next.**

   TIP: In some cases, Windows XP may display a message at this point noting that the files or components that you are about to install are not digitally signed and may not be safe. While many wireless equipment manufacturers ensure that all of their drivers are tested and signed by Microsoft, others do not.

If you are using the drivers provided with your hardware, click the Continue Anyway option to proceed with the installation. If you select the STOP Installation option, the drivers for your hardware are not installed. An example of this warning screen is shown later in this chapter, in Figure 6-16.

6. **At the Completing the Found New Hardware Wizard screen, click Finish.**

   Your wireless network adapter card's drivers are installed!

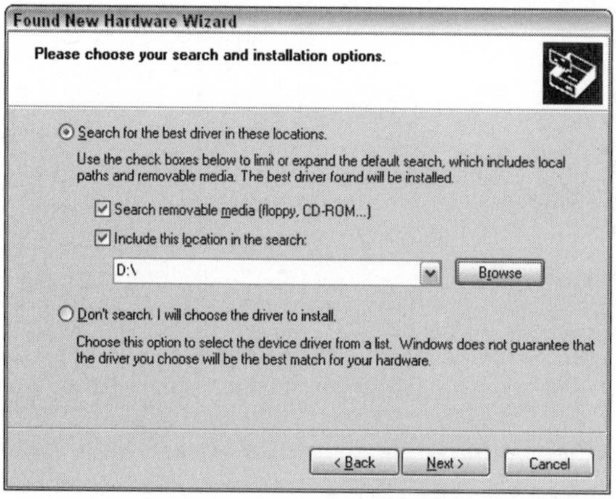

Figure 6-7: Specify your CD-ROM drive letter as the location of the driver files.

Once the drivers for your wireless network adapter card have been installed, Windows XP immediately scans for any available wireless networks within range. If it finds one, it displays another balloon message in the taskbar, as shown in Figure 6-8.

REMEMBER

If Windows XP does not find any wireless networks after your wireless network adapter card has been installed, ensure that your wireless router (or access point) is up and running and that your computer is within range of the wireless network.

To connect to an available network, follow these steps:

1. **Click the Wireless Network Detected balloon.**

   The Wireless Network Connection window appears.

2. **Click the wireless network listed, and then click the Connect button.**

3. **If the Wireless Network Connection dialog box asks whether you want to connect to the unsecured network, click the Connect Anyway button.**

   The connection process includes obtaining an IP address and network settings. Once the process is complete, you should be connected to your wireless network, as shown in Figure 6-9.

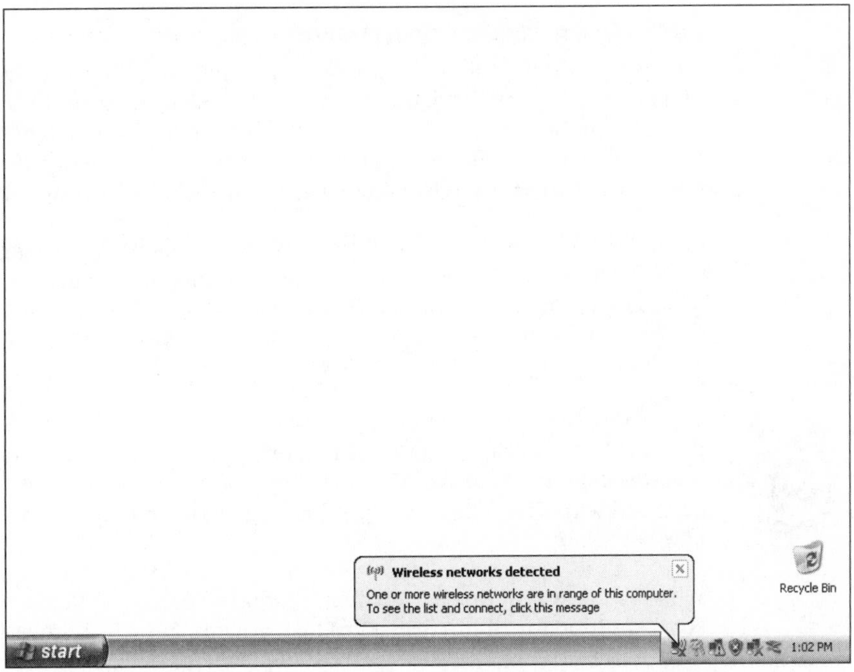
Wireless networks detected
One or more wireless networks are in range of this computer.
To see the list and connect, click this message
Recycle Bin
start
1:02 PM

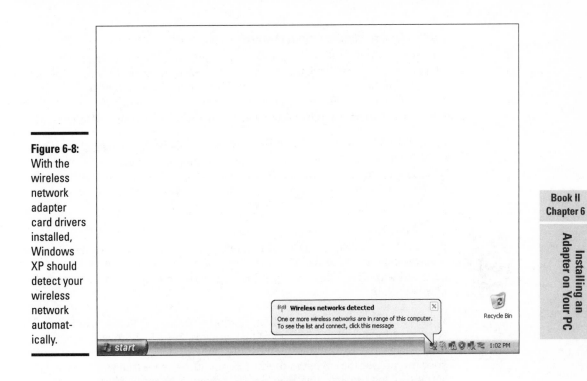

Figure 6-8: With the wireless network adapter card drivers installed, Windows XP should detect your wireless network automatically.

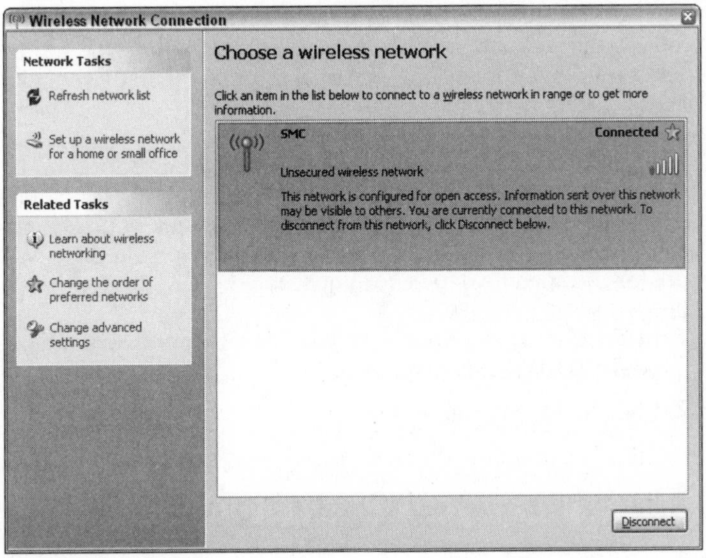
Wireless Network Connection
Network Tasks
Refresh network list
Set up a wireless network for a home or small office
Related Tasks
Learn about wireless networking
Change the order of preferred networks
Change advanced settings
Choose a wireless network
Click an item in the list below to connect to a wireless network in range or to get more information.
SMC
Connected
Unsecured wireless network
This network is configured for open access. Information sent over this network may be visible to others. You are currently connected to this network. To disconnect from this network, click Disconnect below.
Disconnect

Figure 6-9: Connected to your wireless network.

Feel free to tell everyone you know about how well connected you are. They'll certainly be impressed.

Installing adapter utilities

Installing a wireless network adapter card in a computer running Windows XP is usually a straightforward and simple task because of XP's built-in support for wireless networking. Known as *zero-configuration networking,* this feature eliminates the need to install any specialized client software or utilities in order to add wireless networking capabilities to your system.

However, if you're installing your new wireless network adapter card in a system other than Windows XP, you need to install the client software included with your hardware. This software not only includes utilities to configure various wireless networking settings, but also installs the necessary wireless network adapter card driver.

You typically need to install the wireless utility software *prior* to installing the physical network adapter card itself. If you're running Windows 98, Windows ME, or Windows 2000, be prepared to install the software included with your adapter before pulling apart your system to add your new hardware.

While Windows XP doesn't explicitly require you to install any additional software (outside of the driver) to take advantage of its wireless network capabilities, typically nothing stops you from installing the software if that's your preference. Some users prefer to configure their wireless networking settings using the manufacturer's tools, which commonly provide additional tools like signal strength meters, the ability to configure different network profiles, and so forth. At the end of the day, whether you want to use the client program supplied with your adapter or the native capabilities of Windows XP is up to you.

To install the wireless network adapter card utilities for your new hardware, follow these steps. Note that the steps listed here are for a Linksys wireless network adapter card, and that the steps to install your software may be different. When in doubt, using the installation guide supplied with your hardware for the specific details for your model.

1. **Insert the CD supplied with your wireless network adapter card into your CD-ROM drive.**
2. **Click Start➪My Computer.**

   The My Computer window opens.
3. **Double-click your CD-ROM drive letter to open it.**

4. **Look for a file called Setup.exe and double-click it to begin the software installation process.**

   The Setup.exe file may be found as soon as you access the CD, or it may be stored in a folder called Software, Utilities, or similar. When in doubt, check the manuals supplied with your wireless network adapter card.

   The setup program for your wireless network card's utility software opens, as shown in Figure 6-10.

5. **Click the Install link or button.**

Figure 6-10: The setup program for a wireless network adapter card.

6. **Answer the questions asked by the installation program to complete the process.**

   Once the software has been successfully installed, you are prompted to restart your computer.

7. **Restart your computer.**

8. **Log on and look for a new icon for the wireless utility on the taskbar or in your system tray.**

9. **Click the icon to open the program, as shown in Figure 6-11.**

   If the program doesn't appear on your taskbar, attempt to open it from its shortcut under All Programs on the Start menu.

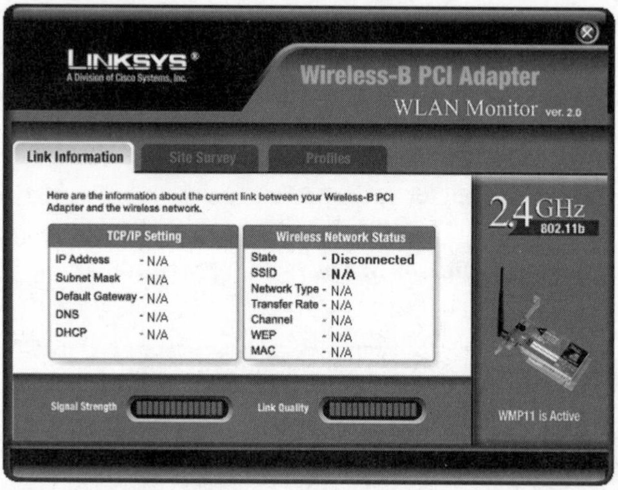

Figure 6-11: The utility for a Linksys wireless network adapter card.

If the wireless utility program opens, it's installed and ready to go! You read more about using the software utilities provided with your wireless network adapter card in Book II, Chapter 7.

If you happen to be running anything other than Windows XP, completing the installation of the software for your network adapter card means that it's time to shut down your system and physically install your hardware. Once the hardware is installed, it should be ready to connect to your wireless network the next time you start up your computer.

Saving Some Time with USB Adapters

If you've never opened your desktop computer's case to install hardware before, the idea can be a little daunting. The good news is that you can avoid getting at your PC's innards completely by opting for an external USB wireless network adapter instead.

USB wireless network adapters make adding wireless capabilities to your PC a snap. All you need is an unused USB port on your computer. Plug in the adapter, install the drivers, and you're off to the races! If you ever change computers, swapping the adapter is as simple as unplugging it from the old one and into the new. No fuss, no muss, and just about as simple as installing any piece of computer hardware could possibly be.

The following sections outline the details of installing a USB wireless network adapter on your computer.

Plug away

Installing a USB wireless network adapter couldn't be easier, but you need a free USB port on your PC. Pretty much any computer manufactured in the last five years will have 2 USB ports available at the back of the system, and maybe even a few at the front. Feel free to use whichever USB port makes you feel most comfortable.

TIP

If you don't have enough USB ports available to connect all of your different USB devices, consider purchasing a USB hub for your system. These devices connect to an existing USB port on your PC, and then add 2 or more USB ports to your system. Usually priced at about $20, USB hubs represent a quick and easy way to extend your USB capabilities.

Of course, if your computer doesn't have any USB ports, that presents a bit of an issue; you won't have anything to plug your adapter into. It's worth noting that you can add USB ports to your PC by installing an internal PCI card, but that's not all that different than installing a PCI wireless network adapter. So, to USB you need USB. Right.

Figure 6-12 shows what a typical USB wireless network adapter looks like. Most of these adapters have a small antenna attached, which you can move from left to right to try to obtain the best signal strength possible.

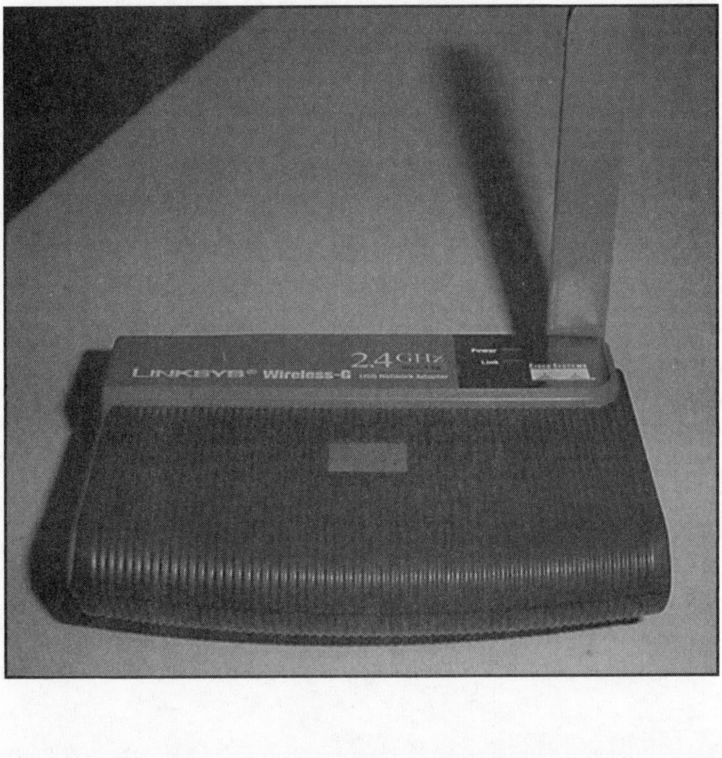

Figure 6-12: A USB wireless network adapter.

1. **With the adapter in hand, start the installation process by plugging the square end of the USB cable into the adapter, as shown in Figure 6-13.**

   This shouldn't be too hard, as only the square end of the cable fits properly. Please don't take pliers to the rectangular end to try and make it fit. That would be bad.

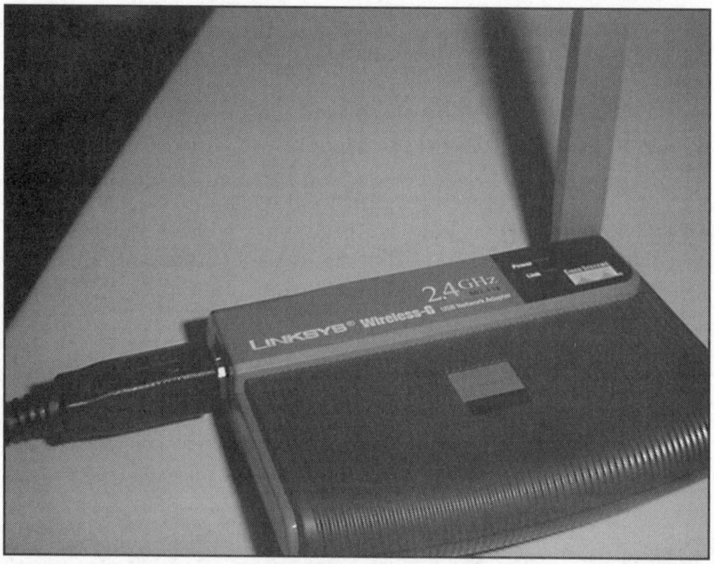

Figure 6-13: Connecting the USB cable to the network adapter.

2. **Plug the rectangular end of the USB cable into an available USB port on your computer, as shown in Figure 6-14.**

That's it. You're done. No, really.

TECHNICAL STUFF

I don't know whether you noticed, but I didn't even mention shutting down your PC. That's because you don't need to when working with USB devices. They're *hot-swappable,* meaning that you can connect or disconnect them without powering down your computer, no damage done. USB is cool, no?

TIP

If you're already well versed in the convenience of using USB devices, you may be experiencing a situation I refer to as *USB overload.* This occurs when you have many USB devices, but too few USB ports. While many newer PCs include 4 or more USB ports as standard equipment, older models generally include only 2. If you want to take your USB setup a little further, consider connecting a powered *USB hub* to your system. These devices add many USB ports to your system and help avoid the need to constantly unplug one device to make room for another. If you're big on USB, you won't have any trouble finding a use for all the additional ports that a USB hub provides.

Figure 6-14: Connecting the USB cable to the computer.

Driving Miss Lazy

Choosing a USB network adapter doesn't make you lazy, it just saves you a whole lot of time. Just plug and go! That means that you have more time to do fun stuff that has nothing to do with your wireless network, like fishing, camping, taking your kids to the park, or cooking a gourmet meal.

While opting for a USB wireless network adapter steers you clear of needing to open your computer, you can't avoid installing a driver. (Sorry!) The good news is that the whole process is quick, painless, and should go off without a hitch.

After you connect the USB wireless network adapter to your computer, Windows XP should detect the presence of a new USB device automatically, as shown in Figure 6-15. Clicking this balloon message opens the Found New Hardware Wizard immediately, but if you wait a few seconds the wizard opens all on its own.

Follow the steps to install the necessary drivers for your USB wireless network adapter:

1. **At the Welcome to the Found New Hardware Wizard screen, select No, Not This Time and click Next.**

2. **When asked what you would like the wizard to do, select Install from a List or Specific Location (Advanced). Click Next.**
3. **At the Please Choose Your Search and Installation Option screen, ensure that your CD-ROM drive is listed under Include This Location in the Search.**
4. **Insert the CD-ROM provided with your wireless network adapter card.**

   If you downloaded the driver files from the manufacturer's web site, be sure to instead enter the drive letter and folder where they are stored on your hard drive.
5. **Click Next.**

   In some cases, the drivers or files that you are installing may not be digitally signed. If this is the case, a warning message similar to the one shown in Figure 6-16 appears.
6. **Click the Continue Anyway button for each of these messages that you encounter.**

Figure 6-15: Windows XP should automatically detect your wireless network adapter when you connect it to a USB port.

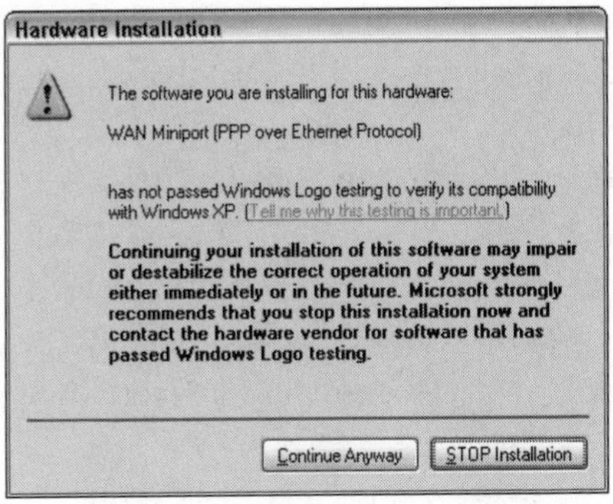

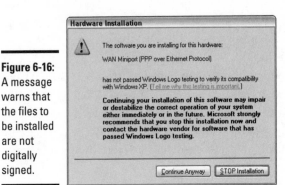

Figure 6-16: A message warns that the files to be installed are not digitally signed.

Once the drivers for your USB adapter are installed, you should see a balloon message stating that your wireless network has been found. Connect to the new network using the steps outlined in the "Who's Driving?" section earlier in this chapter.

Again, utilities

Much like any wireless network adapter, a USB model typically includes a software utility required to use the adapter on non-Windows XP systems. While you don't necessarily need to install this software on a Windows XP system, you can if you want to. Installing the utility not only installs various software components and tools, but also the driver for the wireless network adapter card.

If you're planning to install a USB wireless network adapter on a non-Windows XP system, the same rule applies as with PCI-based models: Install the software first and then connect the adapter to your system. Of course, your best bet is always to follow the instructions that were supplied with your model.

Installing the adapter utilities for a USB wireless network adapter are typically no different than for any other model. Just pop in the CD, open your CD-ROM drive letter in My Computer, and then run the Setup.exe program. Once the setup window opens (as shown in Figure 6-17), use the Install link or button to begin the installation process, and answer the questions appropriately as them come up. See, I told you that installing a wireless network adapter wasn't that difficult!

Figure 6-17: The setup program for a USB wireless network adapter.

Chapter 7: Adapter-ing

In This Chapter

- **Configuring your wireless network adapter**
- **Using Windows XP's Wireless Zero Configuration**
- **Working with your adapter's software utilities**
- **Ensuring that your wireless network adapter functions correctly**
- **Estimating the range your wireless adapter supports**

Installing your wireless network adapter is only half the battle. Although it may be up, running, and ready to go once you have the physical hardware installed or connected, it's still important to be familiar with how the related software components are used and configured. Welcome to a chapter I like to call "Adapter-ing," where you discover all the juicy details of getting under your wireless network adapter's hood.

Configuring Your Wireless Adapter

If you have your wireless network adapter installed, it's time to read more about how to configure its settings. If you're running Windows XP, you can configure your wireless network adapter using its built-in wireless networking capabilities *or* the software utility included with your adapter. If you're not running XP, the good news is that the software provided with your adapter gets the job done.

So as not to be impartial, I show you how to configure your wireless network card using either method. It's two techniques for the price of one!

Starting at Zero

One of the best reasons for using Windows XP as the operating system for computers on your network is its built-in support for wireless networking. Using a feature known as Wireless Zero Configuration, Windows XP has the ability to handle all wireless client settings without the need for any additional software utilities or programs. With other operating systems (such as Windows 2000 or Windows 98), you need to install a utility program supplied with your wireless network adapter card for your computers to connect to a wireless network.

Assuming that you've already installed your wireless network adapter according to the instructions I outlined in Book II, Chapter 6, it's time to get down to the business of configuring your adapter. It may seem like you've nothing left to do, as Windows XP automatically scans for available wireless networks once the adapter card is installed and allows you to connect at the click of a button. However, plenty is going on behind the scenes that you want to be familiar with. The best way to begin is with a little orientation, discovering where to find the settings with which you need to be familiar.

The easiest way to get at your wireless network adapter card's configuration is by clicking the wireless network icon on the Windows XP taskbar. If you hover your cursor over the icon, you are presented with a tooltip that provides the following information, as shown in Figure 7-1:

- ✦ The name of the network connection.
- ✦ The current connection speed.
- ✦ The current signal strength for the connection.
- ✦ The current status of the connection.

Figure 7-1: Viewing the status of your wireless network connection.

Clicking the wireless network icon opens the Wireless Network Connection Status window shown in Figure 7-2.

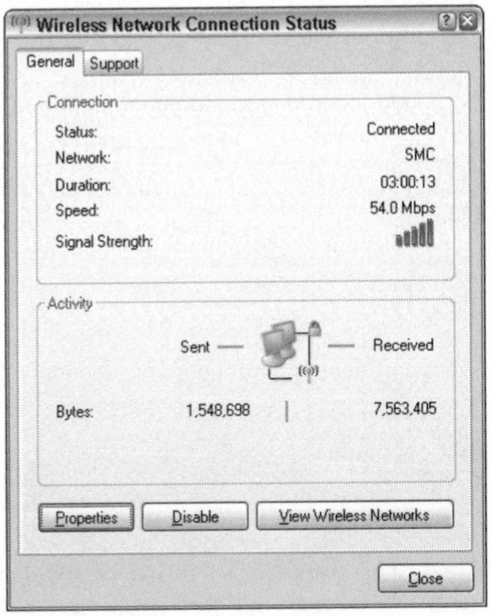

Figure 7-2: The Wireless Network Connection Status window.

The General tab of the Wireless Network Connection Status window provides information about your wireless network, including details of the current connection and any activity (data sent or received) over the wireless link. Furthermore, this tab includes a number of buttons that help you delve deeper into the configuration of your adapter or control its general operation.

You find these buttons on the General tab:

✦ **Properties.** This button takes you to the Properties window for your wireless network adapter, from which general network, security, and wireless settings are configured.

✦ **Disable.** If your wireless network adapter is currently enabled, pressing this button disables it. If the adapter is currently disabled, this button changes to read Enable.

✦ **View Wireless Networks.** Pressing this button opens the window that allows you to scan for wireless networks within range and connect to available networks.

Additionally, the Wireless Network Connection Status window includes a Support tab, as shown in Figure 7-3. This tab's Connection Status section lists details about your IP address and related settings, including how the address is assigned to your computer (manually or via DHCP).

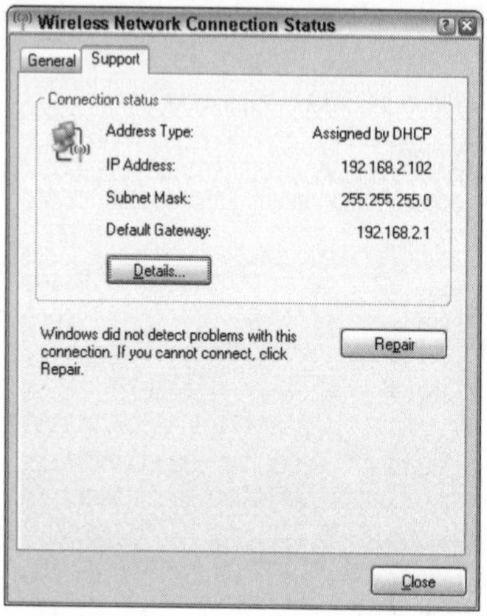

Figure 7-3: The Support tab of the Wireless Network Connection Status window.

The Details button on the Support tab simply provides more information about your wireless network adapter's network settings, as shown in Figure 7-4.

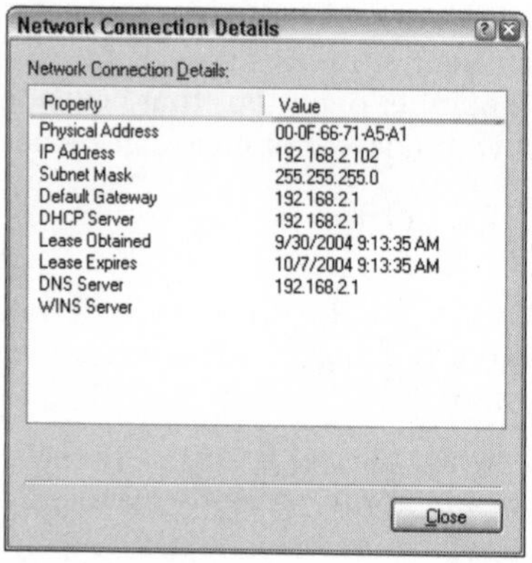

Figure 7-4: Reviewing network connection details.

Finally, the Support tab includes a button named Repair. When you press this button, the wireless network adapter attempts to restore connectivity with the network. This includes going through the process of attempting to renew its IP address and related settings. You read more about dealing with networking connection problems in Book IV, Chapter 3.

Now that you know where to find things, get down to configuring settings for your adapter.

Dances with networks

When your wireless network adapter is first installed, it is configured to obtain an IP address automatically by default. Because your wireless router is configured to distribute IP address automatically by default as well, your wireless adapter should obtain an address without issue as part of connecting to the wireless network.

As you discover in Book II, Chapter 5, you don't necessarily need to have DHCP running on the your wireless network. Instead, you might opt to configure the IP addresses on all of your wireless devices manually. Disabling DHCP on your router stops it from handing out IP addresses to any computer that requests one, including outside users within range of your network.

If you have disabled the DHCP component on your router, configure IP address settings on all of your client systems manually. To do this, follow these steps:

1. **Click the wireless network connection icon on the Windows XP taskbar.**

   The Wireless Network Connection Status window opens.

2. **Click the Properties button.**

   The Wireless Network Connection Properties window opens, as shown in Figure 7-5.

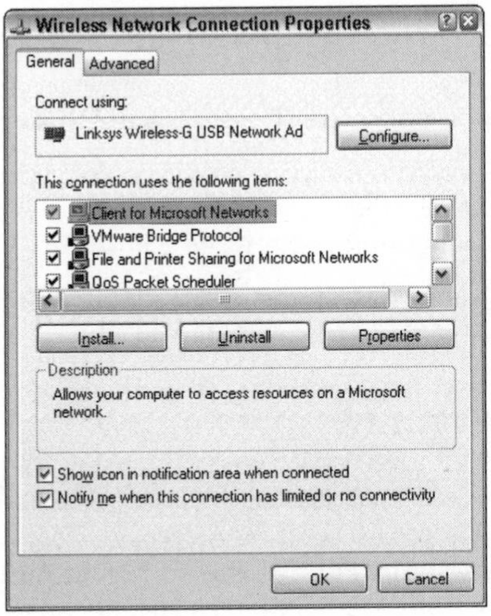

Figure 7-5: The Wireless Network Connection Properties window.

3. **In the This Connection Uses the Following Items section, click Internet Protocol (TCP/IP) and then click Properties.**

   The Internet Protocol (TCP/IP) Properties window opens, as shown in Figure 7-6.

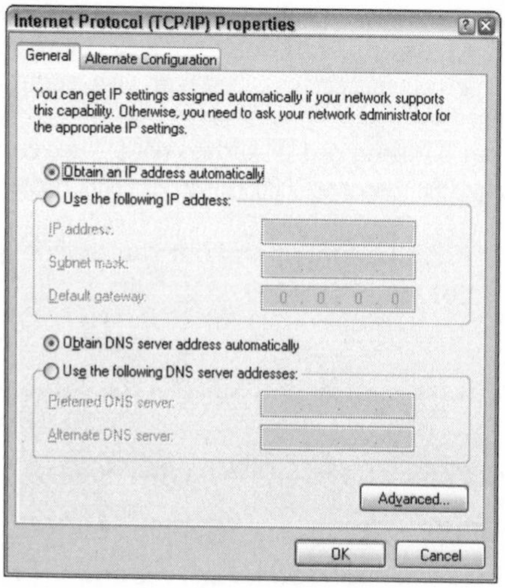

Figure 7-6: The Internet Protocol (TCP/IP) Properties window.

4. **Click the Use the Following IP Address radio button.**

   The text boxes to enter IP address, Subnet mask, and Default gateway values can now be edited.

5. **In the IP Address text box, enter the IP address for this connection.**

   Make sure to use a valid address for your network. For example, if your router uses the IP address 192.168.2.1, a valid IP address for this system is 192.168.2.*x* (where *x* is any number between 2 and 254).

6. **Press the Tab key. A Subnet Mask value of 255.255.255.0 is already entered. You should leave this value as it stands.**

7. **In the Default Gateway text box, enter the IP address of your wireless router (for example, 192.168.2.1).**

   Your IP address settings should now be similar to those shown in Figure 7-7.

   - If necessary, click the Use the Following DNS Server Addresses radio button. In most cases, this step is unnecessary because almost all wireless routers automatically take care of DNS requests on behalf of client systems, with no further configuration.

- If it is necessary for your network, enter the DNS server IP addresses provided by your ISP in the Preferred DNS server and Alternate DNS server text boxes.

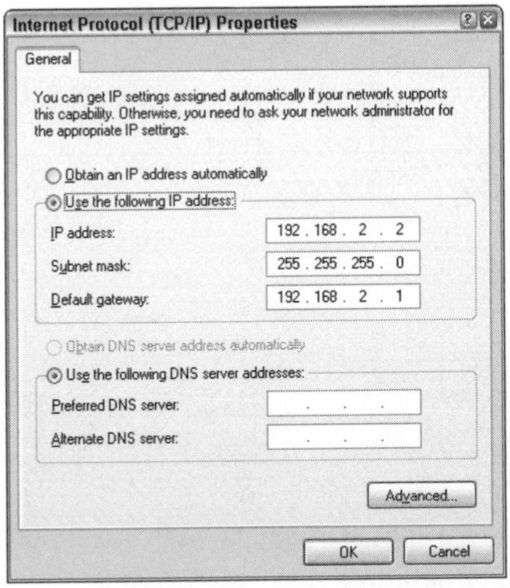

Figure 7-7: Configuring IP address settings manually.

8. Click OK to exit the Internet Protocol (TCP/IP) Properties window. Click OK again to exit the Wireless Network Connection Properties window.

Your manual and unchanging IP address is configured!

WARNING!

Configuring IP addresses manually isn't a bad idea, especially if you're worried about outside users gaining access to your wireless network. However, if you decide to go the manual route, be careful to ensure that each device on your network is assigned a unique address, since a duplicated IP address causes communication problems. You should also disable your router's DHCP component, if only to ensure that you don't run into conflicts between manually and dynamically assigned addresses.

Once you've configured your wireless network adapter card with a manual IP address, you should still be able to connect to other devices on your network (such as your router) without issue. To check the status of your connection, click the wireless network connection icon on the taskbar and then click the Support tab. The Connection status section should show your new address and list the Address Type as Manually Configured, as shown in Figure 7-8.

Don't forget that you can always go back to obtaining an IP address via DHCP by enabling your router's DHCP component, and then changing the settings in your Internet Protocol (TCP/IP) Properties window to the Obtain an IP Address Automatically setting.

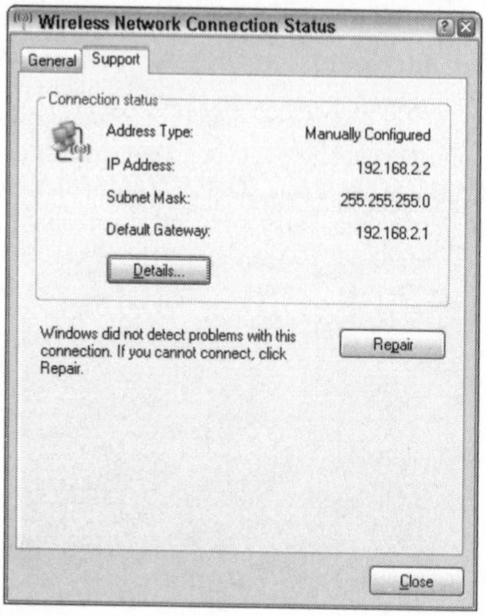

Figure 7-8: Reviewing your connection's status.

Ready for wireless

Once your TCP/IP network settings are configured, it's on to the wireless portion of your program. The primary wireless configuration settings that allow your adapter to connect to a wireless network are accessed via the Wireless Networks tab in the Wireless Network Connection Properties window shown in Figure 7-9.

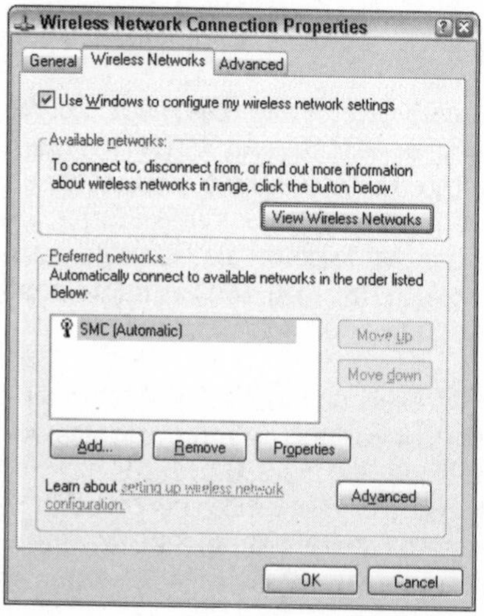

Figure 7-9: The Wireless Networks tab.

The purpose of settings and buttons on the Wireless Networks tab are outlined here:

- **Use Windows to Configure My Wireless Network Settings.** When this setting is enabled, Windows XP uses Wireless Zero Configuration as the method of configuring settings for your wireless network adapter. If this checkbox is cleared, the software utility provided with your adapter must be used to configure wireless network settings.
- **Available Networks.** Clicking the View Available Networks button in this section opens a window that allows you to scan for and then connect to or disconnect from any wireless networks within range.
- **Preferred Networks.** This section allows you to configure your wireless network adapter with the settings required to connect to different wireless networks. The buttons in this section can be used to add or remove networks, as well as configure a network's settings. The Move Up and Move Down buttons allow you to control the order in which Windows XP automatically attempts to connect to the networks you have configured. Networks higher on the list have preference and are the first to which a connection is attempted. The Advanced button in the Preferred Networks section is looked at later in this section.

Assuming that you are currently connected to a wireless network that was discovered automatically, that network should be listed in the Preferred Networks section of the Wireless Networks tab. The listed name for the network is its *Security Set Identifier (SSID),* follow by the word Automatic in brackets. This lets you know both the name of the preferred network and that you did not configure its settings manually.

While your own wireless network may well be the only one you ever intend to connect to, you may need to connect to a different wireless network that requires some manual configuration. Use the following steps to add a preferred network to your adapter's list:

1. **If it's not open already, click the wireless network connection icon in your taskbar, click the Properties button, and then click the Wireless Networks tab.**
2. **In the Preferred networks section, click the Add button.**

   The Wireless Network Properties window opens, as shown in Figure 7-10.
3. **On the Association tab, type the SSID name of the wireless network you want to add.**
4. **In the Wireless Network Key section, select Disabled in the Data Encryption drop-down box.**

While some wireless networks require the configuration of security features like encryption, I'm going to assume that you're connecting to an unsecured network for now. The processes for implementing wireless security and connecting to security networks are looked at in detail in Book IV, Chapter 1.

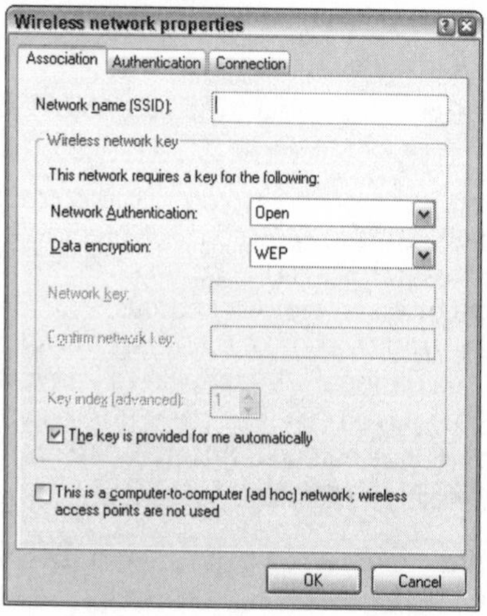

Figure 7-10: Adding a new wireless network.

5. **Click the Connection tab.**

   The Connection tab appears, as shown in Figure 7-11.

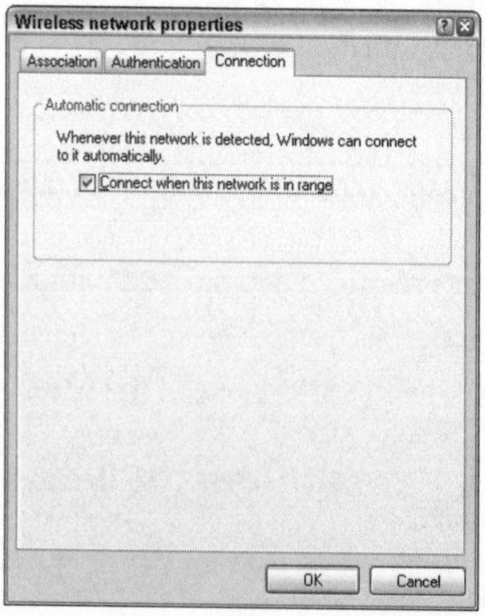

Figure 7-11: The Connection tab in the properties of a wireless network.

6. **In the Automatic connection section, decide whether to select or deselect Connect When This Network Is Within Range:**
   - **Enable it if preferred.**
   - **Disable it if you would rather Windows XP never attempt to connect to this network automatically.**

7. **Click OK.**

   The new wireless network is added to the top of the Preferred Networks list in Figure 7-12.

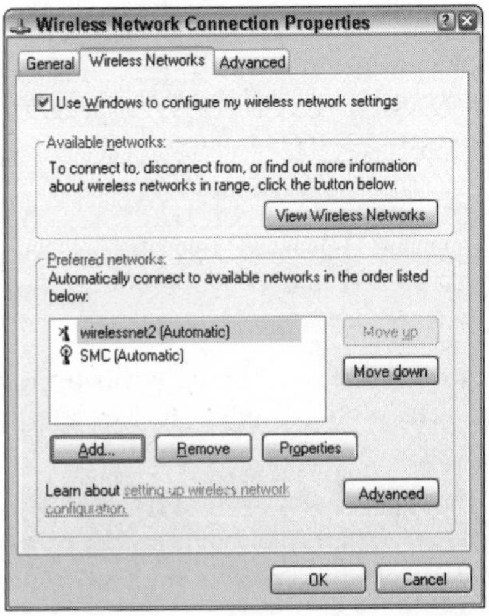

Figure 7-12: The Preferred networks list after adding a new wireless network.

8. **Click the new wireless network in the Preferred Networks list. Click the Move Down button.**

   The new wireless network is now the second entry on your Preferred Networks list, bringing the entry for your own home network to the top of the list.

I did promise to get to it, so you may be curious about the Advanced button on the Wireless Networks tab. Clicking this button opens the Advanced window shown in Figure 7-13.

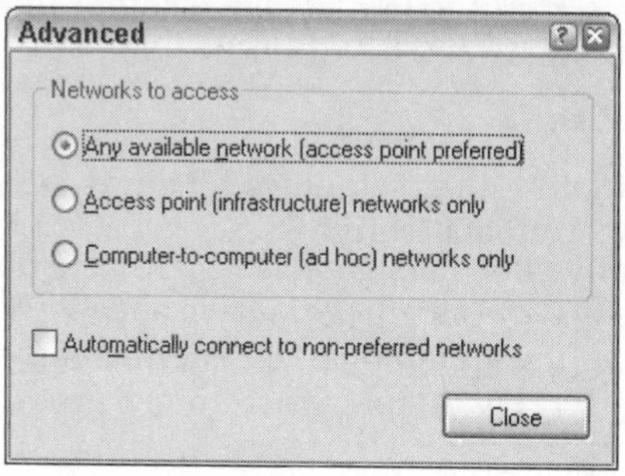

Figure 7-13: The Advanced window accessed from the properties of a wireless network connection.

The settings in the Networks to Access section allow you to control the different types of wireless networks that your wireless network adapter card attempts to connect to. These options are available:

- **Any Available Network (Access Point Preferred).** This option is selected by default and dictates that your wireless network adapter attempts to connect to any available wireless network, but gives preference to wireless networks that use access points.
- **Access Point (Infrastructure) Networks Only.** If this option is selected, your wireless network adapter only connects to wireless networks that use access points.
- **Computer-to-Computer (Ad Hoc) Networks Only.** If you select this option, your wireless network adapter only connects to wireless networks that do not use access points, such as those formed between two computers with wireless network adapters.

As a general rule, stick with the default Any Available Network option to ensure the greatest degree of compatibility with any wireless networks you may encounter.

In the wireless networking work, an *infrastructure mode network* is simply a wireless network where clients connect to each other or the Internet via an access point (or wireless router). An *ad-hoc mode network* is a wireless network without an access point, where computers with wireless connections communicate directly with one another. Most wireless networks work in infrastructure mode, but ad-hoc mode is a great option for transferring files between wireless systems if no access point or router is handy.

Additionally, the Advanced window includes a checkbox called Automatically Connect to Non-preferred Networks. If you enable this option, your wireless network adapter card automatically attempts to connect to any wireless network within range, regardless of whether it appears on your preferred networks list. As a general rule, you should keep this setting disabled, lest you run the risk of connecting to someone else's network without their permission.

Device Manager settings

On top of the settings that must be configured to connect to different wireless networks, most wireless network adapters have advanced properties that can be configured using the Windows XP Device Manager tool. While needing to configure these settings is rare, it's still worth knowing about them and how to get at them should you need to.

Follow these steps to get at the advanced settings for your wireless network adapter in Device Manager:

1. **Click Start, right-click My Computer, and click Properties.**

   The System Properties window opens.

2. **Click the Hardware tab and then click the Device Manager button.**

   The Device Manager window opens.

3. **Expand the Network Adapters section.**

4. **Right-click your wireless network adapter and click Properties.**

   The Properties window for your wireless network adapter opens.

5. **Click the Advanced tab.**

   The Advanced tab for your wireless network adapter is displayed, as shown in Figure 7-14.

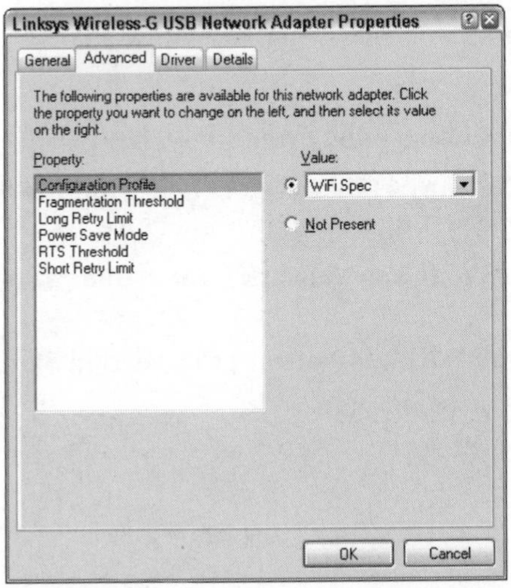

Figure 7-14: The Advanced tab from the properties of a wireless network adapter in Device Manager.

6. **On the Advanced tab, click each of the different items displayed in the Property list. Review the associated values for each.**

   The available property settings for a given wireless network adapter varies from model to model.

7. **Click OK to exit the Properties window for your wireless network adapter, and then close Device Manager.**

Now you know how to get at the advanced properties for your wireless network adapter card should the need ever arise.

Using your wireless adapter's utilities

If your wireless network adapter is installed on a computer running an operating system other than Windows XP, you need to use the software utility included with your adapter to get connected to your wireless network. If you are running Windows XP, you still have the option of using the utility supplied with your adapter, instead of the Wireless Zero Configuration method.

I'm going to assume that you're running Windows XP to begin with, just to walk you through the process of making the switch to the adapter utility instead of the Wireless Zero Configuration. Once that part is sorted, the configuration steps for the utility itself should effectively be the same, regardless of the operating system that you're using. I'm also assuming that you've already installed the software utility for your wireless network adapter. If not, the necessary steps are outlined in Book II, Chapter 6.

Follow the steps to stop Wireless Zero Configuration from being the primary configuration tool for your wireless network adapter:

1. **Click the wireless network connection icon on the taskbar.**

   The Wireless Network Connection Status window opens.

2. **Click the Properties button.**

   The Wireless Network Connection Properties window opens.

3. **Click the Wireless Networks tab. Deselect Use Windows to Configure My Wireless Network Settings, as shown in Figure 7-15.**

4. **Click OK to close the Wireless Network Connection Properties window.**

5. **Click Close to exit the Wireless Network Connection Status window.**

If the software utility for your wireless network adapter isn't already open and running in the taskbar, open it from its shortcut on the Start menu. The program should currently be configured with the settings you specified when you first installed it.

If the program is already running, double-click its icon in the taskbar and select the option to open the program. Since I'm using a Linksys USB adapter for this example, the Linksys Wireless Network Monitor program opens, as shown in Figure 7-16.

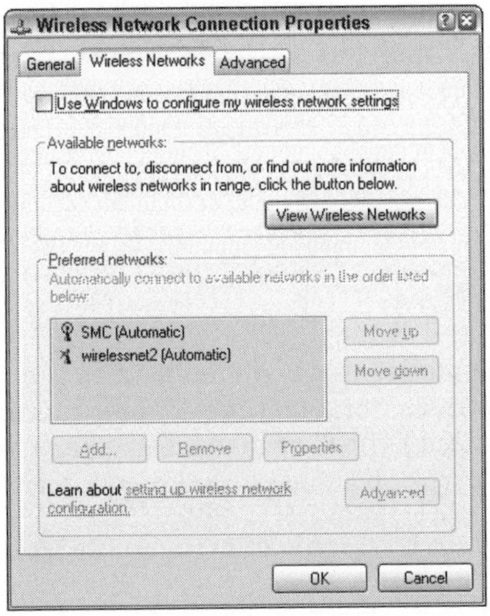

Figure 7-15: Disabling Windows XP from configuring your wireless network adapter.

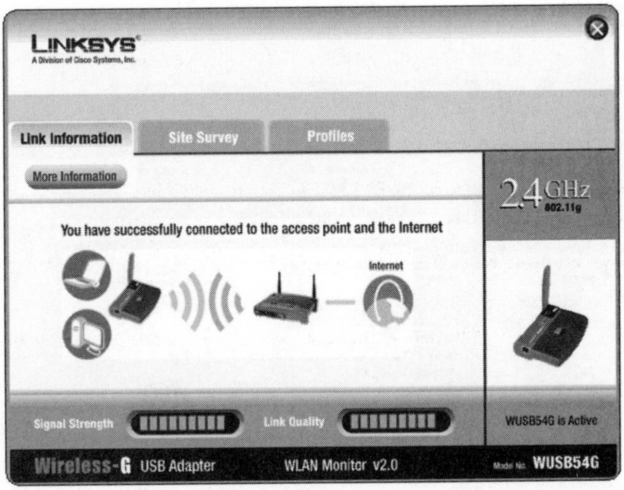

Figure 7-16: The Linksys Wireless Network Monitor utility.

The Linksys Wireless Network Monitor program for my adapter includes three tabs:

- **Link Information.** This tab displays information about the status of the link between the wireless network adapter card and the router, as well as the router's connection to the Internet. The tab also includes information about the strength and quality of the wireless signal from the point of view of the adapter.
- **Site Survey.** The Site Survey tab lists any accessible networks within range, along with basic details about each network. Clicking a particular network name (SSID) displays site information about that network.
- **Profiles.** The Profiles tab configures settings for any existing wireless network, as well as adds settings for additional wireless networks. The idea of a profile on a Linksys router is similar to a preferred network in Windows XP.

To change the settings for the wireless network you configured when you first installed your wireless network adapter's utility software, follow the steps given here.

REMEMBER

The steps for your particular model may be different than the ones listed. These particular steps are relevant for a Linksys adapter running the WLAN Monitor 2.0 utility software. Check the user manual that came with your model for more details on the specific steps for your adapter utility.

1. **Open the Monitor program by double-clicking on its icon in the taskbar if necessary.**

   The WLAN Monitor utility program opens.

2. **Click the Profiles tab shown in Figure 7-17.**

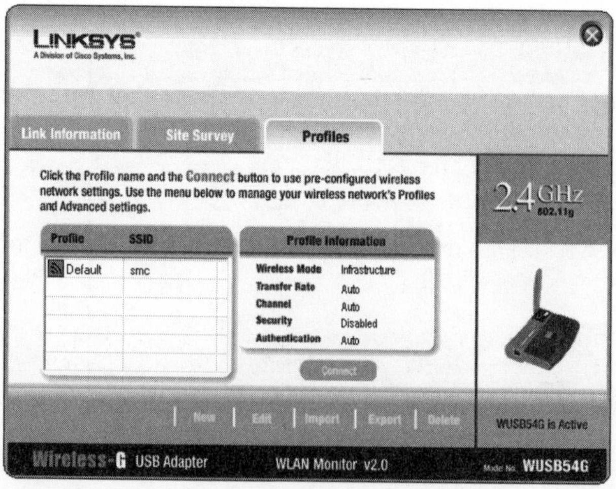

Figure 7-17: The Profiles tab of the Linksys Wireless Network Monitor utility.

3. **Click the Default profile created when you first installed the utility, and then click the Edit button.**
4. **At the Network Settings screen, choose between these two options:**
   - **Use DHCP to obtain an IP address.**
   - **Specify address setting manually, as shown in Figure 7-18.**
5. **Click Next.**

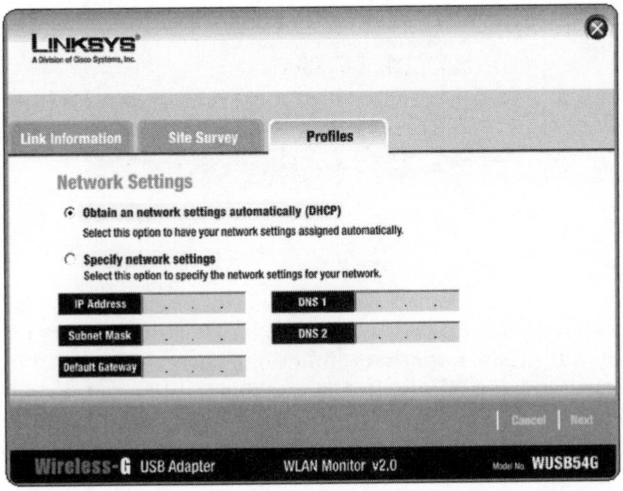

Figure 7-18: Changing networking settings using the Linksys Wireless Network Monitor utility.

6. **At the Wireless Mode screen, select Infrastructure Mode.**
7. **In the SSID text box, enter the SSID name of your wireless network, as shown in Figure 7-19. Click Next.**
8. **At the Wireless Security screen, ensure that Security is set to Disabled. Click Next.**
9. **At the Confirm New Settings screen, ensure that the settings you entered are correct and click Save.**
10. **At the Congratulations screen, click the Connect to Network link to connect to your wireless network.**

    Your adapter is now connected to your wireless networking using its native software utility.

Besides being able to edit your existing wireless network profile settings, you can also add profiles by clicking New on the profile screen (rather than Edit). Some wireless network adapter utilities even include options to import or export the device's configuration settings, making it easier to configure multiple instances of the same adapter on larger networks.

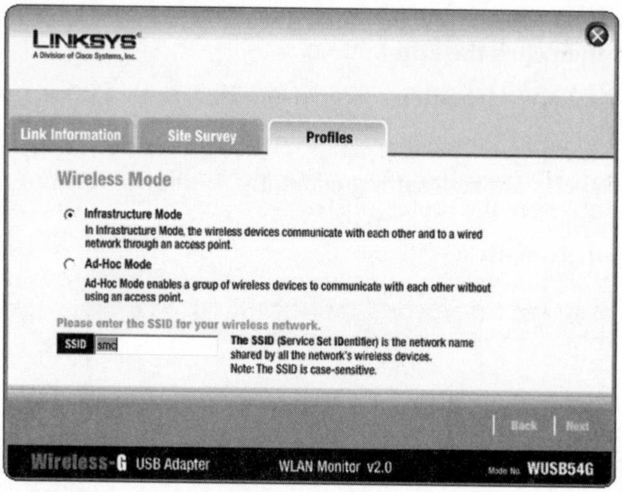

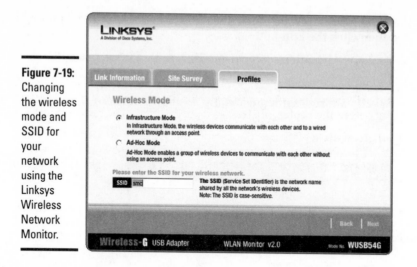

Figure 7-19: Changing the wireless mode and SSID for your network using the Linksys Wireless Network Monitor.

Making Sure It Works

Once you have your wireless network adapter configured correctly, you obviously want to be sure that it functions correctly. In most cases, determining whether your connection is working is as easy as firing up your favorite web browser. If your Internet home page appears, that's a pretty good indication that everything works just fine.

While connecting to the Internet may be proof enough for you (heck, it's always been proof enough for me!), it's never a bad idea to be familiar with some of the more technical methods that can be used to check your connection's status. If nothing else, knowing these techniques adds a few tools to your troubleshooting arsenal, should problems ever arise.

Wireless connection status

Another quick and easy way to test your wireless network connection is to use the Wireless Network Connection Status window shown in Figure 7-20. Recall that to open this window, all you need to do is click the wireless network connection icon on your taskbar.

Use the information in the Connection section of the General tab to ensure that things are working like they should. If your wireless network connection is perfect (or close to it), you should see values similar to these:

- **Status.** The best message to see here is definitely Connected.
- **Network.** This setting should list the SSID name that you configured on your wireless router. If it doesn't, you may be connected to somebody else's network.

✦ **Duration.** This displays how long you've been connected to the wireless network.

✦ **Speed.** In the best-case scenario, the value listed here is equal to the highest possible rate that your wireless network card supports. On an 802.11b network that's 11 Mbps, on an 802.11a or 802.11g network that's 54 Mbps. If this value is lower that the maximum, changes are good that distance from the router, obstructions, or interference are the culprits.

✦ **Signal Strength.** If all five of the signal strength bars are lit green, things are great; you've hit the maximum. Realistically, you can expect lower signal strength the farther the network adapter is from the access point, with obstructions and interference again playing a role.

After you've taken a closer look at the Connection section, shift down to the Activity section. If your wireless connection is working properly, you should see non-zero values under both Bytes Sent and Received. If either of these values is stuck at 0, something is almost certainly not working as it should.

Finally, click the Support tab to take a gander at the Connection status information. If your IP address falls into the same range as the one assigned to your router (typically 192.168.x.x), everything is likely working as it should. If your stuck with an IP address of 0.0.0.0 or 169.254.x.x, your wireless network card isn't receiving an IP address correctly from the router's DHCP component.

You read much more about troubleshooting networking issues like misconfigured IP addresses in Book IV, Chapter 3. Hang tight!

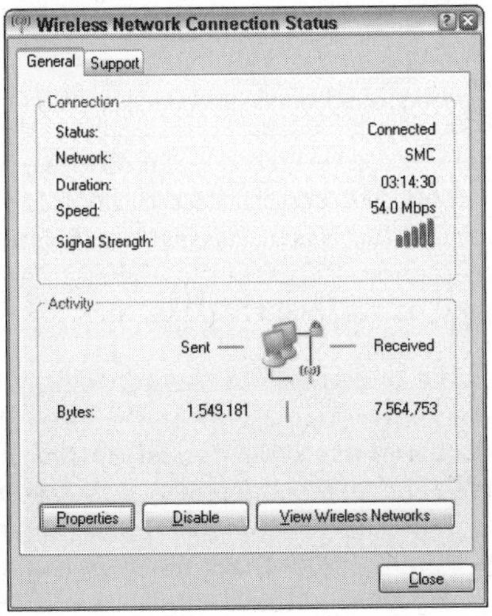

Figure 7-20: Ensuring that your wireless network adapter is connected.

Viewing available wireless networks

Another way to ensure that your wireless network adapter is functioning correctly is to scan for and attempt to connect to wireless networks within range.

1. **Right-click the wireless network connection icon on your taskbar and select View Available Wireless Networks.**

   This opens the window shown in Figure 7-21.

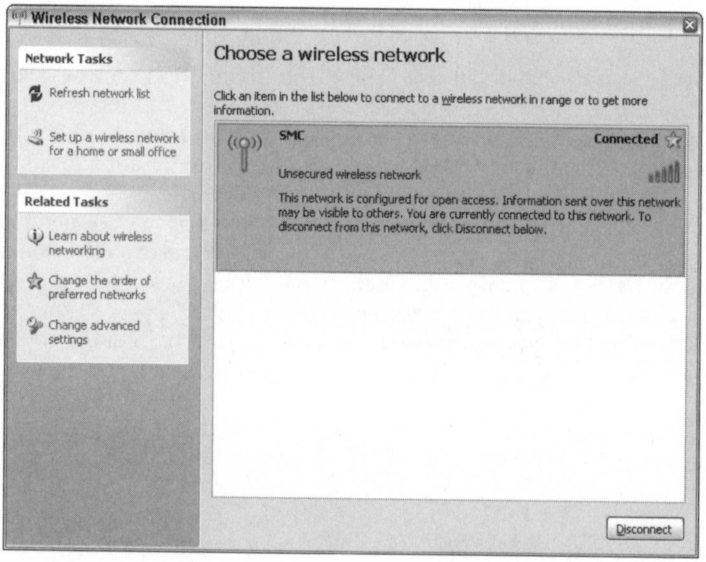
Wireless Network Connection
Network Tasks
Refresh network list
Set up a wireless network for a home or small office
Related Tasks
Learn about wireless networking
Change the order of preferred networks
Change advanced settings
Choose a wireless network
Click an item in the list below to connect to a wireless network in range or to get more information.
SMC
Connected
Unsecured wireless network
This network is configured for open access. Information sent over this network may be visible to others. You are currently connected to this network. To disconnect from this network, click Disconnect below.
Disconnect

Figure 7-21: Viewing available wireless networks within range.

   Any wireless networks that you are connected to (or that your wireless network adapter has discovered) are listed in the Choose a wireless network section. If you don't see the network that you need to connect to, click the Refresh Network List link in the Network tasks menu to scan for new networks.

2. **Once a network is discovered, click it.**
3. **Click Connect. If you're able to connect to the network, you're rocking!**

REMEMBER

If any of the wireless networks listed use security features like Wired Equivalent Privacy (WEP) or Wi-Fi Protected Access (WPA), you need to configure the appropriate security settings for those networks before you can connect to them. You read all about configuring your wireless network adapter to connect to secured wireless networks in Book IV, Chapter 1.

Traveling to utilityland

If you're using the software utility supplied with your wireless network adapter rather than XP's Wireless Zero Configuration feature, use that utility to determine your connection status. The easiest way to do that is to fire up the utility and browse through the information it provides.

For example, the Linksys Wireless Monitor program shows you information about whether your adapter is active and connected to both your wireless network and the Internet from the Link Information tab in Figure 7-22.

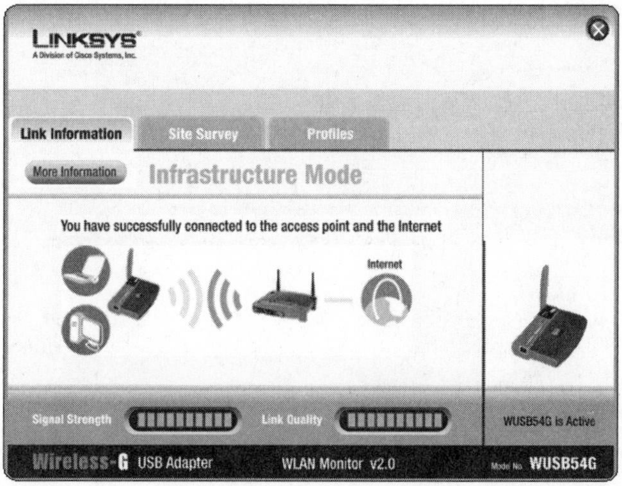

Figure 7-22: Reviewing link information using the Linksys Wireless Network Monitor utility.

From here, you can also click the More Information button to review details of your connection, including its status, as shown in Figure 7-23. As with the tools native to Windows XP, be sure that key elements like your SSID and IP address settings are correct.

Next, click the Statistics button to gather statistical information about packets sent and received, adapter uptime, transmit and receive speeds, and so forth. The Wireless Network Statistics screen for my Linksys USB adapter is shown in Figure 7-24.

Ultimately, the information provided by the Windows XP Wireless Zero Configuration tools and that supplied by your wireless network adapter utility software are very similar. The biggest difference is in where the information is stored or how you find it.

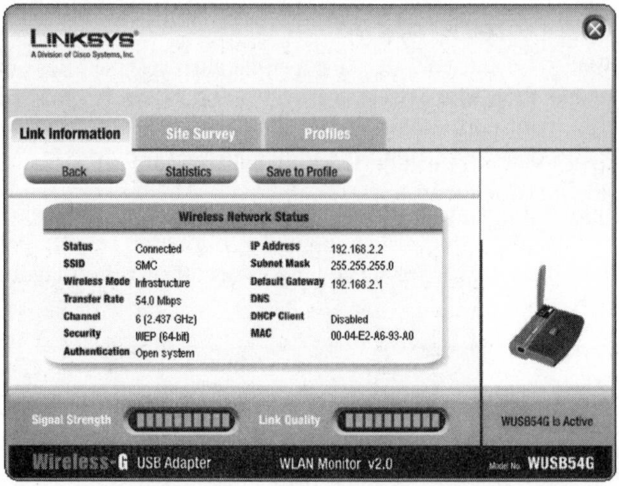

Figure 7-23: Reviewing wireless network status information using the Linksys Wireless Network Monitor utility.

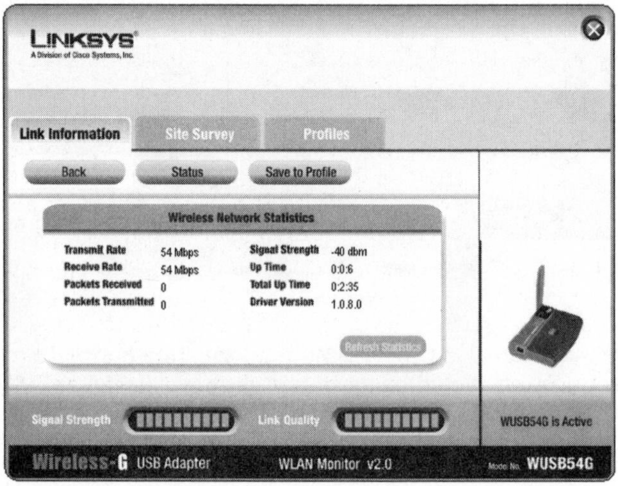

Figure 7-24: Reviewing wireless network statistics using the Linksys Wireless Network Monitor utility.

Estimating Your Range

Estimating the distances that you can span between a computer geared up with a wireless network adapter and your wireless router is a tough call. In truth, it has much to do with your particular environment. Besides distance alone, issues like obstacles and interference have an impact.

As a general rule, as your wireless network adapter gets farther away from your wireless router, signal strength degrades and connection speeds are lower. While you probably obtain the maximum signal strength, quality, and speed when both devices are in the same room, you should expect all of these elements to take a hit as you increase the distance between them. Quite simply, your wireless network takes a bit of a performance hit as it has more elements to work around.

Having said that, don't be surprised if you notice that a wireless network adapter card positioned on the opposite end of your home from your router can only connect at speeds that are a fraction of the maximum. For example, it's not unusual for an 802.11g wireless adapter to connect at speeds of 48, 36, 18, 9, 6, or even 3 Mbps if the distance between the adapter and the router is great. This is a function of the wireless network card and router *adjusting* to a common speed that they can both maintain, based on the quality of the radio signals being passed between them. You read more about dealing with obstacles and interference in Book III, Chapter 5.

In the meantime, use the tools at your disposal to determine the status of your wireless adapter's signal strength. If you're using Windows XP, click the wireless network connection icon on your taskbar and review your signal strength and speed. If both are at the maximum values, then a little celebration may be in order — you've reached peak performance! Most wireless adapter utilities also include signal strength and link quality details, so feel free to gather the information with these tools as well.

If you're finding that your signal strength or link quality is low, take some time to work on positioning your equipment. Are devices like your wireless router in an optimal, centralized location? Can your router and the computer with a wireless connection be placed in a better location than where you currently have them? Have you tried changing the orientation of the devices' antennae to see whether that makes a difference? These are all good questions, and you should take some time to play around with things a bit to see whether different equipment locations or positioning has a positive impact.

Most importantly, don't get yourself down or make any rash decisions if the quality or signal strength of the link to your wireless adapter seems a little low at this point. Rome wasn't built in a day, and your network environment may need nothing more than a little tweaking and tuning to greatly improve performance.

Chapter 8: Troubleshooting Network Hardware

In This Chapter

- Dealing with wireless network adapter card issues
- Upgrading a router's firmware
- Updating a wireless network adapter card driver
- Upgrading wireless network adapter card utilities

You're a do-it-yourselfer, eh? Well, just like anything around the house, your wireless network may need a little fixing from time to time. At the end of the day, though, troubleshooting the hardware on your wireless network has much more to do with the software components of these devices than the physical hardware itself. Having said that, you won't need to have a screwdriver handy and if you're thinking hammer, you should definitely step away from the wireless network!

Some of the more common tasks associated with troubleshooting the hardware on a wireless network include knowing how to reset routers and access points, how to upgrade firmware, and how to deal with device driver issues. Unless you're going to be highly interpretive and overly creative, you shouldn't need much in the way of tools to get these jobs done.

If you're looking for an excuse to run out and purchase some new tools, consider a box of paperclips. You really only need one, but having some spares on hand never hurts.

Shooting Down Hardware Trouble

It's easy to get frustrated when something doesn't work properly. That something could be a noisy fridge, a leaky pipe, or the hardware on your wireless network. Now, I can't help with your fridge or pipes, but I can help you sort issues with your network hardware.

Wireless networking hardware include some common troubleshooting tasks:

- Fixing routers and access points.
- Dealing with network adapter card issues.

Each of these topics is looked at in more detail in the following sections. (Not sure what these things even are? Check out Book II, Chapter 2 for some information before you take out the toolbox.)

Fixing a router

Honestly, not a whole lot can go wrong with your wireless router from a physical hardware standpoint. The only external parts are typically detachable antennae and your AC power adapter.

As a rule, you should *never* attempt to unscrew the external housing on your router to get inside. At best, you immediately invalidate any warranty associated with the hardware. At worst, you could end up with one heck of an electrical shock.

Having said that, if your wireless router won't power up or clearly includes damaged parts (antennae, ports, and whatnot), your best course of action is to return it to the retailer where you purchased it or contact the manufacturer about obtaining a replacement unit. If the router is still within the warranty period, the manufacturer usually ships out a new one without issue.

While you can't do a whole lot about physical damage to your wireless router, I can offer a few tricks for dealing with other issues. One of the most common problems you may come across is being unable to access the router's management interface.

Assuming that the router is powered up and you have a wireless network adapter correctly installed, you should be able to access its *management interface* (the fancy web-based interface from which you configure the router) without issue. However, it's also possible that you changed something in the device's configuration and can no longer connect. If this happens to you, take a look on the back of your router for a Reset button, one of which is shown in Figure 8-1.

In most cases, using a paperclip to hold down this button for a number of seconds (the manual should outline how long exactly) resets the device to its factory default settings. Once complete, you should be able to get at the management interface without a worry.

Outside of configuration issues, the most common issues encountered with wireless routers are connection related. If your router is constantly dropping your Internet connection, the problem may be with your ISP or with the router's firmware. Begin by contacting your ISP to determine the source of the problem. If everything looks alright on their end, you may need to upgrade your router's firmware — a process that I outline in more detail later in this chapter.

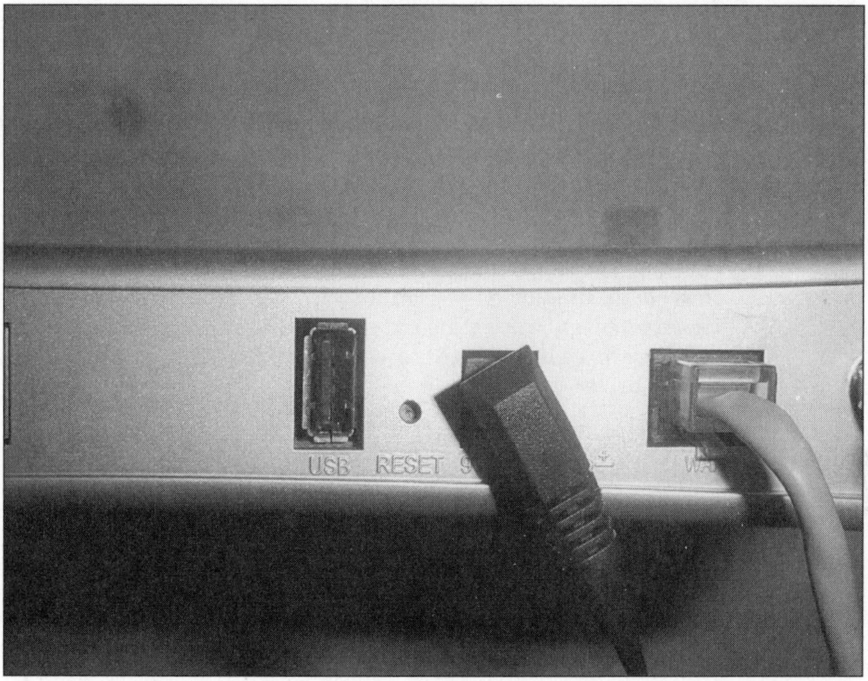

Figure 8-1: You can press the router's Reset button to return it to factory default settings.

If you're having intermittent connection issues between wireless clients on your network and the router, the most likely culprit is interference. Recall that interference comes from a variety of sources including other wireless devices, microwaves, and even your cordless phone. You need to do a little sleuth work to determine which devices are causing the issue, but intermittent issues almost always have a traceable cause. In fact, if everything usually works perfectly and then suddenly doesn't for a short period, you can almost bet the farm that something is causing interference. Now you just have to walk around and find out what that something is!

Solving interference problems on wireless networks is looked at in more detail in Book III, Chapter 5. Methods for dealing with network-related issues get a closer look in Book IV, Chapter 3.

Fixing other access points

Troubleshooting hardware issues with a wireless access point means following the same rules as with a wireless router:

- Never open the external housing.
- Use the Reset button when necessary.
- If connection issues exist, keep an eye open for potential sources of interference.

Working on adapter cards

Getting any network adapter card to function correctly can range from an incredibly simple and straightforward process to what can only be described as an intensely frustrating experience. By and large, most problems with wireless network adapter cards are either related to their physical installation or to the driver that's been installed.

On the physical side of things, begin by checking the following:

- If you're using an internal PCI-based wireless network adapter card on a desktop PC, check to ensure that it's seated in the PCI slot correctly. You shouldn't need to *force* the card into the slot, but it should be seated snugly and firmly if connected correctly.
- If you're using an external USB network adapter, check to ensure that it's properly connected to a USB port on your PC. It's worth noting that the adapter may not function if connected to an unpowered USB hub. If you have the adapter plugged into a USB hub at the moment, disconnect the hub and connect the adapter directly into a port on the PC.
- If you happen to be using a laptop, ensure that your wireless network adapter card is inserted completely in one of its PC Card slots. Check to see whether the edge of the laptop extends too much for the card to be inserted correctly. If this is the case, try installing the adapter in the lower PC card slot.
- If you've installed a mini-PCI wireless network adapter card on your laptop, ensure that it's seated correctly in its slot and that all wires are correctly connected to the device.

If everything on the physical installation side of things looks okay, the problem with your wireless network adapter card is likely software based. Don't assume that you have a physical problem just because the PWR (power), Act (Activity), or Link LED lights on your device aren't lit. In most cases, these won't light up until you have the correct driver installed.

Speaking of drivers, it's amazingly simple to have the wrong driver for your hardware installed, especially if you raced through the driver installation process. I can't begin to tell you how many times I've installed the wrong driver for a device and then wondered why it didn't work. Regardless, I've learned my lesson — after checking the chips (the hardware), the next step is always checking the salsa (um, the driver).

Before you go uninstalling or reinstalling any drivers, it's worth taking the time to do a little preliminary detective work. To determine the current status of your network adapter card, follow these steps:

1. **Click Start, right-click My Computer, and click Properties.**

   The System Properties window opens.

2. **Click the Hardware tab and then click the Device Manager button.**

   The Device Manager window opens.

3. **Expand the Network adapters section to view all network adapters installed on your computer.**

4. **If your wireless network adapter is listed, right-click it and click Properties.**

   The Properties window for your wireless network adapter card opens, as shown in Figure 8-2. If your network adapter isn't listed, follow the instructions for installing a network adapter in Book II's Chapter 6 and Chapter 7.

Figure 8-2: The Properties window for a wireless network adapter card.

5. **Review the Device Status section on the General tab to determine whether any known problems exist.**

   If there is a problem, you are usually presented with an error code that outlines the source of the issue.

For a complete list of the different error codes that you may see in XP's Device Manager, see the online version of the Resource Kit at http://www.microsoft.com/resources/documentation/Windows/XP/all/reskit/en-us/prjk_dec_lgsc.asp.

By and large, the most common error code that you encounter is Error Code 1, which states that the device is not configured correctly. What this means to you is that it's time to search for and install the correct driver, a process that I outline later in this chapter.

It's also worth exploring whether your wireless network adapter *ever* worked in the past, especially if you've made a recent configuration change. For example, perhaps you recently updated the driver for your wireless network adapter. It worked before, but not since the switch. If this is the case and you're using Windows XP, help is close at hand.

Windows XP makes it easy to travel back in time to a previous driver version using a feature known as *driver rollback.* If you have installed an updated driver that isn't working, follow these steps to return to the old version:

1. **Click Start, right-click My Computer, and click Properties.**

   The System Properties window opens.

2. **Click the Hardware tab and then click the Device Manager button.**

   The Device Manager windows opens.

3. **Expand the Network adapters section, right-click your wireless network adapter, and click Properties.**

   The Properties window for your wireless network adapter card opens.

4. **Click the Driver tab.**

   The Driver tab appears, as shown in Figure 8-3.

5. **Click the Roll Back Driver button.**

   If a previous driver is available, you are asked whether you'd like to return to using the previous version. Click Yes to make the switch. Presto: You're back to old, working driver land!

Don't be alarmed if you press the Roll Back Driver button and receive a message stating that no drivers have been backed up for the device. All this means is that you're using the only driver version that you've ever installed. In other words, there's nothing to roll back to.

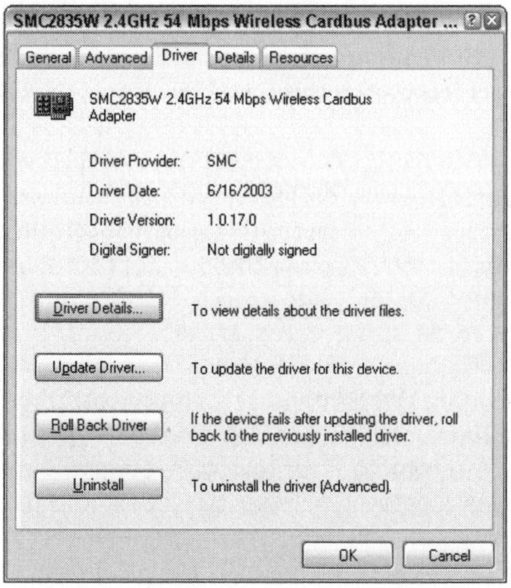

Figure 8-3: The Driver tab in the Properties of a wireless network adapter card.

Taking a Wrench to the Software

As you now well know, fixing your hardware isn't much about messing with the hardware at all, but rather managing the software that makes the hardware do its thing. By updating or upgrading your hardware's software you can potentially eliminate known problems, improve performance, and maybe even add a new feature or three to your wireless devices. The software components for most wireless hardware devices are updated regularly, so if you don't check for new versions, you're almost certainly missing out on something!

Typical ways to take a wrench to the software that makes your wireless hardware run include the following:

- ✦ Upgrading the firmware on your router or access point.
- ✦ Updating the drivers for your network adapter card.
- ✦ Upgrading any software utilities provided with your network adapter card.

All of these marvelous upgrades and updates are looked at in more detail in the following sections.

Upgrading your hardware's firmware

No computer or networking hardware piece is worth much of anything without a little software to make it do something useful. In the world of wireless routers and access points, this software is known as *firmware.* Firmware is effectively the code that acts as a sort of operating system for the router, making different features and functions available. Without firmware installed, the router is nothing more than a fancy paperweight. In a nutshell, the firmware makes the router's hardware run.

When you purchase a wireless router or access point, its firmware is already installed. The version of the firmware included with your router dictates the device's features and capabilities. For example, your router may include a web-based interface, an integrated firewall, and support for various wireless security features. By the same token, your router may not support a few good features, such as the latest-and-greatest wireless encryption standard.

While you could continue using the firmware originally supplied with your wireless router, most manufacturers periodically release updated or revised firmware for their models. Upgrading your firmware typically adds features to your hardware, addresses any known security issues, and fixes any problems with previous versions.

In essence, upgrading the firmware on your router or access point is almost like purchasing a new piece of hardware. You get access to new features and capabilities without spending money on a new unit. On the flip side, upgrading the device's firmware is completely in your hands, and you want to be sure that you do it right. If you make a mistake or run into a serious issue when upgrading firmware, you can easily render your hardware unusable.

Almost all wireless manufacturers make updated firmware releases available on their web site as a download. It's absolutely critical that you install a firmware upgrade that was specifically designed for your router make and model, so have this information handy. In most cases you can determine the exact model number you need from a sticker at the bottom of your router, as shown in Figure 8-4.

Before you hop online looking to download firmware for your device, do a little investigative work and figure out which version you currently have installed. This information is usually accessible from your router's management interface, in a section marked Status or Information. The value you're looking for may be called Firmware version, Runtime code version, or something similar. For the SMC wireless router shown in Figure 8-5, the current Runtime code version is 1.0.0.

With the router's current firmware version in hand, it's time to find out whether any updates are available. The best way to do this is to visit the manufacturer's web site and search for the router via its model number. Once your model is found, look for a link to downloads or driver updates. In the case of the SMC model I'm using, the Drivers and Downloads section for my model lists a firmware version marked 1.956, as shown in Figure 8-6. This firmware release has a higher version number than what I currently have installed, so I download the file.

Figure 8-4: Model information can usually be found on the underside of your router.

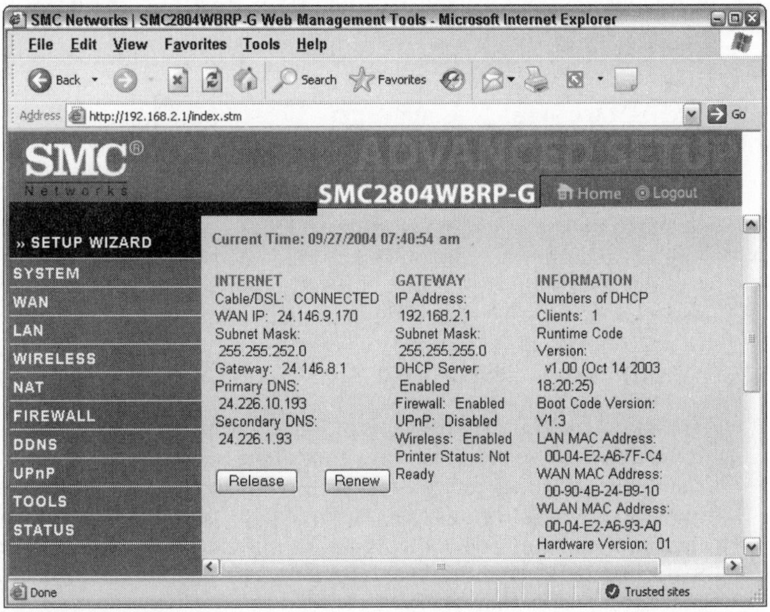

Figure 8-5: Use your router's management interface to determine which firmware version is installed.

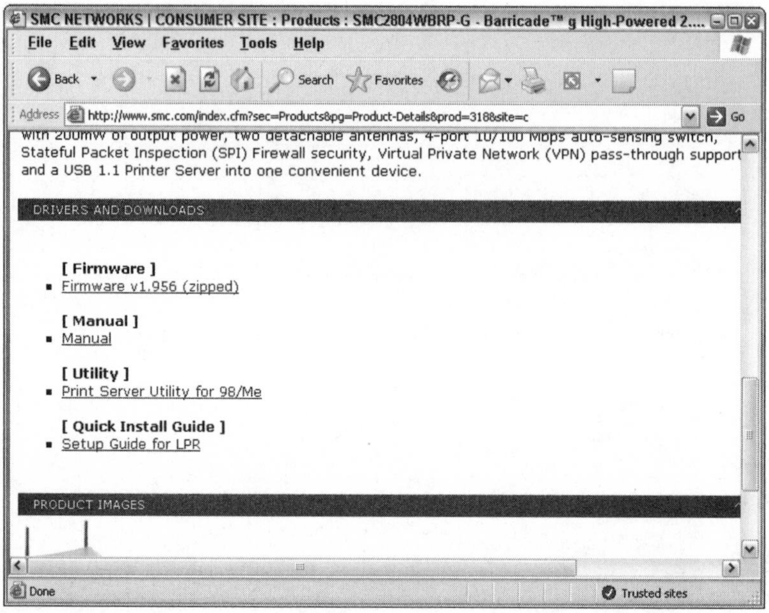

Figure 8-6: Searching for router firmware updates.

Most manufacturers provide a firmware update within a ZIP file. After downloading the file to your hard drive, extract the zipped files to a folder such as C:\firmware. Beyond the actual firmware file itself (usually a file with a .BIN extension), you can expect the ZIP to include a text file that provides installation instructions as well as a history of the firmware release versions.

It's from the text file's release history list that you discover why new versions were released and the specific capabilities they added (or issues that it fixed). You can safely assume that any features added in a previous release are also present in the latest release. Figure 8-7 provides a look at the text file supplied with the firmware upgrade that I downloaded for my router.

WARNING!

Because the specific steps for upgrading a device's firmware vary between models and manufacturers, you should *always* follow the instructions provided with the firmware upgrade to the letter. Don't use a firmware upgrade as a chance to see "what will happen if. . . ." If you don't follow the instructions, there's a good chance you might seriously mess up your hardware to the point that it can't be fixed.

The steps that I list are for upgrading the firmware on my SMC wireless router. Again, the steps for your model probably are different. The model that I'm using has a built-in tool for upgrading firmware, but some models may require you to download and install a special utility on your PC to upgrade your router's code. Again, be sure to follow the manufacturers instructions for your make and model — this is one task where it's definitely better to be safe than sorry.

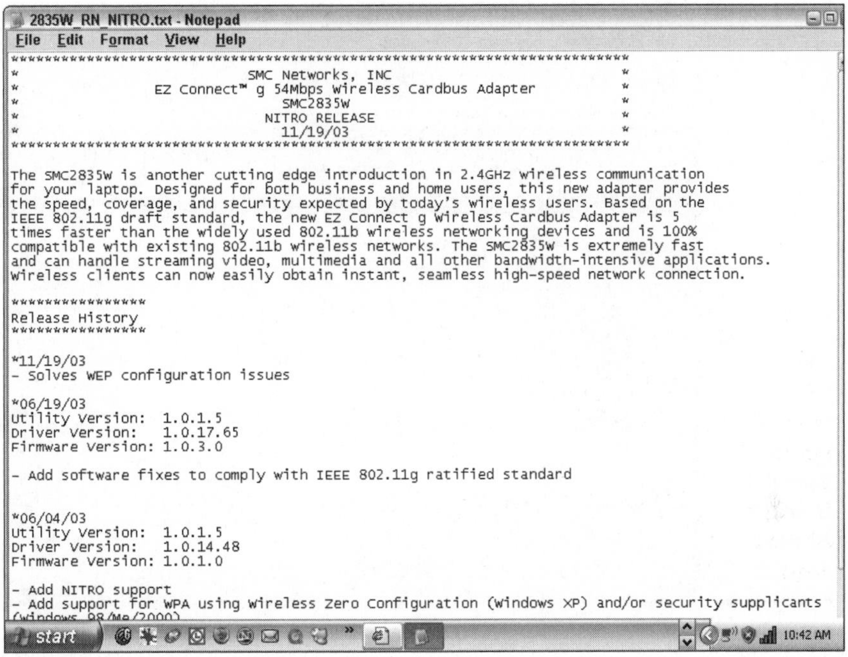

2835W_RN_NITRO.txt - Notepad
File Edit Format View Help
SMC Networks, INC
EZ Connect™ g 54Mbps Wireless Cardbus Adapter
SMC2835W
NITRO RELEASE
11/19/03
The SMC2835W is another cutting edge introduction in 2.4GHz wireless communication for your laptop. Designed for both business and home users, this new adapter provides the speed, coverage, and security expected by today's wireless users. Based on the IEEE 802.11g draft standard, the new EZ Connect g Wireless Cardbus Adapter is 5 times faster than the widely used 802.11b wireless networking devices and is 100% compatible with existing 802.11b wireless networks. The SMC2835W is extremely fast and can handle streaming video, multimedia and all other bandwidth-intensive applications. Wireless clients can now easily obtain instant, seamless high-speed network connection.
Release History
*11/19/03
- Solves WEP configuration issues
*06/19/03
Utility Version: 1.0.1.5
Driver Version: 1.0.17.65
Firmware Version: 1.0.3.0
- Add software fixes to comply with IEEE 802.11g ratified standard
*06/04/03
Utility Version: 1.0.1.5
Driver Version: 1.0.14.48
Firmware Version: 1.0.1.0
- Add NITRO support
- Add support for WPA using Wireless Zero Configuration (Windows XP) and/or security supplicants
start
10:42 AM

Figure 8-7: The text file supplied with a router firmware upgrade.

To upgrade the firmware on an SMC 2804W BRP-G Barricade wireless router, follow the steps below:

1. **Log on to the router's administrative interface.**
2. **Click the Tools menu.**

   The Configuration Tools page appears.
3. **Select the Backup Router configuration option and click Next.**

   REMEMBER

   You should always back up your router's configuration prior to upgrading its firmware.
4. **When the Opening dialog box appears, select Save to Disk and click OK.**
5. **When the Enter Name of File to Save to dialog box appears, choose a folder in which to save the configuration file. Click Save.**

   Your router's configuration has been saved!
6. **Under the Tools menu, click Firmware Upgrade.**

   The Firmware Upgrade page opens, as shown in Figure 8-8.

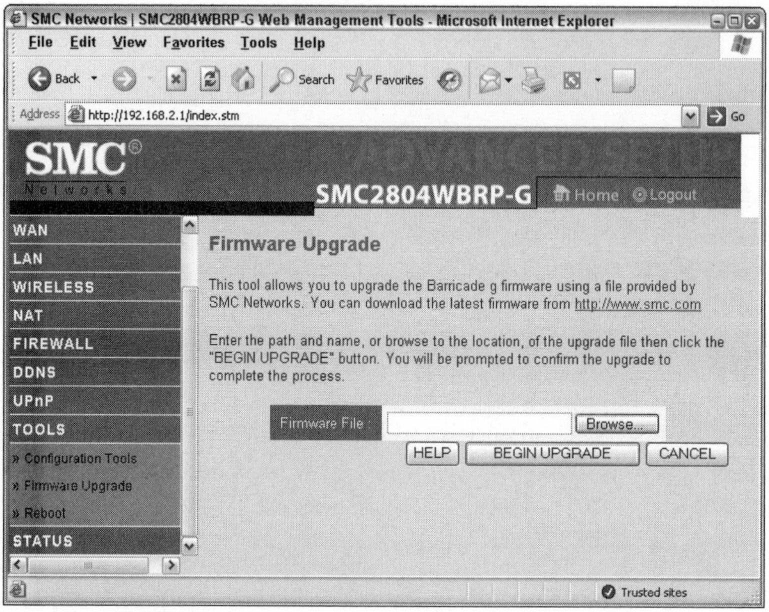

Figure 8-8: The Firmware Upgrade screen on a wireless router.

7. **Click the Browse button and go to the updated firmware file you downloaded from the manufacturer's web site, such as 2804WBRP-G_FWv1956.bin.**
8. **Click the file and click Open.**

   The path and filename of the new firmware file are listed in the Firmware File box.
9. **Click the Begin Upgrade button to complete the process.**

   The firmware upgrade process results in the lights on the front of your router flashing in different sequences. The text file supplied with the router outlines the correct order. Once this process is complete, the firmware on your router should be upgraded to the new version.

   To ensure that the upgrade was successful, review the status screen in the management interface to see whether your router lists the new Runtime code version, as shown in Figure 8-9.

Updating network adapter drivers

In much the same way that firmware gives life to a wireless router or access point, drivers are the heart and soul of a network adapter card. The driver for a particular network adapter card allows an operating system like Windows XP to communicate with the adapter hardware. Without the correct driver installed, your wireless network adapter is just another pretty face.

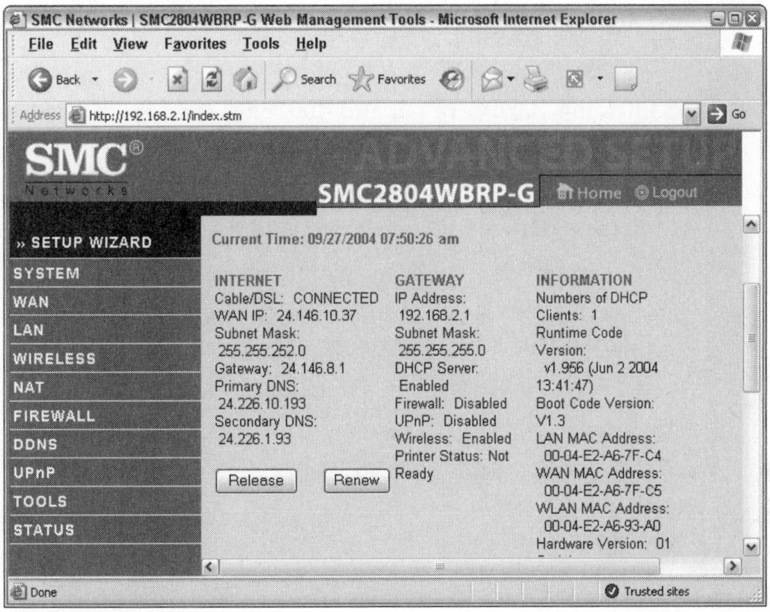

Figure 8-9: Check to ensure that the router is using the updated firmware.

Unlike firmware (which is physically stored in dedicated memory within a router or access point), drivers for a network adapter card are installed on the computer to which the adapter is attached. If your wireless network adapter card is currently working, that is a good sign that you have the right driver installed. However, much like firmware, manufacturers commonly release updated versions of their drivers to fix known problems and add features to their adapters.

The best way to find updated drivers for your wireless network adapter card is to visit the manufacturer's web site and look for updates in their support area. Keep in mind that you need to download the correct drivers for both your specific model, as well as the operating system you're using. In other words, a driver designed for Windows 98 typically won't work with Windows XP, or vice versa.

You can find the model number for your wireless network adapter in a variety of places, including a sticker on the adapter itself, the adapter's box, or the adapter's manual. If the adapter is correctly installed at the moment, you can even find it using the Windows XP Device Manager.

It's never a bad idea to check which driver you already have installed prior to checking for an update. The easiest way to do this is using Device Manager, as outlined in these steps:

1. **Click Start, right-click My Computer, and click Properties.**

   The System Properties window opens.

2. **Click the Hardware tab and then click the Device Manager button.**

   The Device Manager window opens.

3. **Expand the Network Adapters section, right-click the icon for your wireless network adapter card, and then click Properties.**

   The properties window for your wireless network adapter card opens.

4. **Click the Driver tab and note the Driver Version number (as shown in Figure 8-10).**

   You may want to write this number down as a reference.

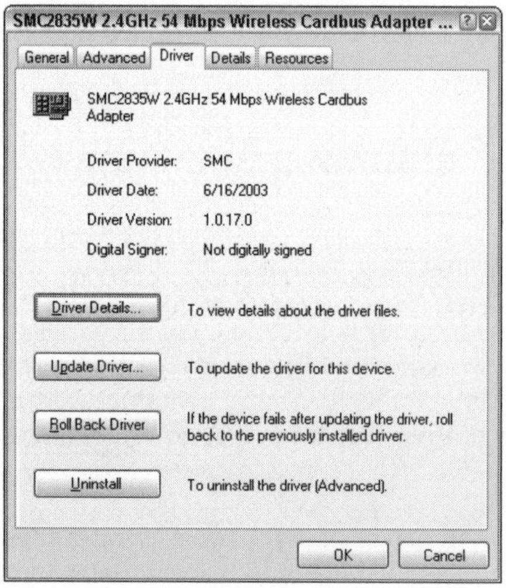

Figure 8-10: Find the version number for an installed network adapter card driver.

Now that you know what driver version you already have, you can head out to check for updates.

1. **If an updated version is available from the manufacturer's web site, download it and extract the drivers to a folder such as C:\Drivers.**

2. **Return to Device Manager and open the properties of your wireless network adapter. Click the Driver tab.**

3. **Click the Update Driver button.**

   This starts the Hardware Update Wizard.

4. **At the Hardware Update Wizard welcome screen, select No, Not This Time. Click Next.**

5. **Select Install from a list or a specific location (Advanced) and click Next.**

6. **Click the Browse button to specify the location of the driver files you just downloaded, such as C:\Drivers.**

   The driver files for your operating system may be stored in a subfolder, such as C:\Drivers\WinXP.

7. **When the correct location is specified, click OK⇨Next.**

8. **When the Hardware Update Wizard finishes installing your new driver, click Finish.**

   You're done. The Drivers screen should list the new version number for the driver you installed.

TIP

If you run into an issue and your wireless network adapter doesn't function correctly after updating its driver, use the Roll Back Driver button on the Driver tab to return to using the previous driver version.

Upgrading adapter utilities

As you discover in Book II, Chapter 7, most manufacturers also include software utilities with their wireless network adapter cards. Although these programs don't necessarily need to be installed for the network adapter to function, they typically provide both diagnostic tools and access to settings that are helpful for both troubleshooting issues and configuring advanced network card properties.

In the same way that manufacturers periodically release updated drivers for their network cards, the same is true of their network adapters' software utilities. Upgrading the client software for your wireless network adapter is never a bad idea, and something that you should consider doing in conjunction with a driver update. In fact, many manufacturers release updated drivers and utility programs at the same time and conveniently package them into a single download.

TIP

As a general rule, you shouldn't expect that installing the newest software utilities for your wireless network adapter card will upgrade the version you already have installed. Most of these software packages are *standalone* in nature, meaning that if you install the newest version, you probably end up with both the new and old versions on your PC. That can make things confusing, so your best bet is to uninstall the current version first.

To uninstall the current version of your adapter's utilities, follow these steps:

1. **Click Start⇨Control Panel.**

   The Control Panel window opens.

2. **Double-click Add or Remove Programs.**

   The Add or Remove Programs window opens.

3. **Find your adapter's utility program in the currently installed programs list.**

4. **Select the utility program. Click the Change/Remove button (as shown in Figure 8-11) and follow the instructions to remove the program.**

   The adapter utilities have been uninstalled. With the previous version of your adapter's utilities removed, tackle these steps:

5. **Visit your network adapter card manufacturer's web site and download the latest version.**

   You typically find it in the model's support section, listed with other available downloads or updates.

6. **Launch the Setup.exe file to begin installation. Follow the onscreen instructions to complete the process.**

   Once installed, the new adapter utility program should be accessible from your Start menu, and may even be configured to launch automatically when you start Windows.

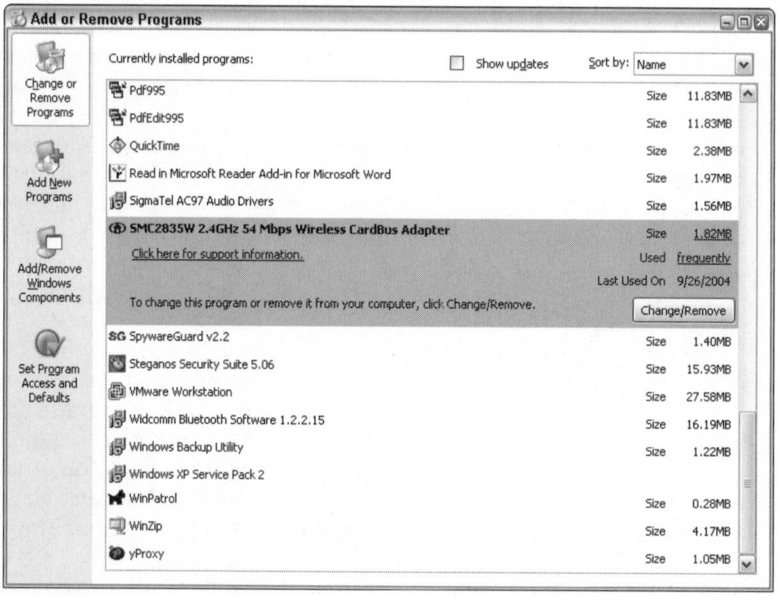

Figure 8-11: Use Add or Remove Programs to uninstall network adapter card utilities.

Book III

Configuring Networks

The 5th Wave — By Rich Tennant

EXPERIMENTING WITH THE
WIRELESS LASER BEAM NETWORK
©RICHTENNANT

"Okay–did you get that?"

Contents at a Glance

Chapter 1: Exploring Window XP Networking 145

Chapter 2: Managing Available Networks 149

Chapter 3: Creating Bridges 159

Chapter 4: Configuring Printers 165

Chapter 5: Confirming Your Network Works 171

Chapter 1: Exploring Windows XP Networking

In This Chapter

- **Windows XP makes wireless easy**
- **Plug and play . . . hopefully**
- **Choosing the kind of network you want**

Before Windows XP, installing any kind of network using Windows computers was often a hassle and usually unpredictable. With the 2001 release of Windows XP, Microsoft introduced an easy wireless network setup and configuration.

If you have a typical setup, which is to say you have a modern PC and networking equipment released in the past one or two years, creating a wireless network should be a snap. If all goes well, you can install a wireless network adapter in your PC and you're almost ready to connect with your chosen wireless network. Now, cross your fingers (I'm watching, as is Microsoft) and venture into the relatively painless world of Windows XP and wireless networking.

Installing Is Child's (Plug and) Play

Most of the work of installing a wireless network is done by the computer as part of the operating system's plug and play feature. That means after plugging in your adapter it should be installed automatically (or close to it).

With modern wireless technology, installing the necessary hardware into your computer is usually so-called *plug and play.* In other words, the process is supposed to be mostly automated: You plug in your *network adapter* (a card that transmits and receives signals over your wireless network) and the operating system is supposed to recognize, install, and configure it.

If you have newer hardware, this should be the case most of the time. If you're trying to use an older or obscure network adapter (stay away from the bargain bins!) or own a computer that you bought more than, say, two years ago, this might not be the case.

And remember that I'm talking about Windows XP here. If you're running an older operating system, all bets are off. My advice: Upgrade to Windows XP before you pursue this course called wireless networking.

Just because Windows XP *can* configure your network adapter doesn't mean you want it to do so. You may find that the utility software that came with the adapter provides more features and better feedback about signal strength and other basics.

In that case, let Windows XP's plug-and-play feature handle the installation and you can look to the network equipment maker for the software to add any extra features that Windows XP doesn't add automatically.

My Network Places

If My Network Places is not already on your Start menu, you can put it there for convenient access. Given the number of times you open My Network Places to take care of network-related functions and configurations, it's a good idea to add it. An update to Windows XP released in fall 2004 includes My Network Places on the Start menu by default.

Adding to the Start menu

Here's how you add My Network Places to the Start menu:

1. **Right-click Start and select Properties.**

   The Taskbar and Start Menu Properties dialog box appears.

2. **Click Customize.**

   The Customize Start Menu dialog box appears.

3. **Select the Advanced tab.**
4. **Under Start Menu Items, scroll down to My Network Places and select the checkbox.**
5. **Click OK.**

Removing from the Start menu

You want to get rid of My Network Places from your Start menu? Hey, I can show you how to do that, too.

1. **Right-click Start and select Properties.**

   The Taskbar and Start Menu Properties dialog box appears.

2. **Click Customize.**

   The Customize Start Menu dialog box appears.

3. **Select the Advanced tab.**
4. **Under Start Menu Items, scroll down and uncheck the box beside My Network Places.**
5. **Click OK.**

Mingling with Different Networks

You can create two kinds of networks with Windows XP:

- **Infrastructure.** Chances are you want to create an infrastructure network, which is the traditional network that uses a DSL or cable modem connecting to your computer directly or through a router.
- **Computer to computer.** You also see this called a peer-to-peer or an ad hoc network. It's a connection made directly between one computer and another.

As always, each has advantages and disadvantages.

Creating an Infrastructure Network

Most likely, when you think of a wireless network, you're thinking about an infrastructure network. Book II, "Planning Your Network," is essentially about creating an infrastructure network. I avoid repeating that information here.

However, anytime you communicate between a wireless access point (such as a wireless router) and a wireless network adapter, you're moving information over an *infrastructure network.* When you're on the road and using a coffee shop's wireless access, you're connecting to an infrastructure network. Your computer is connecting through a wireless access point, which in turn connects to the Internet.

In most cases, it just makes more sense at home to set up and run this kind of network instead of a computer-to-computer network.

Creating a Computer-to-Computer Network

A *computer-to-computer network* means exactly that: Your computer is wirelessly connecting directly to another computer. This is known as an *ad-hoc* network. Both PCs need wireless adapters, of course. Windows XP also will need to be set up to handle a computer-to-computer network connection.

At one time, a computer-to-computer network may have been cheaper to create because you didn't need a router. Instead, one computer can connect to the Internet and the other PC can wirelessly share that connection. Declining hardware costs provide no reason to use a computer-to-computer network when what you really need is an infrastructure network, which requires a router and possibly other hardware.

You can use a computer-to-computer network in your home or on the road, but it usually has specific applications:

- On a business trip, you and a colleague can connect your laptops wirelessly, allowing you to share files without the use of a router or other wireless access point.
- Anytime you're mobile, the network moves with you because you don't have to lug routers or other hardware (aside from your laptop).
- Anywhere an infrastructure network's wireless access point is unreachable, a computer-to-computer network provides an Internet connection, provided one of the computers is connected to the Internet.
- If you don't want to rely on the hardware in an infrastructure network, a computer-to-computer network provides redundancy. If a router goes down on an infrastructure network, the whole network stops working. With a computer-to-computer network, another computer can always share the load. (This assumes more than two computers are in the computer-to-computer network.)

Enabling Internet sharing

Once you have a computer-to-computer network set up, you can configure one computer to share an Internet connection with the other computers. I don't recommend using this fast and dirty way to share broadband access unless you have no other choice. It's slow compared to using an infrastructure network with a router.

If you can, try to build an infrastructure network where a router does the work of divvying out IP addresses to each computer and, most importantly, hides the network behind a firewall.

Chapter 2: Managing Available Networks

In This Chapter

- **Finding out about wireless networks**
- **Adding a preferred network**
- **Watching your network**
- **Setting some advanced preferences**

A good thing about wireless networks is that you don't have those pesky Ethernet cables to tie you up in knots. That doesn't mean that wireless networks are always easy to set up and use. Hopefully, you've made it past the rough spots and are ready to actually transfer 1s and 0s around your home.

Maybe your wireless network is ready to send data between your living room and second-floor bathroom. If so, make sure your PC can see the router and any other access points. That's where Windows XP's Available Networks function enters the picture.

I also discuss some ways to monitor your network's signal strength and capacity. Other chapters discuss similar network troubleshooting and maintenance topics:

- Book II, Chapter 8 gives you some help troubleshooting network adapters.
- Book III, Chapter 5 discusses how you confirm your wireless network is working.
- Book IV, Chapter 3 gives you some tips for solving wireless networking problems.

Finding Out What's Out There

You'll notice the title doesn't say *who* is out there. After all, this chapter's about wireless networks, not dating. If you're looking for relationship advice, please buy *Dating For Dummies.*

Available Networks lets you see what networks are available. *Available* means they're out there, probably close by. The list should include one or more of your own networks, if all goes well.

In some cases, you'll see neighbors' wireless networks. That doesn't mean you can connect to those networks, though. (I tackle that issue in more detail, along with other security topics, in Book IV.)

You likely won't see wireless networks where the owners have intentionally made them invisible to public viewing. The geeks can still discover your network name, but it's one tool in your security toolbox. After I tell you about monkey wrenches and screwdrivers (I'm trying to milk this toolbox metaphor), I talk about how you can make your network mostly invisible in Book IV, "Security and Troubleshooting."

1. **Right-click the wireless network icon in your Windows XP notification area.**

   A menu appears.

2. **Select the View Available Wireless Networks option.**

   You see something like Figure 2-1. The dialog box lists Available Networks. In this case, Dummies is the network and Tunks Home is the neighbor (possibly the one with the barking dog).

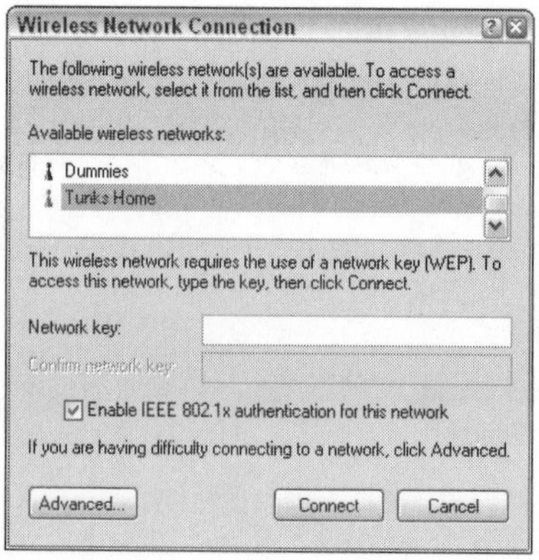

Figure 2-1: If a network requires a network key, you can enter it in this dialog box.

3. **If you have a network key, now's the time to type it in under the list of Available Networks in the Wireless Connection dialog box.**

   Some networks require a *network key,* which is basically a password with so many unrelated letters and numbers that only a *Jeopardy* contestant can remember it.

   What if an available network requires a network key, but you don't have one? If you're sure it's your network or one you've been invited to use, you should ask its administrator for The Magic Key. Unfortunately, "abracadabra" doesn't work here.

4. **If one or more Available Networks don't require network keys, check the box next to Windows XP's caution: Allow Me to Connect to the Selected Wireless Network, Even Though It Is Not Secure.**

   It's a scary check box, I know, but select it for now. I tackle security issues in another chapter. That's it! You're done.

You can do something that ensures almost always having a working Internet connection. In one word, it's called *redundancy.* Say a DSL line now comes into your house. Well, call up the cable company and order its cable modem service, too. Now use one connection for your wired network and the other connection for your wireless network. If one goes down, you can easily switch to the other Internet connection. Too bad you can't do that with electrical service!

What the heck is IEEE?

You mean you don't know what IEEE stands for? Neither did I until I looked it up. It's the Institute of Electrical and Electronics Engineers, an industry group that sets standards for wireless networking and other technologies.

You may have already read about the 802.1b and 802.1g standards, which are essential for making sure your PC's wireless adapter card talks with your wireless router. These standards do all kinds of things, but reading the technical documents makes my head hurt. Suffice it to say they're real important.

The Authentication tab in the Available Networks dialog box mentions 802.1x. That's an x-tra important standard, as it specifies a way for providing authenticated, secure access to wireless networks. If you want to know more about IEEE, and its dizzying array of standards, check out http://www.ieee.org.

Viewing Available Networks

If you followed the previous set of instructions, you've made it past the initial gatekeeper. You can view all available networks now. After following the steps in the preceding section, you find yourself in the Wireless Properties dialog box.

As I mentioned, you may see your neighbors' wireless networks on the list. Ignore them, as it's the right thing to do. Hopefully, they'll do the same for you.

If the stars are aligned, you see your wireless network on the list, as shown in Figure 2-2. Again, in the example the network is dubbed Dummies, which reflects neither on myself, my cat, nor my network hardware.

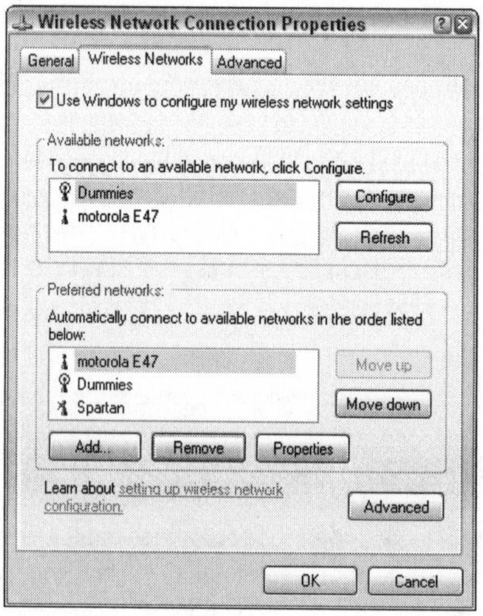

Figure 2-2: Viewing two available networks and three preferred networks.

You can refresh the list of available networks by clicking the — yes! — Refresh button. If you're in a neighborhood with lots of wireless networks, you'll probably see this list constantly change as some networks go live and others shut down.

You can configure an available network from the Wireless Network Connection Properties dialog box. Configuration options include changing the network name (which is also called the *SSID*) and the wireless network key. Here's how you configure an available network:

1. **In the Wireless Network Connection Properties dialog box, select a network listed under Available Networks.**

2. **Select Configure.**

   The Wireless Network Properties dialog box appears, as shown in Figure 2-3.

3. **Select the Association tab, if it's not already selected.**

4. **You can make one or more changes to Association settings:**

   - Change or edit the Network Name (SSID).
   - Toggle Network Authentication between Open and Shared.
   - Change the Data Encryption setting to Disabled or WEP. If you select WEP, you can enter a network key and make other related changes. WEP is discussed in Book IV, Chapter 3, which covers the implementation of wireless network security.
   - Check or uncheck the box beside This Is a Computer-to-Computer (Ad Hoc) Network; Wireless Access Points Are Not Used.

5. **When you're done, you can select the Authentication tab and edit the settings.**

   I'll tell you more about wireless network authentication in Book IV, Chapter 1.

6. **Click OK.**

   Whew! That's it for configuring available networks. Now onward to preferred networks.

Managing Preferred Networks

You also can make an available network a *preferred network.* This gives some networks priority over other networks in case Windows XP has several from which to choose. It also lets you save custom configuration settings so you don't need to make them twice for the same network. When you find yourself in an area covered by a particular wireless network you used in the past, you'll be all set to connect.

The Preferred Networks dialog box is below the Available Networks dialog box. The two network lists look similar except that the buttons are different. Here's what you can do with preferred networks:

- Add a network.
- Remove a network.
- View a network's properties.
- Reorder a preferred network's position.

TIP

Each time you connect to an available network, the network is added to the list of preferred networks. But just because a network appears under Available Networks does not mean it's automatically added to the Preferred Networks list.

Adding a preferred network

Here's how you add a preferred network:

1. **Click the Add button.**

   A Wireless Network Properties dialog box opens.

2. **Enter the network's name and other details.**
3. **Click OK.**

   You're done. That's all there is to adding a preferred network.

Removing a preferred network

This is how you remove a preferred network:

1. **Select the network you want to remove.**
2. **Click the Remove button. It's gone, outta here!**

Viewing a network's properties

It's easy to view a preferred network's properties:

1. **Select a preferred network.**
2. **Click Properties.**

   That now-familiar Wireless Network Properties dialog box appears. Make whatever changes, additions, or deletions you like to properties.

3. **Click OK to finish.**

Reordering preferred networks

Windows XP starts with the first network and moves down. So you'll want your most-used networks toward the top of the list. Here's how to move preferred networks on the list:

1. **Select a preferred network.**
2. **Click either Move Up or Move Down.**

   The preferred network is reordered in the Preferred Networks list, as shown in Figure 2-3.

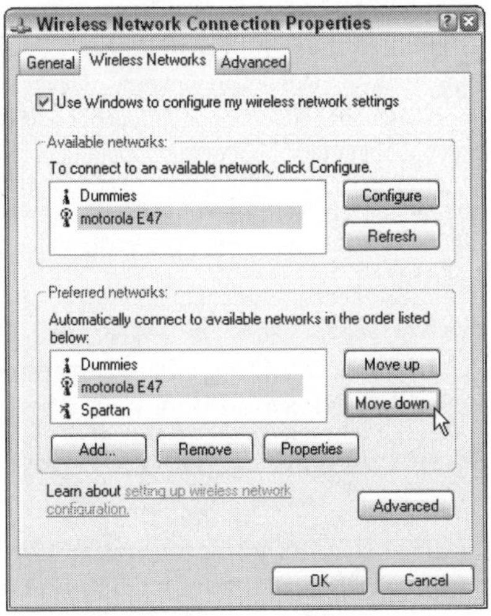

Figure 2-3: Rearranging your preferred networks.

3. **Repeat as many times as necessary to rearrange the order of preferred networks.**

   Now you've reordered your life — or at least your list of preferred networks. It's a good start, though!

Using the Advanced Networking Options

If you dare understand one more level in the increasingly tangled world of wireless networking, you can step up to the Advanced settings. They're reachable from the Wireless Network Connection Properties dialog box.

Here's how you edit advanced settings:

1. **Select Advanced.**

   An Advanced dialog box opens, as shown in Figure 2-4.

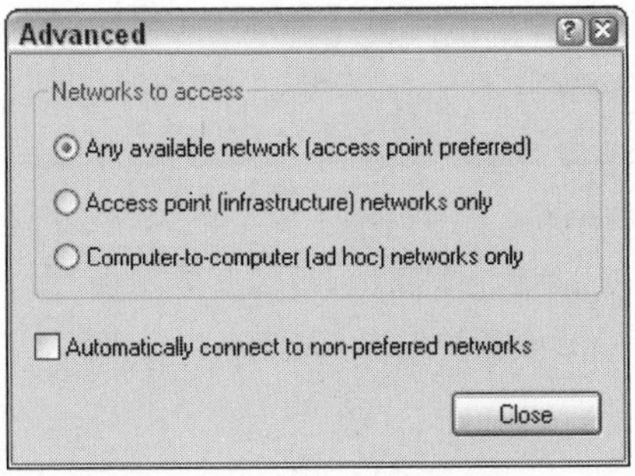

Figure 2-4: You can select the kinds of networks to access.

2. **Select which networks you want to access:**
   - **Any Available Network** means that Windows XP tries to connect to any available network, although it favors a regular, infrastructure network over a computer-to-computer network.
   - **Access Point Networks Only** means that your PC only tries for connections to an infrastructure network. If there's a computer-to-computer network available, it'll skip it.
   - **Computer-to-Computer Networks Only** tells Windows XP to ignore regular networks and only try connecting with computer-to-computer networks (also called peer-to-peer, or ad hoc, networks).
3. **Check or uncheck the box beside Automatically Connect to Non-Preferred Networks.**

   In addition to choosing a network type, you can instruct Windows XP to automatically connect to non-preferred networks. This means that it'll connect to a network even if it's not on your Preferred Networks list.

Connecting with your peers

Most wireless networks are called *access point,* or *infrastructure,* networks. That means your computer connects to the Internet through a wireless router or other access point. Chances are, this is how you'll set up your wireless network.

But there's another way (isn't there always?) you can create a wireless network by connecting two or more computers together. A computer-to-computer network lets you skip wireless network routers and other access points. Instead, PCs talk directly with one another, transmitting and receiving data through their network adapters.

A computer-to-computer network is also known as a *peer-to-peer* or *ad-hoc network.* One name wasn't enough, so the Lords of Geekdom bestowed it with three names.

The obvious advantage is cost: You don't pay for as much networking hardware. One computer usually serves as the gateway to your Internet connection, assuming some of the duties of a dedicated hardware router. Peer-to-peer networking also is handy for connecting a PC to a wireless print server, or networking two TiVo units.

If all you want is to wirelessly connect to PCs in your home, it may be the answer. I discuss the actual set up of these networks in Book III, Chapter 1.

This is handy when you're traveling and you're working with your laptop near networks you've not previously accessed.

4. **Select Close.**

   You're now done with the advanced stuff!

Viewing an Available Network's Signal Strength

You'll be happy to know there's a simple way to view the strength of your wireless network's signal. It doesn't provide a great deal of information, but it's enough to know whether you ought to, say, move your wireless router closer to your computers.

A good time to check your network's signal strength is when you first set it up and anytime you move your PCs or other network hardware. By moving components just a few feet from their original positions, you might find that the signal strength drops. In that case, you can scurry about, putting everything back in place.

Then, with thinking cap firmly applied, you can reconsider where you'll move your equipment.

There are other software and hardware tools for viewing your network's signal strength. I'll discuss them in a later chapter.

To view a simple but helpful visual graphic showing your network's signal strength, just follow these steps:

1. **Right-click the network icon in the Window XP notification area.**

   A pop-up menu appears.

2. **Select Status.**

   A network status dialog box appears.

3. **Select the General tab, if it's not already selected.**

   Under Connection, a small bar graph provides a quick look at the strength of your wireless network's signal, as shown in Figure 2-5. If four or five bars are highlighted, you're enjoying strong, robust signal reception.

   If three or fewer bars are highlighted, you have a pretty weak wireless connection. Read Book IV, Chapter 3, which helps you solve wireless network problems like this one.

On the road again

Many of the topics tackled in this chapter also apply to mobile computing. When you're in an airport, for example, you hopefully see one or more wireless networks available for your use — although some or all may require payment.

When you're in an airport or other public area (or even in one of your company's offices) where you expect to return on a future trip, you can add the network to the list of preferred networks. If you need to make any special configurations for accessing a particular network, you can save them for the next time you connect to the same network.

Monitoring signal strength becomes even more important on the road. Here are some examples:

- By moving just 50 feet to a new location, your airport connection may grow stronger.
- If you're in a strange office, you may not know that the steel walls are blocking a nearby network. By moving around and checking signal strength on your laptop, you find the best spot for (wireless) networking.

4. When you're done viewing your signal strength, click Close.

The Network Connection Status dialog box closes and you know a quick way for seeing how your network is performing.

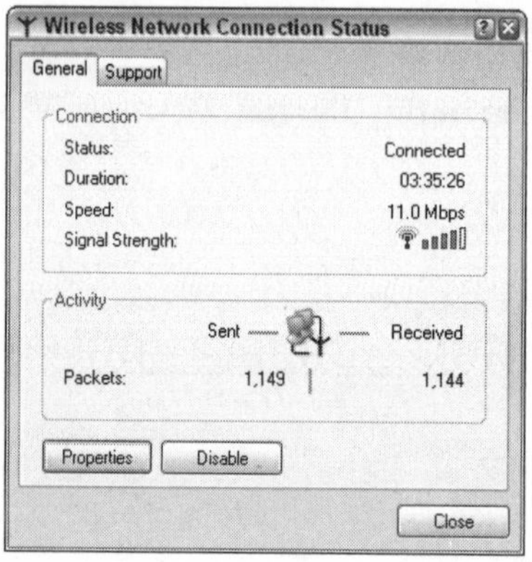

Figure 2-5: With four bars highlighted, this network is cranking.

Chapter 3: Creating Bridges

In This Chapter

- Bridging two or more networks
- Building the bridge with hardware
- Doing what you wish with a bridge

No, this isn't a chapter on civil engineering. And I'm not going to tell you how to build a bridge on the River Kwai, although I may in an upcoming sequel. (Naturally, I'll be playing William Holden's part.) Instead, this chapter is about bridging two or more networks.

Huh? A *bridge* is software or hardware that connects two or more different networks together.

Huh is exactly what I said when I first learned about creating a bridge between, say, a wired Ethernet network and a wireless network. What is it? Why do I need it? Is the Big Bang overrated?

If all goes well, instead of "Huh?" your response by the end of this chapter will be "Duh! These are times when I would want to bridge two or more networks":

- You're adding a wireless network and want it to piggyback on an existing wired Ethernet network. The wireless network has access to the same things — hardware and data — as the wired network does.
- You want to bridge two wired Ethernet networks. This occurs mostly in business environments, but it could occur in a home, too. The wired networks are physically separated and the most convenient way to connect them is by creating a bridge.
- You want to extend the range of a wireless network. By bridging two wireless access points, you can expand the signal range without laying any wires.

You can use a wireless access point as a bridge, if the access point's hardware is equipped to handle the task. Not all wireless access points can be used as a bridge; it must specifically say it can be used as one.

Bridging with Windows XP

Windows XP makes it easy to create a bridge between two or more networks connected to the same computer.

You need a *network adapter,* which serves as a communications point between your computer and the network, for each network you want to bridge. If you're bridging a wired network with a wireless network, your computer needs two adapter cards: one for the wired network and one for the wireless network.

Creating a bridge

Here's how you bridge two networks in Windows XP:

1. **Click Start.**

   The Start menu appears.

2. **Click My Network Places.**

   My Network Places dialog box appears, as shown in Figure 3-1.

   In earlier versions of Windows XP, My Network Places is not located on the Start menu by default. Alternately, you can open it this way:

   1. Right-click the network icon in the task tray.
   2. Select Open Network Connections.

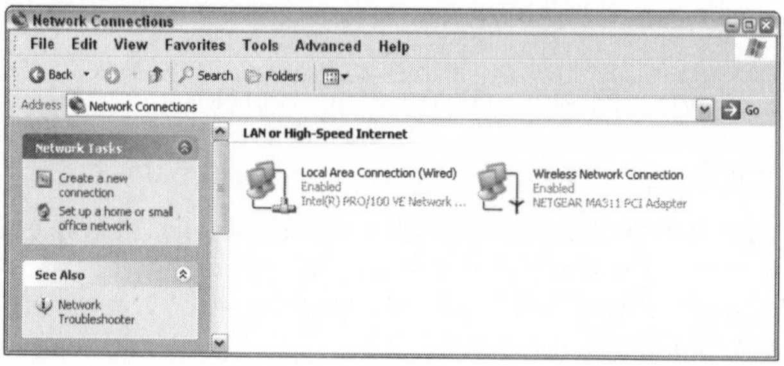

Figure 3-1: My Network Places dialog box.

3. **Select the networks you want to bridge.**

   The networks you select are highlighted. You can select multiple connections by holding down the Ctrl key as you click each network.

4. **Right-click one of the highlighted networks and select Bridge Connections, as shown in Figure 3-2.**

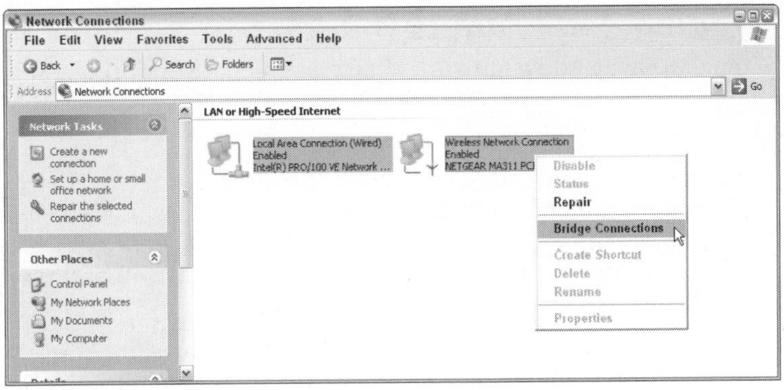

Figure 3-2: Bridging the networks you selected.

Windows XP bridges the connections, as it indicates with the dialog box shown in Figure 3-3.

Figure 3-3: Windows bridging the connections.

The network connections are bridged, as shown in Figure 3-4.

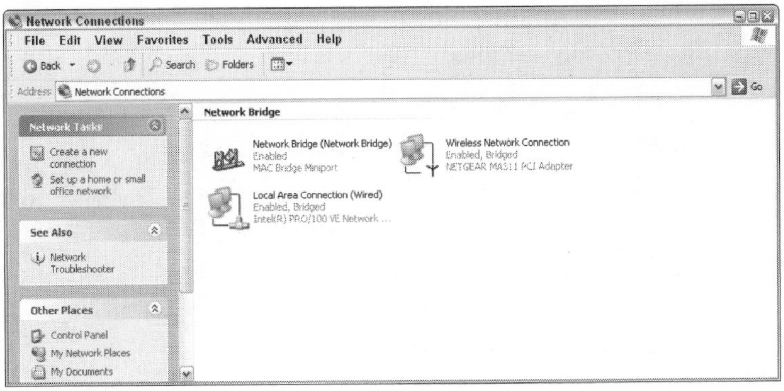

Figure 3-4: These bridges aren't burning.

Adding a network to a bridge

You can easily add a network to an existing network bridge. Just follow these steps:

1. **Click Start.**

   The Start menu appears.

2. **Click My Network Places.**

   The My Network Places dialog box appears.

   TIP In earlier versions of Windows XP, My Network Places is not located on the Start menu by default. These steps are an alternative way to open it:

   1. Right-click the network icon in the task tray.
   2. Select Open Network Connections.

3. **Right-click the network you want to add to the bridge and select Add to Bridge.**

   Windows XP adds the network to the bridge. The Status column in the Network Connections column shows Bridged once the network has been added to the bridge.

Removing a network from a bridge

Maybe you've added a bridge by mistake or maybe you're ready to burn a bridge or two. Follow these steps to get rid of a network from a bridge:

1. **Click Start.**

   The Start menu appears.

2. **Click My Network Places.**

   The My Network Places dialog box appears.

   TIP In earlier versions of Windows XP, My Network Places is not located on the Start menu by default. An alternative way to open it is to follow these steps:

   1. Right-click the network icon in the task tray.
   2. Select Open Network Connections.

3. **Right-click the network you want to remove from the network and select Remove from Bridge, as shown in Figure 3-5.**

   Windows XP removes the network from the bridge.

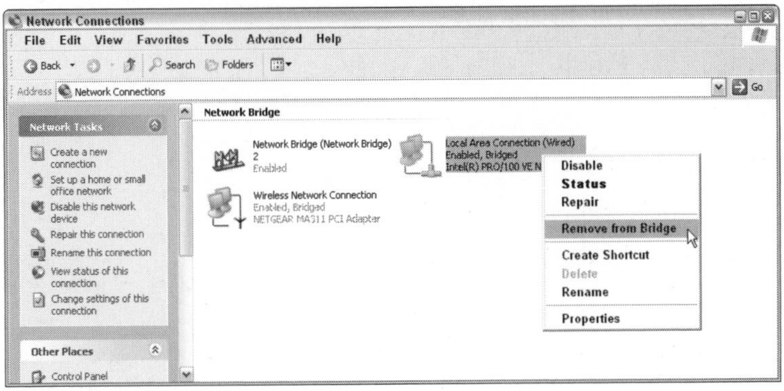

Figure 3-5: Removing a network from a bridge.

Deleting a bridge

If you need to delete a bridge, here are the steps for doing so:

1. **Click Start.**

   The Start menu appears.

2. **Click My Network Places.**

   The My Network Places dialog box appears.

   In earlier versions of Windows XP, My Network Places is not located on the Start menu by default. An alternative way to open it is to:

   1. Right-click the network icon in the task tray.
   2. Select Open Network Connections.

3. **Right-click the network bridge and select Delete, as shown in Figure 3-6.**

   Windows XP deletes the network bridge.

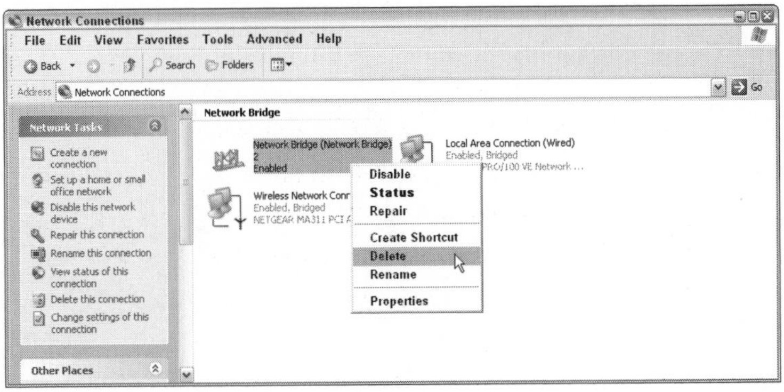

Figure 3-6: Deleting a network bridge.

Chapter 4: Configuring Printers

In This Chapter

- Sharing a printer on your network
- Adding a network printer
- Switching the default printer

A wireless network is about more than just sharing Internet access and your multimedia files. You also can do things like share a printer among all the computers on your wireless network.

In this chapter I tell you how to set up printer sharing across a network, as well as how to add a new printer and change the default printer.

Learning to Share

You can add and select printers for use over your wireless network. For instance, you might be sharing a laser printer on your network and want to add a color inkjet printer that's connected to another computer to your network. Here's how you share a local printer on your entire network:

1. **Click Start.**

   The Start menu appears.

2. **Select Printers and Faxes.**

   The Printers and Faxes dialog box appears.

3. **Do one of the following:**

   - Right-click the printer you want to share and select Sharing.
   - Click Share This Printer under Printer Tasks.

   The Properties dialog box appears for the printer you chose.

4. **Select the Share This Printer button.**

5. **Enter a name for the shared printer, as shown in Figure 4-1.**

   TIP: Try to choose a name that's meaningful to you and to others who use the network. *Printer* is simple, but not very meaningful, especially if you have more than one printer on the network. Better examples include *Upstairs Laser* and *Basement Color.*

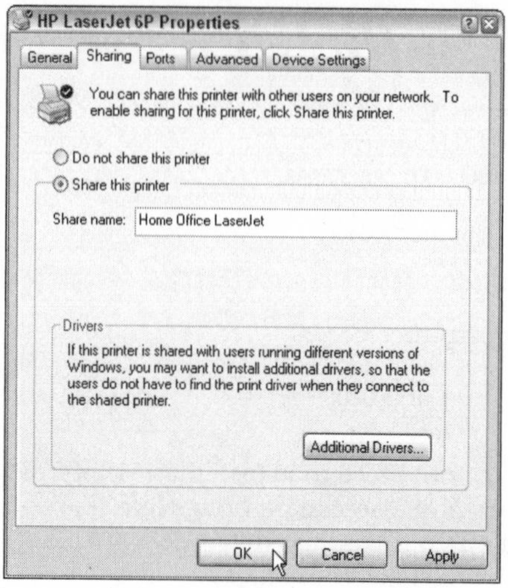

Figure 4-1: A meaningful name is better than a short name.

If you choose a name longer than 12 characters, you receive a warning message: "The share name that you entered may not be accessible from some MS-DOS workstations. Are you sure you want to use this share name?" Unless your network includes computers not running Windows, you can ignore this warning and click Yes.

6. **Click OK.**

An open-palm hand appears superimposed on the printer's icon, as shown in Figure 4-2. (I think the shared icon looks like a guy in a business suit begging for money, but that's me. I may die young from cynicism, but at least there won't be any nasty surprises ahead.)

You're all done here. Move along, move along.

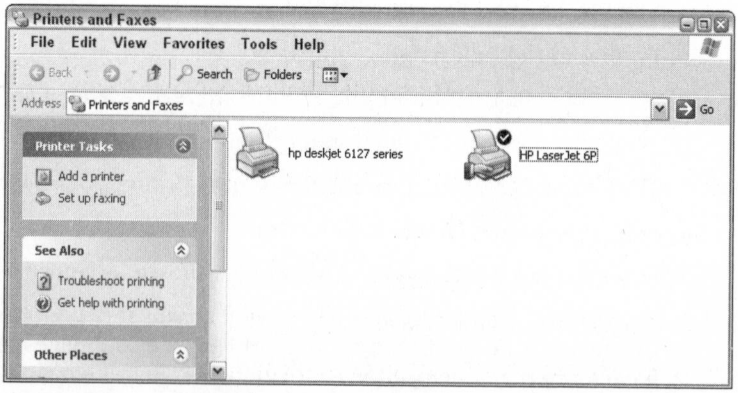

Figure 4-2: Share and share alike: The printer is ready.

Feeling Selfish and Turning Off Sharing

Just as you giveth, you can taketh. If after setting up printer sharing on your network you decide that you no longer want to share the printer, you can easily switch it off. Just follow these steps:

1. **Click Start.**

   The Start menu appears.

2. **Click Printers and Faxes.**

   The Printers and Faxes dialog box appears.

3. **Do one of the following:**

   - Right-click the printer you no longer want to share and select Sharing.
   - Click Share This Printer under Printer Tasks.

   The Properties dialog box appears for the printer you chose.

4. **Select the Do Not Share This Printer button.**
5. **Click OK.**

   The sharing symbol disappears from the printer's icon. That's it for switching off printer sharing. If you want to add a network printer, mosey on over to the next section, please.

Adding a Network Printer

Windows XP automatically usually installs printers for you if you're connecting the printer directly to your PC. If you want to add the ability to use a printer that's connected to another computer on your network, rather than one connected directly to your computer, you need to follow these instructions for each printer you want to add.

REMEMBER

Sharing must be enabled before you can add a network printer. You must enable sharing from the computer that connects to the printer you want to share.

To add a new network printer, follow these steps:

1. **Click Start.**

   The Start menu appears.

2. **Click Printers and Faxes.**

   The Printers and Faxes dialog box appears.

3. **Click Add a Printer under Printer Tasks.**

   The Add Printer Wizard appears.

4. **Click Next.**

   The wizard's Local or Network Printer dialog box appears, as shown in Figure 4-3.

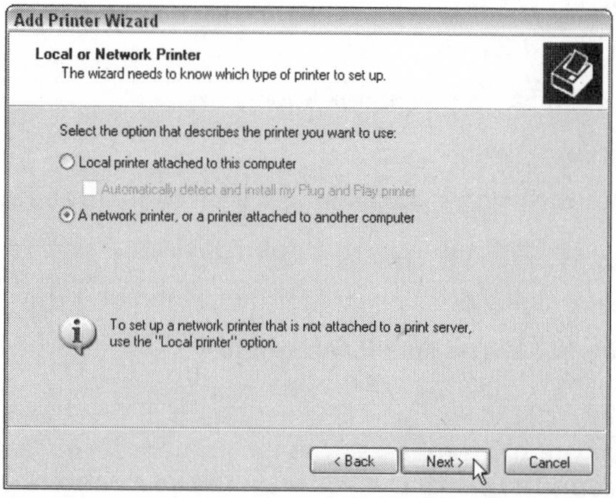

Figure 4-3: Selecting a local or remote printer.

5. **Select A Network Printer, or a Printer Attached to Another Computer.**

6. **Click Next.**

   The Specify a Printer dialog box appears.

7. **Do one of the following:**

   - Select Browse for a Printer if you don't know the printer's name and network address.
   - Select Connect to This Printer if you know the printer's name and network address. Skip to Step 10.

   The Browse for Printer dialog box appears.

8. **Double-click the network (in this case, MSHOME) to expand the menu tree, which is shown in Figure 4-4.**

9. **Select the printer you want to add and click Next.**

   Windows XP displays a warning about the potential hazards of installing a print driver on your machine. If you know it's the correct network printer, you can continue without fear.

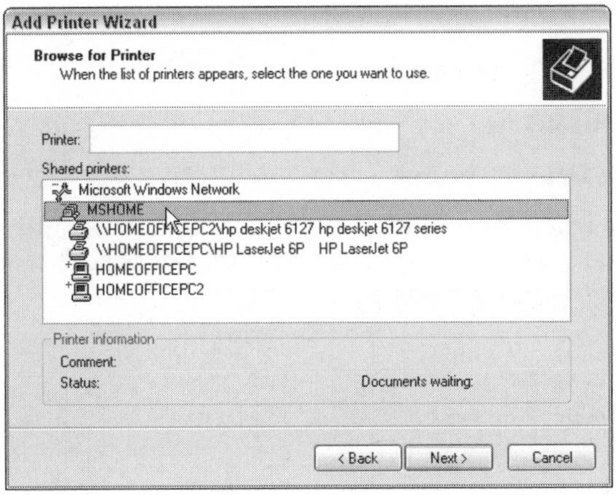

Figure 4-4: Browsing for the network printer you want to add.

10. **Click Yes.**

    The Default Printer window appears. Windows XP installs the appropriate printer driver on your computer.

11. **Do one of the following:**

    - Select Yes if you want the network printer you just added to be your default printer (the printer your jobs go to automatically).
    - Select No if you want to keep your current default printer as is.

    The Completing the Add Printer Wizard dialog box appears.

12. **Click Finish.**

    You just added a network printer to your personal computing arsenal!

Changing the Default Printer

You can change the printer that Windows XP uses as its default printer. The *default printer* is the one where your print jobs automatically go. While you can always choose another printer on the network (if there is one), doing nothing means your default printer handles the job.

Usually, your default printer is your *local printer* (the one hooked up to your computer), but you can choose to make a network printer the default printer. Here's how you do it:

1. **Click Start.**

   The Start menu appears.

2. **Click Printers and Faxes.**

   The Printers and Faxes dialog box appears.

3. **Right-click the printer you want to have as your default printer.**

4. **Select Set as Default Printer.**

   A white checkmark on a black circle appears on the printer icon. It indicates that the printer is now the default printer, as shown in Figure 4-5. You're done.

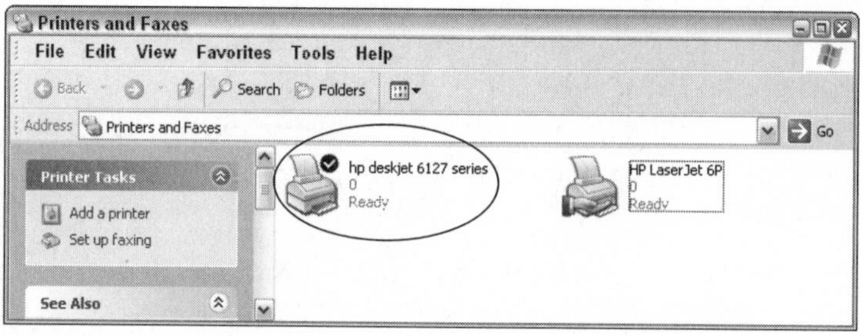

Figure 4-5: This printer's your default.

Chapter 5: Confirming Your Network Works

In This Chapter

- **Checking your signal strength**
- **Monitoring your network's activity**
- **Avoiding possible signal obstacles**
- **Handling interference**

Eureka!" That's what you hope comes out of your mouth after setting up a wireless network. You may want to yell from the tallest antennae that your new wireless network is running without any problems. Hold that thought: First check on your network's health. That includes viewing the signal strength as well as monitoring its *activity* (that is, the network traffic).

Flexing Your Signal Strength

You'll be happy to know of a simple way to view the strength of your wireless network's signal. This method doesn't provide a great deal of information, but it's enough to know whether you ought to move your wireless router closer to your computers.

You should check your signal strength at two different times:

- When you first set up your network
- Anytime you move your PCs or other network hardware

Moving components just a few feet from their original positions may cause signal strength to drop. In that case you can scurry about, putting everything back in place. Then, with thinking cap firmly applied, you can reconsider where you'll move your equipment.

TECHNICAL STUFF

Windows XP has several built-in tools for testing your network. I discuss these in Book IV, Chapter 3.

To view a simple but helpful visual, just follow these steps:

1. **Right-click the network icon in the Windows XP notification area.**

   A pop-up menu appears.

2. **Select Status.**

   A network status dialog box appears.

3. **Select the General tab, if it's not already selected.**

   Under Connection you see a small bar graph that provides a quick look at the strength of your wireless network's signal, as shown in Figure 5-1. If four or five bars are highlighted, you're enjoying robust signal reception.

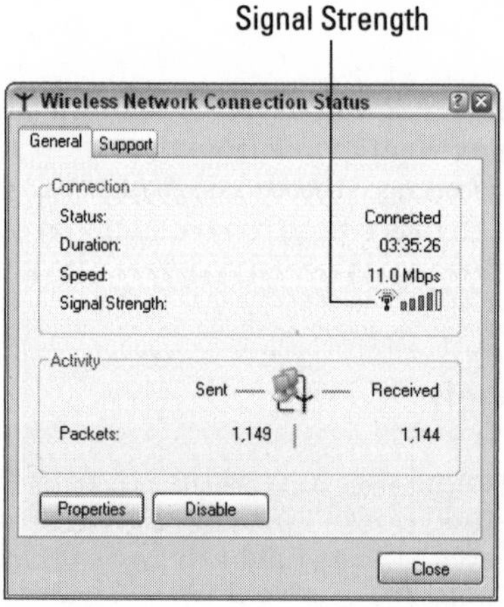

Figure 5-1: With four bars highlighted, this network is cranking.

WARNING!

If only three or fewer bars are highlighted, you have a pretty weak wireless connection. You'll want to read Book IV, Chapter 3, which helps you solve wireless network problems like this one.

4. **When you're done viewing your signal strength, click Close.**

TIP

Would you like an even simpler way to view your signal strength? Move your cursor over the wireless connection icon, located next to the Windows XP clock. A bubble like that in Figure 5-2 pops up and tells the strength with text. Here's how that text breaks down compared to the bar graph:

- Excellent: Your network is just full of energy. This is equivalent to four or five bars.
- From best (which I assume Excellent is) to worst is how I suggest completing the bulleted list.

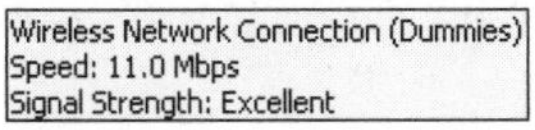

Figure 5-2: Pop-up shows signal strength.

A more sophisticated way of measuring signal strength is discussed a little later in this chapter. Using a third-party software program, you can get a pretty accurate read on the strength of nearby Wi-Fi access points.

Monitoring Your Network

After you've decided which wireless networks you want to connect to, some Windows XP tools can monitor those networks. One of these tools is in the same dialog box that shows your signal strength. Another is a real-time graphical network monitor that's part of Windows Task Manager. In the following sections you learn how to use these tools.

Viewing your network's activity

In the Wireless Network Connection Status dialog box, you can see how much data is moving in and out of a PC over your wireless network.

Here's how you view it:

1. **Confirm that your wireless network is enabled.**

   If it's not, enable it. If you're also running a wired network, disable it.

2. **Right-click the wireless network icon in Windows XP's notification area.**

   A pop-up menu appears.

3. **Select Status.**
4. **Select the General tab if it's not already selected.**
5. **In the Activity area you can monitor data packets sent and received, as shown in Figure 5-1.**

   If there's a number below Sent but a zero is beneath Received, your wireless network may not be working properly. If there are at least three-digit numbers under both Sent and Received, your network should be hunky-dory.

6. **Click OK.**

   That's it for one view of network activity!

Viewing a real-time networking graph

To monitor your wireless network, just follow these steps:

1. **Press Ctrl+Alt+Delete.**

   This is affectionately known by many as the Vulcan death grip. But in Windows XP, instead of immediately rebooting your PC, it displays the Windows Task Manager dialog box.

2. **Select Task Manager.**

   You see several tabs at the top of the dialog box. By default, you are in the Applications tab.

3. **Select the Networking tab.**

   A graph like that in Figure 5-3 shows your wireless network's activity in real time. In this example my wireless network is using about 1 percent of its capacity. The bandwidth I'm using appears consistent because I'm streaming music over the Internet.

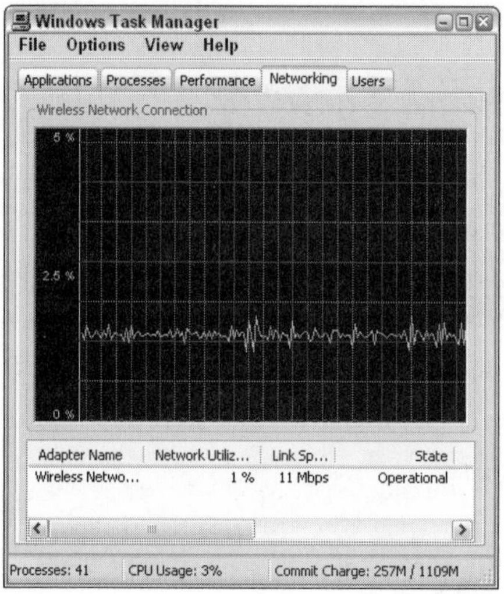

Figure 5-3: A graphics display shows your network's heartbeat, while a text area supplies other useful information.

   If you also have a wired Ethernet network active, you see two graphic windows. One window shows the wired network while the other window shows the wireless network.

   The bottom window shows a bunch of information about your wireless network. For starters you see the Adapter Name, Network Utilization, Link Speed, and several columns displaying your network's *throughput* (how much of the network's capacity is actually being used).

4. **When you're done viewing your wireless network's activity, close the Task Manager.**

   That's it! See how easy it is to monitor your wireless network's activity?

Changing the networking information you see

While viewing the Networking screen in Windows Task Manager, you saw some detailed text information below the glitzy graphical display. It's easy to change the columns displayed there:

1. **In the Windows Task Manager, select View⇨Select Columns.**

   The Select Columns dialog box appears, as shown in Figure 5-4.

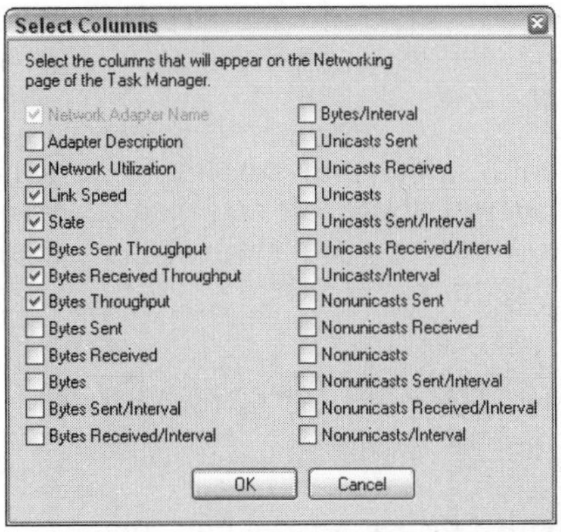

Figure 5-4: Choosing the information you'll see in the networking graph.

2. **Select or deselect the boxes next to columns you'd like displayed.**

   TIP

   The default selections probably do the trick. However, you may want to see something specific or your network administrator may ask you to add columns while diagnosing a problem with your network. For example, you might want to see the number of bytes that were sent or received in order to see exactly how much data has been flowing across your network.

3. **Click OK.**

   Any column changes appear in the text area.

4. **If you added columns, you may need to resize the Windows Task Manager dialog box to see them.**

   Point the mouse over the Task Manager's outline until you see a double-headed arrow and click and drag to resize.

5. **Close the dialog box when you're done viewing the Networking screen.**

   You're done — and you're one step closer to becoming an experienced wireless network administrator.

Stumbling Upon Network Stumbler

While you can get a rough reading on your signal strength from Windows XP and monitor your network, another tool gives you a more detailed view: Network Stumbler. It's free for home users (commercial and government users are encouraged to donate $50 per copy).

Written by Marius Milner, NetStumbler runs under Windows and monitors the signal strength of nearby access points. You can select an access point and NetStumbler displays a real-time graph showing the strength.

You can use it on your desktop PC to see if it's close enough to the transmitter and if the signal is too noisy, which indicates interference or physical obstacles. Better yet, you can install the software on a laptop computer, moving around your house or business to measure signal strength in various places.

Downloading and installing NetStumbler

To download the program, follow these steps:

1. **Point your browser to** http://www.netstumbler.com/.

   The NetStumbler web page loads.

2. **Click Downloads (located on the left side of the main menu).**

   The Downloads page appears.

3. **Click NetStumbler and save the program to your desktop or to another location you'll remember.**

4. **Double-click the downloaded NetStumbler setup program.**

   The Setup dialog box displays the license agreement.

5. **After reading the agreement, click I Agree.**

   The Choose Components screen appears.

6. **Select the type of installation.**

   Complete is the default type, as shown in Figure 5-5.

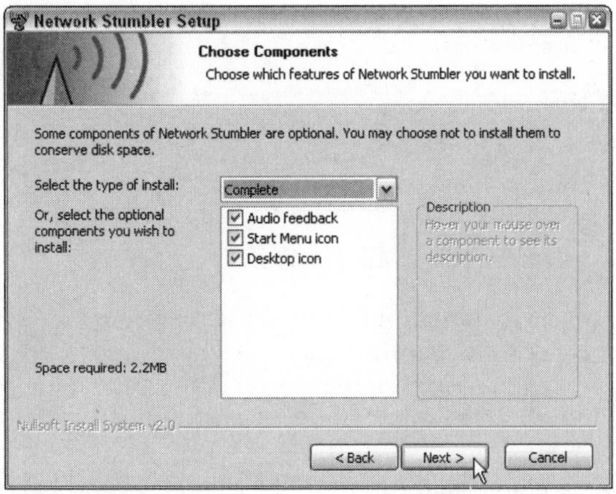

Figure 5-5: Choosing which components to install.

7. **Click Next.**

   The Choose Install Location screen appears.

8. **If the installation directory is acceptable, click Install.**

   You can click Browse to choose another directory. The program installs when you click Install.

9. **When it says Installation Complete, click Close.**

Using NetStumbler

Despite its complicated looks, NetStumbler is easy to use. It displays nearby access points; you choose one to have it displayed as a graphic. From the graphic, you can make some judgments about whether a particular signal is strong.

Here's how you use the program:

1. **Either double-click the program icon on your desktop or click Start, NetStumbler.**

   The program runs and looks something like Figure 5-6. You see the total number of active access points (APs) displayed at the bottom of the screen. One AP is active in Figure 5-6. The device's *MAC (Media Access Control)* number and *SSID (Service Set Identifier)* are displayed in the main window. Each piece of network hardware has its own MAC number, so this helps you identify the specific unit. The SSID is a name that can be used with an access point, but it's not required.

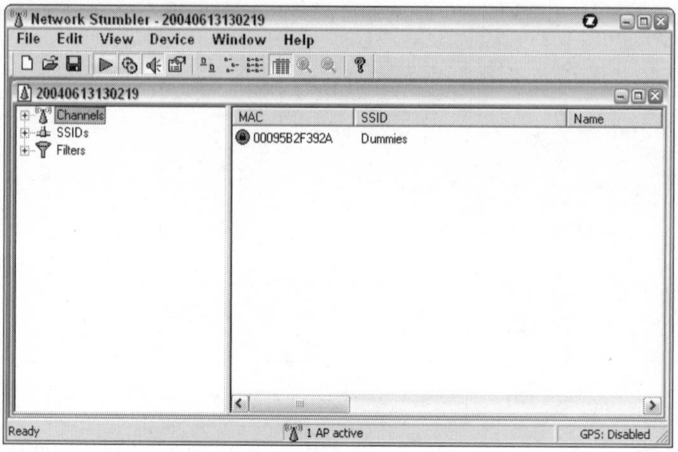

Figure 5-6: NetStumbler displaying nearby access points.

2. **In the left display, click the + beside SSIDs.**

   The directory expands, like you see in Figure 5-7, showing the names of nearby APs.

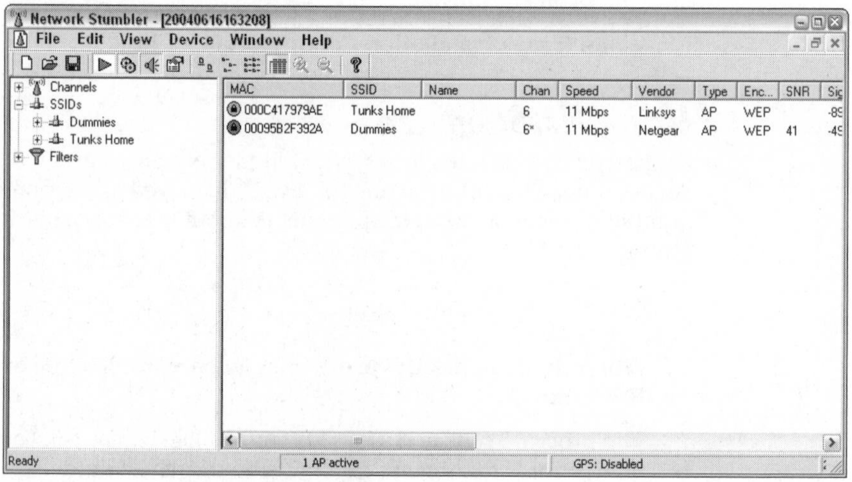

Figure 5-7: The expanded directory shows the SSIDs.

3. **In the left window, click the plus sign next to the AP you want to view.**

   The directory expands one more level, showing the MAC number of the AP you chose, as shown in Figure 5-8. In this example it's 00095B2F392A.

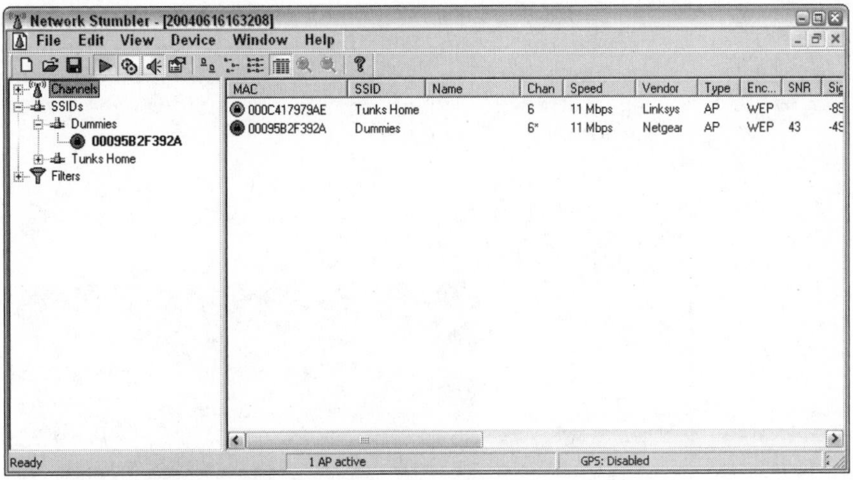

Figure 5-8: The left menu shows the Dummies AP's MAC address.

4. **Click the AP's MAC number.**

   The real-time charting begins, as shown in Figure 5-9. Green bars indicate signal strength. Higher bars indicate a better signal. The red bars indicate signal noise. A good signal should have low red bars. A purple bar, if shown, indicates a loss of signal.

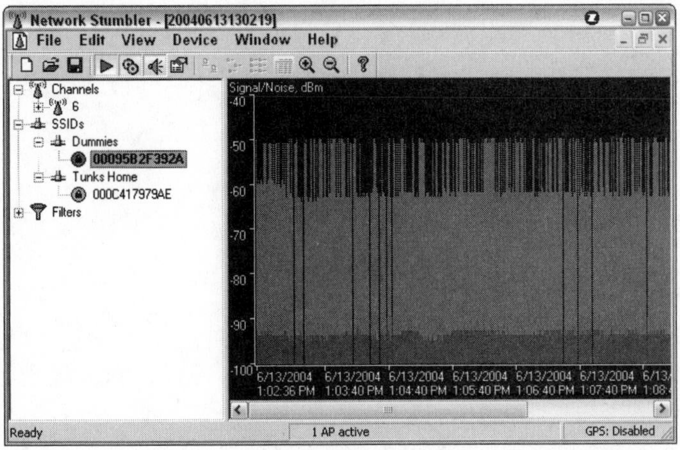

Figure 5-9: NetStumbler displays the signal strength.

The graphic in Figure 5-9 shows a network performing well. The signal has very little noise while it stretches between the access point and my computer's wireless adapter card.

TIP

NetStumbler's Zoom Out function (View⇨Zoom Out) can provide the big picture. By zooming out all of the way, as shown in Figure 5-10, you can compress the period of time shown in the graph. You also even out the signal strength readings, getting a better idea of how your network is performing.

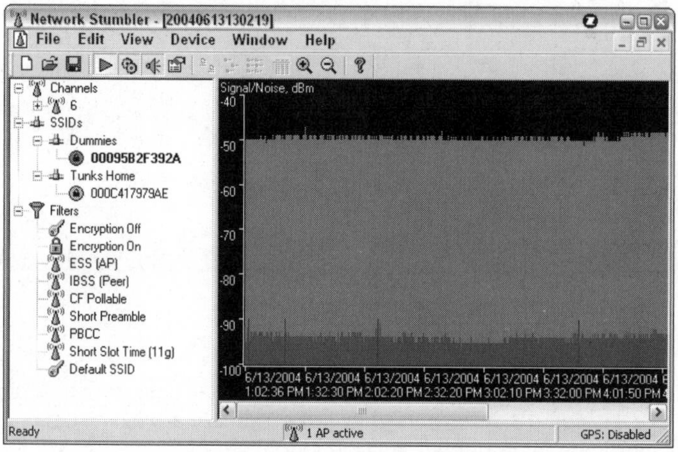

Figure 5-10: Zooming out shows a steady signal over time.

Book IV

Security and Troubleshooting

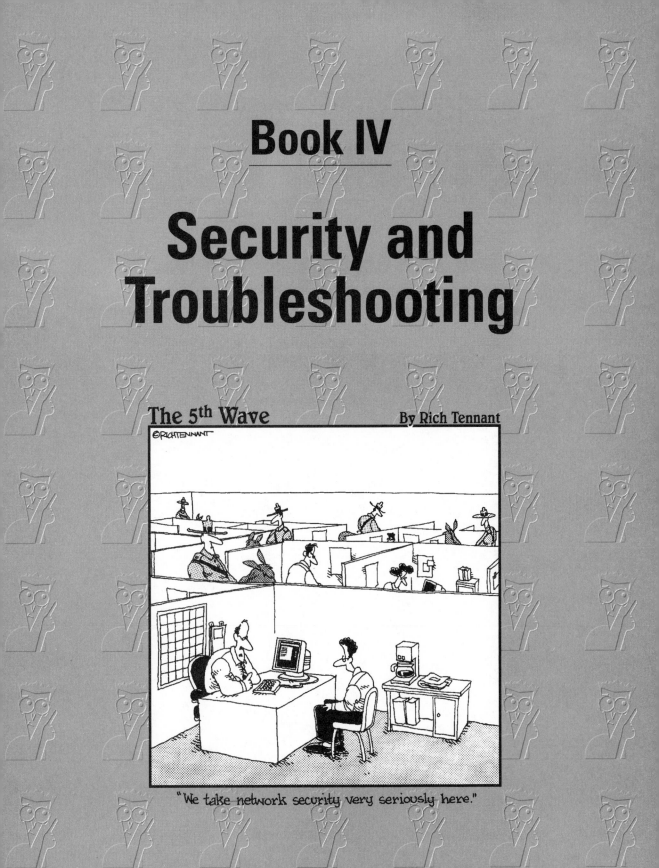

"We take network security very seriously here."

Contents at a Glance

Chapter 1: Using a Safety Net 183
Chapter 2: Managing User Accounts 205
Chapter 3: Solving Network Problems 221

Chapter 1: Using a Safety Net

In This Chapter

- Understanding the dangers associated with wireless networks
- Implementing basic wireless network security
- Setting up encryption on wireless networks
- Taking a proactive approach to wireless hardware and software security

A little safety never hurt anyone, right? When it comes to setting up a wireless network, adding security should always be at (or at least very near) the top of your list. In fact, if you don't secure your wireless network, expect other users within range to connect to your network, "borrowing" your Internet connection, and even rooting through your personal files. If that doesn't sound scary, it should.

Because a new wireless network typically won't have any security features enabled by default, that leaves the job of locking things down in your hands. Well, your hands and mine, as I'm certainly not going to leave you hanging. Actually, if you follow the advice I offer in this chapter, your wireless network will be as secure as possible, and you'll be well on your way to getting a better night's sleep!

Safety First, but Security Firstest

In the wired world, you seldom need to worry about outside users gaining physical access to your network. To do this, they literally need to connect a cable from their PC into a switch or hub on your network. If it did happen, the good news is that you could always just unplug the cable (and then check the locks on your doors and windows).

With wireless networks, gaining physical access is much less an issue. Since there are no wires involved and nothing to plug into, any user within range can potentially connect to your network. Worse still, a firewall does nothing to stop them. The *firewall* is concerned with blocking users attempting to access your network from the Internet, not your front lawn.

Unfortunately, most users install their wireless network and never give a second thought to actually securing it. All wireless routers ship with next to no security features enabled. In simple terms, not securing your wireless network is akin to placing a sign on your house announcing free Internet service for the neighborhood. If you're the least bit concerned about securing your network from outside users, you get down to the business of securing your network immediately.

The good news is that the process of securing a wireless network isn't terribly difficult. You can help to improve the security of your network, quite easily, a number of ways. The more basic methods stop almost all users from being able to connect, while the more advanced methods present a serious challenge to even the most experienced hackers and crackers.

REMEMBER

Some of the different ways that you can improve the security of your wireless network follow:

- Limiting which computers can connect to your wireless router.
- Stopping your wireless router from announcing its presence to the world.
- Encrypting all communications on your wireless network.
- Keeping your wireless software and hardware up to date with the latest and greatest security fixes.

Sure, the list looks like a lot, but the truth is that securing a wireless network isn't nearly a difficult as it sounds. I help you through it; I promise.

Hackers, Crackers, and Slackers

You might be curious as to why anyone would be interested in connecting to your wireless network. The answer is simple — because it exists. With wireless network adapters now built in or easily added to everything from PDAs to laptops, just about anyone can walk or drive around a given area and discover scores of wireless networks.

Even the most honest person is tempted to connect to an available wireless network that Windows XP alerts them to by chance. While wireless networks are often stumbled upon, some people actively seek them out and even chart their locations.

If you've never heard of *war driving,* it can seem almost a little too sci-fi. However, people drive through neighborhoods with their laptops in tow, looking for wireless networks. Many do it out of curiosity, just to see how many networks they *could* connect to if they felt like it. Others are actively mapping out these networks by using a *Global Positioning System (GPS)* connected to their laptops. Some do it for their own reference, while others post the location of unsecured wireless networks on the Internet for all to find.

Hackers and crackers

There's plenty of debate over the use of the terms *hacker* and *cracker.* Most computer professionals see a *hacker* as a skilled programmer who looks for flaws (in system security, for example), with the intent of bringing the issue to light such that it can be fixed. Conversely, a *cracker* is considered the bad guy who attempts to maliciously take advantage of known issues in an attempt to exploit them for personal gain, prestige, or whatever. Most crackers consider themselves hackers, but a real hacker wouldn't take well to being called a cracker. Further confusing the issue is the fact that the media tends to lump both into the hacker category.

If you're interested in reading more about war driving, check out www.wardriving.com. It gives you a better idea of the tools and techniques that people often use to connect to accessible wireless networks.

In most cases, people who engage in activities like war driving (or walking, or jogging) are simply looking for an easy way to "borrow" your Internet connection while within range. Others are more firmly positioned on the dark side, looking for ways to gain access to your home network, computers, and personal information. Regardless of the reason they do it, it's up to you to secure your wireless network. If you don't, you're leaving your wireless network open for anyone within range to access.

As a general rule, it's the hackers and crackers that you want to look out for. Slackers are usually too lazy to be bothered trying to connect to your wireless network.

Plugging Your Security Holes

When trying to secure any network, the most effective way to is to take things one step at a time. With that in mind, I begin by walking you through two easy but effective ways to help secure your wireless network. The first helps reduce the overall visibility of your network, while the second helps control which computers are allowed to connect.

Add some security to your wireless network these two easy ways:

- Stopping your wireless router from broadcasting its SSID.
- Configuring your wireless router to allow connections from your own wireless computers only, by specifying their MAC addresses.

I explain how to configure both techniques in the following sections.

Making your SSID invisible

To make it easy for wireless clients to find your network, wireless routers are configured to broadcast their *Service Set Identifier (SSID)* name by default. Wireless clients listen for these broadcasts and use them to determine which wireless networks are within range and accessible.

Unfortunately, by broadcasting its SSID, the wireless router is making itself known to any wireless client in range. That includes your next door neighbors, the people in the apartment above you, and the strange fellow sitting on your front lawn with his laptop.

One of the easier ways to add a bit of stealth to your wireless network is to disable the SSID broadcast function on your router.

1. **Connect to your router's management interface and pop into the Wireless section.**
2. **Look for a section marked SSID. (This is the same screen from which you configured your network's SSID name back in Book II.)**
3. **Choose to disable SSID broadcasts, as shown in Figure 1-1.**

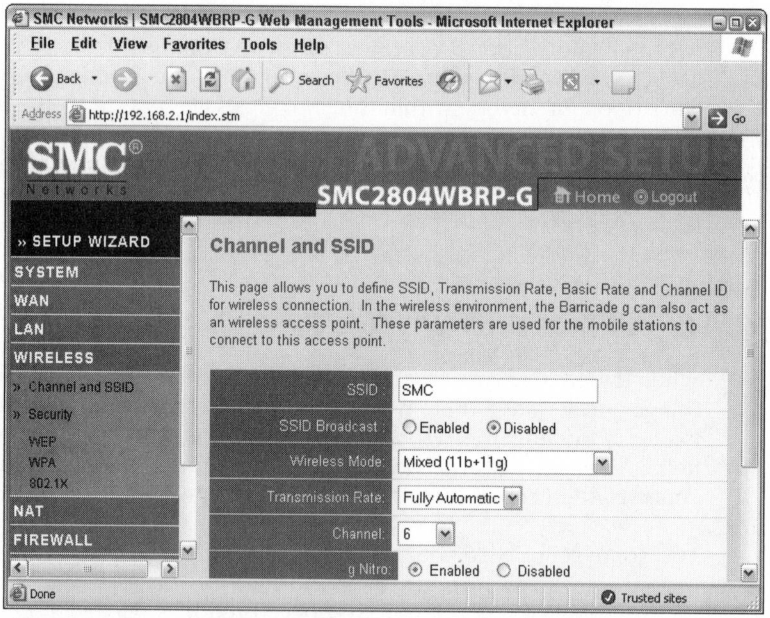

Figure 1-1: Disable SSID broadcasts for better security.

Once you've disabled SSID broadcasts, wireless clients on your network no longer discover your wireless network automatically. As such, you need to configure each client with the correct SSID name for the network manually. To do this, follow the steps:

1. **Click Start, Control Panel.**

   The Control Panel dialog box opens.

2. **Double-click Network Connections.**

   The Network Connections dialog box opens.

3. **Right-click Wireless Network Connection and click Properties.**

   The Properties dialog box for your wireless network connection opens.

4. **Click the Wireless Networks tab.**

   The Wireless Networks tab appears, as shown in Figure 1-2.

Figure 1-2: The Wireless Networks tab in the properties dialog box of a wireless network connection.

5. **In the Preferred Networks section, click the Add button.**

   The Wireless Network Properties dialog box opens.

6. **In the Network Name (SSID) section, type the SSID name associated with your wireless network.**

7. **For now, ensure that the Data Encryption drop-down menu is set to Disabled, as shown in Figure 1-3.**

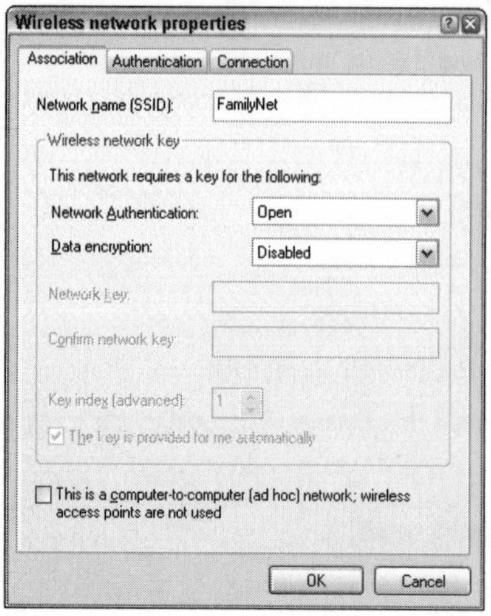

Figure 1-3: With SSID broadcasts disabled on your router, you will need to configure the SSID name on all network clients manually.

8. **Click OK twice to save your new settings.**

Your Windows XP system is now configured with the correct SSID value; you're done!

Tying down the MAC hatch

Another easy and effective way to add a little more security to your wireless network is to exercise some draconian control over which client computers are allowed to communicate with your router. Using a technique known as *MAC security,* you can dictate exactly which client computers are allowed to communicate with your router.

In a nutshell, you implement MAC security by configuring your router with the *MAC* (or physical) addresses of the network cards of client computers on your network. Since each network adapter has a unique MAC address, limiting connections to those from your own computers helps stop outside users from connecting to your wireless router.

Before you can implement MAC security, you need the MAC addresses of the client computers on your network. Follow these steps to obtain them on Windows XP systems:

1. **Open a Command Prompt and type** ipconfig /all.

   TIP

   The physical address value listed for your network adapter card is the string of letters and numbers you're after — something like 00-01-02-03-04-05. Write these down; you need them shortly!

2. **Open your router's management interface and look for a section named MAC security, MAC filter, or similar.**

   This is often found in the Firewall section.

3. **Select the option to enable MAC address control.**

4. **Type in the MAC addresses of the client computers you gathered earlier, as shown in Figure 1-4.**

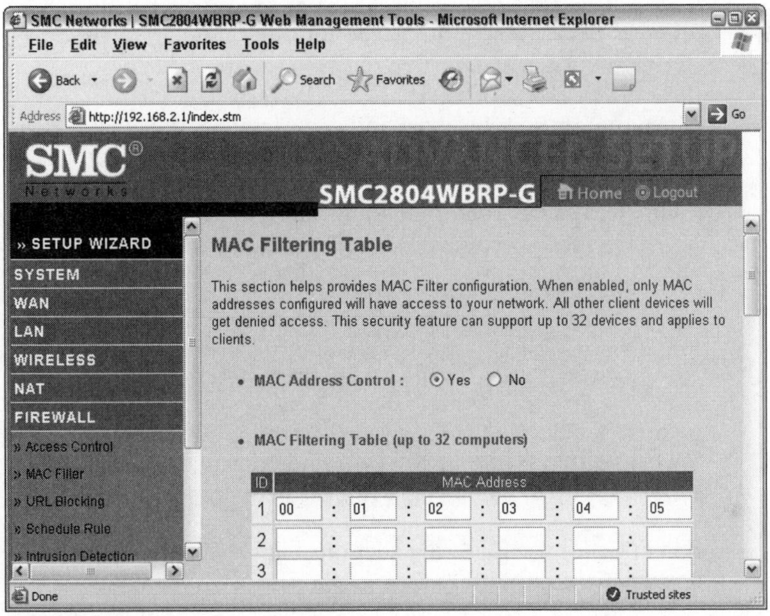

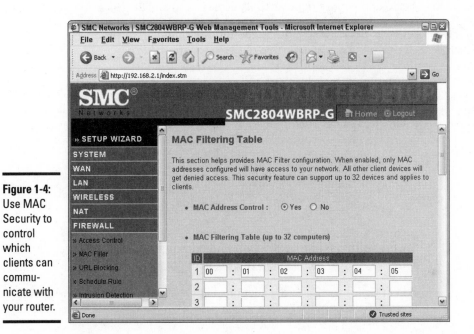

Figure 1-4: Use MAC Security to control which clients can communicate with your router.

Once you've saved these settings, only clients with their MAC addresses listed can connect to your wireless router. Don't forget that if you want to add clients to your network, you need to add their MAC address to this list first.

Introducing WEP, WPA, and Weep

Although reducing the visibility of your wireless network and controlling which computers can access it helps improve security, both methods can only be relied upon up to a point. In the real world, hackers and crackers are not so easily outsmarted. In fact, people who know their stuff employ a range of tools to *sniff out* your wireless network and gather information about it. At the end of the day, you have to remember that your wireless network is transmitting signals, one way or another. Anyone with an appropriate receiver can capture them and gather potentially useful information.

In order to receive signals from your network, hackers typically employ a software tool known as a wireless *sniffer.* When running on a computer or PDA with wireless network capabilities, this software scans the wave for wireless network signals and displays information about the networks it finds. These programs even go as far as to tell the hacker what security methods appear to be configured, the name of your network (stolen from captured packets), and more.

Some of the more popular tools used to find and access wireless networks include Kismet, Network Stumbler, AirSnort, and AiroPeek. A great list of wireless networking utilities and information on how they work can be found at www.networkintrusion.co.uk/wireless.htm.

Given that these tools exist and can easily be utilized by even an inexperienced user, a greater degree of security is in order. Specifically, you want to use encryption to scramble the contents of any transmissions passed across your wireless network. Almost all wireless network equipment (routers, access points, and network adapter cards) support two major wireless encryption standards:

- ✦ An older standard known as Wired Equivalent Privacy (WEP)
- ✦ A newer standard called Wi-Fi Protected Access (WPA)

If you're lucky, all of your wireless gear supports both standards. In the following sections I outline the pros and cons of each encryption standard and how to set them up on your wireless network.

If the title for the following section is misleading, I apologize. There's really nothing to cry about.

Read 'em and WEP

Short for *Wired Equivalent Privacy, WEP* has been around since the 802.11 standards were first released back in 1999. The idea behind WEP was to provide a standard method for encrypting communications over a wireless network — in other words, between devices like your wireless network cards and wireless router or access point.

On the plus side, just about every 802.11 wireless device includes support for WEP. You would be hard pressed to find a wireless network card or router that doesn't support the standard. That means that WEP is a viable encryption option on just about every wireless network, which sounds like a great deal.

Unfortunately, not all encryption techniques are equal, and WEP suffers from design flaws. Without getting too technical (read: boring), the keys used by WEP to encrypt data can potentially be discovered by any user within range who is armed with a wireless sniffing program. Once a few thousand WEP-encrypted packets have been captured, these programs can typically crack the WEP encryption key in use and gain access to the wireless network.

Given its known issues, why would you even consider using WEP? Good question! While WEP may not be completely secure, it's still powerful enough to keep casual users from accessing your network. In the absence of other ways to encrypt transmissions on your wireless network, WEP is better than no encryption at all. However, you need to understand that using WEP still makes your network vulnerable to a motivated hacker who is determined to gain access.

Configuring your wireless network to use WEP involves three main steps:

- Enabling WEP on your wireless router
- Configuring your wireless network adapter cards to use WEP
- Connecting to the new WEP-enabled network

To enable WEP on your wireless router (or access point, for that matter), follow along:

1. **Open WEP's management interface and head for its wireless configuration section.**
2. **Look for a section marked WEP or WEP Security.**

   It's from this page that you configure the key that WEP uses to encrypt communications on your network, as shown in Figure 1-5. Depending on your router's make and model, it may support 40- 64- or 128-bit WEP modes.
3. **As a general rule, select the highest WEP mode available as a longer encryption key will provide better security.**
4. **For home networks, choose Static under Key Provisioning.**
5. **Assuming that you chose the 128-bit mode, enter an appropriate encryption key value. Record the value for later use.**
6. **Use the Key 1 space to type a 26-digit key, in hexadecimal.**

   Before you get all worried about a hexadecimal number, just know that the only valid hex digits are the numbers 0 through 9 and the letters A through F. You ultimately need to enter the same key on all of your wireless network adapters.
7. **With your key value configured, save your settings.**

   Depending on your router, you may need to specify what type of connections the device allows. For example, the Security section on the SMC router shown allows you to select No Security, WEP Only, WEP/WPA, and WPA only as the allowed client types, as shown in Figure 1-6.

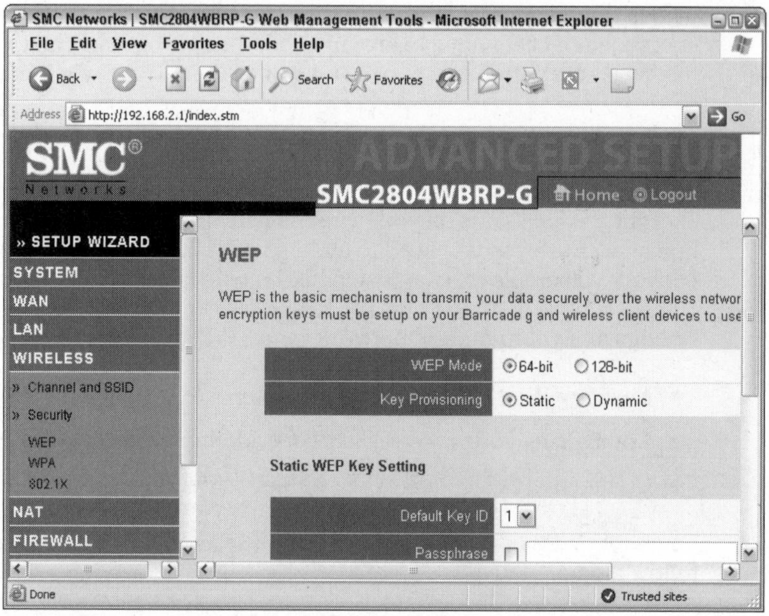

Figure 1-5: Configuring WEP encryption.

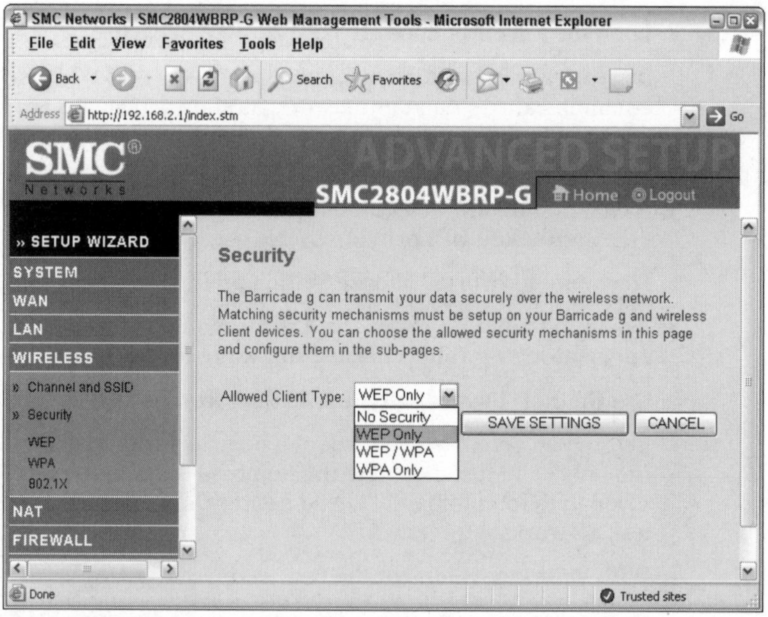

Figure 1-6: Configuring allowed client types on a wireless router.

8. **Assuming that your router gives you a choice, select WEP Only and save your settings.**

TIP

Don't be alarmed when you lose your wireless connection immediately after saving your settings. At this point, your wireless router is configured to require WEP encryption, but your wireless network adapter is still using an unsecured connection.

Get to the business of configuring those Windows XP client systems:

1. **Click Start, Control Panel, and then double-click Network Connections.**

   The Network Connections dialog box opens.
2. **Right-click the wireless network connection icon and click Properties.**

   The Properties dialog box for your wireless network connection opens.
3. **Click the Wireless Networks tab.**
4. **In the Preferred Networks section, click your network's name and click Properties.**

   The Properties dialog box for the wireless network opens to the Association tab.
5. **From the Network Authentication menu, select Open.**
6. **From the Data Encryption menu, select WEP.**
7. **In the Network Key dialog box, enter the 26-digit key value you configured on your wireless router.**
8. **Enter the 26-digit key value again in the Confirm Network Key box shown in Figure 1-7.**
9. **Click the Authentication tab; deselect the Enable IEEE 802.1x Authentication for This Network checkbox.**
10. **Click OK twice to save your settings.**

Your wireless network adapter card is ready for WEP.

Once WEP settings have been configured on both your wireless router and network adapter cards, you're ready to reconnect to your network.

1. **Right-click the wireless network icon in the Windows taskbar.**
2. **Click View Available Wireless Networks.**
3. **On the Network Tasks menu, click Refresh Network List.**

   Your newly secured wireless network should appear on the list, as shown in Figure 1-8.

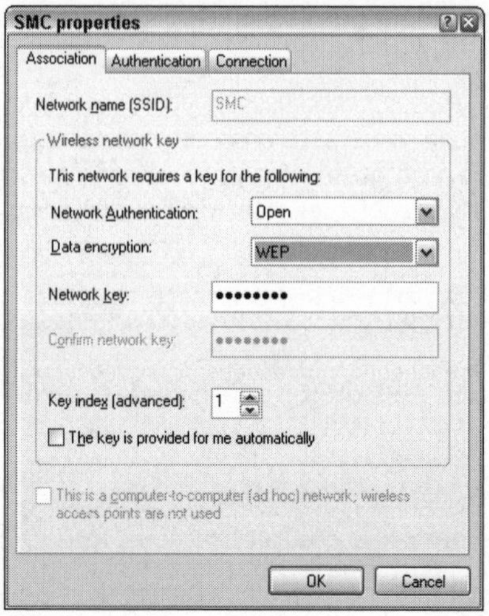

Figure 1-7: Configuring a wireless network adapter card to use WEP encryption.

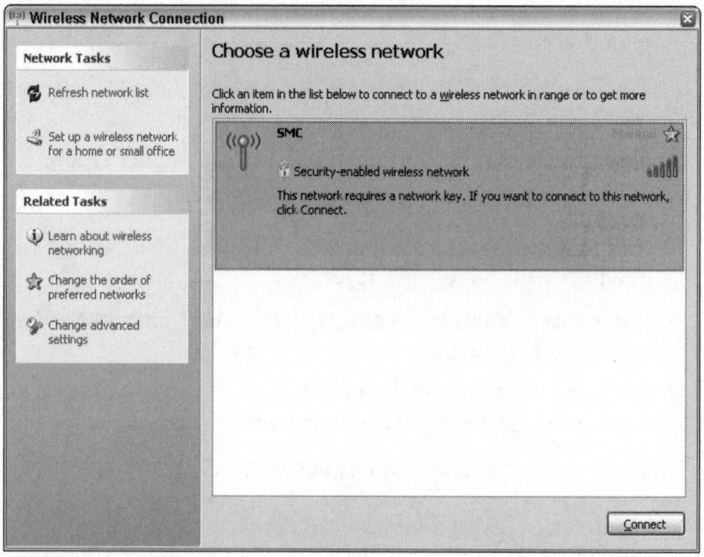

Figure 1-8: Connecting to a WEP-secured wireless network.

4. Click the network and then click Connect.

After a few seconds, you should be connected to your wireless network using WEP encryption.

Upgrading to WPA

Having recognized that WEP isn't secure enough to meet the security needs of wireless networks, manufacturers of 802.11 equipment have agreed on a new wireless encryption method known as *Wi-Fi Protected Access (WPA).* WPA is not an IEEE standard, but rather an interim solution until a new wireless encryption standard is finalized.

The IEEE is the Institute of Electrical and Electronics Engineers, an organization that helps develop technical standards for everything from wireless networks through to consumer electronics. You can read more about the IEEE at their web site at www.ieee.org.

WPA is a much stronger method of encrypting wireless traffic than WEP. Whereas WEP uses the same encryption key for all traffic passed between wireless networking devices, WPA changes the key used to encrypt each and every frame of data sent between devices. The protocol used by WPA to manage and change these keys is called the *Temporal Key Integrity Protocol,* or *TKIP* for short.

Whenever possible, you should use WPA rather than WEP to securely encrypt traffic on your wireless network. Unfortunately, not all wireless devices support WPA by default. In fact, you need to be sure that WPA support is available for each of the following:

- **Windows XP.** WPA support is not included with Windows XP until you install Service Pack 2. If you don't have SP2 installed already, get that sorted first.
- **Your wireless router or access point.** Almost all new wireless access points and routers include support for both WEP and WPA. However, many older devices support WEP only. If your router or access point lacks WPA support, upgrading its firmware to the latest version usually adds it.
- **Your wireless network adapter cards.** In much the same way that many routers and access points lack WPA support, so do many older wireless network adapters. Adding WPA support to your adapters is usually as simple as downloading and installing the latest driver update for your model from the manufacturer's web site.

Once Windows XP and your wireless hardware devices include WPA support, you're ready to set it up. As with configuring WEP, start by configuring WPA on your wireless router or access point:

1. **Log on to your router's management interface and head back to its Wireless Configuration area.**
2. **Look for a section marked WPA or WPA Security, as shown in Figure 1-9.**

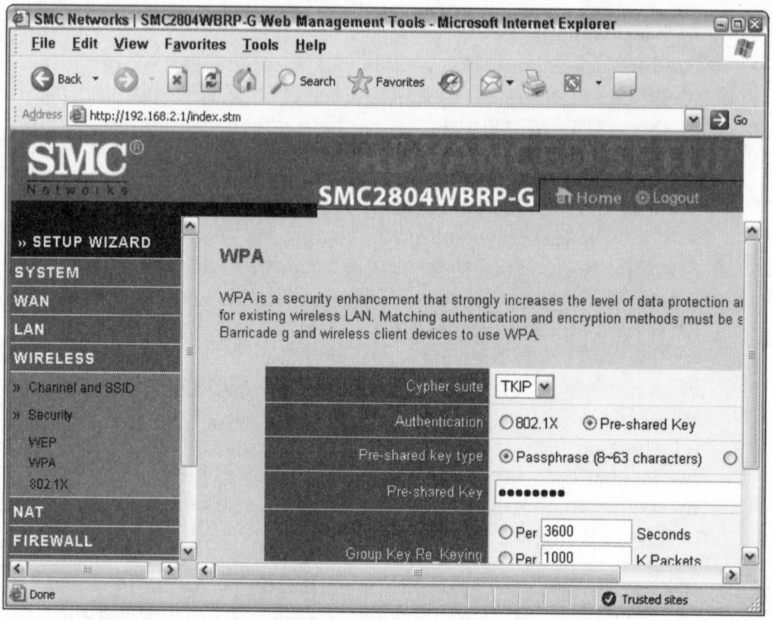

Figure 1-9: Configuring WPA settings.

3. **Ensure that the Cipher suite is set to TKIP and that the Authentication method is set to Pre-shared Key.**
4. **In the Pre-shared Key Type section, choose one of the following as the key:**
   - **Passphrase**
   - **Hexadecimal value**
5. **Type in your key.**

   Again, write it down. You need it to configure your wireless client systems later.
6. **Once you're done, save your settings.**
7. **Head back to the Security section and configure your router to use the WPA Only setting.**

   This limits the router to allowing connections from WPA-enabled clients only.

When you save your settings, you should expect to lose connectivity to your router again.

With your router really to roll, it's time to configure your wireless clients for WPA. To do this, follow the steps:

1. **Click Start, Control Panel, and then double-click Network Connections.**

   The Network Connections dialog box opens.

2. **Right-click the wireless network connection icon and click Properties.**

   The Properties dialog box for your wireless network connection opens.

3. **Click the Wireless Networks tab.**
4. **In the Preferred Networks section, click your network's name and click Properties.**

   The Properties dialog box for the wireless network opens to the Association tab.

5. **From the Network authentication menu, select WPA-PSK.**

   The PSK stands for pre-shared key.

6. **From the Data encryption menu, select TKIP.**
7. **In the Network Key dialog box, enter the pre-shared key value you configured on your wireless router.**
8. **Enter the pre-shared key value again in the Confirm Network Key box shown in Figure 1-10.**

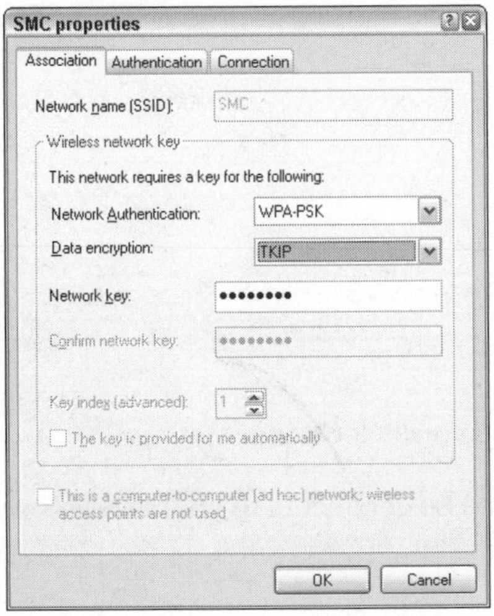

Figure 1-10: Configuring a wireless network adapter card to WPA.

9. **Click the Authentication tab and deselect the Enable IEEE 802.1x Authentication for This Network checkbox.**
10. **Click OK twice to save your settings.**

That's it! Your client is now ready for WPA encryption.

With WPA enabled on your wireless router and network adapter card, you're ready to connect to your wireless network with WPA security.

1. **Right-click the wireless network icon in the Windows taskbar.**
2. **Click View Available Wireless Networks.**
3. **On the Network Tasks menu, click Refresh Network List if necessary.**

   Your newly secured wireless network should appear on the list, as shown in Figure 1-11.

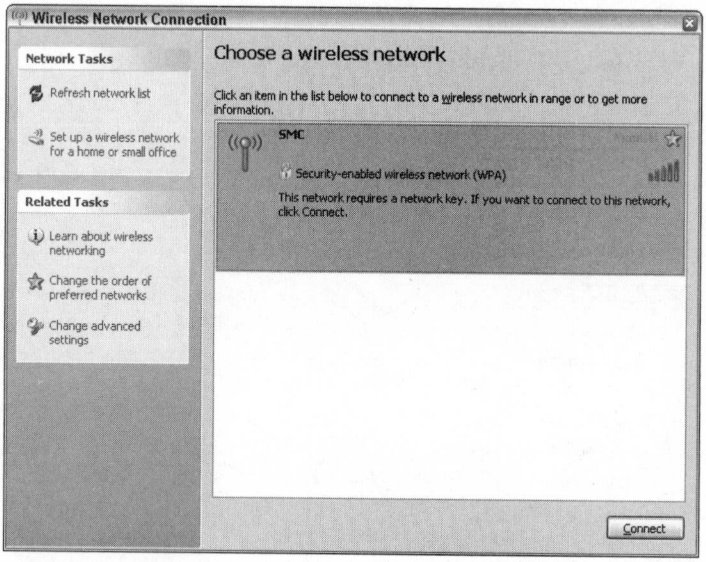

Figure 1-11: Connecting to a WPA-secured wireless network.

4. **Click the network and then click Connect.**

After a short wait, you should be connected to your wireless network using WPA — hip, hip, hooray!

Authenticating with 802.1x

You may be intrigued by a section in your wireless router's configuration called 802.1x authentication, as shown in Figure 1-12. Unfortunately, this section is of very little use to home users. It's really meant for corporate environments where an external server can authenticate wireless users when they attempt to connect to the network.

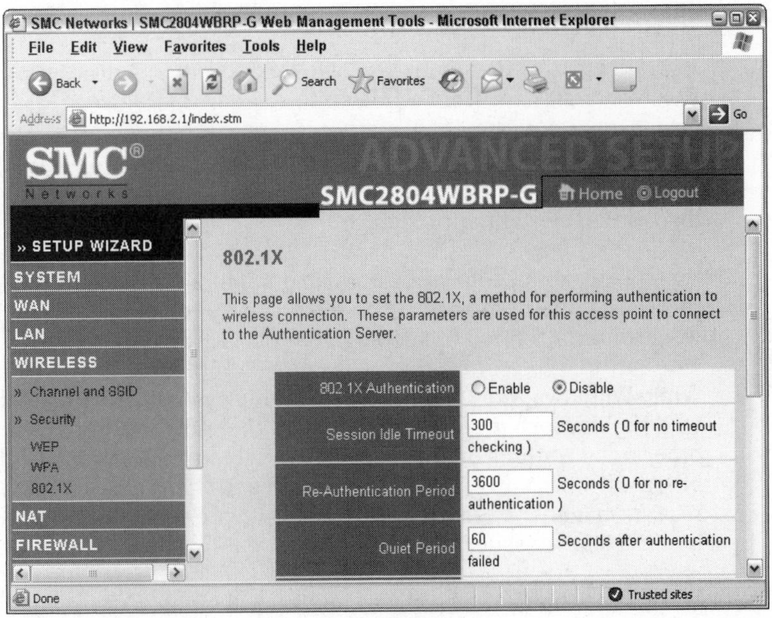

Figure 1-12: Most wireless routers and access points support 802.1x authentication.

The 802.1x authentication capabilities of a wireless router or access point allow it to be used as an intermediary between wireless clients and a RADIUS server. On a corporate network, you configure your wireless router with the IP address of your RADIUS server. Then, when a wireless user passes its authentication request to the access point, the access point forwards the request on to the server. The RADIUS server authenticates the user or computer to ensure that it's allowed to access the wireless network.

Like I said, you really don't need to worry about 802.1x on a home wireless network, so sleep easy.

Fixing Holes Before You Leak

When it comes to securing anything, it's vitally important to remember that security isn't about a set of tasks — it's an ongoing process. As such, one of your goals in attempting to keep your wireless network secure should be to take a proactive approach. In other words, do everything you can to cut off a potential risk at the pass.

One of the best ways to approach security proactively is to stay updated with patches and updates for both your hardware and software. Microsoft releases updates for Windows XP regularly as issues are discovered, while most wireless hardware vendors periodically update drivers and firmware. If you stay ahead of the game, you greatly minimize current (and hopefully future) risks to your network.

Hardening your software

Life can be funny sometimes. While you want to keep your software hard (meaning secure), you definitely don't want to keep your hardware soft (as in not secure). The good news is that keeping your software hard is easy if you take the right approach.

When I talk about *software,* I'm talking about all the non-hardware bits and pieces that your network needs to stay in tip-top shape. In particular, you want to pay attention to keeping Windows XP all patched up.

While Windows XP is a fantastic operating system with great wireless networking support, it's still software, and therefore not perfect. As Microsoft or other organizations uncover security-related problems with Windows XP, Microsoft works away to get them fixed and then releases what are known as *security updates.* A security update is software that you install to patch or repair a known issue.

TIP

You can do things the hard way and keep Windows XP updated by downloading and installing each and every patch manually as they're released. An easier method is to visit the Windows Update Web site regularly (www.windowsupdate.com), scan for updates, and then download and install whatever is considered critical or important. The Windows Update Web site is shown in Figure 1-13.

I know what you're thinking: Isn't having to remember to visit a Web site just as bad as having to remember to check for updates? It sure can be. The good news is that you have another alternative, namely using a feature in Windows XP called Automatic Updates.

If you use Automatic Updates, Windows XP automatically checks for updates regularly and then downloads and installs them without even letting you know. This saves you the hassle of having to remember anything and keeps your system updated as new patches are released. To configure your system to use Automatic Updates, follow the steps:

1. **Click Start, right-click My Computer, and click Properties.**

   The System Properties dialog box opens.

2. **Click the Automatic Updates tab.**

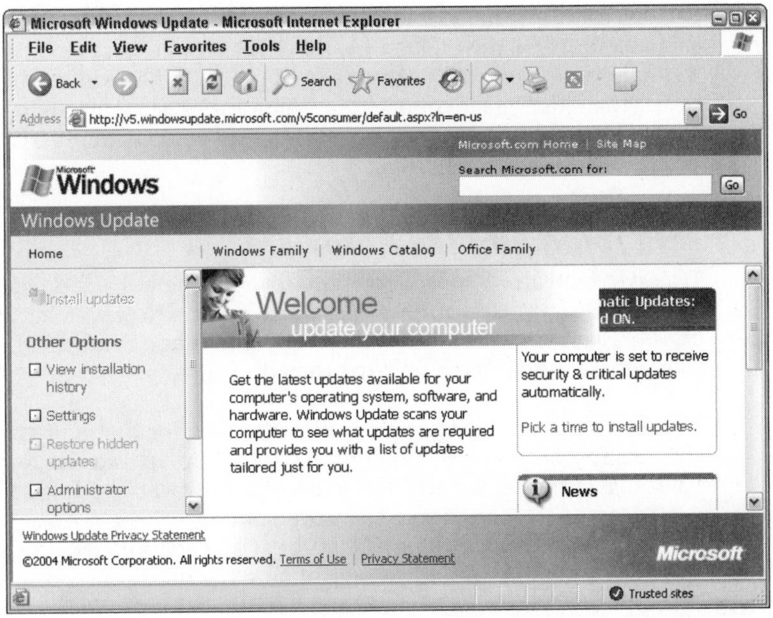

Figure 1-13: If you prefer to do things manually, visit the Windows Update Web site to check for updates often.

3. **Select the option that best meets your needs for updating Windows XP.**

   The best choice is usually Automatic, as shown in Figure 1-14.

4. **Click OK to close the System Properties dialog box. You're done!**

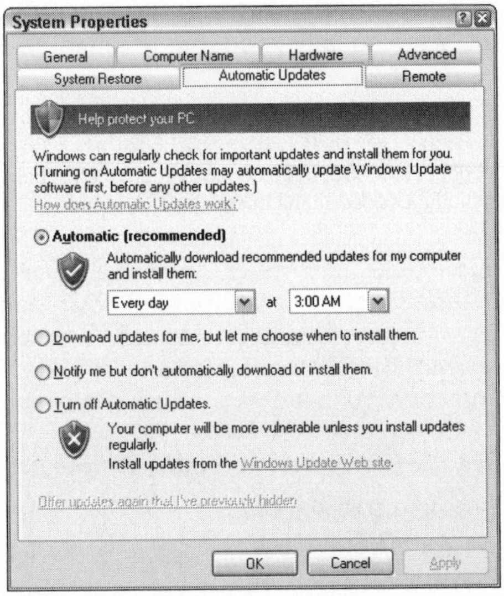

Figure 1-14: Use the Windows XP Automatic Updates feature to keep your computer up to date with the latest patches and security fixes.

Besides downloading and installing critical security updates, the Automatic Updates tool also downloads Windows XP service packs as they're released. A *service pack* is a cumulative group of patches that address many issues, rather than just one. Keeping your Windows XP systems up to date with the latest service pack is important, and should be considered a priority if you're serious about security.

(Un)plugging the hardware

Trying to take apart your wireless hardware is never a good idea and doesn't do anything to make your network more secure. However, hardware devices can be updated by installing newer driver files and firmware, the software elements that help them do what they do.

There's no better way (or really any other way, for that matter) to keep your wireless router or access point updated than to upgrade its *firmware* (the operating system-like code that makes the hardware perform a useful function). Manufacturers release firmware updates or upgrades as a way to add new features to their equipment, address any security issues that have been discovered, and to take advantage of new standards and protocols. A great example is WPA support, which is not found in many older wireless routers and access points, but can typically be added by installing the latest firmware revision. For details on updating your wireless router's firmware, see Book II, Chapter 8.

Much like firmware updates, hardware manufacturers periodically release updated versions of *driver files* (the code that allows the operating system to "talk" to hardware devices) for their wireless network adapter cards to address security issues, make additional features available, and so on. Chances are good that you installed the driver files originally supplied with your hardware, but chances are equally good that the manufacturer has released a few updaters since then.

TIP

If any of your wireless network adapter cards don't include support for WPA, check for an updated driver. Most manufacturers supply updated driver files for network adapter cards that originally lacked WPA support.

To update the drivers for wireless network cards, visit the manufacturer's web site and check their support area for an updated download. You can usually expect these files to be provided in ZIP format. After downloading the file for your model, extract the ZIP to a folder on your hard drive and then follow the instructions here to install the updated drivers:

1. **Click Start, right-click My Computer, and click Properties.**

   The System Properties dialog box opens.

2. **Select the Hardware tab and click the Device Manager button.**

   The Device Manager dialog box opens.

3. **Expand the network adapters icon and right-click your wireless network adapter card's name.**

4. **Click Properties.**

5. **Select the Driver tab and click the Update Driver button.**

   The Hardware Update Wizard opens, as shown in Figure 1-15.

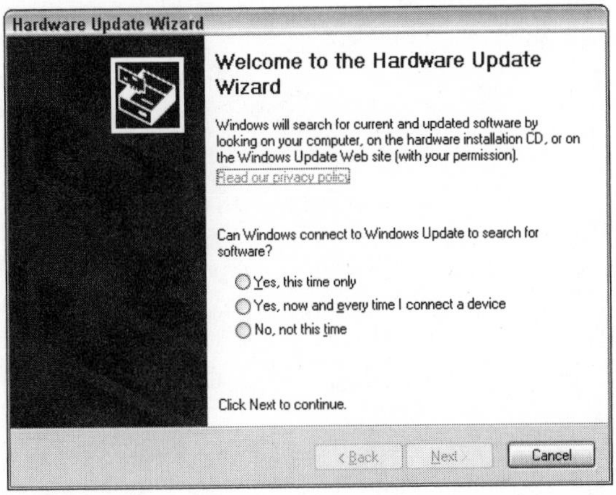
Hardware Update Wizard
Welcome to the Hardware Update Wizard
Windows will search for current and updated software by looking on your computer, on the hardware installation CD, or on the Windows Update Web site (with your permission).
Read our privacy policy
Can Windows connect to Windows Update to search for software?
Yes, this time only
Yes, now and every time I connect a device
No, not this time
Click Next to continue.
< Back
Next >
Cancel

Figure 1-15: Use the Hardware Update Wizard to install updated driver files for your wireless network adapter card.

6. **Select the No, Not This Time option and click Next.**

7. **Select Install from a List or a Specific Location (Advanced) and click Next.**

8. **Click the Browse button. Select the drive and folder location where you saved the updated drivers. Click Next.**

9. **When the Hardware Update Wizard completes, click Finish.**

   Your new drivers are installed.

Chapter 2: Managing User Accounts

In This Chapter

- Choosing an administrator
- Creating, deleting, and changing user accounts
- Disabling the guest account

Like anything else, a wireless network requires a certain number of administrative tasks. Back in the days when I worked in The Corporate World, I'd dread filling out those bloody expense reports, but I knew I had to do it. Think of managing user accounts that way: You may dread it, but it's gotta be done.

User accounts let you manage the people who use your computers and wireless network. User accounts are a security measure that requires people to supply a username and password to log on to a PC, controlling access to your computers and network from both inside (in this case, your home) and outside (anyone in the neighborhood who uses your wireless network to access your computers). As part of managing user accounts, you're responsible for creating new user accounts, changing the accounts' settings, deleting accounts as necessary, and so forth.

Deciding Who Plays Administrator

Computers are great, but they don't run themselves. Someone has to take on the chore of administering your wireless network, even if it's only a small one for your home. Someone — and I bet that's you because you're the one reading my precious words — has to be the alpha and take charge.

Administering your network, especially one with between one to five users, isn't a laborious chore. After all, it's unlikely you have new users coming and going. Mom, Dad, Johnny, and Betsy are pretty much there to stay — at least for a few years. You may have the occasional house guest to add to your network, but things are mostly groovy.

What's the Access Level, Kenneth?

Though it doesn't have a great deal of multilevel security, Windows XP does make a distinction between two of its user account types: *computer administrator* and *limited.* (I talk later about a third account type: *guest.*)

A *computer administrator* can do these things:

- ✦ Install programs and hardware
- ✦ Change things systemwide, such as enabling or disabling the Windows firewall
- ✦ Access and read all files, except those that individual users have marked as private
- ✦ Create and delete user accounts
- ✦ Change other users' accounts
- ✦ Change his own account name or type

A *limited* user can do these tasks:

- ✦ Change his own picture icon
- ✦ Create, change, or remove his own password

It's pretty clear that the capabilities of a limited account are, well, fairly limited. In fact, aside from the silly change-picture feature, limited account users only have control over their own passwords. Limited is so limited that you may want to hand out administrator accounts to several users. Of course, administrators have complete control over a Windows XP system, so think carefully about in whose hands you place that type of power.

A third type of account exists: guest. By default, Windows XP creates one administrator and one guest account. The guest is widely considered a security risk and should be disabled, which I discuss at the end of this chapter.

A guest account does not have a password. Anyone who doesn't have an account on your PC can use a guest account to do things like browse the Internet and read e-mail. The only privilege guest users enjoy, aside from using already installed applications, is changing the guest account picture (the little soccer ball, chess board, or rubber ducky picture that appears next to the Guest name when they log on, as well as at the top of the Start menu).

An administrator has complete access to administrator, limited, and guest accounts.

Creating User Accounts

You can create user accounts as part of installing Windows XP or you can add them later as the need arises. If you don't create any user accounts during installation, Windows XP automatically sets up one administrator account and one guest account. The administrator account is rip, roaring, and ready to go, while the guest account is off *(disabled)* unless you explicitly enable it.

Creating a new user account is pretty straightforward. The hardest part is choosing a name, and even that isn't difficult. To create an account, follow these steps:

1. **Click Start and select Control Panel.**

   The Control Panel appears.

2. **Click User Accounts.**

   The User Accounts screen appears, as shown in Figure 2-1.

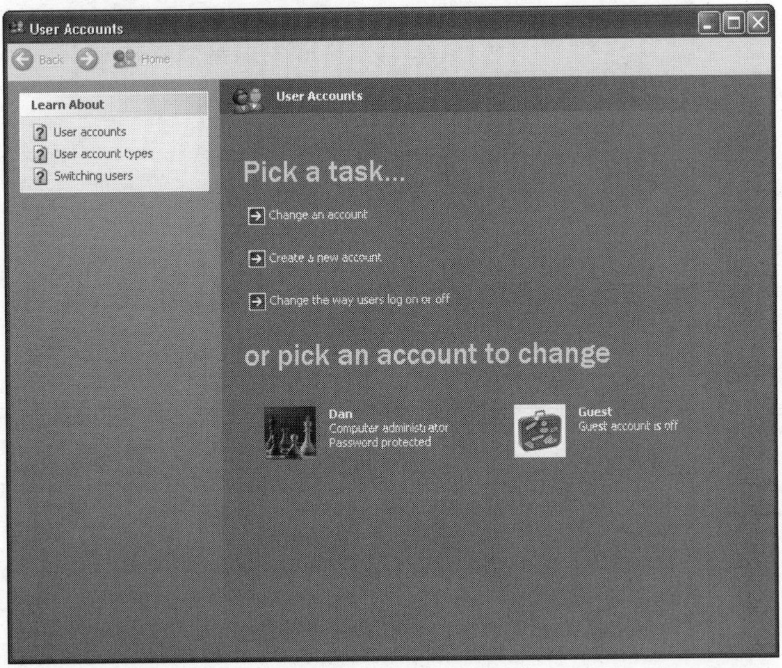

Figure 2-1: The User Accounts screen.

3. **Under Pick a Task, click Create a New Account.**

   The User Accounts screen displays Name the New Account.

4. **Type a name for the account in the form's textbox, as shown in Figure 2-2.**

   When choosing names for your accounts, first names are usually best. However, if you've got two mike accounts to create, simply add the first letter of their last name at the end (for example, mikea or mikeb).

5. **Click Next.**

   The User Accounts dialog box appears. Pick an account type.

6. **Select Computer Administrator or Limited Account, as shown in Figure 2-3.**

7. **Click Create Account.**

   The New Account dialog box shows up on the User Accounts dialog box, as shown in Figure 2-4. You're done!

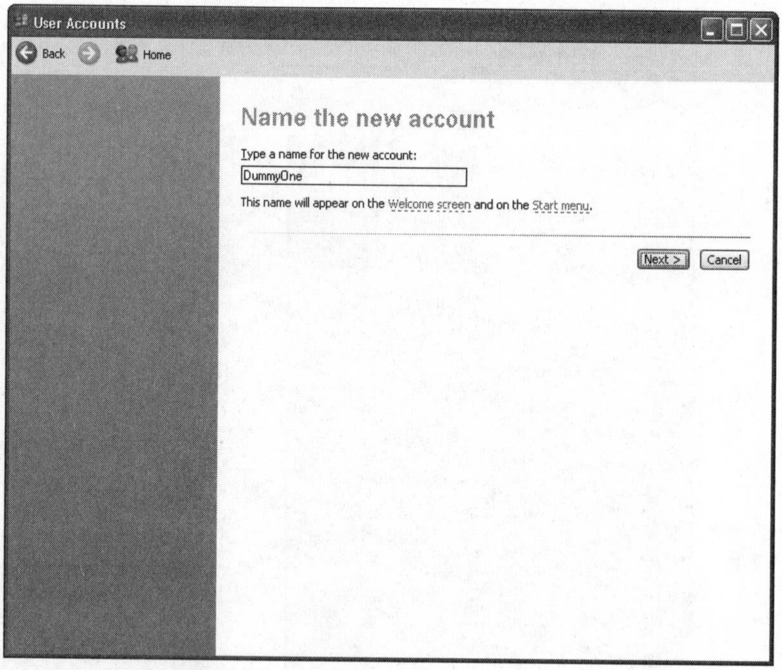

Figure 2-2: I'm typing DummyOne into the new account form.

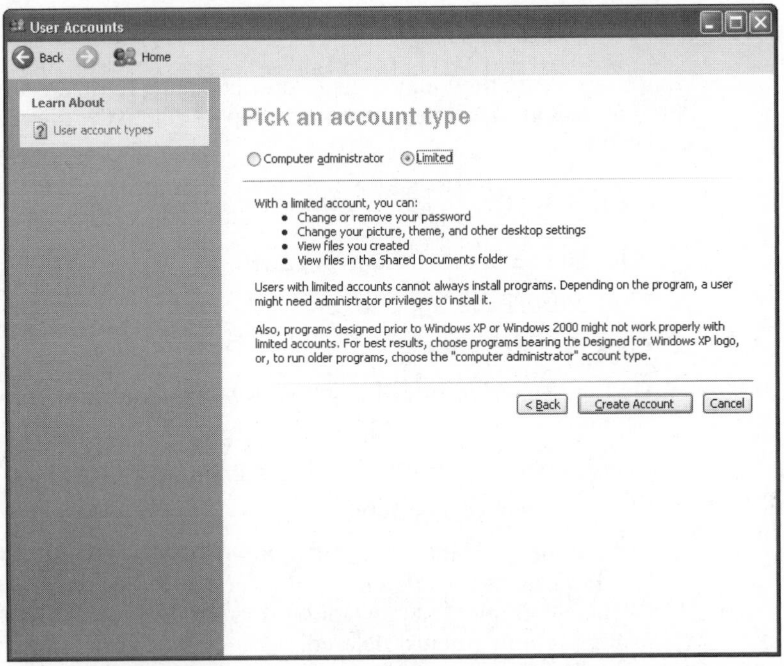

Figure 2-3: Pick an account type.

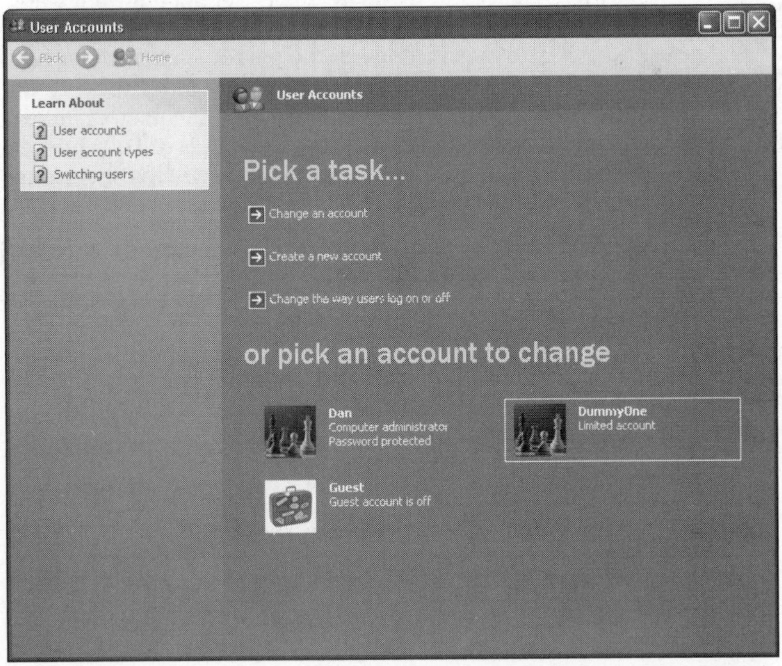

Figure 2-4: Windows XP displays the newly created DummyOne account.

Deleting User Accounts

What thou create thou may delete. After choosing to delete an account, Windows lets you choose whether to keep or delete the files created under the account.

To delete a user account, follow these steps:

1. **Click Start and select Control Panel.**

   The Control Panel appears.

2. **Click User Accounts.**

3. **On the User Accounts dialog box, select the account you want to delete.**

   A new screen asks if you want to keep the account's files.

4. **Choose one of two options:**

   - If you want to keep the files, **click Keep Files**, as shown in Figure 2-5. Windows saves the contents of the account's desktop and My Documents folder to a new folder on your desktop. It has the same name as the account you just deleted.
   - If you want to delete the files and the account, **click Delete Files**, as shown in Figure 2-7. If you delete a user account but want to save all of that user's files (including their favorites and e-mail messages), your best bet is to make a copy of the personal user folder *before* deleting the account. To do this, open My Computer and browse to C:\Documents and Settings. Right-click the folder with the user's name, and copy and paste it to a new location. If you have a CD or DVD burner installed on your computer, burning it to a blank disc helps save some disk space and ensure that you have the files should you ever need them.

5. **Confirm that you want to delete the account by clicking Delete Account. See Figure 2-6.**

   The account is deleted. You're done.

While you can delete any user accounts that you create, you cannot delete the built-in administrator or guest accounts.

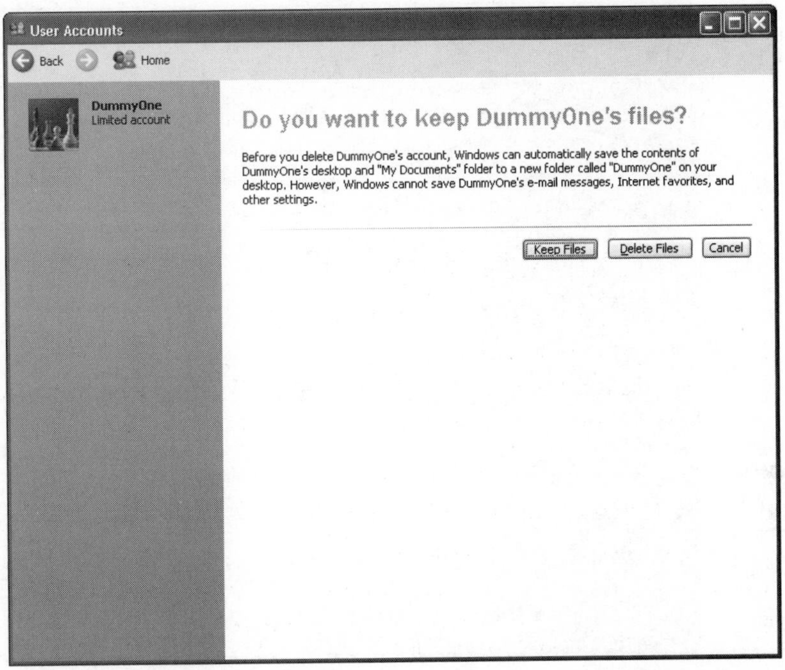

Figure 2-5: Deleting an account while keeping its files.

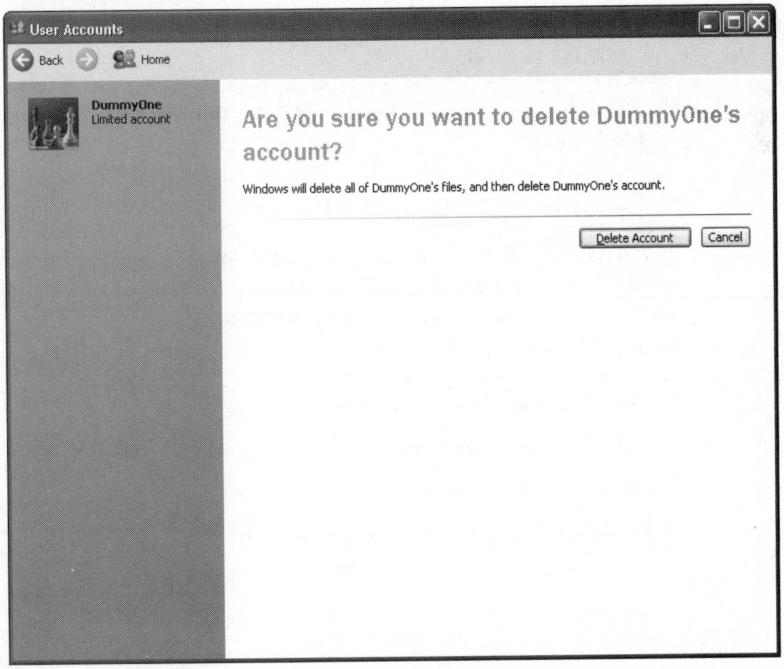

Figure 2-6: Deleting an account *and* its files.

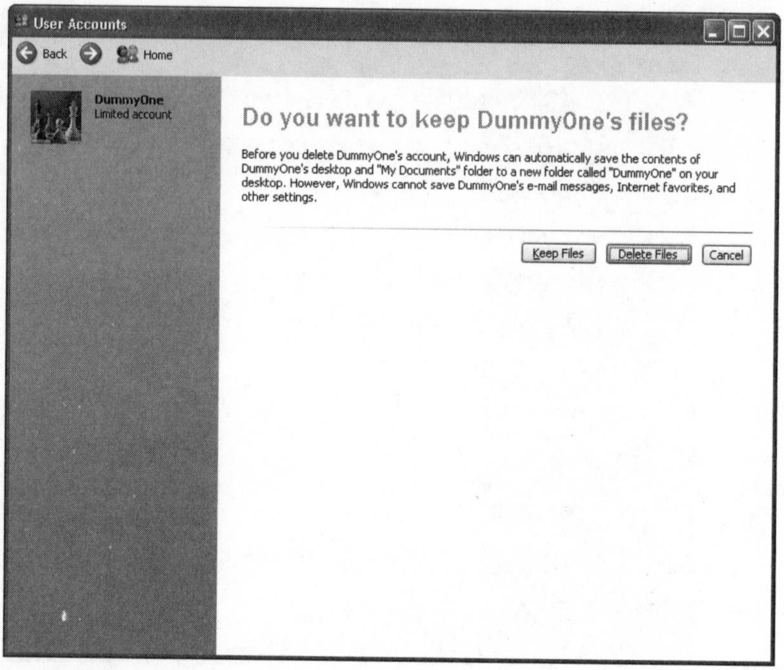

Figure 2-7: Confirming you want to delete the account.

Changing User Accounts

In much the same way that you can create new user accounts, you can alter existing accounts. You can fiddle with the name, password, picture icon, and account type.

Changing the name

While it's not all that common, you might want to change the username for an account. For example, maybe Bob changed his name to Michael, or maybe your friend prefers the username Superstar123 rather than Sarah. Either way, changing the username associated with an account is simple, as outlined here:

1. **Click Start and select Control Panel.**

   The Control Panel appears.

2. **Click User Accounts.**

   The User Accounts dialog box appears.

3. **On the User Accounts dialog box, under Pick a Task, click Change an Account.**

   The Pick an Account to Change dialog box appears.

4. **Select the account you want to change.**

   Windows asks you what you want to change, as shown in Figure 2-8.

5. **Click Change My Name.**

   A screen provides a form for entering the new name.

6. **Enter the new account name, as shown in Figure 2-9.**

7. **Click Change Name.**

   Windows changes the account name. Namely, you're finished. If you made a mistake (such as a typo) in any of the steps, just repeat the steps to fix things up.

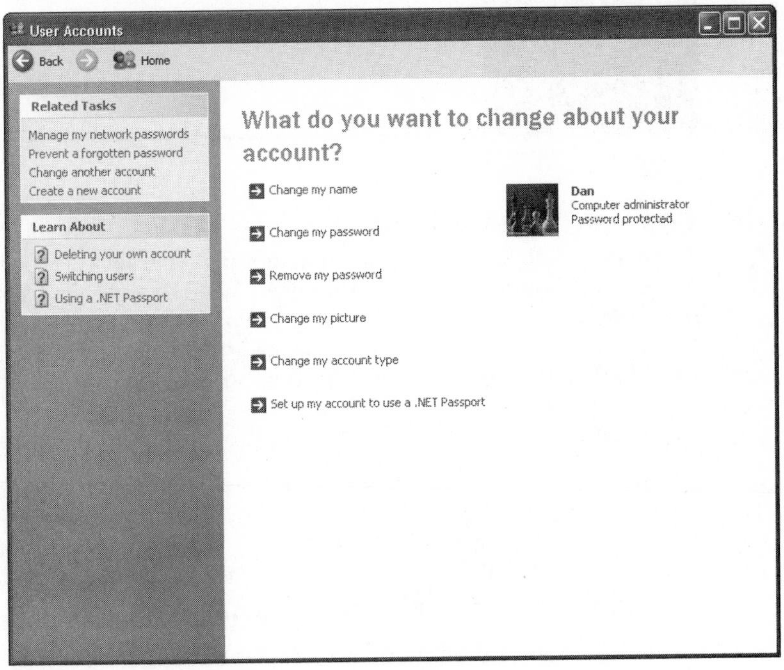

Figure 2-8: A menu of possible changes to a user account.

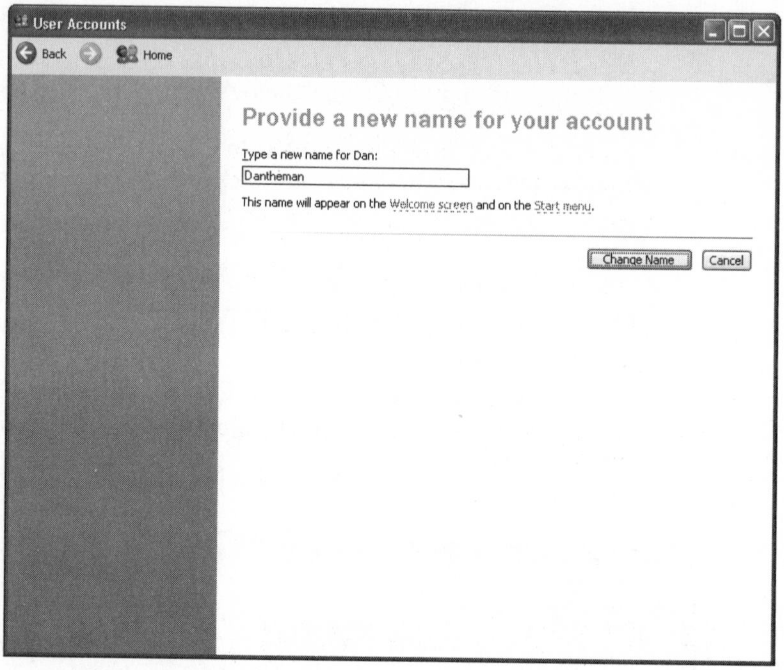

Figure 2-9: Entering a new account name.

Creating a password

When you create a new user account, adding a password is optional. While configuring a password means that users need to supply a password every time they log on, it does add security to your computer. As a general rule, every user account should have a password. If you don't already have a password configured, use the steps here to add one to your account:

1. **Click Start and select Control Panel.**

   The Control Panel appears.

2. **Click User Accounts.**

   The User Accounts dialog box appears.

3. **Under Pick a Task, click Change an Account.**

   The Pick an Account to Change dialog box appears.

4. **Select the account you want to change.**

   Windows asks what you'd like to alter.

5. **Click Create a Password.**

A new screen provides the password-entering form shown in Figure 2-10.

6. **Enter the new password.**

A good password is one that's easy for you to remember, but hard for others to guess. Try to choose a password that is 8 or more characters in length, using a combination of letters, numbers, and symbols. This will make it harder for others to guess.

7. **Enter the password a second time to confirm it.**

8. **Enter a word or phrase to be used as a password hint in case you forget the password.**

If you ever forget your password, this hint is designed to help you remember it. If your password is LakE2005, a good hint might be "good place to swim."

9. **Click Create Password.**

The password is created and you're done.

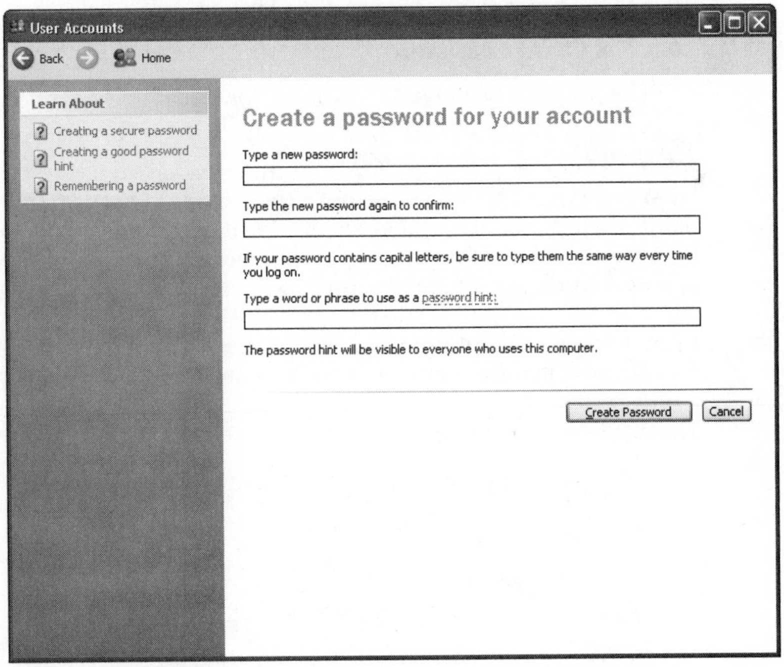

Figure 2-10: Entering a password and a password hint.

Changing a password

For reasons of security or convenience, you may want to change the password assigned to a user account. It's pretty simple:

1. **Click Start and select Control Panel.**

   The Control Panel appears.

2. **Click User Accounts.**

   The User Accounts dialog box appears.

3. **Under Pick a Task, click Change the Password.**

4. **Click Change the Password on the screen where Windows asks what you want to change about your selected account.**

   A password-changing screen appears, similar to that shown in Figure 2-10. You only see the Change Password link if your account already has a password configured.

5. **Enter a new password, confirm by reentering it, and provide a hint that's used in case you forget your password.**

   See the preceding section's steps for hint passwords.

6. **Click Change Password.**

   The password changes and you're done.

Removing a password

I don't recommend that you remove the password from your user account, but if you just can't be bothered entering it each time you log on, Windows XP does allow you to remove it. Once removed, you won't be prompted to supply it when you log on.

Removing a password from an account leaves the account without an important security feature. Think twice before deciding to remove a password.

That said, here's how you remove a password:

1. **Click Start and select Control Panel.**

   The Control Panel appears.

2. **Click User Accounts.**

   The User Accounts dialog box appears.

3. **Click Change an account, and then click the account you want to change.**

4. **At the What Do You Want to Change about the Account screen, click Remove Password.**

   Windows asks that you confirm that you want to remove the password.

5. **Enter your current password and click Remove Password.**

   The password is removed.

Changing the picture

Other than adding some variety to your computing experience, account pictures do little more than let you quickly identify a user's account visually. Here's how you change a picture:

1. **Click Start and select Control Panel.**

   The Control Panel appears.

2. **Click User Accounts.**

   The User Accounts dialog box appears.

3. **Under Pick a Task, click Change an Account.**

   The Pick an Account to Change dialog box appears.

4. **Select the account you want to change.**

   Windows asks what you want to change.

5. **Click Change the Picture.**

   A screen offers 23 pictures from which to choose.

6. **Click a picture.**

   The rubber duck icon is highlighted in Figure 2-11.

7. **Click Change Picture.**

   The picture icon is changed. Quack.

Hey, that's me

Windows XP lets you if you'd rather use a photo as your picture icon, do this. Here's how:

1. Click Start and select Control Panel. Click User Accounts.
2. Click your user account name.
3. Click Change My Picture.
4. At the Pick a New Picture for Your Account screen, click Browse for more pictures.

   An Open dialog box opens.

5. Navigate to the My Pictures folder and select a photo.
6. Click Open.

   You just created a custom user icon, which Windows displays.

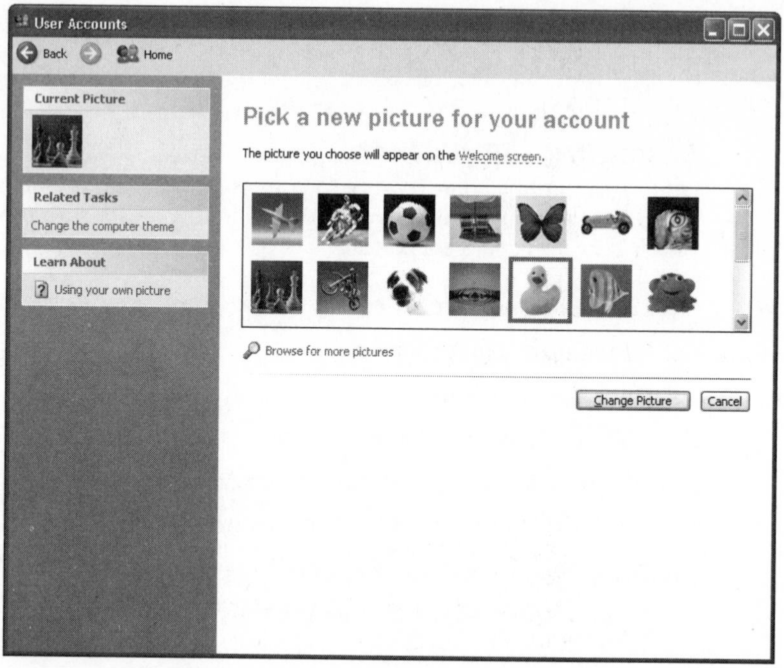

Figure 2-11: Don't put this rubber duck in the bathtub.

Changing the account type

If you originally create a user account as the limited type, Windows XP allows you to change it to a computer administrator, if necessary. This is sometimes required, as in cases where you want a user to install software programs for all users or make changes to other user accounts. You can also change computer administrator accounts back to the limited type, if necessary. Use the steps to change a user account's type:

1. **Click Start and select Control Panel.**

   The Control Panel appears.

2. **Click User Accounts.**

   The User Accounts dialog box appears.

3. **Under Pick a Task, click Change an Account.**

   The Pick an Account to Change screen appears.

4. **Select the account you want to change and Windows asks what you'd like to alter.**

5. **Click Change the Account Type.**

   A screen asks you to pick a new account type, as shown in Figure 2-12.

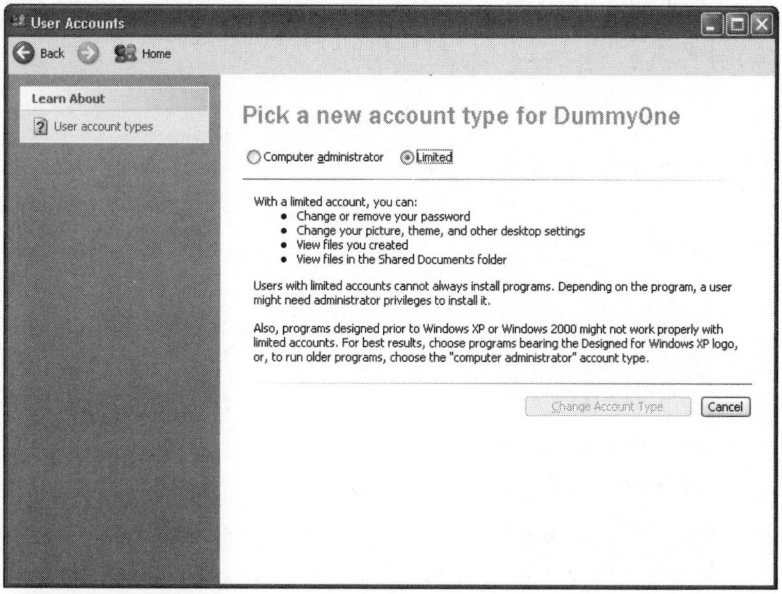

Figure 2-12: Picking a new account type.

6. **Choose either Computer Administrator or Limited.**

   Your only option is to choose the opposite type of the one currently associated with the account.

7. **Click Change Account Type to finish.**

Disabling the Guest Account

WARNING!

Despite Microsoft's recent stepped-up efforts, Windows XP has its share of security holes. One that continues is the guest account, which lets anyone access your PC without a password. The guest account is disabled, or off, by default, but that doesn't stop administrators from turning it on — just another reason to be careful who you make an administrator.

Turning on the guest account couldn't be easier:

1. **Open User Accounts in the Control Panel.**

   The User Accounts dialog box appears. The guest account is under Or Pick an Account to Change.

   If the guest account is enabled, it says Guest Account Is On.

2. **Click the Guest Account area.**

   The screen asks what you want to do change about the guest account. You can see the prompt in Figure 2-13.

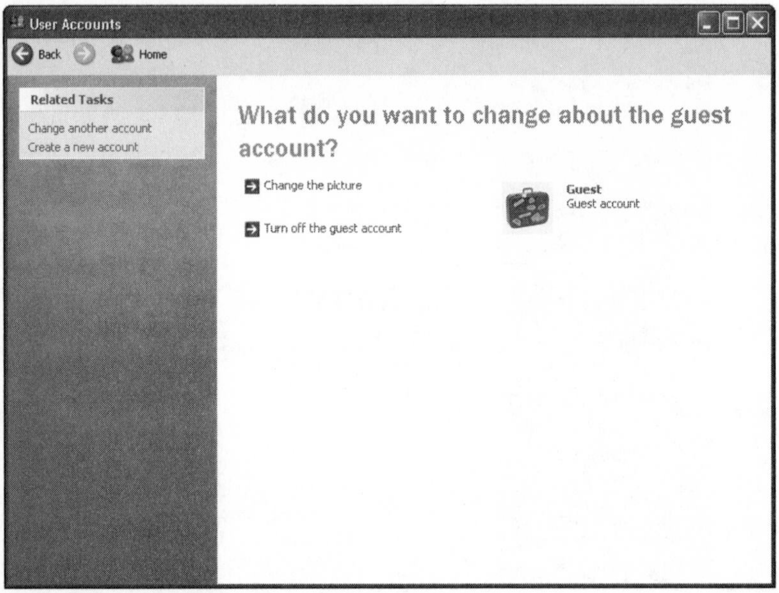

Figure 2-13: Telling guests they're no longer welcome.

3. **Click Turn Off the Guest Account.**

   The screen returns to the one displayed in Step 1. The guest account messages changes to Guest Account Is Off. Fini, mon ami.

REMEMBER

For better or worse, you unfortunately cannot delete the guest account.

Restoring the guest account

If for some reason you decide to override my advice (how dare you!) and want to re-enable the guest account (for example, because you have different friends using your PC and can't be bothered created individual accounts for them), here's how you do it:

1. **Click Start and select Control Panel.**

   The Control Panel appears.

2. **Click User Accounts.**

   The User Accounts dialog box appears.

3. **Click Guest Account.**

   Windows XP asks if you want to turn on the guest account.

4. **Click Turn On the Guest Account.**

   You return to the User Accounts dialog box, which shows the guest account is on. I won't leave you guesting: You're done.

Chapter 3: Solving Network Problems

In This Chapter

- **Taking a systematic approach to network troubleshooting**
- **Solving issues with Windows XP**
- **Dealing with network hardware problems**
- **Using important command-line tools**

In a perfect world, your home network would always hum away without an issue. Unfortunately, with many different devices to install and configure, it's highly likely that you will run into a problem sometime. The good news is that in most cases, you can work your way through the issue to get everything up and running as it should be.

What fun would your network be if you never had to fix anything? Don't think of it as a problem when your network doesn't work, but rather an opportunity to better understand how the whole thing works. How's that for positive thinking?

Houston, We Have a Problem . . .

Network-related problems experienced on a wireless network usually fall into one of the following categories:

- Your wireless systems cannot associate or communicate with your access point or router.
- Your wireless systems discover your wireless network, but cannot connect to it.
- Some of your wireless systems can communicate on your network without issue, while others cannot.
- Systems on your network cannot access the Internet.
- Systems on your network have limited connectivity to the Internet.

If you take a close look at the list of potential networking problems, you notice that all of them have something in common, namely issues with connecting and communicating. Solving network issues is all about just that — getting all devices to interoperate as they should.

Having said that, troubleshooting network issues is often easier said than done. While plenty of tools and techniques can solve different problems, getting to the bottom of those problems means taking a methodical and structured approach. Making a whole pile of changes, hoping that one solves the problem, is pointless. Sure you might get lucky, but you might also mess up something else in the meantime.

I know that this whole troubleshooting process can seem a little daunting, but the good news is that the vast majority of networking problems are easily isolated and even easier to fix. Enough with the theory; time to start looking at some specific steps to help you fix your network!

TIP: Using the steps presented in the following sections can actually help you solve just about any problem, not just those involving your network. For your troubleshooting to be effective, you should follow the steps outlined in the following sections. However, if you decide to use these steps to fix a leaky pipe, add "shut off main water valve" before you get to Step 4. Just another important lesson from a little troubleshooting trial and, um, watery error.

1: Define the problem in a general sense

Defining the problem is often the most difficult step of the entire troubleshooting process, but is by far the most important. For example, is the issue that a wireless system can't communicate with your wireless router, that it can't connect to the Internet, or both? Try not to fall into the trap of thinking of the issue as everything just not working. If something isn't working as it should, it's not working for a reason. Try to start by defining the issue, at least in a general sense.

2: Isolate the problem

Look more closely at your whole network and try to determine whether the problem is universal or limited to a specific system or element. For example, if one of your wireless systems is having trouble connecting to the Internet, you should determine whether other systems on your network are having the same issue. If one can access the Internet and another can't, you know that the Internet service itself is working, eliminating one potential culprit. Or, perhaps all wireless systems cannot connect to the Internet, while wired systems can, again narrowing down the list of suspects.

At this point you should make a list of what works properly and what doesn't. Isolating the problem makes it smaller and more manageable, greatly increasing the probability of solving the issue without pulling your hair out.

3: Define the problem as specifically as possible

After you've isolated the issue to the greatest degree possible, what may have originally begun as "my network doesn't work" hopefully is closer to "my wireless computers cannot access the Internet." While you won't necessarily know *why* you're experiencing the problem at this point, you should have a pretty strong idea of *what* the problem is.

Remember that if you can't define the problem, you have almost no possibility of solving it outside of getting very lucky. While a little luck is handy in fixing any problem, sooner or later it always runs out.

4: Test possible solutions one at a time

As you read through this chapter you discover different techniques and tools that troubleshoot a network. Avoid the temptation to make multiple configuration changes simultaneously. Instead, use a step-by-step approach where you attempt to fix the issue using a given technique, and then test to see whether it solves the problem. If it does, then great. If it doesn't, undo your changes and move on to the next possible solution.

If you attempt to make more than one change at a time, you're actually changing the problem's variables and potentially obscuring the issue at hand or causing other problems. Instead, try to keep everything constant and attempt one fix at a time.

5: Fix the problem and document the solution

When you finally do solve your networking problem, take some time to document how you fixed it. While committing the solution to memory might seem like the best option at the time (of course you'll remember what you did!), writing it down helps ensure that the information doesn't get lost once other fun things like mortgage payments and bills require your undivided attention. Having the solution documented makes dealing with it again in the future a no-brainer. While you might remember what you did to fix the problem a week later, it may not be so easy to recall 6 months down the road.

Starting with Windows XP

Since it's the place from which you're most likely to interact with or experience a problem with your network, start down the troubleshooting path by taking a closer look at your PC. As the most popular user operating system, I'm going to assume that you're running Windows XP in either the Home or Professional Edition variety.

As you no doubt already know, Windows XP includes a number of configurable settings that can impact a network. From the installation of your wireless hardware through to the configuration of network properties, you should be familiar with plenty of settings and tools. In this section I walk you through some of the key Windows XP elements and outline how to use them to help get network problems sorted.

Depending on Device Manager

If your wireless network isn't functioning correctly, that might be the case for no shortage of reasons. However, it's never a bad idea to start the troubleshooting process by ensuring that Windows XP is aware of your wireless network adapter, and that it's installed and configured correctly.

The easiest way to determine whether Windows XP "sees" your wireless network adapter is to fire up Device Manager:

1. **Click Start.**
2. **Right-click My Computer.**
3. **Press the Device Manager button on the Hardware tab.**

   If your wireless network adapter card has been detected, it should be listed under the Network adapters section, as shown in Figure 3-1.

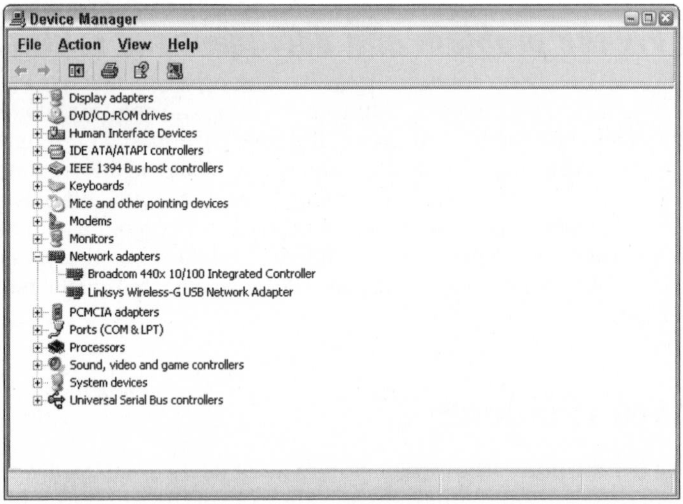

Figure 3-1: Viewing network adapters in Device Manager.

If your wireless network adapter is listed, that's obviously a good sign. The next thing to look for is the style of icon next to your adapter's name. If the adapter is installed correctly, the icon should not include elements like a red X or a yellow warning sign. A red X indicates that the network adapter has been disabled, while the yellow warning sign indicates a problem with the device's driver or configuration.

TIP

If the device icon includes the red X, it likely is the source of your network problem. You can enable a network adapter that has been disabled:

1. **Right-click the network adapter's icon.**
2. **Select the Enable option.**

   If the red X disappears, the device is enabled (though not necessarily configured correctly at this point).

In cases where a yellow warning sign appears over your wireless network adapter's icon, the issue usually has to do with a problem in its configuration. The problem may be that the wrong driver is installed or that another element with the network adapter card is misconfigured. To gather more information, do these things:

1. **Right-click the adapter's icon.**
2. **Click Properties.**

   This opens the Network Controller Properties dialog box for your adapter to the General tab, as shown in Figure 3-2.

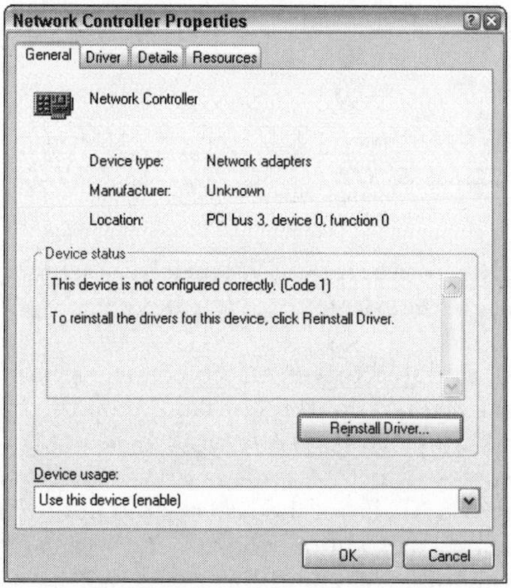

Figure 3-2: Viewing device status information.

Use the information in the General tab's Device Status section to determine the source of the problem. This code and message provided should give you a good source indication and outline what remedies the issue. In the vast majority of cases, problems with hardware are related to the wrong driver being installed.

If it's a driver issue you're experiencing, follow these steps:

1. **Visit the web site of your wireless network adapter's manufacturer to download the correct (or latest) version for your model.**
2. **Download the driver files and extract them to a folder on your hard drive.**
3. **Click the Driver tab.**
4. **Click the Update Driver button shown in Figure 3-3.**

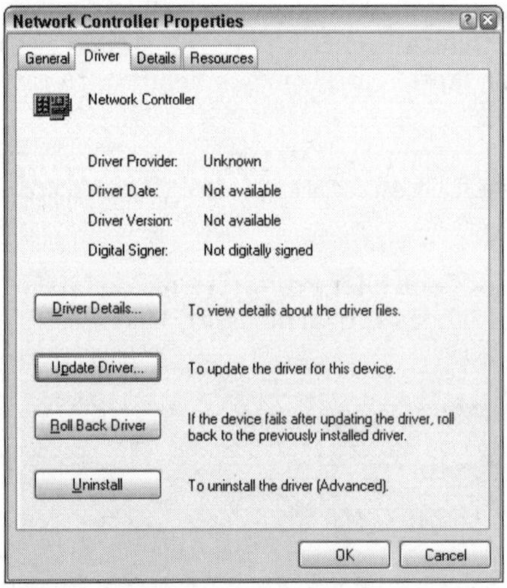

Figure 3-3: Use the Update Driver button to install a new driver for your wireless network adapter.

Ultimately, this opens the Hardware Update Wizard, from which you can walk through installing the correct driver for your device.

In some cases, installing an updated driver may be causing your network problems. If your wireless network adapter worked fine until you installed a new driver and now doesn't function correctly, your best bet is to return to using the old driver. The easiest way to do this is to use the driver rollback feature included with Windows XP. From the Drivers tab in the properties of your wireless network adapter card, simply click the Roll Back Driver button. If an older driver is still available, you can return to using it.

If you don't find any references to your wireless network adapter in Device Manager at all, you can safely assume it hasn't been installed correctly. This may mean that the hardware is not physically connected correctly or that no device driver has ever been installed. The good news is that determining whether the problem is the connection or the driver is generally easy.

In cases where your wireless network adapter is connected correctly but no driver is installed, you can usually tell because Windows XP keeps displaying messages about a new hardware device that's been found, prompting you to install its drivers. You may also see unknown devices listed in Device Manager with a yellow question mark icon, or see devices with a very general name like Network Controller.

If you don't see anything about your wireless network adapter in Device Manager, or if Windows XP isn't prompting you to install drivers for a discovered device, it's usually a safe bet that your adapter isn't installed or connected correctly. In other words, go back and check your connections. In the case of plug-in adapters, be sure they're fully inserted. For an internal PCI adapter card, power down your system, open up your case, and be sure that it's firmly seated in its PCI slot. Book II, Chapter 6 walks through the steps for installing adapters.

Working with wireless network connections

Once you've ensured that your wireless network adapter is installed correctly, it's time to consider different configuration settings that may be affecting your network. These, the most common configuration-related problems, cause issues on a wireless network:

- Incorrect wireless network settings.
- Incorrect TCP/IP settings.
- Incorrect security-related settings.

The follow sections outline each in more detail, as well as specific ways to deal with them.

No wireless networks detected

Assuming that your wireless router (or access point) is powered up and that your wireless network adapter card is installed correctly, Windows XP should automatically detect any wireless networks within range. Messages about the availability of these networks is provided via a balloon message on the Windows XP taskbar. Clicking this message should connect you to the wireless network listed.

If everything is running and you don't receive any messages about available wireless networks, follow these steps:

1. **Right-click the wireless network connection icon on your taskbar.**
2. **Select View Available Wireless Networks.**

   This opens the Wireless Network Connection dialog box shown in Figure 3-4. The Choose a Wireless Network section of this dialog box displays information about any wireless networks that have been detected.

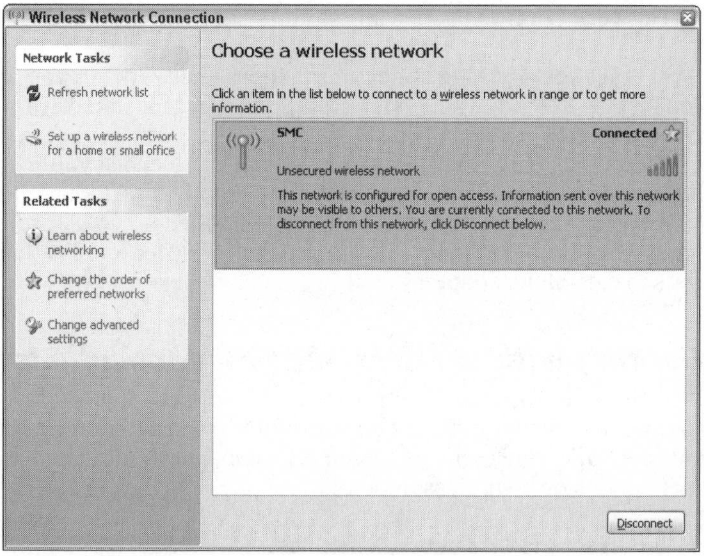
Wireless Network Connection
Network Tasks
Refresh network list
Set up a wireless network for a home or small office
Related Tasks
Learn about wireless networking
Change the order of preferred networks
Change advanced settings
Choose a wireless network
Click an item in the list below to connect to a wireless network in range or to get more information.
SMC
Connected
Unsecured wireless network
This network is configured for open access. Information sent over this network may be visible to others. You are currently connected to this network. To disconnect from this network, click Disconnect below.
Disconnect

Figure 3-4: Viewing available wireless networks.

3. **Act depending on which of these pertains to you:**
   - **You see your network listed: Click it and then click the Connect button.** If everything is working as it should, you are connected to your wireless network (and hopefully the Internet as well) in a matter of a few seconds.
   - **You don't see any networks listed in this window: Click the Refresh Network List link in the Network Tasks section.** XP scans for available networks again, and may find yours.

If your wireless network isn't discovered, a few different possibilities exist:

- **You may be out of range of your wireless router or access point.** If this is a possibility, try moving your computer to a different location to see whether it helps your system discover the wireless network.

- **Too much interference exists between your wireless network adapter and the wireless router.** If this is a potential issue, try to eliminate sources of interference (like an in-use cordless phone) and attempt to connect again.
- **The wireless router may be configured with its SSID broadcast setting disabled.** When a wireless router or access point is configured with SSID broadcast disabled, the network does not announce itself and isn't discovered by Windows XP. If you have disabled SSID broadcast, either enable it or configure your Windows XP system with the necessary SSID manually.

If you installed the client software utility provided with your wireless network adapter on a Windows XP system, that may be the source of the problem. While this software can often be installed on a Windows XP system without issue, it isn't explicitly required and may conflict with the Wireless Zero Configuration feature. If you have installed the utility and are having trouble connecting, try uninstalling the software and using the built-in wireless capabilities of Windows XP instead. If your system discovers your wireless network at this point, you know it was the client software causing the problem.

TCP/IP settings

If Windows XP does detect your wireless network but you still can't seem to connect properly, your wireless network adapter card's IP address settings are likely the issue.

Assuming you haven't done anything to change the adapter's default settings, it should be configured to obtain an IP address automatically. Your wireless router or access point should allocate the required address via its built-in DHCP server. If you haven't changed the default TCP/IP settings on either device, the router should allocate an IP address setting to your computer's wireless network adapter without issue.

The easiest way to check your wireless adapter's TCP/IP settings?

1. **Double-click the wireless network connection icon on the Windows XP taskbar.**

   This opens the Wireless Network Connection Status dialog box.

2. **Click the Support tab to review your current connection status, as shown in Figure 3-5.**

   If everything is functioning as it should, the Address Type section should read Assigned by DHCP. The IP Address setting should be something like 192.168.1.100, the Subnet Mask 255.255.255.0, and the Default Gateway set to the IP address of your wireless router, such as 192.168.1.1.

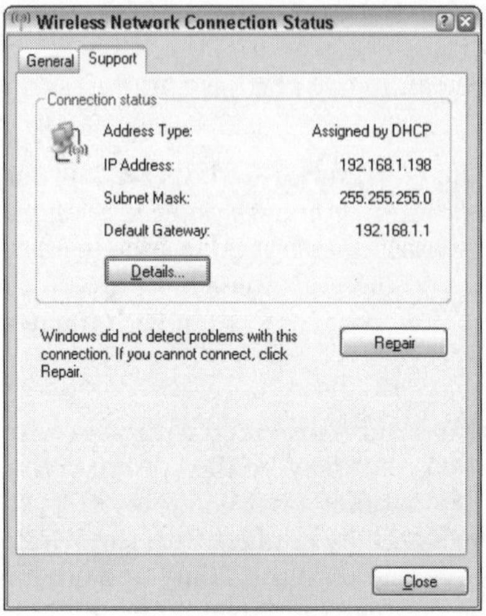

Figure 3-5: Viewing your connection status in the Wireless Network Connection Status dialog box.

If your wireless network adapter can't obtain an IP address from a DHCP server, it automatically assigns itself an IP address. This tell-tale sign indicates that your wireless system cannot contact a DHCP server or that one isn't present on your network. The most common reason is that the DHCP server component on your wireless router has been disabled. Figure 3-6 shows what the Support tab looks like when a wireless network adapter cannot obtain an IP address.

Figure 3-6: The Support screen when a wireless network adapter cannot obtain an IP address via DHCP.

If you click the Details button as this point, you find that your system has allocated itself an address in the 169.254.x.x range, as shown in Figure 3-7.

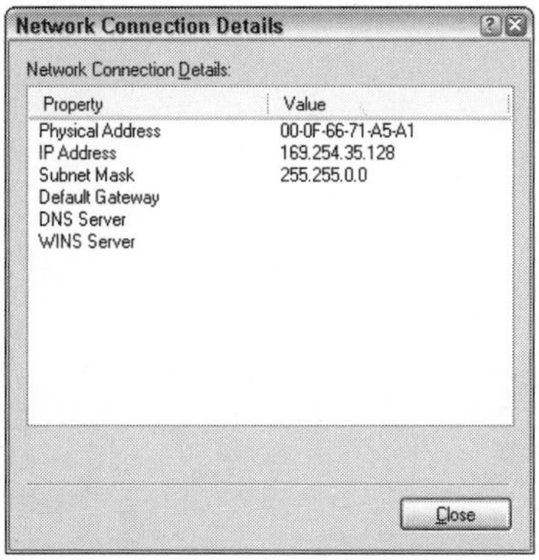

Figure 3-7: Viewing IP address details.

169.254.x.x is the IP address range that Windows XP uses to assign an address to itself when it cannot contact a DHCP server to obtain one. Unfortunately, the address that your system assigns to itself is in a different range than the address in use on your router, so the two devices can't communicate.

In this scenario, you have two choices. First, you could enable the DHCP component on your wireless router. Alternatively, you could assign a manual IP address to your wireless network adapter card. The choice is yours.

If you decide to configure an address for your wireless network adapter manually, be sure that the settings are compatible with those configured on your wireless network, and specifically your router. For example, if your router's IP address is 192.168.1.1, configure your wireless network adapter card with an address starting with 192.168.1.x. The last digit can be anything other than 1, and values up to 254 are valid. Ultimately, the Internet Protocol (TCP/IP) Properties screen for your wireless network adapter card should look similar to the one shown in Figure 3-8.

TIP

While using DHCP certainly makes the TCP/IP configuration process easier, you can run into some issues when using it. Specifically, be absolutely sure that only one device on your network is acting as a DHCP server. If you have two or more systems allocating addresses, there's a good chance that your system could pick up an invalid address from one of these devices. This can also lead to problems with duplicate IP addresses — never fun to troubleshoot.

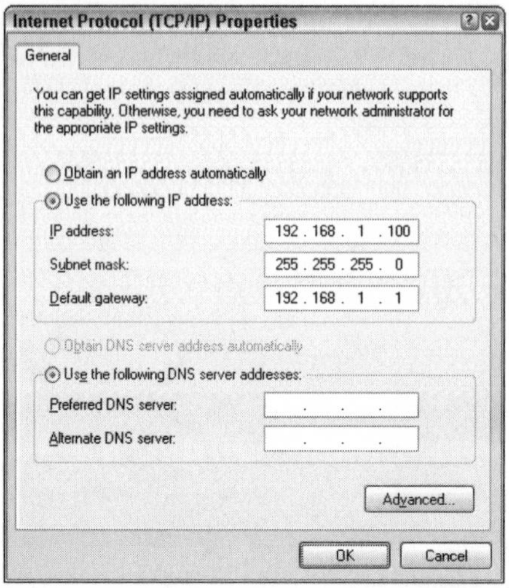

Figure 3-8: Your wireless network adapter card's Internet Protocol (TCP/IP) Properties screen.

The most common mistake leading to more than one DHCP server on a network is adding a wired or wireless router, but forgetting to turn off the Windows XP Internet Connection Sharing (ICS) feature. ICS includes its own built-in DHCP server component, so disable it if you've added a hardware router of any type to your network. If any other devices on your network include a DHCP server component, disable those as well.

You would think that once Windows XP detects your wireless network and your TCP/IP settings are correct that you'd be off to the races, right? Unfortunately, maybe not. There might be a security issue or two to deal with!

Security issues

If your network adapter card is properly installed and your TCP/IP settings are correct, and you *still* can't connect to your wireless network, chances are good a security issue is at hand.

TIP

The most common security-related connection issues that stop you from connecting to your wireless network include the following:

- **MAC address security is enabled on your router or access point.** When MAC address security is enabled on a router or access point, only systems whose MAC addresses appear on the router's list are able to connect. If you have enabled MAC security, be sure that the correct MAC addresses for all of your network systems appear on the list. It's not uncommon to make errors inputting these addresses, so you may want to double-check your list. If you believe this is the issue, disable MAC security and try connecting to the wireless network. If you can connect when MAC security is disabled, try implementing it again with the correct MAC addresses for your network adapter cards.

- **WEP is enabled on your router or access point.** If you've enabled WEP encryption on your wireless router or access point, then WEP must also be enabled and configured on your wireless network adapters. It's usually easy to determine whether a wireless network is protected by WEP, as using the View Available Wireless Networks feature displays protected networks as a security-enabled wireless network. However, to connect you must have your wireless client systems configured correctly and supply the correct key value when prompted. See Figure 3-9.
- **WPA is enabled on your router or access point.** If you've enabled WPA encryption on your router or access point, then you must also enable WPA and configure it on your wireless network adapters. Again, a wireless network secured using WPA is clearly marked as a security-enabled wireless network (WPA) when you use the View Available Wireless Networks feature in Windows XP. Don't forget that Windows XP, your wireless network adapter's driver, and your router or access point must all support WPA for it to function correctly. You also need to supply the correct passphrase when attempting to connect to the WPA-protected network. See Figure 3-10.

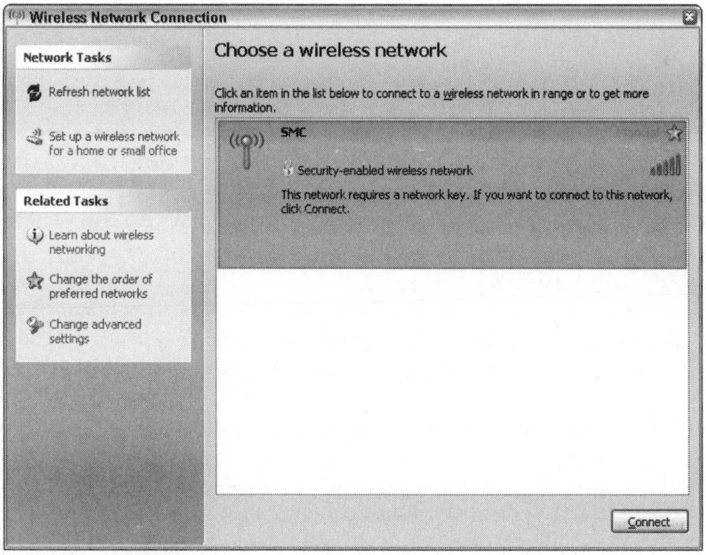

Figure 3-9: A wireless network configured to require WEP encryption, as determined by the network being listed as a Security-enabled wireless network.

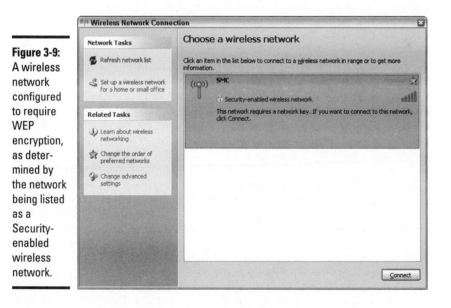

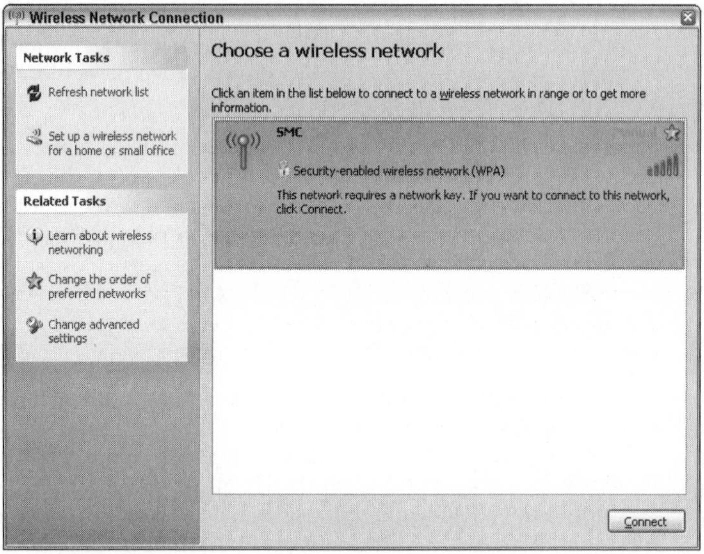

Figure 3-10: A wireless network configured to require WPA encryption.

If you have implemented WEP or WPA encryption on your wireless router (or access point) and are then unable to connect to the device because you've forgotten the required passphrase or key, remain calm. Don't forget that you can always return the device to its factory-default settings by pressing the Reset button. Check your router's user manual to determine how to complete the proper reset sequence for your particular model.

Connecting to other devices

One of the easiest ways to determine whether your wireless network is functioning correctly is by firing up your favorite web browser and attempting to connect to devices on your network or to servers on the Internet. If nothing else, it helps you further isolate any issues.

When making connection attempts as part of troubleshooting your network, your best bet it to take the outside-in approach. In other words, begin by attempting to connect to servers outside your home network, such as a web site on the Internet. If you can connect to the web site, it's generally a good indication that your network is properly configured and functioning correctly.

If you can't connect to any Internet web site, your next step should be to attempt to connect to the management interface on your wireless router or access point. If you can reach this site, then at least you know your wireless network is working and that the problem likely has to do with connecting to the Internet.

If you can't reach your router's management interface, then quite likely the problem rests in the configuration of your wireless network adapter or other devices on your wireless network. If nothing else, attempting to connect to different servers and devices using the outside-in method further helps isolate any issues that you may be experiencing.

Finding the Culprit among Hardware

Once you've sorted any issues related to your wireless network adapter and Windows XP, take a closer look at the setup and configuration of other network hardware devices on your network. You look at these devices in more detail in this section:

- Wireless routers
- Broadband modems
- Other wireless devices like access points and print servers

Feeling router woes

For the most part, your wireless router should perform admirably and without issue. If or when you do run into problems, it's a virtual certainty that the issue has to do with configuration changes you've made. This is almost always the case, since pretty much every wireless router is ready to roll when connected and powered up for the first time.

TIP

Some of the more common router-related issues that you're likely to come across include the following:

- **Inability to access the router's management interface.** If you're unable to connect to your router's management interface at all, ensure that you've entered its IP address correctly in your web browser's address bar. If you can access the router's management interface but can't remember the administrative password that you configured, return the device to its default factory settings (and password) by using its Reset button. Don't forget that completing the reset sequence for the hardware erases any and all custom settings that you may have configured.
- **Incorrect Internet connection settings configuration.** Since different service providers require different connection settings, you may have trouble connecting to the Internet. By default, almost all routers are configured to attempt to acquire an IP address automatically, but this may not work with your provider. When in doubt, consult the documentation provided by your ISP and then manually configure your router with the correct settings to connect to their network.

- **Misconfiguration of wireless network settings.** Common misconfigured settings on a wireless router include its SSID name, SSID broadcast settings, DHCP settings, and the types of clients allowed to connect. For example, if you've configured your router to allow connections for 802.11g clients only, 802.11b clients aren't supported. The router's default configuration typically allows any supported client to connect, so consider returning to the default settings if you're running into issues. If you've disabled DHCP, ensure that all clients on your network are configured with a static IP address. If you've changed the IP address range allocated by DHCP, be sure that the IP address of the wireless router is also changed to fall into the same range.
- **Misconfiguration of wireless security settings.** Misconfigured security settings are among the most common reasons for connection problems with a router. If you've implemented MAC security, be sure that the MAC addresses for clients on your network are entered correctly, and that entries exist for all client systems that need to connect. If you've implemented WEP or WPA, be absolutely certain that the security protocols to be used (TKIP and the like) are configured the same on both the wireless router and wireless client systems. It's also not uncommon to forget the keys or passphrases used for WEP or WPA, so you may need to reset them if these values are forgotten.
- **Incorrect physical connections.** In most cases, the only connection that your wireless router requires is the physical Ethernet cable connection between its *wide-area network (WAN)* port and the *local-area network (LAN)* or Ethernet port on your broadband modem. If you used the cable supplied with your router, you should be able to connect without issue. However, if you used a different cable than the one supplied, it may be the issue. Try testing with another cable in cases where the appropriate lights on the router and modem don't light up when the connection is made.

REMEMBER

If you just can't seem to get to the bottom of an issue with your wireless router, don't forget that you can always just reset the device. Trust me when I say that resetting is often preferable to spending hours or days trying to troubleshoot a device. When the device is reset to its original factory settings, what you get is a clean slate. Even in the worst-case scenario, you're probably only looking at making a few changes to the router and other devices on your home network to get everything back up and running.

Dealing with modem blues

In the vast majority of cases, the modem that connects your network to your broadband Internet service is supplied by your service provider and you don't have access to its configuration interface. The good news is that you typically won't need access to it. Most broadband routers are supplied with a default configuration; all you should need to do is plug it in and make the necessary cable connections.

Most of the time, sorting the connections for your modem is very simple. You usually find one port on the device marked WAN or Internet, which should be connected to the provider's network. This is usually in the form of a traditional coaxial cable or a phone cable, depending on whether you're using a cable- or DSL-based service. The other port on your modem is typically marked LAN or Ethernet and should be connected to the WAN port on your router using the cable supplied with the modem.

If you've connected everything together per the service provider's instructions, your modem should connect to the Internet service without issue. In cases where you cannot connect, a few possible reasons exist:

- **The service provider's network is currently experiencing issues.** Typically, you can't do much here, short of waiting for the problem to be solved.
- **You haven't connected the modem to your network and the service provider's network correctly.** If you follow the instructions provided with the modem and used the supplied cables and equipment, this shouldn't be an issue.
- **Your router isn't configured with proper connection settings for the provider's network.** Many broadband Internet service providers use different connection methods, so follow the instructions provided with respect to setting up your connection. Some providers require you to configure a username and password to connect, while others use encrypted protocols like *Point-to-Point Tunneling Protocol (PPTP).*

In each of these cases, your best bet is to consult the documentation provided by the service provider as a starting point. If you're sure that everything is connected and configured as required and still experience issues, contact the provider's technical support department to try to determine the issue. In most cases, the service provider's staff can remotely test the modem to determine whether it's functioning correctly and capable of connecting the service.

Unfortunately, problems with broadband Internet connections are almost completely out of your hands. All you can really do is configure the modem and connections per the instructions provided and then hope for the best. Don't get too discouraged if your initial connection attempts fail or you run into issues. In many cases, this results from someone at the provider's facilities forgetting to connect or enable the service on their end, and the issue can be quickly remedied.

REMEMBER

It's not uncommon for a service provider to refuse to support your Internet connection if you have a home network set up. This occurs because of the variables that a network introduces into the mix. If you're having trouble connecting to the service provider's network via your router, you should attempt to connect directly from your PC using the instructions that they supplied. Do this before you call tech support, because the person you talk to almost certainly will want to walk through your setup in excruciatingly painful detail. You should be absolutely, 100-percent prepared for questions about whether you've plugged in your modem and whether your computer is turned on. While these questions can be frustrating, just keep in mind that the person at the other end of the phone can't actually see your setup, and therefore can't assume anything.

Fielding problems with other hardware

Certainly a whole range of wireless devices can be added to any network. Examples include access points, wireless print servers, and more. Because these devices can include different configurable settings and capabilities, discussing any specific network troubleshooting strategies is difficult.

TIP

However, problems with the configuration of any wireless device usually fall into the following categories:

- **Physical connections.** Always ensure that any and all physical elements of a device are properly connected as an initial step in the troubleshooting process. This includes power adapters, Ethernet cables, and so forth.
- **TCP/IP settings.** Be sure that the IP address settings configured on any wireless device match those in use on your network. Many devices are initially configured with an IP address as part of their factory default settings, and these settings may be incompatible with the address range in use on your network. Whether your network uses DHCP or manual addressing, be sure that all devices are allocated addresses in the same range.
- **Wireless configuration settings.** Most wireless devices are configured with a default SSID value that probably won't match the one in use on your network. If you're having trouble connecting to or "seeing" a wireless device, ensure that its wireless settings match those in use on your network.
- **Wireless security settings.** If you've implemented wireless security features like WEP or WPA on your wireless network, be sure these settings are configured for other devices like a wireless print server or access point. You should also take care that all the devices on your network support the same standard. For example, if you've implemented WPA on your wireless router and require all wireless connections to use this encryption, a wireless print server that only supports WEP cannot connect.

When in doubt, don't underestimate the importance of the user manual provided with your wireless hardware device. In most cases it provides all the information you could ever need to properly troubleshoot connectivity or configuration issues.

REMEMBER

Don't automatically assume that the small 4- to 5-page setup guide included with your wireless device represents all of the documentation for your hardware. Most manufacturers include a comprehensive user manual on the accompanying CD that includes detailed setup, configuration, and troubleshooting information specific to your model.

Getting Cozy with Network Tools

While you can't deny that the various wireless networking tools included with Windows XP or your network adapter are great for troubleshooting, don't overlook a few oldies but goodies. Specifically, I'm talking about the command-line networking tools that no serious network support person would ever think of leaving home without. The good news is that you don't need to remember to bring them along, since Windows XP includes them.

REMEMBER

I won't keep you in the dark. These three tools absolutely must be in the toolkit of anyone troubleshooting a network:

- ipconfig
- ping
- tracert

If you've never used or worked with the command-line tools included with Windows XP, not to worry. I show you everything you need to know to get them on your side.

ipconfig

When you need to gather information about the configuration of network adapter cards on your computer, turn to ipconfig. Not only does ipconfig display useful information like the IP address, subnet mask, and default gateway configured for a given adapter, but it also tells you the adapter's MAC address, whether it was configured manually or via DHCP, and more.

To use ipconfig (or any of the other command-line utilities you see in this chapter), open a command prompt:

1. **Click Start.**
2. **Select All Programs, Accessories.**
3. **Click Command Prompt.**

   This opens the Windows command-line interface shown in Figure 3-11.

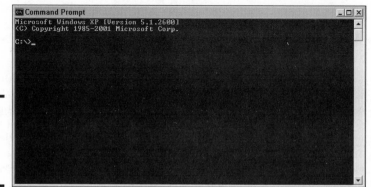

Figure 3-11: The Command Prompt window.

With the Command Prompt window open, you're ready to roll. When entered without any *switches* (the subcommands entered after a / character) or additional information, ipconfig provides basic information about your network adapters installed on your system, like you see here:

```
C:\>ipconfig

Windows IP Configuration

Ethernet adapter Wireless Network Connection:

        Connection-specific DNS Suffix  . :
        IP Address. . . . . . . . . . . . : 192.168.1.198
        Subnet Mask . . . . . . . . . . . : 255.255.255.0
        Default Gateway . . . . . . . . . : 192.168.1.1
```

If you're interested in gathering more complete information about your adapter and its configuration, use the ipconfig /all command:

```
C:\>ipconfig /all
```

```
Windows IP Configuration

        Host Name . . . . . . . . . . . . : xphome
        Primary Dns Suffix  . . . . . . . :
        Node Type . . . . . . . . . . . . : Unknown
        IP Routing Enabled. . . . . . . . : Yes
        WINS Proxy Enabled. . . . . . . . : No

Ethernet adapter Wireless Network Connection:

        Connection-specific DNS Suffix  . :
        Description . . . . . . . . . . . : Linksys Wireless-
    G USB Network Adapter
        Physical Address. . . . . . . . . : 00-0F-66-71-A5-A1
        Dhcp Enabled. . . . . . . . . . . : Yes
        Autoconfiguration Enabled . . . . : Yes
        IP Address. . . . . . . . . . . . : 192.168.1.198
        Subnet Mask . . . . . . . . . . . : 255.255.255.0
        Default Gateway . . . . . . . . . : 192.168.1.1
        DHCP Server . . . . . . . . . . . : 192.168.1.1
        DNS Servers . . . . . . . . . . . : 192.168.1.1
        Lease Obtained. . . . . . . . . . : Tuesday, October
    05, 2004 8:30:23 AM

        Lease Expires . . . . . . . . . . : Tuesday, October
    12, 2004 8:30:23 AM
```

As you can see, adding the /all switch provides a great deal more useful information. In this case, it shows you the adapter's physical (MAC) address, that DHCP is in use, the DHCP server that allocated the address, the DNS server being used, and even when the DHCP address lease was obtained and expired. Ultimately, the ipconfig /all command is the best place to turn when you're looking for definitive information about your network adapter.

Besides simply providing information, you can use the ipconfig command to release or renew an IP address obtained via DHCP. If you want to release your current IP address, use the ipconfig /release command:

```
C:\>ipconfig /release

Windows IP Configuration

Ethernet adapter Wireless Network Connection:

        Connection-specific DNS Suffix  . :
        IP Address. . . . . . . . . . . . : 0.0.0.0
        Subnet Mask . . . . . . . . . . . : 0.0.0.0
        Default Gateway . . . . . . . . . :
```

If you want to obtain a new address, use the ipconfig /renew command:

```
C:\>ipconfig /renew

Windows IP Configuration

Ethernet adapter Wireless Network Connection:

        Connection-specific DNS Suffix  . :
        IP Address. . . . . . . . . . . . : 192.168.1.198
        Subnet Mask . . . . . . . . . . . : 255.255.255.0
        Default Gateway . . . . . . . . . : 192.168.1.1
```

Presto! Your new IP address appears.

ping

No question about it — ping is probably the most useful and popular TCP/IP troubleshooting tool ever developed. Part of the reason is that the tool is so easy to use and provides essential and useful information. By pinging a computer on your network or a server on the Internet, you can immediately determine whether your system can reach and communicate with the system specified.

For example, say you want to see whether the wireless network adapter on your system can communicate with your wireless router. To find out, open a command prompt and ping the router's IP address:

```
C:\>ping 192.168.1.1

Pinging 192.168.1.1 with 32 bytes of data:

Reply from 192.168.1.1: bytes=32 time=3ms TTL=64
Reply from 192.168.1.1: bytes=32 time=1ms TTL=64
Reply from 192.168.1.1: bytes=32 time=1ms TTL=64
Reply from 192.168.1.1: bytes=32 time=1ms TTL=64

Ping statistics for 192.168.1.1:
    Packets: Sent = 4, Received = 4, Lost = 0 (0% loss),
Approximate round trip times in milli-seconds:
    Minimum = 1ms, Maximum = 3ms, Average = 1ms
```

When the ping command is issued, it attempts to contact the address that you specified four times; it expects to receive four replies. In this example, the router replied all four times and 0 percent of *packets* (the small bundles of data sent and received by computers when communicating over a network) were lost. If you received this reply, you can safely say that your wireless network adapter is capable of communication with your router.

Going a step further, you can also ping servers on the Internet. In the following example, I use the ping utility to see whether my system can communicate with the www.google.com server:

```
C:\>ping www.google.com

Pinging www.google.com [64.233.161.104] with 32 bytes of
   data:

Reply from 64.233.161.104: bytes=32 time=51ms TTL=241
Reply from 64.233.161.104: bytes=32 time=52ms TTL=241
Reply from 64.233.161.104: bytes=32 time=51ms TTL=241
Reply from 64.233.161.104: bytes=32 time=52ms TTL=241

Ping statistics for 64.233.161.104:
    Packets: Sent = 4, Received = 4, Lost = 0 (0% loss),
Approximate round trip times in milli-seconds:
    Minimum = 51ms, Maximum = 52ms, Average = 51ms
```

In this example, the Google web site replies, so I can again safely assume that my wireless system can communicate with the server. By extension, when I ping a server on the Internet and receive a reply, I can safely say that communication with my wireless router works. If it didn't, I never would have reached the Internet.

If you can't reach a server or IP address that you're attempting to ping, the response looks something like this:

```
C:\>ping 192.168.1.2

Pinging 192.168.1.2 with 32 bytes of data:

Request timed out.
Request timed out.
Request timed out.
Request timed out.

Ping statistics for 192.168.1.2:
    Packets: Sent = 4, Received = 0, Lost = 4 (100% loss),
```

TIP

In some cases, you may notice that an attempt to ping an IP address or server results in only one or two successful responses, rather than all four. If this happens to you, it generally indicates that some type of issue is present between your system and the one you're trying to ping. In the case of a wireless network, the most likely culprit is interference; it may cause some of the ping packets to be lost or dropped.

tracert

While ping is a great tool in helping determine whether your system can communicate with another over a TCP/IP network, the information it provides is sometimes a little too basic. For example, if you cannot reach the IP address or server that you're attempting to ping, you might immediately assume that something is wrong with your system or the system you're trying to reach.

Unfortunately, large networks like the Internet are seldom that simple. In fact, when you can't ping a particular server, the problem may not be your system or the server, but rather an issue somewhere in between. When you attempt to contact a server on the Internet, the data you send to the server ultimately crosses a number of different networks (and routers), and any of those could be the one experiencing issues.

Because ping only provides basic information, a more robust tool is required. Enter tracert, a tool that not only attempts to contact the IP address you specify, but also every router in the path between your system and the destination server. Ultimately, this information is useful in helping you to determine where a problem exists, if one does.

In this example I use the tracert command to determine the route between my system and the Google web site:

```
C:\>tracert www.google.com

Tracing route to www.google.com [64.233.161.104]
over a maximum of 30 hops:

  1     1 ms     1 ms     1 ms  . [192.168.1.1]
  2    12 ms    14 ms    11 ms  10.72.224.1
  3    18 ms    18 ms    24 ms  d146-0-41.home1.cgocable.net
   [24.146.0.41]
  4    25 ms    25 ms    25 ms  d226-3-241.home.cgocable.net
   [24.226.3.241]
  5    26 ms    25 ms    35 ms  cgowave-hala-
   core2.cgocable.net [24.226.0.166]
  6    25 ms    24 ms    25 ms
   h64-187-46-221.gtcust.grouptelecom.net [64.187.4
6.221]
  7    24 ms    31 ms    25 ms  GE2-0.WANB-
   TOROON.IP.GROUPTELECOM.NET [216.18.63
.5]
  8    45 ms    45 ms    44 ms  POS6-0.WANB-
   MTRLPQ.IP.GROUPTELECOM.NET [216.18.6
```

```
3.198]
  9     45 ms     45 ms     48 ms  66.59.191.178
 10     48 ms     49 ms     48 ms  eqixva-google-gige.google.com
   [206.223.115.21]
 11     50 ms     50 ms     51 ms  216.239.48.78
 12     53 ms     58 ms     53 ms  216.239.47.153
 13     50 ms     62 ms     55 ms  216.239.48.22
 14     52 ms     51 ms     53 ms  216.239.48.190
 15     51 ms     51 ms     52 ms  www.google.akadns.net
   [64.233.161.104]

Trace complete.
```

Notice that tracert begins on my network and then lists each and every router crossed on the way to the Google web site. If a problem had arisen at some point during the process, it would be evidenced by the point at which tracert could not continue. If the tracert command was unable to get past the router on my own network (192.168.1.1), that would likely indicate a problem with my router, or possibly my Internet connection.

At the end of the day, the ipconfig, ping, and tracert utilities included with Windows XP help you gather useful troubleshooting information. Don't be afraid of the command-line interface. It won't bite — promise!

Best of luck with troubleshooting your network. May the force be with you!

Book V

On the Road

The 5th Wave By Rich Tennant

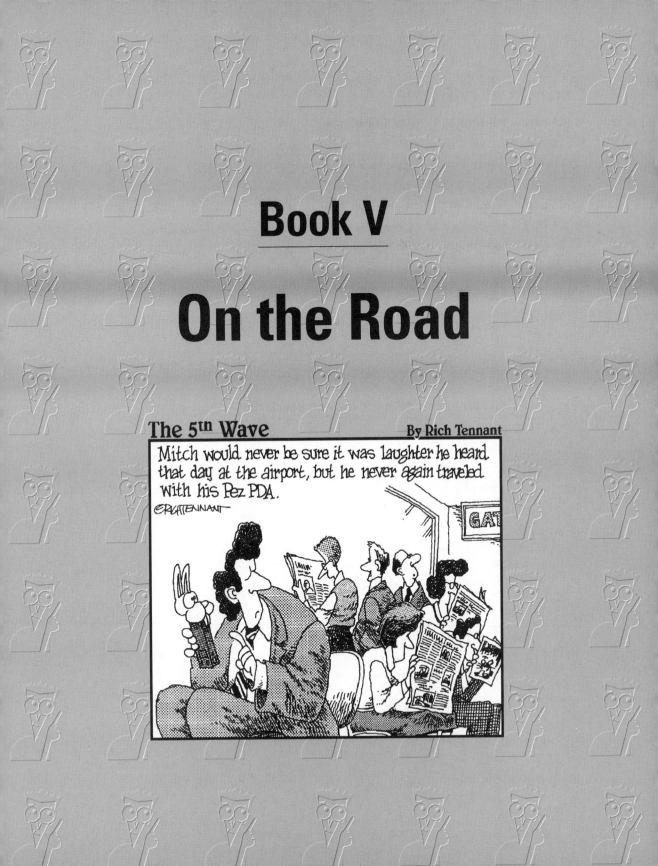

Mitch would never be sure it was laughter he heard that day at the airport, but he never again traveled with his Pez PDA.
©RICHTENNANT
GAT

Contents at a Glance

Chapter 1: Putting a Network in Your Lap(top) 249

Chapter 2: Connecting PDAs to Networks 261

Chapter 3: Synchronizing PDAs over a Network 273

Chapter 4: Picking a Blackberry 287

Chapter 5: Finding Wi-Fi Hotspots 303

Chapter 6: Setting Up a VPN Connection 315

Chapter 7: Strapping on Microsoft SmartWatch 325

Chapter 1: Putting a Network in Your Lap(top)

In This Chapter

- Installing and using a wireless card
- Power backup on the road
- Printing while on the road
- Feeling at home

If you think of the network is only being something that you have in your home, you're missing an awful lot. Having the ability to connect your laptop PC to a network opens up whole new worlds for you. A networked laptop PC not only shares files on your home network, but connecting a networked laptop PC is also far easier while you're on the road. In this chapter you read about a number of options that make your life on the road with a laptop a lot more convenient.

In many ways, a networked laptop PC is identical in operation to a networked desktop PC. Topics such as network security, user accounts, and basic network setup, covered earlier, also apply to a networked laptop PC. Therefore, this chapter concentrates on topics that are specific to your laptop PC and its use while you're away from home.

Discovering Your Options for Wire-Free Access

It's important to remember that connecting on the road is not necessarily the same thing as connecting at home. You have different options that might work better in some circumstances than in others. To some extent, the options that are best for you depend on a number of factors that you have to weigh carefully.

Before choosing your on-the-road connection options, you should ask yourself a number of questions:

- ✦ Do I need to be able to connect wherever I am?
- ✦ How important is my connection speed?
- ✦ Do I need real-time Internet access?
- ✦ What is my budget?

The following sections take a look at a number of options that are based on your answers to these questions.

Choosing the slower but somewhat expensive option

If the most important factor in connecting wirelessly is that you need to connect from pretty much anywhere, you need to consider a solution that provides connectivity through a broad, reaching, wireless service. Most often this means setting up an account with someone like AT&T Wireless, Sprint, or Verizon Wireless. With this type of service you can connect wherever there's cell phone service.

The different service providers use different types of networks to provide wireless data service. These networks have names like CDMA, GSM, GPRS, and EDGE. In addition, a number of these types of networks exist, so it is vitally important that you choose your network provider before attempting to buy the equipment.

What makes this type of connection more expensive than most other options is the service contract that you have to sign with the service provider. What makes this type of connection somewhat slower than most other wireless options is that it uses the cell phone network to communicate. That network was designed for voice, not data.

Choosing the faster but somewhat limited option

If connection speed is the factor that's most important, you probably need to consider a solution that trades off long range to provide higher speed. In this case, a Wi-Fi connection is probably your best option.

Wi-Fi hotspots are pretty easy to find, especially in most large cities. Coffee shops, fast food restaurants, hotels, and even quick print shops offer access. In some cases this access is free, while in others you have to pay a small fee.

If you have a home network, you probably already have all of the equipment you need to connect to a Wi-Fi hotspot. You know that this type of connection provides speed, but that the signal only travels a limited distance. You can't, for example, generally expect to connect several miles away from the hotspot.

Choosing the gimme-it-all option

Okay, I can hear you saying "I want it all." In other words, you want to connect wherever you are and you want high speed, but you don't want to spend a lot of money.

I wish I could offer that option. Unfortunately, the closest I can come to that is to suggest that you may want to subscribe to a cellular data service plan and also make sure that your laptop is equipped to connect to Wi-Fi hotspots. You probably want to carefully monitor your cellular data service plan and only use that service when absolutely necessary.

On the other hand, you may want to keep in mind that Wi-Fi service is becoming more ubiquitous with each passing day, and that the time may soon come when you can get a Wi-Fi signal just about anywhere.

Getting Carded

Installing and using your wireless card is very similar to installing and using any other PC card in your laptop. The process consists of three main steps but the order of those steps depends on a number of factors. The steps (in no particular order) follow:

- Install the necessary driver software in your laptop PC.
- Insert the card into the slot on the side of your laptop.
- Configure your laptop for the selected service.

WARNING!

Reading the user manual that came with your wireless card is extremely important. That manual tells you the correct order for performing the installation steps, and the order is often dependent on the operating system version that's installed on your laptop. That is, you may have to install the software drivers first on some operating system versions and you may have to insert the card first on others — and this is for the exact same wireless card!

Figure 1-1 shows an example of the Sierra Wireless AirCard 775 that is used on many of the modern cellular data services. Depending on your carrier, you may buy the card from your service provider or you may buy it directly from Sierra Wireless (www.sierrawireless.com).

Figure 1-1: The Sierra Wireless AirCard enables you to connect almost anywhere cellular service is available.

TIP

No matter what type of wireless card you use, you can greatly extend the battery life in your laptop PC by either turning the card off or removing it when it is not in use.

Using a wireless cellular data card

If you've ever bought a cell phone, you're probably aware that each device that uses the cellular network has to be activated before it can be used. Buying a wireless cellular data card and installing it into your laptop is only the first part of the task.

Although different cellular carriers follow different procedures, generally once you sign up for service you have to provide the unit ID for your wireless card to the carrier, who activates the card. As is the case with cell phones, the activation is specific to a particular unit ID and this means that if you replace the wireless card you need to cancel the old activation and then activate the new wireless card.

REMEMBER

Wireless cellular data providers offer a broad range of service plans (just as they do for voice service). In general, though, you sign up for either a specific amount of monthly data transfer or a specific amount of connect time. Running over your allocation can become quite expensive, so it's important to not only sign up for the correct plan but also to monitor your usage to ensure that you don't run up huge overage charges.

Depending on the network that you're connecting to, you'll likely find that the wireless cellular data card functions much like a dial-up modem only without wires. That is, you'll use a small dialer-type application to connect to the cellular network as needed and then disconnect once you no longer need the connection.

Using a wireless network card

Using a wireless network card in your laptop is really the same thing as using your wireless home network on any of your PCs. The primary difference with a laptop PC is that it's portable and this enables you to take your laptop places where you can connect to other networks besides your home network. In fact, this means that the whole world of Wi-Fi hotspots becomes available to your wireless networked laptop PC.

TIP

Before you buy a wireless network card for your laptop PC, remember that many laptops now come with a wireless network adapter built in. Also, Windows XP has quite capable wireless networking features built in, so you probably don't need to rely on additional applications to help you locate Wi-Fi hotspots.

You may have read about wireless security in previous chapters. Wireless security when you're on the road with your laptop PC can be somewhat of a mixed bag: Some Wi-Fi hotspots are wide open and others use the full range of available security features. In some cases you may be given a username and password that function for a limited period of time, or you may need to enter a security key to match that in use by the access point.

Even when you have all of the information that you need, making the connection can sometimes be a bit difficult — especially if you need to enter the WEP or WPA security keys because the configuration methods for wireless network cards can be rather confusing. That's where a program like Cirond's Winc, shown in Figure 1-2, can be really handy. Winc not only makes configuring your wireless card's security options easy, but it also helps you identify any available wireless networks.

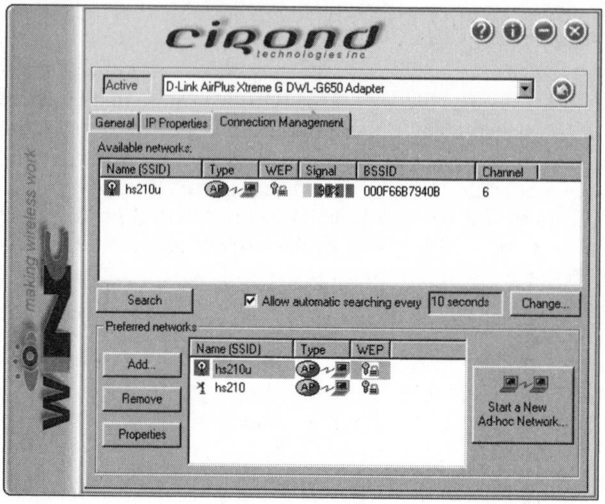

Figure 1-2: Winc is an invaluable tool for the laptop PC road warrior.

Winc remembers the settings that you've created for different wireless networks and then automatically uses those settings when the network is again detected. This makes it very easy for you to configure numerous different wireless networks such as your home network, your office network, and the one at your local coffee shop. You can download a free 30-day trial version of Winc from the Cirond Web site at www.cirond.com.

TIP

If you want to share files with another wireless laptop PC user, you needn't be within range of a wireless network access point. As long as both of you are using Winc you simply need to click the Start a New Ad-hoc Network button in Winc and follow the prompts. An *ad-hoc* network is a simple network where the computers communicate directly without an access point.

Getting Out and About

Laptop PCs are made for travel, but that doesn't mean life on the road is always easy. After all, a lot can go wrong — especially if you're depending on your laptop to help you do business or even just keep you from becoming lost in some strange locale.

I won't bore you by repeating a bunch of pretty obvious information, such as how attractive laptop PCs are to thieves. Rather, look at some topics that can help you get more use from your laptop while you're on that road trip.

Finding Wi-Fi hotspots

Because this book's focus is on wireless topics, it makes sense to begin the discussion on traveling with a laptop PC with the subject of finding Wi-Fi hotspots. Quite simply, Wi-Fi hotspots are likely your primary means of connecting to the Internet and for sending and receiving e-mail.

A number of Web sites have lists of Wi-Fi hotspots. A quick Google search produces hundreds of hits. Some of these sites are better than others, but none of them is up-to-date enough to be your single source of information. Most of these sites depend on information supplied by volunteers, although some use lists of hotspot providers that are in some way affiliated with the site. Still, the lists do give you a starting point.

TIP

If you're going on a road trip you may want to print out a couple of hotspot lists for your destination before you set out. That way you have some idea where to begin looking for an Internet connection.

Once you're in the general area of a Wi-Fi hotspot you have several choices for locating a usable signal:

- ✦ Break out your laptop PC and see if the built-in software can find the Wi-Fi signal and allow you to connect.
- ✦ Fire up your laptop and use a program like Winc (as mentioned earlier in this chapter) to locate any nearby Wi-Fi signals and then to make a connection to one of them.
- ✦ Leave your laptop in its case and pull out a pocket-sized Wi-Fi signal finder like the Hawking Technology Wi-Fi Locator. Once you've found the best signal you can, connect with your laptop.

Of these three options, the last one is by far the most convenient. The Hawking Technology WiFi Locator shown in Figure 1-3 can lock in on a Wi-Fi signal and show you both the strength and direction of that signal from as much as 1,000 feet away — much farther than your laptop's wireless network card is likely to. Because the Hawking Technology WiFi Locator indicates the direction of the signal, you won't waste time driving around trying to find the best possible signal.

Other Wi-Fi finders exist, but the Hawking Technology WiFi Locator has some unique features that greatly increase its usefulness. Because the Hawking Technology WiFi Locator uses a high-gain, directional antenna, it's the only unit I've seen that can find a signal at such a great distance and show you the signal's exact direction. Hawking Technology offers two models of the Wi-Fi Locator: the HWL1 shown in Figure 1-3 and the HWL2. Once you've located the signal with the HWL2, you can connect it to a USB port on your laptop and use the HWL2 to make the connection to the Wi-Fi hotspot. Not only does this eliminate the need for a separate wireless network card, but it also enables you to connect over a much longer distance due to the built-in, high-gain antenna on the HWL2. You can find out more about both models (and a bunch of other really slick Wi-Fi–related products) at the Hawking Technology Web site at www.hawkingtech.com.

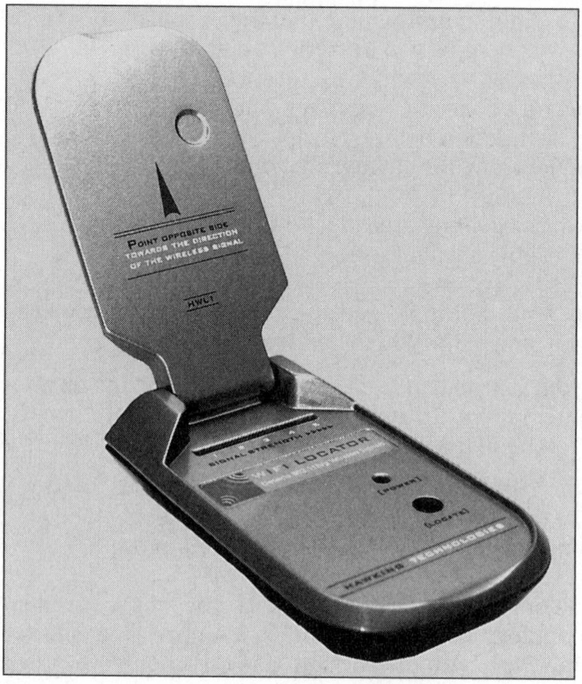

Figure 1-3: The Hawking Technology WiFi Locator quickly finds the direction and strength of Wi-Fi signals.

Power backup on the road

Although not strictly a wireless issue, keeping your laptop powered while you're on the road can be a challenge. Even the most power-stingy laptops don't last through a full day of constant use on battery power, and if you've opted for one of the more power-hungry units you are lucky to get more than about 2 hours on a full charge.

When you're traveling, the weight of all of your equipment can become a real issue. It seems like the longer the trip, the heavier all of those separate little power adapters and cables seem. Sure, each one might weigh just a few ounces, but when you're dragging everything down a long airport concourse to the farthest gate, that can feel like pounds.

One way to cut down on your travel weight is to buy a single power supply that works with all of your portable devices and with the power outlets in your hotel, your rental car, or in an airplane. While it's true that the manufacturer of your laptop probably doesn't offer such a great power supply solution, some companies do. For example, iGo Mobility Electronics, Inc. (www.igo.com) has just such a product. You can see it in Figure 1-4.

If you're really going out to get away from it all (but can't quite give up on your laptop), you might want something like the Notebook Solar Laptop Computer Charger from Sierra Solar Systems (www.sierrasolar.com/prod_store/LAP_laptop.html) shown in Figure 1-5. This handy unit can charge other devices like your cell phone when it isn't powering your laptop and does good things for the planet by using solar power, too.

TIP

You may find that the higher-capacity solar charger is a good investment because it charges your laptop's battery faster.

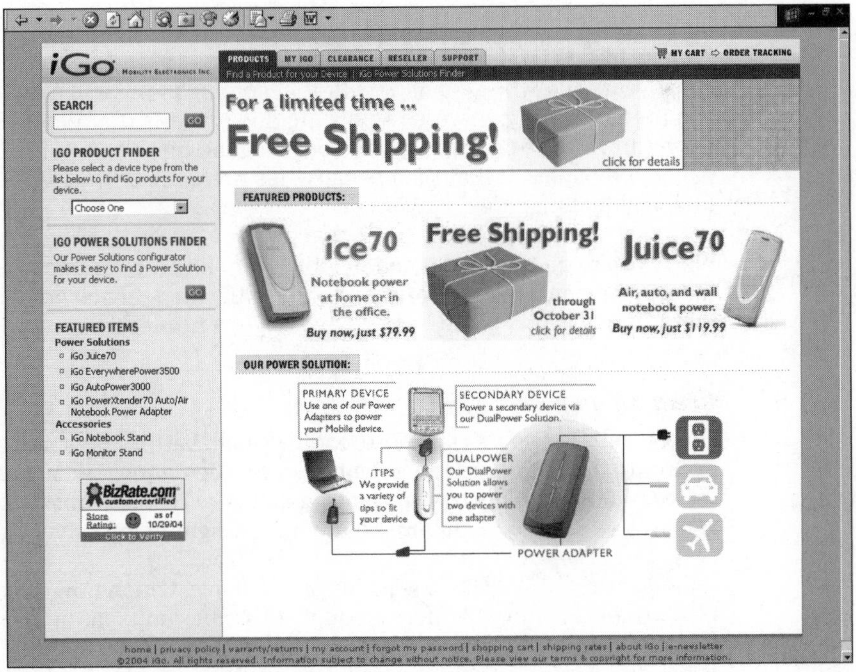

Figure 1-4: The iGo Web site offers power solutions that every road warrior needs.

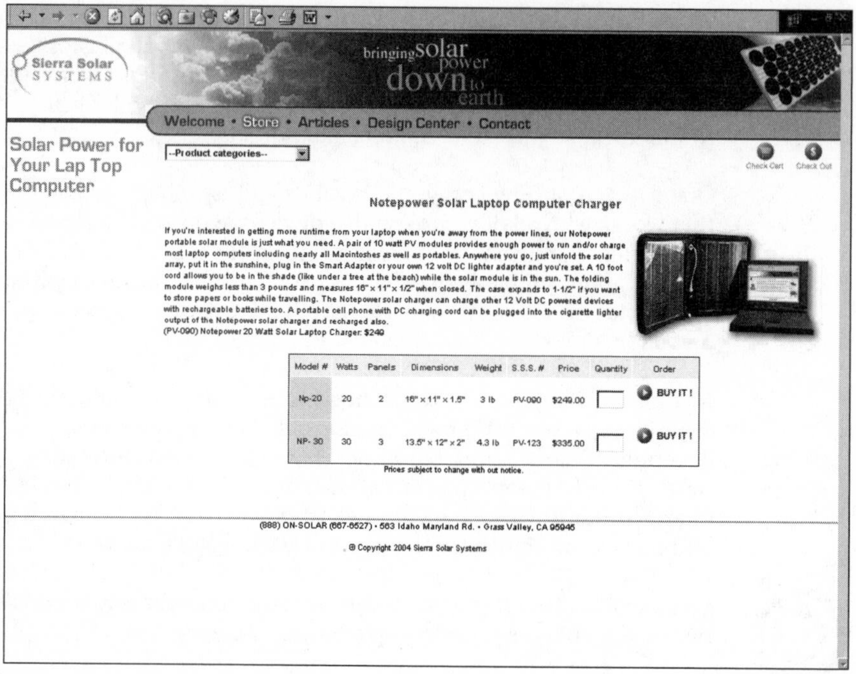

Figure 1-5: Power your laptop from the sun and you never worry about finding an outlet.

Printing while on the road

Some years ago when e-mail was first becoming popular, a number of pundits predicted that we were rapidly moving towards the "paperless office" of the future. It probably would have been a good idea to invest in the stocks of paper companies at that time because it's pretty clear that we're a long way from eliminating paper.

When you're on the road it can be difficult to find a convenient way to print those documents that simply can't wait until you get back home. Sometimes there simply is no choice — you have to get a printout.

Carrying your own printer

For a number of years I've relied upon a small, battery-powered, portable printer to do the job when I'm on the road. The Canon BJC-50 easily fits into the case alongside my laptop, runs on a built-in rechargeable battery pack, and only adds about 2 pounds to the total weight of my travel pack.

Although the Canon BJC-50 is no longer available, Canon now offers the similar i80 Portable Printer. HP offers a couple of similar units in the DeskJet 450CBi Mobile Color Inkjet Printer and the DeskJet 450ci Mobile Printer. The latter offers direct infrared printing from Pocket PCs as well as additional memory for faster print spooling.

You shouldn't expect the sort of print speed or paper-handling capabilities in a portable printer that you take for granted with a desktop printer, but then I really don't want to try packing along my HP Color LaserJet on a trip, either.

Using a printing service

Another on-the-road printing option you may want to consider is a printing service such as PrintMe (www.printme.com). This service is available at some Wi-Fi hotspots and it enables you to print to a printer at the hotspot without loading any printer drivers.

If a FedEx Kinko's print shop is nearby, you may find their printing service pretty handy, too. See www.fedex.com/us/officeprint/main/index.html for more information on getting signed up for this service.

Printing using a USB key

Any office you visit probably has a printer you could use if only you had a way to get your document to that printer. Few people are likely to want to open up their network so you can access it, but there's no reason you can't use a little innovative thinking to get around that problem.

One very simple solution is to use a USB memory key such as the SanDisk MiniCruzer (www.sandisk.com), shown in Figure 1-6, to transfer your document to a PC on the network and print it from that PC. You can even open the document directly from the USB memory key so that you aren't storing a copy of the document on the PC connected to the printer.

Figure 1-6: A USB memory key makes it very easy to transfer data between different PCs.

USB memory keys are extremely handy because they enable you to quickly exchange data between different PCs using a very tiny package that easily fits into your pocket. All modern PCs have USB ports and the USB key simply appears as an additional disk drive. To a great extent USB keys have replaced floppy disk drives and they've become very popular because they hold so much more than a diskette and work with any PC.

Faxing: your last resort

If you can't find any other way to print but absolutely must have a printout of an important document, the desperate have one last resort: sending a fax to a nearby fax machine. True, the quality of the printout probably won't win any awards, but when you're out of options it pays to be resourceful.

To send a fax you either need a modem in your laptop PC and access to a phone line or Internet access and an account with an Internet-based fax service such as eFax (www.efax.com).

Lounging at Home

Thus far this chapter has primarily focused on the mobile uses for a networked laptop PC. However, no law says you can't have a little fun with your laptop when you're at home. Consider the following ways that having a wireless laptop PC might enhance your home life:

- ✦ On a nice summer afternoon when you're stuck working on a report for that boss who always drops a bomb on you just before the weekend, why not take your laptop out to a shady spot in the backyard and work out there? You still can do your online research thanks to your wireless Internet connection, and who knows — maybe the fresh air will inspire you.
- ✦ If you're having some friends over for a cookout on your deck, take your laptop and a set of speakers out, too. Then you can listen to an Internet radio station and never have to worry about changing CDs on your stereo system.
- ✦ It's amazing how much information is available on the Internet these days. If you need to recalibrate your underground sprinkler system, tune up your furnace, or track down the wiring harness layout in your car so that you can add a CD changer, the information is probably online somewhere. If you take your laptop to your job you can view the information onscreen as you work and have easy access in the event you need a bit more detail.
- ✦ When you're absolutely out of ideas what to make for dinner, bring your laptop into the kitchen. With the multitude of cooking-related sites, you can quickly find a whole bunch of ideas for recipes using ingredients you have on hand.

Wireless laptop PCs are awfully handy whether you're a road warrior or simply want a convenient PC that you can move anywhere in your home without a second thought.

Chapter 2: Connecting PDAs to Networks

In This Chapter

- **Connecting a Pocket PC**
- **Connecting a Palm PDA**
- **Making a VPN connection**

If you have a Pocket PC or Palm *personal digital assistant (PDA),* you're in luck. If either one has Wi-Fi wireless capability, you can connect to your network and Wi-Fi hotspots while on the road. In case you haven't heard of them, PDAs let you organize your life. You can keep track of appointments, contacts and to-do lists on them. If your PDA is wireless enabled, you can even grab your e-mail and surf the web from them.

Even if your PDA didn't come with built-in Wi-Fi capability, you often can add this functionality by using a plug-in wireless card. If you have a Palm or Pocket PC that comes with built-in wireless access, so much the better! At first, only a couple Palm and Pocket PC models were Wi-Fi–enabled, but the list is growing. Soon, models without Wi-Fi capability will be in the minority, especially as the number of hotspots continues to grow.

In this chapter I talk about connecting both a Pocket PC handheld computer and a Palm PDA to a wireless network. Once you're on the network, you can do just about anything you can on your desktop computer:

- Check your e-mail.
- Surf the Internet (albeit on a much smaller screen).
- Access PC files located on your network. This includes documents, as well as video and music files.

You also can skip the cradle you normally use to synchronize information between your handheld computer and desktop computer. Instead, you can do it over your wireless network.

Want to check your mail but the ballgame is in the ninth inning? No problem, as now you can connect to your network and access your messages (and the scores of other games) while lying on your couch. It's a rough life and I feel your pain.

Reaching into Your Pocket PC

Connecting your Pocket PC to a wireless network is very easy. If your unit doesn't have built-in wireless access, you can buy a Wi-Fi card that fits into the Pocket PC's CompactFlash (CF) or Secure Digital Input/Output (SDIO) slot.

Here's how you connect your Pocket PC to a network:

1. **Turn on wireless networking if it's not already enabled.**

   This is different for each model. On the Dell Axim 30, you push the far right button to enable or disable wireless access. The device connects to a nearby wireless network with the strongest signal. You know it's connected when the connectivity icon at the top changes from two arrows and an X (as shown in the left in Figure 2-1) to just two arrows (on the right).

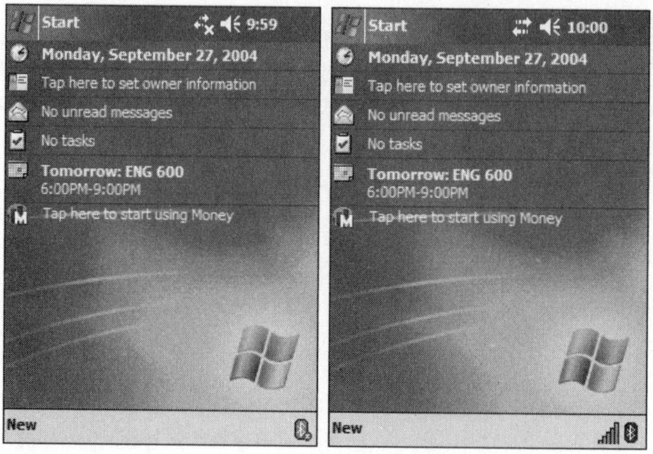

Figure 2-1: The connectivity icon.

2. **From the Start menu, select Internet Explorer.**
3. **Browse to a web page to confirm your wireless connection is working. That's all there is to it.**

When traveling, your Pocket PC can connect to a Wi-Fi network as easily as can Windows XP. Both Windows XP and Pocket PCs running Windows Mobile 2003 share similar *zero-configuration technology,* making it simple for them to detect and connect to nearby Wi-Fi networks.

This saves you the hassle of configuring your Pocket PC every time you're in range of a wireless network. Wi-Fi–enabled Palm PDAs are very easy to connect to wireless networks, too.

Manually configuring your network

You can manually configure the wireless network settings, which is helpful if the automatic network connection feature is not working or you have some special situation. Here's how you access the configuration settings:

1. **Click the selectivity icon at the top of the screen. The icon is shown in Figure 2-1.**

   A connectivity balloon appears, as shown in Figure 2-2.

2. **Click Settings to bring up the Connections tab of the Settings screen.**

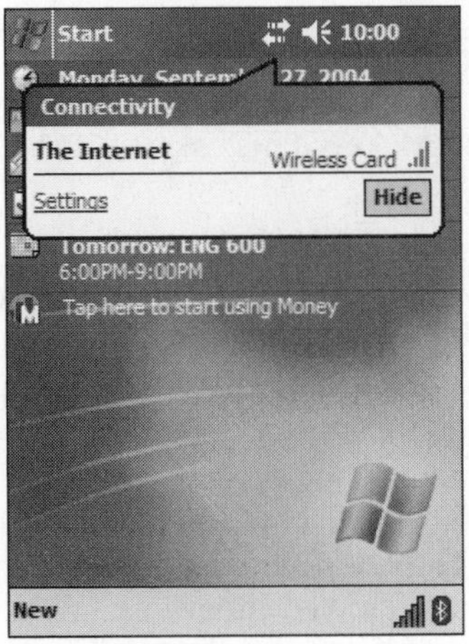

Figure 2-2: The connectivity balloon.

3. **Click Network Cards.**

   The Configure Wireless Networks screen appears, as shown in Figure 2-3.

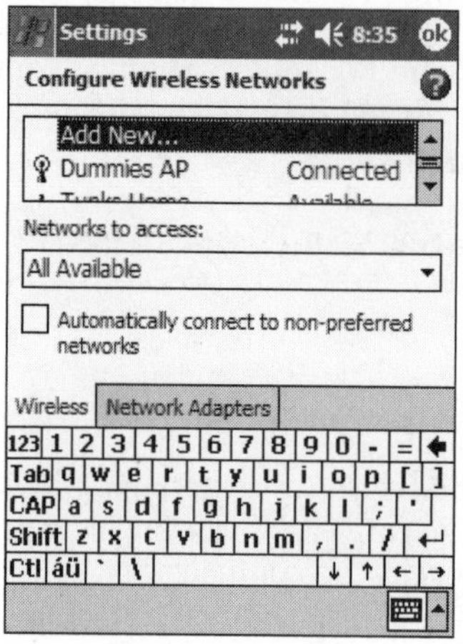

Figure 2-3: The Configure Wireless Networks screen.

4. **From the Configure Wireless Networks screen, you can do the following:**

   - **Add a new network.** Click Add New and enter the appropriate information. Click OK.
   - **Edit an existing network.** Click a network and make changes. Clicking Network Key takes you to the Configure Network Authentication screen. From there you can change the security level from open to secure. You can enter a network key, if necessary. Click OK when you're done.

TIP

You should see one of the listed networks with a Connected or Available status. If not, make sure your wireless networking is turned on and that you're close to a strong Wi-Fi signal.

5. **Click OK to return to the Connections tab of the Settings screen. You're done.**

If necessary, refer to your Pocket PC's manual for troubleshooting tips or contact the manufacturer for help. They're paying me to write a wireless book, not one on all kinds of these new-fangled "deevices." Well, okay, one more bit of help: You might check Microsoft's Pocket PC web site at www.microsoft.com/pocketpc, and despite the crass commercialization of this plug, you might try *Pocket PC For Dummies.* If all else fails, a Pocket PC sails amazingly well from a high-story window. The lesson in gravity and aerodynamics more than makes up for the end result.

Using the Dell WLAN utility

The Dell Axiom 30 comes with a utility that assists you with wireless connections. Among its features is a Site Monitor, which shows you the signal strength of nearby access points. It provides some basic information on signal strength that can help you position yourself in the right spot for best Wi-Fi reception.

Here's you how you get to the Dell utility:

1. **Click the selectivity icon at the top of the screen. The icon is shown in Figure 2-1.**

   A connectivity balloon appears.

2. **Click Settings to bring up the Settings screen Connections tab.**
3. **Click Dell WLAN Utility to bring up the screen in Figure 2-4 and start using at will.**

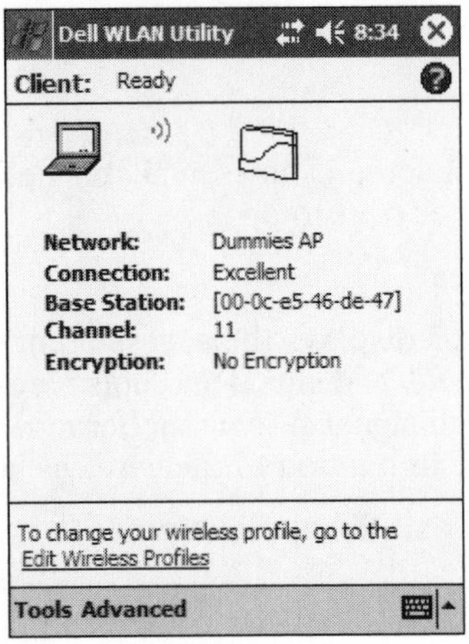

Figure 2-4: The Dell WLAN Utility.

The screen shows the following information:

- The name of the network.
- The quality of the connection. In my example, the connection is excellent.
- A base station identifier.
- The Wi-Fi channel number.
- The status of encryption. In my example, encryption is turned off.

You can use the information for determining a good location to use your Pocket PC while connecting to a wireless network. The data also is helpful for network administrators and others who you may call to troubleshoot your network connections.

Using the Dell Site Monitor

The Dell Axiom 30 comes with a utility that provides a little more information about signal strength than is found elsewhere on the Pocket PC. Here's how you access it:

1. **Select the selectivity icon at the top of the screen. The icon is shown in Figure 2-1.**

   A connectivity balloon appears.

2. **Click Settings to bring up the Settings screen Connections tab.**
3. **Click Dell WLAN Utility to bring up the screen in Figure 2-4.**
4. **Click Advanced (on the bottom of the screen).**

   A menu appears.

5. **Click Site Monitor.**

   The Site Monitor loads. The first screen shows available networks and their type, either infrastructure or peer to peer.

6. **Select a network and click Open.**

   A screen like the one in Figure 2-5 displays the access point's MAC address, *signal-to-noise ratio (SNR),* and signal and noise levels. A high SNR level means you have a good signal! A low number means you may need to relocate your Pocket PC in relation to the wireless access point.

7. **Continue to click OK until you exit the application.**

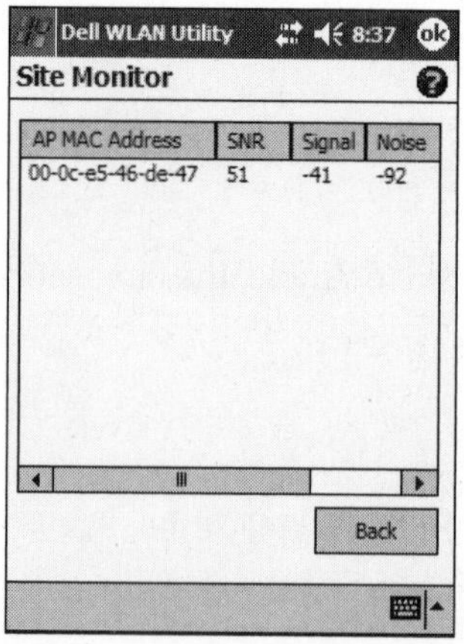

Figure 2-5: Site Monitor displays your signal strength.

TIP

Other models may come with similar utilities. One third-party utility that performs similar functions is called pocketWinc from Cirond (www.cirond.com).

Going Mano y Mano with Palm PDAs

Connecting to a wireless network with a Palm PDA is pretty easy, especially if you own one of the models that has built-in Wi-Fi access. If you don't already own a Palm and are shopping for one, I'd recommend one with the built-in wireless capability. That makes everything easier, as you don't need to use plug-in wireless cards. Instead, because the wireless access is built into the unit, you can fire it up and tell it to connect.

WARNING!

Adding separate components always seems to increase the likelihood that something's going to go wrong — and you spend too much of your precious time figuring out what it is.

While I own the original Palm that I purchased way back in 1999 (when wireless networking and this *Dummies* book were just a twinkle in my eye), the only recent model I use has Wi-Fi access as part of the package. It's called the Palm Tungsten C. Every time I have a strong signal from my wireless network, I can connect with this Palm without any problems. It works beautifully. They're not paying me — though I'm open for negotiations; contact my agent — but I highly recommend it.

Configuring your Palm

Before you try to make a connection, you may want to configure your Palm to ensure that it has all the correct wireless settings.

1. **From the applications launcher screen, select Wi-Fi Setup by clicking the icon.**

   The Wi-Fi Setup screen appears.

2. **Click Next.**

   Your Palm searches for available wireless networks. One of two things occurs:

   - It displays active networks. **You can skip to Step 7.**
   - The list contains no networks. **Click Other to bring up a new dialog box and continue to Step 3.**

3. **Enter your network name. If the network has WEP encryption enabled, check the WEP Encryption box.**
4. **Click Details.**

5. **Choose one of these two options from the pull-down menu:**
   - An access point, or *infrastructure,* connection
   - A peer-to-peer, or *ad-hoc,* connection

   You probably want to make an infrastructure connection, as you probably are trying to connect to your wireless network. If you're trying to connect to a specific PC or another Palm, you should select the peer-to-peer connection. If this makes no sense to you, go with the infrastructure connection, as there's a 95 percent chance that's what you want.

TECHNICAL STUFF

   By clicking Advanced, you can enter a manual IP address and DNS server address instead of using automatic settings for both.

6. **Return to the screen that lists available networks.**
7. **Select a network and click Next.**

   Your Palm makes a connection to the network. If all goes well, the Wi-Fi Setup program displays Wi-Fi Setup is complete. The screen also shows the network name and presents a graphical bar showing signal strength, as shown in Figure 2-6.

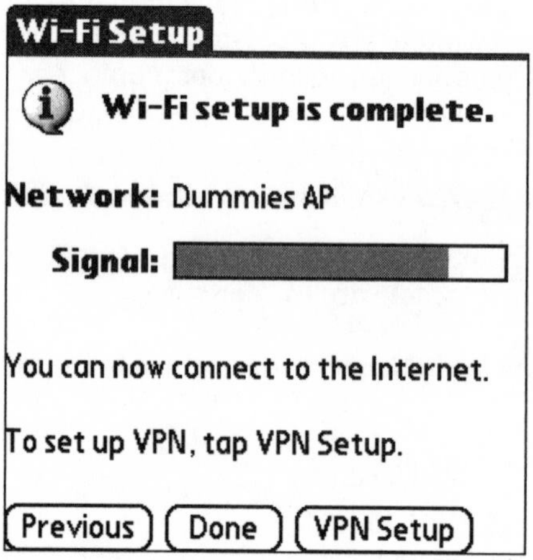
Wi-Fi Setup
Wi-Fi setup is complete.
Network: Dummies AP
Signal:
You can now connect to the Internet.
To set up VPN, tap VPN Setup.
Previous
Done
VPN Setup

Figure 2-6: Your Palm shows the Wi-Fi signal strength.

TECHNICAL STUFF

If it says No Signal beside Signal, click Previous to return to the last screen; then click Next to try connecting to the network again. If you can see the network on the list of networks but still see No Signal, your Palm probably went into sleep mode and then was turned back on, losing the signal, or you have a very weak signal from your wireless access point.

8. **Click Done.**

Confirming your settings

After configuring your Palm's wireless settings, you can quickly take a peek and make sure everything is working correctly. You can do this from the Wi-Fi Preferences screen. Here's how you confirm your settings:

1. **From the applications launcher screen, click Prefs.**

   The Preferences screen appears.

2. **Under Communication, select Wi-Fi.**

   The Wi-Fi Preferences screen appears. From this screen, you can do these things:

   - Turn Wi-Fi on and off.
   - Change the period of time before the Wi-Fi connection disconnects to save battery life. The default is 3 minutes or until the display powers off. You also can choose 5, 10, or 15 minutes.
   - Select the network for connection.
   - View the signal strength.

3. **Click Info.**

   TIP

   The Wi-Fi Info screen appears, displaying detailed information about your network connection, as shown in Figure 2-7. This information is also useful for troubleshooting network problems. This is beyond the scope of this book (and my attention span), but someone who knows what they're doing can get value from it.

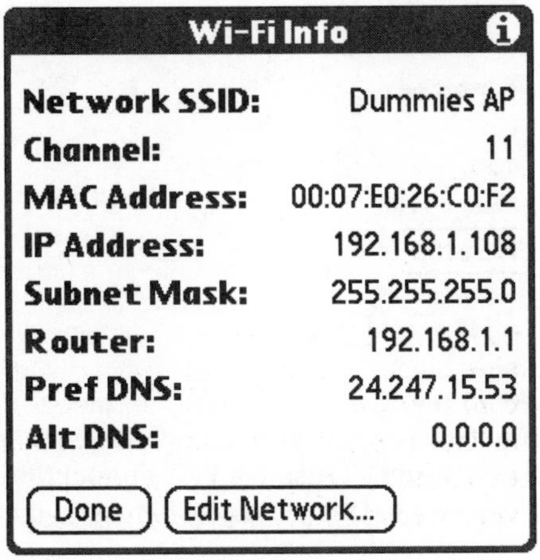

Figure 2-7: The Wi-Fi Info screen.

4. **Click Done.**

   You return to the Wi-Fi Preferences screen.

5. **Click Done to return to the Preferences screen.**

That's it! Now you know where to go to view the important stuff.

Making the connection

Making a wireless connection with a Wi-Fi–enabled Palm is extremely easy. In fact, there's nothing to it: From the applications launcher screen, select an Internet application. You can select Palm's web browser or an e-mail application. You want an application that requires an Internet connection to work. In this example, I have selected the web browser. The web browser loads, your Palm connects to the Internet, and now you can use the Internet application. Figure 2-8 shows the front page of the PalmOne web site, which loads by default unless you change the home page. Browse away or check your e-mail — you're done!

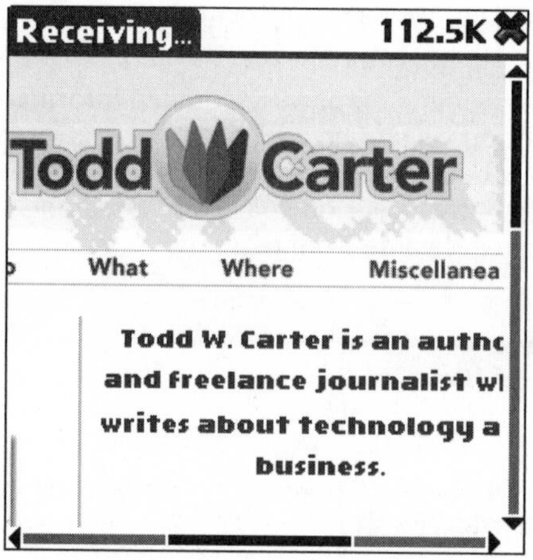

Figure 2-8: Viewing a web page over your new wireless connection.

Making a VPN Connection, Literally

Your Palm can make a *virtual private network (VPN)* connection just like your desktop PC can. VPN connections are secure, encrypted connections that "tunnel" through the public Internet. (I discuss VPN connections for PCs in more detail in Book V, Chapter 6.) In this example, I'm again using my Palm

Tungsten C, so the details may vary depending on which Palm model you're using. The bottom line is that it's pretty easy to set up and make a VPN connection from your Palm to another computer, which mostly likely is one on your company's network.

Configuring your Palm for VPN

You must first configure your Palm for a VPN connection before you can actually connect. Here are the steps for doing that:

1. **From the applications launcher screen, select Wi-Fi Setup by clicking the icon.**

   The Wi-Fi Setup screen appears.

2. **Click Next.**

   Your Palm searches for available wireless networks. It then displays active networks.

3. **Select a network and click Next.**

   The Wi-Fi Setup screen shows network and signal strengths.

4. **Click VPN Setup to bring up the VPN Setup screen.**
5. **Click Next to bring up the VPN Account screen.**
6. **Enter this information:**
   - Account name
   - User name
   - Password
   - VPN server name or address

   If you know what you're doing — and you're a better person than I if you do — you can click Details and change some VPN preferences. Otherwise, I beg you to stay out! Click OK when you're done, returning you to the VPN Account screen.

7. **Click Done.**

   A new screen appears, telling you that VPN setup is complete.

8. **Click Done.**

You're finished configuring the VPN connection. If you have more than one VPN account to create, repeat this process. Rinse.

Connecting a la VPN with your Palm

Now that you configured your VPN account by entering your user name and other information, you're ready to make a secure connection from your Palm to another computer. Here's how you do it:

1. **Click VPN Setup to bring up the VPN Setup screen.**
2. **From the final VPN Setup screen, click VPN Prefs.**

   The VPN Preferences screen appears.
3. **Change VPN from disabled to enabled.**

   The account menu appears.
4. **Choose the correct account from the pull-down menu.**
5. **Click Done. And you're done.**

   The VPN account is used the next time you make a wireless connection. If you're making a VPN connection and then need to disable VPN, just return to the Preferences screen and select Disable from the menu.

Configuring and making a VPN connection with a Pocket PC is a similar process. Please see your Pocket PC manual for more information.

Chapter 3: Synchronizing PDAs over a Network

In This Chapter

- Synchronizing a Pocket PC
- Synchronizing a Palm PDA
- Using AvantGo

I'm assuming that you've successfully connected your Pocket PC or Palm PDA to your wireless network and are ready for the next step: actually using that wireless link to move data across the network. If you're not there yet, check out Book V, Chapter 2, which provides the instructions for connecting.

In this chapter I discuss synchronizing your Pocket PC and Palm handhelds with information on your desktop PC. Naturally, as this is a wireless book, I do everything without wires. That means I don't talk about synching via the handheld cradle; the topic is covered better in other books.

I also tell you how you can add content to these machines from major newspapers and magazines using a service called AvantGo. You can synchronize your handheld computer with AvantGo and take reading material when you travel, or you can update the information from your Pocket PC or Palm while you're on the road.

Getting a Pocket PC to Coordinate

You can synchronize your Pocket PC with your computer two ways:

- Place the Pocket PC into its cradle.
- Connect wirelessly and update your Pocket PC.

I'm going to talk about this last one, leaving you with your Pocket PC manual to read about the first one (which you probably already know, anyway).

You must install Microsoft ActiveSync before you can synchronize your Pocket PC with information on another computer on your network. You can download the latest version of ActiveSync from www.microsoft.com/windowsmobile/downloads/as-dl37.mspx.

Running with ActiveSync

You can use Microsoft's ActiveSync software to wirelessly synchronize information between your Pocket PC and your desktop computer.

Before you can synchronize your Pocket PC, make sure the settings are correct on the ActiveSync software running on your desktop PC.

1. **Click Start, All Programs.**
2. **Click Microsoft ActiveSync.**

   The ActiveSync dialog box appears.
3. **Click File.**
4. **Click Mobile Device.**

   Menu of available Pocket PCs appears.
5. **Select the Pocket PC unit you want to synchronize, as shown in Figure 3-1.**

   In this case, there is only one Pocket PC and it's called Pocket_PC. (Sometimes even computer stuff is easy to follow.)
6. **Click File.**

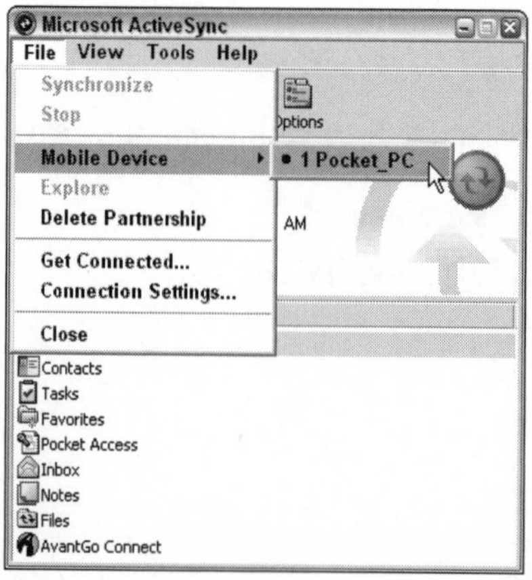

Figure 3-1: Selecting a Pocket PC to synchronize.

7. **Click Connection Settings.**

   The Connection Settings dialog box appears.

8. **Confirm that this choice is selected: Allow Network (Ethernet) and Remote Access Service (RAS) Server Connection with This Desktop Computer.**

9. **Click OK.**

Syncing information from a Pocket PC

Here's how you initiate a synchronization *from* your handheld computer over a wireless network:

1. **Click Start, Programs.**

   The Programs dialog box appears.

2. **Click ActiveSync.**

   ActiveSync dialog box appears.

3. **Click Sync.**

   Your Pocket PC shows Connecting and then Synchronizing, which you see in Figure 3-2.

When it's done, the screen displays Not Connected. The ActiveSync software on both your PC and handheld show the last date and time they connected to each other. If the synchronization is not occurring, make sure you have a working wireless connection and that your Pocket PC is close enough to a wireless access point.

TIP

Make sure Microsoft ActiveSync is also running on your desktop PC.

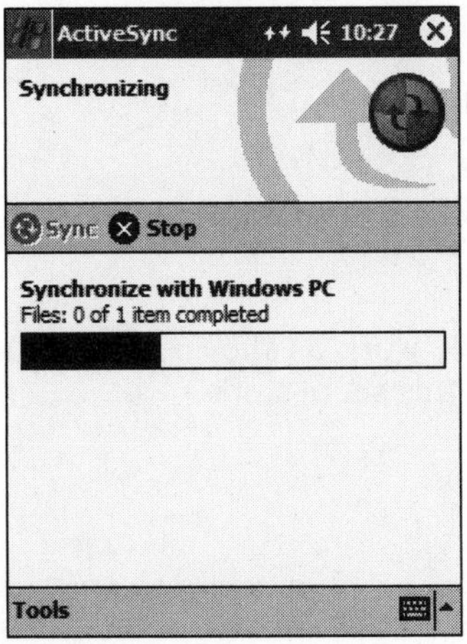

Figure 3-2: Pocket PC synchro-nizing with desktop PC.

You also can synchronize your Pocket PC by using Bluetooth wireless technology instead of a Wi-Fi connection. I discuss Bluetooth in more detail in Book VI, Chapter 5, although I don't discuss how to make connections with PDAs. Your PDA manufacturer should provide that information in a manual or on its Web site.

Bluetooth works over a much shorter range — about 30 feet — but can be an easier way to connect your handheld to your desktop PC at close distances. In addition, with the introduction of more and more Bluetooth-enabled cellular telephones, it's also a way to synchronize information between your Pocket PC and your mobile phone.

Synchronizing a Palm PDA

Just like with the Pocket PC, you can synchronize your Palm PDA with your computer's information in one of two ways:

- You can place the Palm in its cradle and initiate a synchronization.
- You can connect to your computer wirelessly.

Again, I focus on synchronizing via a wireless connection, leaving synchronization using a Palm cradle in your capable hands.

Configuring HotSync on your PC

Before connecting, you need to change an option on the HotSync software running on your desktop PC. It's probably set to connect through local USB or local serial. You want to add a network option so the software knows you are connecting via a wireless connection rather than via USB or serial.

If you don't take these steps, your desktop PC's ActiveSync software won't recognize your attempt to connect for synchronization.

1. **If HotSync is not running, start it.**
2. **Click the HotSync icon.**

   A menu pops up.
3. **Select Network.**

   A checkmark appears beside Network, as shown in Figure 3-3. The menu disappears. You're all set with this set of steps.

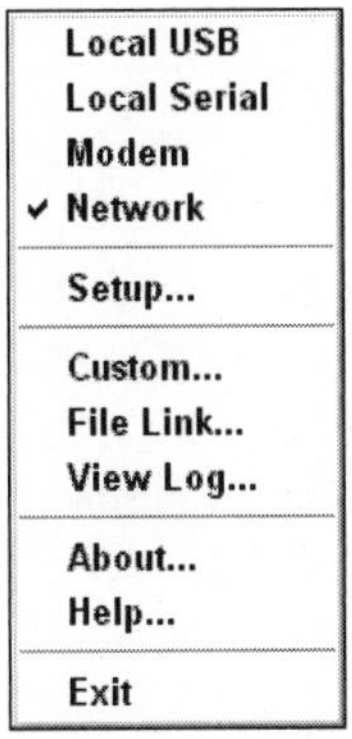

Figure 3-3: Enabling a network connection.

Configuring HotSync on your Palm

After configuring HotSync on your PC, it's time to do the same on your Palm. Just this one last series of steps and you are ready to synchronize wirelessly. Here's what you do:

1. **From the Programs screen, click HotSync.**

   HotSync runs.

2. **Click Network.**
3. **Below the Synchronization button, click the down arrow.**

   A menu appears.

4. **Determine whether your computer is on the list and proceed accordingly:**
   - **It's on the list: Select it.** You can skip the remaining steps and head to the section "HotSyncing your PC to your Palm."
   - **It isn't on the list: Click Select PC.** The Network HotSync Setup screen appears.
5. **Click Next.**

   Your Palm connects, searches for a list of PCs, and then builds the list. A Select a PC screen appears.

6. **Determine whether your computer is on the list and proceed accordingly:**
   - **It's on the list: Select it and click Next.**
   - **It isn't on the list: Click Other.** A new screen appears.

7. **Click Next.**

   A new screen appears.

8. **Click Done.**

   You're returned to the main HotSync screen. You can skip the remaining steps and head to the next section on synchronizing your Palm over your wireless network.

9. **Enter your PC's name or IP address, as shown in Figure 3-4.**

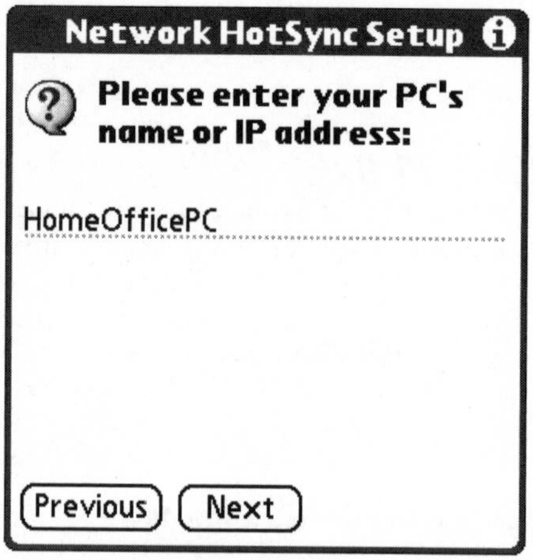

Figure 3-4: Entering your PC's name or IP address.

TIP

Your best bet here is to enter the IP address of the computer with which you're trying to synchronize. You also can enter the computer's name (for example, HomeOfficePC), but the IP address is more precise. If you don't already know the computer's IP address, you can discover it by running a Command Prompt and entering **ipconfig /all**.

Look down and you see IP Address and the number beside it. It probably starts with 192.168.1.1*xx*, where *xx* is the specific address for your computer. ipconfig is discussed in more detail in Book IV, Chapter 3.

10. **Click Next to bring up a new screen.**

11. **Click Done.**

    HotSync returns to the synchronization screen shown in Figure 3-5.

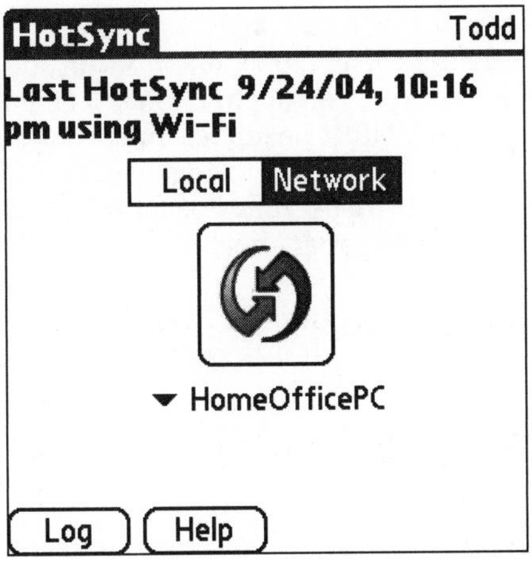

Figure 3-5: Your Palm is ready for a network HotSync.

HotSyncing to your PC from your Palm

You're finally ready to make a wireless connection between your Palm and your desktop PC. Isn't this exciting? I know it is for me. I won't waste any more valuable ink. Here's how you make a HotSync connection from your Palm to your PC:

1. **From the Programs screen, click HotSync.**

   HotSync runs.

2. **Click Network.**

   The default is Local; make sure you change the selection to Network.

3. **Select the correct PC, if more than one is listed.**
4. **Click the Synchronization button.**

Your Palm connects with your desktop PC and synchronizes content. That's it! You're done.

Giving It an AvantGo

AvantGo isn't just a wireless tool. It lets you take information on the road with you, whether or not you have a wireless connection. Part of being wireless is the mobility factor — the ability to access information from anywhere. In this case, the information is already stored on your handheld computer.

With AvantGo, you choose one or more *channels* (each channel is usually a publication) and synchronize between your PDA and AvantGo's servers to update the information. For example, you might choose a channel for *The New York Times* and then grab the latest headlines and articles before you head for the plane. On board, comfortably drinking ginger ale and eating your stale bag of pretzels, you can fire up your Pocket PC or Palm PDA and read a miniature version of the newspaper.

These channels and more are available through AvantGo:

- *The Wall Street Journal*
- *BusinessWeek*
- *Rolling Stone*
- *USA Today*
- *The Sporting News*
- *AccuWeather*
- *Bloomberg*
- *CBS MarketWatch*
- JiWire Hotspot Locator
- Various airlines' home pages (Delta and Northwest)

Setting up and using AvantGo is a long process, but roughly you do these things:

- Register and download the software that's appropriate for your device. (It works with Pocket PCs, Palms, and some smart phones.)
- Install the software on your handheld gizmo.
- Choose the content you want to read.
- Synchronize your device with AvantGo. During this process, old information is removed, current information is left alone, and new information is added.

AvantGo, available at www.avantgo.com, is free, paid for by advertising. After downloading a software program to your PC and your handheld computer, you can synchronize information stored on AvantGo's servers. This way you can carry a bunch of publications in your pocket without it falling on the floor.

1. **Go to AvantGo's web site and click the front page's Get It Now! button.**

   You're taken to the Account Setup page.

2. **Create a username and password.**
3. **Enter your e-mail address, zip code, country, time zone, and preferred language.**

   The zip code enables AvantGo to provide localized content.
4. **Click Continue.**

   The next page is a tedious amount of information that AvantGo requires because the service is advertiser supported. The information you need to enter includes your interests, your age, and gender, and information about your company.
5. **When you're done completing the reader questionnaire, click Continue.**

   The next page, at least for me, consisted of a series of questions about my company's computer purchasing habits. This page may be different for people depending on how they answer the previous questions.

   TIP: The fastest way to answer these kinds of annoying questions is to quickly go through, pull down each menu, and randomly select an answer. It serves the companies right that force us to plow through these time wasters.
6. **When you're done, once again click Continue.**

   The next screen shows AvantGo's Terms of Service and Privacy Statement.
7. **Select both boxes after reading and agreeing to the terms. If you do accept those terms, click I Accept.**

   Finally, you get down to some real business. The following screen offers various devices for use.
8. **Choose the device you own:**
   - **Palm OS**
   - **Palm OS 5**
   - **Pocket PC**
   - **Symbian Series 60 (Nokia 3600 series and the 7650 phones)**
   - **Symbian UIQ (Sony-Ericsson P800/P900 phones)**
9. **Click Continue.**

   For this example, I'm downloading and installing the Pocket PC software. The Download page appears.
10. **Select Click Here to Download.**

11. **When the File Download dialog box appears, click Open.**

    Once the software is done downloading, the installation process begins on your PC.

12. **Walk through the installation, clicking Next and other appropriate buttons.**

Once the AvantGo software is installed, you're ready to synchronize with your Pocket PC or Palm:

1. **Place your Pocket PC or Palm in its cradle and synch it.**

   This is the easiest way to transfer the AvantGo software from your PC to the Pocket PC or Palm, unless you already have a working wireless connection between your handheld computer and your desktop PC.

2. **Go back to www.avantgo.com and click Continue from the Synchronize page.**

3. **On the Configure page, click Configure Device.**

   An Add AvantGo Server dialog box appears.

4. **Walk through that process and click Continue on the Configure screen.**

Now it's time to (yes, once again) synchronize your Pocket PC or Palm with your desktop PC. This updates AvantGo on your handheld computer. At some point in this process, your handheld installs the AvantGo software and updates it each time you synch with your desktop computer.

1. **Go to www.avantgo.com.**

2. **Select the content you want to store and read on your handheld.**

   AvantGo offers you certain channels based on the interests you indicated earlier. For instance, some of my offerings were Reuters, *Rolling Stone* (which I haven't read in 15 years), CBS MarketWatch.com, *Forbes, Salon,* and Wired News.

   You can only download up to 2 MB of content for free at a time. After that, you need to upgrade to a Power User Premium account, which costs $14.95 a year. It lets you access up to 8 MB of content at a time. AvantGo suggests that you can subscribe to six to eight channels without going over the free allotment. Some channels, such as Reuters, *Rolling Stone, Forbes,* and commercial channels like Delta and Northwest Airlines do *not* count toward the content ceiling.

3. **Click the Select button.**

   You see a My Channels area on the web site, shown in Figure 3-6, that reveals your channel capacity and the channels currently synched on your handheld. (Now it's time to synchronize *again*. The U.S. Olympics synchronized swimming team doesn't synchronize as much as you have.)

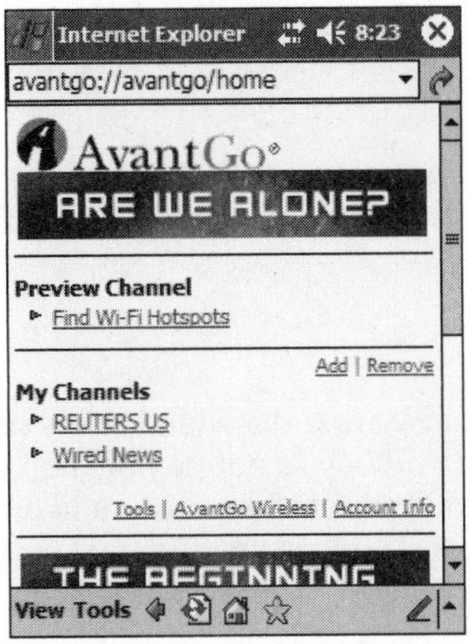

Figure 3-6: AvantGo running on a Pocket PC.

4. **Click any channel to see a list of headlines, as shown in Figure 3-7.**

   By clicking a headline, you can read the story, as shown in Figure 3-8.

Figure 3-7: AvantGo displays news headlines.

Figure 3-8: An AvantGo news story displays on a Pocket PC.

Pretty cool, eh? AvantGo lets you carry around a wide variety of content that's available whenever you are. (No, they're not paying me, but it is pretty cool. in this post-dot–com era, services like this could just as easily not exist. I may as well praise the good ones in an effort to keep them in business.)

Using AvantGo Wireless

In the previous section, I told you how to add and update content to your handheld computer by using AvantGo. One other AvantGo feature may interest you: AvantGo Wireless.

1. **You need to install additional software to use this service: Go to** www.avantgo.com/wireless **to download the software.**
2. **On the page, click Install AvantGo Wireless.**
3. **You see this message: The AvantGo Wireless Feature Is Currently Installed for Your Account.**
4. **To access the service, follow the instructions on the page for syncing from your handheld.**

   From the My AvantGo home page on your handheld, you see the My Wireless link shown in Figure 3-9.

   A list of My Wireless channels appears, as shown in Figure 3-10.

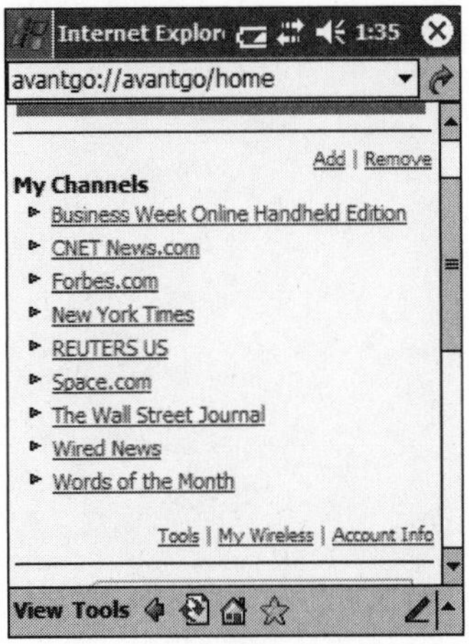

Figure 3-9: The My Wireless link.

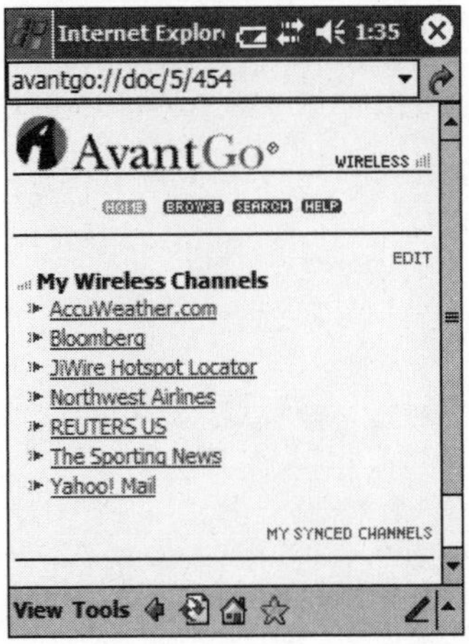

Figure 3-10: My Wireless channels.

TIP

You can edit this list by clicking Edit. Nothing is magical about this list of channels compared to the list of channels discussed in the preceding chapter, but it does allow you to pick a smaller list of channels for AvantGo to update.

This software is helpful when you're using a wireless connection without much bandwidth or with a slow connection. You may have 25 channels to synchronize when your Pocket PC or Palm is connected to your desktop PC, but a much smaller list of only 5 channels under My Wireless. If you're in an airport that has Wi-Fi access, for instance, you can grab your favorite content before boarding the plane, instead of waiting for 25 or more channels to synchronize as you normally would in the comfort of your home or office.

Chapter 4: Picking a BlackBerry

In This Chapter

- Setting up the BlackBerry
- Grabbing your e-mail
- Using BlackBerry as a phone
- Using the Sidekick II

How would you like to access e-mail on the go, from a little device that holsters on your belt like some kind of future phasor gun? It's possible with a BlackBerry. The devise is getting heavy use in corporations but is becoming a more vital tool among consumers, too.

About 1.3 million people subscribe to BlackBerry, so the device certainly has become popular among people who want nonstop access to their e-mail. With the newer BlackBerry models, you can make phone calls and do some rudimentary web surfing.

In this chapter I discuss the BlackBerry and help you figure out how to use its many software applications. I also talk about the Sidekick II, a BlackBerry competitor that is decidedly not aimed at the corporate market.

Avoiding a Raspberry

A BlackBerry is a good way to communicate for several reasons:

- It's wireless, so you can take it with you wherever you go.
- It's small and light, fitting in a holster you can wear on your belt.
- It gives you around-the-clock access to your e-mail.
- It provides 24-hour access to the web, although in a limited fashion.
- It works well with corporate e-mail systems, so workers can easily use their BlackBerrys to stay in touch.
- Newer models provide a mobile phone function in addition to the traditional e-mail access.

You don't buy a BlackBerry directly from its manufacturer, Research in Motion (RIM). Instead, you purchase the device and the accompanying service (you didn't think they'd send you your e-mails for free, did you?) from a cellular phone carrier.

Because the newer models have built-in phones, there's no longer a need to carry a separate cell phone and a BlackBerry. Instead, you get one conveniently combined, sleek unit.

You can read more by visiting the BlackBerry web site at www.blackberry.com.

Which carriers offer the BlackBerry? Here's a short list, which doesn't include smaller telecommunications (or *telecom,* if you want to be sleek, too) providers:

- AT&T Wireless
- Cingular
- Nextel
- T-Mobile
- Verizon

When you subscribe to BlackBerry from one of these services, it's just like subscribing to any other cell phone service. You're purchasing a certain number of minutes of talk time and the right to send messages over your BlackBerry.

Picking a Model, Any Model

The decision about which BlackBerry model to use may be made for you if you have a particular cellular phone carrier in mind. Whichever model that carrier has is the one you will get. They may sell more than one model. (Models with built-in cell phones are similar to the PalmOne Treo 600, which is one of the mobile phones I discuss in Book VI, Chapter 1, Roaming into Cell Phone Territory. They also are similar to the Sidekick II, which I write about later in this chapter.)

Ask yourself some of these questions when deciding which BlackBerry model to purchase:

- Is the newest technology important to me? Or do I just want functionality and can leave the stylish technology to the hipsters?
- Which models are available from my carrier of choice? If you like ABC Wireless, but they don't have the model you want, you may need to go with another carrier or settle with the BlackBerry model they provide.
- Do I want a built-in phone? Or do I want a device that only works with data, including letting me access my e-mail?
- Do I want a color screen or is a monochrome screen okay? Remember that e-mail messages, for better or for worse, read the same either way.

BlackBerry 7200, 7500, and 7700 Series

RIM has different model numbers for what is basically the same device. The numbering gives each phone carrier its own model number (but pretty much the same phone). This is apparently so each carrier can appear to offer its own, exclusive model of BlackBerry. Table 4-1 reveals the model numbers that go with each respective carrier.

Table 4-1 Different Model Numbers and Carriers, Same Old Phone

Model Number	*Carrier*
7230	AT&T Wireless, T-Mobile
7280	AT&T Wireless, Cingular Wireless, Rogers Wireless (Canada)
7510	Nextel, TELUS (Canada)
7730	T-Mobile
7750	Verizon Wireless, Bell Mobility (Canada), TELUS
7780	AT&T Wireless, Rogers Wireless

TIP

The most up-to-date information about the models and the carriers that sell them is at www.blackberry.com/purchasing.

All models weigh about 5 ounces. The screen on the 7700-series models is slightly larger than those on the other phones. Some phones permit international roaming, while others do not. The software applications are similar on all the models in the 7000 series.

The 7200 series, the 7730, and the 7780 are tri-band, which means you have international roaming as you travel with them overseas in Europe and Asia Pacific. The 7510 is designed for Nextel and has an antenna the other models in the 7000 series don't need. While it does have Nextel's walkie-talkie and speaker phone features, it does not allow for outgoing text messages. I discuss SMS messages in Book VI, Chapter 1, Roaming into Cell Phone Territory.

I write about some of the BlackBerry 7200-series models' features later in this chapter:

- E-mail application, including integrated attachment viewing for Microsoft Word, Excel, PowerPoint, WordPerfect, and Adobe file formats
- Web browser applications
- Organizer applications
- 16 MB flash memory, plus another 2 MB of SRAM memory
- Traditional keyboard with backlight
- High-resolution screen supporting 65,000 colors
- Operates on domestic and international (GSM/GPRS) networks
- Battery life estimated at 4 hours talk time, 10 days standby time

BlackBerry 5790

BlackBerry returns to its roots with the introduction of model 5790, which is a data-only handheld that does not have a built-in phone. The most significant difference from the 7000 series is that the 5790 does not have a color screen.

Some of the 5790's features include the following, in addition to what shows up in the 7000 series:

- Screen resolution of 160 × 160
- Operates on Mobitex networks and at the 900-MHz frequency band

Biting into the Main Features

Although some models have different features than others, I'm focusing on the BlackBerry 7230 and 7280, which are the same model offered by different carriers. AT&T Wireless offers the 7230 and 7280, while T-Mobile sells the 7230 to its customers and Cingular Wireless makes the 7280 available. They all are very similar phones.

These applications appear on the 7200-series models shown in Figure 4-1:

✦ E-mail
✦ Phone
✦ Address book
✦ Calendar
✦ Web browsing

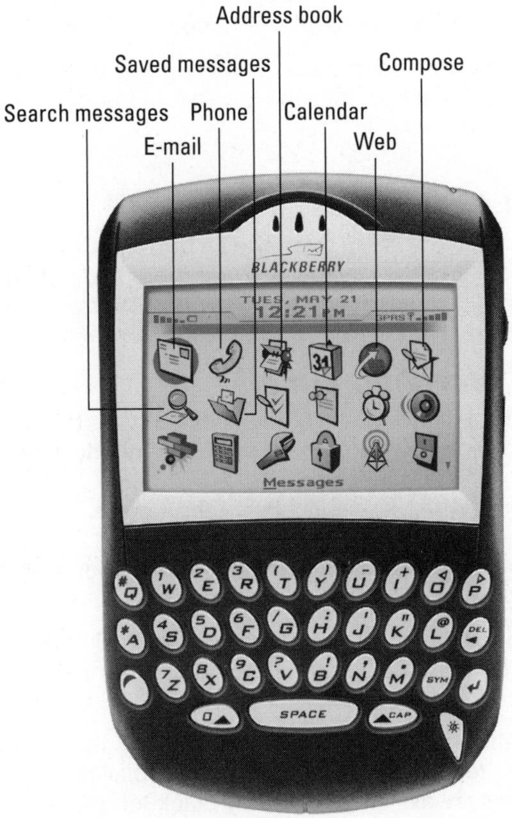

Figure 4-1: The BlackBerry's main applications.

Navigating

BlackBerry owes much of its popularity to its ease of use. Other than the traditionally laid out keyboard — although much smaller, so get those thumbs in shape — the device has very few buttons. It has three non-keyboard buttons:

- **Phone button.** Push this to go to the screen where you either can pick a phone number from your address book or enter a phone number from the keyboard.
- **Trackwheel.** You can whirl the wheel with your thumb and then press when you reach something you'd like to do, like run an application.
- **Escape key.** Press this when you're in an application and want to return to the main menu. Think of it as the key that helps when you get lost: You can escape to safety.

Turning it on and off

Start where all things BlackBerry start: the on button. It's the silver button on the far-bottom right of the keyboard. If you press and hold this button, the BlackBerry turns off. Push it again and the BlackBerry turns on.

Sending and receiving e-mail

Sending and receiving e-mail through the BlackBerry certainly is what has made the brand name synonymous with portable, mobile e-mail messaging.

You can receive e-mail through a BlackBerry three ways:

- Personal e-mail account access through the BlackBerry web client. This is for e-mail addresses like todd@toddcarter.com.
- Business/corporate e-mail access through the BlackBerry Enterprise Server, which lets workers grab their messages from Microsoft Exchange or IBM Lotus Domino.
- BlackBerry e-mail via an e-mail address that looks like mlelrick@blackberry.net. You receive messages through BlackBerry web client. These addresses are assigned to you by BlackBerry.

Reading e-mail messages

E-mail is the first application on the BlackBerry screen, so it's fast and easy to jump right in and check for messages. Just follow these steps:

1. **Making sure the e-mail icon is highlighted, click the trackwheel.**

The e-mail message screen appears, as shown in Figure 4-2.

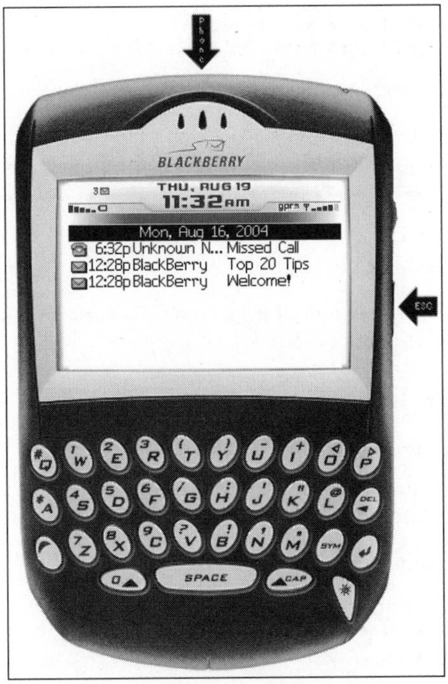

Figure 4-2: The e-mail messages screen.

2. **Double-click the trackwheel to open the message.**
3. **Click the Escape button when you want to return to the main menu.**

   Otherwise, use the menu to perform another function on the e-mail message. That's it.

The first click of the trackwheel opens a menu that, in addition to opening a message, lets you do these things:

- File a message
- Mark a message as unopened
- Save a message
- Reply to a message
- Forward a message
- Delete a message

Taking a shortcut

Sometimes it's okay to take some shortcuts in life. This is one of those times. The two groups of shortcuts I'm including here help you navigate some general areas, as well as another part you will use a lot: messaging.

Composing a message

Now you know how to read your e-mail messages. How do you send one? Just follow these steps:

1. **Scroll to the Compose icon.**
2. **Click the icon using the trackwheel button.**

   A Compose Message screen appears. Click Use Once if the address you need is not listed.
3. **Select E-mail from the menu.**

   One Time E-mail screen appears.
4. **Enter the e-mail address.**

   You can use the spacebar to insert the @ sign into the e-mail address. Clicking the spacebar a second time inserts a period into the address. This lets you enter an address quicker because you don't need to press any special keys to access the symbols and punctuation keys.
5. **Press the Return key.**

   The Subject line appears.
6. **Enter a subject.**
7. **Press the Enter key.**

   The cursor moves to the body of the e-mail.
8. **Enter your e-mail message, as shown in Figure 4-3.**
9. **Click the trackwheel.**

   The menu appears.

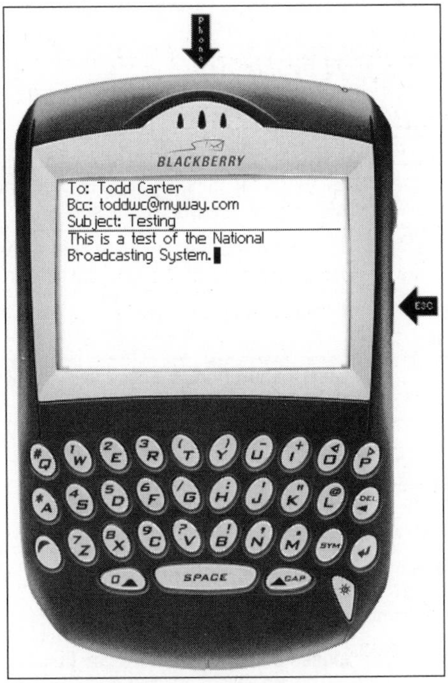

Figure 4-3: Compose an e-mail's address, subject, and message.

10. Click Send. That's how you send an e-mail message with your BlackBerry!

You also can Save Draft or add addresses in the To, Cc, and Bcc fields. If you clicked Send, you are taken to the e-mail screen, which shows your outgoing and incoming messages.

General Shortcuts

Do This	*To Do This*
Press Alt while rolling the trackwheel	Scroll horizontally in any screen where you enter text
Press Alt while rolling the trackwheel	Scroll a screen at a time in the Messages, Address Book, Calendar, Tasks, and MemoPad screens
Type the first letter of an item in an option list or menu	Jump directly to the item
Type the first letters of a name (or the initials separated by a space)	Find a contact in the address book or To screens
Press the Escape key	Exit any screen, menu, or dialog box

Messages Shortcuts

Do This	*To Do This*
Press Alt + I	View all incoming messages
Press Alt + O	View all outgoing messages
Press T	Go to the top message and B to go to the bottom message in the Messages screen
Press N for next, P for previous, and U	Go to next unread message in an open message
Press C in the Messages, Home, and Saved Messages screens	Compose a new message
Press S	Start a search for a message in the Messages and Saved Message screen
Press N for next and P for previous	Learn the corresponding date in the Messages screen
Press R in the Messages screen and in an open message	Reply to the sender with text
Press F in the Messages screen and in an open message	Forward the message
Press G	Return to the last cursor position (if you previously closed a message before you finished reading it)

Making a phone call

You can make a phone call from the BlackBerry a couple different ways. One way uses the dedicated phonecall button on the top of the unit, while the other involves selecting the Phone icon on the device's Home screen.

To use the dedicated phonecall button, follow these steps:

1. **Click the dedicated phonecall button on the top of the BlackBerry.**

   The Phone screen appears.

2. **Select One Time Dial or begin entering the number.**

   The Enter Phone Number dialog box appears.

3. **Enter a phone number.**
4. **Select Call.**

   BlackBerry dials the number.

To place a phone call from the Home screen, follow these steps:

1. **Click the Phone icon.**

   The Phone screen appears.

2. **Select One Time Dial or begin entering the number.**

   The Enter Phone Number dialog box appears.

3. **Enter a phone number.**
4. **Select Call.**

   That phone on the other side should be ringing.

TIP

Clicking a telephone number in an e-mail, for example, makes the BlackBerry call that number automatically. In addition, if you click an e-mail address inside a message, the BlackBerry automatically composes a message with that address. It also works with web addresses; clicking them fires up the browser.

Adding a contact to the address book

You can add a contact to the address book two different ways: Add a contact from scratch or add a contact from a message you received from that individual.

Follow these steps to add a contact from scratch:

1. **From the Home screen, click the Address Book icon.**

   The Find screen appears.

2. **Click the trackwheel to bring up the menu.**
3. **Click New Address.**

   The New Address screen appears.

4. **Enter information into the address book fields, which are shown in Figure 4-4.**

   Press Enter or use the trackwheel to move between fields.

5. **When you're done entering contact information, click the trackwheel to bring up the menu.**

6. Click Save.

The contact information is added to your address book.

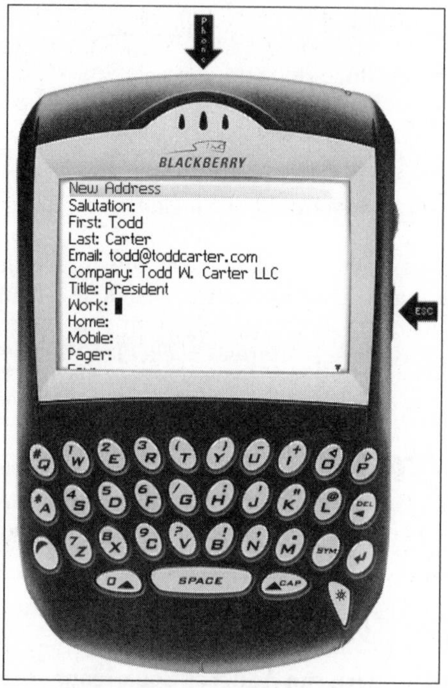

Figure 4-4: Enter information into the address book.

Follow these steps to add a contact to the address book from an e-mail message:

1. **Open the e-mail message.**
2. **Click the trackwheel to view the menu.**
3. **Select Add to Address Book.**

   The New Address screen appears with the e-mail address filled in.
4. **Add any other contact information you'd like.**
5. **Click the trackwheel to bring up the menu.**
6. **Select Save; the contact information is saved in the address book.**

Security help

If you're strolling through Boston's Logan International Airport and you look a little shady to Massachusetts State Police officers, a BlackBerry may be unholstered long before a gun is drawn. The state police are using the devices to perform background checks on suspicious individuals. The BlackBerry connects to a database called LocatePlus, which contains information from various sources about more than 200 million U.S. residents. The database, based on the data, assigns a security rating to everyone. All of this information is available via the BlackBerry.

Browsing the Web

Using a BlackBerry to access the Internet is like using a spoon to dredge the ocean. Most Internet sites are not designed for viewing on such a small screen, although the BlackBerry is a way to read web content in a pinch.

Sadly, I found that many of the web sites I tried to access would not display properly; some of them didn't display at all.

There are several ways to open a web page. Here are the steps for entering a web address in the BlackBerry and visiting that web site:

1. **From the Home screen, click the Browser icon.**

   The Browser Bookmarks screen appears.

2. **Click the trackwheel to view the menu.**

   The menu appears.

3. **Click Go To, which brings up the Go To dialog box.**
4. **Enter the web address.**

   I already told you about the trick of pressing the Space key to insert a key. You also can press Shift + Space to insert a forward slash (/).

5. **Click OK.**

   BlackBerry's browser loads and, hopefully, the web site you requested appears.

Special versions of two popular web sites are designed for small web browsers like the BlackBerry's: www.google.com/wml and mobile.yahoo.com/home. I discuss many of these web services and others in Book V, Chapter 2.

Checking Out the Sidekick II

Two-way pagers have been around for a long time. But they're not quite the same as the BlackBerry because they don't let you send and receive real e-mail messages. Another device has come on the market, however, that performs many of the same data-related functions of the BlackBerry.

It's called Sidekick II (it's actually the third model in the Sidekick series) if you're a T-Mobile customer. It's made by a company called Danger, which manufactures them for different mobile phone carriers. Danger calls them the hiptop2; check out Figure 4-5.

Apparently, teenagers are some of the biggest users. The newest unit began selling in fall 2004, costing about $300 plus $20 for the accompanying T-Mobile data service.

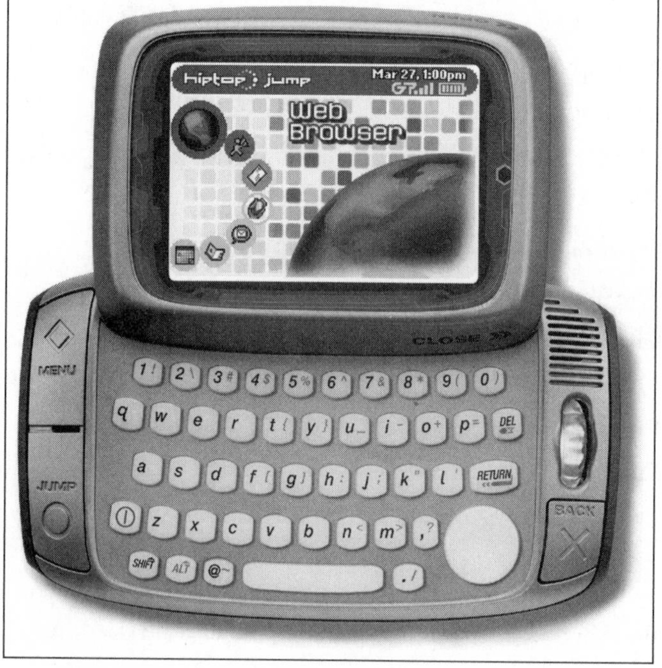

Figure 4-5: The Sidekick II or, as some call it, hiptop2.

Compared to the BlackBerry, the Sidekick II is a little more bulky. One reviewer described it as the size of a bar of bath soap. He said the previous version was more like a bar of hand soap. (If you tied a rope to it, think what you could have!) Anyhow, Danger has made improvements that make the Sidekick II easier to use, as well as boosting the signal of the cell phone it contains.

Some of the Sidekick II's features include:

- Phone
- E-mail
- Instant messaging (AOL and Yahoo!)
- Web browser
- SMS/text messaging
- Built-in camera
- Calendar, address book, and other software applications
- Speakerphone
- Traditional keyboard
- 32 MB RAM
- International roaming

Chapter 5: Finding Wi-Fi Hotspots

In This Chapter

- Using Wi-Fi directories
- Dreaming about airports, hotels, and clouds
- Thinking about security

Your laptop is set up for wireless networking and you're restless to connect to the Internet somewhere outside your home or office. You've heard about *hotspots,* which are places with public Internet access. How can you find them?

Luckily, you can turn to several places for this information before venturing from home. In this chapter I talk about Wi-Fi directories, as well as some public projects that are trying to make wireless access available to everyone.

Getting Thee to a Directory

How do you find Wi-Fi heat in the spots you plan to travel? The quickest way is to do some homework before you leave, searching one of several large databases on the Internet for hotspots. Table 5-1 describes some of the largest online directories. *WAP* is a security protocol that scrambles your wireless communications to keep them from prying eyes.

Table 5-1: Online Wi-Fi Directories

Site	*URL*	*Description*
JiWire	www.jiwire.com	This large online directory of worldwide hotspots lists more than 43,000 hotspots in 65 countries. You can search for a hot spot using several criteria. A search results page is shown in Figure 5-1. A group of mini directories separates free hotspots. Offline versions are available. You can download Windows, Macintosh, and Linux versions from www.jiwire.com/hotspot-locator-laptop.htm. A third version for WAP-enabled cell phones connects live with the JiWire directory.

(continued)

Table 5-1 *(continued)*

Site	*URL*	*Description*
Wi-Fi Zone Finder	www.wi-fizone.org	Maintained by the Wi-Fi Alliance, an industry group, the listings include all service providers that use Wi-Fi–certified equipment. A directory customized for viewing on WAP-enabled cell phones is at www.wap.wi-fizone.org.
Wi-FiHotSpotList.com	www.wi-fihotspotlist.com	Calls itself the definitive list of hotspots. I'll let you decide whether it really is. When I tried it, I experienced a long server delay in displaying the search results.
The HotSpot Haven	www.hotspothaven.com	Counts 24,432 hotspots in its directory. Of those, 9,800 are in the United States. Yet the city with the most is London, with 737, compared to New York City's 320 and San Francisco's 312.
The Wi-Fi Free Spot Directory	www.wififreespot.com	As you might guess, this is a directory of free hotspots throughout the world. If the previous entry didn't include your local library, you might want to visit Wireless Librarian. The web address is a bit long, but the typing is worth it: people.morrisville.edu/~drewwe/wireless/wirelesslibraries.htm.
Wi-Fi Marine	www.wifimarine.org	Do marinas float your boat? Then you might check out this site. It covers everything related to boaters and wireless Internet access.
Web In-Flight	www.webinflight.com	Has information about Wi-Fi service available on airlines.
NodeDB.com	www.nodedb.com	If you're heading overseas, NodeDB.com seems to be one of the largest directories that focuses on hotspots outside the United States.
WiFiMaps.com	www.wifimaps.com	This site was a little slow for me. But the site is a little different from the others in that it displays hotspots on interactive U.S. and world maps. You can search by station name, U.S. state, or by geographic region.

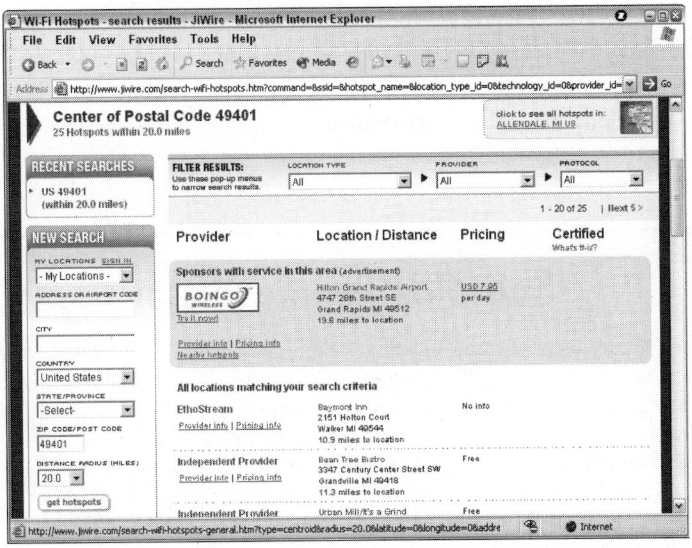

Figure 5-1: Search results for hotspots within 20 miles of a zip code.

Paying for the Goods: Commercial Providers

I wish everything were free (except this book!), but sometimes you need to turn to commercial Wi-Fi providers when you travel. I present you with a list of the major ones:

- **T-Mobile at www.t-mobile.com/hotspot/.** The nation's largest public hotspot provider sells Wi-Fi access at 4,200 locations, including Starbucks, FedEx Kinko's copy centers, and Borders bookstores. It also provides service in some major airports, as well as the frequent-flyer club lounges for Delta Air Lines, American Airlines, and United Airlines. As I write this, T-Mobile has three different ways to pay for access:
  - Unlimited national. The subscription includes unlimited minutes for $29.99 a month if paid a year in advance or $39.99 a month if paid month to month.
  - DayPass. You can purchase this prepaid access for no minimum commitment. It costs $9.99 for 24 continuous hours.
  - Pay as you go. It costs $6 an hour, with a minimum user session of 60 minutes, with additional minutes costing 10 cents each.
- **Boingo Wireless at www.boingo.com.** This large provider of hotspots boasts more than 8,500 locations. Boingo charges $21.95 a month for unlimited connection time.

- **Wayport at www.wayport.com.** Coverage includes six major airports, as well as McDonald's and UPS Stores. It has several types of payment plans:
  - Single hotel connection. This costs $9.95 for a period that ends at midnight.

Searching made easier

T-Mobile offers a free software utility aimed at making it easier to find one of its 4,200 hotspots. Called Connection Manager and shown in the accompanying figure, the Windows software automatically detects a hotspot and logs customers into the service. It includes a hotspot locator tool. Enter your state, city, zip code, or area code to see a list near you. You don't need to be online to use this directory. You can download it at http://client.hotspot.t-mobile.com/.

Boingo Wireless has similar software available for Windows computers and Pocket PCs. You can download it from www.boingo.com/download.html. It also helps you connect to Boingo's virtual private network (VPN) service, which means you make a secure connection to the company's network so that all of your Internet traffic is encrypted (read: jumbled and hence safer). It's a virtual loincloth for public hotspots.

A handy feature that both utilities share: They detect all nearby Wi-Fi signals, whether or not they're part of the companies' network. You can easily connect to any of these detected hotspots.

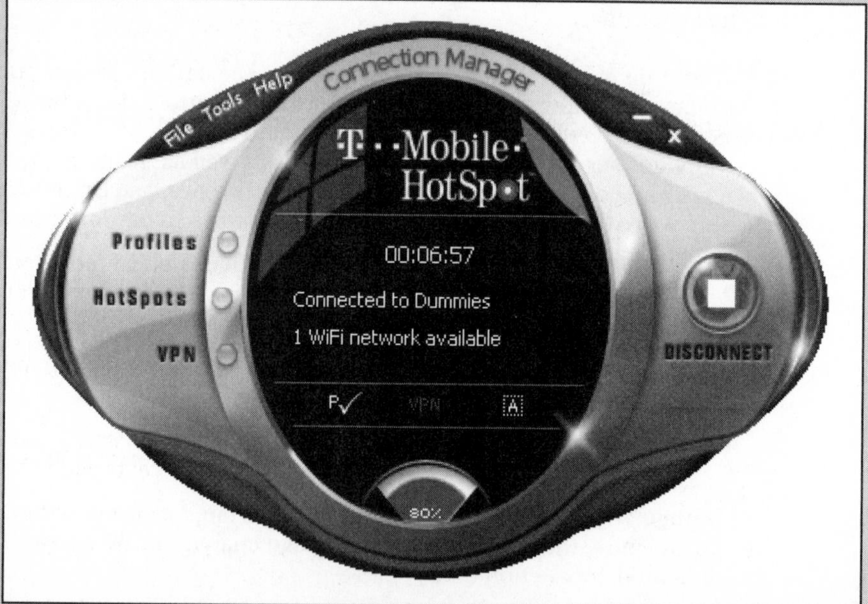

- Single airport connection. This plan runs you $6.95 for a period ending at midnight.
- Prepaid connection cards. Three connections are $25; eight are $50; 20 connections is a cool $100.
- Annual membership. The monthly rate with a one-year agreement is $29.95. Month-to-month service is $49.95 per month.

✦ **Verizon Wireless at www.verizonwireless.com.** It offers Wi-Fi access service in some airports and hotels. It costs $34.99 a month or $6.99 for a 24-hour period.

✦ **Sprint PCS at www.wifi.sprintpcs.com.** Sprint's hotspot list is a combination of its own Wi-Fi locations and those of partners. Sprint is charging $49.95 a month or $6.95 for a 24-hour period.

Going Public

The beauty of Wi-Fi networking is its mobility. It gives you the freedom to wander far from home and still have a solid connection to the Internet. You can find Wi-Fi hotspots around the globe, with the United States, Europe, and Asia leading the way as they add thousands of new access points every year.

In airports

Second to your hotel room, where do you spend most of your time during a business trip? It's probably not in the meeting or at the conference. More likely, it's the airports you pass through, especially with the increased security that forces you to arrive earlier and stay longer. Of course, layovers add to the fray.

That's why it's a good idea to know, before you leave on your trip, which airports offer what Wi-Fi services. Some may offer free access, a combination of limited free access and commercial access, or commercial access only.

As one example, Sprint PCS Wi-Fi offers service in the Kansas City, Salt Lake City, and Louisville airports. It charges $9.95 for 24 hours or $49.95 per month for unlimited service. If you're stuck in one of these airports for several hours, ten bucks may seem like a bargain as you pull out your laptop to check your e-mail.

Here's a list of major airports and some of the wireless Internet services they offer:

✦ **Chicago O'Hare International.** About 15 or so hotspots are spread across the airport, mostly in individual airlines' frequent-flyer lounges. T-Mobile, Telia HomeRun, and iPass are among the service providers.

✦ **Los Angeles International Airport.** Boingo Wireless, iPass, and T-Mobile all offer Wi-Fi service. Boingo covers six terminals.

- **Dallas-Ft. Worth International Airport.** Boingo, T-Mobile, iPass, and Wayport provide coverage in various areas throughout the airport.
- **Atlanta Hartsfield International.** T-Mobile and iPass provide most of the wireless access, which is located mainly in airline lounges.
- **Denver International Airport.** iPass, T-Mobile, and AT&T Wireless are the mile-high Wi-Fi providers.

Obviously, any of these services can change in an Internet minute. However, these snapshots of Wi-Fi access available in the larger airports at least gives you an idea of what's out there. As with other hotspots, you can check availability on one of the hotspot directories listed in Table 5-1.

In hotels

It was a big deal when in 2000 I found a hotel offering high-speed wired Internet access. It beat a slow dial-up connection and I was able to work better in my hotel room.

Now it's almost expected, especially among mid- to high-end hotels, that you'll have wireless Internet access from your room and possibly the lobby, too. For example, these large hotel chains offer some services:

- **Hyatt.** Most of the chain's more than 200 hotels have Wi-Fi access. The service is available in the lobby, other public areas, and some guest rooms. T-Mobile provides the service.
- **Marriott.** More than 1,200 of Marriott's hotels have wireless Internet access. Hotels include Marriott Hotels & Resorts, Renaissance Hotels & Resorts, Courtyard, Residence Inn, TownePlace Suites, Fairfield Inn, and SpringHill Suites. Access is available in hotel lobbies, meeting rooms, and public spaces.
- **Hilton.** More than 50 Hilton hotels have Wi-Fi access. Many of them are centered in New York City, Chicago, and throughout California.
- **Sheraton.** Owner Starwood Hotels & Resorts has Wi-Fi connectivity in more than 150 Sheraton, Westin, and W hotels in the United States. It also provides access to about 40 properties in 10 countries and regions across Asia Pacific.
- **Omni.** More than 30 U.S. Omni hotels provide Wi-Fi access in guest rooms. More hotels will be added, and guests without a wireless card can rent "wireless bridges" though the front desk. I assume this means you rent a USB access point, which you then plug into your laptop's USB port.
- **Best Western.** Yep, you read that right. Even the lower end of the hotel industry is embracing Wi-Fi. And how: Best Western plans to install wireless access in 2,300 properties throughout North America.
- **Microtel Inns & Suites.** More than 200 of the chain's hotels offer free Wi-Fi access. (The deal's even better: They offer free local calls and free

long-distance calls within the continental U.S. Could this be the beginning of the end of the industry's notorious guest phone bills?)

- **Choice Hotels.** Wireless access is a standard feature for the company's Clarion Hotel and Comfort Suites brands. The two chains have more than 600 hotels.

In the (city) clouds

A new movement is equipping many city centers with Wi-Fi access. The Wi-Fi service areas, called *city clouds* or *hot zones,* are a way for cities to differentiate themselves from other business and tourism centers. In many cases, the hot zones are dual use, with police and fire workers using it along with residents and visitors.

It's good PR: If you can check your e-mail on your Wi-Fi–enabled laptop or PDA while visiting a city's downtown, aren't you more likely to remember your visit and have good feelings about the hospitality? Covering several or more blocks beats isolated hotspots at coffee houses and other limited locations.

Here's a small selection of cities and states offering wireless access:

- **New York City, New York.** In the Big Apple, thinking big is part of living. Officials are planning a Wi-Fi network for public safety employees. The price tag: a staggering $500 million to $1 billion.
- **Washington, D.C.** You can get free Wi-Fi access from the front of the Supreme Court, the Library of Congress, and the Capitol visitors' site. The nonprofit group deploying the network hopes to have a hot zone stretch from Capitol Hill to the Washington Monument by 2005.
- **Seattle, Washington.** If you're sleepless in this city, sometime in the future you might be able to access what city officials hope will be border-to-border wireless Internet access. Of course, this city has what seems like a limitless number of coffee shops ready to provide you with Wi-Fi coverage in the meantime.
- **Spokane, Washington.** Its dual-use Wi-Fi network covers a 100-block area that is a mile long and a third of a mile wide.
- **Rio Rancho, New Mexico.** When completed, this city's network will cover 103 square miles.
- **Austin, Texas.** A volunteer effort is underway here to keep Wi-Fi free.
- **Grand Haven, Michigan.** Just down the road from your humble author's abode, this small city along Lake Michigan has a wireless network with 6 square miles of coverage. Wi-Fi access is available 20 miles into Lake Michigan. (Yes, that's over the water!) Residential service begins at $20 per month.
- **St. Cloud, Florida.** The city is offering free Internet access, with its hot zone covering an area about 20 city blocks.

Hot cities and countries

Not surprisingly, the United States is the nation with the most hotspots. In fact, it has more hotspots than the next nine nations on the worldwide top-ten list combined. The source of this list, JiWire (www.jiwire.com), counts nearly 44,000 hotspots worldwide.

- United States: 21,723
- United Kingdom: 7,947
- France: 2,226
- Germany: 1,702
- Japan: 1,261
- Canada: 897
- Australia: 664
- Taiwan: 643
- Spain: 620
- Brazil: 604

When it comes to U.S. cities with the most hotspots, New York City tops the list. Interestingly, half of these cities are in either California or Texas, as the map shows.

- New York City, NY: 1,020
- San Francisco, CA: 596
- Seattle, WA: 467
- Chicago, IL: 441
- Houston, TX: 318
- Washington, D.C.: 296
- Austin, TX: 292
- Atlanta, GA: 289
- San Diego, CA: 275
- Dallas, TX: 247

McWireless and others

What's left after the other locations? In many places, such as Seattle, Wi-Fi–equipped coffee shops are all the rage. (If you live in Seattle, check out the Caffeinated and Unstrung web site at www.seattle.wifimug.org.) Wireless Internet access is also making inroads to fast-food restaurants and sports venues.

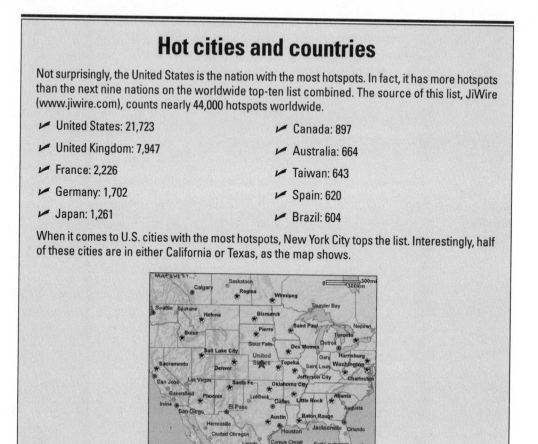

Retailers

Schlotzsky's Delis, Apple retail stores, Panera Bread, and Krystal Restaurants are among the national chains that have Wi-Fi in at least some of their locations. Not only can you buy goods and services from these places, you can go online:

- **Starbucks.** While this national coffee shop famously keeps its customers wired, it also offers Wi-Fi access. The company says that Wi-Fi users stay in its stores longer, with the average wireless session lasting about 45 minutes. Now it's safe to drink and (hard) drive.
- **McDonald's**. I'm not sure how many people take their laptops or PDAs to a McDonald's to get some work done, but 6,000 of the restaurants will have Wi-Fi access by the end of summer 2005. I'll have a salad, a large fry — and my e-mail, please.
- **FedEx Kinko's.** It took T-Mobile six months to wire (unwire?) this copy center's 1,000 U.S. locations. They welcome your use of the stores as surrogate offices.
- **UPS Stores and Mailboxes Etc.** Working with SBC Communications, UPS hopes you see Wi-Fi access in 1,500 of its stores soon. It'll then continue with another 1,800 locations shortly thereafter.

Stadiums and arenas

During baseball game broadcasts, I'm surprised how many people I see in the stands chatting on their cell phones. Maybe providing wireless Internet access is the next logical step? The San Francisco Giants is offering free Wi-Fi access to its baseball fans. Now you can attend a day game while checking your e-mail, making it appear you're working. You also can check on scores and stats — anything you can do at home is available. The Charlotte Bobcats basketball team will have a similar service when its new arena opens in 2005. Other stadiums and arenas have toyed with the idea, too.

On the road

You can be between points A and B and still get online:

- **Airplanes.** German airline Lufthansa has on-board Wi-Fi access. Other international carriers have some plans, but currently no domestic U.S. airline is planning on offering the service anytime soon. However, several U.S. airlines do provide e-mail and instant messaging through seatback phones.
- **Truck stops.** Truck drivers need Wi-Fi access, too. There's family to e-mail and paperwork to file. Offering access differentiates one truck stop from the other, providing a competitive advantage.

- **Highway rest areas.** Texas, Iowa, and Maryland think they know how to encourage tired drivers to stop more often at highway rest stops: Offer them wireless Internet access from the comfort of their vehicles. It's especially a boon to truckers and RVers. With the security lines in airports being so long, the highways may become an important alternative to business travelers.
- **Campgrounds.** Near where I live, the state of Michigan is installing Wi-Fi access in a state park campground. It plans to do this in other state parks, as well. I'm sure this is happening elsewhere, too. My idea of roughing it is watching TV on anything other than a big screen, so battling insects in a tent and foot fungus in the shower is not within my definition of reality. Yet I understand many folks like this return to pre-civilization days. Now they can swat the mosquitoes while surfing the web. Progress!

Clenching Your Security Blanket

WARNING!

Most, if not all, of the public hotspots I discuss in this chapter provide unsecured wireless Internet access. That means you're out there naked, baby. The guy with the tall latte at the next table can easily access your laptop or PDA files if you're not careful. Use a firewall and buckle down your file access, as I discuss in Book IV, Chapter 1. If you're connecting to a corporate network, do so through a virtual private networking (VPN) connection, which I discuss in Book V, Chapter 6.

REMEMBER

Don't send out personal information like credit card numbers unless you're connecting to a web site that encrypts the data before sending it. You can tell if it's a secured site by the web address, which usually begins with https and a closed padlock icon appears in your browser.

T-Mobile, which operates hotspots in Starbucks locations, is very clear that you're on your own when it comes to security. "The T-Mobile HotSpot network is based on evolving wireless technology and is not inherently secure," it says in a security statement posted on Starbucks' web site. "We therefore cannot guarantee the privacy of your data and communications while using the HotSpot service." The statement cautions that an unexplained loss or deterioration of your connection *could* mean that a nearby hacker has gained free access to the Internet using your HotSpot username and password. If you suspect that's the case, logging out knocks the freeloading hacker off the Internet. T-Mobile suggests you then call its customer service department.

REMEMBER

While I cover many of these security issues elsewhere, they're worth mentioning here as you consider connecting to a public hotspot. There's no need to be paranoid (believe me, I know), but vigilance is diligence. T-Mobile makes these security recommendations:

- Don't leave your computer or device unattended. (Duh! The worst security is a stolen laptop.)
- Don't loan your computer or device to someone unfamiliar to you. (You might be a Dummy, but you're not an idiot.)
- Watch for over-the-shoulder viewing of your login, credit card number, or other personal information.
- Properly log out of web sites by clicking Log Out instead of just closing your browser or typing in a new Internet address.
- Passwords should be a combination of letters and numbers, and they should be changed frequently. (This is always good advice.)
- Keep passwords and account numbers secure; don't store them on your computer or device or share them with anyone.
- Avoid using web-based e-mail or instant messaging that uses clear, unencrypted text to send confidential information.
- Remove or disable your wireless card if you're working offline and you are not planning to connect to a hotspot.

Any way you sip it, it's worth letting this advice brew and considering it the next time you connect to the Internet through a public Wi-Fi hotspot.

Chapter 6: Setting Up a VPN Connection

In This Chapter

- **Creating a VPN connection**
- **Using VPN to connect to a faraway computer**
- **Putting together an incoming VPN connection**

Wireless networking security is an evolving area. Though wireless networking has some built-in security features, you can't be as confident with it as you can with wired networking. What if you want to wirelessly move information from your PC to a computer located elsewhere? You're in an airport, using public Wi-Fi access, and you want to connect to an office computer — and don't want anyone to see the information you're sending. How can you pull this off? I'm glad you asked.

I show you how to create and use what's called a *virtual private network (VPN)* to move your data safely over a public network such as the Internet. When you create a VPN connection, you're creating a virtual tunnel. Everything moving through this tunnel is encrypted, or scrambled, so it's safe from prying eyes. Once the data reaches the computer on the other end, the information is decrypted so users can see what you sent.

Setting Up a VPN Connection

Follow along with these steps and you find it's pretty easy to set up a VPN connection (one of which is shown in Figure 6-1). If you have set up other network connections using Windows XP's New Connection Wizard, it is even easier for you.

Figure 6-1: Data moving through a secure VPN tunnel.

Here's how you set up the VPN connection:

1. **Click the Start menu and select Control Panel.**

   The Control Panel opens.

2. **Click Network and Internet Connections.**

   The Network and Internet Connections dialog box appears.

3. **Under Pick a Task, click Create a Connection to the Network at Your Workplace.**

   Figure 6-2 shows this being done. The Network Connection dialog box appears.

   REMEMBER: Despite the menu selection's name, the VPN connection can be made anywhere, not just to a company network.

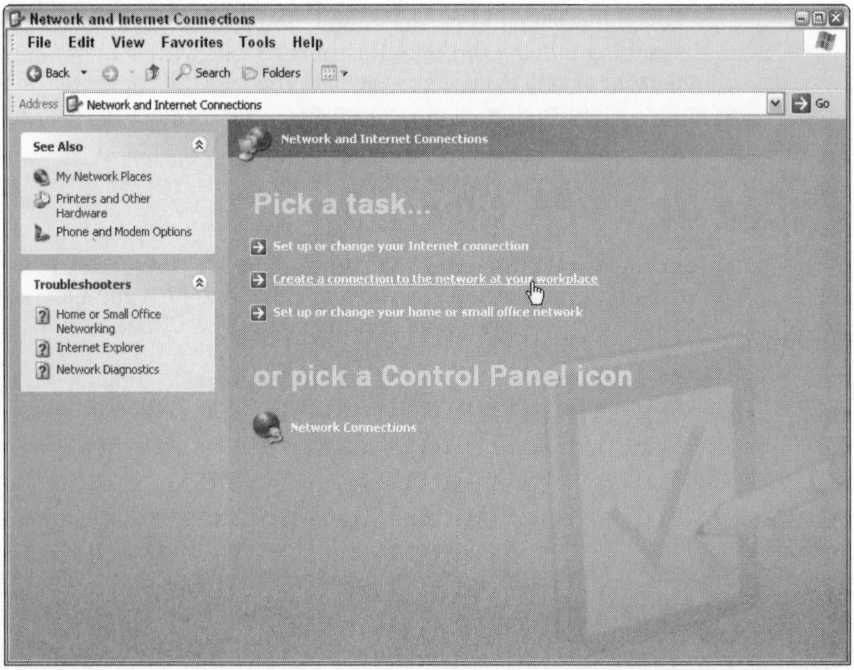

Figure 6-2: The first step in creating a VPN connection.

4. **Select the button beside Virtual Private Network Connection, as shown in Figure 6-3.**

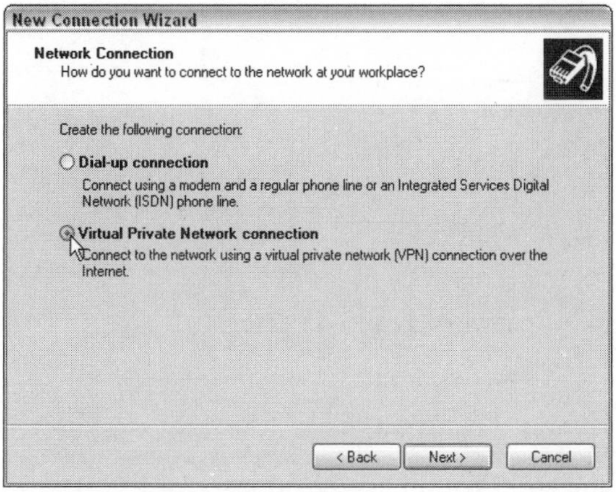

Figure 6-3: Selecting a VPN connection.

5. **Click Next.**

   The Connection Name dialog box appears.

6. **Enter any name for the VPN connection, as shown in Figure 6-4.**
7. **Click Next.**

   The VPN Server Selection dialog box appears.

8. **Enter the domain name or IP address of the computer to which you are connecting, as shown in Figure 6-5.**

   You can get this information from your network administrator.

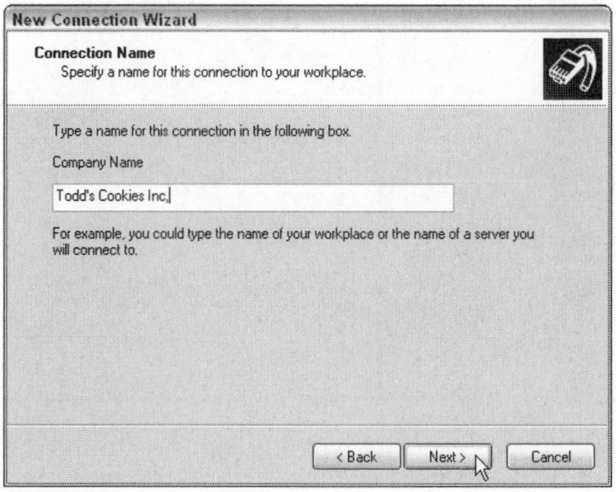

Figure 6-4: Entering a VPN connection name.

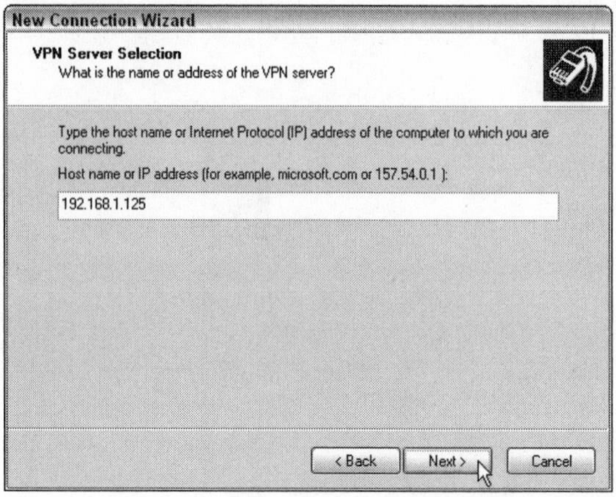

Figure 6-5: Entering a domain name or IP address.

9. **Click Next.**

   The New Connection Wizard screen appears.

10. **Click Finish.**

    Your new VPN connection appears in the Network Connections dialog box, as shown in Figure 6-6.

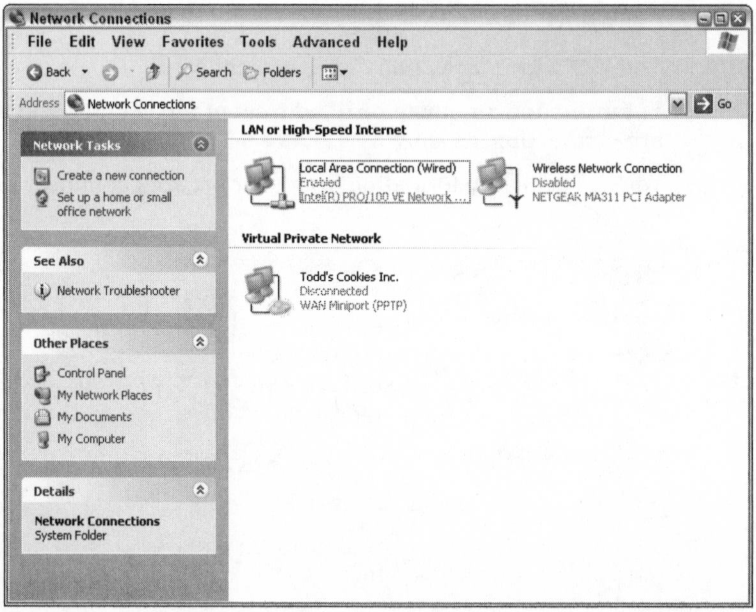

Figure 6-6: You created a VPN connection.

Connecting to a Remote Computer Using VPN

If you've set up a VPN connection on your computer, you can connect to a remote computer that accepts incoming VPN connections. Ask your network administrator whether a remote computer accepts VPN connections. (In the next section I show you how to create an incoming connection for a Windows XP machine.)

Here's how you connect to a remote computer using VPN:

1. **From the Network Connections dialog box, double-click the VPN connection.**

   A connection dialog box appears.

2. **Enter the remote computer's username and password, as shown in Figure 6-7.**

   You can get this information from your network administrator.

Figure 6-7: Entering a username and password.

If you select Save This User Name and Password for the Following Users, everyone with access to your PC can connect to the remote computer. The username and password are saved on your computer, so users won't need to know that information to connect.

3. **Click Connect.**

   You see the Connecting dialog box shown in Figure 6-8.

   If the connection is a success, your Virtual Private Network icon in the Network Connections dialog box says Connected.

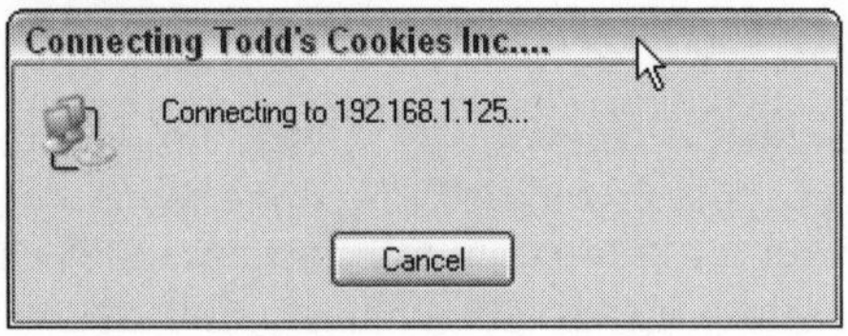
Connecting Todd's Cookies Inc....
Connecting to 192.168.1.125...
Cancel

Figure 6-8: Connecting with a remote computer.

TIP

You can disconnect a VPN connection by right-clicking the VPN connection icon and selecting Disconnect. You can use the icon to reconnect whenever you want by clicking it.

Creating an Incoming VPN Connection

Windows XP lets you create an incoming connection so that other users — maybe even yourself while on the road — can connect to your computer using a VPN connection.

REMEMBER

The Home edition of Windows XP can only accept one incoming VPN connection at a time. The Professional version allows multiple incoming connections.

These steps create an incoming connection:

1. **In the Network Connections dialog box, click Create a New Connection.**

   The New Connection Wizard dialog box appears.

2. **Click Next.**

   The Network Connection Type dialog box appears.

3. **Select Set Up an Advanced Connection, as shown in Figure 6-9.**

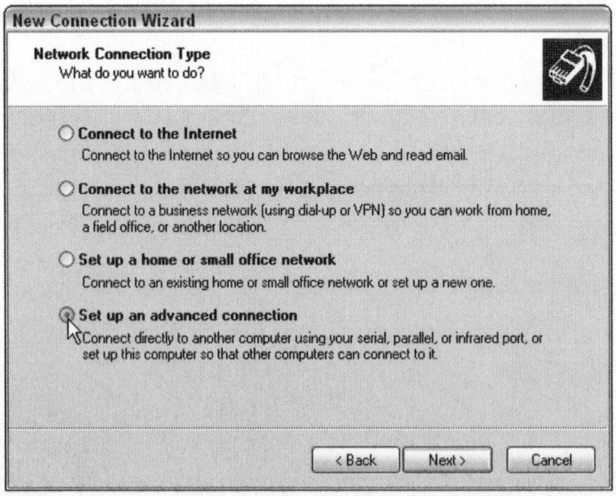
New Connection Wizard
Network Connection Type
What do you want to do?
Connect to the Internet
Connect to the Internet so you can browse the Web and read email.
Connect to the network at my workplace
Connect to a business network (using dial-up or VPN) so you can work from home, a field office, or another location.
Set up a home or small office network
Connect to an existing home or small office network or set up a new one.
Set up an advanced connection
Connect directly to another computer using your serial, parallel, or infrared port, or set up this computer so that other computers can connect to it.
< Back
Next >
Cancel

Figure 6-9: Network Connection Type dialog box.

4. **Click Next.**

   The Advanced Connection Options dialog box appears.

5. **Select Accept Incoming Connections, as shown in Figure 6-10.**

New Connection Wizard
Advanced Connection Options
Which type of connection do you want to set up?
Select the connection type you want:
Accept incoming connections
Allow other computers to connect to this computer through the Internet, a phone line, or a direct cable connection.
Connect directly to another computer
Connect to another computer using your serial, parallel, or infrared port.
< Back
Next >
Cancel

Figure 6-10: Accepting incoming connections.

6. **Click Next.**

   The Devices for Incoming Connections dialog box appears. You can ignore this dialog box.

7. **Click Next.**

   The Incoming Virtual Private Network (VPN) Connection dialog box appears.

8. **Select Allow Virtual Private Connections, as shown in Figure 6-11.**

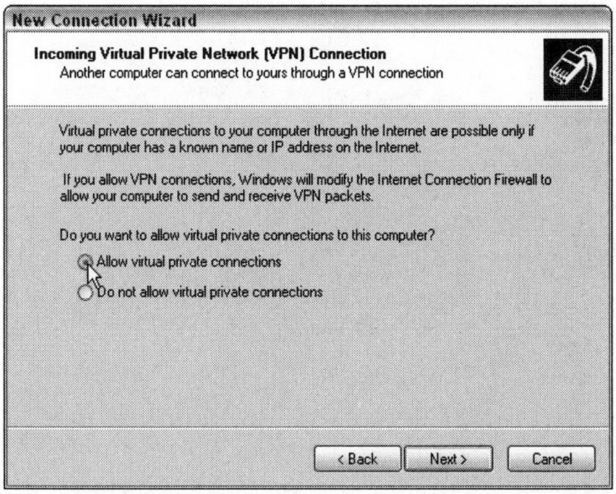
New Connection Wizard
Incoming Virtual Private Network (VPN) Connection
Another computer can connect to yours through a VPN connection
Virtual private connections to your computer through the Internet are possible only if your computer has a known name or IP address on the Internet.
If you allow VPN connections, Windows will modify the Internet Connection Firewall to allow your computer to send and receive VPN packets.
Do you want to allow virtual private connections to this computer?
Allow virtual private connections
Do not allow virtual private connections
< Back
Next >
Cancel

Figure 6-11: Be sure to select this option.

9. **Click Next.**

   User Permissions dialog box appears.

10. **Select each user who's allowed to connect to your computer, as shown in Figure 6-12.**

    The Networking Software dialog box appears.

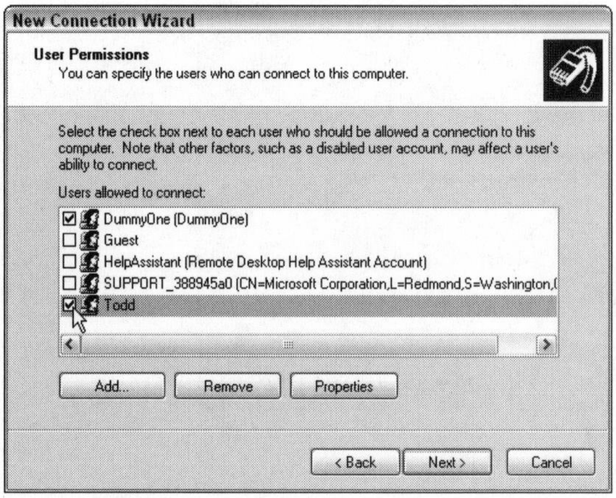

Figure 6-12: Giving users permission to connect.

11. **Select the types of networks that can connect to your computer.**

    Most importantly, make sure that Internet Protocol (TCP/IP) is selected, as shown in Figure 6-13.

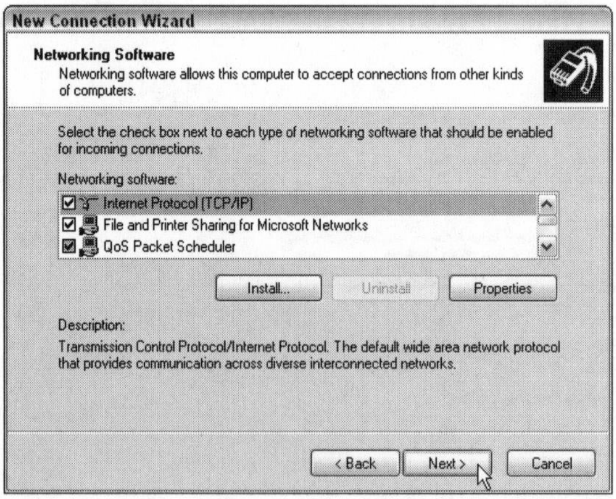

Figure 6-13: Make sure Internet Protocol (TCP/IP) is selected.

12. Click Next.

The Completing the New Connection Wizard dialog box appears.

13. Click Finish.

Your new incoming connection shows up in the Network Connections dialog box like you see in Figure 6-14. That's it: You just set up an incoming VPN connection.

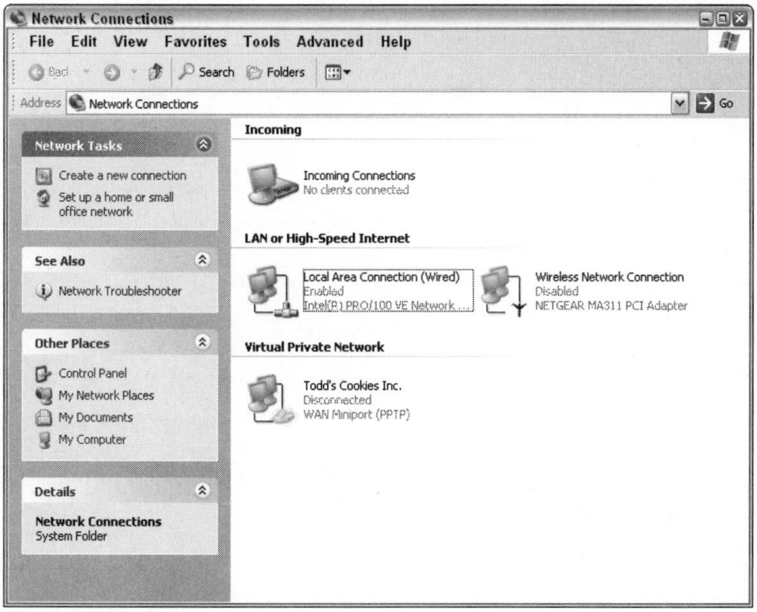

Figure 6-14: Success! The incoming connection is shown.

Chapter 7: Strapping on Microsoft SmartWatch

In This Chapter

- Watching what's on your watch
- Registering your watch with MSN Direct
- Personalizing the information you receive

Did you ever wish you could look at your watch and see something other than the time? Probably not — but the technology industry often finds a solution before you recognize a need. That brings you to Microsoft SmartWatch technology, a cool implementation of wireless technology. In this chapter I talk about Microsoft SmartWatches, which are made by several manufacturers in cooperation with Microsoft. The software giant operates the MSN Direct network which makes it possible to receive news, sports, weather, and other information on your watch.

I talk about choosing a watch, registering your watch with MSN Direct, installing software that lets you synchronize Microsoft Outlook appointments with your watch, and selecting the services that you want to receive on your watch.

Despite its coolness factor, critics exist. My main complaint is that my watch has the darndest band. Maybe I need an intravenous infusion of caffeine, but I can't figure the thing out. Others complain about the technological implementation and I'm still struggling to fit the thing on my wrist.

Picking and Choosing

Aren't you tired of technology writers hauling out the Dick Tracy metaphor whenever there's some kind of miniature gadget that fits on your wrist or in your pocket? Me, too. Despite that, it's a good comparison in this case.

Two companies — Fossil and Suuntro — sell several SmartWatch models that work with the Microsoft service. One of them is a Dick Tracy model. The small screen shows a picture of Dick (May I call him that?) talking to his watch — or at least checking the time.

Fossil makes the $199 Dick Tracy model, along with two other models for $179 each. In addition, it sells the lowest priced watch of the bunch (the Abacus) for about $110. A second company, Suunto, sells a more expensive model that comes with a $299 price tag. Any or all of these prices may change by the time you read this.

All SmartWatches have the same wireless features, which I describe in this chapter. Extras abound, though: Suunto has separate gadgetry and the Dick Tracy displays theme graphics that others don't. They all can receive the same information from MSN Direct, so choosing is really a matter of taste and budget.

TIP

The watch battery, which comes with your watch, lasts two or four days. Place the watch on its recharger for a fillup. Recharging your watch every night is a good idea and should spare you dead battery problems.

Beaming the World

The SmartWatch technology is delivered by an MSN Direct service. MSN, of course, is owned by Microsoft. It partnered with watch manufacturers to make the watches, and a slew of broadcasters across the country to deliver the FM subcarrier band that carries all the news, sports, stock quotes, weather, and lottery numbers.

That last part about forming a broadcasting network is pretty amazing, even for a corporate behemoth like Microsoft. WristNet is based on Microsoft's SPOT, or Smart Personal Objects Technology.

Microsoft installed equipment at the radio stations that enables the broadcasters to send out this data to MSN Direct subscribers. This ad hoc network covers a good portion of the country. Figure 7-1 shows how the network broadcasts news and other information to SmartWatch owners.

TIP

The spot to stop

If you're interested in gathering with other users of Smart Watches and the MSN Direct service, there's a place for you. SpotStop.com includes the latest news on the watches and forums where you can discuss everything about this new technology.

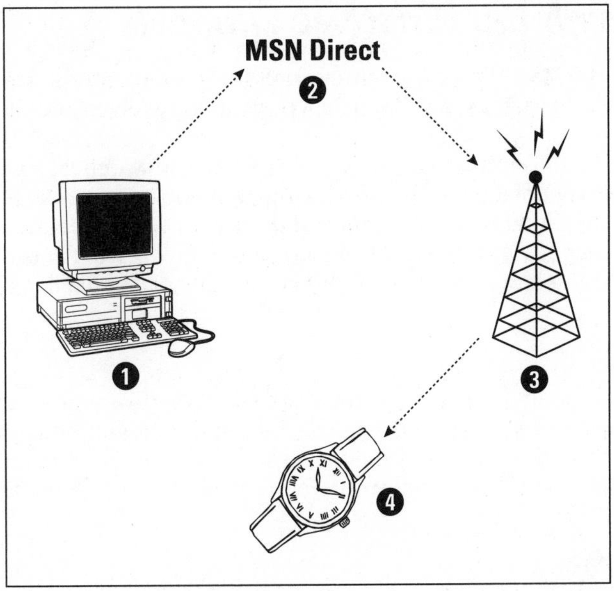

Figure 7-1: Local radio stations form the WristNet network.

But the first thing you want to do is check the coverage map. The service covers at least 100 U.S. and Canadian cities. You don't want to buy one of these watches and find out you can't receive the darn signal! You can review the coverage areas at http://direct.msn.com/about/coverage.aspx by entering your zip code.

One caveat: You need to visit MSN Direct's web site every time you plan to travel so that the service knows where you are within the broadcasting network. Otherwise, if you travel, even to another covered area, you won't receive the service's personal information: instant messages and Outlook calendar appointments. It's an odd peculiarity, as cell phones have long moved across the country with ease, checking in automatically with the cellular network.

If you do travel from one covered area to another covered area, the watch automatically adjusts its time to reflect the local time zone. And the watches are always showing the correct time when they're in a covered area because MSN Direct uses an atomic clock as its time standard.

Flipping through the WristNet Channels

By using the MSN Direct web site, which I talk about later in this chapter, you control what services, or channels, your watch receives and displays.

The time functions are obviously a big part of the watches, so they're already on by default. (Duh! right?) However, you can choose to activate a feature that sends you a different watch face now and then. If you like it, you can keep it. Otherwise, it's erased from your watch. (This, like all these services, is included in the MSN Direct monthly or annual fee.)

Calendar

The calendar requires the installation of a small software program on your PC. The software synchs up to the next six days of your Outlook appointments with your watch. When it's time for an appointment, your watch displays most of the text you originally entered in your Outlook calendar.

Horoscopes

You don't really believe in horoscopes, right? But maybe you like to read them anyway. And it's something to do while you're waiting in the grocery lane. I'm a Capricorn, which means the stars were aligned when I was born, spelling out a future as a *Dummies* author.

News

I'm a news junkie, so this is my favorite channel. Or maybe I should say channels, as news is really comprised of a number of subcategories, letting you decide the kind of information you receive. Here are your choices (and you can choose them all if you want):

- Local news based on your current location
- National stories
- International news
- Business updates, including market trends
- Entertainment headlines
- Health information
- Travel headlines and updates

One-way Instant Messaging

While MSN Direct does not have any kind of e-mail features (yet), you can receive messages another way on your SmartWatch. Someone first needs to have MSN Messenger (or third-party software that connects to MSN). Then they add you to their buddy list and can send short messages directly to your watch. "Instant" messages can take about five minutes to reach your watch. But if it was really important, wouldn't they call your cell phone?

Lottery results

You can choose which daily and weekly drawings you want to receive. I just want to be clear about one thing: If you discover from looking at your watch that you won the lottery, I'm entitled to a handsome percentage. After all, I told you about this service, right? I think 20 percent is fair. This feature only works in states that have lotteries.

Sports

The sports channel was a little slow to launch, but it's finally playing ball. ESPN provides the sports information, which includes everything from pre-game stories to score updates.

The channel includes:

- Game progress and score updates after each inning, period, or quarter of a game
- Team standings for professional sports
- Start times, television schedules (where available), and pre-game stories
- Post-game summary and final score
- Team standings and national rankings (for college teams)
- Leading scorers for basketball; pitching statistics for baseball (wins, losses, and saves)
- Top 25 ESPN rankings for college sports

Stocks

Taking stock of your financial situation doesn't stop when you leave your desk. So MSN Direct delivers quotes for market indices (like the Dow Jones Industrial Average) and individual stocks.

Weather

You can see weather information for up to ten U.S. and international cities. Of course, you can view your local weather conditions and forecasts, too. Here's the information you can tell MSN Direct to send to your watch:

- Current conditions
- Three-day forecast
- Humidity
- Barometric pressure
- Ultraviolet (UV) index
- Sunrise and sunset information

Adding Daily Diversions

Beyond all the mostly serious news and other hard information you can read on your watch, there are a few things you can receive that are mostly for your entertainment. Collectively, MSN Direct calls these Daily Diversions. The content comes from the MSN Encarta encyclopedia.

Quote of the Day

If coffee doesn't get you going in the morning, maybe glancing at an inspirational quote on your watch will.

This Day in History

I like to look at the events that occurred in history on my birthday. With this feature, you can see a list of historical events for every day.

Born on This Day

The name says it all. If it's your birthday, however, chances are your name's not on the list.

TIP

More news, please

You can change the maximum number of news stories to store at one time. The option is on the News Options menu under News and you can decide among 5, 10, 15, and 20. In the same menu you can erase all the current news and start afresh. It's like throwing away your newspaper and awaiting for more to arrive. It takes a few minutes for your watch to receive new stories.

Word of the Day

I like this feature. It helps me discover new words I can use in my books. Alas, I can't think of any right now.

Registering Your Watch

Did I tell you there's a fee for using the MSN Direct service? Well, nothing's free, but the price is manageable. It's $9.95 a month or $59 a year. If you do the math (I just did), you pay double the annual fee if you pay by the month. In any case, I think MSN Direct delivers quite a bit of information for sixty bucks (probably for even $120), but that's something for you to decide.

Before you can use your watch (other than to tell the time), you need to register it on MSN Direct's web site. It's pretty easy. Following these steps gets you registered in no time:

1. **Point your web browser to** direct.msn.com.

   The MSN Direct web page appears, as shown in Figure 7-2.

2. **Click Begin Activation.**

   Welcome to MSN Direct! page appears.

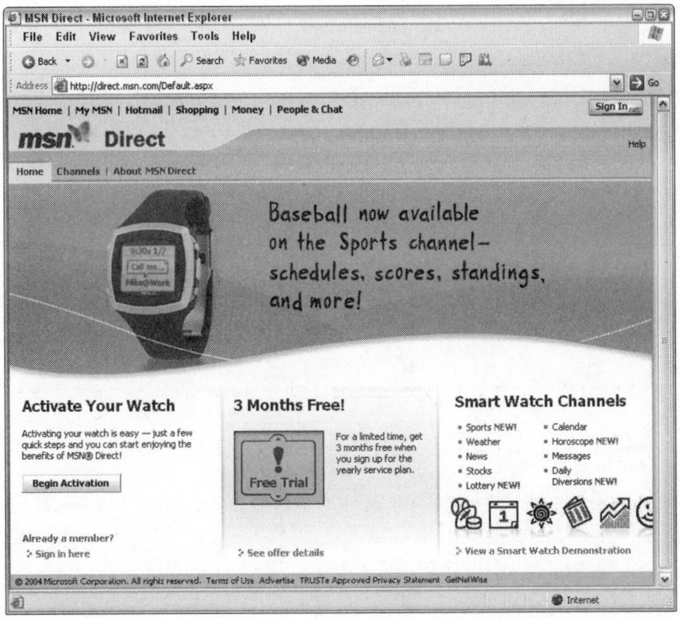

Figure 7-2: The MSN Direct web site.

3. **Click Begin Activation.**

   Yes, they make you click two "Begin Activation" buttons. A web page asks if you have a Microsoft .NET Passport.

4. **Select Yes if you have a Passport (you have one if you have an MSN or Hotmail account) and click Next.**

   If you don't have a Passport, select No and click Next. You can set one up before moving to the next step.

   The .NET Passport Sign-In screen appears.

5. **Sign into your .NET Passport.**

   A web form appears where you can enter your watch ID.

6. **Enter your 16-character ID and click Next.**

   Your watch ID is in the form of XXXX-XXXX-XXXX-XXXX. The Enter Your Location screen appears.

7. **Select your country, state, and metro area and click Next.**

   A map of your coverage area appears, as shown in Figure 7-3.

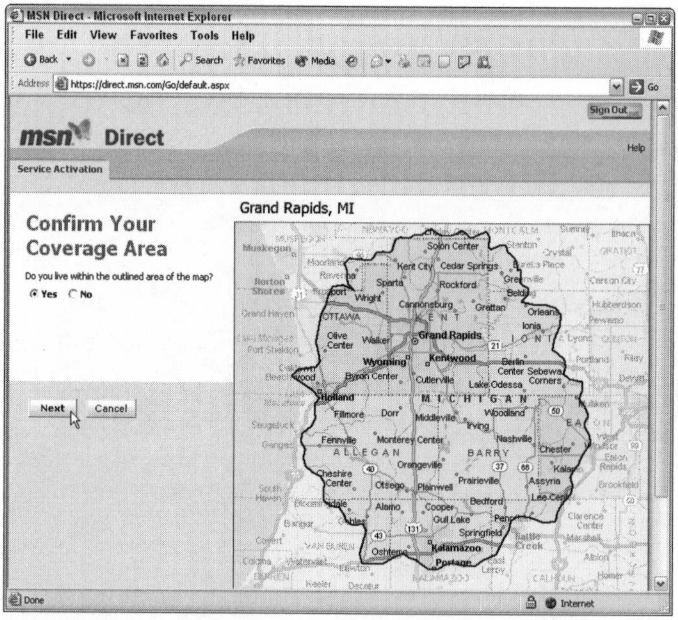

Figure 7-3: Confirming MSN Direct serves your location.

8. **Select Yes to confirm you live within the map's outline and then click Next.**

   The Choose a Service Plan screen appears.

9. **Select the annual or monthly payment plan and click Next.**

   Offer Details text appears.

10. **After reading the offer details, click Next.**

    A billing information page appears.

11. **Enter your billing information, including credit card number and billing address. Click Next.**

    A billing summary page appears.

12. **Click Next if you agree with the billing summary.**

    The Terms of Service page appears.

13. **If you agree with the terms of service, select I Accept and click Next.**

    The Done! page appears. You're finished with registration. If you want to continue and personalize your MSN Direct service, jump to the next section.

REMEMBER: Your watch receives a welcome message after you register it. The watch then continues to receive some other setup information.

Getting Personal with MSN Direct Service

Now that your watch is registered, you can choose the services you want MSN Direct to deliver directly to your wrist. Follow these steps to begin personalizing the service:

1. **From the MSN Direct home page, click Sign In if you're not already signed in.**

   A .NET Passport Sign-In page appears.

2. **Enter your Passport e-mail address and password. Click Sign In.**

   A welcome page appears.

3. **Toward the top, below the MSN Direct logo, click the Channels tab, as shown in Figure 7-4.**

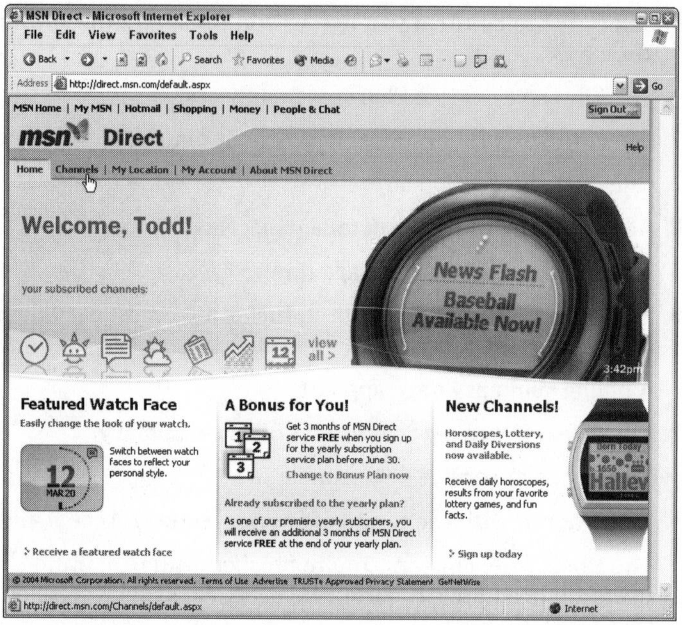

Figure 7-4: Selecting the Channels tab.

My Channels page appears, as shown in Figure 7-5.

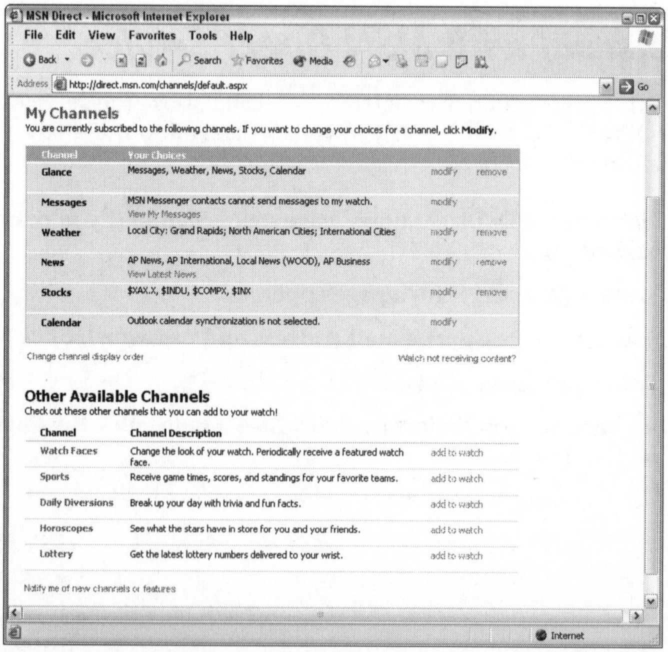

Figure 7-5: My Channels page shows subscribed channels.

4. **As an example, click Modify for the News channel.**

   The channel's default settings are displayed, as shown in Figure 7-6.

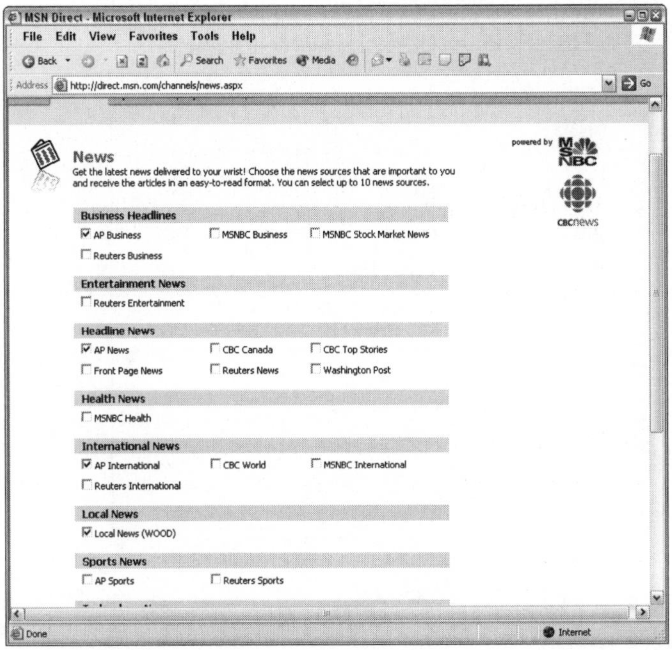

Figure 7-6: News channel displays default settings.

5. **Select or unselect additional news sources by clicking the corresponding box.**

   You can choose up to ten news sources.

6. **Click Save when you're done choosing news sources.**

   Change Confirmed page appears.

7. **Click OK.**

   You return to the My Channels page.

8. **Click a channel's Modify link to change the content you receive.**

   - Remove a channel by clicking Remove.
   - Beside Messages you can click View My Messages to see any instant messages sent to you.
   - Click View Latest News to see the news recently to your watch. On the Latest News page, you can read the short blurb sent to your watch, as well as the full story by clicking the Read Full Article link.

- Change the order channels are displayed. Click Change Channel Display Order at the bottom of the channels list. From the Channel Display Order page, as shown in Figure 7-7, click the up or down arrow to reposition a channel.
- Add other channels by clicking the Add to Watch link beside a channel listed under Other Available Channels.

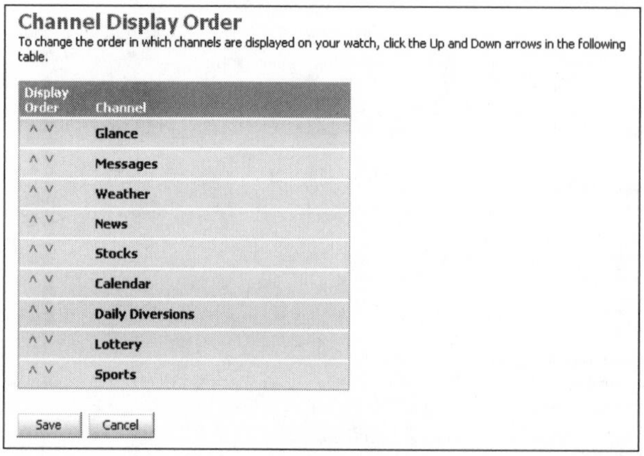

Figure 7-7: Changing the channel display order.

Installing the Outlook Software

In order for the Outlook e-mail client feature to work, you need to download a small software program that acts as the intermediary between Outlook and MSN Direct. It synchs your Outlook calendar items with your watch. That way, you can miss appointments while staring at your nifty high-tech watch.

You first need to download and install the MSN Direct Calendar Add-in for Outlook. Follow these steps:

1. **From the My Channels page, click Modify for the Calendar channel.**

   Calendar channel appears.

2. **Select the box beside Allow Outlook Calendar Synchronization with My Watch.**
3. **Click Download the MSN Direct Calendar Add-in Now.**

   A File Download dialog box appears.

4. **Click Save.**

   A Save As dialog box appears. Save the file to your Desktop or somewhere else where you can find it.

5. **Double-click the download file icon.**
6. **Follow the instructions for installing the add-in application.**

   Installation completes.
7. **Run Outlook.**

   MSN Direct Calendar dialog box appears.
8. **Enter your .NET Passport e-mail address and password. Click Sign In.**

   MSN Direct Calendar dialog box appears, as shown in Figure 7-8.

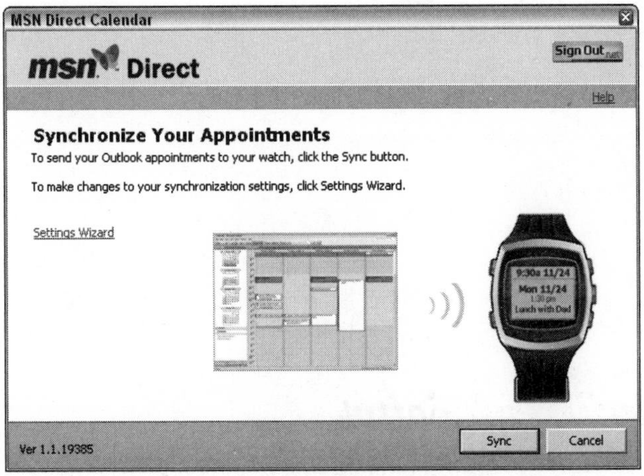

Figure 7-8: Synching your appointments with your watch.

9. **Click Sync to synchronize your Outlook calendar appointments with your watch.**

   A Sync Successful dialog box appears, listing the number of calendar changes sent to your watch.

TECHNICAL STUFF

From the MSN Direct Calendar dialog box, which you also can reach by clicking the MSN Direct icon on your Outlook toolbar, you can change settings by clicking Settings Wizard. Some of the options are listed here:

- Choose On Demand (manual) updates or Automatically (made any time a change is made to your calendar).
- Send only appointments you have created or accepted or accept all appointments.
- Select filters to exclude one or more of the following words or phrases: FW:, Tentative:, Updated:, and *Person Name* on behalf of.

Taking a Glance at This Feature

The watches also have a Glance mode, which cycles through as many of the following channels as you select. It's a cool way to see the information on your watch without pushing buttons. Still, you can press a button when you see an interesting headline and read the details. Everything has a downside, right? In this case, it's that Glance mode and its cycling through content drain the battery faster than leaving your watch on the time screen.

Book VI

Networking Technologies

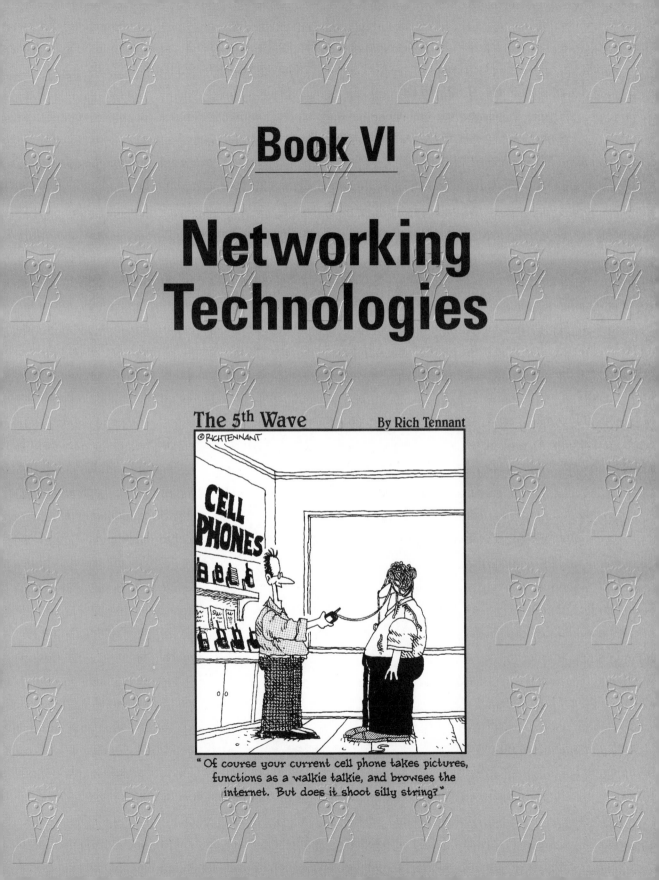

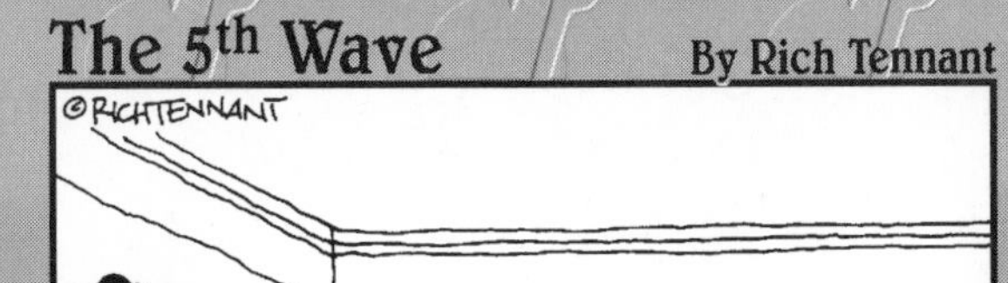

"Of course your current cell phone takes pictures, functions as a walkie talkie, and browses the internet. But does it shoot silly string?"

Contents at a Glance

Chapter 1: Roaming into Cell Phone Territory 341
Chapter 2: Choosing and Using Cordless Phones 351
Chapter 3: Gathering around the Family Radio Service 359
Chapter 4: Picking Peripherals 363
Chapter 5: Cutting Your Bluetooth 371

Chapter 1: Roaming into Cell Phone Territory

In This Chapter

- Selecting a plan
- Choosing a phone: Do I really need those fancy things?
- Health concerns
- Number portability

Does it sometimes seem as though everyone else in the whole world (except for you, of course) has a cell phone? If it seems that way, I've got some good news for you. There actually are one or two other people who don't have cell phones and they get along quite nicely, thank you. It's true that one of them is a hermit and the other one lives on an isolated desert island, but so what?

In reality, a lot of people don't have cell phones. Many reasons exist, including a lot of confusion about cell phone service plans and the multitude of available cell phone models. In this chapter you discover more about how to choose the cell phone and service plan that's right for your needs.

Selecting a Plan

The vast array of cell phone service plans seems rather astounding: prepaid plans, local plans, regional plans, nationwide plans, and who knows how many other variations on these themes? Just about the only thing that all of the different cell phone service plans seem to share is that they are carefully crafted to make it nearly impossible for you to do an accurate comparison between different plans.

Several large companies provide cell phone service throughout the country. From this, you might assume that it is easy to go to their web sites and get a listing of their servers' plans. You would be wrong to make this assumption. Rather, what you find is that the first question you are asked when you want to research service plans is your zip code. In other words, even though these are national companies, they typically don't offer the same plan to people in different areas. If you happen to live in a highly competitive market, you probably can get a much better deal on cell phone service than can someone who lives in a less competitive market.

TIP

Still, it's possible to make certain generalizations about the types of plans that might be available to you:

- Prepaid plans typically cost more per minute of air time than most other plans. Also, the minutes on prepaid plans typically expire after a certain amount of time. So, if you don't use them, you lose them.
- Some plans include hundreds or even thousands of off-peak minutes, but your definition of peak times may be considerably different than the one used by the cell phone company. It pays to check out this little detail before you get too enamored with a plan that only allows you to make cheap calls at times when you'll be waking anyone you call.
- It's important to understand exactly what the cell phone company means by *in-network* and *out-of-network* calling areas. Otherwise you may end up with a bill that is hugely inflated with roaming charges.
- Going over your allocated plan minutes can get to be very expensive. Generally, you simply lose any minutes you don't use, but you pay by the minute for extra time that you use.
- Many plans include long distance calling at no extra charge.
- In most cases any incoming calls are counted against your plan's air time. Thus you end up paying not only for calls that you make, but also calls that you receive.
- Cell phone companies typically try to lock you into a two-year service plan, but if you have very good credit they're sometimes willing to give you a one-year service plan contract. Remember, though, that there is almost always a very hefty early cancellation charge no matter how long the contract.

Because every major cell phone service provider requires your zip code before giving you a listing of the service plans they offer, it's really impossible to give you any usable advice about which plan might be best for you. Rather, it's probably best to simply give you a listing of the major national cell phone service providers so that you can check for yourself. The following list includes the most well-known national cell phone service providers at the time of this writing, but you should be aware that the industry is constantly evolving, companies are merging, and sometimes they even change their names. So, without further adieu, here are some places to begin your search:

- **Cingular Wireless** at www.cingular.com
- **Verizon Wireless** at www.verizonwireless.com
- **T-Mobile** at www.t-mobile.com
- **Sprint** at www.sprintpcs.com
- **Nextel** at www.nextel.com
- **Cellular One** at www.cellularone.com

In addition to these national cell phone service providers, you may well find smaller, local companies offering cell phone service. Obviously, you have to find them on your own.

Choosing a Phone: Do I Really Need Those Fancy Things?

In addition to choosing a service plan, you need to decide which cell phone is right for you. That's probably going to be a lot harder than you can imagine. It seems like every cell phone manufacturer is going all out to try and one up all of the other cell phone manufacturers. The trend probably started with Motorola and their flip phones, but today those phones wouldn't get a second glance from most consumers. Cell phones have become loaded down with so many features; it's amazing that some models are so tiny they seem almost impossible to use without a magnifying glass.

Take a look at some of the features of cell phones so you can get a better idea what to look for when you go shopping. Oh, by the way: Don't forget that your cell phone service provider is almost certainly the best place to buy your cell phone because they typically subsidize the selling price of most units.

TIP

When you sign up for cell phone service, be sure to ask if your provider offers free replacement phones every year or two. Because cell phones pack so much into such a small package, they really start showing their age in a fairly short period of time. In addition, after a couple of years you'll probably be lusting after one of the newer, fancier models that will no doubt be released almost immediately after you get your cell phone.

Size

Believe it or not, it is possible for a cell phone to be too small. If you can't read the display without putting on reading glasses or if the keypad is so small that you have trouble dialing phone numbers, you probably aren't going to have too much fun trying to use a minuscule cell phone.

One way around the problem of too-small cell phones is to go for a *flip phone.* These units have a hinge in the middle so you can open them up when you want to use them, and still fold them into the tiny size that fits into your pocket.

Talk time

When it comes to a cell phone, nothing is more frustrating than having your battery die in the middle of conversation. A number of factors determine how much talk time you can get from your cell phone. Certainly features like color displays and built-in cameras drastically reduce your talk time, but the two main factors that seem to make the biggest difference are the battery capacity and the type of signal your cell phone is using.

The cellular network typically offers two primary types of signals. The older analog signals couldn't accommodate nearly as many cell phone calls from a single tower as the newer digital signals do. The biggest difference between these two types of signals as far as most cell phone users are concerned is that their cell phone battery provides much greater talk time using a digital signal rather than an analog signal.

Many cell phone models have user-replaceable batteries, and in some cases offer the option of a higher capacity battery. It's usually a good idea to at least consider getting a spare battery so you can continue talking when your primary battery runs down.

Cameras

Probably one of the hottest trends in the cell phone industry in the past few years has been the addition of built-in cameras. The first camera phones were probably more of a novelty than anything else, due to their low resolution and poor picture quality. The newer models, however, offer much better picture quality.

People use picture phones for many different and interesting purposes. A real estate agent might use one to send a quick image of a hot new property he's just listed to a potential client. Insurance adjusters use them to send in an image so that someone in their office can help determine the value of a loss. Someone who is on vacation might send back a photo of her beachfront resort in order to make everyone back at the office jealous.

As handy as picture phones are, they're not welcome everywhere. Many health clubs now ban them, and anyone who works in a facility where any type of confidential research is being performed probably won't find themselves very welcome when they whip out their picture phone. Needless to say, picture phones aren't for everyone.

One thing that you may want to keep in mind if you do get a picture phone: Unless the person on the other end of the line also has a picture phone, you can't exchange photos. Oh sure, you could e-mail the photo, but that seems a little lame compared to seeing the image live on your phone.

Headsets

Many areas now ban the use of cell phones while you are driving unless you're using a hands-free option. This certainly makes a lot of sense because it's awfully scary watching someone carry on a highly animated cell phone conversation while they're speeding down the highway driving a two-ton automobile.

Cell phone service providers also understand how dangerous it can be to engage in a phone call using a handheld cell phone while you are driving. Because of this, many cell phone providers throw in a hands-free headset when you buy a new phone and sign up for service. Even if they don't, you should consider a headset to be absolutely essential and buy one yourself — your safety and that of everyone else on the road around you depends on it!

Games

Okay, so I may not be the best judge of this, but I really can't see how playing games on the tiny screen on a cell phone could be much fun. But hey, if that's your thing, don't let me stop you. (Just don't try it while you're driving, okay?)

Web enabled

It's not very likely that anyone would say that the limited screen area on a cell phone is ideal for surfing the Net, but there certainly are times when being able to access the Internet from your web-enabled cell phone might come in handy:

- You're stuck in a traffic jam that hasn't moved for 15 minutes. Accessing the Highway Department's traffic report web site might enable you to figure out how long you're going to be stuck and if there's an alternative route you should consider.
- You've just arrived in a strange town late in the afternoon on business and discovered that an important client wants to meet with you immediately. A quick check of your favorite restaurant review site would help you choose an appropriate place to invite the client for dinner.
- On a whim you've just stopped at a garage sale where the elderly owner has several paintings stacked next to a table. You think they might be valuable, but you'd like to be sure before you make an offer. A web search on your web-enabled cell phone could help you determine a reasonable price and avoid running home and giving someone else a shot at the artwork.
- You've set out on a hike but around mid-morning some heavy-looking clouds seem to be popping up. The weather service web site tells you that an unexpected storm is developing and you'd be wise to cut your hike short.

TIP

Many web-enabled cell phones allow you to download *ringtones* to replace the standard ring. One site where you find free ringtones for download is Free Ringtones Galore (www.ringtonesgalore.co.uk/).

Messaging

When is a cell phone not exactly a cell phone? When it's a messaging device, of course. That is, cell phones are often used to send and receive text messages as well as other types of messages. The cell phone industry even has fancy names for such messages:

- **SMS:** Short messaging service
- **MMS:** Multimedia messaging service

Basically, the two types of messaging services are similar in that they allow you to send messages that are not voice messages. SMS messages are text only, while MMS messages can include still images, video, or even audio clips.

Several factors determine if you can use either or both of these types of messaging with your cell phone. These include the capabilities built into your cell phone as well as if your cell phone service provider offers messaging services. In some cases, the messaging services are included in your standard service plan, but in others you may find that you pay an extra charge for each message. It pays to know what is included in your plan.

Staying Healthy

Cell phones use two-way radios to send and receive your telephone calls. These radios operate at a fairly high frequency and many studies have shown that concentrated radio waves can be harmful to human health. The question is, are you in danger when you use a cell phone? I don't pretend to have the answer to that one. Instead, I refer you to the web site shown in Figure 1-1. This site (www.fda.gov/cellphones) is the Food and Drug Administration's official site dealing with the safety of cell phones.

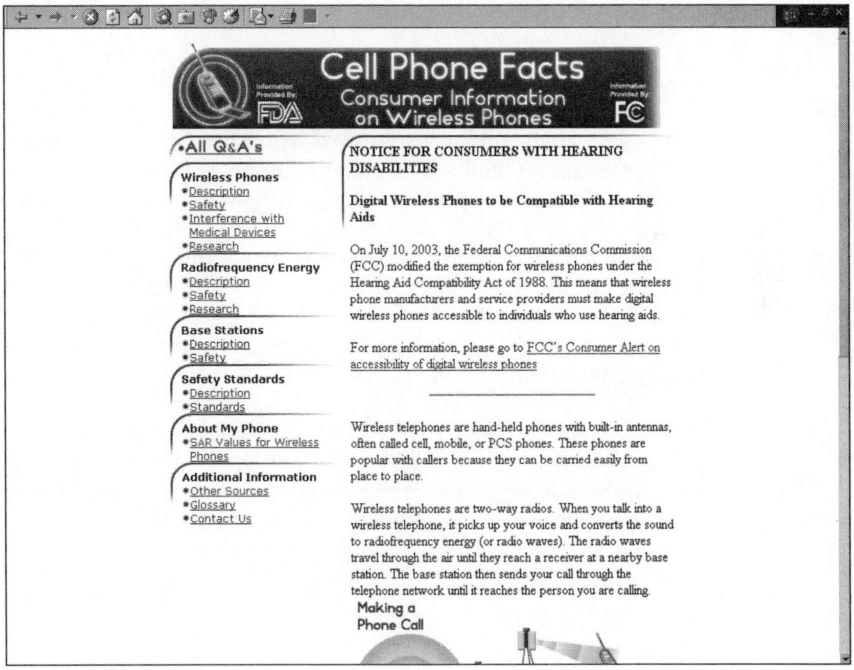

Figure 1-1: The FDA offers this consumer information site dealing with the safety of cell phones.

Personally, I'd just as soon have those radio waves as far away from my head as possible. That's another good argument in favor of using a headset with your cell phone.

Putting Your Number on the Move

In years past, your cell phone's telephone number was completely under the control of the cell phone service provider. If you changed to a new provider, you ended up with a new telephone number. This was quite a hassle, so lots of people stuck with a cell phone service provider they didn't like simply because they didn't want to lose the phone number they had been using and that everyone knew.

In late 2003 the Federal Communications Commission (FCC) agreed upon a regulation that enabled people to keep the same phone number when they switched carriers. This regulation also made it possible for people to eliminate their regular landline phone and switch their phone number to a cell phone. This made it possible for people to have a cell phone as their only telephone.

Figure 1-2 shows the FCC web site (www.fcc.gov/cgb/NumberPortability/), which explains how number portability works. As you would expect with almost any government program, the number-portability program does have some unexpected kinks. For example, many cell phone service providers charge a monthly fee to "cover the costs of the number portability program." In addition, carriers can also charge a fee to transfer your phone number to a new carrier even if you've been paying a monthly fee for this. It's important to note that these fees are not government mandated nor are they taxes that the cell phone service provider pays to the government. They are, plain and simple, just another method that cell phone service providers use to extract money from their customers.

It can take several days to transfer your phone number from a landline phone to a cell phone. The process should only take a few hours going from one cell phone to another cell phone, but some carriers may attempt to drag out the process in order to convince you not to switch. Regardless, you should be aware that your telephone number may be out of service for a period of time during the transition.

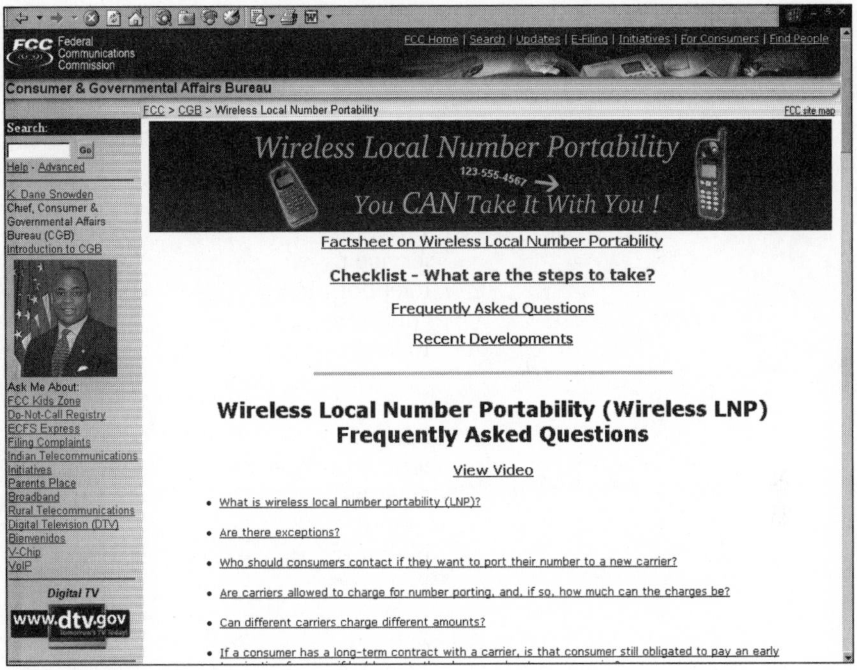

Figure 1-2: The FCC provides this information site to answer your questions about number portability.

Chapter 2: Choosing and Using Cordless Phones

In This Chapter

- **Distinguishing the difference between analog and digital**
- **Selecting your hertz: 900, 2.4, or 5.8**
- **Getting someone to speak up (or move things out of the way)**

It's bad enough that buying a cellular phone and wireless networking equipment is so complicated. Now, with new options for cordless phones, even that once straightforward purchase is forcing you to reach for the aspirin. Consider me the aspirin — and you don't even have to call me in the morning. In this chapter I discuss the different kinds of cordless phones, the advantages of one over the other, and a technology term or two.

Cutting the Cords

If you're over 35, you probably remember the days when one of the only telephones in the house was a corded model mounted on the wall. The only way to increase your distance from the phone was to purchase a longer cord. While it might be possible, wrestling with a 300-foot cord so you can chat as you garden is a bit impractical.

Around 1990, when the FCC assigned bandwidth in the 900 MHz frequency range, cordless phones first became a real alternative to corded telephones. The newer frequencies were a big jump in clarity and range from the old 43–49 MHz band.

As manufacturers began making digital models, cordless phones grew even more practical; they were more secure (less eavesdropping) than analog versions. Also, more channels are available for use by the cordless phone to communicate between the base station and handset, which means less interference:

- 10 to 25 channels for inexpensive 900-MHz phones.
- 20 to 60 channels for most 900-MHz phones.
- 50 to 100 channels for high-end 900 MHz phones and for 2.4- and 5.8-GHz phones.

Table 2-1 breaks down the megahertz and gigahertz by range.

Table 2-1 Cordless Phone Ranges

Frequency Band	*Range*
900 MHz	75 to 400 feet
900 MHz with DSS	200 to 1,500 feet
2.4 GHz with DSS	300 to 2,000 feet
5.8 GHz with DSS	300 to 2,000 feet

Analog phones

Analog cordless phones act like a plain, old AM/FM radio. They convert sounds waves into radio waves, transmitting them between the cordless phone and its base station. Anyone with a converter and a radio scanner can eavesdrop. (Selling police and fire radio scanners that pick up 900-MHz transmissions is illegal; 2.4-GHz and 5.8-GHz phones are out of range of most radio scanners.)

What is this DSS?

Many new cordless phones — and I recommend making sure this is true of the one you purchase next — use a technology called *DSS,* or *digital spread spectrum.* The *digital* part of DSS means your conversation is converted from analog sound waves to digital 1s and 0s. (You can buy a digital phone that does not use DSS, however.) The *spread spectrum* part is less clear, though I figure it has something to do with the radio spectrum. This technical term is vague until you discover what it is, how it works, and why you want it.

First, why you want it: DSS-equipped phones are much more secure than analog and plain digital phones. In fact, it's nearly impossible to listen to a conversation taking place on a DSS phone because the listener only hears quick bursts of data that transmit very quickly across multiple frequencies. Imagine that your favorite AM radio talk show uses spread spectrum: You would need to change among multiple stations many times a second to keep up with the broadcast. Everything happens so fast that it's impossible to follow conversations sent with DSS unless you have the right equipment. You can feel pretty confident that the credit card information you reveal during a telephone call on this phone is safe.

Second, phones using DSS suffer from less interference. Depending on different factors, they may also have a greater range than similar phones that don't use DSS technology. In addition to being more secure, DSS is a more efficient use of the radio spectrum.

A DSS phone may also be referred to by *frequency hopping spread spectrum* or *FHSS.*

When you and an analog handset get too far from the base station, you hear static over the conversation until you can no longer communicate with the base station. These phones also are prone to static from interference. Figure 2-1 shows analog versus digital communications methods.

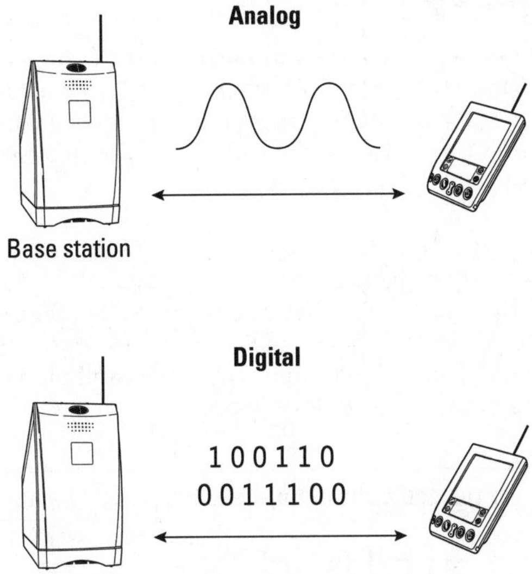

Figure 2-1: Analog and digital phones work differently.

Digital phones

Digital phones convert sound waves into digital signals, which consist of a lot of 1s and 0s. If you tune into a conversation transmitted digitally, you can't hear it without using equipment that converts the output into something humans can understand. When you go out of range with a digital phone, the conversation simply ends with dead air. Digital phones offer no gray area between a good signal and a lousy signal. Their existence shows up on the timelines in Figure 2-2.

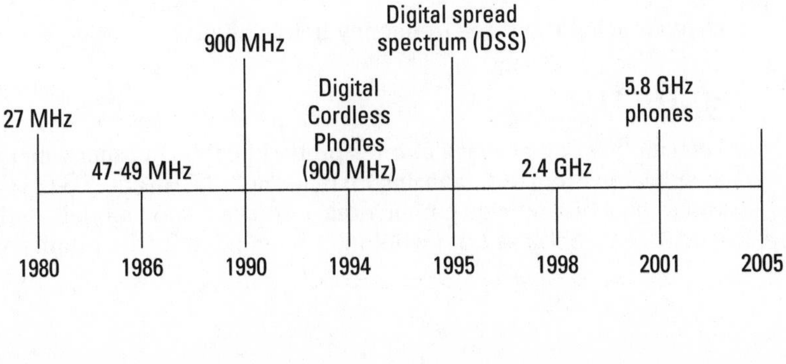

Figure 2-2: A timeline of cordless phone frequency band use.

Some digital phones use something called *digital spread spectrum (DSS)*. See the "What is this DSS?" sidebar in this chapter for further information. Not all digital phones have DSS, but all DSS phones are digital.

Choosing Your Frequency

Can you imagine if when purchasing a cell phone and a calling plan, you had to tell the company what technology you want to use? Of course, you have some choices when it comes to handsets and choosing a particular carrier for its network. You don't have to tell the cell phone provider at what frequency you want the phone to operate.

You must do exactly that when choosing a cordless phone for your home or office. When shopping for cordless phones, you choose the frequency and sometimes whether the radio signals are analog or digital. Shopping for the phones in a store does little to narrow your decision-making, other than deciding on the look and feel of the phone. Table 2-2 can help you start your comparison shopping before you set foot in a store.

Table 2-2 Pros and Cons of Cordless Frequency Bands

Band	*Pros*	*Cons*
900 MHz	Cheap, won't interfere with Wi-Fi	Usually little or no security
2.4 GHz	Price is right, can be secure	Possible conflicts with Wi-Fi
5.8 GHz	Clear, likely more secure	More expensive

You have an array of choices when purchasing a cordless phone. The important option is the frequency band on which the phones operates. Cordless phones are available in 900-MHz, 2.4-GHz, and 5.8-GHz models. Generally, as the frequency goes higher, so does the maximum distance you can take the handset from the base station. Conversation clarity also improves as you venture into higher-frequency bands. This assumes no interference from other sources of radio waves, physical structures like walls, and the weather.

Here are what the three frequency bands offer.

900 MHz

You can buy one of these phones pretty cheaply, but many manufacturers are phasing them out, favoring instead the 2.4-GHz and 5.8-GHz models. If you're on a budget, you can buy one of these analog models for less than you paid for this book — but I wouldn't recommend it (the phone, not the book).

Why? The prices of 2.4-GHz phones are very reasonable and cover a larger area with less likelihood of interference. Also, with the use of a simple converter gizmo, it's very easy for someone to overhear your conversations on a 900-MHz phone using a radio scanner.

You can expect to pay about $20 for a basic analog phone and up to $50 for one that uses DSS technology.

2.4 GHz

Quality and price meet here. This is the sweet spot for cordless phones; most of them made today operate in this frequency range. They offer more clarity and range than you get with a 900-MHz phone.

Given the number of 2.4-GHz models, you can find them in a wide variety of configurations, choosing the features you want and not paying for ones you don't need. You can buy 2.4-GHz phones in analog and digital models. These phones are also available in multiple-handset models, which let you add more handsets as you need them. Some models let you have as many as eight — seemingly enough for every room of your house. While the additional phones need a nearby AC outlet, they don't each need a phone jack.

The downside? Phones operating in the 2.4-GHz range have a good chance of interfering with your Wi-Fi (802.11b and 802.11g, but not 802.11a) network.

5.8 GHz

You see more and more models using this frequency band. At first, there were few and the price tags were high. These phones have an exceptionally notable advantage over the other two kinds of phones: The 5.8-GHz band is less populated. Along with an increase in clarity and distance, cordless phones using this frequency are the perfect fit for a home that has a Wi-Fi network and other interference on the 2.4-GHz band.

It seems that manufacturers have focused first on 5.8-GHz phones loaded with a number of features, including the ability to add multiple handsets, rather than cheaper models with fewer features.

Featuring Cordless Phones

If the confusion over frequencies isn't bad enough, you have to decide between a myriad of features when shopping for a cordless phone. From caller ID displays to multiple-handset models, you have much to discover before plopping down your greenbacks.

You find some of the features on cordless phones:

- **Caller ID.** If you subscribe to caller ID service through your local phone company, this feature is a must. If the phone's not enabled for caller ID, subscribing doesn't make any difference. When you get an incoming call, the caller's phone number and possibly the name (if you pay for this service) appears on the handset's display.
- **Call waiting ID.** I hate call waiting. I think it's partly responsible for the decline of western civilization — but there you have it: Most people seem to love it. (Hi, mom!) Nonetheless, call waiting ID is a cool feature. While you're on the phone with someone else, you can see who is trying to reach you. If you want to take the new call, you select it — and hopefully not before you tell the current caller bye bye.
- **Answering machine.** I thought everyone who needs to record calls signed up for call waiting through their phone company. I guess not. Long gone are the days of cassette tapes; the answering machines built into these phones are digital, which have far less recording capacity. One benefit is that long-winded callers have fewer seconds to leave their messages, sparing you some rambling.
- **Multiple handsets.** You can do several things with these phones:
  - Add up to eight handsets (depending on the model) for use throughout your home.
  - Answer a call using any one of the phones.
  - Transfer a call to and from a handset.
  - Page a handset, making the setup similar to an intercom system.
  - Plug each handset's cradle into a power outlet; they don't require separate phone jacks.
- **Two-line phones.** These models can handle multiple phone lines so you can answer an incoming call from either line. If you have a second line in your home, consider this feature.
- **Speakerphone.** This feature is always handy, especially when stuck on hold with a credit card company or other sadistic entity. You can push the appropriate button and leave the handset in its cradle, using the speakerphone located in the base station. The sound quality varies, so consider it in person, while shopping. Some cordless phone handsets also have a speakerphone feature.

Avoiding Interference

As I mentioned earlier, if you have a Wi-Fi network in your house, I don't recommend the purchase of a 2.4-GHz cordless phone. If your household is constantly using a baby monitor, that could be a problem, too. Even microwave ovens, which operate on the same frequency, can create problems. If your analog phone has interference, you hear it as static and hisses. A digital phone will probably fade in and out or have a shorter range.

TIP

The best way to eliminate or reduce these kinds of interference problems is to move the phone's base station around the house, seeing if a different location makes any difference. If you already have a Wi-Fi network and purchased a 2.4-GHz phone without reading my wise admonitions beforehand, you still have hope. Just turn off the network when you're using the phone and vice versa. However, you may find the two coexist peacefully.

Chapter 3: Gathering around the Family Radio Service

In This Chapter

- Using Family Radio Service radios
- Improving communications at Disney World
- Increasing your range with GMRS radios

You've probably seen those cute little Family Radio Service radios in the electronics aisle, packaged in a tiny pair and priced right. They're *two-way radios* (ones that both transmit and receive) that operate on bandwidth set aside for the *Family Radio Service (FRS).*

These radios are basically walkie talkies with 14 channels. Press a button when you want to talk and let it go when you want to listen. Some of the radios are so small — the size of a lighter — that they might get lost in your pocket. You don't need a license to use them and they come in very handy at places like huge amusement parks. FRS radios are like a short-range version of the CB radios that took off in the late 1970s (as if the whole CB radio craze wasn't painful enough, with the country music industry producing more dreary songs).

Calling All Radios

In a generous moment in 1996, the FCC created FRS and put aside a set of frequencies for this new service aimed specifically at — you guessed it — families. Small businesses can use FRS radios to conduct business.

Mind your manners: Though you don't need a license, the FCC can revoke your right to use the FRS band.

This option is great if you don't want a radio weighing you down. With prices in the $20 range for a pair, they're much cheaper than communicating with a cell phone that you may end up losing.

The radios broadcast on something called *narrowband FM* (that's for the propeller heads) and their power is limited to 0.5 watt. That's enough, if all conditions are right, to transmit up to two miles. You should count on something less, though. They're usually best when everyone with a radio is within a half mile or so of each other.

Some models are capable of transmitting and receiving on both the FMS band and another area of radio spectrum set aside for GMRS bands. (You need a license from the FCC to operate a General Mobile Radio Service [GMRS] radio. I discuss that in this chapter's "Distancing Yourself with GMRS" section.)

FMS according to the FCC

You share FMS channels with others, so don't monopolize a channel with a lengthy soliloquy. If someone announces that she has an emergency, you must get off the channel so she can communicate.

In its rules, the FCC details the proper uses of FRS radios. Feel free to do this stuff:

- Call another person to establish communications.
- Send an emergency message. This means someone's life is in jeopardy, not that Kohl's is having a half-off sale on tennis shoes.
- Make a voice page.

The FRS is part of America's Citizens Band Radio Services. The radios operate on a band of radio spectrum that stretches from 462.5625 MHz to 467.7125 MHz. FMS is covered in Part 95.191-95.194 of the federal Code of Federal Regulations (CFR). If you're a real wireless geek, you can read more about the service on the Federal Communications Commission's web site at wireless.fcc.gov/services/personal/family/.

Keeping the family unit intact

I think Disney World in Orlando, Florida, has the largest concentration of FMS radios in use. I've never heard more radios in use than when I was there. For good reason. FRS radios are good at keeping your family or other group in contact at amusement parks and other large, populated places (or large, unpopulated places, like a national forest).

Why not use a cell phone to do the same? I anticipated that question and created this list of why FRS radios are better:

- **No cell phone roaming charges**. If you've ever ventured outside your calling area, you know how much these charges are and how fast they accumulate.

- **Costs less than a cell phone and no service fees**. Uncle Sam welcomes your free use of FMS frequencies.
- **Less valuable than a cell phone**. I'd rather lose an FMS radio than my cell phone. Aside from the charges that result if the finder makes unauthorized calls, you probably have names and numbers stored on your phone. You might not have a backup and the time it takes to reenter the information is time you could be doing something else (like standing in line at Space Mountain).
- **One pair costs as much as one cell phone**. Unless you're planning on talking to yourself, you need at least two cell phones. FMS radios are usually sold in pairs, so you're ready to go out of the box.
- **No worries about coverage area**. While you know how fickle cell phones are in a partially served area, FMS radios work just about anywhere. In fact, it's national parks and other out-of-the-way places where reliable communications are most important.

Distancing Yourself with GMRS

General Mobile Radio Service (GMRS) is FRS' big brother. While you don't need a license to operate FMS radios, you do need one to use a GMRS radio, which is part of the land-mobile radio service. You submit an application to the FCC and, if you pay your taxes and vote Republican, you're issued a five-year license. (I'm kidding about the taxes part.)

Everyone in your family can use the radio too, even though the license is under your name. The FCC is very generous with the definition of *family,* including in it spouse, children, parents, grandparents, aunts, uncles, nephews, nieces, and in-laws. That just about covers everyone.

In exchange for the hassle of applying for the license, you get greatly expanded range. Instead of FMS' two miles, your GMRS range increases to up to five miles. Table 3-1 compares the two further.

Table 3-1 Comparing FRS and GMRS

	FRS	*GMRS*
Range	2 miles	5 miles
Power	0.5 watt	1–5 watts
License?	No	Yes
License fee	$0	$75 for 5 years

I know where you are!

What happens if you combine an FRS/GMRS radio with a global positioning service (GPS) receiver? Now you can talk with someone *and* track his whereabouts.

The Rino models (from GPS receiver maker Garmin), shown in the accompanying figure, track you with the GPS component, sending your location to the other radios in your party. At the same time, you can see on a map display where your partners are. It's really a cool way to combine two wireless technologies.

The radio uses the FRS band to transmit your exact location to another Rino user who is within two miles. When you want to talk to each other, the radios use GMRS for a five-mile range. You can read more about GPS in Book VIII.

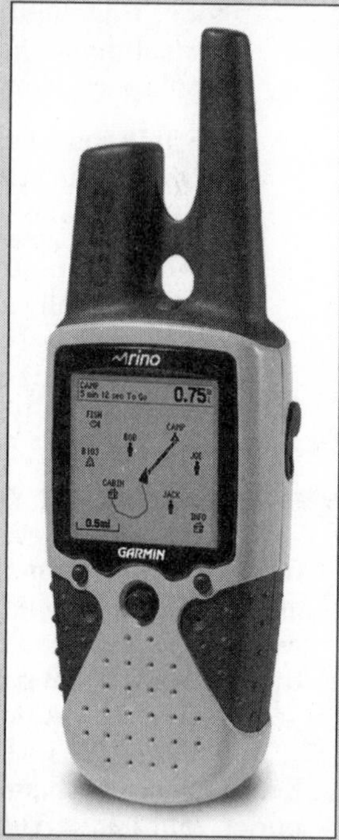

Garmin's Rino combines GPS with FRS/GMRS.

You can apply online for a license through the FCC's web site or fill in Form 605 and mail it. You can read more about the licensing process at http://wireless.fcc.gov/services/personal/generalmobile/.

GMRS radios operate in the 462-MHz to 467-MHz band and usually transmit with 1 to 5 watts of power. The old name for the GMRS service was Class A of the Citizens Radio Service. Rules governing the service's use are in CFR Part 95.1-95.181. More information about GMRS is available on the FCC's web site.

Chapter 4: Picking Peripherals

In This Chapter

- Cleaning off your desk
- Choosing wireless peripherals

You may be focusing on Wi-Fi and Bluetooth networks and forgetting some of the more peripheral uses of wireless technology. In this chapter, namely, I'm referring to peripherals for your computers.

A *peripheral* is really anything that's not included as part of your desktop or laptop computer. This includes keyboards, mice, trackballs, and game controllers. (It also includes printers, but they're covered in Book III, Chapter 4.) While these all once were tethered to your PC via wires, more and more of them are sold in cordless versions. In this chapter I highlight a few of the cordless peripherals you can buy.

Unplugging Your Desktop

Logitech, one of the largest manufacturers of cordless mice and keyboards, recently boasted that it shipped more than 50 million cordless peripherals worldwide, including keyboards, mice, and trackballs.

You may see peripherals called *cordless* or *wireless.* I guess I like wireless because this book isn't called *Cordless All-in-One Desk Reference For Dummies.* It's a good thing, too, as I picture a cordless phone disguised as a *Dummies* book. I'd love the looks — I'll gladly take a black-and-yellow phone any day — but holding a book to my head for an hour could be tiring.

Of course, cordless peripherals still come with cords. The base stations usually plug into a USB port (found on the back or front of your computer) on your computer and then sit somewhere on your desk — but probably out of the way and out of sight. Lucky you, though: No wires get between your mouse/keyboard and your PC.

Seems logical

Logitech introduced the first radio-frequency cordless mouse in 1991 and the first cordless keyboard-and-mouse combination in 1998. Logitech cites a study showing that 8 out of 10 US consumers know about cordless peripherals.

It's a sizeable market, with Logitech estimating that retail sales of cordless mice and keyboards total $230 million a year. That's a growth rate of nearly 50 percent. It seems I'm not the only one cutting the cords and opting for a wireless desk.

One of the most irritating things — and I have a long list of irritating things, which I'll save for when I write a self-help tome — about a regular, corded mouse is that the wire gets hung up on something on your desk or you want to move the mouse and get stuck because of the short cord. You know how Tony the Tiger sounds when he gets his favorite cereal? Well, add some bravado and a little more testosterone, and you might imagine the growl I make when I'm at the end of my cord.

Just thinking about this gets me upset. In fact, I may not be able to continue writing this book. *Long pause.* Alas, my accountant again says I must continue.

Cordless Mice in Seattle

Actually, Microsoft is located in nearby Redmond. The headline is clever, though, don't you think? Microsoft and Logitech are two of the largest makers of cordless mice. Various other companies manufacture similar cordless peripherals, including game controllers, which are described later in this chapter.

Microsoft mice

Both the IntelliMouse Explorer and Optical Mouse (www.microsoft.com/hardware) work up to six feet from their base stations. They operate on the 27-MHz band, which is the same frequency on which some of the original cell phones operated. This band has four available channels for wireless peripherals. Two are set aside for wireless mice and two are slated for wireless keyboards.

Bluetooth peripherals work similarly to the cordless mice and keyboards I mention in this chapter, although the maximum distance between peripheral and base station is higher. A regular wireless mouse or keyboard can work several feet from its base station; the same peripherals using Bluetooth can communicate up to about 30 feet away. A Bluetooth base station also can simultaneously interact with several devices, including appropriately equipped cell phones and handheld computers. I discuss mice and keyboards that use Bluetooth wireless technology in Book VI, Chapter 5.

IntelliMouse Explorer

The mouse in Figure 4-1 is the one I use day in and day out. I love it, except for the annoyance of swapping rechargeable batteries every couple weeks. (It uses regular batteries, too.) Microsoft advertises longer battery life, so maybe the problem I'm having with frequent battery changes is solved. Supposedly, these new models have a battery life of up to six months.

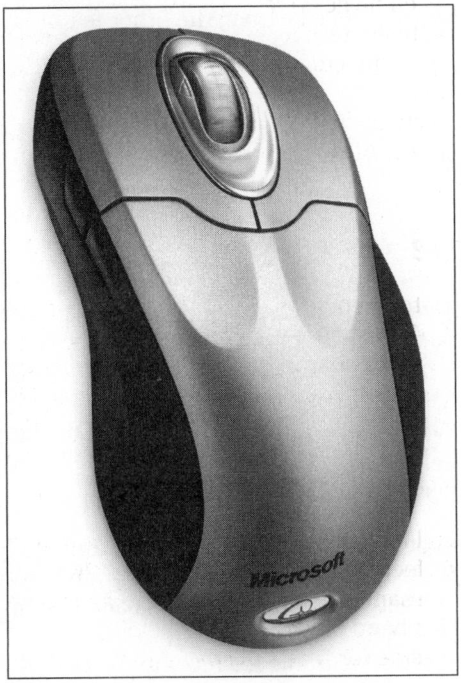

Figure 4-1: Microsoft's wireless IntelliMouse Explorer.

I like this mouse because it's made for surfing the Web. It has two small buttons on the left side that let me go forward and backward when using my Web browser. Of course, it has the two regular mouse buttons, as well as a small wheel that makes it easy to scroll pages. It's an optical mouse, so no ball in the bottom is attracting gunk that slows down its movements.

The newest models now have something called Tilt Wheel Technology. You can move the mouse wheel left and right, as well as rotate it back and forth for up and down movements. The actual retail price is as low as $40.

Cut the cord and consider this mouse.

Optical Mouse

The Optical Mouse is basically the same as the IntelliMouse Explorer, but without the front and back buttons for controlling a Web browser. It costs only a little less than the other mouse, so I'm not sure of the advantages of picking this one. The street price is around $35. For five more bucks, you can get the Web browser controls while keeping the other features.

Logitech mice

Logitech has a range of wireless mice — many more than Microsoft. You can order them online at www.logitech.com.

MX 700 Cordless Optical Mouse

The MX 700 seems to be the granddaddy of Logitech's non-Bluetooth wireless mice. The company says this model uses what it calls Fast RF cordless technology to give the same response as a corded mouse. The MX 700 is shown in Figure 4-2.

It has buttons galore (wasn't that a James Bond movie?), including some similar to those on the Microsoft IntelliMouse Explorer for moving back and forward through Web pages.

In addition, it has Cruise Control buttons for scrolling through long Web pages and documents. It also has a Quick Switch Program Selector button that lets you switch views between active programs and documents.

The base station also serves as a cradle for recharging the MX 700, which has a street price ranging from $45 to $65.

Figure 4-2: The Logitech MX 700 Cordless Optical Mouse.

Cordless Optical Mouse for Notebooks

A basic cordless mouse, the Optical Mouse for Notebooks is small so you can easily take it with your laptop on the road. You plug a transmitter into your laptop's USB port to use this mouse, which communicates with the transmitter, eliminating the larger base stations found on other cordless mice. You can buy this for about $35.

Cordless Presenter

It's not chiefly used as a mouse, but Logitech's Presenter is wireless. It's designed to give you remote control of a presentation from just about anywhere in the room. It includes a built-in laser pointer and also functions as a two-button optical mouse.

It's not cheap: Its street price is, the $175 range. If you need one of these, you probably have an expense account anyhow.

Trackballs

I'm no expert, but I'd say *trackballs* are a niche market. If you haven't seen one, it's basically a mouse with the ball on the top rather than the bottom. The unit stays in place as you move the ball (and hence, the onscreen pointer) with your fingers.

Trackballs are good for precision work (graphical work) and games. However, if you don't know if you need one, you probably don't. Go ahead and buy one; see if I care.

Logitech has two wireless trackballs. One is the Cordless Optical TrackMan and the other is the Cordless TrackMan Wheel. The Optical TrackMan is the fancier of the two and costs about $50 on the street. The TrackMan Wheel has a street price of about $40. Both models have lots of buttons. The TrackMan Wheel has its ball on the left side instead of on top. You use your thumb to operate the ball, rather than your fingers.

Finding the Home Row: Keyboards

You also can find keyboards that are wireless. Want to know more? Read on!

Microsoft wireless keyboards

Microsoft sells wireless keyboards and mice as a set. It offers about five sets; a sixth one is Bluetooth enabled. The sets have different features depending on the price tags. They range from a basic set to an elite set.

One of the keyboard sets comes in an ergonomic model, which I prefer and use every day. If you don't know what *ergonomic* means, you probably have seen one of the keyboards anyway: The keys are split into two groups, positioned at angles that more closely mimic the normal angles of your wrists. They cut down on injuries to your wrist.

Logitech wireless keyboards

You can get a wireless keyboard from Logitech for about $30. It's called the Cordless Access Keyboard and you can see it in Figure 4-3. It's like a normal keyboard but comes with enhanced function keys. (Those are the ones that start with F1 and go to F12.) It also has some keys for controlling multimedia files. One of the wireless keyboard/mouse sets, the Cordless Comfort Duo, has an ergonomic keyboard.

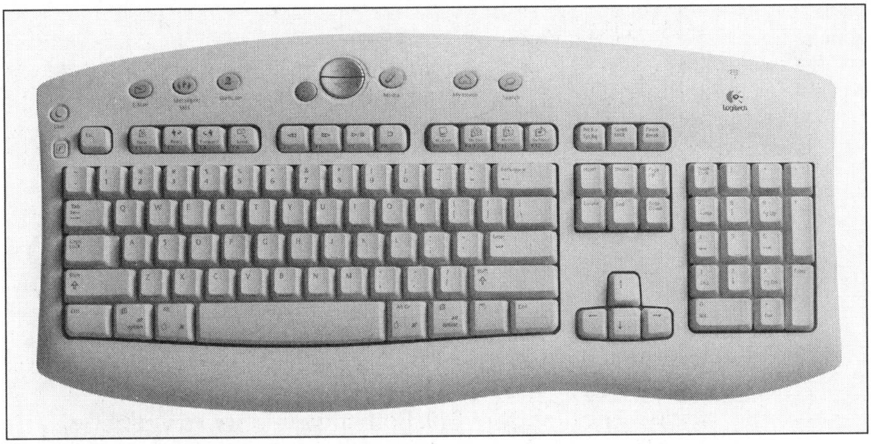

Figure 4-3: Cutting the cord with Logitech's Cordless Access Keyboard.

Getting with the Game Controllers

Logitech sells a couple of wireless game controllers for the PC. While the two controllers I discuss here are pretty durable and feature rich, I'm betting that a real gamer would insist on a corded model to avoid something called *latency,* which I discuss in the nearby sidebar.

Cordless RumblePad

The Cordless RumblePad, shown in Figure 4-4, is similar to the game controllers you get when you buy video game consoles like PlayStation2. It's two way: It transmits your commands while receiving information that's translated into vibration feedback effects.

TECHNICAL STUFF

Oh, latency; time escapes me

If you use cordless game controllers, you should get to know this word: latency. *Latency* is the delay between the time you select a button on the game controller and when the computer actually receives the command. With wired controllers, your PC instantly knows you want to shoot the bad guy in Doom. Cordless controllers can have some degree of latency, which affects your response time, even if you're the fastest gunslinger alive.

Like so many other things, there's a tradeoff: You gain the freedom of playing games without wires, but you may lose some response time. Wireless mice and keyboards have latency issues, too, but they're minimal when running most everyday home and business applications.

Figure 4-4: Gaming without wires.

It operates on the 2.4-GHz frequency band, the same as many cordless phones and Wi-Fi networks, but Logitech says interference problems are minimal. It uses a trick that makes the signal between controller and base unit hop among frequencies at a rate of 250 times per second.

You can use up to eight controllers at a time without causing interference problems, Logitech says. The Cordless RumblePad has a street price of about $40.

Freedom 2.4 Cordless Joystick

The 2.4 in the name stands for the 2.4-GHz frequency band that this joystick uses to communicate with a base station. This game controller has many, many buttons. (Not a very in-depth review, but I don't play games much.)

This peripheral is probably perfect for gamers that fling a joystick around the room as they battle the bad guys. The same battle can turn deadly with a corded model, as the hero suffocates from what becomes a garrote.

Chapter 5: Cutting Your Bluetooth

In This Chapter

- **Exploring Bluetooth**
- **Using peripherals**
- **Making the connections**
- **Staying safe with Bluetooth**

The history of Bluetooth is growing a little long in the tooth. For much of the time (since 1998 to be exact), the industry group behind the technology was singing the blues — Bluetooth was slow to catch on. Now with its introduction in cell phones, cell phone headsets, and other popular devices, the interest is rising.

Bluetooth is very similar to Wi-Fi technology, except that it works over a much shorter range. Bluetooth is designed to work within about 30 feet or so, although it can go as far as around 300 feet in some cases. The technology really is a substitute for cables, so a short range isn't a problem.

The coalition of companies behind Bluetooth, the Bluetooth Special Interest Group, has been pushing the technology for years. Ericsson, IBM, Intel, Microsoft, Motorola, and Nokia are among its members. They came up with a short-range communications standard that works throughout the world on an unlicensed radio spectrum. You can read more about the Bluetooth Special Interest Group on its Web site at www.bluetooth.com.

In this chapter I talk about Bluetooth technology and how it works. I also walk you through some sample applications, including making a connection between a Pocket PC and a desktop computer and using a headset with your cell phone.

Opening Wide

Bluetooth is a way to cut the cords between gizmos and gadgets and let them all chat with each other. Think short range when you consider the possibilities of the technology. This isn't something that's likely to work between a computer in an upstairs room and a printer in the basement. Your Wi-Fi network is for situations like that.

Instead, you might use Bluetooth to exchange information between a handheld computer and a desktop PC. A popular use and one that most people probably don't even realize utilizes Bluetooth: connecting a headset with a cell phone for hands-off use. Of course, you need a Bluetooth-enabled cell phone and headset for this to work.

Almost any kind of short-range wireless communications is a good use for Bluetooth. Rather than *local access networks (LANs),* Bluetooth can create *personal area networks (PANs).*

Getting to the nitty-gritty

Bluetooth is supported and used in products in more than 3,000 companies. Many of these products are cell phones. The Zelos Group predicts that nearly half of all mobile phones sold in the United States by 2006 will include Bluetooth technology.

Yet Bluetooth is not just an add-on technology for cell phones. Some of its many uses are shown here:

- Connecting your laptop to your desktop computer.
- Connecting a Pocket PC or Palm PDA to your desktop or laptop PC.
- Connecting your Mac to your PC for a quick transfer. (If you're going to do this on a long-term basis, you're better off connecting these together via a Wi-Fi network.)
- Exchanging electronic business cards with someone who also has a Bluetooth-enabled handheld computer.
- Synchronizing your Bluetooth-enabled cell phone address book with your Mac or PC.
- Moving files, such as photos, from your cell phone to your computer.
- If you're on a data network, use your Bluetooth cell phone as a modem, creating a temporary Internet connection for other devices.
- Connecting a headset to your cell phone for hands-free driving. You can answer your phone without touching your cell phone, which can be stowed away in a nearby briefcase.

- Sending *short messaging service (SMS)* messages via your PC rather than via the small screen and keyboard of a cell phone. (Logitech, for one, has a free application that lets you do this with its Bluetooth hub.)
- Connecting a Pocket PC, Palm, or laptop to a Bluetooth-enabled *global positioning system (GPS)* receiver. You can keep the small GPS receiver on your dashboard while your laptop uses GPS software and maps to provide verbal directions. You also can mount a handheld computer on the dashboard for viewing a map without the need to connect the GPS receiver to the PDA. Book VIII talks about GPS in depth.

Connecting to various and sundry devices

Before you can use Bluetooth, you obviously need some way for your computer to access other Bluetooth devices. Recently, more and more computers come equipped with built-in support. These computers include the following:

- Pocket PCs.
- Palm PDAs.
- BlackBerry 7290.
- PC laptops.
- Mac iBooks and PowerBooks. Bluetooth is an option on the iBook, but it comes with the PowerBook. You can use iSync to synchronize your calendar and other information among other Bluetooth devices. Check your Mac manual or help files for more details.

For computers that don't have built-in support, you can add Bluetooth technology a few different ways:

- USB adapters. These simply plug into your computer's USB port. You can use them in either a desktop or laptop PC. A USB adapter that works up to 300 feet is slightly more expensive than one that has a range of up to 30 feet. A pretty blue light blinks on the Belkin USB adapter I use.
- PC card. These slide into your laptop's PCMCIA slot. Some PDAs accept these cards, also.
- Compact Flash card. You can plug this card into your PDA if it has a Compact Flash slot. Converters are available so you can plug a Compact Flash card into a PCMCIA adapter and use the CF card in your laptop, too.

Why Bluetooth?

So far I've saved you from the bad puns about blueberry-stained teeth, yada yada (well, I did do a couple puns, but I hope you'll forgive me). Do you want to know the real origin of the name Bluetooth? I'm no historian, but this much I can tell you: Once upon a time, in a land far, far away, there lived a Danish king named Harald Blatand, which in English is Harold Bluetooth. The 10th-century king helped unite warring factions in parts of what are now Norway, Sweden, and Denmark.

The special interest group behind Bluetooth (the technology, not the king) liked the parallels between Harold's maneuverings and the technology's aim of allowing collaboration among different industries. The name stuck. If Harold weren't already famous — you knew who he was, right? — he will be soon. The Bluetooth Special Interest Group's logo is shown in the accompanying figure.

Exploring its insides

Bluetooth operates on unlicensed radio spectrum in the 2.4-GHz frequency band. It uses something called spread spectrum frequency hopping. That's a pretty fancy name to associate with a technology with a silly name like Bluetooth! Anywho, *spread spectrum frequency hopping* means that the Bluetooth signal jumps around among 79 different frequencies at an amazing rate of up to 1,600 times a second. All of that hopping is designed to reduce interference. Remember that Wi-Fi, for one, operates on similar frequencies in the 2.4-GHz band. Also sharing the spectrum are cordless phones, microwave ovens, and baby monitors.

Bluetooth can move information at speeds up to 723 kilobits per second. Bluetooth has several versions, one with a range of 10 meters (or about 30 feet) and another having a range of 100 meters (or about 330 feet). The difference, other than the distance, is the amount of power the device expends sending out the signal.

They each have their place. For instance, you don't need a 300-foot range for a keyboard and mouse, where 30 feet is more than enough. Pumping out enough power to hit a range of 300 feet is great for wirelessly connecting a printer to your PC. Table 5-1 shows the three power levels.

Table 5-1 Bluetooth Power and Ranges

Type	*Power Level*	*Operating Range*
Class 3	100 mW	Up to 100 meters (333 feet)
Class 2	10 mW	Up to 10 meters (30 feet)
Class 1	1 mW	0.1 to 10 meters (0 to 30 feet)

These distances are what I call *paper distances,* as they are what the manufacturers or the Bluetooth Special Interest Group declare as the range. Your mileage may vary, and likely will. Don't expect to get 300 feet out of Bluetooth every time, unless you're a very lucky person. (You're probably the kind of person who wins three sweepstakes in a year, when I've never won one.)

Up to seven slave devices can connect to a master device. The *master* device is just the device that happened to start the party rolling; the *slave units* are the followers. A master device and one or more slave units is enough to create a *piconet*. You can join up to 10 piconets and create something called a *scatternet*, which means you can have up to 80 devices connected all at once.

Styling and profiling

There are 13 possible uses *(profiles)* for Bluetooth connections. These profiles are universal and manufacturers use them to ensure that a Bluetooth device works with other Bluetooth devices. They are basically technical specifications. Instead of *profiles,* you might think of them as *services* — things you can do once you have a Bluetooth connection in place.

For two or more devices to communicate via Bluetooth and do something, they must all support the same profile. If you want to transfer files between your PDA and desktop PC, for instance, both computers must support the profile designed for transferring files. Some of the profiles are very technical. The most obvious ones, where the name basically tells you what the specification does, include the following:

- **Headset.** This lets a headset communicate with another Bluetooth device. This is how cell phone headsets talk to a nearby Bluetooth phone.
- **File Transfer.** This is pretty obvious, too. This profile is used so that file transfers can occur between two Bluetooth devices.
- **Synchronization.** This synchronizes contact list and calendar information between two Bluetooth devices.
- **Dial-Up Networking.** Specifies how a Bluetooth device connects to a modem or cell phone.
- **Hardcopy Cable Replacement.** That's a fancy way of saying this is the profile for communicating with printers.
- **Human Interface Device.** This defines how Bluetooth keyboards and mice communicate.
- **Intercom.** This specifies how two Bluetooth phones can connect directly with each other.
- **Cordless Telephony.** This outlines the way a cordless phone is created using a Bluetooth device. *Telephony* is a fancy word for telephone services.

Using Peripherals

In Book VI, Chapter 4, I cover the use of wireless peripherals like keyboards and mice — but I left out the peripherals that operate over Bluetooth frequencies, saving them for this chapter.

For now, only a few desktop peripherals — which basically includes keyboards and mice — use Bluetooth as their communications medium. It's a robust technology, barring any interference issues, so you might find that using such a keyboard or mouse is better than what you've experienced in the past when using wireless peripherals. There's the added benefit of creating a Bluetooth access point. For example, the Logitech diNovo Media Desktop incorporates a Bluetooth access point into the mouse recharging cradle.

Here's a selection of Bluetooth-enabled peripherals:

- **Logitech.** Logitech has two keyboard-mouse combinations and one mouse that run on Bluetooth. The diNovo Media Desktop includes a thin keyboard, MediaPad (which is a number keypad that also controls music and other multimedia), a mouse, and a Bluetooth hub. The Cordless Desktop MX for Bluetooth includes a keyboard, mouse, and Bluetooth hub. Finally, the MX 900 Bluetooth Optical Mouse is just that: an optical mouse with Web surfing buttons that operates via Bluetooth.
- **Microsoft.** The Optical Desktop Elite for Bluetooth is a combination of keyboard and mouse. The IntelliMouse Explorer for Bluetooth mouse is available separately. In both cases, the Microsoft Transceiver for Bluetooth works as a Bluetooth hub. Microsoft has a chart of cell phones, PDAs, and printers compatible with its Bluetooth hub at www.microsoft.com/hardware/mouseandkeyboard/bluetooth_compat.mspx. A Bluetooth-enabled keyboard and mouse are shown in Figure 5-1.
- **Apple.** They have a Bluetooth keyboard and mouse. Used with the iMac, you can go almost entirely wireless by eliminating all but the power cord. The keyboard and mouse are $69 each.
- **Think Outside.** This company makes the Stowaway Bluetooth Wireless keyboard, with models for the Pocket PC, Palm, and Symbian (for cell phones that run the Symbian operating system).

REMEMBER

Bluetooth is a cross-platform technology. In other words, a Bluetooth keyboard works on both PCs and Macs. The whole point of Bluetooth is to allow interoperability among devices, no matter what they are or who makes them.

Figure 5-1: A Bluetooth keyboard and mouse.

Making Your Devices Discoverable

Before one Bluetooth device can find another Bluetooth device, the device needs to be *discoverable.* That means, in basic English, that you want a Bluetooth-enabled gizmo to be found by other Bluetooth devices. If you don't want anyone to know a device exists, then you can turn off the discovery setting. In that case, you're hidden and other people cannot see you. However, if they know you exist, they still can connect to you.

In Windows XP, here's how you confirm that the discovery setting is on:

1. **Right-click the Bluetooth icon in the notification area of your system tray.**
2. **Select Open Bluetooth Settings.**

   A Bluetooth Devices dialog box appears. The Devices tab displays the Bluetooth devices that have already connected to your PC. These are paired devices, which I discuss in the next section.
3. **Select the Options tab.**
4. **Check the Turn Discovery On box if it's not already checked. See Figure 5-2.**

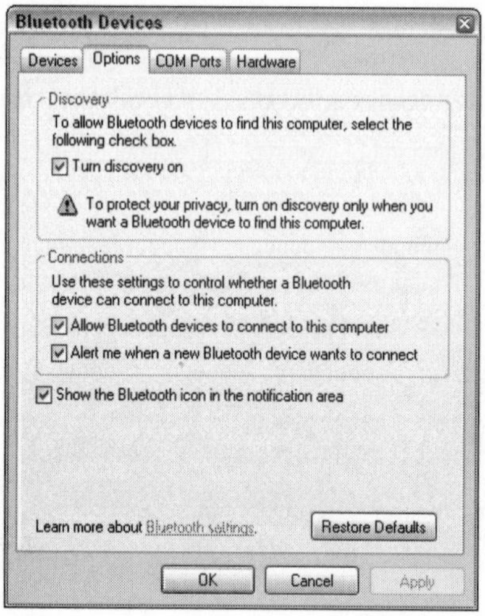

Figure 5-2: Turning on discovery so your PC is seen by other Bluetooth devices.

5. **Under Connections, confirm that the options are selected:**
   - **Allow Bluetooth Devices to Connect to This Computer**
   - **Alert Me When a New Bluetooth Device Wants to Connect**
6. **Click OK to finish.**

Pairing Your Devices

Before two Bluetooth devices can communicate, they must go through something called *pairing.* Any number of four digits (or so) is entered and exchanged between the devices. The number is a one-time deal and you can forget it after pairing is completed. (Thank goodness you don't have something else to remember, eh?)

Essentially, pairing means that the Bluetooth devices are authenticating one another. They're saying, "Hey, do you want to connect? If so, send me that four-digit number our owners agreed on earlier."

After you initiate the Bluetooth connection, the first device asks for a number. After you enter the number, the second device asks for the same number. After both devices have the same numbers, they are officially paired. After a device pairs with another device, that specific pairing can be permanently stored in a paired list so that the exchanging of PINs is no longer necessary.

Installing a USB Bluetooth Adapter

Installing a USB Bluetooth adapter is one of the easiest ways of connecting a laptop, desktop PC, or Mac to a Bluetooth network. You simply plug the thin, two-inch–long adapter into an open USB port and install the software.

REMEMBER

The Windows XP examples in this chapter use Windows XP Service Pack 2 (SP2). Microsoft added some Bluetooth support in SP2. If you're using an earlier version of Windows XP, you may see differences in some of these examples.

This example uses the Belkin Bluetooth USB Adapter (F8T001) shown in Figure 5-3. The installation and setup of other USB Bluetooth adapters is likely to be different.

Figure 5-3: A Belkin Bluetooth USB adapter.

Do not insert the USB adapter until Step 7.

1. **Insert the CD that came with your USB adapter into your computer's CD-ROM player.**

   The installation menu automatically appears. If it does not, find the file start.exe on the CD and run it.

2. **Place your mouse cursor over Install and then click Click Here, as shown in Figure 5-4, to start the installation wizard.**
3. **Click Next.**

   The License Agreement screen appears.

4. **Read the license agreement and, if you do, select I Accept the Terms in the License Agreement. Click Next.**

   The Destination Folder screen appears.

5. **If the folder destination is OK, click Next. If not, click Change and select a different folder before continuing.**
6. **Click Install to install the software.**

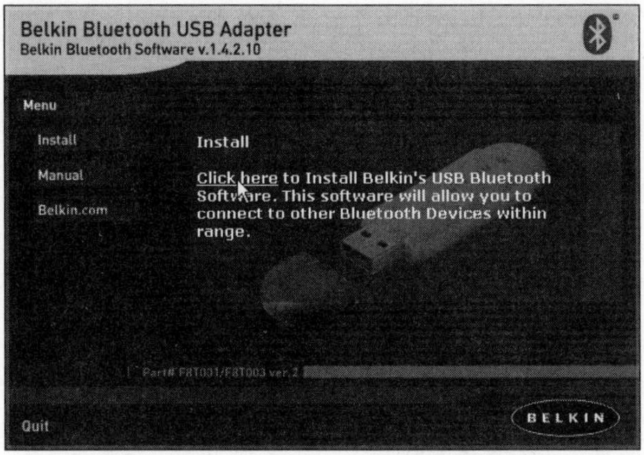

Figure 5-4: Beginning the installation.

You may see a Driver Signature Notice informing you that the drivers are not certified by Microsoft because Microsoft does not have a Bluetooth certification program in place. Click OK.

The software places a My Bluetooth Places icon on your desktop, as shown in Figure 5-5, and the Bluetooth Device Not Found dialog box appears.

Figure 5-5: The My Bluetooth Places icon on your desktop.

7. **Insert the USB adapter into one of your computer's USB ports.**
8. **Click OK.**

   The installation continues.

9. **Click Finish.**

   A Bluetooth icon appears in the notification area of Windows XP's task tray. You're done installing your USB adapter.

Moving Files between a PC and Mac

If you want a quick way to transfer files between a PC and a Mac, Bluetooth might be the answer. You can relatively easily set up a Bluetooth connection between the two computers; creating a Wi-Fi network that includes PCs and Macs can be more difficult. In fact, the first Bluetooth-enabled device I saw when I started playing around with the technology was my Mac laptop. It discovered the Mac almost instantly and I was able to view a directory of files over a Bluetooth connection.

Admittedly, this book is PC-centric; I'm writing this from the perspective of the PC, not the Mac. Here's how you connect your Bluetooth-enabled laptop or desktop PC to your Mac:

1. **On your PC, right-click the Bluetooth Devices icon in the system tray's notification area.**

   A pop-up menu appears.

2. **Select Show Bluetooth Devices.**

   The Bluetooth Devices dialog box appears.

3. **Click Add under the Devices tab, as shown in Figure 5-6, to bring up the Add Bluetooth Device Wizard.**

Figure 5-6: Adding a Bluetooth device.

4. **Turn on the device you're trying to add, make it discoverable, and give it a name you can recognize.**
5. **Select My Device Is Set Up and Ready to Be Found.**
6. **Click Next.**

   Your computer searches for all Bluetooth devices. If it doesn't find the device you are attempting to add, double check that the device is on; then click Search Again. Figure 5-7 shows three Bluetooth devices: a Mac, a Dell Axim 30 Pocket PC, and a Nokia 6600 mobile phone.

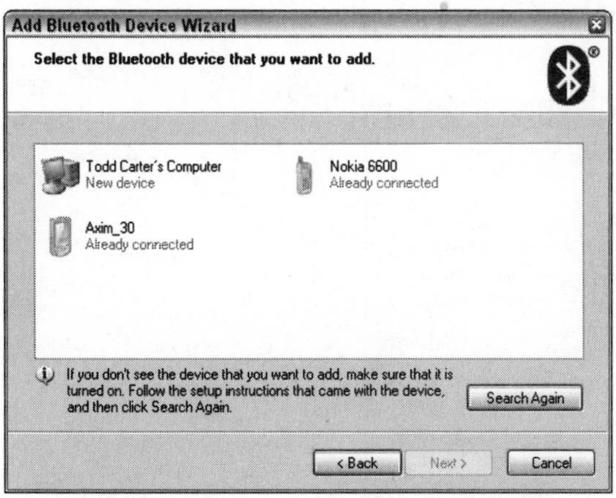

Figure 5-7: Selecting your Mac.

7. **Click the icon that represents your Mac.**
8. **Click Next.**

   A passkey dialog box appears.
9. **Select one of these options:**
   - **Choose a Passkey for Me.**
   - **Let Me Choose My Own Passkey.** If at home or somewhere else where you're less concerned about security, select Let Me Choose My Own Passkey. Then enter something like 0000. If you let your computer choose, the number is relatively long and difficult to remember. This is a one-time number that you can forget after entering it into both devices.

A balloon pops up in the notification area telling you that new hardware was installed. This is another way of saying that you have a connection with your Mac. (Yell at the folks in Redmond, not me!)

10. **Click Finish.**

    The Bluetooth Devices dialog box lists the Bluetooth device you just paired with (in this case, a Mac laptop called Todd Carter's Computer, as shown in Figure 5-8).

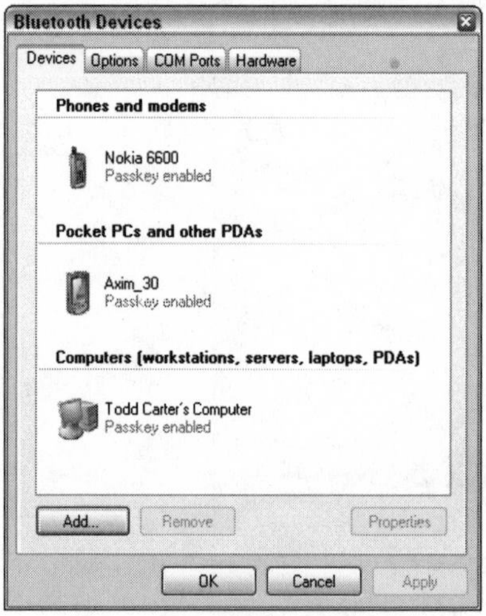

Figure 5-8: This dialog box displays all of your paired Bluetooth devices.

11. **Right-click the Bluetooth icon in the notification area of the system tray.**

    A pop-up menu appears.

12. **Select Send a File to bring up the Bluetooth File Transfer Wizard.**
13. **Click Browse (which is beside Send To).**

    Your computer searches for and displays Bluetooth devices.

14. **Select the Mac computer.**
15. **Click OK.**
16. **Click Next.**

17. **Beside File Name, click Browse and select a file to send, as shown in Figure 5-9.**

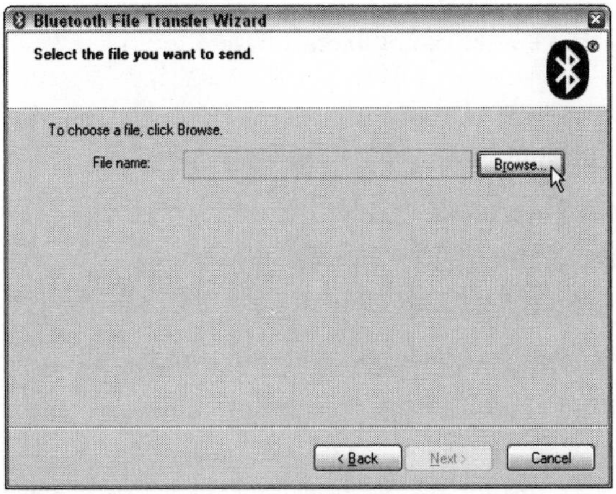

Figure 5-9: Select Browse to find a file to send.

18. **Click Next.**

    Your Mac informs you that you have an incoming file and asks you to accept or decline it.

19. **Click Accept.**

    The file is transferred via Bluetooth.

20. **On your PC, click Finish.**

You can use the same technique to transfer files from your PC to other Bluetooth devices, if Bluetooth on those devices supports file transfers and if the device can handle the file type and size. Moving files between two PCs via Bluetooth is similar to the steps I outline for moving files between a PC and a Mac.

Moving from Tooth to Pocket (PC)

A Bluetooth-enabled Pocket PC can make a quick connection to a number of devices, including printers, another Pocket PC, a Mac, and, of course, to a PC. You can transfer and print files. If you're connecting a Bluetooth-enabled cell phone to your little network, you also can use your Pocket PC to synchronize information.

I'm using a Dell Axim 30 Pocket PC that has both Wi-Fi and Bluetooth access built in. (The only way to fly!) I'm connecting to a Bluetooth access point that connects to my network. You also can connect directly from your Pocket PC to any one of a number of Bluetooth-enabled devices, including a desktop PC. I'm going to connect to the network and then view files on the network, which confirms that I'm really connected.

1. **Turn on your Pocket PC.**
2. **In the bottom-right corner, click the Bluetooth icon.**

   A pop-up menu appears.
3. **Click Bluetooth Manager.**
4. **At the bottom left, click New.**

   A menu of Bluetooth connection types appears, as shown in Figure 5-10.
5. **Select the kind of connection you want to make.**

   In this example, I'm selecting Connect to a Network. Possible connections appear on the screen, as shown in Figure 5-10. In this example, my desktop PC and a Belkin Bluetooth access point appear on the list.

TIP

You can view a list of services (also called profiles) that each nearby, discoverable Bluetooth device supports by selecting New⇨Explore a Bluetooth Device. In the next screen, select the device of which you want to view its services.

Figure 5-10: A Pocket PC displays a list of available Bluetooth devices and networks.

6. **Select a device from which to connect to a network.**

   You are offered an opportunity to create a shortcut for the connection. I select the Belkin access point in this example.

7. **Name your shortcut anything you want.**

   I call my shortcut Todd's AP.

8. **Click Finish.**

   A list of devices appears. You may see duplicates if you've made connections multiple times to the same Bluetooth device.

9. **Click Start⇨Internet Explorer. Browse to a site like www.yahoo.com or www.google.com to confirm that the Bluetooth connection is working.**

If your Pocket PC also has Wi-Fi access, disconnect your Wi-Fi access points during these steps to ensure you are making a Bluetooth connection and not a Wi-Fi one.

TIP

By double-clicking a device in the list, a window showing signal strength appears, as shown in Figure 5-11. In this example, the signal strength is Just Right.

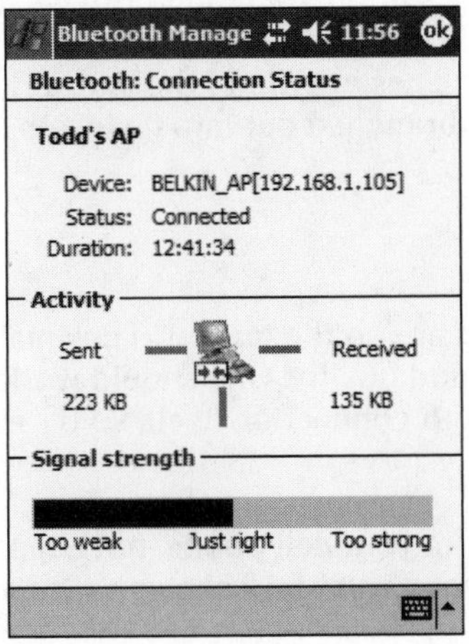

Figure 5-11: The status of a Bluetooth connection.

In this example I'm using a Pocket PC to connect to other devices. But you also can do the same thing with a Palm handheld computer that has Bluetooth capability. While I don't go into the step-by-step procedures for making a connection in this book, they are similar to the ones used for Pocket PCs. Please check your Palm owner's manual or the Palm Web site for more information.

Moving within Earshot of Your Cell Phone

I predict that one of the most popular uses for Bluetooth will be as a method connecting a headset to your cell phone. It's a marvelous idea because the cords tying the headsets to the cell phones are always getting in the way and, frankly, they look kind of silly. (So do some of the headsets currently for sale, but that's for a separate book on fashion.)

Connecting the two devices is exactly what Bluetooth was designed to do. It's a short-range task that requires a strong connection. Cell phone coverage is bad enough; you don't need reception problems with the Bluetooth connection, too.

In my example, which gives you an idea of how a cell phone and headset work together over Bluetooth, I'm using a Nokia 6600 phone and a Logitech Mobile Bluetooth Headset. Logitech's interest in Bluetooth clearly grew from its focus on keyboards, mice, and other peripherals. While it sells some other wireless peripherals, the Bluetooth ones are top of the line, at least as far as price. From there, the company branched out into headsets and other Bluetooth devices.

Setting up the headset

More and more Bluetooth headsets are on the market. They mainly differ in design, weight, battery life, and sound quality. One should work like any other when it comes to the Bluetooth connection itself, so try each one on your ear and see which fits best.

The headset works up to 30 feet from your cell phone, but expect to stay much closer to your phone than that. Figure 5-12 shows a Bluetooth-enabled headset.

Figure 5-12: A Bluetooth-enabled headset for mobile phones.

Using my Logitech headset as the guinea pig, here's how you connect to your Bluetooth mobile phone:

1. **Turn on the headset by pressing the multifunction button above the earpiece for seven seconds.**

   The headset begins to flash red and blue.

2. **Release the button.**

   The headset continues to flash for two minutes, indicating that it's ready to communicate with another Bluetooth device.

3. **Follow the instructions for connecting your Bluetooth phone to the headset. Make sure your phone is discoverable.**

   The Logitech headset appears to other Bluetooth devices as Logitech HS01. Its passkey is 0000. If the connection is successful, the headset blinks blue every three seconds.

Sending a Photo to Your PC

Mobile phones with cameras (or is it cameras with mobile phones?) are all the rage, so I want to show you how to transfer a photo from your phone using Bluetooth. I'm using a Bluetooth-enabled Nokia 6600 mobile phone for this example, so your phone may differ in how it handles the same chore.

1. **Right-click the Bluetooth icon in your system tray's notification area.**

   A pop-up menu appears.

2. **Select Receive a File.**

   The Bluetooth File Transfer Wizard appears, as shown in Figure 5-13.

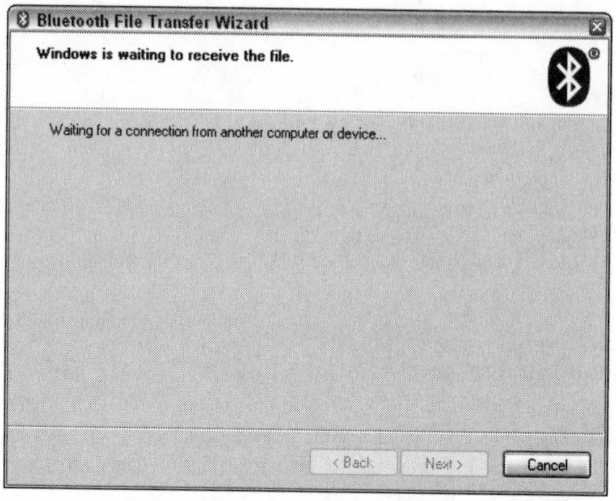

Figure 5-13: Windows waits for an incoming Bluetooth file transfer.

The wizard displays Windows Is Waiting to Receive the File.

3. **Turn on your phone.**
4. **Press the Menu key to bring up the menu.**

   These are instructions for the Nokia 6600 phone. The exact steps for your Bluetooth-enabled phone may differ. Please check your manual for details.
5. **Select Connectivity to bring up the Connectivity screen.**
6. **Click Bluetooth.**

   The Bluetooth screen appears. Confirm Bluetooth is turned on and that My Phone's Visibility is set to Shown to All.
7. **Press the Menu key to bring up the Menu screen.**
8. **Select Gallery.**

   The Gallery screen appears.
9. **Select the Images folder.**

   The Images folder opens, displaying photos taken by the Nokia 6600.
10. **Select an image and open it.**

    The image appears.
11. **Click the Options button.**

    The Options menu pops up.

12. **Select Send and then select Via Bluetooth.**

    The photo is sent (hopefully)!

13. **On your PC, you are prompted to save the received file, as shown in Figure 5-14.**

    Click Browse and choose another location if you don't like the one displayed.

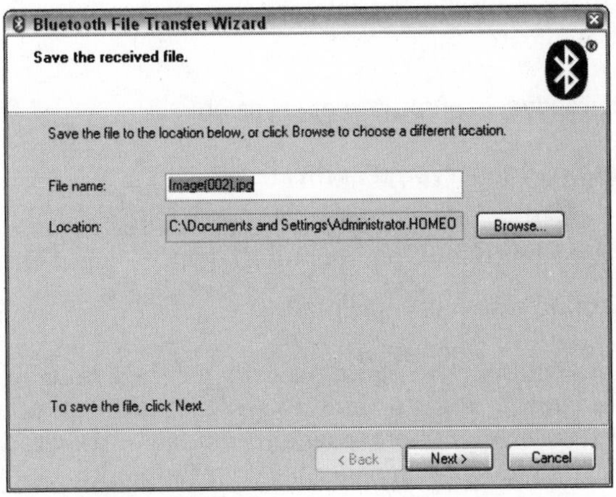

Figure 5-14: Saving a received file.

14. **Click Next.**

    The Bluetooth File Transfer Wizard indicates the file transfer was a success and displays the following:

    - Which device sent the file
    - Filename
    - File size

15. **Click Finish. You just received a photo over Bluetooth! You're done.**

TIP

If you have problems, please check your owner's manual or contact the manufacturer. There are too many Bluetooth devices, especially cell phones, to address all of the possible problems that can arise. Still, it's a fairly easy technology to use, so I don't think you will have many problems.

Staying Safe with Bluetooth

Like all communications technologies, Bluetooth has its share of potential security risks. Admittedly, they are less severe than Wi-Fi security problems because Bluetooth signals travel such a short distance. With most of the devices working only within a 30-foot radius, it makes it more difficult to eavesdrop or otherwise cause havoc.

Still, knowing the potential security problems is important. I'm sure as Bluetooth grows in popularity, hackers will find even more loopholes that engineers must eliminate.

Bluetooth has three levels of built-in encryption:

- **Mode 1:** Nothing is encrypted at this level.
- **Mode 2:** Information sent to a single Bluetooth device is encrypted. However, data sent to multiple Bluetooth devices is not encrypted.
- **Mode 3:** All information is encrypted.

WARNING!

Overall, Bluetooth exhibits two major security glitches: bluejacking and bluesnarfing. *Bluejacking* is not so much a security problem as an invasion of your privacy. It involves someone sending you an unsolicited message that may or may not be polite. In order for your Bluetooth-enabled phone to be hijacked this way, however, it first must be discoverable by others.

Bluejacking

In essence, a bluejacker creates a contact in his phone address book that contains the message (rather than name, address, and other information) he wants to send. He selects this contact and then tells the phone to send it via Bluetooth. The phone searches for Bluetooth phones within 30 feet. The owner then sends the message anonymously to one of the phones on his list.

TIP

How can you protect yourself from this annoyance? You can try one of these:

- Make your phone hidden from other Bluetooth-enabled devices.
- Ignore the messages, unless you're expecting one.
- Turn off the Bluetooth feature.
- Turn off the phone when you're in a busy area where bluejacking is more likely to occur.

Bluejacking has a positive side: It's also a way to send free text messages to friends and business associates. If you want to use this feature, then ignore the list of ways to protect yourself against it.

Bluesnarfing

While bluejacking is irritating, bluesnarfing is nefarious.

Bluesnarfing is the stealing of your private information without your knowing it. That's right. Someone can connect to your Bluetooth phone without your phone letting you know about the connection. She can transfer a copy of your address book, calendar, electronic business card, and other information. This can happen while your Bluetooth phone is tucked away inside your jacket, briefcase, or purse! Someone can completely suck out your most important information without your knowing about it.

TIP

How can you stop bluesnarfing? Try these tips:

- **Make your phone hidden.** This may not matter on some phone models, where you're vulnerable to bluesnarfing whether you're discoverable *or* hidden. You can view a list of vulnerable phones at www.thebunker.net/release-bluestumbler.htm.
- **Turn off Bluetooth**. This is your best bet. Turn it on only when you need it to transfer files, synchronize your contact list, and so on.
- **Turn off your phone.** This is the least practical, but a guaranteed way to keep it safe (assuming you don't physically lose it).

Remember, wireless technology is inherently unsecure. Only things like encryption, due diligence, and other precautions make it as secure as possible — and then there still might be loopholes. So be careful out there!

Book VII

Home Technology

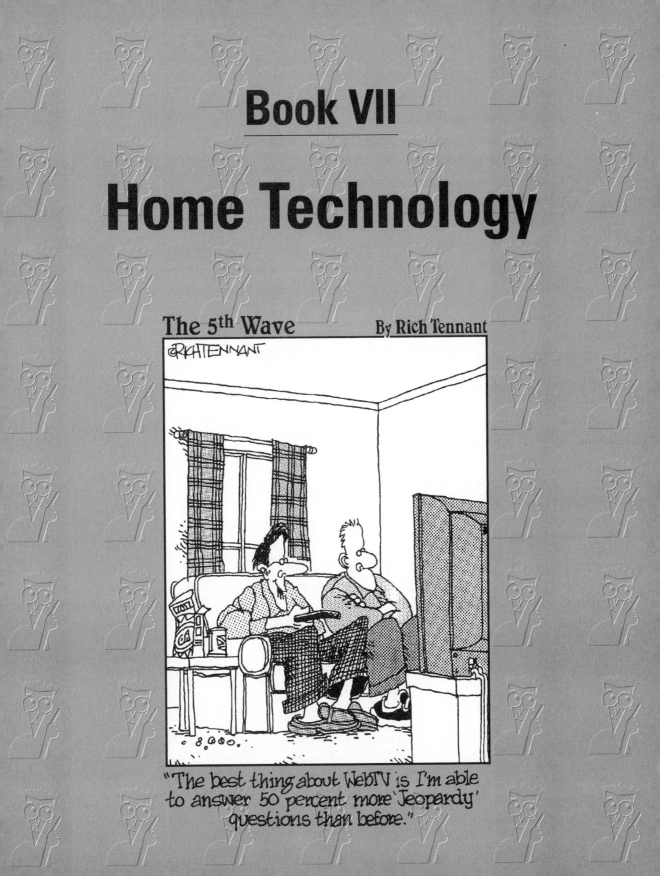

The 5th Wave By Rich Tennant

"The best thing about WebTV is I'm able to answer 50 percent more 'Jeopardy' questions than before."

Contents at a Glance

Chapter 1: Your Entertainment Center 397
Chapter 2: Setting Up Gadgets 409
Chapter 3: Chatting with Motorola's IMfree 419
Chapter 4: Sharing Multimedia Files with Windows XP....................437
Chapter 5: Using TiVo's Home Media Features 447
Chapter 6: Exploring Digital TV and Satellite Radio 461
Chapter 7: Forecasting from Your Patio....................469
Chapter 8: Security in the Air via Motorola 483

Chapter 1: Your Entertainment Center

In This Chapter

- **Linking your network with your entertainment center**
- **Checking out the latest multimedia player products**
- **Looking at other gadgets**

You've got your wireless network set up throughout your house. You're moving around files wirelessly, surfing the Web with your laptop from the couch. Maybe you're streaming some music from one PC to the other wirelessly or from a PC to your laptop.

There must be something else, right? What about all this talk about the PC serving as your entertainment hub, connecting your files with your stereo and your television set?

This chapter discusses just that. I'm going to talk a little about how your wireless network can help you view photos and video on your TV set and listen to music on your stereo. Then I'm going to provide some short summaries of several media players currently on the market. Some are better than others, but you'll have some basic information designed to help make an informed purchase decision.

TIP

In this chapter I call these devices *media players,* but you'll hear them called several other names:

- ✦ Multimedia servers
- ✦ Media hub
- ✦ Digital media receivers
- ✦ Music streaming devices

In the next chapter I pick three multimedia gizmos, including a wireless camera, and walk you through setting them. Even if you don't purchase one of those items and instead choose another,

Entertaining the Wireless Way

The entertainment gadget experience falls somewhere between listening to audio on your $20 computer speakers and having a full-featured home media PC running a special version of Windows XP. With the former, you get poor sound, but few set-up hassles. With the latter, you must invest much more money — at least around $1,000 — to get a computer that directly feeds music, photos, and videos into your home entertainment center. (In fact, the home media PC becomes part of your home entertainment center.)

Most of the products I list are a compromise between those two extremes. You get the advantages of a dedicated device that (hopefully) does a few things very well with minimal hassle, but the disadvantage of easily costing a Ben Franklin or more. Figure 1-1 shows a typical media player configuration on a wireless network.

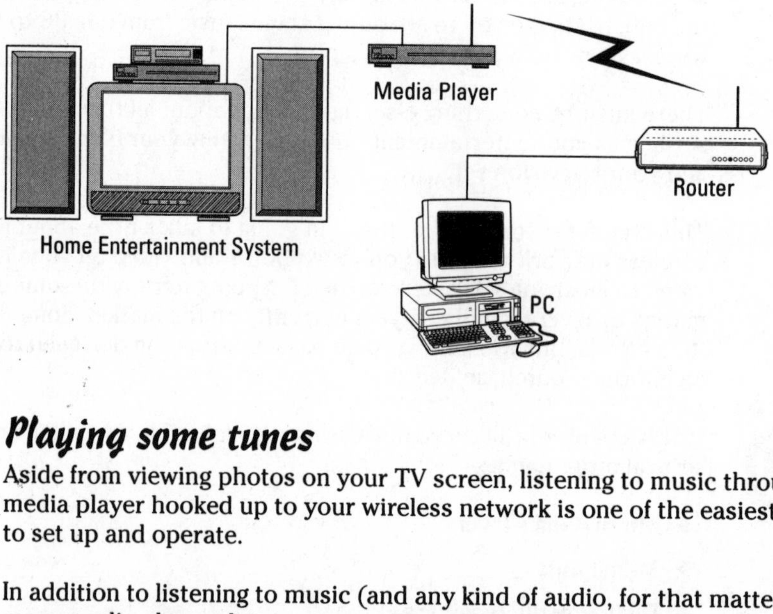

Figure 1-1: A simple connection between a wireless network and a media player.

Playing some tunes

Aside from viewing photos on your TV screen, listening to music through a media player hooked up to your wireless network is one of the easiest things to set up and operate.

In addition to listening to music (and any kind of audio, for that matter), many media players let you stream Internet radio stations to your stereo. My favorite is www.digitallyimported.com, which plays while I write.

Some of the most popular formats include the following:

- ✦ Audio CD
- ✦ MP3
- ✦ WMA
- ✦ AAC
- ✦ WAV

REMEMBER

To the best of my knowledge, none of the media players I discuss in this chapter play files that are encrypted in a scheme called *digital rights management (DRM)*. In other words, when you purchase a song online and download it, you probably can't play it on these media hubs. The players simply are not set up to handle these DRM files the way iTune or Windows Media Player are — but you still can play music that you ripped from your own CD collection.

You can make playlists of your songs so that groups of tunes play together, one after the other. You might make a playlist called Jazz Standards and another one called 1980s New Wave. Of course, you can make hundreds of these lists if you want.

These playlist formats are some of the most popular:

- ✦ M3U
- ✦ PLS
- ✦ WPL

Did I really look like that?

You know that big box of photos you have somewhere that you are going to organize any day now? Well, that day has arrived. Now that you can view your photos on your TV screen, why not take the time to scan in your photos so they're available for use by these gizmos?

Both Windows and the Macintosh have some fine software packages that help you organize your photos. You can scan them on a scanner, make some changes (like eliminating that dreadful red eye that happens when you use a flash), and organize them.

Photo management programs include Adobe Photoshop Album (www.adobe.com; about $50) and Google's free Picasa (www.picasa.com) software. The popular formats for photos include the following:

- JPEG
- TIFF
- BMP
- PNG

TIP

Do you own a TiVo? If you do, some of these photo and music features are already built into the newer Series 2 units. I talk about connecting TiVo to your wireless network in Book VII, Chapter 5.

Hollywood on a hard-drive platter

Video and wireless are not quite like water and oil, but they're close. If you're going to move around video files on a wireless network, you need the bandwidth to handle them. That probably means scrapping 802.11b equipment, if you've already purchased it, and moving up to the only slightly more expensive 802.11g gear. Book II, Chapter 2 talks about 802.11 options in depth.

The throughput differences between the two technologies (b and g) are striking and you'll definitely see an improvement with 802.11g networking equipment. If you're streaming video in real time you almost certainly need 802.11g equipment.

What kind of video can you watch on media players? Just about anything your media player can read. You may want to watch some home movies you've converted into digital format, for instance. One online service "rents" movies for download and watching.

More video services are sure to follow, especially given Hollywood's concern about content transferring illegally over peer-to-peer networks. As Apple's iTune music store has shown, people will pay for content. They're willing to go the legal route as long as the options are there.

Some of the more popular video formats include the following:

- MPG (MPEG-1, MPEG-2, MPEG-4)
- WMV
- ASF
- AVI
- Xvid

More wireless media players play only music than play both music and video. That's partly because manufacturers — at least until recently with the growing popularity of 802.11g — probably felt they couldn't meet the expectations of non-geeky consumers. After all, video takes substantial bandwidth, which wired Ethernet and, in most cases, 802.11g can deliver.

REMEMBER

Finally, as far as video streaming goes, I have a bit of wisdom. I call it Carter's Theorem: The coolest way isn't always the best way. If it's easier to simply buy a DVD burner, burn a DVD with some video, and then play it on a DVD player, think about doing so rather than investing large sums trying to figure out how to smoothly stream it over your wireless network.

What's important is that it works. Your friends and relatives watching the video probably don't care how you managed to get it to the TV set.

Looking at the Latest Gadgets

Some cool gadgets can move multimedia content between your wireless network and your stereo and television. For obvious reasons, I only include media players that work with wireless networks, but some others run on a wired Ethernet network (and many of the devices listed here give you the option of using them over a wired network, too).

Media players require you to first load some software onto your PC. The gadgets then make a connection with your computer and request the photo or video files you want to see on your TV set or the music files you want to listen to on your stereo.

You usually navigate using a remote control with a user interface that uses one of these three things:

- **An LED or LCD screen on the front of the media player box.** This provides minimal information, but then, you don't need a TV set to display information if you're only going to listen to music. Hence, your television doesn't need to be in the same place as your stereo (because you're not missing much on its readout, anyway).
- **Your TV screen.** The media player displays information on your television in the same way that TiVo and similar devices do. More information in larger text makes these user interfaces easier to navigate.
- **The remote control itself.** In a few cases, a media player displays information on the remote control unit. It's easier to see because it's right before your eyes, but the amount of information that can be displayed at one time is limited to a few lines.

As I've hinted at earlier, make sure your network is running at peak performance before trying these at home. A strong signal is necessary for getting the fastest speeds, which in turn are needed to pump out those huge video and audio files. Otherwise, you're going to be disappointed, and that's the last thing I (and my publisher) want.

Some of these devices use 802.11b technology, while others use 802.11g technology. You can mix and match these two technologies, but remember that introducing a 802.11b device into an otherwise completely 802.11g network degrades the throughput. In some cases, I mention which technology the media player users. For others, you can find out by visiting the product's Web site.

Netgear Wireless Digital Music Player

Named the MP101 because it's supposed to be as easy as a 101-level class to install and use, the Netgear Wireless Digital Music Player is one of the cooler looking gizmos in this chapter. It has a plain metal box with a four-line LCD screen and a remote control. You get the feeling that it's all business inside that box.

Its software finds music files on your PC, sorts them by title, artist, album, genre, or playlist, and collects them into one database. You use a remote control to navigate through the music, whose titles display on the LCD screen. It also works with Internet streaming radio stations, as well as the Rhapsody Digital Music Service; a 30-day free trial to the service is included. You can listen to music on your stereo, boom box, headphones, or powered speakers. It works with both 802.11b and 802.11g networks. This device (www.netgear.com) amazed me by how fast it detected and connected to my wireless network.

Linksys Wireless-B Music System

This is the only media player I know of that's meant to be portable around the house (and garage and yard, I suppose, if your network has the range). The Linksys Wireless-B Music System (www.linksys.com) looks like a boom box, with two detachable speakers that you can use when you're not hooking up the media player to your home stereo system. It comes with a remote control that you use to navigate the LCD menus, which let you browse the music on your home PCs. You also can access the Rhapsody Digital Music Service (you get a free trial with purchase) and you can listen to Internet radio stations. As the name suggests, the music system uses 802.11b technology.

In the next chapter I walk through the steps for setting up and using these Netgear and Linksys products. This chapter is simply a review of some of the most promising devices for moving multimedia information around your home wireless network.

D-Link MediaLounge Wireless Media Player

D-Link's MediaLounge DSM-320 Wireless Media Player (www.dlink.com) is the slimmest media player in the lot. You can listen to music on your stereo and view digital photos, slideshows, and videos on your TV set. It supports the MP3, WMA, and WAV audio formats; JPEG, BMP, PNG, TIFF, GPEG2000, and GIF image formats; and the MPEG 1, MPEG 2, MPEG 4, Xvid, and AVI video formats. It also handles M3U and PLS audio playlist formats. It has an impressive array of output jacks: RCA audio, RCA video, S-Video, component video, optical digital audio, and coax digital audio. MediaLounge retails for about $160.

Sound Blaster Wireless Music

You can connect up to four Sound Blaster Wireless Music receivers to your wireless network at one time. Sound Blaster says the player either connects automatically to your wireless network or with a "simple USB setup."

You view and choose songs and playlists on the remote control's built-in LCD screen. The remote is also unusual from other players in that it uses radio frequency transmission rather than line-of-sight infrared technology. That means you don't have to be in the same room as the receiver to change songs and do other things. It works on both 802.11b and 802.11g networks.

Gateway Connected DVD Player

You can stream music, photos, and video using Gateway's (www.gateway.com) wireless DVD player. Oh, and you can watch DVDs on it, too. Using 802.11g technology, Gateway lets you watch home movies and MPEG video files stored on your PC. It comes with a remote control and uses your TV set for the user interface. Gateway sells the Connected DVD Player for $199.99.

PRISMIQ MediaPlayer

The PRISMIQ MediaPlayer (www.prismiq.com) is one of the originals. Its features go beyond just moving multimedia files, though it does a pretty good job with that. It also browses the Web and displays news and weather.

It's a pretty easy device to hook up and configure. Wireless access doesn't come built in, as you need to insert a PC card (the same kind you use on laptops) into a slot on the back. You need to see for yourself how well video files move around wirelessly from your PC to PRISMIQ, as it uses the slower 802.11b technology. You may find that wireless is good for moving around audio and photos, but that a wired Ethernet connection is better for transferring video files. This media player retails for about $200.

Apple AirPort Express

This player works with iTunes software and an iPod. You plug the small AirPort Express, shown in Figure 1-2, into an electrical outlet and then connect your stereo or set of powered speakers via either an optical digital or analog audio cable. Everything is automatic (or so Apple says). The iTunes software detects the connection and displays it on a menu (and other AirPort Express units) throughout your house. You can choose the location that you want the music to play and then click Play on iTunes. You can have as many of these gizmos in your house as you can afford, one for each room (and don't forget the closets, both water and otherwise).

Figure 1-2: The Apple AirPort Express.

Roku SoundBridge

Roku's SoundBridge plays PC or Macintosh music files from anywhere in the house, and even can play songs directly from iTunes without additional software. The large display shows most of the information you get from competing units that use the TV screen as the user interface.

Roku offers two SoundBridge models. The M1000 has a 7-inch display that can show two lines of text. The M2000 has a 12-inch display that can show up to four lines of text.

TIP

If you want more information on a product, check out the company's Web site: www.rokulabs.com. Not only do you find the basics (and not so basics), but many of the product manuals are available for download, usually in Adobe Acrobat PDF format.

Other media players

Some other media players are not as high profile as those covered in the earlier section.

Play@TV

The Play@TV (www.playattv.com) NMP-4000 plays music and displays pictures and video, but it uses a 802.11b network rather than the faster 802.11g. Still, according to one magazine review, the video files play almost flawlessly. Play@TV is very similar to the PRISMIQ MediaPlayer except that it doesn't have the Web-browsing capability. Supported file formats include MP3, WMA, and WAV for audio; JPEG and BMP for photos; and MPEG-1, MPEG-2, MPEG-4, ASF, and WMV for video. The list price is $199.

Linksys Wireless-B Media Adapter

This is similar to Linksys' Wireless-B Music System, but it doesn't have the built-in speakers. It moves photos and music from your PC to your home entertainment center. Using the remote control and your TV set, you can browse through photos on your computer by folder, filename, or thumbnail picture. It supports JPG, GIF, TIFF, and BMP photo formats. For music, it can handle MP3 or WMA formats. You can navigate by title, artist, genre, or playlist. You also can play music in the background while viewing photos.

Rockford Omnifi DMS1 Digital Media Streamer

Like the Netgear and Linksys music players, Omnifi's device works with the Rhapsody online music service. You can hook up multiple DMS1s to play different music in different rooms, using the same computer. Made by Rockford Corporation (www.omnifimedia.com), the DMS1 lists for $300.

Combining the uncategorizable

Some wireless gadgets don't neatly fit into the category of a media player.

- **Linksys Wireless-G Game Adapter.** This gizmo lets you connect a PlayStation2, Xbox, or GameCube console game system to your wireless network. Those consoles all allow wired connections, but this game adapter cuts those wires so you don't need an Ethernet jack in the same room in which you play video games.
- **AlphaSmart Dana Wireless.** AlphaSmart (www.alphasmart.com) is known for its simple, text-based word processor used by students, writers, and others. It's a very simple laptop with a very long battery life. It offers no frills, but it keeps on doing what it does best for a long time. The company now has a wireless version of the device built on top of the Palm operating system. You can surf the Web on the small, monochrome screen, but I'm not sure that's the best use. Instead, having a fast way to transfer your files between it and your desktop PC, as well as the ability to check your e-mail, are probably the reasons to buy one of these, which sells for $429.
- **Linksys Wireless-B Internet Video Camera.** You can connect this video camera to your wireless network and then view its video from a Web browser anywhere in the world. It has MPEG-4 video compression that produces a 320×240 video stream. The downside is that video really should move over an 802.11g network, not an 802.11b one.
- **D-Link Securicam DCS-5300G Internet Camera.** Operating at 802.11g speeds, you can control the camera from a Web browser. It delivers audio and video, and you can pan, tilt, and zoom by using Web-based controls. As I write this, Securicam retails for about $475 — not exactly a hobbyist's plaything.
- **D-Link DVC-1100 Wireless Broadband Video Phone.** While wireless, this one is a little unusual in that it doesn't require a PC to operate. Instead, it wirelessly connects to your broadband connection (so you need at least a router). You and someone with the same unit located in a different place can conduct a videophone conference. One retails for about $230.

Wi-Fi'ing to Your Car Stereo

Did you think that using your wireless network to enjoy the multimedia splendors lurking on your hard drives was limited to inside your house? It isn't. In fact, brilliant scientists in their secluded laboratories are working on technology that extends your Wi-Fi network into your garage.

Namely, your wireless network soon will let you transfer audio files to your car stereo. You can already use wireless networks inside automobiles. For example, as I discuss Book VI, Chapter 4, you can drive along with a headset that communicates — sans wires — with your cell phone. That's basically an ad hoc network running in your car.

One company, the previously mentioned Rockford Corporation, sells the Omnifi DMP1, a mobile digital media player that lists for $600. Some of its fine features include the following:

- Wireless transfer of music, audio news, and information updates from your PC or the Internet.
- A 20-GB hard drive that stores about 300 hours of audio files in MP3 and WMA formats. You can remove the hard drive from your vehicle.
- Surface-mounted controller with an LCD display for your dashboard.
- SimpleCenter software manages your music and can transfer hours of music to your car in minutes.

Auto supplier Delphi already has a prototype of a Wi-Fi–enabled car stereo installed in a 2004 Lincoln Aviator SUV. In addition to the regular buttons on the stereo, there is a synchronization button. By pressing it, music files on your computer travel over your Wi-Fi network and are stored on a memory drive in the stereo. You might see this for sale in 2006 models.

Chapter 2: Setting Up Gadgets

In This Chapter

- **Oh, do we have gadgets!**
- **Adding a media server to your home**
- **Seeing your way with Internet video cameras**

The term *gadget* is one of those words that people use even though it doesn't really provide a good definition of a specific item. After all, just what is a gadget, anyway? Well, it's probably not really necessary to be awfully precise about this because for most people a gadget is something they know when they see.

In this chapter you read about some devices that some people would probably call *gadgets,* while other people would probably call them useful and fun additions to their wireless home entertainment environment. Regardless of what you call them, these gadgets may not be a part of your home yet, but they may well end up on your short list for the near future.

Exploring Gadgets Galore

Many different things, of course, deserve to be called gadgets. Certainly when TV remote controls were first introduced most people thought of them as gadgets. Today hardly anyone can imagine using a TV without a remote. All this really says is that gadgets do become a part of ordinary life and when they do, people stop thinking of them as gadgets.

Consider the following list and see how many you think will be so successful that they'll lose their gadget status:

- **TV-B-Gone** at www.tvbgone.com. This unit serves as a universal remote control with only one purpose — turning off any TV set within the immediate area. Want some peace and quiet instead of some blaring sports show?
- **Cell-Block-R** at www.cell-block-r.com/CellBlockR.htm. This gadget prevents the use of cell phones within an area such as a church, an auditorium, or even a restaurant. Tired of some bore at the next table blabbing into a cell phone while you're trying to have a nice, quiet dinner?

- **Laserpod** at www.laserpod.com/laserpodIntro.asp. A modern version of the lava lamp, the Laserpod gives your home or apartment a light show of "ever-changing organic lightforms of profound beauty." Want some 60's music with that?
- **Sony AIBO** at news.sel.sony.com/pressrelease/5228. Who wouldn't want a robot dog with its built-in digital camera and the ability to dance as it plays your favorite music? Just think: No need for a pooper scooper, either!
- **Peugeot Quark** at www.peugeot-avenue.com/index.asp?num_page=433&langue=en. A fuel cell-powered concept vehicle. Who wouldn't want an electric ATV?
- **Jens of Sweden Excentrique** at www.jensofsweden.se. A 24-carat gold-plated MP3 player. Who wants one of those plain old iPods when you can go for the gold?

Okay, so maybe these gadgets are a little off the wall, but I bet that at least one of them got you thinking that you'd like to have one. Well, that's the point. You may not quite yet feel the need to run out and buy the gadgets you see in this chapter, but take the time to see what they can do — you may change your mind tomorrow.

Adding a Media Server to Your Home

A *media server* is a gadget that serves to deliver music, video, still images, and possibly other types of entertainment in your home. As the *server* part of its name implies, a media server is a computer-based gadget and primarily provides electronic media content that's stored on or delivered through a computer.

What is a media server?

Different manufacturers have different definitions of what a media server is, but in general you find some combination of the following content options available:

- **Music.** From audio CDs, MP3s, Windows Media Audio (WMA), and possibly from online music sources such as Rhapsody, Napster, or iTunes.
- **Images.** Photo albums from digital cameras as well as scanned images. Often these are available as automated slide shows and, in many cases, can be accompanied by music.

- **Video.** Recorded or streaming video such as TV programs or movies. Because of Digital Rights Management (DRM) issues, this generally does not include commercial DVDs.
- **Internet radio.** A selection from the thousands of streaming radio feeds available on the Internet. This feature uses your existing Internet connection. In some cases you also need a subscription to a specific Internet service such as AOL, but other models do not require any ongoing payments.
- **Web browsing.** Some units enable you to surf the Web on your TV.
- **Web-based e-mail.** Some units also provide access to Web-based e-mail services.
- **Chat.** A few models also support online chat.

I can see you thinking that you can easily do all of these things (and a whole lot more) with just about any PC. Well, that indeed is true, but I'm talking gadgets here. Besides, do you really want some ugly, noisy PC in your living room?

Media servers are made for the living room. They're small — the PRISMIQ MediaPlayer mentioned a bit later in this chapter is actually a little smaller in most dimensions than this book! They're quiet because they typically don't have noisy components like hard drives or fans, and they're usually equipped with a handy remote control rather than a keyboard (although you can add a keyboard to some models).

Who makes media servers?

As I mentioned earlier, the exact definition of a media server depends to a great extent on who is doing the defining. With that in mind, I offer the following short list of some of the currently available products that fit into a loose categorization of media servers:

- **Toshiba RS-TX20 Digital Media Server** at www.tacp.toshiba.com/dvr/product.asp?model=RS-TX20
- **Kenwood Entré Entertainment Hub** at www.kenwoodusa.com/product/product.jsp?productTypeId=147&sortBy=price&productId=2357
- **Linksys WMLS11B Wireless-B Music System** at www.linksys.com/products/product.asp?grid=33&scid=38&prid=631
- **D-Link MediaLounge DSM-320 Wireless Media Player** at www.dlink.com/products/?pid=318
- **PRISMIQ MediaPlayer** at www.prismiq.com/products/product_media player.asp

Even though these products are available as this is being written, you can be sure that some will be replaced by newer models and others may simply disappear over the next several years. Still, this sampling does show that there are a number of manufacturers who take the idea of media servers seriously enough to believe that they'll become a mass market success.

Moving Some of Everything with PRISMIQ MediaPlayer

The PRISMIQ MediaPlayer serves as an excellent example of a home media server. This unit has built-in Ethernet to connect directly to your home network, and it also supports many popular PC card wireless network adapters. This section looks at some of its features to give you a better understanding of how a media server works in your home.

The PRISMIQ MediaPlayer functions along with the PCs on your home network to deliver video, audio, and images from your PCs to your home entertainment system and TV set. It also includes several features that enable you to browse the Web, listen to Internet radio, send and receive e-mail, and engage in chat rooms from the comfort of the sofa in front of your TV. PRISMIQ also offers an optional wireless keyboard for those times when the included remote control might not be optimal — such as for chat or e-mail.

Setting up the PRISMIQ MediaPlayer

To begin using your PRISMIQ MediaPlayer you must first install the included Media Manager software on one of the PCs on your network. Ideally you install this on a PC that has a TV tuner because that enables you to make full use of the SnapStream Personal Video Station application, which you can optionally install. The SnapStream software enables you to record live TV and then stream it on your network.

The PRISMIQ Media Manager application scans your PC to locate any of the many supported types of media content. Once this content is logged in to the Media Manager's records, you can view it using the PRISMIQ MediaPlayer.

TIP

Be sure to have the PRISMIQ Media Manager application scan all of the PCs on your network so that any media they contain is also available for viewing. Also, the PC that runs the PRISMIQ Media Manager application must be on whenever you want to play any of the content using the PRISMIQ MediaPlayer. You can turn off that PC's monitor to save energy, however.

After the Media Manager application is installed, you're ready to add the PRISMIQ MediaPlayer to your network. If you're using an Ethernet connection, you can simply plug in the included network cable. If you want to go wireless, you need to read the PRISMIQ MediaPlayer setup manual to see how to configure your wireless card. You also need to connect the PRISMIQ MediaPlayer to your TV or home entertainment center receiver using the included cables.

Figure 2-1 shows how the PRISMIQ MediaPlayer display appears on your TV screen once the unit is installed and ready to use.

Figure 2-1: The PRISMIQ MediaPlayer is ready to use.

Using the PRISMIQ MediaPlayer

Using the PRISMIQ MediaPlayer is actually very easy. The remote control has dedicated buttons for the most often used functions and it has a large navigation button to move the cursor on your TV screen. Of course, you have to spend a few minutes getting used to a new remote control, but you can ace it in no time.

Take a look at some of the screens you see as you use the PRISMIQ MediaPlayer. Figure 2-2 shows how the display appears when you're playing music tracks from an audio CD that you've copied to the hard drive of your PC. Notice that the screen shows the name of the CD, the track title, the name of the artist, the length of the track, and (in some cases) the *bit rate* that was used to copy the track to your PC. Some of this information may not appear if you didn't allow your PC to obtain the information from the Internet when you copied the tracks to your hard drive.

Figure 2-2: Playing audio tracks using the PRISMIQ Media Player.

Figure 2-3 shows how the display appears when you are selecting digital photos to display on your TV. When you click an image, that image displays full screen on your TV. You can also choose to run a slide show of all the images in a folder or to play an audio track along with the images.

Finally, Figure 2-4 shows the screen that appears when you choose the Web option either by clicking or by pressing the Web button on the remote. The PRISMIQ MediaPlayer includes the fairly simple Web browser shown in the figure, but you'll probably want the optional wireless keyboard if you plan on doing too much surfing from your sofa.

These examples have barely touched on the ways that you can use the PRISMIQ MediaPlayer as a part of your home entertainment options. Even so, you probably are already thinking about exactly where you want to add this gadget to your life.

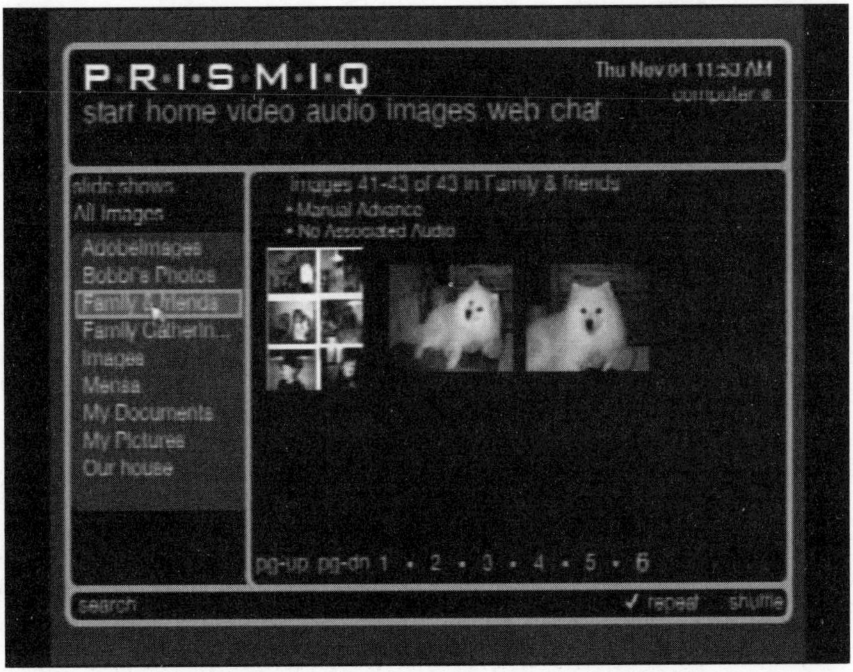

Figure 2-3: Selecting images to display on your TV with the PRISMIQ Media Player.

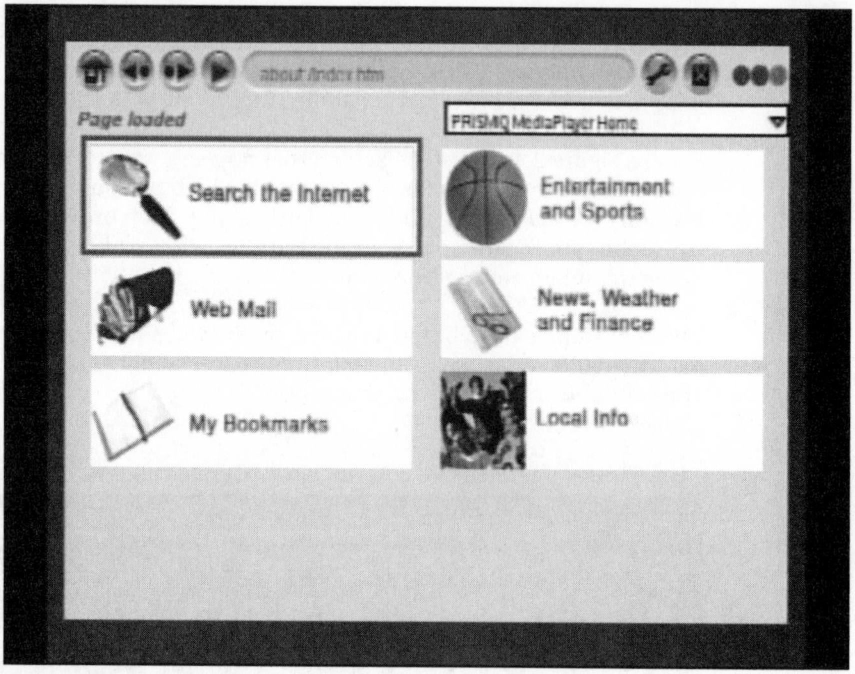

Figure 2-4: You can surf the Web on your TV with the PRISMIQ Media Player.

Looking into Internet Video Cameras

Internet video cameras — commonly called *webcams* — are another of those gadgets that you probably don't really need, but that you may decide that you really want. Webcams are used for many different purposes and one of those purposes could be just what you've been looking for.

Here are a couple of ways that people use webcams:

- ✦ The Nevada Department of Transportation (NDOT) has three webcams that enable the public to follow the progress of a major highway extension project. These cameras show the construction of the longest concrete arch span in the U.S. You find them at factory.oxblue.com/client/galena/.
- ✦ You can view current traffic conditions at various locations in California at the Caltrans Web site at video.dot.ca.gov/.
- ✦ Want to see what's going on in Rome right now? Try the Capitolium.org webcam at www.capitolium.org/eng/virtuale/webview.htm.
- ✦ For a live view of the current conditions at the South Pole, visit the Climate Monitoring and Diagnostics Laboratory Web site at www.cmdl.noaa.gov/obop/spo/livecamera.html.

- Are you stuck in a drab and dreary spot but would like to pretend that you're on the beach? Try the AllAboutCabo.com webcam at www.allaboutcabo.com.
- Worried that Mount St. Helens might blow up and ruin your vacation to the Northwest? Try the Forest Service's webcam at www.fs.fed.us/gpnf/volcanocams/msh/.

People also aim webcams at their fish tanks, their cats, and even at the grass growing in their yards. Some people use private webcams to monitor their homes when they're away. You can also use a webcam to create a video phone!

Many different webcams are available. Here's a listing of some places to look for a webcam:

- Logitech has several webcam models. You can find the details at www.logitech.com/index.cfm/products/productlist/US/EN,CRID=20.
- D-Link also offers a wide variety of webcams. See /www.dlink.com/products/category.asp?cid=58&sec=1 for more information.
- Linksys has the WVC54G Wireless-G Internet Video Camera, which you find at www.linksys.com/products/product.asp?grid=33&scid=38&prid=650.
- Labtec offers some very inexpensive webcam models at www.labtec.com/index.cfm?countryid=1001&languageid=1&page=gear/listing&crid=30.
- Finally, Hawking Technology produces a line of excellent webcams that you can find at www.hawkingtech.com/prodList.php?FamID=15.

TIP

For more options than you find with the software that typically comes with webcams, check out Active WebCam from PY Software (www.pysoft.com). You can download a free trial version that supports multiple webcams and includes many security-related features.

WARNING!

If you intend to place a webcam in a location aimed outdoors, be aware that aiming the camera so that it looks directly into the sun will likely damage the camera. Sure, that sunset shot may be beautiful, but in the long run it's probably going to destroy the image sensor in the camera. (Don't ask me how I know this.)

Are you ready to add some interesting new gadgets to your life? This chapter has given you some places to begin your quest to become the technology gadget king of your neighborhood.

Chapter 3: Chatting with Motorola's IMfree

In This Chapter

- **Instant messaging moves to the couch**
- **Getting ready for IMfree**
- **Mastering emoticons and abbreviations**

Are you addicted to instant messaging? Perhaps you know a certain teenager who is? Would you like to chat without being tethered to your computer? If you do know such a teenager, would you like to use your computer while letting the chatting continue? Thanks to Motorola, the maker of the instant messager called IMfree, these things are possible.

You don't need a paid America Online (AOL) account to use IMfree. You can get an account for free. However, if you subscribe to AOL, your existing account does work with IMfree.

Getting Ahold of Your Messager

IMfree, which at the time of this writing costs about $75, looks like a two-way pager with a display and a small keyboard. Shown in Figure 3-1, you hold it in two hands, your thumbs tackling the standard-layout keyboard.

IMfree wirelessly connects to your PC using 900 MHz unlicensed digital spectrum. Motorola says you can use IMfree up to 150 feet from the base. This range depends on a number of factors, including the location, walls, and outside interference, the latter of which I discuss later in this chapter.

You can use up to seven handhelds at once with each base, which sounds crazy to me. It could be a perfect solution for the Brady Bunch, however. (Yes, I'm assuming that Alice would use one, too.) Each of those handhelds can handle six IM chats simultaneously. That's up to 35 ongoing conversations through one base unit! (Motorola doesn't sell the handheld unit separately, so you need to purchase the whole setup even though you won't use more than one base unit per computer.)

Figure 3-1: Send and receive instant messages (aka IMs).

Setting Yourself Up for Freedom

One technology writer described it best: IMfree looks like a slice of bread. It might be a little more accurate to say it's like a slice that includes a generous amount of crust. It also comes with a base antenna, which resembles a coaster with a USB cord attached, and a power adapter.

Don't you hate it when you're all ready to play with a new electronic toy and discover that you must charge the battery first? IMfree needs to charge for 16 hours the first time, but you can use it while it's plugged in and charging. (Still, as you find throughout this book, batteries are your best friends in the wireless, mobile world.) Motorola estimates the battery life is four hours of continuous use. IMfree goes into sleep mode after about two minutes of inactivity, which helps extend battery life. Subsequent rechargings take up to 10 hours.

Installing software on your PC

Before you can use IMfree's handheld, you need to install software on your PC that communicates with the base unit, which in turn talks to the handheld.

The IMfree handheld can't talk with the base station unless the PC client software is running.

Just follow these directions for installing the software:

1. **Insert the CD-ROM that Motorola packages with IMfree.**

   A Welcome to the MX240a Setup Wizard dialog box appears, as shown in Figure 3-2.

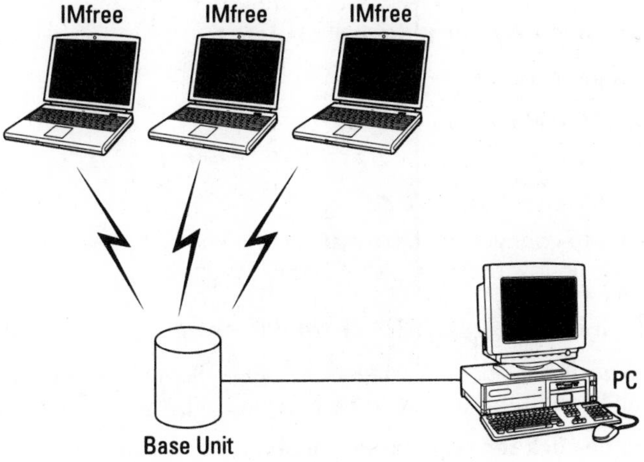

Figure 3-2: Installing IMfree's PC software.

2. **Click Next.**

   A Motorola license agreement appears.

3. **If you agree, select I Agree and click Next.**

   An AOL Instant Messenger license agreement appears.

4. **Read the license agreement and click Next.**

   A User Information dialog box appears, and may have your name and organization filled in.

5. **If the Full Name and Organization fields are blank, enter the information.**

6. **Click Next.**

   A Shared File Access dialog box appears.

7. **Decide whether you want other people who use your computer to access this software.**

8. **Click Next.**

   A Select Installation Folder dialog box appears.

9. **If the installation folder location is okay, click Next. Otherwise, click Browse to select another folder.**

   An Options dialog box appears.

10. **Decide if you want to add a shortcut icon to the desktop and if you want the application to start each time Windows starts.**

    A Confirm Installation dialog box appears.

11. **Click Next to confirm the installation.**

    The application installs.

12. **Click Finish and you're done.**

Running the software

You've got to connect the base station to your computer before you can rev the engine. Follow these steps to connect them:

1. **Plug the base station's USB cord into one of your PC's USB ports.**

   The ports are about ½" wide and 3⁄16" high. Some PCs have them on the front in addition to the two that virtually always are on the back.

2. **Double-click the application's icon on your desktop.**

   The PC client software loads. If the software is running and the base is connected, you see a green icon in the Windows XP notification area. If the base disconnects from your PC — you pull the USB plug from your PC, for instance — you see a red triangle icon in the notification area.

   If you're connected to the Internet, the software checks for the latest version. If a newer version is available, a dialog box asks if you'd like to update the software.

3. **Click OK and you're done.**

Powering up and registering

If your PC client software is running and the IMfree base is plugged into your computer, you can register the handheld with the base station.

When you first turn on the handheld unit, you hear a pleasant tune and see a message:

> Before you can use this device you must first register it with your base unit. Your base ID may be found on a label on the bottom of your base unit.

These steps get you up and registered:

1. **Turn on the handheld with the power button located on the top right.**

   You see the base ID message. If you don't see the message, press the Menu button and then press the Option button (below Regstr).

2. **Enter the base station ID into the handheld.**

   The ID is a series of six letters.

3. **Press Send.**

   The handheld looks for a nearby base station. Upon finding one, it asks you to return to the PC and accept the registration shown in Figure 3-3.

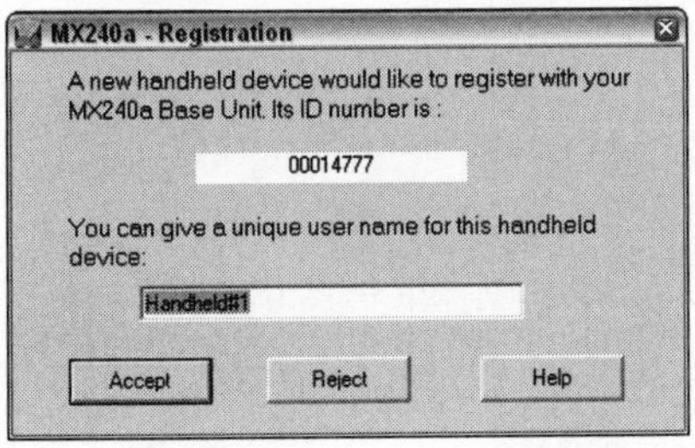

Figure 3-3: Accepting the registration of a handheld unit.

4. **Delete the default and enter a name for the handheld.**

   The default name for the first handheld is Handheld#1.

5. **Click Accept.**

   The handheld is registered with your base station.

Setting up your PC

After your handheld is registered with the base station, you need to configure the software options for the client software.

1. **Start the client software if it's not already running.**

   You should see a green icon in the notification area.

2. **Right-click the green icon.**

   You see the menu shown in Figure 3-4.

3. **Select Setup.**

   A Setup dialog box appears.

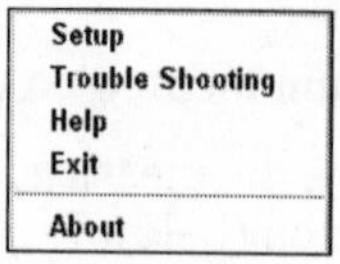

Figure 3-4: The client software's right-click menu.

4. **Select the handheld you want to set up from the pull-down menu shown in Figure 3-5.**

   Remember, you have to register the handheld first.

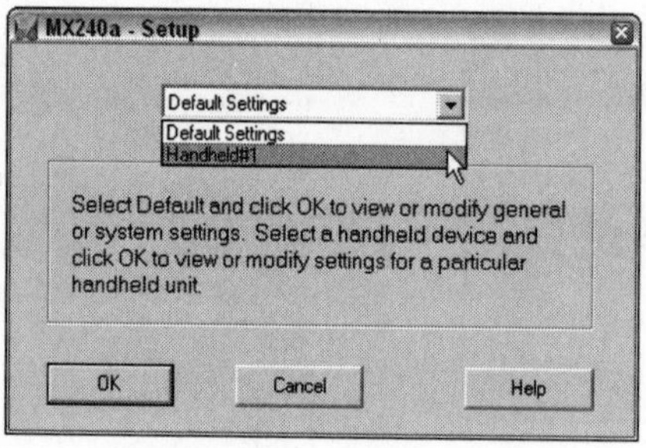

Figure 3-5: Selecting your handheld in the client software.

5. **Click OK.**

   A new dialog box displays the Security tab shown in Figure 3-6.

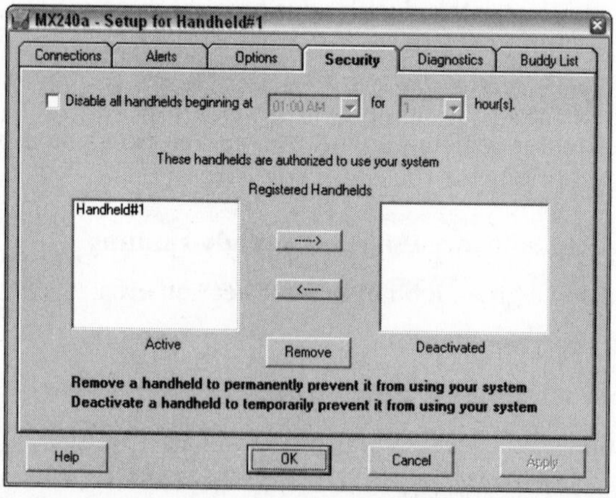

Figure 3-6: Tabs show groups of options.

6. **Click OK when you're done with the setup dialog boxes.**

You can do various and sundry things on different tabs:

- **Security**. You can add to and remove from the list of units authorized to use your base station. You also can disable all handhelds beginning at a certain time and lasting for a certain number of hours. You may want to use this feature to keep your children off IMfree during certain hours.

  If you remove, rather than deactivate, a handheld, you must reregister the handheld with the base station.
- **Connections**. You can select your Internet connection type, the type of modem connections, and enter information about a proxy server, if you use one.
- **Alerts**. Choose the handheld sounds you want to associate with nine alerts. If you want silence, check the Disable Alert on Handheld box for each alert you want to disable. You can listen to the sounds by clicking the blue play button. Using the music editor, you can modify an alert sound's play rate, scale, note duration, and volume.
- **Options**. You can choose who can contact you. You can create allow and block lists or block all incoming chat invitations.
- **Diagnostics**. Click Start Test to run four different tests:
  - Internet connection.
  - Base to handheld link.
  - USB link.
  - IM network service.
- **Buddy List**. You can click the Buddy button to add *buddies,* which is AOL's term for chat partners. You can click Group to add a new group, which holds a number of buddies. Clicking Remove does just that. Motorola recommends you organize your buddies into five or fewer groups for better display on your handheld. You can't work with the Buddy List until you create an AOL Instant Messenger screen name, which you embark upon in the next section.

You can manage your buddies and groups through the AOL Instant Messenger (AIM) software. Any changes made to the Buddy List in either the IMfree or AIM software are reflected in the other list when you next log in.

Creating an AIM screen name

Before you can use AOL Instant Messenger (AIM), you must create a screen name. It can be just about anything, assuming someone else doesn't already have it. For this book, I chose the screen name WirelessDummies. Funny, but no one else had chosen it before me, so it's mine, mine, mine.

Here's how you create an AIM screen name:

1. **Use your PC to browse to** www.aim.com.

   You see the AOL Instant Messenger web site shown in Figure 3-7.

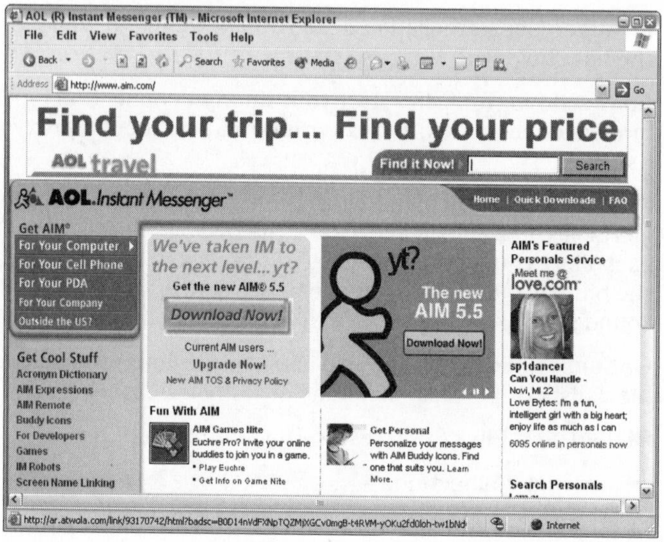

Figure 3-7: AOL Instant Messenger web site.

2. **Click the Download Now icon.**

   A new web page appears.

3. **Click New Users Click Here.**

   The first of two pages about creating screen names appears, as shown in Figure 3-8.

4. **Enter a screen name in the Desired Screen Name form.**

   Millions of screen names are already taken. Finding an unused screen name may take a while.

5. **Enter a password and then confirm it by reentering.**

6. **Enter your e-mail address.**

7. **Select your birth date.**

8. **Type the word you see in the image.**

   This prevents automated screen name creation by spammers.

9. **Click Submit.**

   A second web page confirms your screen name, as shown in Figure 3-9. If your screen name is already taken, you need to select another one.

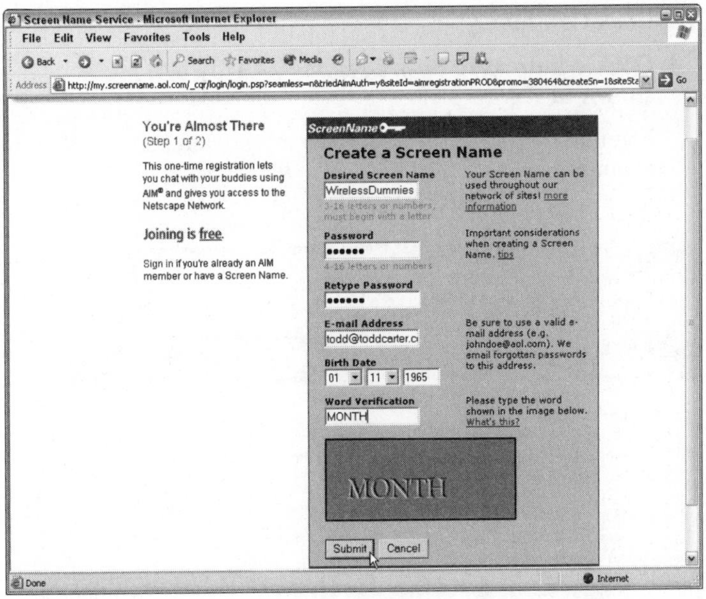

Figure 3-8: Entering information for creating a screen name.

10. **Select your gender and enter your zip code and country.**

11. **Click Submit.**

A Congratulations dialog box appears.

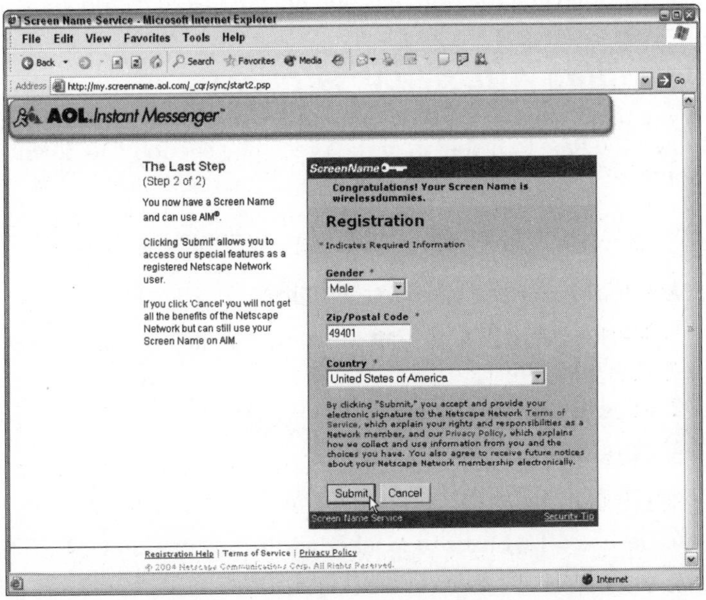

Figure 3-9: Completing the screen name registration.

12. **Click Continue.**
13. **Click Windows to download the AOL Instant Messenger software shown in Figure 3-10.**

    If you're using a Mac, select Macintosh. I'm using a Windows PC for this example.

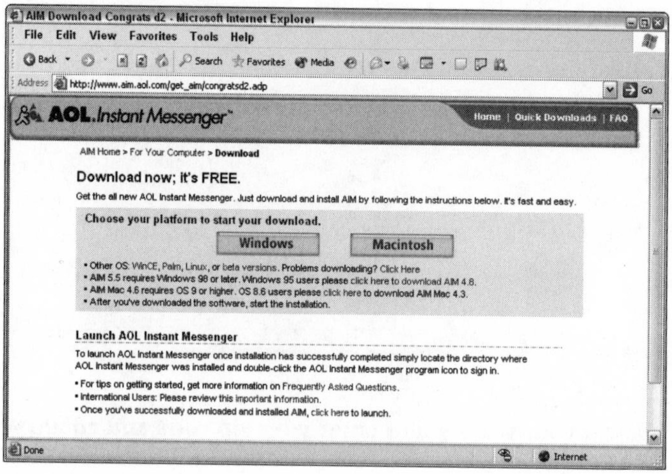

Figure 3-10: Downloading the AIM software.

14. **Save the file to a location you'll remember.**

    The following section tells you how to install the downloaded file.

Installing AOL's AIM software

If you don't already use AOL Instant Messenger software on your computer, now's the time to install it. In the preceding section you download the AIM software.

Follow these steps to install the software on your computer:

1. **Double-click the downloaded file.**

   The Installing AOL Instant Messenger dialog box and a licensing agreement appear.
2. **Click Yes to start setup.**
3. **Click Next.**

   The AOL Instant Messenger Install Components dialog box appears.
4. **Deselect the boxes to disable additional components, if desired.**
5. **Click Next.**

6. **If the default installation directory is okay, click Next.**

   You can change the install directory by clicking Browse and choosing another folder.

7. **Select whether you use a modem or a LAN for your Internet access.**

   If you have a broadband connection such as DSL or cable, select the LAN button.

8. **Click Next.**

9. **Select your country, enter your zip code, and decide whether you want to make www.netscape.com your home page.**

10. **Select where you want icons to appear, if at all.**

11. **Click Next.**

    Finally, the actual installation is about to begin!

12. **Click Next.**

    The software installs and a Screen Name dialog box appears.

13. **Enter your screen name.**

14. **Click OK.**

    The software loads, waiting for you to enter your username and password.

15. **Enter your username and password.**

16. **Click Sign On.**

    If all goes well you're signed onto AOL's Instant Messenger service, as shown in Figure 3-11.

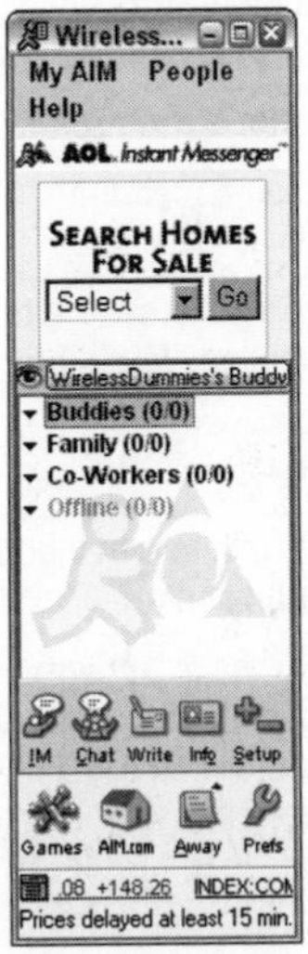

Figure 3-11: Connected to AOL's Instant Messenger service.

No, you can't get rid of that big ad on the top. Too bad, eh? But the service *is* free.

Using IMfree

If you've set up everything and the handheld unit is charged, start using the darn thing. If you're like me and love to play with gadgets, you probably thought this moment was beyond reach. Fret not, as it's here.

First, a quick checklist:

- Is your base station plugged into your PC?
- Is the client software running on your PC?
- Do you have the handheld turned on?

Yes, yes, yes? Great, great, great!

The keys to chatting

Most of handheld's keys are basic: letters, numbers, that kind of thing. Some others may not be immediately recognizable. Table 3-1 breaks down functions.

Table 3-1 IMfree's Keyboard

Key(s)	Where It Is	What It Does
Option	Six of them line the bottom of the dialog box	The keys are blank, as their functions are determined by the text just above them. The text changes as you move from one menu to the next.
↑ and ↓	Top left	Move you around the dialog box.
Menu	Second key to left of space key	You do a bunch of stuff with this key.
Who's On	Left of Menu key	Press to switch to the Who's Online Now dialog box.
Talk	Far-right bottom corner	Press to switch to the Talk dialog box.
Bye	Left of Talk key	Press to wave goodbye (in the virtual sense).
Sym	Right of space key	Press to activate symbols. It's like a shift key, activating the top characters on each key. Press the key twice to lock it on; press once more to turn it off.

Key (s)	Where It Is	What It Does
Send	Large key on far right, second row from bottom	Press to send information. It's like the Enter key on a keyboard.
↑	Left of the space key	Capitalize letters.

Getting a move on

If you've followed all the steps in the "Setting Yourself Up for Freedom" section in this chapter, get ready to chat.

1. **Press the power button on the upper right.**

   The handheld turns on. If it finds the base station, it displays Select a Service.

2. **Press the option button below AIM.**

   The option button is the gray button on the keyboard directly under the dialog box. AIM is the only service IMfree currently supports.

3. **Enter your screen name into the handheld and press Send.**
4. **Enter your password.**

   The Who's Online Now dialog box appears.

5. **Press the number that corresponds with the buddy with whom you want to chat.**

   A chat session begins. Send messages by entering text and pressing Send when you finish. Press the Bye button to end an IM session.

You can have an IM session on your PC as long as it's separate from the one on your handheld. To do this, you must log in using different screen names. Also, IMfree doesn't support Buddy icons or custom fonts. Instead, all text is sent and received in AIM's default text format.

Avoiding interference

IMfree uses frequencies in the 900 MHz range, so it may fall victim to the same kinds of interference you may experience while using your cordless phone. These include cordless baby monitors, cordless headphones, and cordless speakers. If you're having problems, you may experience the same with IMfree. (However, Motorola says IMfree uses 900 MHz *digital* unlicensed radio spectrum, so it shouldn't interfere. This section helps if that turns out not to be the case.)

If you hear static and other kinds of noises (not including those emanating from your conversation partner) on your cordless phone, you probably suffer from some interference in that frequency band.

Of course, you won't hear static on IMfree, but you may find you're not receiving all of your messages or that your chat partner is not receiving any of your messages. More likely, you must decrease the distance between the handheld unit and the base. In other words, you don't have enough signal strength to sit 100 or 150 feet away from the computer connected to the IMfree base.

Now for something completely similar

Once upon a time, not too many Internet minutes ago, AOL was the only place the masses could chat online. Now that online America increasingly finds itself outside AOL's walls and on the Internet at work and home, people have many other venues for chatting with those who use poor grammar and spelling.

Yahoo! and MSN both have chat clients similar to AOL. Software programs, like Trillian, work with all three services. In the case of Trillian, shown in the accompanying figure, it also works with ICQ and Internet relay chat (IRC). ICQ is easy to use (and also owned by AOL). IRC is the original instant messaging environment. It's usually populated by the more technically literate, although Trillian, for one, makes the task of connecting to and chatting on IRC channels easy.

While this chapter focuses on a gadget that only works with AOL, that's not an endorsement. If there were other, similar doodads that worked with Yahoo!, MSN, or IRC, I'd happily cover them. At least AOL (just like the others) doesn't require you to subscribe to its online service in order to use the chat technology. It's more like a loss leader to possibly draw you into the pay services. (There's nothing wrong with the old-fashioned landline telephone, by the way. It's still a reliable means of chatting and there's only poor verbal grammar to endure. As far as I know, you can't misspell words during a one-on-one voice conversation.)

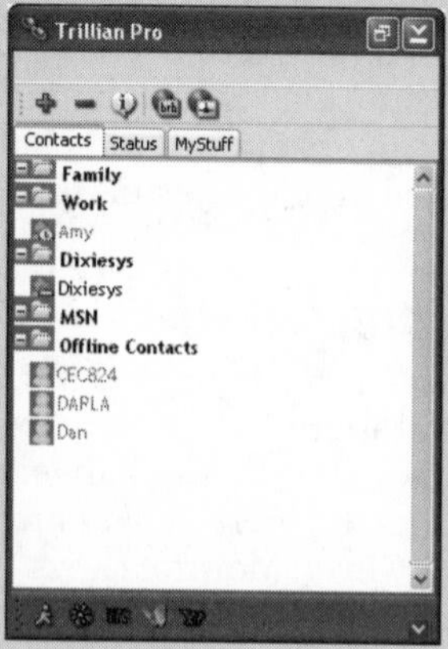

Trillian communicates with all major chat services.

Swearing off the smiley

A related but admittedly irrelevant tale: In January 2003 I pledged to myself, in one of those silly bouts of new year's resolutionisms, to stop using smileys in my e-mail correspondence. The resolution lasted but six weeks, which is certainly longer than any dieting pledge I've made. For me, the smiley was a necessity to prevent some sentences from coming across as sarcastic or mean spirited.

TIP

The best solution is making sure everything else in the same frequency range is turned off. If that solves the problem, great. If not, you may have interference that's outside of your control or signals that just can't penetrate any walls between you and the base.

I don't suggest you tear down walls just to get better range, although swinging a sledgehammer is not a bad way to spend a Saturday afternoon. Instead — and I know this is a cop out — you may need to bow to the technology gods and simply sit closer to the base unit. Problem solved. Probably.

Emoticoning and abbreviating

I'm told writing is the best kind of confessional. So it's true: I wear my heart on my sleeve (which makes for some very nasty stains come laundry time) and I'm prone to expressing my emotions now and then. How do you convey emotions in the anonymous forum of instant messaging?

The pioneers have already sowed that land, my dear reader. Through years of trial and error (and a reluctance to type even one more character than necessary), the IM faithful produced a shorthand for communicating emotions during online chats.

You often must crane your head sideways to see what these symbols represent, but most of them are one take or another on a *smiley,* which looks like a smile and lets the other person know you're being lighthearted). These *emoticons* prevent misunderstandings by adding the visual cues that online communications take away. Of course, you probably have seen these emoticons used in e-mails, too.

Maybe my eloquent prose convinced you that IMfree is the perfect complement for online chatters, even though you've never uttered an instant-messaged word in your life. Trying something new is good for your soul (and, in this case, Motorola's revenues).

Getting the device hooked up and working is just the beginning. If you've never chatted online, you need a quick lesson in online world lingo. You can forget most of the English you know, as you find the worst grammar and spelling imaginable during online chats (at least those conducted between teenagers, if the ones I've seen are a fair indication).

Many chatters use these abbreviations:

- AFAIK As Far As I Know
- BAK Back At Keyboard
- BBL Be Back Later
- BCNU Be Seeing You
- B4N Bye For Now
- BRB Be Right Back
- BTW By The Way
- F2F Face To Face
- FWIW For What It's Worth
- FYA For Your Amusement
- FYI For Your Information
- GFY Good For You
- GGBB Gotta Go Bye Bye
- GL Good Luck
- GMTA Great Minds Think Alike
- G2G Got To Go
- GTGB Got To Go, Bye
- ILU Love You
- IDK I Don't Know
- IMHO In My Humble Opinion
- IMO In My Opinion
- INALB I'm Not A Lawyer, But. . .
- IOH I'm Outta Here
- IOW In Other Words
- IRL In Real Life
- ITS I Told You So
- KIT Keep In Touch
- LOL Laughing Out Loud
- LTL Let's Talk Later
- LTNC Long Time No Chat
- LTNS Long Time No See
- MAYB Maybe
- NM Nothing Much
- NP No Problem
- NRN No Reply Necessary
- NYO Need Your Opinion
- PDQ Pretty Darn Quick
- PLS Please
- PMFJI Pardon Me For Jumping In
- POS Parent over shoulder, change subject
- POV Point Of View

- ROTFL Rolling On the Floor Laughing
- RSN Real Soon Now
- TIA Thanks In Advance
- TMI Too Much Information
- TTFN Ta Ta for Now
- TTYL Talk To You Later
- TTYS Talk To You Soon
- TU Thank You
- TX Thanks
- TY Thank You
- TYVM Thank You Very Much
- YMMV Your Mileage May Vary
- U You
- U2 You, Too
- WB Welcome Back

Chapter 4: Sharing Multimedia Files with Windows XP

In This Chapter

- **Moving multimedia files on your wireless network**
- **Sharing your files with others**
- **Keeping your secrets safe**
- **Assigning a drive letter to a network folder**

The fun of having a home network is that you can share files among your various computers. If you have family photos and videos everyone enjoys viewing or watching on their own PC, you don't have to store them on each individual computer. Instead, you can store them on one computer and then access them from anywhere on the network. All you need to do is make sure that the files are enabled for sharing.

In this chapter I talk about sharing your files — all kinds, including video and music — on a network, blocking access to files, and mapping a network drive to make it easier to reach files stored on a remote computer.

In Book VII, Chapters 1 and 2, I talk about some hardware gadgets, generally called *multimedia servers,* that help you move photos, music, and video from your computers to your home entertainment system. This chapter discusses how you can transfer these kinds of files among your networked computers using nothing more than Windows XP.

Tuning In to Sights and Sounds

Maybe you live a state away from your grandkids. You need photos of the youngins, and how better to get them than online, right? Or maybe you're a college student who's ready to pitch his Discman and pledge allegiance to MP3s. Here's the trashcan; you can move music files until the cows come home (or at least until finals start). Finally, perhaps you're the struggling director who works on his movies at home on her PC. You need video ability and I'm going to tell you how to get there.

You may or may not fit into one of these scenarios for sharing music over your network:

- Listening to music stored on a hard drive on a networked computer.
- Listening to music stored in one place, where a computer is acting like a dedicated server.
- Streaming music or other audio from the Internet over your network so that all computers have access to the stream.

Taking a looksee at video

Moving video across your network is the most trying of the three kinds of multimedia files I've mentioned. Video and movie files can be huge, weighing in at the multigigabyte level. Photos and music files are a blip on the bandwidth screen compared to large video files.

TIP

If you're planning on moving a lot of large video files between the computers on your network, consider one of these alternatives to wireless networking:

- I know it's blasphemous to say in a 700-page book on wireless technology, but you might want to consider using a wired network for this chore. The files will move much quicker, getting close to 100 Mbps if you're running a Fast Ethernet (100 Mbps as opposed to a 10 Mbps) network.
- If you're still keen on a wireless network to transport your ripped DVD files and other largess, you definitely should go with an 802.11g network rather than the slower 802.11b network. The prices of the faster 802.11g equipment are falling fast.
- You might try buying the "turbo," or faster, versions of 802.11g equipment that some manufacturers make. You won't get the Fast Ethernet speeds they suggest, but the access points and network adapters likely will get you an improvement in speed. With huge video files, every little bit helps.

Sharing Your Files on a Network

I've said it before and I'll say it again: Windows XP makes it easy to share files across a network. In fact, one folder on each computer is already shared with everyone on the network. It's called the Shared Documents folder and every Windows XP computer has it automatically turned on for sharing.

Other folders can be shared on the network, but you must make a special effort to enable them for sharing, so they can be shared with other users on your network. If you have files and folders you don't want to share on the network, disable the feature. I talk about this later in this chapter.

The computer that's sharing the files and folders must be connected to the network. And, of course, it must be turned on.

Here's how you share a folder with others on your network:

1. **Navigate to the folder you want to share.**
2. **Select the folder.**
3. **Do one of the following:**
   - Click Share This Folder under File and Folder Tasks.
   - Right-click the folder and select Sharing and Security.

   The folder's Properties dialog box appears.
4. **Select the Share This Folder on the Network checkbox, which is under Network Sharing and Security.**
5. **Enter a name in the Share Name box, like that shown in Figure 4-1.**

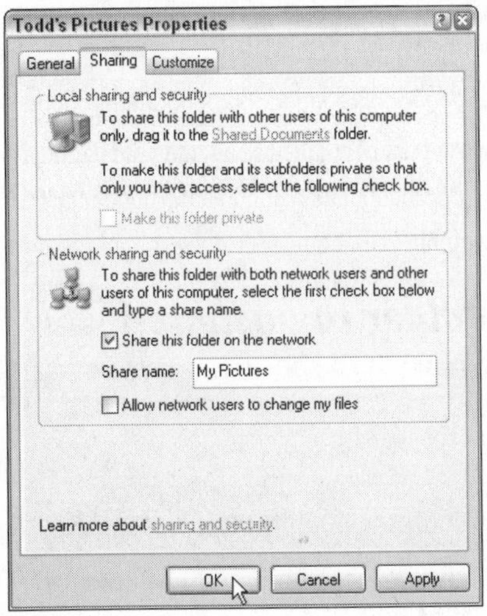

Figure 4-1: Entering a share name.

6. **Click OK.**

   The folder's icon changes to show a hand, indicating it's now being shared. That's all there is to sharing your folders.

Unless you're a masochist (hey, we all need a hobby) or are the only one using your network, I don't suggest selecting Allow Network Users to Change My Files. Otherwise, you may find, say, your word processing documents changed without your permission.

REMEMBER

Folder-sharing limitations

You have some limits to the files and folders you can share on your network. You can't share files in these folders:

- Documents and Settings (C:\Documents and Settings, for example)
- Program Files
- Windows

Not selecting this also protects you to some extent if during a security lapse an intruder gains access to your wireless network. At the worst, the intruder could only read the file, not write to it. However, anyone can copy files from a shared folder. They cannot change the files, but they can snag copies and store them on their PC (and then change versions of that saved file).

Blocking Access to Files

Just as you can open the doors to your file treasures with Windows XP, you also can close them. You can stop others on the network from accessing your files.

Changing a shared folder to unshared

1. **Navigate to the folder you want to share.**
2. **Select the folder.**
3. **Do one of the following:**
   - Click Share This Folder under File and Folder Tasks.
   - Right-click the folder and select Sharing and Security.

   The folder's Properties dialog box appears.
4. **Deselect the Share This Folder on the Network checkbox, which is under Network Sharing and Security.**
5. **Click OK.**

   The folder's icon changes so it no longer shows the sharing hand symbol.

Monitoring shared folders

You can monitor shared folders on your computer to see which ones are being accessed from the network. Here's how you do that:

1. **Click Start.**

   The Start menu appears.

2. **Click Control Panel.**

   The Control Panel appears.

3. **Click Performance and Maintenance.**

   The Performance and Maintenance dialog box appears.

4. **Click Administrative Tools, an icon located toward the bottom of the screen.**

   The Administrative Tools window appears.

5. **Click Computer Management.**

   The Computer Management dialog box appears.

6. **Click the plus sign (+) beside Shared Folders.**

   The Shared Folders menu tree opens.

7. **Click Shares.**

   Shared folders display in the main window, as shown in the accompanying figure.

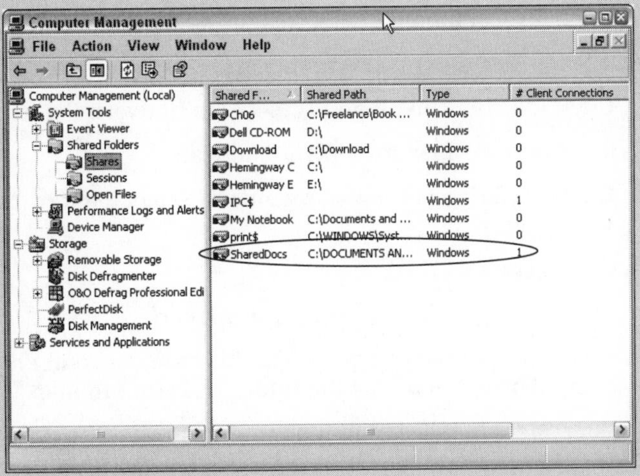

You can see which folders have connections by looking under # Client Connections. In this example, another computer on the network is connecting to the SharedDocs folder. You can monitor your shared folders whenever you want. Just don't use it to spy on what others in the household are viewing (wink, wink).

Hiding a folder from others

Windows XP has a trick for hiding a folder from others on the network: Add a dollar sign to the end of the folder name.

It works pretty well, unless someone on the network knows the folder name and adds the dollar sign or can guess the folder name and then appends the dollar symbol when he's searching for the folder.

Assigning a Drive Letter to a Network Folder

Rather than navigating to a network folder every time you want to access it, you can create a direct link to the folder. It's called assigning, or *mapping*, a drive letter to a network folder. It's easy to set up and use.

After setting it up, you can connect to the network drive the same way you access a hard drive on your own computer. Just follow these steps:

1. **Click Start.**

   The Start menu appears.

2. **Click My Computer.**

   The My Computer window appears.

3. **Click the Tools menu and select Map Network Drive.**

   The Map Network Drive Wizard appears.

4. **Click the Drive pull-down menu and select a letter to assign the network folder.**

5. **Click Browse.**

   The Browse for Folder dialog box appears.

6. **Double-click the workgroup (in this case, Mshome) that contains the computer that contains the folder you want to map.**

   Computers in the workgroup are shown.

7. **Double-click the computer that contains the folder you want to map.**

   Folders that are available for sharing appear.

   Only folders that have been enabled for sharing on the networked computer are shown. If the folder you want to map is not shown, you'll need to enable its sharing from the networked computer.

8. **Select the folder you want to map, as shown in Figure 4-2.**

   In this example, the folder is called SharedDocs and it's located on the Homeofficepc2 computer.

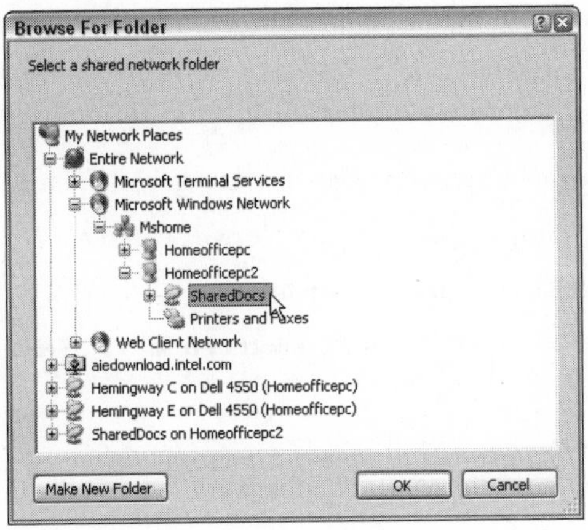

Figure 4-2: Selecting a folder to map.

9. **Click OK.**

   The folder's network path appears in the Folder: pull-down menu.

10. **Click Finish.**

    The SharedDocs folder on Homeofficepc2 is now a network drive, with a drive letter of X, as shown in Figure 4-3. Now you can access this folder quickly and easily. And you're finished.

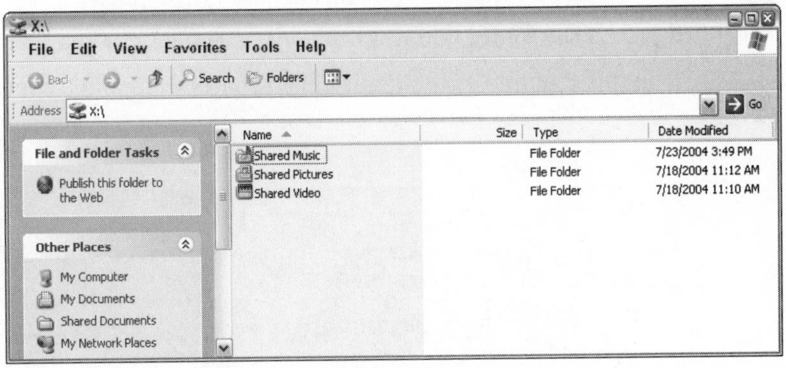

Figure 4-3: X marks the spot.

Switching off automatic connections

When you assign a network drive letter to a network folder, as I explained in the last section, Windows XP automatically tries to connect to that network drive every time you log in to your computer.

However, you can turn that feature off, which can make the log in process faster. Long delays can occur if the computer that has the network drive is turned off or otherwise unavailable.

1. **Click Start.**

   The Start menu appears.

2. **Click My Computer.**

   The My Computer window appears.

3. **Click the Tools menu and select Map Network Drive.**

   The Map Network Drive Wizard appears.

4. **Click the Drive pull-down menu and select a letter to assign the network folder.**

5. **Click Browse.**

   The Browse for Folder dialog box appears.

6. **Double-click the workgroup (in this case, Mshome) that contains the computer that contains the folder you want to map (and off to grandmother's house we go).**

   Computers in the workgroup are shown.

7. **Double-click the computer that contains the folder you want to map.**

   Folders that are available for sharing appear.

   REMEMBER: Only folders that have been enabled for sharing on the networked computer are shown. If the folder you want to map is not shown, you'll need to enable its sharing from the networked computer.

8. **Select the folder you want to map, as shown in Figure 4-3.**

   In this example, the folder is called SharedDocs and it's located on the Homeofficepc2 computer.

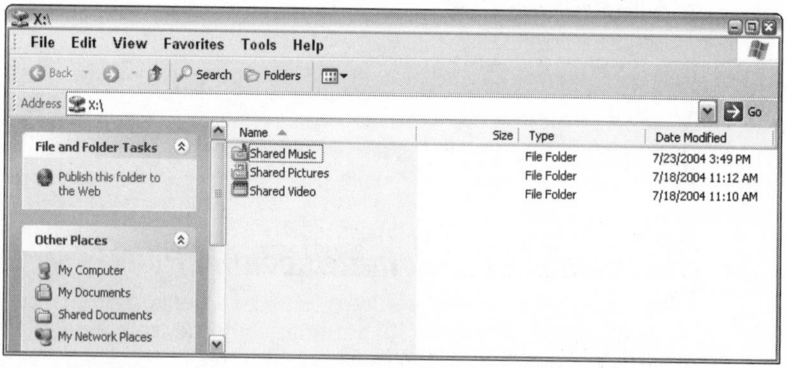

Figure 4-3: Selecting a folder to map.

9. **Click OK.**

   The folder's network path appears in the Folder: pull-down menu.

10. Deselect the box beside Reconnect at Login before clicking Finish.

11. Click Finish.

The SharedDocs folder on Homeofficepc2 is now a network drive, with a drive letter of X, as shown in Figure 4-4. Now you can access this folder quickly and easily. And you're finished.

Now Windows XP won't try to connect to the network drive every time you log in.

Disconnecting from a mapped network drive

If there's a way to connect to a network drive, there must be a way to disconnect, right? Of course. You don't think Bill Gates earns all those billions for nothing, do you? (And I don't earn all of my millions for doing nothing, either.)

1. **From My Computer, double-click the network drive you want to disconnect.**

   The network drive window appears, showing the folder's content.

2. **Click the Tools menu and select Disconnect Network Drive.**

   The Disconnect Network Drives dialog box appears.

3. **Click on the network drive(s) you want to disconnect, as shown in Figure 4-4.**

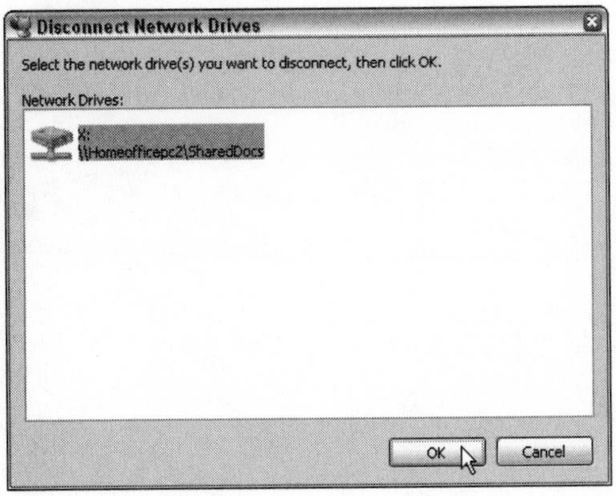

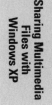

Figure 4-4: Disconnecting a network drive.

4. **Click OK. You are done!**

Browsing Your Network

After you make certain files and folders accessible to everyone, you may want to browse your network to confirm which folders are actually available. If a folder you thought was made available for public access on the network, but you don't see it, you'll want to return and make sure you correctly walked through the steps for sharing it.

Otherwise, you may want to browse your network simply to find something or to see which computers are on the network. Just follow these steps for browsing the network:

1. **Click Start.**

   The Start menu appears.

2. **Click My Network Places.**

   If My Network Places is not on your Start menu, see Book III, Chapter 1, for instructions on adding it.

   My Network Places appears.

3. **Double-click a network folder to see its contents.**

   The shared network folder opens, showing its contents. You can navigate around a network folder as you would one on your own computer. That's all there is to browsing your network. Simple, eh?

Chapter 5: Using TiVo's Home Media Features

In This Chapter

- Getting into your TiVo
- Hooking it up
- Troubleshooting the connections

If you haven't heard about TiVo yet, you will. I guarantee it (and I don't just mean from reading this chapter). This unit, which is basically a small computer that sits near your television and digitally records shows, is going to change the way everyone watches TV.

Fortunately for you, TiVo can connect to the Internet and other TiVos in your home via wireless connection. Setting them up for wireless access is fairly easy. This chapter helps you connect your TiVo to a broadband connection and, if you have two TiVos, to each other.

Turning on the TiVo

I don't spend much time with my TV, but I do like watching baseball games and *Judge Judy* (not necessarily in that order). These programs air during times that I'd rather be writing this book. (Yes, working and watching TV just about explain my life — but I *do* still have my hair at 40.)

So what do I do? I tell TiVo to record these programs and I watch them after a long day slogging at my computer for Wiley. It does so obediently and then I decide when to watch them, not when the network schedulers say I should.

TiVo, which is pictured in Figure 5-1, goes beyond just recording what I tell it to record. It also watches how I watch TV and suggests programs I might like to view based on my history. I help it out by rating shows good or bad by pressing a green thumbs up button when I like a show and a red thumbs down button when I don't.

The ABCs of DVRs

Technically, TiVo is a *digital video recorder (DVR).* You also see them called *PVRs* or *personal digital recorders.* Take your pick, though the first moniker seems more popular. While this chapter focuses only on TiVo and its wireless capabilities, TiVo is not the only DVR out there.

The race was mostly between TiVo and its rival, ReplayTV. ReplayTV's ownership change and the zeal of TiVo fans seem to have all but eliminated that contest. Satellite TV operator Dish Network has its own models of DVRs, which do basic recording but aren't smart enough to suggest programs you might like to watch. DirectTV has a version of TiVo that combines the technology with its satellite receiver box; it just released a version of its TiVo unit that records high-definition television (a hot technology topic that I discuss in Book VII, Chapter 6).

Cable TV companies also are releasing their own versions of digital recorders, which are a hot selling point for consumers deciding whether to spend their entertainment dollars with the cable TV industry or the satellite TV folks.

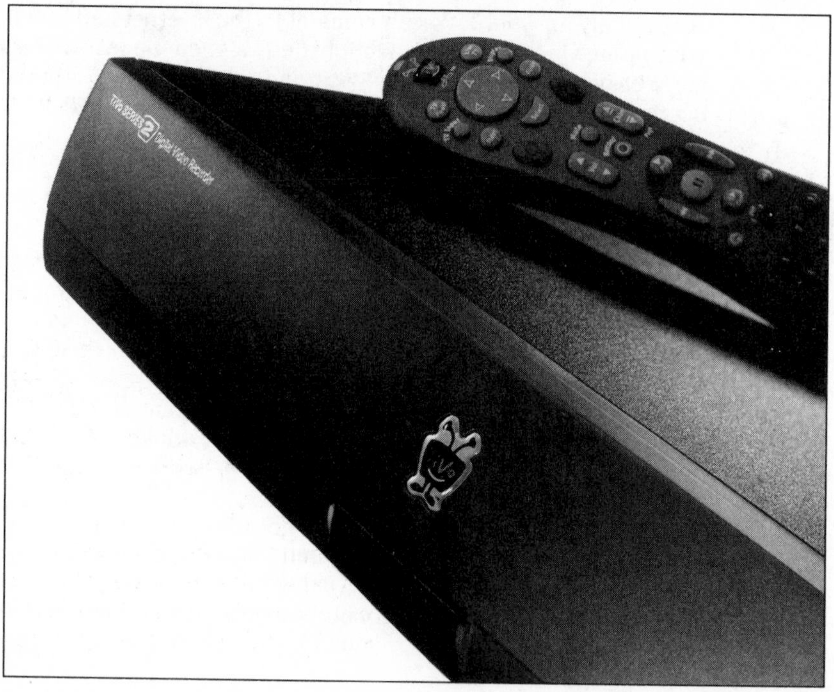

Figure 5-1: The TiVo Series2 with its remote control.

It combines my viewing history, ratings, and anonymous information it collects from others' viewing habits to suggest programs. If I haven't specifically told it to record something during a certain time period, either by a one-time recording command or an ongoing Season Pass, which records all of a program's showings, and it thinks there's a program airing that might interest me, it records a program for me to consider. I can watch it or, if it's obvious dreg, quickly delete it.

Sometimes the suggestion is a hit, like a great classic movie, and other times it's a big miss, like *Sewing with Suzanne.* (Not that there's anything wrong with sewing, mend you.) In any case, using TiVo is a whole lot better than trying to figure out those (dying) VCR machines.

Making a Connection

Where's the wireless angle with this TiVo doodad, you ask? I was just getting to that. Several angles exist, actually:

- You can connect a TiVo wirelessly to your wireless router, providing your DVR with a broadband connection to the Internet. Every night, TiVo makes a dial-up phone call to headquarters and downloads program information. A broadband connection is a faster way for TiVo to grab this data. (Of course, you can do this and the following items with a wired network, too, but this, as you might have noticed, is a book about wireless.) Figure 5-2 shows a TiVo connected to a wireless network.

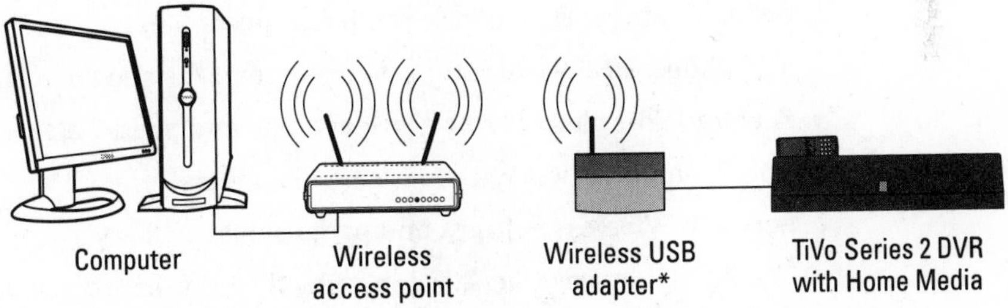

Figure 5-2: TiVo connected to a home wireless network.

- Even if you don't have a broadband Internet connection, you still can connect your TiVo to an internal wireless network. This lets you use TiVo's Home Media Features to move photos and music from your PC to your TiVo for viewing on your TV and listening on your stereo.

✦ You can connect two TiVos together using a peer-to-peer wireless network. By doing this, you can use TiVo's multi-room feature, which lets you record a program on one TiVo and watch it on another.

Configuring your TiVo

Whether you want your TiVo to connect to the Internet to download TiVo's program information or to move photos and music from your PC to your TiVo, you first need to configure its wireless networking settings. This all takes place on the TiVo, using the remote control.

If you want to connect two TiVos together wirelessly, without using a router or computer, you need to create a peer-to-peer network, which I cover later in this chapter.

Here's how you set up and configure TiVo for wireless networking:

1. **Connect a USB wireless adapter, from TiVo's recommended list of adapters (see sidebar), to the back of the TiVo. You plug in the USB cable into one of TiVo's USB slots.**

   Now it's time to configure your TiVo.

2. **From TiVo Central, scroll to TiVo Messages & Setup and press Select.**

   The TiVo Messages & Setup screen appears.

3. **Scroll to Settings and press Select.**

   The Settings screen appears.

4. **Scroll to Phone & Network Setup and press Select.**

   The Phone & Network Setup screen appears, as shown in Figure 5-3.

5. **Scroll to Edit phone or network settings and press Select.**

   The Phone & Network settings screen appears.

6. **Scroll to Wireless Settings and press Select.**

   You see a Wireless Checklist, showing the information you need for the next few steps.

7. **After reading the information, press Select.**

   You see a list of available wireless networks, as shown in Figure 5-4.

8. **Scroll to the network you want to use and press Select.**

   If your network is not on the list, select Connect to a closed wireless network. You then enter your wireless network name.

   Otherwise, after choosing an existing network, you see the Wireless Settings screen.

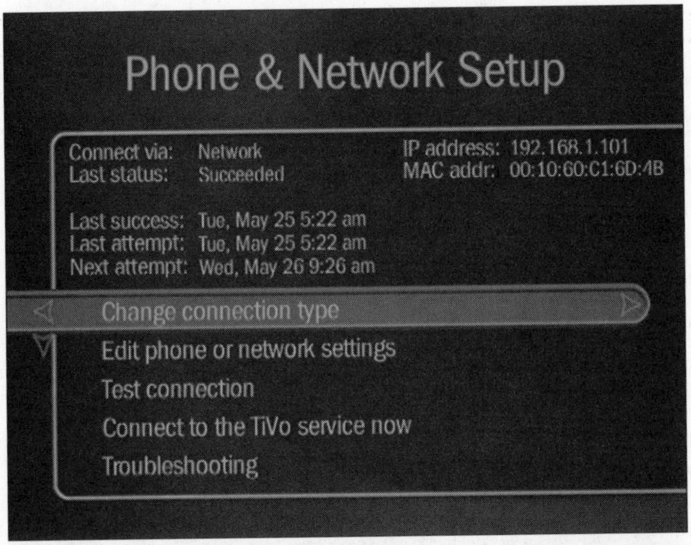

Figure 5-3: The Phone & Network Setup screen.

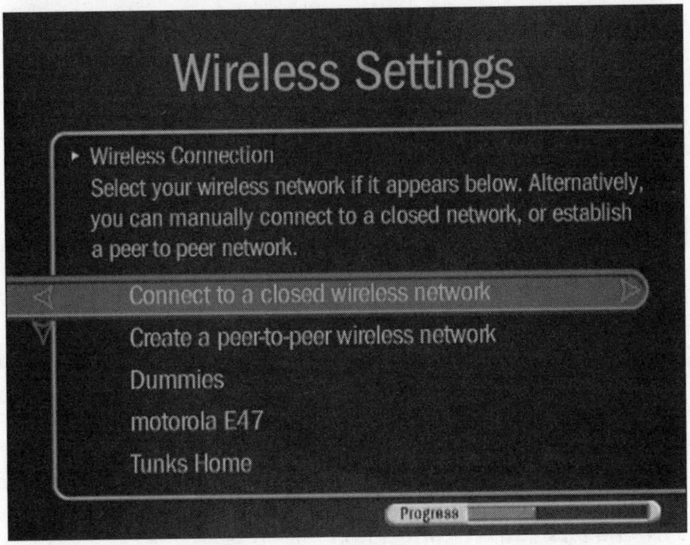

Figure 5-4: TiVo lists available networks.

9. **Choose one of the following:**
   - **Enter password with alphanumeric characters**
   - **Enter hexadecimal password**
   - **The wireless network doesn't use a password**

TiVo recommends you use a password with hexadecimal characters.

Enter the password and the select Done entering text.

10. **Choose from the encryption levels shown here and press Select:**
    - **40 or 64 bit**
    - **128 bit**

    A screen appears showing your network name, password and encryption level.

    TiVo says whether the network is found. If you entered a password, it may tell you that the network is found but that the password may be incorrect — from my experience, even if you entered the correct password. You can return to the previous screens to change your settings.

11. **If everything is OK, select Accept These Settings.**

    You return to the Phone & Network Settings, which you last left in Step 6. You can return to the previous screen (which shows current network information, including your signal strength) or continue to TCP/IP Settings, which I cover in the next section.

Configuring TCP/IP settings

If you're among the vast majority of home networking users, this part of TiVo's wireless settings should be painless. To configure TiVo's TCP/IP settings:

1. **From the Phone & Network Setup screen, scroll to Edit phone or network settings and press Select.**

   A second Phone & Network Setup screen appears.

2. **Scroll to TCP/IP Settings and press Select.**

   The TCP/IP Settings screen appears.

3. **Choose one of the following and press Select:**
   - **Obtain IP address automatically**
   - **Specify static IP address**

   You probably want to choose Obtain IP address automatically. If you need to specify a static IP address, skip to step 6. Otherwise, continue to Step 4.

4. **Enter a DHCP Client ID.**

   You probably don't need to do this. In which case, select I don't have a DHCP Client ID.

A screen appears where you can confirm settings. A message should appear that says These settings appear to be valid.

5. **Select Accept these settings or Restore the previous settings.**

   If you select Accept these settings, you're done! If you select Restore the previous settings, the changes you just made to the TCP/IP settings are cancelled and you can start over.

6. **If you need to specify a static IP address, choose that option from the TCP/IP Settings screen.**

   A screen containing a static IP address checklist appears. You may want to jot down the items before continuing.

7. **Press Select to continue to the next step.**

8. **Enter a static IP address for TiVo and press Select.**

   If you're using a static address, you probably know what you're doing here. If you're lost, you may want to buy a router that has a built-in DHCP server.

   A screen where you enter the subnet mask appears.

9. **Enter your subnet mask and press Select.**

10. **Enter your gateway/router IP address and press Select.**

11. **Enter your DNS (domain name server) address and press Select.**

    A confirm settings screen appears. If your settings are successful, TiVo says These settings appear to be valid.

12. **If the settings are valid, press Access these Settings.**

    You're done.

13. **If the setting were unsuccessful, go back to previous screens to confirm you entered everything correctly.**

Switching to broadband access

If your TiVo connects to your wireless router, which then connects to the Internet, you need to tell TiVo to switch from a dial-up connection to the much faster broadband connection.

TIP: You can connect TiVo to the Internet using a broadband connection. By doing this, TiVo connects to the Mother Ship using the Internet rather than a very slow dial-up phone connection.

Here's how you switch over to a broadband connection:

1. **On the TiVo Central screen, scroll to TiVo Messages & Setup and press your remote control's Select button.**

   The TiVo Messages and Setup screen appears.

2. **Scroll to Settings and press Select.**

   The Settings screen appears.

3. **Scroll to Phone & Network Setup and press Select.**

   The Phone & Network Setup screen appears.

4. **With Change connection type highlighted, press Select.**

   The Connection Type screen appears.

5. **Scroll to Network and press Select.**

   The check mark beside Phone moves to Network, as shown in Figure 5-5.

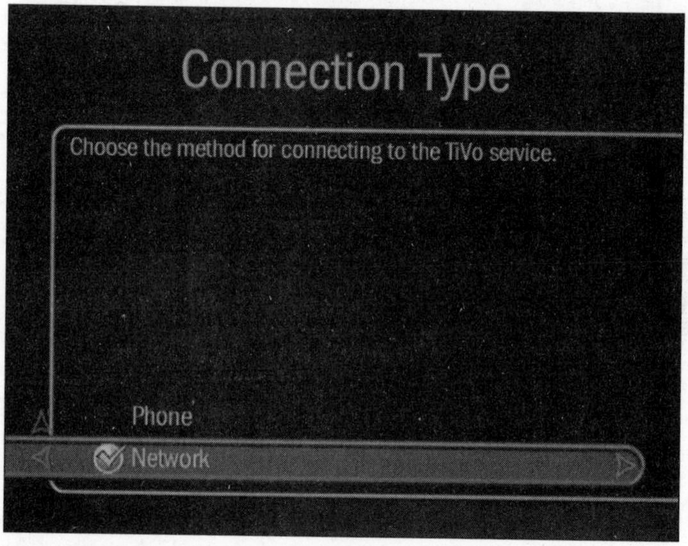

Figure 5-5: Switching from a phone to network connection.

That's it! Your TiVo connects to TiVo headquarters over your Internet connection rather than via your phone line.

Testing the connection

There's a quick way to find out if your TiVo's broadband connection to the Internet is working:

1. From the Phone & Network Setup screen, scroll to Test connection and press Select.

The Test Connection screen appears.

2. Press Select to test your network connection.

TIP

Your DVR attempts to connect to the TiVo server. If all goes well, the test takes about 15 seconds. It could be longer if there is network congestion or problems on TiVo's end. If the test is a success, you see a Connection Succeeded message, as shown in Figure 5-6.

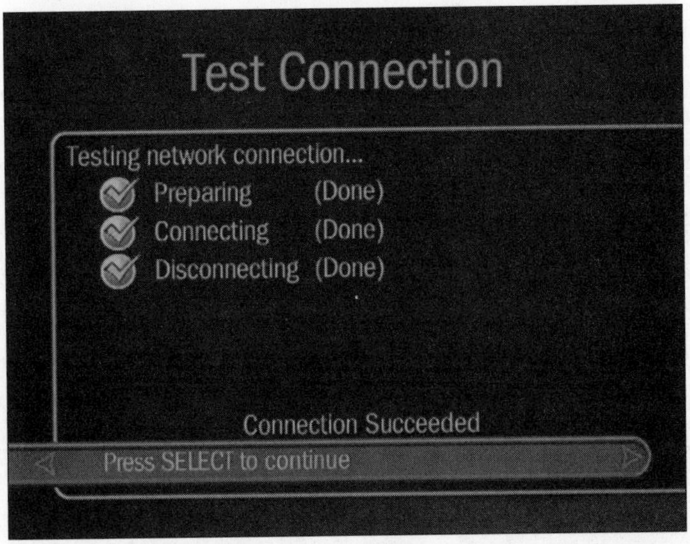

Figure 5-6: Testing your network connection.

3. Press Select to return to the Phone & Network Setup screen.

From here, you can do things like make a real (not test) connection to the TiVo service to update your DVR's information and edit your network settings.

If you're done with this screen, you can return to TiVo Central. Hey, after a successful test, you deserve some time watching a recorded show on your TiVo. That's if you're not having trouble with the connection. In that case, you want to see the next section.

Troubleshooting the connection

TiVo provides some general tips for fixing an ailing network on the Network Troubleshooting screen. You reach that screen from the Phone & Network Setup screen. Select Troubleshooting.

In addition to general networking troubleshooting tips, which I let you read for yourself, TiVo makes several suggestions for troubleshooting a wireless network:

- ✦ Check your signal strength on the Phone & Network Setup screen. Improve this strength with these methods:
  - Move the adapter away from the TiVo to avoid interference.
  - Move the adapter to a higher location.
- ✦ Provide a better line of sight to your wireless router. As you probably know, walls and wireless signals aren't the best of friends. Anything you can do to move the adapter closer, or at least in eyesight, of your router is a good thing.
- ✦ If your wireless network uses a password, try a hexadecimal one instead of an alphanumeric one.
- ✦ Try turning off the sometime-enemies of wireless networks: microwave ovens, cordless phones, and other wireless gizmos. If they're off and your network suddenly works, you have a pretty good idea of the culprit(s). You have a working network, even if you do need to toss the cordless phones and microwave oven (your stove and oven cook better, anyhow).

TiVo is PiCkY

TiVo is not very forgiving when it comes to USB wireless adapters. An official list of recommended adapters work with the DVR — and then there's just about everything else.

If things aren't going well as you hook up your TiVo to a wireless network (or to another TiVo with a peer-to-peer connection), please check TiVo's web site to make sure your wireless adapter is guaranteed to work. The list is at http://tivo.com/adapters. One thing you won't see is 802.11g adapters. TiVo only supports 802.11b adapters.

Of course, in a perfect world — call it Technology Utopia — all USB wireless adapters would work with TiVo. But this, I'm sorry to tell you, is not a perfect world. Thus, the following USB adapters are the only ones TiVo specifically recommends for all Series2 DVRs:

- Linksys WUSB11 version 2.6
- Linksys WUSB11 version 2.8 (Only if your TiVo is running the current software version)

You still have hope if you don't own those models. TiVo says it has "positive reports" of five other models working with the Series2 DVRs:

- Netgear MA101 version B
- D-Link DWL-120 version E (but not DWL120+)
- SMC 2662W version 2
- Belkin F5D6050
- Belkin F5D6050 version 2000

Peer to Peer, Yes Sir!

You don't need a router and all of that other highfalutin (I've always wanted to use that word) wireless networking equipment and a computer to use TiVo's multi-room feature. Instead, you can purchase two USB wireless adapters and connect two TiVo's together.

This is called a peer-to-peer wireless network, which means the TiVo's talk directly to each other rather than relaying their messages through a router. It's cheaper. Is it easier? It can be. But this is *wireless* networking, so problems are always a possibility. If they weren't, you wouldn't need this book, and I'd be out peddling vacuum cleaners door to door.

If your TiVo's are connected via a peer-to-peer network they aren't connected to the Internet. But they still can call into TiVo corporate headquarters by using an old-fashioned dial-up phone line connection.

Here's how you create a peer-to-peer network:

1. **From TiVo Central, scroll to TiVo Messages & Setup and press Select.**

   The TiVo Messages & Setup screen appears.

2. **Scroll to Settings and press Select.**

   The Settings screen appears.

3. **Scroll to Phone & Network Setup and press Select.**

   The Phone & Network Setup screen appears.

4. **Scroll to Edit phone or network settings and press Select.**

   The Phone & Network settings screen appears.

5. **Scroll to Wireless Settings and press Select.**

   You see a Wireless Checklist, showing the information you need for the next few steps.

6. **Select Create a peer-to-peer wireless network.**

   Wireless Settings' Peer-to-Peer Wireless Channel screen appears.

7. **Select a channel to use for your network.**

   TiVo suggests you try channel 11 first, and that is the default setting.

8. **Press Select to continue to the next step.**

   The Wireless Network Name screen appears.

9. **Enter the name, or SSID, of your wireless network and then select Done entering text.**

   Both TiVo's must have the same network name, or SSID.

   Believe me when I tell you that entering a network name, or SSID, with a remote control is tedious. With this in mind, you may want to choose a short network name for both TiVo's to use when making a peer-to-peer connection.

   The Wireless Password Format screen appears.

10. **Choose one of the following selections:**

    - Enter password with alphanumeric characters
    - Enter hexadecimal password
    - The wireless network doesn't use a password

11. **If you choose to enter a password, you see a screen for entering it. Select Done entering text when complete. If your network doesn't require a password, go to step 13.**

    The Wireless Encryption screen appears.

12. **Select the level of encryption used on your network:**

    - **40 or 64 bit**
    - **128 bit**

13. **On the Confirm Settings screen, select Accept these settings if everything is OK. Otherwise, select Restore the Previous Settings and make changes to the appropriate settings.**

You return to the Phone & Network Settings screen. You can move one screen backwards and test the connection. If all is well, you can view the network's signal strength. Otherwise, change the appropriate settings until the test connections works.

If your peer-to-peer connection is working, you see the other TiVo listed at the bottom of your TiVo's Now Playing on TiVo screen, as shown in Figure 5-7. In fact, this is also a good way to see if two TiVo's are communicating over a regular wireless network.

In both cases, you're ready to watch a program recorded on another TiVo. Figure 5-8 shows a program as it begins to stream from one TiVo to the other.

Figure 5-7: Your other TiVo appears on Now Playing on TiVo screen.

Figure 5-8: *Judge Judy* begins to stream to another TiVo.

Chapter 6: Exploring Digital TV and Satellite Radio

In This Chapter

- **Understanding digital TV**
- **Deciphering the HDTV lingo**
- **Listening to satellite radio**

Until recently, it seemed that the digital revolution had bypassed the staidly broadcasting industry, which has transmitted analog signals to television viewers and radio listeners for more than a half century.

Then a funny thing happened on the way to the broadcasting tower. The federal government set a deadline for TV stations to begin transmitting on a digital channel, paving the way for an eventual shift from analog to digital broadcasting. Many of these stations use their newfound digital radio spectrum to broadcast some of their programming in *high-definition TV* or *HDTV*.

Meanwhile, two satellite radio broadcasters continue to add subscribers, frightening over-the-air radio stations, which are making a slow move into their own digital broadcasting.

Wanting My HDTV

Some people have compared the differences between HDTV and analog broadcasting to another technological advance in television broadcasting: color TVs largely replacing black and white sets. For now, TV stations are broadcasting both the old-fashioned analog signals and the new digital signals. As I write this, over 1,000 TV stations in 200-plus U.S. markets are broadcasting a digital channel. This covers 99.69 percent of U.S. TV households, according to the National Association of Broadcasters (NAB).

It's a stark contrast, with HDTV providing the fine detail, wide screens, and CD-quality surround sound that once were reserved for the movie theater. You can watch the Super Bowl and actually see the individual leaves of grass on the field (unless it's fake, of course), see a wider view of the game, and hear the crowd noise around you.

You can check which of your local stations are broadcasting digitally and on which channel by going to www.digitaltvzone.com. The NAB-operated site lets you click your state to see listings by market.

Remember: If you don't have a digital TV with an over-the-air tuner, you can't view these digital channels. You just see static-filled screens on an analog TV set. An *over-the-air tuner* lets you grab digital signals for free by using an antenna instead of paying for cable or satellite TV service.

Digital TV is *not* necessarily the same thing as HDTV. The Federal Communications Commission requires broadcasters to transmit a digital signal, but it does not insist they use this digital radio spectrum for broadcasting high-definition programming. However, most do, as the national networks are moving toward an increasingly impressive schedule of HDTV simulcasts of prime-time shows and sporting events.

Understanding All Those Terms

HDTV, like just about any new technology, comes with its own menu of seemingly indecipherable and indigestible terms and acronyms. Hopefully, I can help make everything fall in place for you. You can download a free guide to HDTV from the Consumer Electronics Association at www.ce.org/hdtv. I list more HDTV resources in the Internet Directory.

First, HDTV has three resolutions:

- **1080i.** The i stands for *interlaced,* indicating how the TV displays horizontal scan lines. It's a high-definition format that excels when displaying static images. Most of the broadcast networks use this format.
- **780p.** The p stands for progressive scan, which is favored for fast-action programming, like Monday Night Football. This makes sense, as ABC is the only network using this format, although Fox is expected to follow.
- **480p.** This isn't really high definition, but it is widescreen and it's still much better than standard TVs can deliver. It's called *enhanced definition* and is the resolution level that DVDs deliver. (Yes, HDTV broadcasts are much better looking than even the best DVDs, at least for now.)

One more aspect of HDTVs: *aspect ratios.* In human language, this means the TV screen's shape. There are two aspect ratios:

- **4:3.** This means a screen measures four units across and three units down. This is the squarish screen of traditional TVs. It was the size of movie theater screens until about 1950.

✦ **16:9.** This is 16 units across for every 9 units down. This is the widescreen shape of the modern movie-theater screen. When you watch widescreen movies from DVD with this aspect ratio, you won't see the black bars on the top and bottom that you see now with regular TV sets. You do see them on the left and right sides when watching anything broadcast in 4:3 aspect ratio. If you watch a sporting event with this screen, you see things on both sides that viewers with a standard TV cannot.

Going Shopping for a High-Definition TV Set

The prices of HDTV sets have dropped considerably and likely will continue to do so. In the beginning, HDTVs cost thousands and thousands of dollars. You still can get some of those, but why pay a lot for technology that is constantly changing and coming down in price.

Now you can find entry-level sets — which are like old-fashioned TV sets but high definition — for well less than $1,000. Rear-projection TVs that use old-fashioned cathode-ray technology (CRT) to project an image from the back of the TV onto its large screen cost anywhere from about $1,000 to $2,000.

More sophisticated models use LCD rear-projection or digital light processing (DLP) technology. DLP sets use a computer chip with 500,000 tiny mirrors to create a picture. Both LCD rear-projection and DLP sets are coming down in price and now cost in the $2,000 to $3,500 range.

Table 6-1: Modeling the HDTV Experience

Technology	*Pros*	*Cons*
Direct-view CRT	Great picture	Heavy, screen size limited
CRT rear projection	Cheaper	Picture can lose alignment, very heavy
DLP	Crisp images, light	Expensive, some can hear whirling sound
LCD rear projection	Slim, lighter	Expensive
LCD flat panel	Slim, can hang on wall	Expensive, limited size
Plasma	Thin, bright images	Expensive (up to $18,000!), limited life span
Front projection	Large, theater-like image	Difficult to install, dark room best

Built-in tuner

HDTV manufacturers need to focus their energies here, in my opinion. Would you purchase an analog TV that didn't come with a built-in, over-the-air tuner? I wouldn't. Yet, that's what many TV set makers want you to do when they sell HDTV-ready models.

The arguments against including an over-the-air tuner is that it keeps a TV's price lower. After all, manufacturers have argued, each satellite TV and cable TV provider require its own *set-top boxes,* or receivers, to receive their HDTV signals. Many of these set-top boxes have over-the-air tuners built in.

This means that many consumers purchase an HDTV set, bring it home, set it up — and find they can't receive any digital channels! (The TVs do usually have analog tuners built in, but you didn't pay extra for a digital TV so you could come home and watch the same old, same old.)

HDTV ready

You may also see this type of set called an *HDTV monitor* or a *HDTV-ready set.* They all mean that the TV is ready to display high-definition video, but it first needs one of the tuners I discussed in the preceding section. This can be a set-top box from a cable or satellite TV company or an over-the-air tuner. Without one of these, your brand-new digital TV only receives old-fashioned analog signals.

REMEMBER

Consider this tuner need when shopping, as a lower-priced HDTV-ready set may, in the end, be costlier after you add a $300 or so over-the-air tuner.

However, if you plan to use the TV with a satellite or cable TV box, this may be the way to go — especially if that box includes an over-the-air tuner. That way, if you lose cable or satellite TV service due to a storm or other reason, you still can grab local signals.

Blown Away by My Reception

You can receive HDTV programming several ways: over the air from an antenna that receives the digital signals, from a satellite TV provider, or from your local cable TV company.

Receiving HDTV over the air

An irony of digital TV is that this high-tech service can require the same kind of old-fashioned antennae that once adorned every rooftop. As cable and satellite TV gained viewers, those antennae started coming down, either intentionally or from an act of rust.

In black and white

An interesting tidbit about digital TV signals: Unlike analog broadcasts, where poor reception means static and other problems, you either can receive a digital signal or you cannot. There's no in between. If you're too far away from the broadcasting tower, you see a black screen.

With the introduction of digital TV, many people are returning to those antennae (at least, to the modern version of them) to receive digital signals from their local broadcasters. Depending on your location, you may be able to use an indoor antenna.

After all, local broadcasts are still free, even in their HDTV splendor. If there's enough on network television to entrance you, you may decide to ditch cable or satellite TV service.

If you want some detailed information about your distance from local broadcasting towers and the kind of antenna that's best to receive those signals, check out www.antennaweb.org. Enter your full address, indicate possible nearby obstructions, and select whether you have a single- or multiple-story home.

Given this information, the web site provides a wealth of data. It includes a suggested antenna type and the compass directions and distances of local broadcasting towers. You can choose to show only digital stations, making the listing easier to read.

Receiving HDTV via satellite TV

Both local and cable channels broadcasting in HDTV are available from two satellite TV service providers, DirectTV and Dish Network. For an additional fee, you subscribe to these local stations, receiving them via your satellite provider rather than over the air.

Along with cable TV providers, satellite TV services are offering a package of HDTV content that goes beyond these local stations. They include new channels, such as ESPN HD, Discovery HD, HDnet (movies), HBO HD, and Showtime HD. Table 6-2 lists some of these channels and their main content; Note that these channels are in addition to local network stations.

You usually need to purchase a new set-top box that receives HDTV content. This investment is on top of the one you make for the high-definition TV. In addition, DirectTV has released a version of its TiVo-enabled receiver that can record and play HDTV programming. Dish Network has its own version of a TiVo-like device that records high-definition programming. (You can read more about TiVo in Book VII, Chapter 5.)

Voom is a new satellite TV service devoted to HDTV programming, although it also carries some basic cable channels.

Table 6-2: Some HDTV Channels

Channel	*Programming*
Bravo HD+	Arts and entertainment
Cinemax HD	Movies
ESPN HD	Sports
Discovery HD Theater	Science and nature
HDnet	Movies
HBO HDTV	Movies
Playboy Hot HD	Adult
Showtime HD	Movies
Starz HD	Movies
TMC HD	Movies
TNT in HD	Drama and sports

Receiving HDTV over cable TV

Receiving HDTV programming over cable TV is similar to getting it from a satellite TV provider. In some cases, you could have trouble receiving all of the local HDTV channels because of negotiation problems.

More HDTV TV sets are beginning to include CableCARD slots. With one of these cards, you can bypass the set-top box and plug the coaxial cable into your TV. You insert a card into a CableCARD slot, which carries information about the services you are allowed to view, as well as any limitations on the programming you can record. These TVs are labeled *cable ready.*

Grabbing for the Heavenly Sound

If you're tired of listening to the same five FM radio stations in your area, you'll be elated to hear about satellite radio. The two services now providing news, talk radio, sports, and music channels direct from their satellites to your mobile or home receiver are more likely to carry the niche programming difficult to find on local radio.

Their programming is CD quality, which you can't get from old-fashioned terrestrial radio broadcasters. Sirius and XM Radio are both steadily building their customer bases. Table 6-3 briefs you about the charges, which are based on August 2004 prices.

Both services require you to buy a receiver that you can hook up to your car stereo or replace. You can buy models for receiving satellite radio in your home. XM Radio has a $50 receiver that works with your PC, feeding the audio through your sound card. You select channels using software downloaded for free.

Table 6-3: Charting Satellite Radio

Service	*Monthly Fee*	*Additional Radios*	*Notes*
Sirius	$12.95	$6.99	More sports programming, NPR
XM Radio	$9.95	$6.99	Investors include GM, American Honda, DirectTV

But Sirius-ly, folks

At one time, Sirius had an advantage over rival XM Radio because it broadcast music channels without commercials. Now both services do that. The differences between the services are relatively minor unless you are a sports fan: Sirius has an exclusive arrangement with the NFL to broadcast its games. You can also hear play-by-play broadcasts of some NBA and NHL games. If you're a fan of public radio, Sirius is the only one to broadcast National Public Radio and Public Radio International.

TECHNICAL STUFF

For the technically inclined, Sirius boasts that it has three satellites at a high-elevation geosynchronous orbit, providing better line-of-sight coverage in the continental U.S. It says XM Radio only has two geostationary at a low elevation angle; Sirius argues this makes XM Radio's signal more susceptible to obstruction.

TIP

Sirius' music channels, but not its talk radio and news programming, are available for free to many Dish Network satellite TV subscribers. You also can listen to the channels on the Sirius web site at www.siriusradio.com.

XM marks the spot

After serving commercials on its music channels, XM Radio woke up one day and decided to remove them, matching Sirius. It also has a sizeable audience, topping the two-million mark.

XM Radio also broadcasts individual weather and travel reports for more than 20 metro areas. (Sirius broadcasts similar information for about the same number of cities.) For an additional $2.99 per month, you can subscribe to XM Radio's Playboy Radio channel.

Chapter 7: Forecasting the Weather from Your Patio

In This Chapter

- **Setting up a wireless weather station**
- **Generating graphics from data**
- **Publishing your weather data online**

Like just about everyone else, I get my weather information from the TV, newspapers, or the Internet. Wouldn't it be cool to have your own weather station, where the information you collect is accurate for you because you're getting it in your backyard?

I thought so, too. (Okay, so label me a geek!) I set off to find a home weather station that was affordable, easy to install, and, of course, wireless.

A number of wireless weather stations are out there. The one I use in this chapter is called Professional Weather Station 2310, made by La Crosse Technology (www.lacrossetechnology.com). It costs about $300. It doesn't require you to run any wires into your home, thus the wireless part of the weather station.

Taking the Station Out of the Box

You get these goodies, pictured in Figure 7-1, with this weather station:

- Weather base station with LCD screen that displays these gems:
  - Relative pressure.
  - Indoor and outdoor temperature and humidity.
  - Wind speed and direction.
  - Sunny, cloudy, or rainy icons.
  - *Tendency,* which indicates by up or down arrow the air pressure forecast.
- Base station power adapter.

- PC cable that connects the base station to your computer's serial port.
- Thermo-hygro sensor, which senses temperature and humidity. It also collects data from the wind and rain sensors before transmitting it to the base station.
- Wind sensor, which picks up wind direction and speed.
- Rain sensor.
- CD with software for your PC.

The sensors stay in touch with the base station wirelessly. The data displays on the LCD screen as well as the software you install on your PC, which provides another way of viewing your weather information.

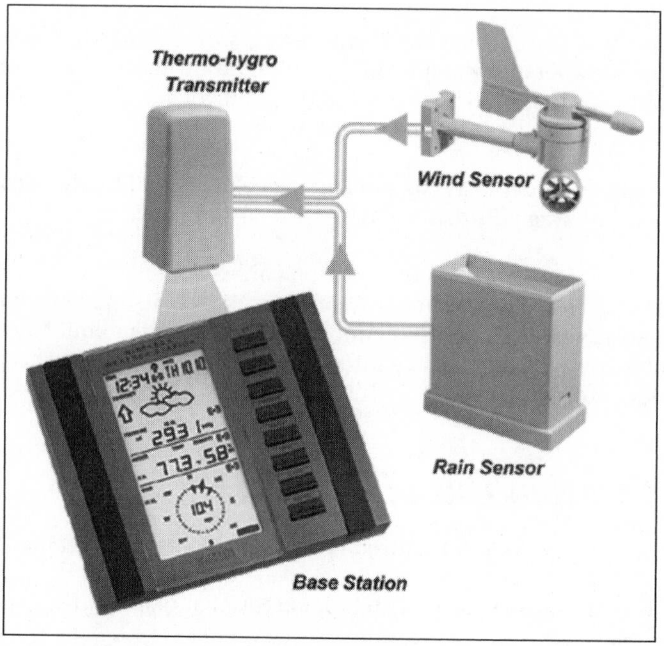

Figure 7-1: La Crosse Technology's 2310 weather station.

TECHNICAL STUFF

The 2310 weather station transmits on the 433-MHz frequency. Data from the sensors, which are connected via cables, is updated as often as every 16 seconds. The base station receives updates more frequently when the wind speed is constantly shifting or there is heavy rainfall.

TECHNICAL STUFF

Here comes the sun

La Crosse Technology and other companies sell completely wireless weather stations. The difference is that each sensor is solar powered and transmits directly to the base. The 2310 model I'm using requires you to string telephone line-like cable between each module. The main module then transmits its signals to the base station. However, you pay a premium for eliminating those two or three cables between sensors, as the solar-powered systems cost significantly more.

First I walk through the hardware set-up process and then I walk you through the installation and configuration of your software. Finally, I show you how to publish data that your weather station generates to your web site.

Here's how you set up the hardware:

1. **Decide on an outdoor location to install your weather station.**

   A deck or rooftop are two possible locations. All the sensors must be mounted within the distance of the cables that tie them together.

2. **Install the wind-vane/wind sensor on a pole so it has access to an unobstructed wind path.**

   Most of the hardware you need for installation comes with the weather station.

3. **Mount the rain sensor on a horizontal surface about two to three feet above the ground.**

   WARNING!

   Make sure the rain sensor's in an open area, away from trees and or other coverings. Do not install it under a spout or anything else that artificially increases the actual rain fall. While you're at it, make sure someone is there to spot you if you fall while you're mounting all this equipment, and watch out for power lines.

4. **Mount the thermo-hygro sensor on a wall beneath the extension of the roof.**

   TIP

   Your weather station's instruction manual provides more detailed information on the proper mounting and locating of the sensors.

5. **Connect cables from the wind and rain sensor to the thermo-hygro sensor.**

6. **Install a fresh set of batteries in the thermo-hygro sensor.**

   These AA batteries should last about 1 year.

7. **Inside your home, near your PC, connect the AC adapter to the base station.**

8. **Connect one end of the PC cable to your computer's serial port (this is a D-shaped connector on the back of your PC and it has 9 pins) and the other end to the base station.**

9. **If the PC is turned on, reboot so that the PC cable is recognized. If the computer is off, turn it on so you can begin installing the software.**

You're done with the hardware end of your weather station. Now it's time to start installing one of three software packages that come with the weather stations so you can get the most out of your system.

You don't need to install software to use your wireless weather station. The base station is capable on its own of showing you the results of the weather data the sensors are transmitting. By installing the software, however, you can display more weather information, manipulate it graphically, and publish the data to your Web site.

You can set a dozen weather alarms with the La Crosse Technology weather station:

- Indoor temperature high and low
- Outdoor temperature high and low
- Indoor humidity high and low
- Outdoor humidity high and low
- Wind chill high and low
- Dew point alarm high and low
- Rainfall 24-hour
- Rainfall 1-hour
- Pressure high and low
- Wind speed high and low
- Wind direction
- Storm warning

Please see your weather station's manual for instructions on how to set alarms.

TIP

Checking your forecasts

You can check local weather forecasts and current conditions at plenty of places on the Internet. This can come in handy as a way to see how close your weather station reflects what the pros are doing. One of the most popular sites is www.weather.com, operated by the Weather Channel. Two others are the Weather Underground at www.wunderground.com and AccuWeather at www.accuweather.com.

However, my favorite is My-Cast at www.my-cast.com. In most metropolitan areas, it provides frequent forecasts for 4-mile-wide areas. That compares to 20-mile-wide forecasts from the National Weather Service. It's almost like having your own weather station — but not quite, as you know from reading this chapter.

Installing and Using Weather Software

La Crosse Technology provides three free computer software packages that enhance the information you receive on the base station's LCD screen:

- **Heavy Weather.** This displays real-time weather information that the sensors collect and transmit to the base station. You're essentially jacking into the base station to pull out the information and display it on your PC's monitor. You can receive up to 175 different kinds of weather information recorded by the base station. You can export the information to Excel to generate statistics and charts.
- **Heavy Weather Review.** This program lets you further manipulate the weather information that the base station receives so you can view its history in a graphical format.
- **Heavy Weather Publisher.** This software takes the information you receive from the base station and uploads it to your web site so others can view it.

That's heavy . . .

Heavy Weather is the basic part of a three-part software package that lets you extend your wireless weather station features. After you install the software, you can use it to visualize the data your weather station is collecting.

As I'm writing this, you need to download an updated version of La Crosse Technology's Heavy Weather software from its web site at www.heavy weather.info rather than install the software that comes with the weather station. If you don't install this newer beta version of the Heavy Weather software, you cannot use the other two free software packages that allow you to generate detailed graphical reports and publish data to your web site.

Installing the software

First, you need to download and install the Heavy Weather software:

1. **Point your browser at www.heavyweather.info/new_english_us/index.html.**
2. **Go to the Software Downloads page and choose your model from the appropriate drop-down list.**
3. **Click Heavyweather.**
4. **Click Download Heavyweather Software — V2.0 Beta.**

   A File Download dialog box appears.
5. **Click Run or Open, depending on the version of Windows XP you have installed.**

   The file downloads.
6. **If you receive a security warning, click Run.**

   A WinRAR Self-Extracting Archive dialog box appears.
7. **Click Install.**

   A HeavyWeather Installation dialog box appears.
8. **Click Finish.**

   The software installs on your computer.
9. **Click OK.**

The Heavy Weather software is installed.

Using the software

Now you can run the software and view the weather data stored on your weather station's base station. Click Start⇨All Programs⇨HeavyWeather⇨Heavy Weather. The Heavy Weather software loads, as shown in Figure 7-2. That's all there is to it!

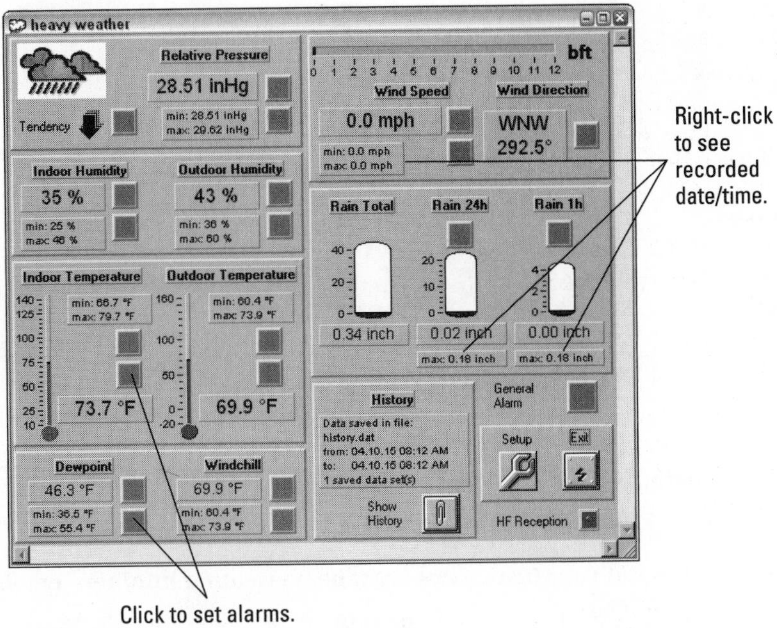

Figure 7-2: Heavy Weather's control panel displays current weather conditions in real time.

You can right-click min. and max. gauges to see the time and date they were recorded, as shown in Figure 7-3.

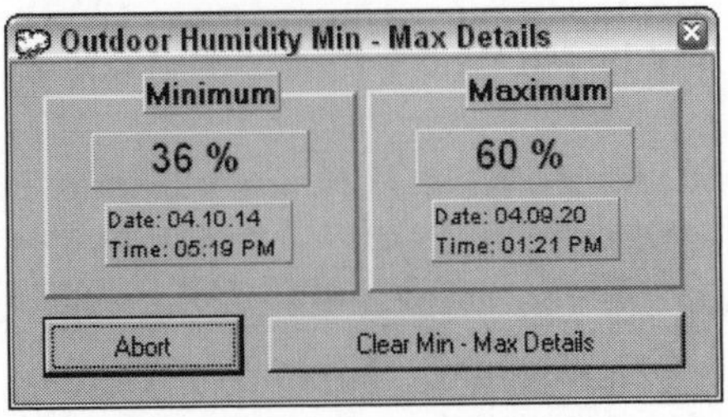

Figure 7-3: Viewing minimum and maximum details for humidity.

You can right-click the gray boxes in each section to set alarms, which I'm doing in Figure 7-4.

Getting graphic about it

The next step is to download, install, and run the Heavy Weather Review software. The review software works with Heavy Weather to provide graphical representations of your weather data.

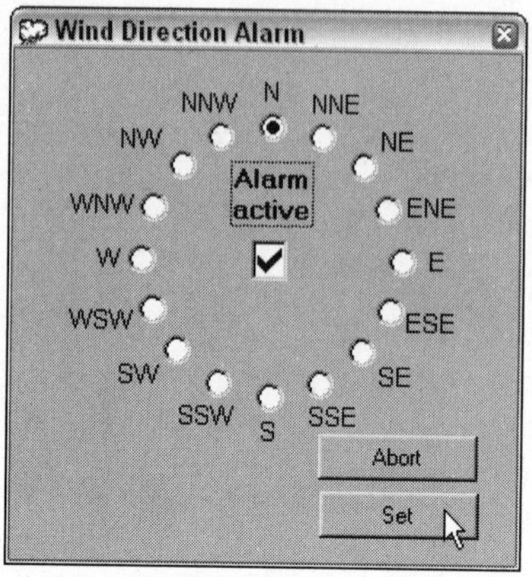

Figure 7-4: Setting an alarm for wind direction.

Installing the software

Here's how you install the software:

1. **Point your browser at www.heavyweather.info/new_english_us/index.html.**
2. **Go to the Software Downloads page and choose your model from the appropriate drop-down list.**
3. **Click Heavy Weather Review.**
4. **Click one of two links, depending on what applies to you:**
   - **You've already downloaded some other Heavy Weather software: Click Download and Install Heavy Weather Version 2.0 Beta Release.**
   - **You haven't downloaded any other Heavy Weather software: Click Download the Heavy Weather Version 2.0 Beta Release Installer.**

   A File Download dialog box appears regardless of which you choose.
5. **Click Run or Open, depending on the version of Windows XP you have installed.**

   The file downloads.
6. **If you receive a security warning, click Run.**

   The Heavy Weather Review Setup Wizard appears.
7. **Click Next.**

   The Select Destination Location window appears.
8. **Click Next.**

   The Select Start Menu Folder dialog box appears.

9. **Click Next.**
10. **Click Install.**
11. **Click Finish.**

    The Heavy Weather Review application is installed.

Using the software

Once you have the Heavy Weather Review software installed, you can begin using it.

If you just installed your weather station, you may get a warning that says Not Enough Data Points in History File. In that case, while you wait a few days for more information to accumulate in your weather station's base station, you can use the program's demo template. I used that file to generate the figures in this section. You can read the help file to determine how to display your own data.

1. **Double-click the HeavyWeather Review icon on your desktop.**
2. **Double-click Demo Template.hwg.**

   A graph of indoor temperature and dew point appears, as shown in Figure 7-5.

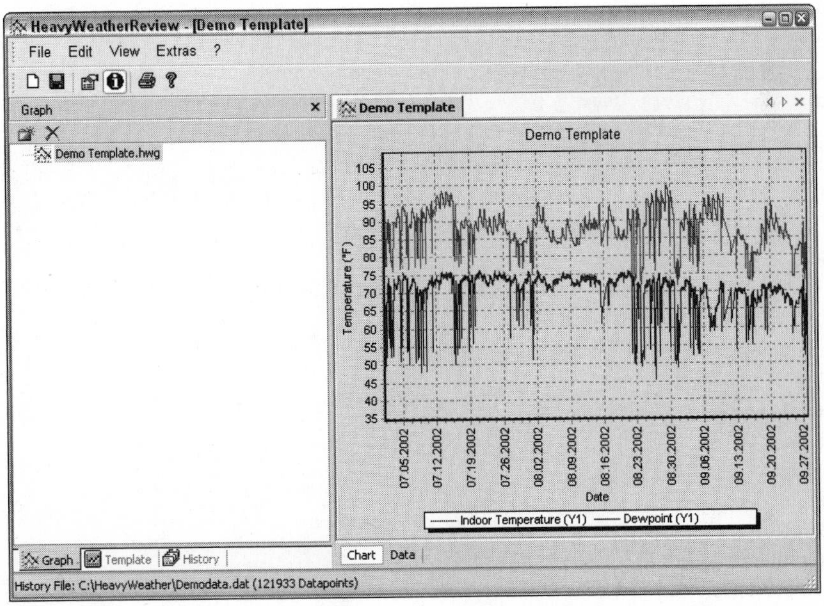

Figure 7-5: Heavy-Weather Review's graph of weather conditions.

3. **At the bottom of the screen, click Data to see the information used to build the graph.**

   The data points are shown in Figure 7-6.

4. **Under File, you can choose to save the graph or to print it.**

5. **By selecting File ➪ New Template, you can change the information used to build the graphs.**

   You can view any data that your sensors and base station collect. A new template dialog box is shown in Figure 7-7.

6. **Click OK when you're done.**

If you open a new template, give it a name in the Title text box. You can exert a lot of control over the table setup, determining what's in each axis — and which is which, by the way; I can never recall which is x and which is y. You can just ignore the weather that's too extreme for you: Set a minimum and maximum for the data. If in the midst of all this science you're feeling creative, choose a graph background color and decide among fonts.

Telling the web about your weather

Now that your weather station is collecting detailed information about inside and outside conditions, it's time to share it with others on your own Web site. That's where the Heavy Weather Publisher module comes into play.

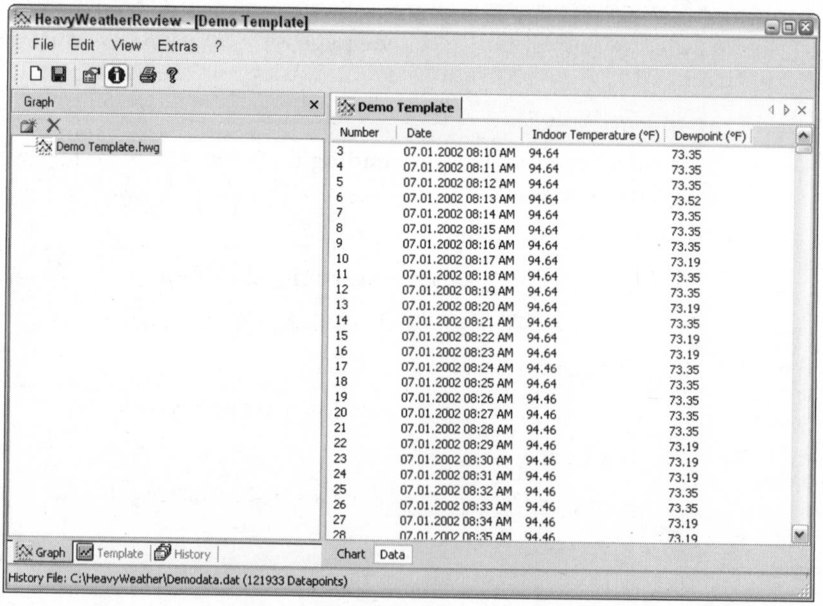

HeavyWeatherReview - [Demo Template]
File Edit View Extras ?
Graph
Demo Template.hwg
Demo Template
Number Date Indoor Temperature (°F) Dewpoint (°F)
3 07.01.2002 08:10 AM 94.64 73.35
4 07.01.2002 08:11 AM 94.64 73.35
5 07.01.2002 08:12 AM 94.64 73.35
6 07.01.2002 08:13 AM 94.64 73.52
7 07.01.2002 08:14 AM 94.64 73.35
8 07.01.2002 08:15 AM 94.64 73.35
9 07.01.2002 08:16 AM 94.64 73.35
10 07.01.2002 08:17 AM 94.64 73.19
11 07.01.2002 08:18 AM 94.64 73.35
12 07.01.2002 08:19 AM 94.64 73.35
13 07.01.2002 08:20 AM 94.64 73.19
14 07.01.2002 08:21 AM 94.64 73.35
15 07.01.2002 08:22 AM 94.64 73.19
16 07.01.2002 08:23 AM 94.64 73.19
17 07.01.2002 08:24 AM 94.46 73.35
18 07.01.2002 08:25 AM 94.64 73.35
19 07.01.2002 08:26 AM 94.46 73.35
20 07.01.2002 08:27 AM 94.46 73.35
21 07.01.2002 08:28 AM 94.46 73.35
22 07.01.2002 08:29 AM 94.46 73.19
23 07.01.2002 08:30 AM 94.46 73.19
24 07.01.2002 08:31 AM 94.46 73.19
25 07.01.2002 08:32 AM 94.46 73.35
26 07.01.2002 08:33 AM 94.46 73.35
27 07.01.2002 08:34 AM 94.46 73.19
Graph Template History
Chart Data
History File: C:\HeavyWeather\Demodata.dat (121933 Datapoints)

Figure 7-6: Dates, indoor temperatures, and dew points.

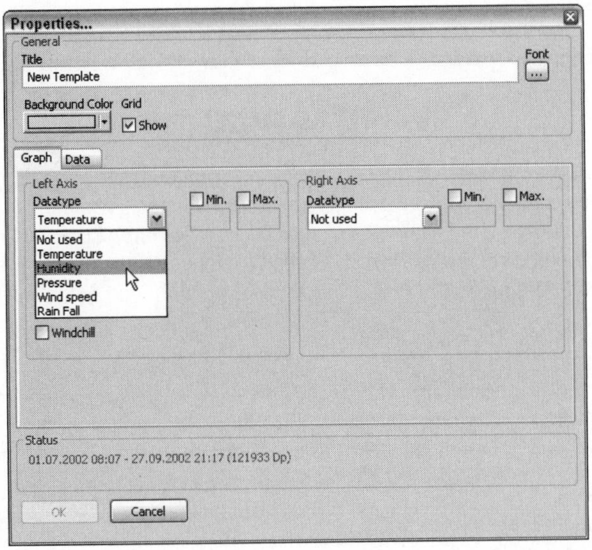

Figure 7-7: A new template for choosing the weather data to display.

Installing the software

You've got to get this done before you can publish your findings and thrill the world over with your weather statistics:

1. **Point your browser at www.heavyweather.info/new_english_us/index.html.**
2. **Scroll to the bottom of the page and click Download Heavyweather Publisher Software.**

   A File Download dialog box appears.
3. **Click Run or Open, depending on the version of Windows XP you have installed.**

   The file downloads.
4. **If you receive a security warning, click Run.**

   The Heavy Weather Publisher Setup Wizard appears.
5. **Click Next.**

   The Select Destination Location window appears.
6. **Click Next.**

   The Select Start Menu Folder dialog box appears.
7. **Click Next.**
8. **Click Install.**

TIP

Sharing is nice

It's great that you can view your weather information and maybe even share it with others online, but what about becoming a real weather station, where your information serves as a mini National Weather Station bureau?

That's where Weather Underground's network of personal weather stations comes in. Rather than relying solely on the professionals, who forecast for large areas, Weather Underground's personal weather stations cover much smaller areas.

You can see personal weather stations near my zip code by going to www.wunderground.com/cgi-bin/findweather/getForecast?query=49401#PWS. Just replace your zip code for 49401 and you see local personal weather stations (assuming your area has one). Click Add Your Weather Station to add your weather station. Compatible software uploads its data to the Weather Underground site, which displays it for all to see.

The network works only with software packages that may not support your weather station. In fact, from what I can gather, no software that works with the La Crosse Technology 2310 weather station is compatible with the Weather Underground's personal weather station network.

9. **Click Finish.**

Windows has installed the Heavy Weather Publisher application!

Using the software

Figure 7-8 shows one of the three graphics you can display on your Web site. You can click the box beside the example to make it active — that is, making it the graphic that automatically uploads to your Web server at an interval you choose. The *interval* is the length of time between information updates. You can choose the interval under the Export tab on the right side of the screen. There, you also enter your FTP server's name, username, password, target file path, and filename. If you're unfamiliar with FTP, ask your Web hosting company for more information or check out some reliable FTP sites online.

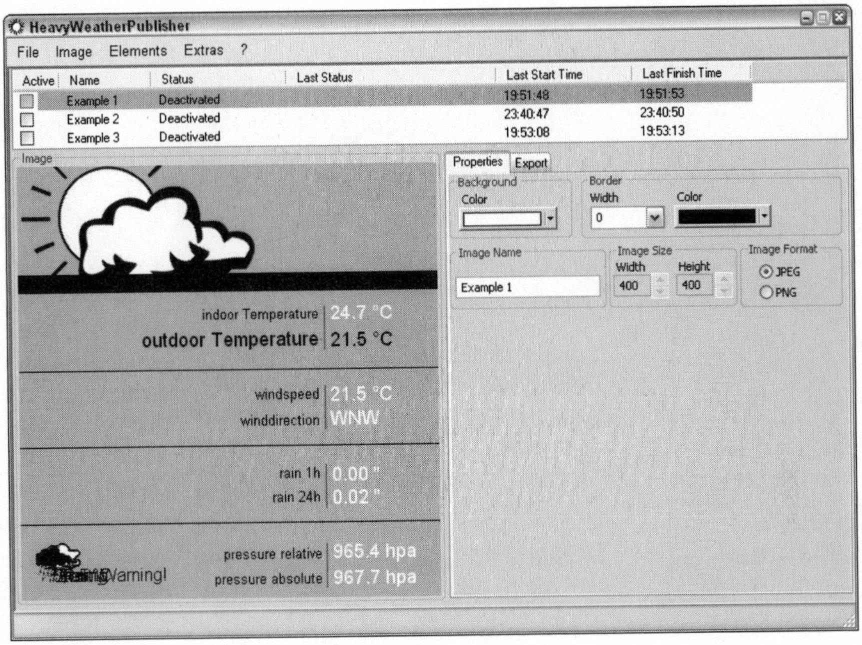

Figure 7-8: Choose a graphic, any graphic.

Chapter 8: Security in the Air via Motorola

In This Chapter

- **Setting up the system**
- **Looking at events and archives**

Wouldn't you like to know what goes on at home while you're away? In this chapter, I talk about the wireless Motorola Home Monitoring and Control System. Basically, it lets you monitor your home from afar through the use of a wireless camera and sensors. The system also performs these feats:

- ✦ Sends real-time notifications when there's trouble.
- ✦ Sends photos, videos, and text alerts so you can view them remotely, from a web browser or a cell phone.
- ✦ Stores video so you can watch it anytime from your computer.
- ✦ Archives things like temperature changes.

WARNING!

Motorola is careful to call this a *home monitoring and control system,* rather than a home security system. In its warranty information — in bold, capital letters — Motorola says, "This product is intended only for use to facilitate home monitoring and control and is not intended to be a substitute for a home security system." You've been warned!

Digging Through the Goodies

It all starts with Motorola's Easy Start Kit, which has a suggested list price of $300 and is shown in Figure 8-1. It includes a USB gateway/controller that connects your computer with the wireless components, a wireless camera, and power adapters for both.

You can purchase other components separately:

- ✦ Additional wireless cameras. Hey, why not have one in every room of the house? Plus the garage? And maybe the shed?
- ✦ Wired cameras. You can have up to three.
- ✦ Wireless door/window sensor. This alerts the system when a door or window opens.

- Wireless temperature sensor. This lets you monitor for temperatures that rise or fall rapidly, indicating problems like fires or freezing temperatures. The sensor, shown in Figure 8-2, is especially handy if the home you monitor is a vacation residence.
- Wireless water sensor. A good way to monitor basements, this sensor tells you when it detects — can you guess? — water.

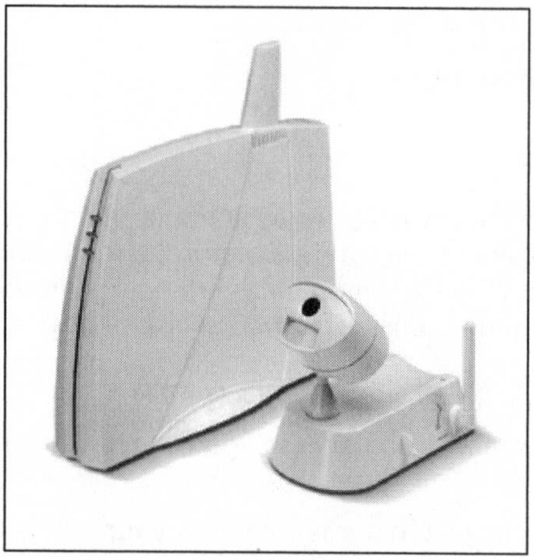

Figure 8-1: The Home Monitoring and Control System's controller and wireless camera.

The sensors work 60 to 80 feet from the *gateway* (the device that attaches to your computer), so it's best to place the gateway (and its PC) in a central location. The sensors can transmit through walls, ceilings, and floors, but the range is limited. The gateway and sensors transmit and receive on the 418-MHz frequency.

The example system I'm using in this chapter includes these things:

- USB gateway
- One wireless camera
- One wireless door/window sensor
- One wireless temperature sensor
- One wireless water sensor

TIP

The system can handle up to eight sensors; I'm using three. There's enough capacity left to add sensors to many of your doors and windows. You may want to use some of that capacity for additional temperature and water sensors, however. It also can handle up to three wired cameras and up to six wireless cameras.

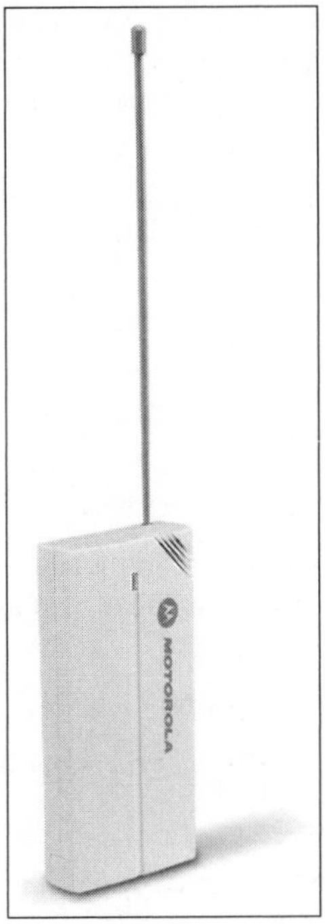

Figure 8-2: The system's temperature sensor.

The system has a remote service that costs about $20 per month. It lets you monitor and control your system from afar, using a Web browser. However, the Shell HomeGenie service was unavailable at the time I wrote this chapter. You can read more about the service at www.shellhomegenie.com.

TIP

You can download the latest drivers and other software for Motorola's system at (are you ready for this?): www.broadband.motorola.com/consumers/support/default.asp?SupportSection=HomeMonitoring.

Setting Yourself Up for Security Success

Before you can begin using your new security system, you need to set up the hardware, install the software, and configure the system. The following sections show you how to do these tasks.

Setting up the hardware

Setting up everything is easy. Get the hardware ready to go:

1. **Remove the Easy Start Kit and sensors from the packaging.**
2. **Some assembly required: Attach an antenna to each sensor.**

3. **Insert batteries in each sensor.**

   Battery life is 1 year with normal usage.

4. **Install the sensors in the appropriate locations.**

Please see the instruction manual for each sensor. You can have up to eight sensors.

Installing the software

Software installation is a lengthy but fairly simple process:

1. **Load the CD-ROM that comes with the Easy Start Kit.**

   The installation program automatically loads. A license agreement screen appears. If the license screen does not appear, run launch.exe from the CD-ROM.

2. **Read the license agreement and if you do, click I Agree.**

   A welcome screen appears and Figure 8-3 shows you what it looks like.

3. **Click Install Required Software.**

   The Motorola Home Monitor Installation Wizard appears.

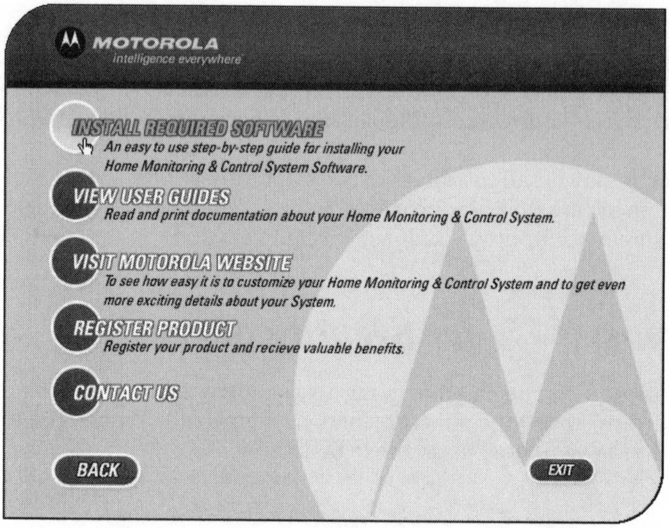

Figure 8-3: Starting the software installation.

4. **Click Next.**

5. **Choose a directory in which to install the program by clicking Browse. When you're done, click Next.**

   The Select Program Folder screen appears.

6. **Click Next.**

7. **Plug the USB cord of the system controller into a USB port on your PC.**

   The USB ports are about ½" wide and 3/16" high. You find at least two on the back of your PC and may find some on the front, as well.

   The Found New Hardware Wizard appears. Windows asks if it can connect to Windows Update to search for software.

8. **Select Yes or No and then click Next.**

   The next installation screen appears.

9. **Click Next.**

   If you receive a warning that the software has not passed Windows compatibility testing, click Continue Anyway. Windows installs the software.

10. **Click Finish.**

11. **Return to the Motorola software and click Next.**

12. **Click Finish.**

    The Home Monitor software launches. The Motorola Home Monitor Setup Wizard appears.

13. **Click Next.**

    If you have any wired cameras, connect them to the controller.

14. **Click Next.**

    TIP

    The wizard explains that you must push the discovery button on each wireless device that's part of the monitoring system. You can use the discovery tool that comes with the Easy Start Kit or use something like a paper clip to reach the indented button. The discovery tool looks like an elongated paper clip.

15. **Click Next.**

    The Device Discovery screen appears.

16. **Push the discovery button on each device so the controller knows the device is part of the system.**

    Each device appears on the screen as the controller discovers it, as shown in Figure 8-4.

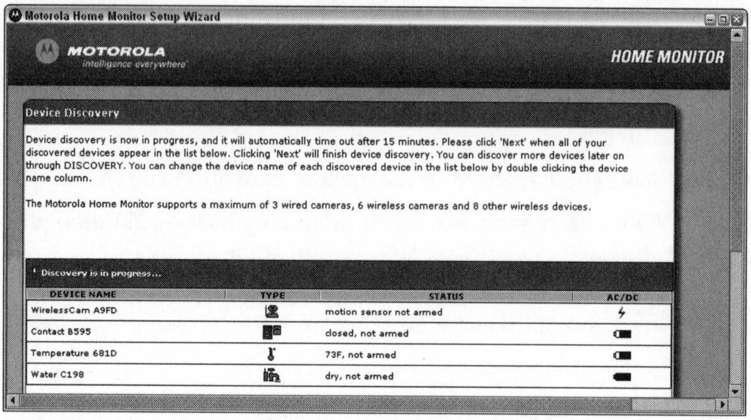

Figure 8-4: Discovering the system's sensors.

17. **When you're done with device discovery, click Next.**

    The Wi-Fi Information screen appears, asking whether you have a Wi-Fi network.

18. **If you have a Wi-Fi system, click Yes. If not, click No.**

    If you have a Wi-Fi system, the software asks what channel the Wi-Fi network uses. Select it in the pull-down menu. If you don't know, leave the default, Don't Know, selected.

19. **Click Next.**

    A congratulations screen appears.

20. **Click Finish.**

    The software begins running, showing the status of discovered devices and displaying live camera images, as shown in Figure 8-5.

Configuring the software

After installing the software and hardware, it's time to configure your home monitor software.

REMEMBER

Check frequently for software updates. Click Start⇨All Programs⇨Motorola Home Monitor⇨Motorola Updates. Be sure to update the software. If you don't update, you may not be able to use the Shell HomeGenie remote web features, which were not yet available when I wrote this chapter.

Editing sensor parameters

The cameras and sensors all have parameters that you can change from the control panel. Click Edit beside the device you want to change. Some of the choices for the parameters include the following:

- ✦ Wireless camera:
  - Quiet period before rearming: 5, 10, 20, 30, 60 seconds
  - Capture video clip length: 5, 10, 20, 30, 60 seconds
  - Brightness, contrast, and quality controls
- ✦ Door/window and window sensor. You can change the power mode from normal to save, which makes the batteries last longer.
- ✦ Temperature sensor. The default thresholds for triggering an event are 41F and 113F. You can change the thresholds to anywhere from –40F to 135F. You can change the power mode from normal to save, which makes the batteries last longer.

TECHNICAL STUFF

Depending on lighting conditions, your wireless camera can view larger objects from up to 200 feet away with a viewing angle of 80 degrees. The motion sensor detects objects up to 12 to 14 feet away with a field of view of 80 degrees. The camera's microphone picks up normal conversations from 6 to 10 feet away.

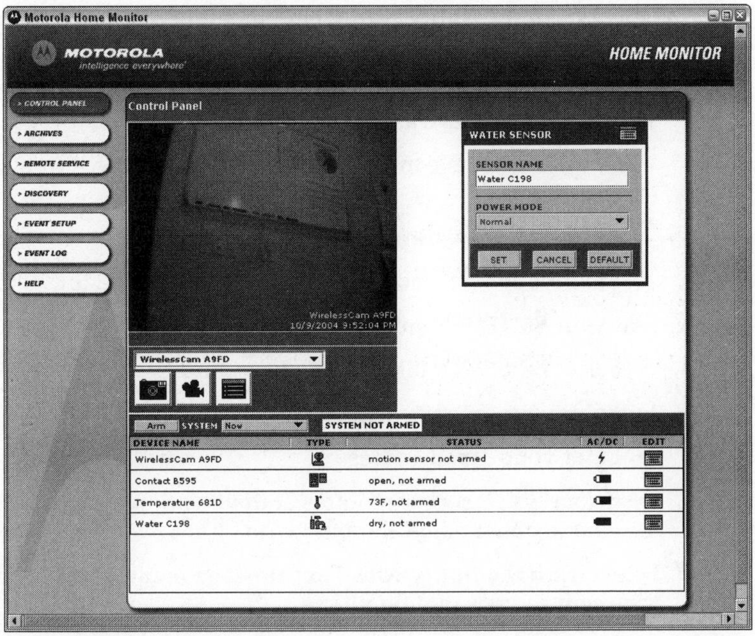

Figure 8-5: The control panel shows live video and the status of other devices.

Setting alerts

Events can also be called *alerts.* An *event* is triggered when a certain event happens. For instance, when the temperature probe registers a temperature above a certain threshold, the software can send you an e-mail or text message. You also can tell the camera to take an image that goes into the archive and which can be sent to you as an e-mail attachment.

Here's how you set an event:

1. **In the Home Monitor software, click the Event Setup menu button.**

   The Event Setup screen appears.

2. **Choose a sensor device from the pull-down menu.**

   For this example, I chose my wireless camera.

3. **Chose an event.**

   The event is different for each sensor. I chose Motion Detected.

4. **Choose Action Device.**

   This is usually one of the cameras. I chose Wireless Camera.

5. **Choose between Actions:**

   - **Capture Video**
   - **Capture Image**

6. **Select from the Notify with E-mail menu if you want an e-mail notification.**

   I selected my e-mail address and selected With Image as Attachment. This sends the image as an attachment.

   You must create an e-mail or text message profile before you can use those options:

   1. Click Edit E-Mail Profiles or Edit Text Profiles.
   2. Enter your e-mail address, as shown in Figure 8-6.

7. **Edit your SMTP (outgoing e-mail) information:**

   - Select Edit SMTP Info.
   - Enter your outgoing e-mail address. (It often begins with smtp.)
   - Enter your e-mail address.
   - If your SMTP server requires authentication (ask your ISP), enter your account name and password.

8. **Select from the Notify with Text Message menu if you want a text message sent to your mobile phone.**

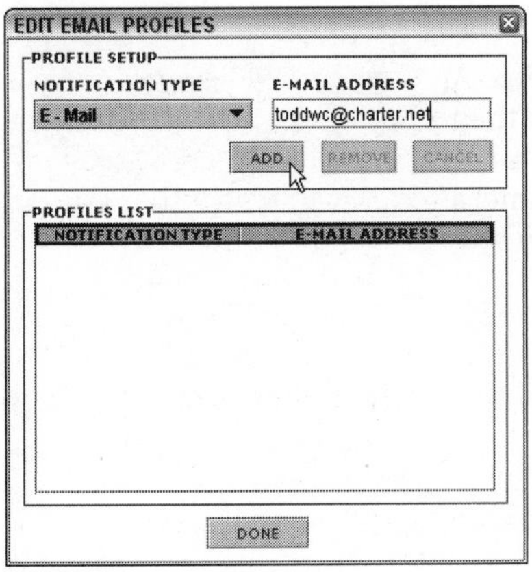

Figure 8-6: Editing an e-mail profile.

9. **Select Update.**

That's it! You just created an event. You now can create one or more events for each of your sensors.

TIP: The software floods you with e-mails if you pick a frequently occurring event, such as when the camera detects motion. After a short rest period each time, the event continues triggering indefinitely as long as the camera senses motion. Keep this in mind as you create events.

Viewing the event log

Home Monitoring and Control System keeps a running tally of noteworthy events, such as temperature changes (if you're using the temperature sensor) and other changes to the sensors. From the control panel, click Event Log. Figure 8-7 shows an event log.

Digging though the archives

The software keeps an archive of images and video. You can view its contents by clicking the Archives menu button. You can delete all or selected images and videos.

Arming the system

Lastly, after you're done configuring the home monitor, you're ready to arm the system. The Arm button is on the control panel. You can arm the system immediately, or in 1, 5, 10, 15, or 30 minutes. You also can disarm the system once it's armed. You see either System Is Armed or System Is Not Armed.

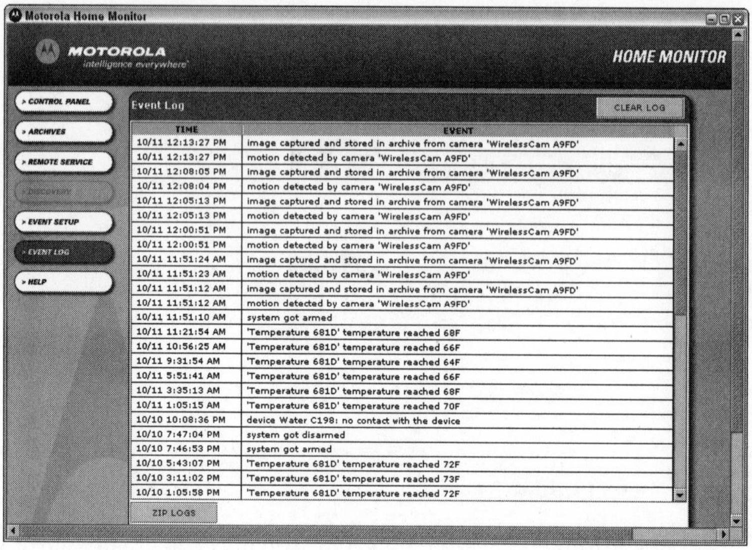

Figure 8-7: An event log lets you keep tabs.

Book VIII

Global Positioning Systems

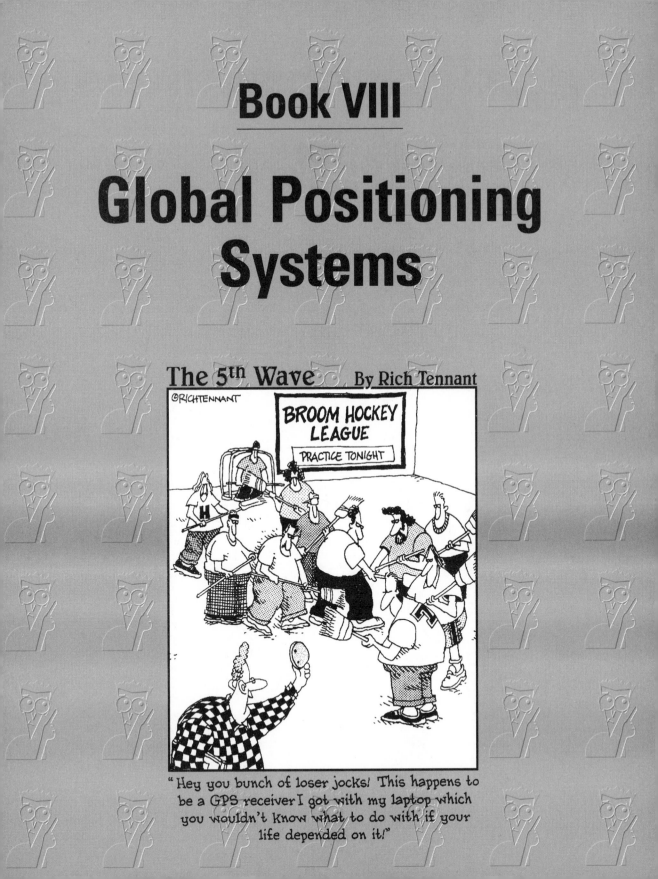

The 5th Wave By Rich Tennant

"Hey you bunch of loser jocks! This happens to be a GPS receiver I got with my laptop which you wouldn't know what to do with if your life depended on it!"

Contents at a Glance

Chapter 1: Getting Uncle Sam to Ante Up 495

Chapter 2: Finding Your Way with GPS 507

Chapter 3: Exploring with the Rest of GPS 519

Chapter 1: Getting Uncle Sam to Ante Up

In This Chapter

- **Getting a handle on your position**
- **Knowing your options**
- **To map or not to map**
- **Making a connection with your PC**

Every once in a while, the U.S. federal government gives its citizens — and sometimes the entire world — a gift. When the government financed, launched, and began running the *Global Positioning System (GPS),* it did just that: gifted us.

GPS is a system for finding your place anywhere in the world. As long as you have a fairly clear view of the sky, where the two-dozen (or so) satellites orbit the Earth, you have a pretty good chance of getting a GPS reading and finding your way to where you want to go.

Its uses are almost limitless:

- Navigate the roads, letting more advanced GPS receivers lead you along street by street. Some models even speak the directions so you can keep your eyes on the road and not on the receiver's display. You also know which direction you're traveling in and how fast you're driving.
- Find a remote fishing hole — and then find your way back to your car. You can even keep your favorite hot fishing spot a secret because with GPS you've no need to leave any sort of marker that might tip off other anglers.
- Hike in the woods without getting lost. Or at least if you do get lost, your GPS receiver helps you get un-lost. It's the modern version of *Hansel and Gretel,* but the bread crumbs in this case are virtual, displayed on your GPS receiver as waypoints.
- Find a lost child who is wearing a GPS receiver on his or her wrist.
- Run or jog and collect precise information about your workout.
- Make an emergency call with your new GPS-equipped cell phone and help the 911 dispatcher locate you even if you aren't sure of your precise location.

Knowing Where You Are

Where are you? I know you're there because you're reading this book. You have to be somewhere to do that. But where are you really? In precise terms.

I can tell you where I am in precise terms:

N 42.96506 W 085.92599 Elevation: 744 feet above sea level

That's with an accuracy of about 30 feet. Just enough to throw off a stalker or an angry editor. (I'm just kidding about the stalker part.) In the next chapter, I explain how to understand that reading, but for now I just want you to see how accurate GPS can be.

How'd I get this reading? By using a very inexpensive GPS receiver called the Garmin eTrex. It was a $79 Christmas gift. It doesn't talk to me and doesn't display any maps other than a very rudimentary one, but it's enough to get a basic reading from the GPS system. Figure 1-1 shows the eTrex. You can find out more about Garmin GPS receivers at www.garmin.com.

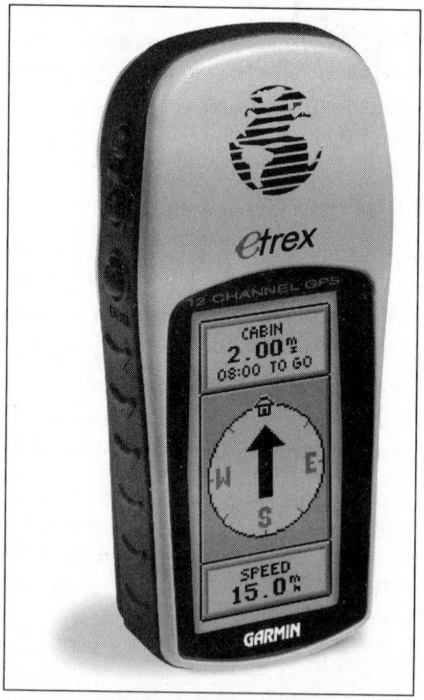

Figure 1-1: Garmin's eTrex GPS receiver is inexpensive.

Many other GPS receiver models do show quite detailed maps. For example, DeLorme (www.delorme.com) sells a broad range of GPS receivers and mapping programs that work with laptop PC, Pocket PCs, and many Palm OS PDAs. The DeLorme GPS receivers and mapping programs not only tell you where you are, but they can tell you the best route from where you are to where you want to go. Figure 1-2 shows the DeLorme BlueLogger GPS receiver that not only shows your current position but can also keep a log of where you've been for later playback. With it you can prove that you only went down to the hardware store and didn't stop at the local pub on the way.

Figure 1-2: The DeLorme BlueLogger GPS receiver can store a complete log of where you've been.

Achieving Missile Precision — Almost

Do you have a chimney somewhere in the world where you'd like the U.S. military to fire a long-distance missile? Using GPS, they can do it. Assuming all goes well, the missile will find the chimney, make a downward turn, and take a ride straight down. GPS is relatively new, although Santa Claus has been using a similar technique for years.

How the military uses GPS

How do you think the U.S. military makes those precision strikes during confrontations? Soldiers take a GPS reading of the target, transmit it to artillery and air forces, and get the heck out of the way. The GPS coordinates and very expensive ammunition does the rest — at least it does if no one in the area is using one of the GPS jammers available from Russia.

The military has an advantage over civilian GPS users: It uses some additional information to gain even more precision in GPS readings. The information is encrypted so that civilians — read: enemies — can't get the same precision. The U.S. military uses GPS in its missiles, its tanks, and other ground and air resources, and probably in ways that if I knew about they'd have to kill me.

Being selective

On May 1, 2000, President Bill Clinton signed an order turning off the *Selective Availability* feature of the GPS system. Selective Availability was designed to degrade the GPS signal that was received by non-military users so that the location information provided by civilian GPS units would be less precise than that of military GPS receivers. The U.S. military still has the ability to use a similar *Selective Deniability* feature in war zones or when there is a global terror alert, but this feature is targeted at specific areas rather than affecting all civilian users worldwide. See the article on GPS at wordiQ.com (www.wordiq.com/definition/Global_Positioning_System) for more information on GPS precision.

Civilians can find their way, too

The precision the U.S. military achieves when using GPS for its guidance systems isn't quite as precise when a civilian uses the service. It's close enough for finding a fishing hole or navigating your way out of the woods, though.

The difference is so small, at least from a civilian perspective, that if I gave you the GPS coordinates for my front door, you might wind up at my back door — just enough precision to foil enemies without harming hapless hikers lost in the woods.

Actually, even civilian GPS receivers can have extremely precise measurements using a system known as *Wide-Area Augmentation System (WAAS).* This system relies upon ground-based transmitters whose position is very precisely known. These transmitters broadcast a signal that is matched with the satellite transmitted GPS signal so that the normal positioning errors are reduced to such an insignificant degree that a WAAS-enabled system can be used to land an airplane in zero-visibility conditions. The WAAS system currently is only available in North America, but WAAS-enabled GPS receivers provide normal GPS accuracy even when they're used in areas where WAAS isn't available.

Most GPS receivers enable you to monitor the current signal to determine how accurately your position is being reported. Typically this information is reported using the following values:

- **PDOP** (Position Dilution Of Precision): A number representing the relationship between the error in user position and the error in satellite position using three coordinates. Smaller values are better.
- **HDOP** (Horizontal Dilution of Precision): A number similar to PDOP, but relating only to your horizontal position.

✦ **EHPE** (Expected Horizontal Position Error): The error in horizontal position, which you can assume under current conditions. For example, Figure 1-3 shows that the GPS receiver is probably accurate to within about 27 feet when I captured the image.

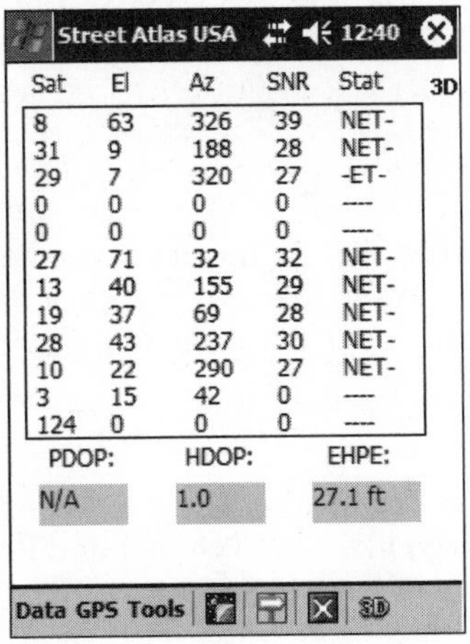

Street Atlas USA 12:40
Sat El Az SNR Stat 3D
8 63 326 39 NET-
31 9 188 28 NET-
29 7 320 27 -ET-
0 0 0 0 ---
0 0 0 0 ---
27 71 32 32 NET-
13 40 155 29 NET-
19 37 69 28 NET-
28 43 237 30 NET-
10 22 290 27 NET-
3 15 42 0 ---
124 0 0 0 ---
PDOP: HDOP: EHPE:
N/A 1.0 27.1 ft
Data GPS Tools

Figure 1-3: The GPS receiver has my position located within about 27 feet of my actual location.

Some other satellite navigation systems exist (almost)

Even though the GPS system is the best-known satellite navigation system, it's not the only such system — well, almost, that is:

✦ The Russians had their own system called GLONASS (Global'naya Navigatsionnaya Sputnikovaya Sistema or Global Navigation Satellite System), but the system was pretty much defunct by 2001 and is considered virtually useless for navigation.

✦ The European Union and the European Space Agency is intending to launch their own alternative to the GPS system called Galileo, but it won't be functional until at least 2008. Galileo is interesting because it is compatible with the next-generation GPS system, which is set to begin operation in 2012. Once the two systems are both in operation, GPS accuracy will be greatly improved through the use of 58 total satellites.

✦ The European Space Agency, the European Commission, and EUROCONTROL are also developing the European geostationary navigation overlay system (EGNOS) as a precursor to Galileo. EGNOS is intended to supplement GPS and allow position to be determined to within 5 meters.

✦ Finally, the People's Republic of China has launched satellites for their Beidou navigation system (unlike the other satellite navigation systems, Beidou is not an acronym but rather the Chinese name of the Ursa Major constellation). The Beidou system relies upon stationary satellites, which limits its usefulness to those locations in Asia that have a view of the satellites.

Even though some other satellite navigation systems exist, GPS is really the only viable option for most people today. The GPS receiver you buy now can certainly provide the navigation services you need for the foreseeable future.

Using GPS

What can you do with GPS and its receiver? As the list at the beginning of this chapter shows, the number of ways to take advantage of this free service are numerous. Here I go into detail on a few of the more popular uses.

Taking a hike

A GPS receiver is a must-have accessory for the outdoors type among you. It helps get you to where you want to go like a map cannot and prevents panic when all of those trees start looking alike.

WARNING!

Still, as my Garmin manual cautions, it's important to carry an old-fashioned compass and map with you whenever you hike in new territory. If your batteries die or the trees prevent you from getting a good lock on the satellite signals, your GPS receiver isn't much help. Also, if you're trekking into some back country or there's a possibility that the weather might turn sour, be sure to tell someone where you're planning on going so they know where to start looking for you if you don't return when you told them you'd be back.

If I was an outdoors person, and I'm not (although I do go outside to get the daily mail), I would buy one of the fancy new two-way radios that combines a communications transceiver with a GPS receiver. I discuss these in Book VI, Chapter 3, which is about Family Radio Service and other two-way radios.

On the road again

I have a horrible time getting to new destinations. Actually, I have a horrid time finding places I've already visited, too. I don't know how many times I've driven to some strange city and found myself in the less glamorous parts of town rather than where I should be, safely in my friend's driveway.

GPS to the rescue!

Instead of relying on memory and getting all of those numbered highways mixed up in my head, I can rely on a GPS receiver to provide turn-by-turn directions. I tell the receiver where I'm going — it knows where I am, of course — and it tracks my direction and speed and lets me know when it's time to make a turn onto another highway or road.

If you're hungry on the way, some advanced models can tell you where the nearest restaurant is located. The DeLorme Street Atlas programs include information on literally thousands of *points of interest* including restaurants, gas stations, parks, campgrounds, and so on to make your trip far more enjoyable.

On a bike ride

It might not seem obvious at first, but a portable GPS receiver (or a Pocket PC with a GPS accessory receiver) can be a wonderful addition for your bicycle. This is especially true if you set off on a road trip, but even mountain bikers can appreciate the way that a GPS receiver helps them find the trail in rugged back country.

If you do decide to bring along your GPS receiver on your bike, keep in mind that a bike presents something of a challenge to fragile electronic gear. Your local bike shop can probably supply a strong handlebar mount for the GPS receiver, but you may also want to shop carefully for a GPS receiver that's rated for rugged use.

It's a bird, no, it really is a plane

Private pilots travel in a world where the ordinary landmarks simply look a whole lot different than they do from ground level. It's awfully hard to read road signs from several thousand feet in the air, so getting a little extra help in determining exact position is really important to a pilot.

GPS technology has become a very important tool for pilots over the past several years. Products like Anywhere Map from Control Vision (www.controlvision.com) have simply revolutionized the general aviation world because they've made it possible for virtually every flyer to realize the benefits of GPS mapping at a fraction of what it would have cost even a few years ago.

Just for fun

In the next chapter I talk about two other fun uses of GPS: finding goodies in a hobby called geocaching and finding your ancestors and their haunts in genealogy. I just mention them here briefly so you can decide whether you want to read more details in the next chapter.

Geocaching

By using your wits and a cheap GPS receiver, you can participate in something called *geocaching.* It's really a high-tech treasure hunt. The treasure, or *cache,* is usually inexpensive items, but the fun is in the chase. With coordinates in hand, you can drive to nearby locations, finding your way to the cache with GPS receiver in one hand and perhaps a can of bug spray in the other.

Genealogy

The use of GPS technology is just starting to catch on in the hobby of *genealogy,* which is the search for your family roots. With a GPS receiver, you can make the drive to old family homesteads easier and even find relatives' graves. Instead of requiring other researchers to retrace your steps on their own, you can provide precise GPS coordinates to make their hunt for family information and physical remnants easier.

Exploring Your Options

A wide variety of GPS receivers are available in all kinds of styles and with different levels of features. What you buy mostly depends on what its main use is, because a hiker's GPS receiver must be much smaller than one meant to rest on your vehicle dashboard.

Choosing a portable unit

When choosing a portable unit, these are some of your choices:

- **Magellan** at www.magellangps.com/en/
- **Garmin** at www.garmin.com
- **Cobra** at www.cobra.com

Each of these manufacturers offers an assortment of models aimed at different types of users. You probably want to look at several different GPS receivers before choosing because the extra features that are included in the slightly more expensive models can greatly improve the convenience of using a portable unit.

TIP

If you intend to use your portable GPS receiver with your laptop PC, be sure to buy a unit that includes the necessary cables or adapters. These are typically not included with the least expensive models.

Driving around with a vehicle GPS unit

In the car, you have lots of options for using GPS:

- You can buy a new car that has a fancy built-in navigation system. This is by far the most expensive option, of course, but it's the only one that's guaranteed to impress the neighbors (or make your boss start wondering if you're being paid too much). Built-in navigation systems often have a hidden cost your dealer may "forget" to mention, though. In most cases you need to buy expensive map add-ons if you want maps for the entire country.

- If you like the idea of a built-in GPS navigation system but aren't in the market for a new car, the manufacturers of portable GPS receivers offer aftermarket units that can be added to your existing car. While these might not have quite the caché of a factory-installed GPS navigation system, they're a lot more affordable and you can move them to a new vehicle in the future.
- You can also use a Bluetooth or another GPS receiver with a laptop PC and carry it along in your car. This option is far less expensive than the other two vehicle options I mentioned, and it has one feature that trumps both of them in a big way — the laptop PC's screen is far bigger than that on any built-in vehicle GPS system. In addition, GPS mapping software for your laptop is far less expensive to update, so it's far easier on your wallet when you want to know about the newer roads.
- If you want the small size of a portable GPS receiver but you also want most of the advanced mapping options available with laptop PC GPS mapping software, you might want to consider pairing up a GPS receiver with a Pocket PC. I talk about using a GPS receiver with a Pocket PC shortly, but this is an excellent choice in many cases.

WARNING!

No matter what type of GPS navigation system you use in a vehicle, it can be very dangerous to you and everyone else on the road if you don't take the time to get to know the unit before you begin driving. In fact, unless the GPS navigation system uses voice prompts to tell you when and where to turn, it's far safer to have a passenger handle the navigation duties than to try to watch the screen while you're driving.

Merging your laptop with GPS

I've already mentioned how you can use your laptop PC for navigation in your vehicle. This is a very popular option among RV owners because they usually plenty of room for the laptop and at least one passenger who can handle the navigation while driving. In addition, GPS mapping software for laptops generally includes the locations of RV parks so you may not need a big, printed RV park directory.

Another way to use GPS with your laptop is to combine your search for WiFi hotspots, which I discuss in another chapter, with GPS. Using your laptop, you can drive around, essentially mapping hotspot locations. To aid in this quest you may want to download a trial version of Winc from Cirond (www.cirond.com/winc.html). This extremely handy program quickly identifies all WiFi connections within an area and helps you determine if you can connect to them. Cirond even offers a Pocket PC version called pocketWinc, shown in Figure 1-4.

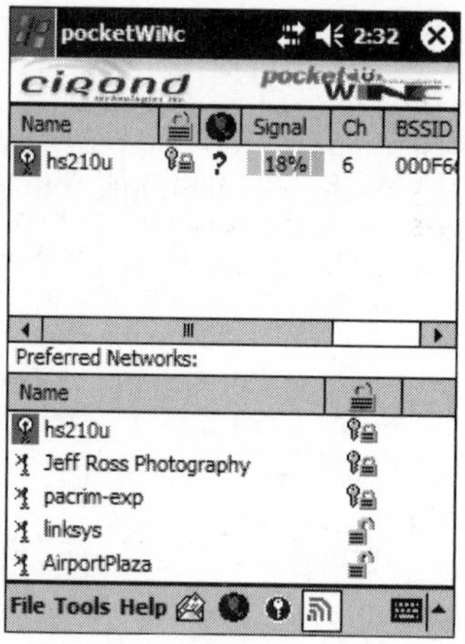

Figure 1-4: Winc and pocketWinc enable you to easily locate and connect to WiFi hotspots.

Using GPS with a Pocket PC

I've mentioned several times that a Pocket PC and a GPS receiver make an excellent pairing. With the two, you have most of the size advantages of standalone portable GPS receivers and a whole raft of capabilities that you won't find in most portable GPS units. (You may want to pick up a copy of *iPAQ For Dummies* or *Pocket PC For Dummies* — both written by Brian Underdahl and published by Wiley Publishing — to read more about what you can do with a Pocket PC.)

Because different Pocket PC models offer different expansion options, you find several types of GPS receivers that work with various Pocket PCs. I recommend checking out the products that are available from the following:

- **DeLorme** at www.delorme.com
- **Pharos GPS** at www.pharosgps.com
- **Teletype** at www.teletype.com
- **PocketMapStore** at www.pocketmapstore.com
- **ALK Technologies** at www.alk.com

In each case you should specify the type of Pocket PC you own so you can get the proper GPS receiver.

TIP

GPS maps can eat up a lot of memory on a Pocket PC. If you don't already have a Pocket PC, try to get one with built-in Bluetooth so you can use the expansion slot for a memory card to hold your maps.

Using a GPS-enabled cell phone

Nextel has a service called TeleNav that provides audible driving directions, automatic notification when you've gone off course, and locations of nearby businesses like gas stations and restaurants. You can read more at www.nextel.com/about/enterprise/wbs/gps/navigate.shtml. Other carriers have similar services. Visit your carrier's web site or call to see if they sell any GPS-enabled phones.

Saying Goodbye to AAA?

Some of the least expensive GPS receivers don't display maps. Instead, they display your location on the screen, comparing where you are to where you want to go. The more expensive units, on the other hand, do allow you to upload maps so they're displayed on the GPS receiver.

I recommend you don't take AAA or any other paper map out of the loop just yet, especially when you're using a GPS unit in the car. There's still the chance the map data you upload is not up to date, that your batteries will go dead, or that you'll have some other technical problem. Having a map gets you to the Grand Canyon long after your GPS receiver stops working. If you're hiking, a compass and a map are essential, even if you have the best GPS receiver available. In that case, your life is possibly at stake and you don't want to rely on an electronic gizmo to get out of the woods and back home.

GPS mapping programs for laptop PCs generally offer the option to print out both ordinary maps and those that show your selected route. These printed copies can serve as an excellent backup for your GPS unit and save you a trip to the auto club office.

Making a Connection with Your PC

There are quite a few reasons why I think you'll find that having a connection between your GPS receiver and your PC awfully handy. Examine a few of them.

Upgrading software and maps

As I mentioned in the previous section, once you move beyond the most basic portable GPS receivers you quickly get into units that display maps rather than simply numbers to indicate your position. You may have noticed, however, that maps have a certain amount of obsolescence built in. For some reason people want to build new roads, change the course of old ones, or even just rename existing roads. That's one reason many GPS receivers offer the option to connect to your PC — so you can update the maps in the GPS receiver.

Downloading your life's movements

Virtually all GPS units can store some record of where they've been. By downloading this tracking information to your PC you can map out the route you took in getting somewhere. Here are some possible uses for this type of information:

- ✦ Imagine how useful it would be to be able to print out maps of the trail to some hidden but beautiful picnic spot so that you could share those maps with your friends.
- ✦ If you have a consulting business where you must visit your client's locations, you could use your GPS track to justify the travel expenses you bill to the customers or that you claim on your tax returns.
- ✦ Because the GPS track also includes information about the speed of travel, you might try to beat an unwarranted speeding ticket by convincing a judge that the GPS track is an accurate representation of how you were driving. I don't think I'd bet on that working, but you're welcome to try. (Just don't blame me if the judge throws the book at you — remember, I'm not offering anything resembling legal advice here.)
- ✦ You could put your GPS receiver in your car before you let your teenager drive to the library and remind him or her that the unit tracks both speed and location. Who knows? It might just make your kid drive a bit more carefully.

Using your GPS with your laptop

Don't you just love it when you can get the best of both worlds out of a product? Well, when it comes to GPS, it's entirely possible for you to do so. There's no reason why you can't buy a small, portable GPS receiver that's perfect for taking on hikes and then connect that same GPS receiver to your laptop PC to use with the far more comprehensive PC-based GPS mapping software for trip navigation in your vehicle.

Sure, you'll probably have to buy a portable GPS receiver that's slightly above the bottom of the line, but virtually any of the portable units that include a PC connection cable as standard equipment can likely do the job. (You can check the PC-based GPS mapping software manufacturer's web site to verify if a particular portable GPS unit is considered compatible.)

TIP

GPS receivers work the best in vehicles when the receiver has a clear view of the sky. The optimal location in most cars is at the front of the dashboard as close to the windshield as possible. A small piece of rubberized drawer liner (like you find in the housewares section at your local store) goes a long way toward preventing the GPS receiver from sliding around as you drive.

Chapter 2: Finding Your Way in the World

In This Chapter

- A quick mapping course
- Coordinating your coordinates
- Deciphering a GPS display
- Understanding waypoints

In the preceding chapter I give you an overview of the *global positioning system (GPS).* Hopefully, that chapter gives you a good understanding of what GPS is, how you can use it, and how to pick a GPS receiver. It also shows you a number of different options to fit different circumstances so you also realize that GPS isn't something just for a few dedicated hobbyists.

Now I'm going to take you to the next step, which is understanding how to read a GPS display. Most importantly, I give you a quick lesson in longitude, latitude, and related mapping terms so you know what your GPS receiver is telling you. You probably learned most of this in school, but if you're like most people, didn't pay very close attention to something you thought you'd never use.

Still, while this information is interesting and (hold your applause) delightfully presented, it's more important to understand your GPS receiver so you can figure out how to get un-lost. After all, it's unlikely a latitude and longitude reading will help much when you're lost in the middle of the forest without a clue about which way to get out.

Giving Some Latitude to Your Longitude

You probably remember latitude and longitude from geography class. It's an international way to indicate your location in the world. You probably don't think in international terms too much, though, so take a few minutes to review what latitude and longitude mean.

Figure 2-1 shows a world map divided by latitude and longitude lines. If you know the latitude and longitude values of any location on the planet you can use those values to find that location on the map.

A GPS receiver does its magic by listening to signals from the GPS satellites and then tells you where you stand, also in the geographic sense, by determining your precise latitude and longitude. In fact, that's how a GPS receiver is able to display your location on a map. It simply takes your latitude and longitude numbers and figures out where that position is on the map.

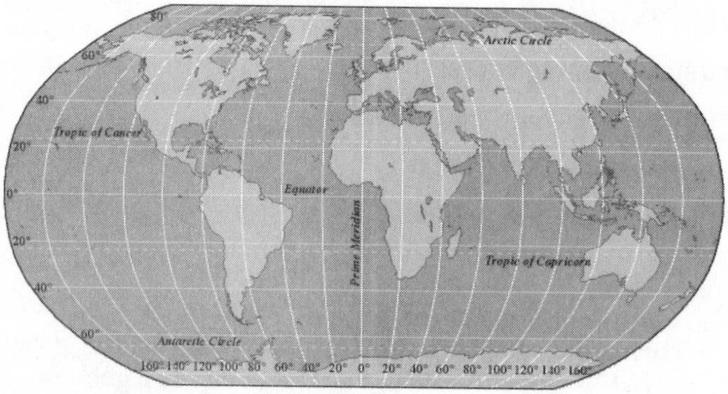

Figure 2-1: Latitude and longitude lines help you find your location on Earth.

A Quick Course on Mapping

This isn't a book on mapping or geography or even GPS, so this is a very short introduction to the three things you should know about: latitude, longitude, and elevation. Even so, this basic information should enable you to begin using your GPS receiver for simple navigation. It also helps you remember a few easily confusing facts.

A bit of simple geometry

Okay, you knew this was coming, didn't you? Yes, it's necessary to have just a brief review of geometry to make certain that we're all speaking the same language:

- ✦ When you divide a circle into degrees, there are 360 degrees in a complete circle.
- ✦ Both latitude and longitude are measured in degrees, which is often shown using the ° symbol.
- ✦ For the purposes of navigation, the earth is considered to be essentially round. Flat earth societies pretty much gave up their fight a long time ago.
- ✦ Because latitude and longitude both indicate a position on a round planet, the total number of degrees around the earth in either latitude or longitude is 360 (even though, as you discover shortly, the values are expressed a bit differently, they do add up to 360).

- Fractions of degrees are measured in minutes, with 60 minutes in 1 degree. The symbol for minutes is '.
- Likewise, fractions of minutes are measured in seconds, with 60 seconds in a minute. The symbol for seconds is ".
- Sometimes, though, fractions of degrees are expressed using decimal values rather than minutes and seconds. The results are the same, but just a bit of math is involved in converting between the two. For example, 39 degrees and 30 minutes could also be shown as 39.5 degrees (because 30 minutes is one half of a degree). It could also be shown as 39° 30'.

That wasn't too bad, was it? Now that you've got the simple geometry out of the way, see how it applies to latitude and longitude.

Latitude

The lines of latitude run east and west around the globe. Latitude is shown as degrees north in the Northern Hemisphere and as degrees south in the Southern Hemisphere. Starting at the equator, when you go north, the north latitude rises to 90 degrees when you reach the North Pole. When you go south of the equator, the south latitude reaches 90 degrees when you hit the South Pole.

So, for example, Reno, Nevada is located at approximately 39 degrees and 30 minutes north latitude, while Los Angeles, California is at about 34 degrees north latitude. From these two values you can tell that Reno is farther north than Los Angeles — and that's without looking at a map.

Longitude

The imaginary lines of longitude run north and south. The zero-degrees longitude line runs through Greenwich, England, which is called the *prime meridian.* If you went west of the prime meridian and a friend went east, you'd eventually meet up at the International Date Line, which has nothing to do with romance. You would go 180 degrees in both directions. (Remember how I told you the numbers would add up to 360?)

In the Eastern Hemisphere, the longitude is given as degrees east. In the Western Hemisphere, longitude is given as degrees west. You may also see west longitude expressed as a negative value. That is, W119° is the same as –119°.

Going back to the earlier example, you find that Reno is at about W119° 50' while Los Angeles is approximately W118° 15'. Hey, wait a minute! That puts Reno west of Los Angeles, doesn't it? Well, yes it does, and that's exactly why understanding a little bit of geometry is so important. (Go ahead, look on a map and you see that Reno actually is farther west than Los Angeles — you can win a bar bet with this one.)

Elevation

Elevation is when you magically float in the air, with nothing holding you. No, wait. That's *levitation*. What I'm talking about here is *elevation,* which is basically the distance you're standing above sea level. If you're on a high mountain, you're obviously at an elevation much higher than sea level.

When using a GPS, you must receive signals from a fourth satellite to measure your elevation. You only need three visible satellites if all you need is your two-dimensional position in the world. GPS receivers typically display 2D to indicate a two-dimensional fix and 3D to indicate a three-dimensional fix. A *fix* is simply the navigational term for knowing your precise location.

Coordinating Your Coordinates

Latitude lines are always parallel to the equator and to each other. Longitude lines, however, are not really parallel to each other because they meet at the north and south poles.

One important result regarding the difference between latitude and longitude lines is that a one-degree change of latitude is always equal to the same distance (ignoring elevation differences, of course), but a one-degree change of longitude varies. Look at how this can be:

- Going directly north or south changes your latitude but not your longitude. One degree of latitude change equals just about 70 miles. You could figure out the circumference of the earth and divide that by 360 to verify this, but your number comes pretty close if you do.
- Going one degree east or west at the equator changes your longitude but not your latitude. Again, if you're at the equator, one degree of longitude change is also about 70 miles (because the earth is round, so the circumference around the equator is virtually the same as it is on one of the longitude lines).
- Now, imagine that you are standing exactly at the north pole. Take one step south (that's any direction from where you are). That places you about three feet away from the north pole, so if you stay the same distance out and walk all the way around the pole you'll go about 20 feet. But that 20 feet brought you all the way around the world so you traveled through 360 degrees of longitude. A little math tells you that one degree of longitude change here is a bit less than an inch. How can this be? Well, the latitude lines are parallel (running east and west,

remember) so the circles going entirely around the world are much shorter than they are at the equator. Because the longitude lines all meet at the poles, each of them is exactly the same length.

It's easy to see how this could be confusing, so aren't you glad that your GPS receiver does all of the math for you? And aren't you glad that I went to the north pole to do the measurements so you wouldn't have to?

Explaining How GPS Works

I'm not an engineer or anything close, but I think I can describe in simple terms how the GPS system works. Sure, in this case it really is rocket science, but the general idea is fairly easy to understand.

Imagine for a moment that you have found three posts pounded into the ground in a triangular pattern somewhere in your yard. One day you're down at the library and you come across some historical records that mention that the town recluse used to live on your property and that before he died he told someone that he had buried some treasure exactly 100 feet from the posts. Can you figure out where to dig without ruining all of the landscaping you've so carefully added to your yard?

Actually, that's a pretty simple problem because there's only one solution. If you tie a 100-foot string to each post and then see where the three ends meet, you've found the spot because there is no other place that's exactly 100 feet from all of the posts (as shown in Figure 2-2).

The GPS system works something like those three strings. By precisely measuring the distance from several satellites in orbit around the earth to your location, it's possible to determine exactly where you are, like you see in Figure 2-3. The rocket scientists figured out how to calculate the precise position of each GPS satellite at each point in time and they know that radio signals travel at the speed of light, so throw in a little fancy math and bingo!

TECHNICAL STUFF

Have you been wondering why it takes at least four GPS satellites to produce a 3D fix? It's because you need one more measurement than the number of dimensions to rule out multiple positions in the remaining dimension. In the example of using three strings to find the buried treasure in your yard, you assumed that where the three strings touched the ground was where the treasure was buried. If you held onto those three strings and raised them up above the ground, you would find that they would still meet even if you held them above your head. The same thing happens with the GPS satellite signals, but once you add a fourth signal there's only one point that can be your location.

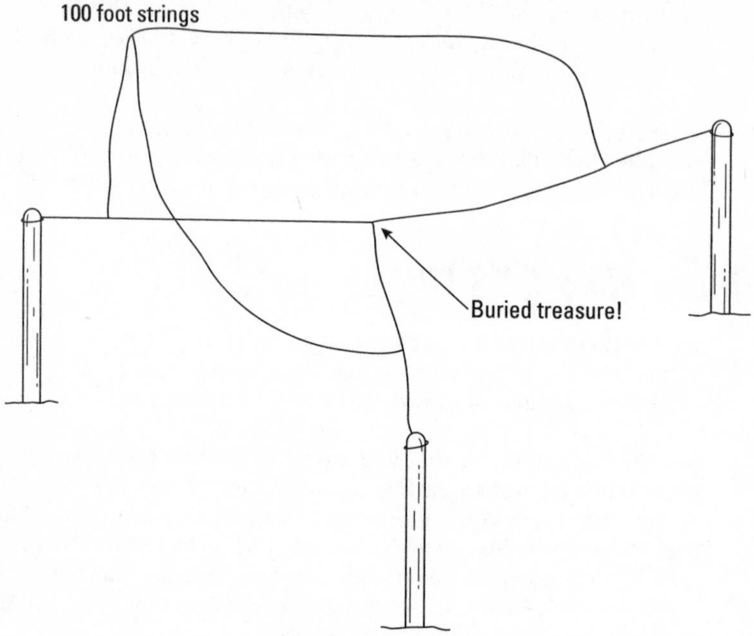

Figure 2-2: You can locate a point by carefully measuring the distance from known points.

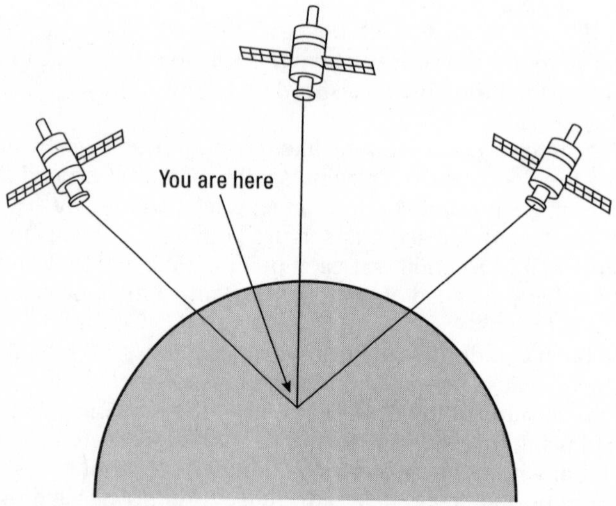

Figure 2-3: You can locate your position by carefully measuring the distance from the GPS satellites.

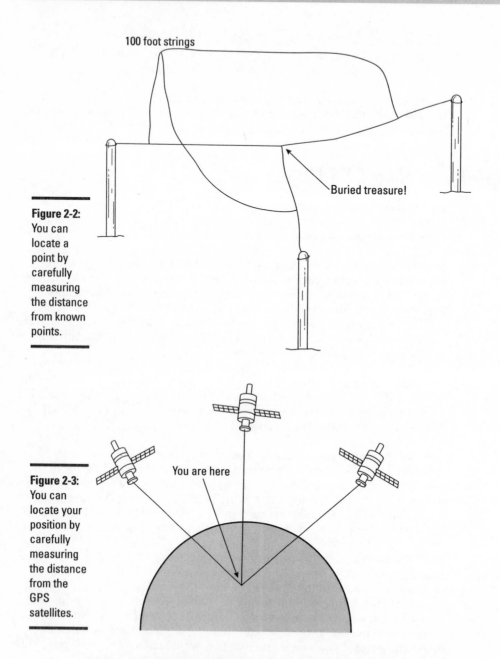

Figure 2-4 shows an example of how a GPS receiver shows a display of the satellites that are being tracked. In this case the display symbols indicate that four satellites are being used for navigation and the 3D indicator near the upper right of the display tells you that the unit has a 3D fix. GPS receivers often have more satellites in view than are being used for navigation simply because the data from some of the satellites might not be coming through reliably enough for navigation purposes.

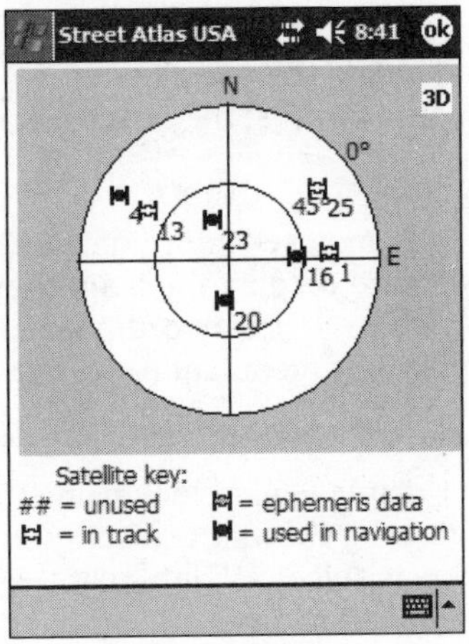

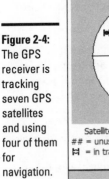

Figure 2-4: The GPS receiver is tracking seven GPS satellites and using four of them for navigation.

Reading a GPS Display

I own a Garmin eTrex GPS receiver. Like most modern GPS receivers, you can choose how to display your coordinates. That is, you can choose degrees, minutes, and seconds or you can opt for degrees and decimal fractions.

For example, my location in a digital format, according to the display on my GPS receiver, is this:

N 42.96506 W 085.92599

Using the degrees, minutes, and seconds display, the following represents the same location:

42° 57' 54.4" N 85° 55' 33.6" W

That means I'm in the Northern and Western hemispheres. To be exact, I'm in this location:

42 degrees, 57 minutes and 54.4 seconds north of the equator

85 degrees, 55 minutes and 33.6 seconds west of the prime meridian

That puts me in West Michigan. If you look at the digital equivalent of my location you can see how the 42 degrees, 57 minutes, and 54.4 seconds were simply converted to 42.96506:

N 42.96506 W 085.92599

The same was done with the second half of the coordinates. It's 57 minutes of one way and 0.96 of the other. In other words, they're the same coordinates, just expressed differently.

TIP

That's important to know because you may see coordinates expressed one way, but your GPS receiver may be set to display them another way. Usually, you can make a quick conversion to the coordinates of your choice by going into your receiver's setup menu and selecting Units or something similar.

Figure 2-5 shows how a GPS receiver display might look using the degrees and decimal degrees option and Figure 2-6 shows the display when the degrees, minutes, and seconds option is selected. Note that these two readings do not show precisely the same location.

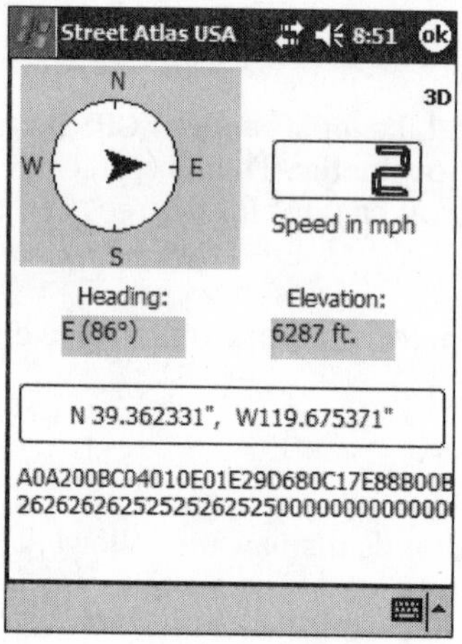

Figure 2-5: The GPS receiver is displaying coordinates using degrees and decimal degrees.

WARNING!

Due to rounding errors, you may not get precisely the same values when you try to convert between the two types of display. It's always best to pick one method and stick with it to avoid these types of errors.

Figure 2-7 shows one very good reason why you may prefer to use a GPS receiver that displays your position on a map rather than using latitude and longitude coordinates. I don't know about you, but it's a lot easier for me to determine my location by looking at the map display than by reading the coordinate display.

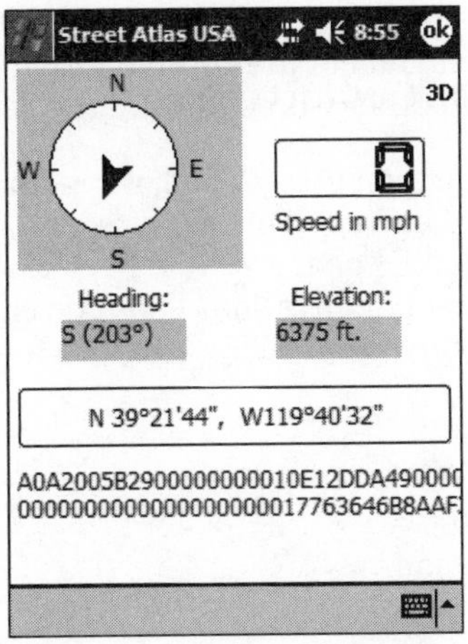

Figure 2-6: The GPS receiver is displaying coordinates using degrees, minutes, and seconds.

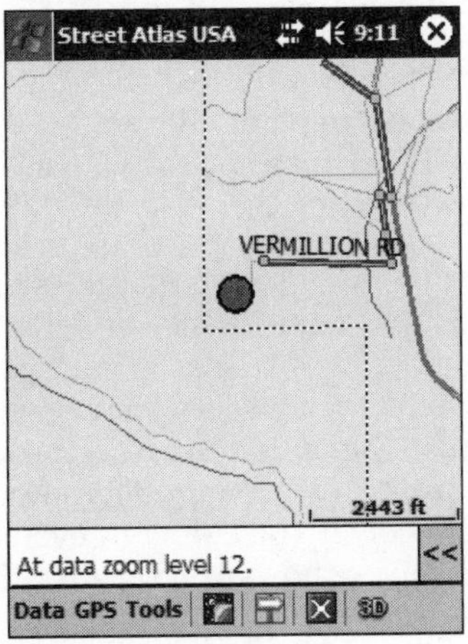

Figure 2-7: The GPS receiver is my current location using a map display.

Finding Your Waypoints

Waypoints are the essence of basic GPS navigation. At the simplest level waypoints are just the various points along the route between where you are and where you want to go. Even if you've never used a GPS receiver before, you've certainly used waypoints — you probably just didn't use that name for them.

Understanding how waypoints work

To understand how waypoints work, consider the following set of directions:

1. Take Highway 395 south to the junction of Highway 341.
2. Turn left on Highway 341.
3. Turn left at the intersection with Cartwright Road.

Those directions seem clear enough, don't they? Well, waypoints work pretty much the same way except that waypoints are often indicated using geographical coordinates in place of the names or numbers of roads or other physical objects. In fact, that same set of directions could be expressed using two waypoints (because the directions tell you to turn in two places) as in the following:

1. Go to N39° 24' 10.1", W119° 44' 46".
2. Go to N39° 21' 59.1", W119° 39' 59".
3. Turn left.

Although it's true that both sets of directions get you to the same place, the directions that use waypoints offer one distinct advantage over the directions that use highway names and numbers. Can you spot the important difference? The first set of directions is pretty useless without additional information — such as an assumed starting point. The sets of directions using waypoints need no other details because anyone with a GPS receiver can follow them no matter where the trip began.

Even though this example only uses two waypoints, that doesn't mean that you necessarily want to set off on a cross-country hike directly between the two waypoints. You might find a number of obstacles in your path that prevent that sort of straight-line approach. If you use a GPS receiver that displays maps, you might want to choose the option to create a route that uses roads rather than to create a direct route. (The method for choosing this varies according to the type of GPS receiver you use.) But even if you choose the direct route option, your GPS receiver shows you the distance and direction to your next waypoint, just as you see in Figure 2-8. This means that if you have to navigate around a steep hill, a lake, or even a large building, your GPS receiver shows you how to reach the waypoint.

Creating waypoints

You can create your own waypoints a number of ways. The precise methods depend on your particular GPS receiver, of course, but generally you'll probably find that you have at least some of these options available:

- Enter waypoints manually by entering latitude and longitude coordinates before you set out with your GPS receiver. This method requires that you know the coordinates, of course, but it allows you to set very accurate waypoints.

- The manual process may also be as simple as clicking points on an on-screen map. This generally won't be quite as accurate as entering specific latitude and longitude values, but it's far more convenient.
- Most GPS receivers allow you to manually set waypoints at your current location. This method is very handy if you're out for a walk in a strange city and want to be sure that you can find the way back to your starting point.
- Many GPS receivers offer an automatic tracking option. Typically this option creates waypoints at specific time intervals so you can later play back a record of your travels. If you use this option it's a good idea to learn how to set the recording interval. That way you can set a value appropriate to your mode of travel — shorter intervals for vehicular travel and longer intervals when you're on foot.

WARNING!

Portable GPS receivers typically have a limited amount of available memory. If you set the recording interval too short you can lose your earlier recorded waypoints when the memory becomes full. As you can imagine, this could make it difficult for you to backtrack in unfamiliar terrain.

The popularity of GPS receivers has generated a whole new hobby — exchanging lists of useful and interesting waypoints. Web sites such as GPS Waypoint Registry (www.waypoint.org) are dedicated to collecting and sharing lists of these waypoints.

This chapter has helped you understand a bit more about how to use your GPS receiver. Although there wasn't room for an entire course on the finer points of GPS usage, I'm sure that you're far more comfortable about how you can use your GPS receiver to get from where you are to where you want to be.

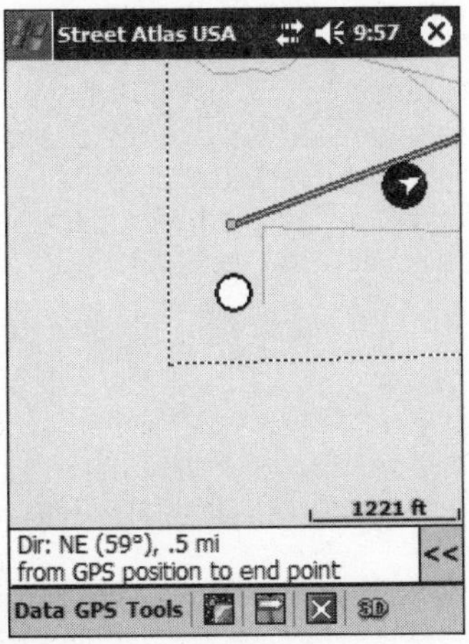

Figure 2-8: The next waypoint is a half a mile to the northeast from my current position.

Chapter 3: Exploring with the Rest of GPS

In This Chapter

- **Exploring geocaching**
- **Using GPS to find cemeteries**
- **Finding your ancestors' homesteads**

A fast-growing hobby called *geocaching* uses your GPS receiver to track down plots of small prizes hidden around the globe. *GPS* stands for Global Positioning System and can be used for more than simply finding your way out of the forest.

The second use is a more practical one. You can use GPS coordinates in genealogy research, both for finding cemeteries (and even specific gravestones) and your ancestors' old homesteads, schools, churches, and other sites.

Seeking and Hiding with Geocaching

GPS is not only about using the technological equivalent of bread crumbs to find your way out of the forest. It also helps provide the basic navigational tools for geocaching, helping you pinpoint within feet the location of hidden caches that others have left for you to find.

When you've mastered the seeking, you may want to try the hiding part. You can create your own caches, maybe right in your backyard, that others can seek. There are even groups and Web sites — such as www.geocaching.com — dedicated to this hobby.

Going for the cache

(Going for the cache! Get it? I knock myself unconscious coming up with these things. Which is probably why it takes me so long to write them.)

Given the choice, you probably would rather go for the cash. But geocaching leads to its own treasures, many of them you keep while others you take to the next cache location and exchange for something else. You can do this on and on, traveling across the United States and other countries (but mind the oceans, lest you find yourself with some wet cache).

Playing it safe while playing

Having fun shouldn't lead to forgetting about good old common sense. Consider these things before heading off:

- Travel in pairs.
- Let someone know where you're going if you go out to look or hide a cache.
- Carry ID, water, and a flashlight if you're hiking.
- Make sure you get permissions to hide a cache on property if it's not yours.
- Make sure you know what the park rules are for hiding things.
- Follow your instincts and don't do something if your gut is saying not to.

For those who love technology, the outdoors, and a good quest, it's a perfect hobby. It's a little like a modern-day version of scouting, where you might have earned an orienteering badge for your skills with a map and compass. Now you're using your map, compass, and GPS navigational skills. You can do it with friends and family; you breath the clean air of mostly remote areas and improve your navigational skills for the day you might need them. (On the other hand, staying inside is safer and dryer. But I'm assuming you *like* the outdoors.)

In most instances the hidden caches are tucked away in a hidden location in a public place. Don't expect to be digging for buried treasure in someone's yard — if you do, you're probably looking in the wrong place.

You don't need an expensive GPS receiver for geocaching. An inexpensive model (like the Garmin eTrex receiver) costs $75 and is enough to get you going. Later, if you want a GPS receiver that displays maps and has other features, you always can spend a little more money ($150 to 200) for an advanced model. See Book VIII, Chapter 1 for more information about your options in buying a GPS receiver.

You can find nearby caches by searching on the www.geocaching.com web site. You can search by zip code, state, country, and other variables. Once you find a cache you want to find, www.geocaching.com has some suggestions for hunting it down:

- **Research the cache location.** Buy a topographical map for remote cache locations. Use services like MapBlast (www.mapblast) or MapQuest (www.mapquest.com) to get driving directions for more easily accessible ones.

- **If you're familiar with the area, navigate there using mostly the readings from your GPS unit.** www.geocaching.com doesn't recommend this for first-time hunters. However, you may need to use a combination of all three strategies to find a cache. Bringing along a compass is a good idea, too.
- **Drive as close to the cache location as you can.** When you get within 300 feet, check your GPS receiver's margin of error. It could be between 25 and 200 feet. The smaller the error, the more you can rely on your receiver's reading. For the last 30 feet or so, circle the area to find the cache. For higher error rates, the circle is larger.
- **When you find the cache, at least write your name in the enclosed log book.** If you want to take an item from the cache and replace it with another, that's great, too. This is all done under the honor system, of course. You're not supposed to find the cache, take all the loot, and run off for an early retirement.
- **When you leave your car, mark your waypoint on your GPS receiver.** This way you can find your way back to the car. Otherwise, you may need to wait for the next person who finds the cache so they can lead you back to civilization. (For more information on waypoints, see Book VIII, Chapter 2.)

If you have a Family Radio Service (FRS) radio, you can receive two channels that geocachers use to see if anyone is nearby at cache locations. Channel 2 is the primary channel and channel 12 serves as the alternative. I cover FRS radios in Book VI, Chapter 3.

Hiding the bounty

Once you have mastered the art and science of geocaching, you may want to try your hand at hiding your very own cache.

As for goodies, you can put just about anything in your cache. Yes, even cash — which would make you a very popular person indeed on the geocaching circuit! Many caches contain inexpensive toys, CDs, and any other knickknacks you can imagine and that fit into the container. Some people even include disposable cameras, asking all the finders to take a photo of themselves.

www.geocaching.com makes these recommendations for hiding your own cache:

- **Research the location.** Look for someplace that may require some hiking, rather than an easy-to-find place close to well-traveled areas where someone may discover the cache accidentally.

TIP

Letterboxing: Geocaching sans batteries

What do you get if you take geocaching and substitute the GPS receiver with a compass? *Letterboxing,* a low-tech version of geocaching. And, no, it's not a heavyweight bout between the ABCs.

Instead of taking a trinket and leaving one, as you do in geocaching, letterboxing involves leaving your mark at every treasure location by stamping a log book with your own customized rubber stamp. You use another rubber stamp, stored in the cache box, to stamp your own book, like a passport.

If you wake up one Saturday morning and find your GPS receiver's batteries are dead, a similar hobby awaits you. That is, if you're handy with a compass.

You can read more about letterboxing at www.letterboxing.org.

- **Prepare your cache.** Your best bet is a waterproof container. You can place the actual items inside sealable plastic bags like those you use for sandwiches. Include a *log book* (small spiral notebook) and pen or pencil so seekers can record their find. Consider including a goodie that finders can take with them. Finally, mark the container with the average waypoint and consider enclosing a note, one of which is shown in Figure 3-1, explaining what the cache is all about.
- **Hide the goods.** This is where you use your GPS receiver. Get the cache's coordinates by taking a waypoint reading. For better accuracy, you should average the waypoints. If you're using a low-end GPS model, this may require taking a waypoint up to 10 times — you take a waypoint and then walk away, returning to do another one — and then finding the average waypoint measurement. This average is what you write on your container and in the log book, keeping a copy for the next cache you find.
- **Report the cache.** This involves filling out an online form on www.geocaching.com. Information includes cache type, size, coordinates (of course!), overall difficulty and terrain ratings, a description, and optionally, hints.

> **GEOCACHE SITE - PLEASE READ**
>
> **Congratulations, you've found it! Intentionally or not!**
>
> What is this hidden container sitting here for? What the heck is this thing doing here with all these things in it?
>
> It is part of a worldwide game dedicated to GPS (Global Positioning System) users, called Geocaching. The game basically involves a GPS user hiding "treasure" (this container and its contents), and publishing the exact coordinates so other GPS users can come on a "treasure hunt" to find it. The only rules are: if you take something from the cache, you must leave something for the cache, and you must write about your visit in the logbook. Hopefully, the person that hid this container found a good spot that is not easily found by uninterested parties. Sometimes, a good spot turns out to be a bad spot, though.
>
> **IF YOU FOUND THIS CONTAINER BY ACCIDENT:**
>
> Great! You are welcome to join us! We ask only that you:
>
> - Please do not move or vandalize the container. The real treasure is just finding the container and sharing your thoughts with everyone else who finds it.
> - If you wish, go ahead and take something. But please also leave something of your own for others to find, and write it in the logbook.
> - If possible, let us know that you found it, by visiting the web site listed below.
>
> Geocaching is open to everyone with a GPS and a sense of adventure. There are similar sites all over the world. The organization has its home on the Internet. Visit our website if you want to learn more, or have any comments:
>
> **http://www.geocaching.com**
>
> If this container needs to be removed for any reason, please let us know. We apologize, and will be happy to move it.

Figure 3-1: A copy of a letter you can leave in your cache box.

Finding Your Ancestors

GPS receivers can help you find your way, plot your course, and always let you know where you stand in the world. One thing it can't do is help you find your soul. That's beyond the scope of this book and is the reason my next project is *Finding Your Soul For Dummies*.

Alright, so I'm not writing that book. But I have something pretty close, and that's discovering your past by tracking down where your ancestors have tread. Even if you know where deceased relatives lived, it's often difficult to find their old homesteads.

A very grave matter

Speaking of souls, you can use your GPS receiver to find burial sites. Some kind people have already logged the latitudinal and longitudinal positions of some cemeteries and share them with others on a web site called The U.S. GeoGen Project (www.geogen.org).

In many cases, it's an even more difficult task to find old cemeteries, some of which aren't as preened and tended to as those where our closest relatives rest. They may be in heavily wooded areas. Or, worst of all, vandals or developers may have tipped over or removed headstones so that you're not even sure what you're visiting is a cemetery. If you have a map that lists the cemetery, have jotted down its longitude and latitude coordinates, and are heading there with a GPS receiver, you have a much better chance of actually finding it, like the person shown in Figure 3-2.

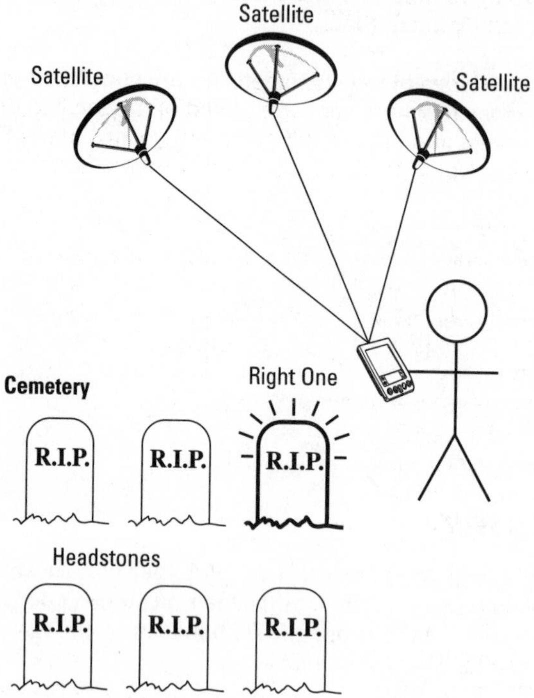

Figure 3-2: Your GPS receiver can help find an ancestor's grave or homestead.

Now think how great this would be if you had the GPS coordinates of a specific ancestor's gravestone? Not too long ago, I enlisted my adventuresome mother in a quest for a great-grandfather's grave. We knew the cemetery, but not the location of the gravestone.

I had the cemetery's name, so I bet you're thinking the rest was easy. Far from it. It was a large cemetery. There were thousands of gravestones, many of them flat against the ground so you can see them only after walking up to each and every one.

And just finding the cemetery wasn't easy.

Now imagine you have the GPS coordinates for the cemetery and that, maybe from another genealogist's efforts, you even have the latitude and longitude of the actual grave. Now that's something! Imagine the time you'd save. Even with GPS readings that have a margin of error of 20 feet or so, you have narrowed down the search considerably.

This isn't a book on genealogy and I'm assuming you know how to narrow down your search of cemeteries where your ancestors may be buried. GPS technology isn't going to help you find these sites unless you know they are places to look for family headstones.

Once you have a good idea of which cemeteries are good bets, either because they are close to where ancestors lived or are located on the family land, you can use maps and other tools to find the coordinates. From there, it's a matter of using your GPS navigational skills to reach each one and check them out.

TIP

In addition to the U.S. GeoGen Project's web site mentioned earlier, a good place to look for coordinates of cemeteries is the Geographic Names Information System (GNIS). The GNIS contains information about nearly two million U.S. physical and cultural geographic features. Many of these include associated latitudinal and longitudinal coordinates to enter into your GPS receiver to help you find them.

Here's how you do a quick search of the GNIS:

1. **Point your browser at www.geonames.usgs.gov.**

   The GNIS home page appears.

2. **In the left menu, under Query GNIS, click U.S. and Territories.**

   A query form appears.

3. **You can search many different ways. To search for cemeteries within a county, as shown in Figure 3-3, do the following:**

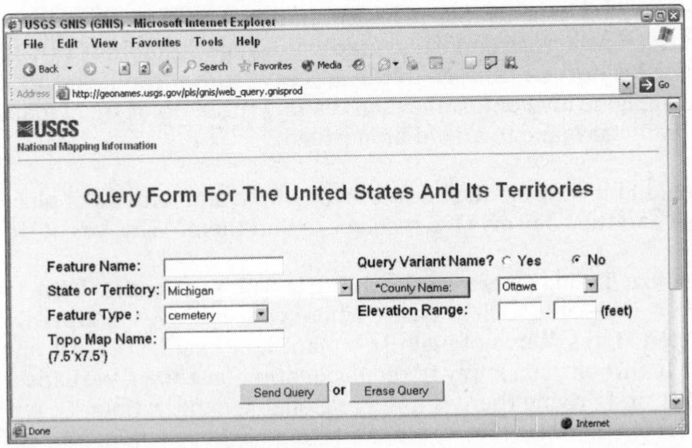

Figure 3-3: Searching for a county's cemeteries.

- Select a state.
- Click County Name.
- Select the county name from the pull-down menu.
- Select Cemetery under Feature Type.
- Click Send Query.

The site displays a list of search results, as shown in Figure 3-4.

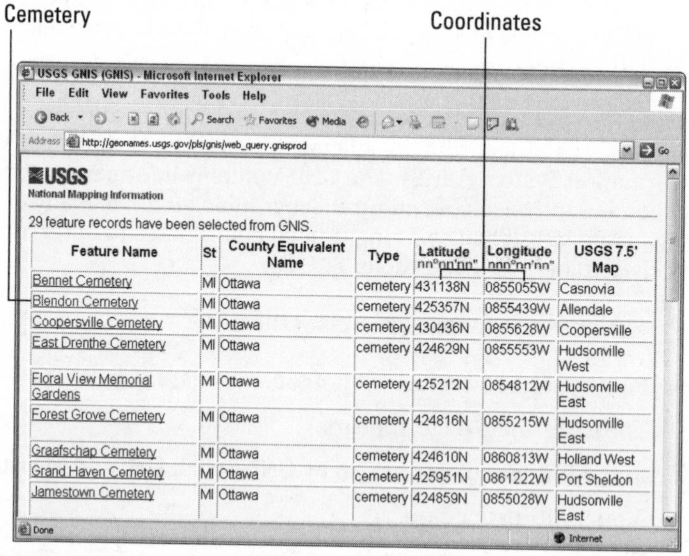

Figure 3-4: A list of cemeteries in Ottawa County, Michigan.

Where is (old) home sweet home?

As I do a bit of genealogical research to find the source of my genes, I sometimes come across confusing maps showing where this or that ancestor made his home. I can't go to the grocery store without getting lost, so you can imagine my confusion when reading these homestead maps, let alone actually traveling to an old homestead.

Wouldn't it be easier if I knew the longitude and latitude of places I want to visit and then use my GPS receiver to find them? Why, yes, it would be easier.

Just like finding cemeteries with Uncle Sam's (celestial) help, you can use GPS coordinates to help locate where your relatives migrated within the United States. Why not just use a map? Like I said, I get lost on the way to the bathroom, so simply finding a location on a map, perhaps in another state, and driving there is not a reasonable expectation.

Instead, you can use the GPS navigation skills you discovered in the preceding chapter to travel to locations you want to visit as part of your genealogy research. Remember, these towns may be so small that they are difficult enough to find on a map. By using your GPS receiver, especially one designed for automobile use, you can find those homesteads quicker by following the coordinates.

REMEMBER

Don't forget to write down and make available the locations' coordinates to genealogists, homesteads, farms, county courthouses, and local libraries.

Glossary

802.11 series: Wireless standards that include 802.11a, 802.11b, 802.11g, 802.11i, and other current and future related standards. Generally, 802.11b and 802.11g are used for Wi-Fi hotpots.

802.1x: An authentication scheme for Wi-Fi. Mostly used in corporate environments.

access point: A wireless device that serves as a communications hub for Wi-Fi clients.

ad-hoc mode: A mode in Wi-Fi networking where one computer connects directly to another computer, bypassing a central access point.

analog: Something that is not digital.

antenna: A metal rod or wire used to transmit and receive radio signals. All wireless technologies use some kind of antenna, even if it's so small you cannot see it.

band: A group of frequencies.

BlackBerry: A handheld device made by Research in Motion (RIM) that lets you access your e-mail and browse the web anywhere there is wireless coverage.

Bluetooth: A wireless technology operating in the frequency range of Wi-Fi communications, but has a much shorter range. Mostly used as a substitute for cables on the desktop (keyboards, mice) and in cell phone applications (wireless link between a headset and phone).

bridge: Lets you connect two or more networks together. For your purposes, it usually means connecting a wireless network to a wired network.

cable modem: A device that connects between your cable TV company's Internet connection and your network or computer. It enables you to send and receive information over the Internet using a coaxial cable that runs into your home.

cellular phone: A mobile telephone that uses a network of short-range transmitters to communicate with the landline phone system.

coaxial cable: Cable used for cable TV and some other applications.

cordless phone: A wireless phone usually used inside the home or yard that operates over one of three frequency bands: 900 MHz, 2.4 GHz, or 5.8 GHz.

cracker: Someone who hacks into a network with malicious intent.

DHCP: The dynamic host configuration protocol provides a way to automatically allocate IP addresses to computers on a network.

digital: Something, such as wireless signals, composed of 1s and 0s.

driver: Software that allows hardware to communicate with your computer's operating system. Each piece of hardware, such as a network adapter, has its own driver. The manufacturer usually provides the driver.

DSL: Digital subscriber line. This is one way to get broadband Internet access.

DSL modem: A device that connects between your telephone company's DSL connection and your network or computer. It enables you to send and receive information over the Internet using a telephone line that runs into your home.

encryption: Scrambling information as a way to secure it.

Ethernet: A network that connects two or more computers together.

firmware: A small software program inside hardware, such as routers, that controls the hardware.

GHz: Gigahertz.

Global positioning system: Worldwide network of satellites operated by U.S. Defense Department that enables civilian and military users to pinpoint their location on Earth.

GPS: *See* global positioning system.

hacker: An individual who attempts to break into computer systems and networks. *See* cracker.

HDTV: High-definition TV.

hotspot: A wireless access point.

hub: A hardware device used to connect two or more network devices.

infrastructure mode: A mode in Wi-Fi networking where computers connect through one or more access points. This is the most popular way of creating a wireless network.

instant messaging: IM. A technology that allows for real-time, two-way text communications between two or more individuals. Yahoo!, MSN, and AOL operate the largest IM networks.

interference: Electrical noise or conflicting radio signals that cause a deterioration in the radio signal in Wi-Fi and other wireless communications.

IP address: A number in the format *xxx.xxx.xxx.xxx* that designates a host address on the Internet. Each domain name, such as www.google.com, has one or more associated IP addresses.

KB: Kilobytes.

Kb: Kilobits.

kHz : Kilohertz.

LAN: Local access network.

MAC address: Media Access Control. A wireless hardware device's unique number that identifies it on a network.

MB: Megabytes.

Mb: Megabits.

Mbps: Megabits per second.

mini-PCI adapter: A wireless network adapter that can be installed in newer laptops that include a mini-PCI slot, freeing the laptop's PC card slot for other uses.

multimedia: One of many forms of media. Can include photos, video, and music.

network: A way to connect two or more computers.

network adapter card: A wireless device that allows a laptop, desktop, or handheld computer to connect to a Wi-Fi network. Also called a network interface card (NIC), a network adapter card transmits and receives data over the network.

network interface card: NIC. *See* network adapter card.

number portability: The ability to keep your current cell or landline phone number when you either switch carriers or move to a new residence.

PC card: An adapter inserted into a laptop slot to allow the computer to receive and transmit Wi-Fi radio signals.

PCI adapter: An adapter card inserted inside a desktop computer to allow the computer to receive and transmit Wi-Fi radio signals.

PDA: Personal digital assistant.

peer-to-peer mode: *See* ad-hoc mode.

peripheral: A device that connects to a computer.

RF: Radio frequency. Electromagnetic waves that operate on frequencies from about 3 kHz to 300 GHz. Every wireless device uses a frequency.

router: A device that sits between your cable modem and your network, routing Internet traffic to its proper destination.

Service Set Identifier: SSID. An identifier that a Wi-Fi network transmits so that nearby receivers know of its presence in the area. The SSID can be disabled as a first-level security precaution.

SmartWatch: A wristwatch produced by one of several manufacturers that can receive news and information using a wireless network. Created by Microsoft.

SMS: Short message service. A text service offered on phones using the GSM digital cellular telephone system. The messages are limited to 160 alphanumeric characters.

SSID: *See* Service Set Identifier.

streaming: The process of sending multimedia information between two or more computers.

TCP/IP: Transmission Control Protocol/Internet protocol. A protocol for sending information over the Internet and local networks.

universal serial bus: USB. A standard for sending and receiving data between a computer and a peripheral device, such as a wireless access card. USB 1.1 moves data at up to 12 Mbps, while the newer version (2.0) can handle up to 480 Mbps.

USB: *See* universal serial bus.

virtual private network: A technology that permits secure communications between two points. A VPN tunnels through the public Internet, sending and receiving encrypted information.

VPN: *See* virtual private network.

WAN: Wide-area network.

WEP: *See* wired equivalent privacy.

WPA: *See* Wi-Fi protected access.

Wi-Fi: Wireless fidelity. Wi-Fi permits communications over the 2.4-GHz band within a radius of up to 300 feet. Wi-Fi is used to create wireless networks and hotspots, allowing anyone with the proper wireless equipment to connect.

Wi-Fi protected access: WPA. A newer encryption standard for securing Wi-Fi networks that replaces the vulnerable wired equivalent privacy (WEP) standard.

wired equivalent privacy: WEP. An older encryption standard, vulnerable to hackers, for securing Wi-Fi networks. WPA is now supported by most manufacturers and is preferred over WEP.

Windows XP: Microsoft's latest operating system, which provides many built-in wireless networking functions.:

wireless: Communications that use radio waves rather than wires.

Internet Directory

In this directory . . .

A web directory saves you time and aggravation and can help you succeed in your never-ending search for more knowledge (or for things to purchase). This directory leads you to articles, whitepapers, shopping, downloads, and a plethora of wireless information.

In these pages, you find an extensive list of web resources:

- Wi-Fi hotspots
- Networking, including components and troubleshooting
- Windows XP
- Home entertainment options, including HDTV and satellite radio
- Cellular and cordless phones
- Global positioning system information

About This Directory

To use the directory, use the heading to find what topics you're looking for, read the site descriptions, and visit the sites that have what you're looking for. To help you discern whether a site may be useful to you, this directory includes some miniature icons (otherwise known as *micons*). Here's an explanation of what each micon means:

- This site leads you to hotspots, where the public can get wireless Internet/LAN access.
- You can download software or other files from this site.
- Information about electronic commerce or shopping-cart software is available at this site.
- Wireless devices, such as a tablet PC, can be found at this site.
- Here you can find services that support wireless devices.

Adapters

Adapters are various devices that connect a computer to a network.

About

http://compnetworking.about.com/cs/wirelessproducts/a/howtobuildwlan_4.htm

This article explains how to configure your adapters after setting up a wireless router or access point.

BULLETPROOF NETWORKS

http://support.bulletproof.it/vpn/w9x/adapter_install.shtml

If you want to install a VPN adapter, this site gives you step-by-step instructions. The steps are fortified with figures so you can follow along.

Cisco Systems

http://www.cisco.com

This extensive web site offers thorough information on any number of its wireless products, including access points, bridges, and routers. You can view presentations, white papers, and data sheets; the demos are a high point. Security notices are a nice offering as well.

CramSession

http://learn.serebra.com/cramsession/

The courses offered at this site lay out topics and requirements at the start so you know what you need. You can search by keyword for a course list, which includes certification in several areas and a good assortment of networking topics.

Dev2dev

http://edocs.bea.com/wli/docs81/upgrade/

If you need assistance installing upgrade utilities and the wizard, this is a good site for you. They tell you how to purchase and take a CD or online course also, since this may be the first time for some visitors and the experience is different from live classes.

KEYSPAN

http://www.keyspan.com/products/usb/pdaadapter/

Keyspan is the manufacturer of, among other things, a high-speed USB serial adapter that works for PDAs or Pocket PCs. This site offers the product's features and tells you what you need on your end before it'll work. You can get downloads from the site and elect to be updated with new information.

Microsoft TechNet

http://www.microsoft.com/technet/prodtechnol/winxppro/maintain/wifisoho.mspx

If you just didn't get what you needed in this book, this article may have what you're looking for. Read how to configure Windows XP to create a wireless network for your home.

O'REILLY WIRELESS DEVCENTER

http://www.oreillynet.com/pub/a/wireless/2003/10/31/WinXPUnwired.html

This site helps if you want to "improvise" a wireless network instead of buying new equipment. For those who learn best visually, clear figures portray how to configure a wireless adapter. Reader feedback is offered at the end of the article if you want to get an idea about how useful the information is before getting started in earnest.

Replacing or Installing Server Net Adapter Plug-In Cards (PICs)

http://cssi.nonstop.compaq.com/Customer/procedrs/MSEBs-n-PICs/snda/pro00001.htm

If you're mucking about inside your computer, you may wind up needing help from this site. Here is where you can get help using the right precautions and read up on the standard operating practices (SOPs). This site helps you lower the amount of time the enclosure door is prone to overheating.

SIS

http://www.seminarinformation.com/details.cfm?id=19954&sp=918,1133&row=1

Want to get out of your home and network with some people? Here you can find out about seminars, classes, and conferences that cover all sorts of networking topics (or locations, if travel is what intrigues you most). Just enter search criteria — topics, locations, or event dates narrow your options.

USB Gear

http://www.usbgear.com/

USB Gear manufactures wireless products including hard drives, adapters, and infrared. Who doesn't want something that's infrared? You can buy these products online at your leisure.

WebSphere

http://publib.boulder.ibm.com/infocenter/wsphelp/index.jsp?topic=/com.ibm.wesm.doc/wesmdev-installingtheadapteronwindows.htm

This site offers a description of the steps to installing the adapter on Windows.

Blackberry

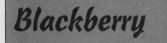

Can't get enough news about Blackberries, the very popular handheld device that synchronizes with a computer? Check out these sites.

Alternative Networks

http://www.alternativenetworks.com/media_pr.asp?PRID=37&PRYR=0

With more and more businesses finding that their boundaries have extended well beyond the desktop, the need for a viable remote working tool is abundantly clear.

DirectMobileAccessories.co.uk

http://www.directmobileaccessories.co.uk/default.php?cPath=671

This site has information on Blackberry models and accessories.

On The Go

http://www.onthegosolutions.com/?ref=google

Here is a Blackberry shopping site.

PDAStreet

http://www.pdastreet.com/forums/showthread.php?threadid=49825

Here are discussions of problems and solutions regarding the Blackberry.

Shopzilla

http://www.shopzilla.com

Here you can find information on Blackberry models and accessories. Simply search under Blackberry.

Bluetooth

Bluetooth technology enables seamless voice and data connections between a wide range of devices through short-range digital two-way radio.

Apple

http://www.apple.com/bluetooth/

Bluetooth technology is a cutting-edge open specification that enables short-range wireless connections between desktop and notebook computers, handhelds, personal digital assistants, mobile phones, camera phones, printers, digital cameras, headsets, keyboards, and even a computer mouse.

Bluetooth

http://www.bluetooth.com/

You can connect wirelessly everywhere. This site is a good place to start.

CNET Reviews

http://reviews.cnet.com/Sony_Ericsson_T608/4514-6454_7-20912596.html

The Sony Ericsson T608 phone represents a new look and palette of features for CDMA (Code Division Multiple Access) mobiles, including integrated Bluetooth.

Ericsson

http://www.ericsson.com/bluetooth/

Here is the company web site for Ericsson Technology Licensing highlighting Bluetooth wireless technology and Bluetooth intellectual property solutions.

Howstuffworks

http://electronics.howstuffworks.com/bluetooth.htm

This article looks at a completely different way to form the connections, called Bluetooth. This gadget is wireless and automatic, boasting a number of interesting features.

MS Mobiles.com

http://www.msmobiles.com/news.php/1498.html

Here is more Bluetooth news.

Outpost

http://www.outpost.com/product/3854717

Logitech's stylish cordless keyboard and rechargeable optical mouse combined with a fully functional Bluetooth hub is all you need to put your Bluetooth devices to work for you right now.

Palowireless

http://www.palowireless.com/bluetooth/

Here is the original and definitive Internet guide to Bluetooth technology.

Time.com

http://www.time.com/time/gadget/20031203/

People have been talking about Bluetooth for the past few years. It has been described as a miracle technology that can eliminate wires from your daily life.

ZDNet.uk

http://news.zdnet.co.uk/communications/wireless/0,39020348,39145881,00.htm

A security flaw has been discovered in Bluetooth that lets an attacker download all contact details along with other information from a vulnerable phone, while leaving no trace of the attack. Unlike bluejacking, which is where users can send a message to Bluetooth phones without authorization, this latest discovery allows data, such as telephone numbers and diary entries, stored in a vulnerable device to be stolen by the attacker. The new exploit is called bluesnarfing.

Cell Phones

Cell phones can store information, make lists, track appointments, do simple math, send or receive e-mail, play games, integrate other devices, and access the Internet.

ABC News

http://abcnews.go.com/Technology/story?id=44664

Be the first to know what's going on around the world by signing up for SMS (Short Message Service) alerts on breaking news and politics delivered straight to your cell phone.

CELL-PHONE-ACCESSORIES.com

http://www.cell-phone-accessories.com/

Enjoy the ease and comfort of online shopping for cell phones here.

CellUpdate.com

http://www.cellupdate.com/

This site helps you sort through the many new plans, changing rates, and special features.

C/NET

http://reviews.cnet.com/5208-7817-0.html?forumID=74&threadID=37625&messageID=441030

Here is a cell phone forum and phone shop.

Ericsson

http://www.ericsson.com/mms/

Action and excitement play an important part in today's mobile lifestyle. With Multimedia Messaging Service (MMS) people can capture the moment and share it instantly with friends and relatives.

IST

http://web.mit.edu/ist/services/telecommunications/guidelines.html

This web page is intended to assist in the decision-making process around what equipment and service provides the best options and pricing for the user.

Mobile MMS.com

http://www.mobilemms.com/default.asp

The Multimedia Messaging Service (MMS) is, as its name suggests, the ability to send messages comprising a combination of text, sounds, images, and video to MMS capable handsets.

NBFAA

http://www.alarm.org/Portability_Act%20.html

The Wireless Local Number Portability Act includes the ability for consumers to not only change cell phone carriers without changing their telephone number, but also to move their home wired telephone number to cellular phones.

Nokia

http://www.nokia.com/nokia/0,,400,00.html

MMS stands for Multimedia Messaging Service, a technology that allows you to create, send, and receive text messages that also include an image, audio, and/or video clip.

Photobucket.com

http://photobucket.com/results.php?mt=cell+phones

Shop here to choose from a large selection of cell phones and virtually build your own cell phone by selecting the features you need at the price you want.

Search Bug

http://www.searchbug.com/peoplefinder/landline-or-cellphone.aspx

Go to this site to verify if a phone number is a cellular number or a regular landline number.

Soyouwanna.com

http://www.soyouwanna.com/site/syws/cellphone/cellphone.html

Here is a humorous but informative site regarding cell phones.

Cordless Phones

Cordless phones give individuals the flexibility to move around an office or home while staying on a call.

AHERN

http://www.ahernstore.com/cordless-phones.html

Here are cordless phones, headsets, recorders, conference phone equipment and more.

Consumer Search.com

http://www.consumersearch.com/www/electronics/cordless_phones/

ConsumerSearch.com reviews the reviews of cordless phones, as well as hundreds of other products.

Howstuffworks

http://electronics.howstuffworks.com/cordless-telephone.htm

Someone remarked that although cordless phones have been around for about 20 years, lately they're a lot more sophisticated.

Wi-Fi Planet

http://www.wi-fiplanet.com/tutorials/article.php/2191241

The majority of cordless phones in use today are 2.4-GHz models. These phones, innocent as they may seem, reap devastating effects on 802.11b WLANs.

Wireless Communications

http://www.privacyrights.org/fs/fs2-wire.htm

Wireless phones are very popular, and the number of people who use them is steadily growing. But even though wireless devices have many advantages, privacy is not one of them.

DHCP

Dynamic Host Configuration Protocol (DHCP) is a network component that provides a common address so all the computers on a network can access the network's resources.

Ask Leo

http://ask-leo.com/what_is_dhcp.html

Here Leo breaks down dynamic IP addresses for readers, explaining how they're assigned on the fly. Leo also has kindly provided a DHCP FAQ and links to DHCP titles on Amazon.com.

CREATIVEPRO

http://www.creativepro.com/story/feature/16146.html

This article tackles the debate between dynamic and static IP addressing. The author talks in a way that's down-to-earth, revealing some of what users consider loftiness.

DHCP FAQ

http://www.dhcp-handbook.com/dhcp_faq.html

This minimalist site gets to the heart of any and all DHCP questions you might have, including those about implementation. Don't know what DHCP spoofing is? Log on to the DHCP FAQ and find out. What freeware DHCP servers can you get for yourself? Come to the DHCP FAQ and discover that, too.

IP Address Assignment Behavior and Specs

http://www.stanford.edu/group/networking/netdb3/specs/ipaddr.html

The site approaches the assignment of DHCP addresses as well as their specifications. A series of figures and point-by-point analyses help you understand more.

E-Mail

E-mail can be wireless. Don't believe me? Read more at these sites.

Looksmart Findarticles

http://www.findarticles.com/p/articles/mi_m0IGV/is_2_3/ai_71561827

The pocket-sized Talkabout T900 provides EarthLink subscribers with an extension of their primary EarthLink e-mail and allows them to send and receive messages without being tied to their PC.

Metrocall Wireless

http://storefront.metrocall.com/texan/2way_main.asp

Two-way messaging devices are sold here. The compact unit fits in the palm of your hand and is ideal for exchanging e-mail messages with coworkers.

Network Services

http://www.networkservices.net/products/twoWay.asp

This company will help you send and receive e-mail, manage your contacts and calendar, and receive important messages.

SkyTel

http://www.skytel.com/products/skywriter.htm

2Way Messaging means real communication from the palm of your hand. It's the perfect solution for workgroups, emergency notification systems, and companies with specialized wireless data needs like field dispatching or remote network management.

Fixed Wireless Access

Fixed wireless access replaces copper wire with radio signals and allows you to access the Internet.

The Edge

http://www.nwfusion.com/edge/research/fixedwireless.html

This site contains a good overview of wireless cable, industry regulation, new developments, system architecture, and elements. You get articles as well as editorials and forums, which allows you to glean a lot of perspectives. If online research doesn't appeal as much to you, subscribe to their paper.

EETIMES

http://www.eetimes.com/printableArticle.jhtml;jsessionid=OFZKB3XBBSMIIQSNDBGCKH0CJUMEKJVN?doc_id=OEG20020412S0061&_requestid=111643

Wireless Internet service providers and their equipment providers are becoming more popular and this article talks about those providers in detail.

Forbes

http://www.forbes.com/2000/04/18/feat.html

With all the talk of the broadband wars focused on the battle between cable and DSL services, the technology known as *fixed wireless* is easy to miss. Despite that, it may still become a popular alternative to Internet access. This article explains.

Hawking Technology

http://www.hawkingtech.com/

Hawking manufactures several wireless goodies, including routers and adapters. They also build a Wi-Fi locator whose unique features they tout stem from its high-gain, directional antenna. The site offers a product search and featured products. One of its strong suits is its online support and tutorials. If after checking out the site you're interested in purchasing one of their products, you can search for a nearby supplier.

ISP-Planet

http://www.isp-planet.com/fixed_wireless/

ISP-Planet boasts a full archive of wireless-related articles, news, a glossary, and different newsletters. It also has a pretty handy search tool and directories if you really want to drill down to specific information.

Mobile Enterprise

http://www.mobileenterprisemag.com/APCM/templates/columns_template.asp?Articleid=1120&Zoneid=20

Newer, faster wireless technologies promise wide-ranging connections for the unwired.

NetworkWorldFusion

http://www.nwfusion.com/

This site offers resource articles, newsletters, reviews, and primers. A search allows you to look for a specific topic and late-breaking IT news keeps you up to date in the meantime.

Wi-Fi-FreeSpot

http://www.wififreespot.com/

Whether you're a local resident or a business traveler or vacationer just passing by, The Wi-Fi–FreeSpot Directory helps you find all types of free Wi-Fi locations, including laundromats, auto repair shops, and RV parks.

GPS

A Global Positioning System (GPS) receiver uses signals from satellites to pinpoint its exact location, anytime, anywhere. You cannot hide.

About

http://genealogy.about.com/cs/cemetery/a/gps.htm

If you have narrowed down the area where your ancestor died, but still aren't sure in which cemetery they are buried, turn to maps and GPS for assistance.

ALK

http://www.alk.com/

This site offers solutions for in-vehicle GPS navigation, fleet management, shipment tracking, or customized systems.

Anywhere Map

http://www.controlvision.com/

Anywhere Map is a unique tool for today's pilot. It combines an advanced color GPS moving map, high-resolution terrain map, obstacle avoidance with a robust flight management system, flight planning, airport guide, flight calculator, clearance recorder, and co-pilot.

Buxley's Geocaching Waypoint

http://www.brillig.com/geocaching/

Simply put, geocaching is treasure hunting for the 21st century. Armed with a GPS receiver, a set of coordinates that tell you the location of a cache and a healthy sense of adventure, players go out and look for caches of goodies.

Cerritos College

http://www3.cerritos.edu/earth-science/tutor/Latitude_Longitude/calculating_latitude_and_longitude.htm

A definition: The system of latitude and longitude is the grid system used to uniquely locate any point on the surface of a sphere.

Chaeron Corporation

http://www.chaeron.com/gps.html#GPSml

There is a growing need for standard GPS location sharing between different systems and users.

Cobra

http://www.cobra.com/

The NAV ONE unit is a specialized, portable navigation system for use in vehicles. It provides turn-by-turn route guidance.

DPC

http://democrats.senate.gov/~dpc/pubs/108-2-002.html

In 1973, the Department of Defense was looking for a foolproof method of satellite navigation. Based on previous department experience with satellites, the concept of a Global Positioning System (GPS) was developed.

Family Tree Magazine

http://www.familytreemagazine.com/articles/apr04/gps.html

You've just learned where your great-great-grandfather is buried, and you'd like to make a trip to the grave site. But you've never visited the cemetery, and trying to read a map (especially one with tiny print) while you drive can be a little scary. Thanks GPS technology, you don't need a good sense of direction or an extra set of eyes to find your destination.

Garmin

http://www.garmin.com/

Garmin is a leader in Global Positioning System (GPS) technology and an innovator in consumer electronics. They serve both the aviation and consumer markets. Their products are used in flying, boating, driving, hiking, and many other activities. They're customer-focused and committed to producing quality products that improve people's everyday lives.

Geocaching

http://www.geocaching.com/

A GPS device and an urge to travel are the things you need for high-tech treasure hunting. Here you can find the latest caches in this fun and exciting sport.

GPS World

http://www.gpsworld.com/gpsworld/article/articleDetail.jsp?id=39281

Discussion at the podium and in the hallways reflected a more cooperative tone among U.S. and European officials and favorable attitudes toward dual GPS-Galileo receivers.

GpsPasSion

http://www.gpspassion.com/forumsen/topic.asp?TOPIC_ID=12597&whichpage=5

Here is discussion on upgrading Belkin Clipon GPS.

Howstuffworks

http://www.howstuffworks.com/gps1.htm

When people talk about "a GPS," they usually mean a GPS receiver. Here, the site explains how the system is a bunch of satellites. The U.S. military developed the satellites network as a military navigation system.

Howstuffworks

http://science.howstuffworks.com/question356.htm

Trying to measure the sea level and just can't get the darn ocean to sit still? This web site feels your pain.

DeLorme

http://www.delorme.com/

There are many GPS receiver models that show quite detailed maps. DeLorme sells a broad range of GPS receivers and mapping programs that work with laptop PC, Pocket PCs, and many Palm OS PDAs. The DeLorme GPS receivers and mapping programs not only tell you where you are, but they can tell you the best route from where you are to where you want to go.

Magellan

http://www.magellangps.com/en/

At this site you can find YOUR adventure.

Mapsite for Magellan

http://www.gmsts.org/operations/content/documents/mapsite-mag.html

This site explores downloading Magellan GPS data.

Mindbranch

http://www.mindbranch.com/listing/product/R155-024.html

Mindbranch wonders if the United States can afford to continue upgrading GPS.

Navicache.com

http://www.navicache.com/

This site breaks down the current trend of geocaching, which it explains was originally referred to as a "stash hunt." Now that there are thousands of caches hidden all over the world, it has become a little more sophisticated. Some participants are really creative when making their caches.

NEXTEL

http://www.nextel.com/about/enterprise/wbs/gps/navigate.shtml

Now you can spend more time driving and there is no need to ask for directions. Thanks to TeleNav, you know where you're going, even if you aren't where you thought you were.

Pharos

http://www.pharosgps.com/

Because different Pocket PC models offer various expansion options, several types of GPS receivers work with different Pocket PCs.

PocketMap Store

http://www.pocketmapstore.com/

Here are the ultimate GPS bundles.

Reading Topographic Maps

http://www.map-reading.com/

This site offers a word to the wise: GPS devices are wonderful instruments but before you start using said instrument to travel in earnest, you need the skills to find your way with a simple map and compass. Study up.

Teletype GPS

http://www.teletype.com/

This site assists navigation on land, air, and water.

WordIQ

http://www.wordiq.com/definition/Global_Positioning_System

GPS was designed by the United States Department of Defense and they control it, too. Anyone can use it. The best part is it's free to use it.

Zaurus User Group

http://www.zaurususergroup.com/forums/index.php?s=b46baaa2fd1685c12487a4832a42b60c&showtopic=7968&st=0&#entry49142

Here is information on downloading to a Zaurus device.

HDTV

High-definition television (HDTV) has roughly double the number of vertical lines and horizontal lines when compared to conventional systems.

About

http://hometheater.about.com/library/weekly/aa021102a.htm

The controversy regarding the future of HDTV is resurfacing among industry professionals and consumers. Manufacturers ponder their degree of commitment to producing HDTVs and related products, and consumers who own HDTVs reflect on the wisdom of their purchases.

AnandTech

http://www.anandtech.com/video/showdoc.aspx?i=2089

With HDTV slowly becoming the standard in broadcast television, every company making TV tuners has started to make the shift.

EDG

http://www.edgonline.com/newsletter/Mar_04/service_center-0304.htm

Here is a newsletter discussion on the difference between HDTV-compatible and HDTV-ready. HDTV-ready indicates that you do not need a set top box for the HDTV signals, the tuner is inside. HDTV-compatible indicates just the opposite; you need a set top box, or receiver, to get HDTV programming. These terms are being used incorrectly in the industry.

Epinions.com

http://www.epinions.com/content_2933301380

The writer of this opinion (epinion) is confused over possibilities, but suggests getting the HDTV and getting on with life.

Home Theater Magazine

http://www.hometheatermag.com/hdtvtuners/86/

The writer of this article feels that the amazing choices could drive any self-respecting videophile to drink.

KOIN.com

http://www.koin.com/koin/receivehdtv.asp

Since digital TV stations aren't often available on local cable systems, you should get yourself a good, old-fashioned antenna.

News Channel 9

http://www.wixt.com/business/consumerreports/story.aspx?content_id=5FF23BD3-AD26-452B-B208-84A3387E9458

These days, there's more high-definition television programming than ever. In addition to satellite and cable programs, now much of the prime-time lineup is broadcast in high definition.

PBS Online

http://www.pbs.org/opb/crashcourse/

The history of television may be short, but compared to the telephone and the computer, it hasn't kept up with the advance of technology. HDTV is going to evolve television and take it into the next century.

Sound and Vision

http://www.soundandvisionmag.com/article.asp?section_id=1&article_id=639&page_number=2&preview=

You have many options for making the video connection between an HDTV tuner and monitor.

StreetPrices.com

http://www.streetprices.com/Electronics/Consumer/TV/HDTV/HDTV_Compatible/

Here are some HDTV-compatible choices.

TV Predictions Newswire

http://www.tvpredictions.com/hdtvprice092904.html

Best Buy, the electronics retailer, was selling the HDTV-ready set for a very good price.

VideoHelp.com

http://www.videohelp.com/forum/archive/t229740.html

Want to know some scoop? This forum reveals a dirty secret in the consumer electronics industry. Many of the so-called HDTV-ready sets can't display HD resolution but can take in an HD signal.

Home Entertainment

Much of the vision of the home entertainment network is coming from manufacturers who want to sell all-in-one gateway products to cable and satellite service providers. Some are just beginning to ship first-generation, wireless-ready products.

Dig It

http://dig-it.com/102,1153,modules.php

If you reach this site, chances are you're a digital lifestyle guru. If we snooped through your hard disk, we'd find a treasure trove of media files.

Engadget

http://features.engadget.com/entry/6336778455600767/

There might not be anything new but after reading this information you can rest assured that numerous combinations of different technologies exist. This web site may have those great combinations.

LINKSYS

http://www.linksys.com/press/press.asp?prid=142

A new wireless home solution offered by this manufacturer connects your home entertainment center and your network together. That way you get access to the Internet and to digital content.

LINKSYS

http://www.linksys.com/products/product.asp?grid=33&prid=658

The Media Center Extender, manufactured by LINKSYS, shows homemade (or otherwise made) digital movies and photographs on your TV. If you have a digital music collection, you're free to pull them away from those tinny computer speakers. Play them through your woofers and tweeters.

Motorola

http://commerce.motorola.com/cgi-bin/ncommerce3/ProductDisplay?prrfnbr=247536&prmenbr=126&bcs_cgrfnbr=230509&zipcode=

IMfree lets instant messengers roam almost anywhere around the house, up to 150 feet from an Internet-connected PC and base station, so your teens can chat with up to six buddies at a time from the comfort of wherever.

PC Magazine

http://www.pcmag.com/article2/0,1759,904324,00.asp

The vision of the PC industry places a computer at the center of the networked home, controlling outlying devices, but consumer electronics companies think the best way is to place some type of media server at the center of the network.

PC Magazine

http://www.pcmag.com/article2/0,1759,1388944,00.asp

This article persuades you to step away from your savings account, stop considering buying another computer just so the kids can IM each other, and consider instead buying Motorola IMfree.

PRISMIQ

http://www.prismiq.com/

The PRISMIQ MediaPlayer lets you dig on a vast array of digital media (movies, music, and pictures). You also get access to the Internet through TVs, stereos, and entertainment centers anywhere in your house.

Remote Central.com

http://www.remotecentral.com/

If you have a universal remote control, this article's author feels for you, because you're bound to experience some confusion.

Replacement Remote Controls

http://www.xdiv.com/remotes/

The only problem (besides having to buy one, period) with replacement remote controls is that the codes hold the key. You need to know the codes remotes you want to reproduce, and the codes are usually in the manual. Here is where you can get some help.

SMARTHOME

http://www.smarthome.com/6329.html

The D-Link DSM-320 802.11g Wireless Media Player unites your network with your home entertainment center, allowing you to share, access, and enjoy your digital media, whether music, videos, or photos — in the comfort of your living room.

SnapStream Media

http://forums.snapstream.com/vb/showthread.php?t=11932

In this forum, a person feels that having one media server with media players in each room seems to be the way to go.

The TECHZONE.com

http://thetechzone.com/?m=show&id=60

These people updated their wide screen, implemented time shifting, and went wireless, all to avoid the dreaded flag that would prevent them from burning their recorded shows to DVD.

Universal Remote Control

http://www.universalremote.com/

This is a leading manufacturer of wireless remote control devices for the consumer (Home Theater Master brand), OEM, and Cable TV markets.

WebElectric Magazine

http://www.webelectricmagazine.com/99/2/uirr.htm

We know how these remotes go; after a year or two, the buttons get dirty, or lose their conductivity. So we open the unit, clean the buttons, and put it back together.

Laptops

Laptop computers can go everywhere you go.

About

http://mobileoffice.about.com/od/businesstravelersadvice/bb/hotelinternet.htm

This site offers travelers advice: Office professionals who are on the move need to know they can find good Internet access while staying in hotels. Good Internet access is defined here, in case you're not sure what to expect.

About

http://mobileoffice.about.com/cs/laptops/bb/byblaptop.htm

Mobile workers need laptops that have long battery lives. Even better are laptops that allow you to add an extra battery. You never know if your mobile work will take you to places where electricity is not an option. Traveling by air, rail, or bus are prime examples. It's also worth looking at how long it takes to recharge your laptop batteries.

Amazon.com

http://www.amazon.com/exec/obidos/tg/detail/-/B00007KDVK/102-4715655-4121732?v=glance

Now you can buy the first high-speed wireless networking PC card for laptops to use the 802.11g standard, which is four times faster than the current standard.

Apple

http://www.apple.com/batteries/

Apple says that you can recharge a Lithium-ion battery whenever convenient, without the full charge or discharge cycle necessary to keep Nickel-based batteries at peak performance.

Expansys

http://www.expansys.com.au/forumthread.asp?code=110680&thread=18

This is a forum thread on the "small" problem of a wireless card freezing a laptop. Every time the card is inserted into the slot, the laptop freezes after a couple of seconds.

Geek Pragmatique

http://www.geekchic.com/practi10.htm

A tongue in cheek reference on this site tells you that the tan lines resultant from what is now commonly known as Laptop Lounging Latency are far from an embarrassment; they are becoming the most sought-after fashion accessory around.

How to Buy a Laptop in 2004

http://www.cyberwalker.net/columns/aug03/how-to-buy-laptop-2004.html

The rule of thumb is aim at a 4 lb or less notebook for frequent air travel. A 4 to 6 lb device is ideal for back and forth mobility with occasional airport travel. Choose a 6 lb or heavier machine for occasional portability.

Macopinion

http://www.macopinion.com/columns/roadwarrior/01/08/21/

In this opinion, the limiting factor of laptops remains battery life when you're out of range of some place to plug in the AC adapter.

NetworkWorldFusion

http://www.nwfusion.com/news/2003/1117wifivpn.html

Some of the largest service providers that cater to multinational customers are readying Wi-Fi-to-VPN access services that will span the globe.

Notebook-Battery-For-Less.com

http://www.notebook-battery-for-less.com/

This is one of the major distributors for replacement laptop batteries.

O'Reilly Wireless

http://www.oreillynet.com/pub/a/wireless/2000/11/03/wavelan.html

This article proposes if you have gone to a trade show in the last year, you've probably seen one of these funny looking cards sticking out of the side of many an excited geek's laptop.

The Raymond Sarrio Company

http://www.sarrio.com/sarrio/12voltlaptop.html

This site has an abundance of technical information. For instance, products called the Powerbase and Powerbase, Jr. do not have regulated voltage supplies. As a result, these two batteries put out 15 Volts when fully charged, but when near discharge, their voltages drop to around 8.5 Volts.

Sierra Solar Systems

http://www.sierrasolar.com/prod_store/LAP_laptop.html

Here is where to buy a Notepower portable solar module if you are away from power for long periods of time. A pair of these modules will provide enough power to run and/or charge most laptop computers, including nearly all Macintoshes as well as portables.

Tek n Toys

https://estore.shopplex.com/app/storefront.aspx?cat_id=51&modid=30214092059015

This shopping site offers laptop and tablet accessories.

Wireless Laptop Tips

http://www.udel.edu/topics/wireless/closing-instructions.html

Here are Wireless Laptop Tips for smooth operation.

Microsoft SmartWatch

Here is a convenient way to get local news, weather, sports, international and business news, plus the closing figures of the three stock indexes on a watch.

Computer Buyer

http://www.comp-buyer.co.uk/buyer/news/64906/swatch-turns-to-microsoft-smart-watch-technology.html

Swatch has announced its Paparazzi watch featuring Microsoft's Smart Watch technology that wirelessly feeds in data via a U.S. network of FM radio signals.

Harvard Business Online

http://harvardbusinessonline.hbsp.harvard.edu/b02/en/common/item_detail.jhtml?id=504004

Harvard Business Online wonders if this is the next big thing for Microsoft or is it a waste of money and resources?

Microsoft Office Online

http://office.microsoft.com/en-us/assistance/HA011196241033.aspx

The network sends two types of signals to your watch: Broadcast information, such as news stories, sports information, financial information, and current weather conditions and personal information, such as your messages and calendar appointments.

PDAntic.com

http://www.pdantic.com/reviews/smartwatch.htm

A certified gadget geek feels that there are some situations where it is in bad taste to pull out a PDA or Smartphone, while nobody takes offense if he glances at his wrist.

Mobile Society

The changing workplace and major changes in the home have pushed the development of wireless, easily moved, technical devices.

Apple

http://www.apple.com/airportexpress/onthego.html

As long as your current location is wired for broadband, AirPort Express lets you create your own wireless network . This site explains how to do that. You also get the lowdown on AirTunes, including what they are and how to set them up. The Tech Specs page gives you all the numbers you need to know to get things going (or at least what you need to get to get things going).

AT&T Wireless

http://www.attwireless.com/

The newly joined AT&T and Cingular Wireless let you can peruse wireless plans and cell phones here before subjecting yourself to a live salesperson. If you're already a user and want to get into some of the superfluous fun stuff, get your mitts on ringtones and graphics. The FAQs help you sort out what phones offer what services and extras.

Bluetooth

http://bluetooth.weblogsinc.com/entry/4732841284116141/

This unofficial site offers updated information on all the names, acronyms, numbers, and brands, of wireless technology in "layreader" terms. There's also a directory of other blogs and archives for your retrieval.

CEA

www.ce.org/hdtv

The Consumer Electronics Association (CEA) site offers lots of market research and the latest news, including legislation. When you become a member (and there are different levels for different fees and corresponding privileges) you are privy to this information and more, including what initiatives CEA is working toward and, if you want it, a big membership directory. If you want to shop at this site you have to register.

CNN

http://www.cnn.com/SPECIALS/2004/wireless/

This page offers a gateway to several wireless goodies: charts, a glossary, interactive information about security, and a gallery that shows your options for various wireless pursuits. You can read articles about various aspects of wireless and sign up to get alerts about Bluetooth, PDA's, WiMax, or Wi-Fi.

IDA

http://www.ida.gov.sg/idaweb/wireless/infopage.jsp?infopagecategory=factsheet:wireless&versionid=6&infopageid=I875

The Infocomm Development Authority of Singapore (IDA) is charged with creating a competitive information communications industry in Singapore. Along those lines, this article boasts the benefits of wireless networking.

Intel

http://www.intel.com/personal/do_more/wireless/stories/promo_intro_3.htm

Intel's site has all the bells and whistles that all big-time computer players have, including product support and in-depth information about its products. One of the most interesting parts of the site is an article you can find by searching for "Exploring the Wireless Life." It explores the goings-on of four people who were each given an Intel IBM ThinkPad T40. Read about their trials and tribulations and whether they'll go back to wired computing.

MSNBC

http://msnbc.msn.com/id/6011606/

MSNBC offers up this *Forbes* articles about cell phones and working wirelessly. The author explains how you plug a network card into a laptop computer, which dials into the cellular network and connects anywhere a user can get a signal. AT&T seems to be the forerunner in this technology, but other bigwigs are right behind them.

PCWorld

http://www.pcworld.com/news/article/0,aid,89424,00.asp

The Cellular Telecommunications and Internet Association show is a big deal, and this PC World article talks about what even bigger issues will take center stage at this years show. Boingo is, in part, sponsoring the event in hopes its exposure will help the startup.

Sierra Wireless

http://www.sierrawireless.com/

This site is mostly geared toward business owners needing the ubiquitous "solutions," but a home wireless networker can benefit from the available support and downloads, which include AirCards and network coverage maps. You can shop for Sierra Wireless' PC cards, software, and accessories here as well. If you're really into them you can sign up to receive quarterly newsletters that alert you to new product releases.

Wi-Fi Net News

http://wifinetnews.com/

In addition to articles both recent and archives (and which you can search by category), this site links you to hotspot directories and other sites housing wireless communities. If you like, you can sign up to receive daily e-mails containing user posts.

WirelessWeek

http://www.wirelessweek.com/

This wireless-industry site offers in-depth coverage and breaking news on mobile business, technology, regulations, information, analytics, and data. You can seek out information on specific types of wireless topics, including networking and accessories. There are even some wireless industry classifieds in case you're looking for things from anywhere to tower space to software.

PDAs

PDAs are portable computers of small size designed as organizers, note takers, or communication devices.

About

http://webdesign.about.com/library/weekly/aa060500a.htm

With the Palm VII wireless Internet, cell phones that offer Web access, and other pocket-sized computers, it is getting more and more important to think about how your Web site "displays" on the palm-sized computers and internet devices.

Afterdawn.com

http://www.afterdawn.com/news/archive/625.cfm

This is a popular PDA site with current information.

BargainPDA

http://www.bargainpda.com/default.asp?newsID=1167&showComments=true

For something fun, go here for NASCAR information and mini Valentine's Day cards to send to Pocket PC and Smartphone owners in addition to e-mail.

Brian's PDA Optimized Web Site List

http://www.cantoni.org/palm/links.html

This is a very complete PDA web site list.

EMailman

http://www.emailman.com/pda/

This is an award-winning mail server which includes server-based antivirus protection, spam filtering, rule-based content filtering (avoiding unwanted messages), web-based access to e-mail and much more.

IEEE

http://csdl.computer.org/comp/trans/tm/2003/01/h0040abs.htm

Modern Personal Digital Assistant (PDA) architectures often utilize a wholesale data transfer protocol known as "slow sync" for synchronizing PDAs with Personal Computers (PCs).

Inq7.net

http://www.inq7.net/mobile/mobileservices.htm

This site accommodates the needs of mobile users of handheld computers, the mobile version containing the full text of all the day's stories on INQ7.net, including breaking news.

Microsoft

http://www.microsoft.com/windowsxp/expertzone/meetexperts/bridgman.mspx

Got streaming wants and desires? This site could help. Expert Zone columnist Galan Bridgman explains how to use Windows Media Encoder to convert live audio and video to Windows media format.

Mobile Industry News

http://www.btinternet.com/~andy.nott/industrynews.htm

Go here to watch news clips, music videos, film trailers, and much more.

Omega One

http://www.omegaone.com/news/default.htm

Synchronizing news is now faster; Pocket PC owners can access local and global weather, news, and stocks.

Palm Infocenter

http://www.palminfocenter.com/view_story.asp?ID=6464

The European browser manufacturer, Opera, has announced they have developed a new medium screen resolution, or MSR, optimized browser, based on their existing technology. The company says it will ship with several as of yet unannounced products in the near future.

PC WORLD

http://www.pcworld.com/news/article/0,aid,111553,00.asp

Good Technology has launched the latest version of its GoodLink wireless e-mail software along with a partnership with Handspring (handheld devices) to bring the GoodLink software to the Treo 600 (smartphone).

PDA Toolbox Webring

http://l.webring.com/hub?ring=kwhipp

This webring's (online community) purpose is to increase awareness and development of PDA Toolbox applications.

PDAlive

http://www.pdalive.com/

In this article, PalmOne (PalmSource's biggest customer and maker of the Treo 650) might be planning to use Microsoft's WindowsMobile OS in its Treo line of SmartPhones.

Pocket PC Thoughts

http://www.pocketpcthoughts.com/articles.php?action=expand,13897

This article helps you synchronize content from the Internet from top content providers such as MSNBC, USA Today, NPR, Comedy Central and others so you can watch or listen when you have the time.

PocketPCSoft.net

http://www.pocketpcsoft.net/php/newresults.php?type=music

Your Pocket PC becomes a live audio effects machine with the help of this site's goodies. This program adds a live echo, flanger, slicer, and other sound effects to your audio input and you get to hear it in real time.

PocketSolutions

http://www.thepocketsolution.com/pocketpcaccessories/prods/PSI-217.html

This simple Sync & Charge (PDA cradle and AC adapter) cable allows you to power your Sony from the USB (Universal Serial Bus) port, while synchronizing your contacts, e-mail, and files without the bulk of a hefty cradle.

Popular Mechanics

http://popularmechanics.com/technology/telecom/2002/10/sidekick/

The Sidekick, designed by Danger, is a wireless device that gives you access to e-mail, SMS (Short Message Service), the web, and AOL Instant Messenger. It's also a GSM (Global System for Mobile Communications) cell phone and has PDA functionality. Want to know even more? Check out this site.

Sessionware

http://www.sessionware.com/partners.htm

This powerful architecture , a fast, reliable and highly secure mobile computing platform, is designed to provide a rich user experience across popular devices and networks with the built-in flexibility to support evolving technologies and standards.

Slipstick Systems

http://www.slipstick.com/addins/olpda.htm

This site is devoted to synchronizing Microsoft Outlook (e-mail) with a PDA.

Sun Microsystems

http://docs.sun.com/db/doc/806-1360/6jalch364?a=view

The Personal Digital Assistant Synchronization (PDA Sync) application enables you to synchronize data from Sun applications, such as Calendar Manager, with data in a similar application on your PDA. It also enables you to install applications and databases from your workstation or server to your PDA.

Web Developer's Journal

http://www.webdevelopersjournal.com/articles/think_pda.html

PDAs (Personal Digital Assistants) led by the Palm Pilot, are hugely popular even without Net connections. Now that they are getting wired, expect them to become inescapable. For Web content providers this is both an opportunity and a problem.

Peripherals

It is likely that the most common wireless peripherals are the wireless keyboard and the wireless mouse. Not sure what other devices qualify as peripherals? Read on.

Amazon.com

http://www.amazon.com/exec/obidos/tg/browse/-/172496/102-4715655-4121732

Go here for a long list of wireless mice.

Apple

http://www.apple.com/keyboard/

The Apple wireless keyboard and wireless mouse give a degree of freedom from physical restraint that you can't even imagine until you try it.

GEEK.com

http://www.geek.com/news/geeknews/2002Jul/bga20020709015306.htm

Get your geek news at this site.

HardCOREware

http://www.hardcoreware.net/reviews/review-125-1.htm

This site considers the attitude of gamers toward wireless mice.

Microsoft

http://www.microsoft.com/hardware/mouseandkeyboard/productdetails.aspx?pid=014

This site gives you mouse and keyboard product details.

PalmOne

http://www.palmone.com/us/products/accessories/peripherals/

Adding keyboards and other add-ons to your handheld can take you beyond the basic functions built into every PalmOne handheld. Use them to boost your business productivity, enhance creativity, and make the most of your leisure time.

That Computer Guy's Help Forum

http://forums.thatcomputerguy.us/lofiversion/index.php/f6.html

Here is a forum of questions, some humorous, that include gaming.

Satellite Internet Access

This section covers the use of satellites in gaining access to the Internet.

Bentley Telecom

http://www.bentleytelecom.co.uk

Star Pro is a scalable, high-performance satellite IP terminal that delivers broadband access with a high-speed return channel. This site explains this terminal as well as tells you more about its manufacturer and about satellite broadband in general. A nice FAQ on the About Satellite Broadband page may address some of your questions.

Forbes

http://www.forbes.com/2001/05/03/0503satellite.html

With all the talk of the broadband wars focused on the battle between cable and DSL services, the technology known as *fixed wireless* is easy to miss. Despite that, it may still become a popular alternative to Internet access. This article explains.

Satellite Signals

http://www.satsig.net/ivsat.htm

Need a list of satellite Internet access service providers? You can get that here. And this site isn't only for the United States. You can get North, South, and Central American and Caribbean information here, in addition to Europe and more. The site offers coverage maps and a link to a forum for which you don't even have to register to participate.

Satellite - TV - Store

http://www.satellite-tv-store.com/

Need satellite Internet products? This site includes items for sale for your satellite TV, TiVo, and HDTV systems. The site offers name brands like DIRECTV, TiVo, Sirius, and Direcway. You can search by category and get a brief summary, which then links you to a different site that offers further information and the option to buy.

XILINX

http://www.xilinx.com/esp/wired/optical/net_tech/satellite.htm

Always-on broadband connections to the Internet via satellite access system is explained here. In addition to reading about this topic, you can dig up articles about other satellite access topics, including virtual LANs, TCP/IP, and networking equipment.

Satellite Radio

Satellite radio gives subscribers greatly improved sound quality and a vast array of options, including lots of stations without commercials. However, it requires the use of equipment far more complicated than simple AM or FM radio.

Howstuffworks

http://www.howstuffworks.com/satellite-radio.htm

If you travel too far away from the source, the signal breaks up and fades into static on most stations since radio signals can only travel about 30 or 40 miles. On long trips, you might have to change radio stations every hour or so as the signals fade in and out.

SIRIUS

http://www.siriusradio.com

SIRIUS feels they do it right. That means 65 channels of music and no commercials. Plus they give more than 50 channels of sports, news and entertainment programming, much of it exclusive to SIRIUS.

XM Satellite Radio

http://www.xmradio.com

One big idea can change everything and XM Satellite Radio is one big idea. America's most popular satellite radio service gives you the power to choose what you want to hear — wherever and whenever you want it.

Security

Security is a crucial part of wireless networking and its devices. These sites offer security solutions, software, or general heads ups for both companies and individuals.

Certicom

http://www.certicom.com/index.php?action=sol,lp_wireless&c1=AdWords&Source=Wireless&kw=Ad1&wt.srch=1

Security is the name of the game at Certicom, whose Certicom Security Architecture (CSA) for Mobility crosses platforms in an effort to help mobile handset manufacturers make more secure products. You can download an article that discusses this technology. If you register you gain access to more resources, including the company's whitepapers.

CRN

http://www.crn.com/sections/features/features.jhtml?articleId=50900253

This article may help ease your fears. It walks readers through all the things that are helping make wireless a more secure option these days. Wavelink and AirMagnet specifically are discussed, and if you want to respond to the article, click Start a New Thread.

Practically Networked

http://www.practicallynetworked.com/support/wireless_secure.htm

This site offers an overview of tactics for making your home network safe and cozy. Some of the tips offer links to further information, and if you have further questions after reading these ideas, you can search for more security information.

Security Web Page

http://www.drizzle.com/~aboba/IEEE/

The administrators of this site attempt to provide accurate information about current standards (as well as glitches they see with them) and the most up-to-date solutions for fixing problems. This page also offers whitepapers and standards. You can easily pick out the most recently added information via the New! icon.

Symantec

http://enterprisesecurity.symantec.com/products/products.cfm?ProductID=237&EID=0

Symantec helps make your Pocket PC or Palm more secure. You can buy some of the software directly from the site or, if you're still researching your options, read about the benefits Symantec software offers, by way of reviews and documentation.

Wireless LAN Security FAQ

http://www.iss.net/wireless/WLAN_FAQ.php

This site isn't pretty, but it sure is functional. Get the latest version of Wireless LAN Security FAQ. If you're so inclined and are on the cutting edge yourself, e-mail the web site's administrator with updates you know about.

Testing

Some companies offer a way to test what you're working with in wireless. These services will likely appeal to those of you with a business.

Agilent Technologies

http://we.home.agilent.com/USeng/nav/-536885380.536892774/pd.html

This company provides something called the QoS Manager to monitor, report, and test basic and advanced wireless services. With it you can validate a service's quality as it goes over various wireless voice and data networks.

Dynamic Telecommunications, Inc

http://www.dynamictelecommunications.com/Presentations/why%20scanner%20july2002%20.pdf

This information is provided to you in a presentation-type format, with succinct points about testing wireless devices and accurately measuring signal strength.

Elliott Laboratories

http://www.elliottlabs.com/services/services_wireless.htm?source=google&campaign=wireless&group=1&creative=text

This company can test your wireless devices, consul with you about them, and offer certification services. In particular they're on the ball about 802.11 Wi-Fi, WiMax, and Bluetooth. If they offer a service you need, you can get a price quote from them online.

ExtremeTech

http://www.extremetech.com/

This site offers lots of wireless articles, especially in the area of home entertainment, where there's information galore, including audio, gaming, and HDTV. If you get tired of looking at articles and crave some interaction, go to the forums.

HomeNetHelp.com

http://www.homenethelp.com/web/howto/firewall-test.asp

Security is a relentlessly important wireless issue and firewalls are a crucial part of that security. When you have a firewall in place (and you should), you might want to check how well it is working. You can get your hands on a lot of scanning options here, as well as user feedback and opinions.

Howstuffworks

http://computer.howstuffworks.com/vpn.htm

Virtual private networks (VPNs) are explained here, from what components make up a VPN to their security to tunneling. The information is broken down into a table of contents-type organization so you can skip around to the information you're specifically looking for.

MAXPC

http://www.maxpc.co.uk/tutorials/default.asp?pagetypeid=2&articleid=17851&subsectionid=705

This tutorial breaks down wireless networks and tell you how they work. Other tutorials are there at your fingertips.

MET Laboratories

http://metlabs.com/pages/wireless&radio.html

This FCC-designated Telecommunication Certification Body (TCB) tests and certifies that your wireless goodies are working the way they're supposed to. You can request an online quote if you'd like to find out fast how much dough you might have to put down to get this information.

MOBILEROBOTS.com

http://www.mobilerobots.com/wireless.html

Companies might benefit from testing and monitoring their Wi-Fi networks. This company's PatrolBot could be just the thing they're looking for to perform those tasks.

NETGEAR

http://kbserver.netgear.com/kb_web_files/n101311.asp

Widening your wireless device's range is one thing many users find themselves interested in doing. When you implement one of the changes proposed on this site, make sure it's been improved (and how). This site encourages you to test in your actual environment.

Operative Software Products

http://www.operativesoft.com/html/network.htm?source=google

This site offers products that perform high-level services including network analyzation and monitoring. If you need your gigabytes analyzed, this is the place to be.

WindowsNetworking.com

http://www.wown.com/articles_tutorials/Introduction-Wireless-Networking-Part1.html

Here you can read further about the different types of wireless networks, including WLANS (wireless local-area networks) and WWANS (wireless wide-area networks), as well as different security approaches (WEP, SSID, and MAC). You can get Bluetooth- specific information while you're here, too.

TiVo

TiVo automatically finds and digitally records up to 140 hours of programming. Your favorite show, movies, home improvement programs, cartoons — whatever you choose — is recorded while you're out living life.

DealDatabase.com

http://www.dealdatabase.com/forum/showthread.php?t=38350

Here is a forum discussing the problems occurring when TiVo programs are moved to a PC.

PC World

http://www.pcworld.com/reviews/article/0,aid,110993,00.asp

With TiVo's new Home Media Option software upgrade, owners of the company's Series2 digital video recorders can stream music and photos from PC to TV using the popular service's oh-so-friendly remote-controlled interface.

TiVo Hacks for Beginners

http://lists.saigon.com/vault/tivo/

This page contains TiVo hack links found while the writer was learning his machine.

TiVo Support

http://customersupport.tivo.com/knowbase/root/public/tv1159.htm

This site has customer support for TiVo questions.

TiVo to DVD

http://tivo.30below.com/jdouglass/

The writer feels that getting stuff from TiVo to DVD is tricky. The writer also encourages corrections in a humorous way.

Tivo Upgrade Instructions

http://kpog.com/tivo/

TiVo is actually a small PC. It runs the Linux Operating system and has a processor, memory, IDE connections and a hard drive.

WIRED NEWS

http://www.wired.com/news/technology/0,1282,59088,00.html

This site has a tongue-in-cheek approach to TiVo and ReplayTV.

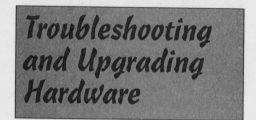

Troubleshooting and Upgrading Hardware

This section addresses those times when a computer system hangs mysteriously, when conflicts between components need resolution, or when components need replacement.

Cyberdrive.com

http://www.cyberdrive.com.tw/Firmware.htm

Here is more information on upgrading firmware. You also get specifications for different operating systems and the chance to download the necessary goods.

DIGITALHOME

http://www.digitalhomemag.com/wireless/howdoisetitup4.shtml

Here you have some basic setup tips and troubleshooting ideas for wireless and Wi-Fi. The article covers configuration, security, and troubleshooting. A glossary might come in handy as well.

D-Link

http://support.dlink.com/faq/view.asp?prod_id=966

If you're getting ready to upgrade firmware, check out this information. D-Link first warns readers that most of the time, upgrading firmware resets all the settings to default. That means you lose all your settings, including your password. Get past that and you have a nicely laid-out set of instructions taking you through an upgrade.

Foundry Networks

http://www.foundrynet.com/services/faqs/upgradingSoftware.html

Foundry offers solutions for wireless networking, including access points, a WLAN software upgrade, and an application suite. This high-level site talks about lower "cost of ownership" and "leveraging." It may be more intense than what you're interested in.

LiveVault

http://www.livevault.com/support/knowledge/technote/tn039.asp

This site offers information backup and recovery, as well as news and reviews.

MacInTouch

http://www.macintouch.com/panfirmware.html

This site offers what it considers to be Macintosh firmware traps. Lots of real-world examples from ordinary people just like yourself are found on this site, and some of them offer ideas and help for some of the presented problems.

U.S. Nuclear Regulatory Commission

http://www.nrc.gov/site-help/eie/chngsw.html

Check out this site if you want to use your digital ID with more than one browser or e-mail application (with Netscape Navigator and Microsoft Internet Explorer, for instance). You're taken through the importing and exporting steps for both programs. It's short and sweet.

Your Window To

http://www.yourwindow.to/security-policies/ref040202.htm

If you've had a disaster, you may need to recover. This site might offer the help you need. You can download a template to get started on the road to recovery. If security is your bag, try checking out the information security policies, also downloadable.

ZD Net UK

http://insight.zdnet.co.uk/hardware/servers/0,39020445,2126152,00.htm

If you need help troubleshooting your wireless local-area network (WLAN), this site can help. You're told how to ascertain the effectiveness of the access point and your hardware, and you're given further suggestions for checking signal strength and changing channels. Other wireless topics are offered at the end of the article if you want to seek more information.

Troubleshooting Wireless Networks

What do you do when your wireless networks don't work? You find tips here.

About

http://compnetworking.about.com/od/homenetworking/tp/commonproblems.htm

The author helps you avoid the typical home-networking troubles people run into. Of course, you have this book on your side as well, so you may never need to visit this site. But if you feel like it, go read about slow networks and unsecure networks (and then come back here and read those sections that talk about those topics in more detail).

DUX Computer Digest

http://www.duxcw.com/

What causes most network problems? Visit this site and find out. Reviews, forums, how-tos, FAQs . . . you know the deal. One of the nice features is questions everyday-type users ask when they're getting started.

Microsoft

http://support.microsoft.com/?kbid=826942

Microsoft lists is Windows XP package, which includes "hotfixes" and updates. The things included in this package are also included in Windows XP Service Pack 2. You can download the things you need from this site.

PRACTICALLY NETWORKED

http://www.practicallynetworked.com/tools/wireless_articles.htm

If you're looking for technical articles on Wireless networking, try these.

TechRepublic

http://techrepublic.com.com/5100-6255-1055909.html

If you've been working on your wireless network and feel pretty comfortable with is (but find it's still having trouble of one kind or another), try the troubleshooting tips you find on this site. The "How to Troubleshoot Your Wireless Network" discusses hardware, WEP, and DHCP. The list of potential problems is thorough.

TEK-TIPS FORUMS

http://www.tek-tips.com/viewthread.cfm?qid=582449

This document describes the reasons for wireless connection loss after Windows update in Windows XP machines and the ways to overcome it. Don't be surprised by all the pop-ups that appear as you hover over links.

WildPackets

http://www.wildpackets.com/products/airopeek

This site, while geared toward businesses, can be of use to home wireless networkers. You can peek at the various products, learn the technical specifications, and download demos.

WIRED NEWS

http://www.wired.com/news/wireless/0,1382,63705,00.html

This article tackles the issue of Wi-Fi, its users, and Windows XP. The author posits from evidence that the frequent loss of wireless connections for Windows XP users stems from XP's Wireless Zero Configuration. There's a workaround offered at the end of the article if you are having similar troubles.

Wireless Tools for Linux

http://www.hpl.hp.com/personal/Jean_Tourrilhes/Linux/Tools.html

This down-to-business web site a smattering of information about Linux' wireless tools, as well as links to source code.

Video and Music

It is possible to see and hear anything, anywhere, with wireless technology.

About

http://compnetworking.about.com/b/a/091858.htm

Baby monitors and security cameras are nothing new. With a wireless network, though, these devices suddenly become much easier to physically install.

theCarStereo.com

http://www.thecarstereo.com/

Find the products that fit your vehicle here.

HomeTech Solutions

http://www.hometech.com/video/camnet.html

This is a breed of cameras that are network ready. Just connect (with a Category 5 cable) to your internal network and view the images from anywhere on your network. If you have a router and an always-on internet connection, you can access the camera from any computer in the world with an internet connection.

LINKSYS

http://www.linksys.com/products/product.asp?grid=33&scid=38&prid=566

The Linksys Wireless-B Internet Video Camera sends live video through the Internet to a web browser anywhere in the world. This small unit lets you keep an eye on your home or your rugrats. Or you can watch the paint dry in your living room while you're at work.

Microsoft

http://support.microsoft.com/default.aspx?scid=kb;en-us;Q316992

This article discusses the multimedia file types that Microsoft Windows Media Player supports and provides a sample of most of these file types.

MobileVideoZone.com

http://www.mobilevideozone.com/?source_ID=google

Now you can add TV or video accessories to any car, SUV, van, or boat.

Windows XP Beta Test Site

http://windowsxp.devx.com/articles/article3/default.asp

Windows XP has many new specialized folders to help the user organize and retrieve documents and multimedia files.

VPNs

VPNs (virtual private networks) are a way to communicate safely (as if in a tunnel) over the Internet.

About

http://compnetworking.about.com/library/weekly/aa010701d.htm

VPN technology is based on the idea of tunneling. Network tunneling involves establishing and maintaining a logical network connection.

Cisco

http://www.cisco.com/univercd/cc/td/doc/product/vpn/client/rel4_0/osxguide/connect.htm

This describes how to establish a VPN connection with a private network.

Howstuffworks

http://computer.howstuffworks.com/vpn15.htm

In a remote-access VPN, tunneling normally takes place using PPP (Point to Point Protocol). Part of the TCP/IP (Transmission Control Protocol/Internet Protocol) stack, PPP is the carrier for other IP protocols when communicating over the network between the host computer and a remote system. Remote-access VPN tunneling relies on PPP.

Microsoft Tech Net

http://support.microsoft.com/default.aspx?scid=kb;en-us;305550&sd=tech

This shows how to configure a VPN connection to your corporate network in Windows XP Professional.

Setting up a VPN connection using OpenBSD

http://www.drijf.net/vpn/

OpenBSD (mail filtering) can make home computers seem part of the office intranet.

Troubleshooting VPN Connections

http://edserv05.its.yale.edu/ras/vpn_trouble.htm

Here is more advice on connecting to VPN within Windows.

WindowsITPro

http://www.winnetmag.com/Windows/Article/ArticleID/8290/8290.html

Here is an article discussing VPN and the need to troubleshoot it.

WindowsNetworking.com

http://www.wown.com/j_helmig/vpn.htm

Here is more information on Virtual Private Networks.

Weather

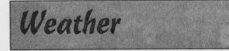

Everybody talks about the weather, but nobody does anything about it.

Hall Mall

http://hallmall.com/

Search for weather stations (under the Home and Garden category) and get all sorts of goodies that measure barometric pressure, temperature, humidity, rainfall, wind speed and direction, and much more. If you decide to pursue an item, you wind up at Amazon.com.

Torka

http://www.torka.com/Weather_Stations/Weatherstations_main.html

This manufacturer produces various and sundry weather goodies, from barometers to thermometers. You can see their weather stations by clicking that category on the left side of the home page. Most of the site is currently under construction but they do offer customer service phone and fax numbers, as well as an e-mail link.

Wi-Fi Hotspots

Hotspots are fixed, wireless, high-speed Internet access in convenient public locations.

About

http://mobileoffice.about.com/od/mobileperipherals/gr/mobileedgewifi.htm

This site acknowledges that when you are looking to use a hotspot and wish to work from the privacy of your own vehicle nothing is more frustrating than guessing where you might get a Wi-Fi signal.

Google Directory

http://directory.google.com/Top/Computers/Data_Communications/Wireless/802.11/

This directory includes computer, communication, and wireless data.

Hotspot Haven

http://www.hotspothaven.com/locations.asp?state=CO

This global Wi-Fi hotspot directory touts an interactive guide that helps you find wireless locations. You can also get information about wireless Internet service promotions and products that help you set up a Wi-Fi hotspot.

Intego

http://www.intego.com/wiFiLocator/

A good source for finding wireless networks anywhere.

Intel

http://intel.jiwire.com/wi-fi-wireless-hotspot-london-gb-l-amandine-18612.htm

Here are details on the Wi-Fi hotspot at L'Amandine, 40 Haven Green, Ealing, London, GB.

Jiwire

http://www.jiwire.com/

This site lets you search for Wi-Fi hotspot locations and reveals the hottest hotspots throughout the United States and the world. If you become a member you can get an updated directory and a weekly newsletter. Also gives you some product reviews for when you're looking to build a network at home.

NodeDB

http://www.nodedb.com/

The Node Database Finder lists people who are interested in running or are already running a wireless network. If you don't have a wireless network but are interested in setting one up, add yourself! This site covers the continents. If you select Locate Internet you're prompted to enter your location information. You also get to decide whether you want to see all the sites in your area or just the free ones.

PalmZone.net

http://www.palmzone.net/modules.php?name=News&file=article&sid=263

Riverwalkmobile.com revived the WiFi Hotspot Directory, a database covering public wireless internet access locations throughout the United States and Canada.

PatronSoft

http://patronsoft.com/firstspot/index.html?src=ot

FirstSpot is a Windows-based Wi-Fi hotspot management software (sometimes also known as *hotspot access controller* or *wireless gateway*). It tracks and secures your WLAN visitor-based networks or hotspots in a centralized way. Based on captive portal technology, FirstSpot lets your hotspot users log in via web browser.

Wi-Fi Hotspotlist.com

http://www.wi-fihotspotlist.com/

To find hotspots near a location, enter a complete or partial address. By default, all locations within 1 mile are shown.

Wi-Fi Networking News

http://wifinetnews.com/

This site gives daily reporting on Wi-Fi and the whole IEEE 802.11 family of standards.

Wi-Fi ZONE Finder

http://www.wi-fizone.org/zoneFinder.asp?TID=7

Search for a Wi-Fi ZONE sites here and become a member to glean benefits like participation in Wi-Fi Alliance events. This site also helps you build your wireless network; answer questions to get a wireless network tailor-made for you.

WiFiMaps

http://www.wifimaps.com/

This is a good location-based Wi-Fi directory. After entering just a few tidbits of information (including SSID and MAC numbers), you can search for your access point. Pick your state to explore interactive maps of Wi-Fi usage. It distinguishes between free and paying hotspots and those with WEP or no WEP. Heck, this site is interesting even if you're not after Wi-Fi location information and are an appreciator of maps.

Wi-Fi Marine

http://www.wifimarine.org/

Are you a boater and a wireless user? (That would be one long extension cord if not, right?) This web site's builders are interested in wireless Internet solutions for the boating community. This site also helps you locate hotspots.

WiFinder

http://www.wifinder.com/

This site is directed at hotspot owners. There is a directory for easy worldwide searching and statistics for those interested in minutiae. You can rate the best — or worst — hotspots.

WiMax

WiMax (Worldwide Interoperability for Microwave Access) is just part of the ever-evolving world of wireless. This is technology for so-called wireless broadband and could make things even faster and more powerful than they already are.

COMPUTERWORLD

http://www.computerworld.com.au/index.php/id;1044277208

Here you get a look at how WiMax works, what it works with, and the standards by which it operates. It also tells you how users will benefit when the operators take on this "Wi-FI on steroids."

Mobile Enterprise

http://www.mobileenterprisemag.com/APCM/templates/columns_template.asp?Articleid=1120&Zoneid=20

This columnist talks about new wireless technologies and approaches (including WiMax) and some of his experiences with them. You can find further information (including a Buyer's Guide) at the Mobile Enterprises site via links and category tabs or via a keyword search.

NetworkWorldFusion

http://www.nwfusion.com/

This site is an abundance of resource articles, newsletters, reviews, and primers. A search (especially for WiMax) allows you to look for a specific topic and late-breaking IT news keeps you up to date in the meantime.

WiMAX Trends

http://www.wimaxtrends.com/

You can get all the traditional information presentation formats here: articles, news briefs, and press releases. You can subscribe to a biweekly newsletter or join the forums (which you can search) if you want to stay really current on the issues.

WiMAX World

http://www.wimaxworld.com/

WiMAX World is the only United States conference focused on WiMAX and next-generation wireless broadband. You can get conference details and dates here as well as order conference proceedings if want to see something you missed. You can even view video of the conference.

Windows XP

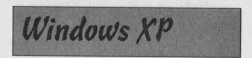

This section is devoted to operating wirelessly within a Windows XP environment.

Microsoft

http://www.microsoft.com/whdc/device/network/wireless/wirelesstech.mspx

Windows and wireless go hand in hand according to Microsoft, and some of the scenarios are offered here. If in doubt about whether one of these (or any) pertain to you, read the handy table and then check out the industry standards. These scenarios cover wireless communications and handheld devices.

SuperSite for Windows

http://www.winsupersite.com/showcase/windowsxp_networking.asp

This site details the Windows XP RTM release. Click the hackers link and get exported to a site that attempts to sell security software.

University of Minnesota

http://www1.umn.edu/adcs/network/wirelessxp.html

The author has detailed how 802.11b technology lets WLAN card-equipped computers to join a wireless network. Then you are introduced to the steps for configuring your computer with Windows XP to use its wireless card. Links let you jump to a specific spot in the steps.

Updatexp.com

http://www.updatexp.com/upnp.html

Universal Plug and Play is explained here for those wholly unfamiliar and lets you in on how it benefits you as a user. The site author has done his due diligence by way of providing security information.

Wi-Fi Networking News

http://wifinetnews.com/archives/002454.html

This article digs into Microsoft patches for its wireless friends. Here you see what the big patch fixes and how you can get the patch for yourself.

WindowsNetworking

http://www.windowsnetworking.com/kbase/WindowsTips/WindowsXP/AdminTips/Security/WindowsXPUniversalPlugandPlaysecurityquagmire.html

Want to know more about the debate on Windows XP's Universal Plug and Play? What? You say you didn't know such a debate existed? Well, look no further. Here you get to read about whether the feature is a security hazard, whether it's buggy, or if you should just disable it altogether.

Wireless Network Security

Wireless Network security is absolutely necessary, and this section is devoted to that.

ARUBA

http://www.arubanetworks.com/products/whitepapers/secure-wireless/index.php?pg=2

Here is what vendors don't tell you about the real challenges of making your corporate network invisible.

BA

http://www.ba.be/security/wireless.html

This site tells of a scene straight out of the latest Hollywood blockbuster: A creepy figures stops his car in front of a corporate HQ, gets out his laptop, puts an antenna on the roof, and 10 seconds later he logs in to the network inside the building.

BBC News

http://news.bbc.co.uk/1/hi/technology/2202653.stm

It seems hackers have taken the practice of looking for open wireless networks to new heights.

Broadband Reports.com

http://www.dslreports.com/forum/remark,11457754~mode=flat

At this site, people discuss SSID (Service Set Identifier) and the general consensus is disabling it does nothing for making your network more secure.

Cirond

http://www.cirond.com/winc.html

Winc (Wireless Internet Networking and Communications) allows users of mobile and desktop PCs to easily find and connect to wireless networks. They can manage customized wireless connections in a more efficient way, enjoy improved performance, find support for a wider range of wireless network adapters, and more quickly get to work with their wireless network of choice.

CREDANT

http://www.credant.com/?src=overture&OVRAW=wireless%20security&OVKEY=wireless%20security&OVMTC=standard

This site describes CREDANT Technologies, a market leader in providing software that enables organizations to control security enterprise-wide for mobile workers.

CNN.com

http://www.cnn.com/2004/US/06/30/security.gap/

Here is an article on why homeland security is vulnerable to wireless hackers.

COMPUTERWORLD

http://www.computerworld.com/securitytopics/security/story/0,10801,93625,00.html?f=x2365

In this article, a person claims to be a parasite. He doesn't pay for the bandwidth he's using, he doesn't ask for permission to use it, and it's mostly because he doesn't even know whom to ask.

DevX

http://archive.devx.com/wireless/articles/WAP/WAPjp112000.asp

This is a good source of wireless articles. WAP stands for Wireless Application Protocol, and is a set of specifications for developing web-like applications that run over wireless networks.

EWeek

http://www.eweek.com/article2/0,1759,1627206,00.asp

In this article, WLANs have been exposed by a hack.

Fluke Networks

http://www.flukenetworks.com/wireless

Here is more troubleshooting advice. With the wireless option, you can analyze 802.11 a/b/g WLANs just like you analyze your wires.

Forbes.com

http://www.forbes.com/technology/2004/06/14/cx_ah_0615securewifi.html

Since wireless home networks are the latest craze for busy executives, the "default install" can create nothing short of a nightmare for corporate information technology personnel charged with keeping a company's data secure.

International Engineering Consortium

http://www.iec.org/online/tutorials/wap/

Positioned at a high level, this tutorial serves as an introduction to WAP, explaining its basic concept, benefits, architecture, and future.

LINKSYS

http://www.linksys.com/edu/page10.asp

Here is more information on MAC. With MAC address filtering enabled, wireless network access is provided solely for wireless devices with specific MAC addresses. This makes it harder for a hacker to access your network using a random MAC address.

Lots of Good Books

http://law.lotsofgoodbooks.com/us_law-item_id-0072227877-search_type-AsinSearch-locale-us.html

Experts say that SSIDs were never designed to be passwords.

MANCHESTER ONLINE

http://www.manchesteronline.co.uk/business/scienceandinnovation/s/133/133221_no_protection_from_wireless_hackers.html

It's a little depressing to know that there is no protection from wireless hackers.

Microsoft

http://www.microsoft.com/security/guidance/modules/default.mspx

Get assistance with key security issues in these self-contained blocks of guidance that take a comprehensive approach to specific issues. Whether you're looking for information on hardening file servers or design guidelines for enhancing the security of Web applications, you'll find it here.

NetMotion Wireless

http://www.netmotionwireless.com/product/

From security to reliability to support for every type of wireless connection, NetMotion Mobility is the industry's most complete solution for enabling mobile computing.

NetStumbler.org

http://www.netstumbler.org/archive/index.php/t-1468

Here is what you need to do to make a Cisco access point (security sensor) invisible.

NetworkWorldFusion

http://www.nwfusion.com/reviews/2004/1004wirelesswep.html

This reviewer states that the most egregious issue with WEP is its lack of key management. You pick an encryption key, give it to your users and then, typically, never change that key. Anyone who can recover your key can then decrypt all WEP traffic you've sent using it, compromise the privacy of your network, and get a good handle on its access controls.

News.com

http://news.com.com/Catching+wireless+hackers+in+the+act/2100-1033_3-956126.html

Here is an article on how it has been a cinch for vandals with an eye on Internet mischief to launch attacks by co-opting an unsecured wireless network. Fortunately, such break-ins may not go so unnoticed now.

PCSTATS

http://www.pcstats.com/articleview.cfm?articleID=1489

This article states that there are settings that will free the user from needing to change single settings on any of their other wireless hardware.

Security.itworld.com

http://security.itworld.com/4361/NWW010423119898/

A new version of wireless connectivity software from NetMotion Wireless will run on Windows CE-based devices and include the Rijndael encryption algorithm (set of steps) being proposed for the federal government's Advanced Encryption Standard.

Simplywireless

http://www.simplywireless.com.au/security.htm

Here is an article on how to simply secure an 802.11 WLAN.

Tech Republic

http://techrepublic.com.com/5100-6264-5283472.html

This site states that Media Access Control (MAC) is often ignored because it's not spoof-proof. But it is another brick in the wall: It's essentially another address filter, and it clogs up the works for the potential hacker. It limits network access to registered devices that you identify on address-based access control rosters.

TechRepublic

http://techrepublic.com.com/5100-6264_11-5320778.html

TechRepublic tells you to put your in-house people to work poking holes.

THAT Technical Bookstore.com

http://www.booksmatter.com/b0131840274.htm

Here is information on how to protect computers from hackers and lawyers.

WAP

http://www.hippy.freeserve.co.uk/wap.htm

Wireless Application Protocol, is a collection of protocols and transport layers (data transfer) which allow mobile and portable communication devices such as mobile phones and Personal Digital Assistants (PDAs) to receive information over the airwaves much as personal computer users obtain information over the Internet.

Webopedia

http://www.webopedia.com/TERM/W/WEP.html

This is a good place to go for definitions. WEP, short for Wired Equivalent Privacy, is a security protocol for wireless local area networks (WLANs) WEP is designed to provide the same level of security as that of a wired LAN. LANs are inherently more secure than WLANs because LANs are somewhat protected by the physicality of their structure, having some or all of the network inside a building.

Windows Security

http://www.aspfree.com/c/a/Windows-Security/Hardening-Wireless-LAN-Connections-Part-2/

All the hardening steps you have undertaken to secure your WAP and define who can connect to it are pointless exercises if you do not also harden the wireless connections themselves.

Wireless LAN Security Site

http://www.drizzle.com/~aboba/IEEE/

Have you read all about the security problems with WEP? Here are the papers and presentations that lay out the problem in detail.

Wireless Security

http://forum.homenethelp.com/Wireless_Security/m_14581/tm.htm

You can manually type in the MAC addresses of the wireless NICs (Network Interface Cards – adapters) that are allowed to use your wireless network.

WSJ Online

http://www.joejava.com/wsjthebestway.htm

All access points let users create a unique name called an SSID, a service set identifier for their Wi-Fi networks. For a computer to gain access to the network, its Wi-Fi adapter card must be set up with the network's SSID. The adapter card's settings typically are reached through an icon for the card on your computer. Once the SSID on the card is set to match the SSID on the access point, the computer will automatically connect with the network each time you use it.

Wireless Networks

Wireless technology was once a patchwork of incompatible systems from different vendors. With new wireless hardware and industry standards, wireless networking was born.

About

http://compnetworking.about.com/b/a/2003_10_26.htm

This mini article gives you the bare-bones facts about what you need to get a wireless network off the ground. Of course, About.com offers further information on wireless (and a plethora of other topics).

Amazon.com

http://www.amazon.com/exec/obidos/tg/detail/-/B00007KDVJ/104-4044056-0443120?v=glance

Here's another great place to read product reviews, compare prices, and shop. You can start broadly, in the Electronics section, or you look at products or brands. You can even get used products from this site.

Apple

http://www.apple.com/hardware/

This site offers, among other things, an explanation of the 802.11g base station, which gives you wireless Internet, printing, and bridging. AirPort Express, PowerBooks, and Bluetooth are tackled here in terms of how they relate to your Macintosh.

Arescom

http://www.arescom.com

Arescom offers digital broadband solutions for home users. At their web site you can read about their "residential solutions" and then move on over to read about their products, which include routers and adapters. They offer support for their products and sales help as well.

Ask Dr. Tech

http://www.askdrtech.com/?goto=1

Become a member and get help and technical support from an expert for your PC or Macintosh. Dr. Tech is a Microsoft-certified solutions provider. There are levels of help, so those people working on home computers don't get stuck buying enough support for an entire company.

Ask Leo

http://ask-leo.com

This site lets you search for questions that technical expert Leo Laporte has answered or write in with your own questions. Apparently Leo has more than two decades of computer experience, so it can't hurt to ask, right? You also get to search archives and see what the most frequently asked questions (and their answers) are. Better take a look at those before shooting off an e-mail to Leo.

AT&T Wireless

http://www.attwireless.com/business/built/enterprise.jhtml;dsessionid=MQUK0PSTLV021B4R0G1CFEY

Small business at home? Check out this site, which describes wireless technology to help you manage your wireless environment efficiently and drive down total cost.

Birkbeck

http://www.bbk.ac.uk/ccs/docs/wam/"wifihardware.htm

This page is designed as a guide for the tested hardware and does work on the Birkbeck wireless LAN. This site warns you against PC cards that do not work.

Bitpipe

http://www.bitpipe.com/data/plist?t=pd_10_20_72&src=googleprod

Need information about wireless computing products? This site has it. You get whitepapers as well as case studies. Less partial information but still potentially useful? Product literature. You can search by hardware or system when you're looking for information here. You can also register to be a member — for free! — and sign up for newsletters. Becoming a member allows you to save information and receive e-mail alerts.

BizRate

http://www.bizrate.com/buy/superfind__cat_id--4,keyword--wireless,lp--1,mkt_id--16838405,rf--ggl,sfsk--1.html

This site helps you compare hardware prices from different stores for when you're researching what it'll cost you to set up your home network. You also get to see product ratings.

Blogcritics

http://blogcritics.org/archives/2003/01/26/135101.php

The archives hold information about wireless that you might find interesting. This article tries to assert that wireless will eventually allow users to have essentially free broadband Internet access.

Broadband Reports

http://www.dslreports.com/

This source bills itself as the bible for information on DSL, cable, and other high-speed Internet services. You get links to the latest news and the day's hottest forum topics are listed on the home page also. If you want to chat it up with other like-minded users, you can do that, and a plethora of reviews are available for you to wade through. There's a portion of the site that helps you find broadband service and you can review any potential providers at your leisure.

Buffalo

http://www.buffalotech.com/products/wireless.php

This site offers products including adapters and access points. They offer incredibly helpful diagrams for installing wireless networks in an apartment or hotel (you know, in case you're building such a structure). You can't buy their goods online, but they offer a retailer list in case you're interested in pursuing their brand.

Business Know-How

http://www.businessknowhow.com/manage/wireless.htm

This author talks about her struggle to set up a network in her home and then how surprisingly easy it was setting up a wireless network. She touches on the hardware that helped her, as well as links you to more information about that hardware (and talks prices, too).

Cisco Systems

http://www.cisco.com

Search for AVVID (Architecture for Voice, Video and Integrated Data) and find out about this intelligent network Internet infrastructure. Cisco AVVID is the industry's only enterprisewide, standards-based network architecture and it lets you combine business and technology strategies.

CNET

http://reviews.cnet.com/Networking/2001-3243_7-0.html

This site offers product reviews for all sorts of wireless components, as well as shopping on the spot. If you really feel like doing your homework, you can look up various articles, compare prices, and dig into the forums while you're at it.

Comcast

http://faq.comcast.net/faq/answer.jsp?name=18073&cat=Connection&subcategory=1

Cable provider Comcast offers high-speed Internet with home networking. This network allows you to share access to the Internet, files, CD drives, and printers across the network (but you already knew that after reading this book). This FAQ may be able to offer answers to even more of your wireless networking questions.

COMPUTERWORLD

http://www.computerworld.com/news/2000/story/0,11280,45079,00.html

This article tackles how new technologies change the way we live and work. In particular the author discusses how wireless technology fits into our current lives and perspectives.

Computing.Net

http://www.computing.net/networking/wwwboard/forum/22418.html

This wireless router connection discussion might pull you in, but if not, a number of other computing topics just might. You can search for wireless topics in the areas of software, different operating systems, security, or hardware, among others. The Novice Section is nice for someone just getting started (just starting with computing, period) and includes information about how to use AOL's Instant Messager.

Connect - It

http://www.connectitwireless.net/index.htm

This shows Tower components and mounting hardware for the wireless industry. You can download a catalog, request information, and apply for credit.

Covad

http://www.covad.com/blp/dsl/

Covad offers DSL subscriptions. You can read about the different offers (one is geared toward home users and another toward business owners) and compare the rate speeds, prices, contract times, and installations. You can either install the DSL yourself or have someone come out and install it for you. They offer support, a newsletter, and your standard persuasive argument about why they're the best solution for you.

DEMOmobile.com

http://www.idgef.com/demomobile2/

This wireless conference site allows you to seek out the dates, schedule, and venue details for next year's conference as well as peruse photographs and videos of what happened at the most recent conference. A list of the speakers is available, as well as detailed information about their expertise and qualifications. The conference sponsors are linked to, of course, and the list includes heavy hitters.

Distributed Systems Online

http://dsonline.computer.org/0209/d/w5icon.htm

This article's author claims that most wireless devices will interconnect across networks within a few years. The software that gets in on all the action is mentioned, as well as what drives developers to do what they do (read: develop).

D-Link

http://www.dlink.com/

You can shop for wireless products from this manufacturer, who also offers support and case studies. Build a wireless network by following along with the Network Configurator and answering questions. Get there by clicking Configurator. The site offers specials as well, but if you're not into buying this stuff online, you can find local retailers.

DSL Cable

http://cable-dsl.home.att.net/

Do you have a cable modem or DSL? This site offers ways you can increase speed, enhance security, and fix problems. The site is broken down into a table of contents that links you directly to the information you need. Though this site offer detailed information about a number of scenarios and the site author offers his e-mail address for comments and suggestions, he warns that he can't offer one-on-one technical help.

DSL/Cable Webserver

http://www.dslwebserver.com/

If you need information about setting up and maintaining your own web server on a DSL or cable connection, you've come to the right place.

The Elder Geek

http://www.theeldergeek.com/kbi_user_accounts.htm

Search here for your computer-related questions. Search for Windows XP user accounts and you get to an impressive list of articles. Some of them detail how to configure active directory accounts and groups for wireless access in Windows 2000. Some also show you how to create and configure user accounts in Windows XP.

Enterprise

http://www.esgresults.com/wcm.htm

Enterprise Solutions Group helps organizations control wireless spending through a best practices approach. They educate groups about RFP and contract negotiations, rate plan analysis, wireless use policies, and monitoring.

EZLAN.net

http://www.ezlan.net/bridging.html

Connecting two parts of one or two networks is something many people do at home now with their computers. This site tells you how to avoid long wires of CAT5e.

Freesoft

http://www.freesoft.org/CIE/Topics/30.htm

This bare-bones site offers information about bridging a network. Once you read this summary you can compare bridging to routing by following the available link at the beginning of the description. If you feel you want to know more about other (or heck, all) wireless topics, go to the Topics page and search through the available list.

Gartner

http://www3.gartner.com/research/spotlight/asset_102069_895.jsp

This site has a wealth of articles for your perusal, one of which tackles the evolution of public network infrastructure. The site asserts that a rigorous framework will result in "lower costs, simplified operations, and greater visibility." Read this analysis and decide whether you agree.

Hewlett-Packard

http://h71036.www7.hp.com/hho/cache/8932-0-0-225-121.aspx

Security remains a big issue for wireless users. This Hewlett-Packard site provides tips that can help you develop a security strategy, and not just for your PC — also for your Pocket PC. The page also provides links to other sites of interest, from wireless basics to firewalls.

Hewlett-Packard

http://h10010.www1.hp.com/wwpc/us/en/sm/WF02a/18972-236253-396578.html

This is a summary of all HP wireless network print servers currently available for purchase and recommended for small and medium business.

HomePCnetwork

http://www.homepcnetwork.com/

You have a network on your home PC? This is the site for you. It is devoted to home users who are building and maintaining their networks. You can take advantage of a FAQ, a forum, glossary, and how-tos, among several other resources geared toward your ilk.

Home Toys

http://www.hometoys.com/htinews/jun99/articles/allied/allied.htm

This author talks about the potential barriers to wireless home networking and provides a table that lays out different technologies' raw data rates and whether they're open standard, proprietary, or industry consortium.

Howstuffworks

http://computer.howstuffworks.com/wireless-network.htm

Want to know how Wi-Fi works? This site explains that mystery and lets you approach the topic by general working knowledge, what you need to create a Wi-Fi network, and how to set one up in your home. But hey, you already know how to do that after reading this book, so check out the other Howstuffworks topics like money or people.

IBM

http://www-1.ibm.com/industries/wireless/doc/jsp/solution/

IBM offers a lot of information that you may or may not understand after wading through the computerspeak. It offers related links after you search for something specific, so perhaps if you don't find what you're looking for on one page, another can help.

iGo

http://www.igo.com/default.asp

The "Power Solutions configurator" helps you if you've run into a snag. You pick your product (from a list that includes PDA and mobile phone), manufacturer, and model, and then tell iGo how you're powering that thing. Poof, up comes a product recommendation complete with price and a link that lets you buy it on the spot.

ISP-Planet

http://www.isp-planet.com/fixed_wireless/business/2002/urban_bol.html

Here's a brief ditty that airs some stories about difficulties users have dealt with while rolling out Wi-Fi networks in urban areas. The article offers links afterward to other Wi-Fi topics.

ITtoolbox

http://wireless.ittoolbox.com/documents/document.asp?i=1328

This wireless whitepaper discusses the obstacles to 3G wireless. The paper talks about the design tools and methods to overcoming these obstacles.

KNOWLEDGESTORM

http://www.knowledgestorm.com/

If you go to this site you can search by keyword, company name, or title. A search for wireless brings up articles, reports, whitepapers — and "sponsors." The site offers related topics in case you can't find what you're looking for in the initial category you try.

LINKSYS

http://www.linksys.com/

Linksys is a part of Cisco Systems, Inc. and is provides wireless and Ethernet networking for consumer and small office/home office (SOHO) users. You can get an up close and personal look at their products at this site, and after doing that inspect the product's user guide (which you might need to have FTP to look at). If something interests you, find out where you can buy it. If this is jumping ahead some for you, check out the Education page, which provides basics about networks, including an acronym list so you can swim through the alphabet soup.

Looksmart

http://www.findarticles.com/p/articles/mi_m0BRZ/is_12_22/ai_98977153

Storage area networks (SANs) continue to attract attention while businesses look to reduce management costs and increase storage asset use. Distributing storage resources over a network, consolidating management, and letting multiple applications and users share disks are appealing propositions. This article talks more about this prospect.

Low Cost Long Range Wireless Network

http://www.accelenet.net/wireless.html

Want a low-cost, high-speed wireless network? Only need a range of three miles? This site describes just that. Oh, and you have to be based in "normal terrain." Whatever that means.

Macosxhints Forums

http://forums.macosxhints.com/showthread.php?s=&threadid=20186

These forums are imminently searchable but you must register before you can really participate. The subjects are specific and intuitive, but if you want to be a good little forum user, check out the FAQ before doing anything.

Microsoft

http://support.microsoft.com/default.aspx?scid=kb;en-us;Q318750

This site explains configuring active directory accounts and groups for Windows 2000 wireless access. The information is broken down into steps so you can easily follow along and then further information is offered after. You get to provide feedback regarding how useful this page is.

Microsoft

http://www.microsoft.com/hardware/mouseandkeyboard/bluetooth_compat.mspx

Here is a list of devices and their compatibility rating with the Microsoft wireless transceiver for Bluetooth. You also get access to associated how-to documents. The matrix is regularly updated with new devices.

Microsoft TechNet

http://www.microsoft.com/technet/security/guidance/peap_int.mspx

Wireless Local Area Network (WLAN) technology in business is a controversial topic. Security is an issue, but so is the possibility of losing benefits if a WLAN isn't used. There is still a good deal of confusion about whether a WLAN is safe to use for corporate computing. This article helps you choose a security strategy for your business, if you have one.

NETGEAR

http://www.netgear.com/

This powerhouse offers wireless products and if you can't find what you're looking for in their impressive drop-down Product Finder, type in something else. You can get routers, gateways, and other wireless ephemera at this site, and they've broken down the categories into nice, easily understandable groups on the Products page. Of course they offer technical support and the forums may come in handy if you're willing to look before typing in your support question. Again, you can either buy online at this site or retrieve a list of available retailers.

NetworkClue

http://www.networkclue.com/hardware/network/wireless/antennas.php

Antennae are a crucial part to some parts of the wireless world, and choosing the right one is important. This site helps explain concepts like Fresnel zone and polarity and then breaks down the different types of antennae.

NetworkWorldFusion

http://www.nwfusion.com/newsletters/itlead/2004/0308itlead1.html

According to Aberdeen Group estimates, the average Fortune 500 Company spends $116 million a year on telecom services. This may not apply to your home network, but it could apply to your work laptop. Check out this article and, if you like, sign up for more information via a newsletter.

Office of Information Technologies

http://www.oit.umass.edu/network/bridge.html

You may want to do the opposite of what most sites offer to help you do. Maybe you want to disable a network and stop the bridging madness? Then here's the place to be. This page takes you through the steps necessary to turn off what may be automatically enabled on your laptop. If this isn't the topic you're interested in or need help with, search further topics, including switching from wired to wireless networks and virtual private networks (VPNs).

Overclockers Club

http://forums.overclockersclub.com/?showtopic=32161

This site offers a heavily populated forum, which you must register for, with categories split by hardware and software. You also get access to articles and downloads, in addition to product reviews and the Overclockers store (no wireless products here, just good, old-fashioned tchotckes.

PRACTICALLY NETWORKED

http://www.practicallynetworked.com/

Here you get all the basics laid out in a very understandable way: product reviews, price reviews, and daily news. (If you're looking to compare prices, make sure you've narrowed down your needs and desires. If you go into any one category you'll be overwhelmed with the number of prices to compare.) The forums or user opinions might be of interest to you as well, considering they tackle everything from routers to print servers to Bluetooth. If this is too large a place to start from, use the site's search engine to find what you're looking for.

The Register

http://www.expansys.com

The Register is a UK-based wealth of information about wireless networking, including PDAs, Pocket PCs, and cellular phones. Luckily they offer a link to other country-specific information (including the United States, France, and Italy) so there's no need to convert pounds when determining product price. You can also get Bluetooth and GPS product information here, as well as more general wireless goods, including cables. There's a Deal of the Day and a Clearance section if you're looking for super bargains. Anytime you inspect a product other, related items and accessories are offered up as well.

Seattle Wireless

http://www.seattlewireless.net/index.cgi/HardwareComparison

This community compares hardware so you can do some investigating while figuring out what wireless components to buy. A table nicely breaks down the information for digestive ease and if you have trouble converting dBm to mW, a link takes you to a downloadable converter.

Small Business Computing

http://www.smallbusinesscomputing.com/webmaster/article.php/3287631

This site gives the goods about overcoming wireless network configuration obstacles. If you're setting up your network at home and are running into trouble, you might benefit from checking out this site at large. There's a good search engine, a forum, and a glossary.

SMC Networks

http://www.smc.com/index.cfm?action=home_page

This manufacturer develops network interface cards (NICs), hubs, and switches for Ethernet and fast Ethernet. A veritable stash of wireless goodies at your fingertips! Pick what you're interested in, read more about it, and decide whether you want to buy it on the spot or continue shopping around. SMC also has home entertainment products for video and audio interests.

SpeedGuide

http://www.speedguide.net/

A large section focuses on cable modems and DSL technology. The approach is fast paced and geared toward someone who knows his or her stuff already. You can get your usual news and review here, as well as very thorough broadband help by way of downloads, patches, and "registry tweaks." You get even more services if you become a SpeedGuide member and obtain a Premium account.

StarMicoTech

http://www.starmicrotech.com/

Your basic wireless hardware needs are here: Shop away! You can narrow your choices down by item or seller, there's a special-of-the-day, and if you want to see what the Joneses are buying, check out the top sellers.

Studiowhiz.com

http://www.studiowhiz.com/forums/index.php?showtopic=4956

Participants in this forum discuss the fact that with the network bridge, you've no need to purchase an additional hardware-based bridge device. If you get tired of reading about this, you can search for industry or site news, reviews, and tutorials.

Tech Support Guy

http://forums.techguy.org/showthread.php?p=1024077

This forum lets you scope out users who have questions similar to yours or register and ask your own questions. One such question is this: "I thought I could connect two PCs with wireless network cards on an ad-hoc basis like this. The two PCs are in two rooms, one above the other, so are not too far apart."

Tom's Networking

http://www.tomsnetworking.com/

SmallNetBuilder and Tom's Hardware Guide have started Tom's Networking. Lucky you! Check out the available whitepapers and articles or get down to the nitty gritty and start comparing prices right off the bat. Tom's Low Price Finder is bound to help you get what you need at the price you want, right? The Top Tens (top ten most recent FAQs, top ten most-read articles published in the last 90 days, and so on) are nice if you want to just glance at the information and catch up quickly.

UNIX

http://ap-utils.polesye.net/

This site offers a set of wireless access point utilities for UNIX. These utilities help you configure and monitor wireless access points under UNIX using a protocol referred to as SNMP. You can download the source code from this site and screenshots help those of you who are more visual learners.

Using a UNIX Computer as a 802.11 Wireless Base Station

http://www.live.com/wireless/unix-base-station.html

This explains how to use a UNIX computer as a base station. The article offers links to setting up a Wi-Fi connection at a place called Dana Street Roasting Company, source code for building an 802.11 access point with Linux, and the home page to the manufacturer that made ORiNOCO.

Verizon

http://www22.verizon.com/ForHomeDSL/Channels/DSL/bridge/standard.asp?promotion_code=VZBNR/W28&variant=

This site has many things that pertain to wireless living and working, but this particular page takes you to the DSL versus cable debate. (Then you get to read why Verizon DSL is your alleged absolute best option, period, hands down.) They provide a FAQ and a kit to help aid installation if you decide not only to take them up on their offer but to put the DSL in yourself. Not even sure you are DSL eligible? There's a spot where you can enter your phone number to verify coverage.

Wi-Fi Planet

http://www.wi-fiplanet.com/wimax/article.php/3089781

This article discusses Niverville, Manitoba and its philosophy about building a wireless network structure for business' (and the province's economy's) sake.

Wi-Fi Planet

http://www.wi-fiplanet.com/tutorials/article.php/1453261

This tutorial helps you think through the necessary steps and components before you jump in with both feet. You can compare a wireless LAN with an Ethernet alternative or provide budget information if you're proposing a solution to management. The tutorial tackles access points and components, as well as provides links to further information about those topics and others related to wireless networking. Related articles are offered as well.

Wikipedia

http://en.wikipedia.org/wiki/Wireless_access_point

This site is loaded with definitions of all sorts of things. Come here and type in the word or phrase you need to understand more about and Wikipedia offers it up, along with lots of links to further information.

WindowsITPro

http://www.winnetmag.com/Windows/Article/ArticleID/40051/40051.html

The author of this article has received e-mail from readers, including administrators, who have problems when creating or managing user accounts. The author reviews creating and managing user accounts and shares some tips to make creating and managing easier.

Wireless Business & Technology

http://www.sys-con.com/wireless

This technology publisher offers a plethora of articles and editorials about wireless products and the industry at large. You can also sign up for a free newsletter at this site.

ZDNet

http://news.zdnet.com/2100-9595_22-993803.html

This article's author explains that employees are more productive in a more flexible environment, which is what wireless networks (and technology) offers. Here you can see the author tackle issues such as bandwidth, applications, and security.

Wireless Printers

People on the move need to print and this is how it's done.

Apple

http://www.apple.com/airportexpress/

Get all the goods on Apple's AirPort Express, a handy gadget that lets you get online, print, and stream music (iTunes, of course) to any room in your home. The system requirements are provided and downloads are available if you do purchase this technology.

Envy News

http://www.envynews.com/index.php?ID=683

Get a description, specifications, and installation and configuration instructions for a product that lets you print wirelessly from your Bluetooth. Sounds tasty, no?

FedEx Kinko's

http://www.fedex.com/us/officeprint/main/index.html

You can print to a Kinko's via your laptop; just enter your zip code to find the closest location. The site takes you through some basic questions to get you started uploading both the necessary software (and then your file). Easy as pie.

McGill

http://www.mcgill.ca/ncs/products/soho/networking/printer/

Here is where you can get instructions for how to install a printer on a Windows 95/98 network.

PC Magazine

http://www.pcmag.com/article2/0,1759,1618347,00.asp

If you are considering sharing a printer via network, read this article. The author asserts that anyone with more than one computer should probably do so.

PC World

http://www.pcworld.com/howto/article/0,aid,15273,00.asp

If you're traveling and forget your printer (and there's nary a FedEx Kinko's in sight and you haven't purchased PrintMe), use this great tip to get around the problem.

PrintMe

http://www.efi.com/products/printme/

PrintMe is a printing service available at some Wi-Fi hotspots. It lets you print to a printer at the hotspot without loading any printer drivers. Read about how it works, learn what one of its stations includes, make comparisons to its competition, and find out where you can buy the service. If you're unsure whether PrintMe is for you, check out the FAQ.

SanDisk

http://www.sandisk.com

Hold on there, partner! Before you even get to see the site you're asked whether you want to download the software. Maybe Don't Install is the best choice for right now, eh? After you cozy up and learn that SanDisk offers data storage cards (PC cards yes, and USB flash drives as well), you might think it wise to get that stuff onto your computer.

Waterwheel.com

http://www.waterwheel.com/Guides/how_to/Printers/install_Printers.htm

If you need to install a printer, this site can help you do that.

Wi-Fi Planet

http://www.wi-fiplanet.com/news/article.php/1483091

Here's a brief study of Hewlett-Packard's partnerships announcement. Adobe, Cisco Systems, and Research In Motion (among others) all partnered with HP to get printers to mobile workers.

WindowsITPro

http://www.winnetmag.com/Articles/Print.cfm?ArticleID=40399

Some older laptops don't have a conventional printer port. Motion Computing is a company that offers what it calls the Motion M1200 FlexDock. However, one reader says that seems like a heavy option.

Index

Numerics

2.4 GHz frequency band
  Bluetooth, 374
  cordless telephones, 29, 355
3G (third-generation) networks, 17
4:3 aspect ratio on HDTV, 462–463
5.8 GHz frequency band cordless telephones, 355
16:9 aspect ratio on HDTV, 462–463
418-MHz frequency for Motorola Home Monitoring and Control System, 484
480p resolution on HDTV, 462
780p resolution on HDTV, 462
802.1x authentication, 198–199
802.11b, 802.11g, and 802.11a Wi-Fi standards. *See also* Wi-Fi standard
  choosing among, 35–38
  choosing for movie/video file transfers, 438
  described, 13
  inadequate bandwidth for wireless video file handling, 400, 401, 402
  indoor range, frequency, speed and compatibility comparison, 28, 35
  multi-standard devices, 37–38
  possible conflict with 2.4GHz frequency band cordless telephones, 355
  TiVo units supporting 802.11g, 456
  "turbo" versions, 438
900 MHz cordless telephones, 354–355, 431
900 MHz digital unlicensed radio spectrum, for IMfree instant messaging, 431
1080i resolution on HDTV, 462

A

AAC music format, 399
abbreviations used by chatters, 433–435
access points
  adding additional to extend range or coverage, 64, 81
  Bluetooth for Logitech diNovo Media Desktop, 376
  as bridge connecting wireless to wired networks, 62, 159
  configuring for wireless routers, 63–64
  configuring WPA Security, 195–196
  described, 27
  determining IP address assigned, 82
  DHCP server feature, 73–74
  DHCP settings, 64, 76–78
  firmware upgrades, 43, 133–138, 202
  firmware upgrades for WPA support, 195
  monitoring signal strength with NetStumbler, 176–180
  password for, 63–64
  resetting with Reset button, 129–130, 234, 235, 236
  resetting SSID, 63, 236
  security settings, 64, 195–196
  TCP/IP settings, 64
  troubleshooting, 129–130
  as wireless hub component, 31, 62
accessories. *See also* GPS (global positioning service) receivers; media players; Palm PDAs; peripherals; Pocket PCs
  AlphaSmart Dana Wireless word processor, 406

cordless game controllers, 369–370
D-Link DVC-1100 Wireless Broadband Video Phone, 406
D-Link Securicam DCS-5300G Internet Camera, 406
HDTV, 461–466
headsets for cell phones, hands-free and Bluetooth-connected, 345, 372, 388–389
home monitoring and control systems, 483–492
IMfree instant messaging, 419–435
Laserpod, 410
Linksys Wireless-B Internet Video Camera, 406, 417
Linksys Wireless-G Game Adapter, 406
radio, 10, 11, 260, 326–327, 359–362
Sony AIBO robotic dog, 410
TiVo units, 447–460
TV-B-Gone, 409
weather forecasting, 469–482
webcams, 416–417
Active WebCam from PY Software, 417
ActiveSync, 274
activity
customizing display, 175–176
described, 171
monitoring, 173–175
ad-hoc mode (computer-to-computer or peer-to-peer) networks, 114, 147–148, 156, 254
adapters. *See also* wireless network adapters
mini-PCI, 31, 33
multi-standard devices, 37–38
network, 160
PC cards, 31, 32, 33
PCI (peripheral component interconnect) adapters
compared to adapter-style cards, 86
described, 31, 33
installing, 86–89
installing adapter utilities, 94–96
installing client software *prior* to physically installing card, 94–96
installing drivers, 89–93
troubleshooting, 130
two styles of, 86, 87
troubleshooting, 130–133
USB wireless network adapters
advantages, 96
for Bluetooth, 373, 379–381
described, 32
disadvantages, 85
as hot-swappable, 98
installing, 96–98
installing driver, 99–101
installing utilities, 101–102
on non-Windows XP systems, 101
Add Bluetooth Device Wizard, 382–383
Add Printer Wizard, 168–169
Adobe Photoshop Album, 400
Advanced Connection Options dialog box, 321
AIM (AOL Instant Messenger), 425, 428–430
AirCards, for wireless Internet connection, 13–14
airlines
Web In-Flight hotspot Web site, 304
with Wi-Fi hotspots, 311
AiroPeek, 190
AirPort Express (Apple), 404
airports
with hotspot Internet services, 307–308
Sprint hotspot sites, 307
T-Mobile hotspot sites, 305
Wayport hotspot provider, 306
wireless networks in, 158
AirSnort, 190
"Allow Network Users to Change My Files" option, 439
AlphaSmart Dana Wireless word processor, 406

analog phones, 352–353
answering machine feature on cordless telephones, 356
antennae
detachable, on routers, 43
directional, 45, 46
omnidirectional, 45
for range of wireless networks, 44–45
repositioning for better reception, 125
Anywhere Map (GPS mapping) from Control Vision, 501
AOL Instant Messenger (AIM), 425, 428–430
AOL subscribers and IMfree, 419, 432
Apple. *See also* Mac users
AirPort Express, 404
Bluetooth-enabled peripherals, 377
iTune music store, 400, 404
ASF video format, 400
aspect ratios on HDTV, 462–463
Association settings, editing, 153
AT&T Wireless Network, 14, 250
Atlanta Hartsfield International airport hotspots, 308
auction sites, online, 32, 40
Audio CD music format, 399
Austin's Wi-Fi hotspots, 309
authentication
editing settings, 153
802.1x, 198–199
enabling WEP, disabling IEEE 802.1x, 193
enabling WPA, disabling IEEE 802.1x, 197–198
pre-shared key method, 196
Automatic Updates, configuring Windows XP for, 200–202
AvantGo
advantages, 273, 279–280
channels available through, 280
Power User Premium account, 282
registering and downloading software, 280–282
synchronizing with handheld device and desktop PC, 282–284
AvantGo Wireless, 284–285
AVI video format, 400

B

baby monitors as source of interference with wireless network signals, 357
backwards compatibility of 802.11g wireless standard devices, 37
bandwidth, fair use policies of satellite service Internet access, 20
batteries
and charging for IMfree instant messaging, 420
Motorola Home Monitoring and Control System, 486
Professional Weather Station, 472
rechargeable, 12, 365
stocking up on, 12
battery chargers, 12
Belkin Bluetooth USB Adapter (F8T001), 380–381
Best Western hotels with Wi-Fi hotspots, 308
.BIN file type, 136
bit rate, 14
Blackberry
address book, 297–299
advantages, 14, 287
choosing model, 288–290
e-mail, 292–295
main applications of 7200-series models, 291
navigating, 292
on/off button, 292
phone calls, 296–297
shortcut keys, 295–296
Web browsing, 299

Bluejacking, 392–393
bluesnarfing, 393
Bluetooth
  advantages, 372
  Bluejacking, 392–393
  bluesnarfing, 393
  described, 276, 371
  discoverability and Windows XP discovery setting, 378–379
  frequency, power, and range, 374–375
  hubs and peripherals, 376–377
  installing Bluetooth USB adapter, 379–381
  interoperability, 377
  master device, slave units, piconets, and scatternets, 375
  moving files between PC and Mac, 382–385
  moving files and synchronizing information to Pocket PC, 385–388
  My Bluetooth Places icon, 381
  origin of name, 374
  pairing of devices, 379
  possible uses, 372–373
  profiles (services or uses), 375–376
  range for peripherals, 365, 375, 388
  security considerations, 15
  security risks, 392–393
  sending photos to PC, 389–391
  Windows XP support in Service Pack 2 (SP2), 379
Bluetooth Devices dialog box, 378–379, 382
Bluetooth File Transfer Wizard, 384–385, 389–391
boaters, Wi-Fi Marine hotspot Web site, 304
Boingo hotspot finder utility, 306
Boingo Wireless hotspot provider, 305
Borders bookstores as T-Mobile hotspot sites, 305
Born on This Day feature of SmartWatch, 330
brick, as obstacle for wireless networks signals, 29
bridges
  access points as, 62, 159
  adding/removing networks, 162–163
  for connecting different types of networks, 61–62, 159
  creating, 160–161
  deleting, 163
broadband Internet access, 17, 38
broadband modems, 39–40
browsers, router configuration for Web-based, 42
buddies (chat partners), 425
burial sites and cemeteries, genealogy with GPS, 523–526

C

cable modem Internet access, 17, 38, 236–238
cable TV
  companies' versions of digital recorders, 448
  offering HDTV, 464, 466
  transmitters, wireless, as sources of interference with wireless network signals, 29
CableCARD slots, 466
Cabo San Lucas, Mexico, webcam view, 417
Calendar Add-in for Outlook (SmartWatch), 336–337
calendar feature of SmartWatch, 328
Call Waiting ID feature on cordless telephones, 356
Caller ID feature on cordless telephones, 356
Caltrans, webcam view of traffic conditions, 416

cameras. *See also* Motorola Home Monitoring and Control System
  D-Link Securicam DCS-5300G Internet Camera, 406
  Linksys Wireless-B Internet Video Camera, 406
  webcams, 416–417
campgrounds, with Wi-Fi hotspots, 311
Canon portable printers, 258
car stereo
  DMP1 mobile digital media player (Rockford Omnifi), 407
  from Sirius and XM Radio satellite radio services, 467
cards. *See* adapters; PC cards
cathode-ray technology (CRT), 463
Cell-Block-R, 409
cell phones. *See also* cordless telephones
  advantages, 10
  advantages of frequent free replacement, 343
  advantages of purchase from service provider, 343
  cameras, 344–345
  changing telephone numbers or switching landline number to cellular service, 348–349
  comparison to Family Radio Service (FRS) two-way radios, 360–361
  considerations for talk time, signal type, and batteries, 344
  downloadable free ringtones, 346
  flip phone style, 344
  games, 345
  GPS-enabled, 505
  hands-free and Bluetooth-connected headsets, 345, 372, 388–389
  in-network and out-of-network calling areas, 342
  messaging services, 346–347
  radio waves and health considerations, 347–348
  roaming charges, 342, 360
  safety considerations, 345, 347–348
  selecting among features, 343–347
  selecting among plans, 341–343
  synchronizing information with Bluetooth, 385
  Web-enabled, 346
cellular-based packet data networks, 17
Cellular One, national cell phone service provider, 343
cemeteries and burial sites, genealogy with GPS, 523–526
channels, 280
chat rooms, through media servers, 411
Chicago O'Hare International airport hotspots, 307
China's global navigation system, 499–500
Choice Hotels with Wi-Fi hotspots, 308–309
Cingular Wireless, 288
Cirond's Winc for configuring laptop security options, 253–254, 255
Citizens Band Radio Services, 360, 362
city clouds in city centers (hot zones of Wi-Fi hotspots), 309–310
Clarion Hotels with Wi-Fi hotspots, 308–309
clocks. *See* SmartWatch
cloning of MAC address for routers, 58–59
clutter, eliminating with wireless peripherals, 11, 27
Comfort Suites Hotels with Wi-Fi hotspots, 308–309
Command Prompt, 240
Compact Flash cards for Bluetooth, 373
computer administrators, 205–206
computer-to-computer (or peer-to-peer or ad-hoc mode) networks, 114, 147–148, 156, 254

computers. *See* PCs
concrete arch highway extension project, webcam view of, 416
concrete, as obstacle for wireless networks signals, 29
Connected DVD Player (Gateway), 403
Connecting dialog box, 319–320
Connection Manager T-Mobile hotspot finder utility, 306
coordinates, longitude, latitude and geometry (GPS technology), 508–511
cordless telephones. *See also* cell phones
- advantages, 9
- analog style, 352–353
- blocking with Cell-Block-R, 409
- D-Link DVC-1100 Wireless Broadband Video Phone, 406
- digital style, 353–354
- DSS (digital spread spectrum) technology, 352
- features available, 355–356
- 5.8 GHz frequency band, 355
- frequencies and range, 352
- 900 MHz frequency range, 354–355
- obstacles and interference considerations, 29, 229, 352, 353, 354, 355, 357, 456
- pros and cons of available frequency bands, 354–355
- security considerations of DSS, 352
- as source of interference with wireless network signals, 29, 229
- as sources of interference with wireless network signals, 29
- technological advances, 351–352
- 2.4 GHz frequency band, 355

crackers and hackers, 185, 189–190
CRT (cathode-ray technology) HDTV sets, 463

D

D-Link devices
- DVC-1100 Wireless Broadband Video Phone, 406
- MediaLounge Wireless Media Player, 403, 411
- Securicam DCS-5300G Internet Camera, 406
- webcams, 417

Dallas-Ft. Worth International airport hotspots, 308
Danger's hiptop2, 300
date, time, and time zone information for routers, 54–55
DCS-5300G Internet Camera (D-Link Securicam), 406
default printer, 169
degrees, minutes, seconds and geometry (GPS technology), 508–509
Dell Axim 30 Pocket PC, 262–266
Dell Site Monitor (for Pocket PCs), 266
Dell WLAN utility (for Pocket PCs), 265–266
DeLorme BlueLogger GPS receiver, 497
Denver International airport hotspots, 308
detachable antennae on routers, 43
Device Manager, 115–116, 131–133, 139–140, 224–227
DHCP clients log (DHCP setting on wireless router), 77
DHCP (Dynamic Host Configuration Protocol), 73
DHCP servers
- described, 42, 74
- included in ICS (Internet Connection Sharing) feature, 232
- settings for access points, 64
- troubleshooting, 229–231

troubleshooting automatic private address problems, 79–80
troubleshooting duplicate in ICS (Internet Connection Sharing) feature, 232
Windows XP automatic private IP address default, 79–80
dial-up versus high-speed wireless connection to Internet, 9, 17, 38
digital light processing (DLP) technology, 463
digital media receivers, 397
digital rights management (DRM) encryption, 399
digital spread spectrum (DSS) technology for cordless telephones, 352
digital style cordless telephones, 353–354
digital subscriber line (DSL) Internet access, 17, 38, 39
digital TV, 462. *See also* HDTV (high-definition TV)
digital video recorders (DVRs), 448
diNovo Media Desktop, 376, 377
directional antennae, 45, 46
DirectTV (satellite TV operator), 448, 465
DirecWay (formerly DirecPC), 20–21
discoverability of Bluetooth devices, 378–379
Dish Network (satellite TV operator), 448, 465, 467
DLP (digital light processing) HDTV sets, 463
DMP1 mobile digital media player (Rockford Omnifi), 407
DMS1 Digital Media Streamer (Rockford Omnifi), 405
DNS server (DHCP setting on wireless router), 77
doggie, robotic, Sony AIBO, 410
Domain Name (DHCP setting on wireless router), 76
door/window sensors. *See* Motorola Home Monitoring and Control System
driver rollback, 132, 226
drivers
configuring for print servers, 70–71
described, 90, 202
determining current version number, 140
installing for PCI adapters, 89–93
installing for USB adapters, 99–101
returning to previous version (driver rollback), 132, 226
troubleshooting, 132, 138–141, 225–227
updating, 140–141, 202, 226
DRM (digital rights management) encryption, 399
DSL (digital subscriber line) Internet access, 17, 38, 39, 236–238
DSS (digital spread spectrum) technology for cordless telephones, 352
DVC-1100 Wireless Broadband Video Phone (D-Link), 406
DVDs, Connected DVD Player (Gateway), 403
DVRs (digital video recorders), 448
Dynamic Host Configuration Protocol (DHCP), 73. *See also* DHCP servers
dynamic IP addresses, 75, 76–80

E

e-mail. *See also* IMfree instant messaging
from Motorola Home Monitoring and Control System, 490, 491
through media servers, 411
eFax (Internet-based fax service), 260

EHPE (Expected Horizontal Position Error), 499
802.1x authentication, 198–199
802.11b, 802.11g, and 802.11a Wi-Fi standards. *See also* Wi-Fi standard
  choosing among, 35–38
  choosing for movie/video file transfers, 438
  described, 13
  inadequate bandwidth for wireless video file handling, 400, 401, 402
  indoor range, frequency, speed and compatibility comparison, 28, 35
  multi-standard devices, 37–38
  possible conflict with 2.4GHz frequency band cordless telephones, 355
  TiVo units supporting 802.11g, 456
  "turbo" versions, 438
elevation (GPS positioning), 510
emoticons, 433
encryption
  digital rights management (DRM), 399
  of GPS signals, 498
  uses for, 190
  WEP (Wired Equivalent Privacy) protocol support on routers, 43, 122, 190
  WPA (Wi-Fi Protected Access) protocol support on routers, 43, 122, 190
End IP (DHCP setting on wireless router), 76
enhanced definition of HDTV, 462
Entré Entertainment Hub (Kenwood), 411
ergonomic keyboards, 368
Ethernet cables, 149, 236
Ethernet networks
  and media players, 401
  for movie/video file transfers, 438
Ethernet ports
  integrated four-port switch, 42, 61–62
  modems, 40
Europe's global navigation system, 499
Excentrique MP3 player (Jens of Sweden), 410
expandability of wireless networks, 27

F

fair use policies of satellite service Internet access, 20
Family Radio Service (FRS) two-way radios
  advantages, 10, 359
  channels for geocachers, 521
  combining with GPS, 362
  comparison to cell phones, 360–361
  FCC's rules, 359, 360
  and GMRS (General Mobile Radio Service), 360, 361
  range, 360
fax services, 260
faxing document when from home, 260
FedEx Kinko's print shops
  printing service, 259
  T-Mobile hotspot sites, 305, 311
FHSS (frequency hopping spread spectrum)
  with Bluetooth, 374
  for cordless telephones, 352
file sharing with Windows XP. *See also* media players
  caution against "Allow Network Users to Change My Files" option, 439
  advantages, 437–438
  alternatives to wireless networks for huge video files, 438
  assigning drive letter to network folder, 442–443
  blocking access to files, 440, 442
  browsing network, 446
  disconnecting from a mapped network drive, 445
  hiding folders, 442

monitoring shared folders, 441
specifying folders to be shared, 439
switching off automatic connections, 443–445
unsharable folders, 440
firewalls, 42, 183
firmware, of routers and access points, 43, 133–138, 202
5.8 GHz frequency band cordless telephones, 355
fixed wireless Internet access, 17
foreign travel, NodeDB.com hotspot Web site, 304
Fossil SmartWatches, 325–326
"Found New Hardware" message, 90, 99
Found New Hardware Wizard, 91–92, 99–101, 487
4:3 aspect ratio on HDTV, 462–463
418-MHz frequency for Motorola Home Monitoring and Control System, 484
480p resolution on HDTV, 462
frequency hopping spread spectrum (FHSS), 352, 374
front projection HDTV sets, 463
FRS (Family Radio Service). *See* Family Radio Service (FRS) two-way radios
fuel cell-powered concept car, Quark by Peugeot, 410

G

games
advantages of static IP address, 81
cordless controllers, 369–370
online, unavailable over StarBand residential services, 20
Garmin eTrex GPS unit, 496
Garmin's Rino GPS (global positioning service) receivers, 362
Gateway Connected DVD Player, 403
gateways, 75, 484
genealogy with GPS, 502, 523–527
General Mobile Radio Service (GMRS), 360, 361
geocaching with GPS, 501, 519–523
Geographic Names Information System (GNIS) site, 525–526
geometry, longitude, latitude and coordinates (GPS technology), 508–511
Global Positioning Service. *See* GPS (global positioning service) receivers
GMRS (General Mobile Radio Service), 360, 361
GNIS (Geographic Names Information System) Web site, 525–526
Google Picasa photo organizer software, 400
GPS (global positioning service) receivers
caution: carry old-fashioned compass and map, 500, 505
caution against forgetting common sense when geochaching, 520
caution against using while driving, 503
caution on dead batteries or obsolete maps, 505
caution on leaving trip information with someone, 500
advantages, 11
bicycles with handlebar mount, 501
with cell phones, 505
civilian uses, 495, 500–502
combining with Family Radio Service (FRS) two-way radios, 362
connecting Pocket PC, Palm, or laptop with Bluetooth, 373, 503
DeLorme BlueLogger GPS receiver, 497
EHPE (Expected Horizontal Position Error), 499
elevation, 510
Garmin eTrex unit, 496
genealogy, 502, 523–527

GPS (global positioning service) receivers *(continued)*
- geocaching, 501, 519–523
- as government funded satellite system, 495
- HDOP (Horizontal Dilution of Precision), 498
- hobbyists' GPS Waypoint Registry Web site, 517
- how it works, 511–513
- with laptops, 503–504, 506
- longitude, latitude, coordinates and geometry, 508–511
- manufacturers, 504
- military uses, 497
- other nations' systems, 499
- paper maps, 505
- PDOP (Position Dilution Of Precision), 498
- with Pocket PC, 504
- points of interest, restaurants, gas stations, parks, campgrounds, etc., 501
- portable units, 502, 506
- portable units' limited memory, 517
- precision/accuracy considerations, 496, 497–499
- reading display, 513–515
- satellites used for, 511–513
- Selective Availability and Selective Deniability, 498
- upgrading software and maps, 505
- used by hackers/crackers, 185
- uses for downloaded tracking information, 506
- vehicle units, 502–503
- waypoints, creating and using, 515–517
- Wide-Area Augmentation System (WAAS), 498

Grand Haven, Michigan's Wi-Fi hotspots, 309
guest accounts, 206, 219–220

H

hackers and crackers, 185, 189–190
Hardware Update Wizard, 140–141, 226
Hawking Technology
- webcams, 417
- WiFi Locator, 255–256

HDOP (Horizontal Dilution of Precision), 498
HDTV (high-definition TV)
- aspect ratios, 462–463
- cable-ready with CableCARD slots, 466
- with cable or satellite service provider, 464
- free guide, 462
- growing popularity, 461–462
- HDTV monitors or HDTV-ready sets, 464
- lack of built-in tuners, 464
- local antenna/range information Website, 465
- need for tuner or set-top box, 464
- packaged channel offerings, 465
- range considerations, 465
- receiving over cable TV, 466
- receiving via antennae, 464
- receiving via satellite, 464, 465–466
- recorded by TiVo unit, 448
- shopping for sets, 463
- TiVo-enabled receivers, 465, 466

headsets for cell phones, hands-free and Bluetooth-connected, 345, 372, 388–389
Heavy Weather Publisher for sharing reports on Web site, 478–481
Heavy Weather Review software for graphical representations, 475–478
Heavy Weather software for real-time information display, 473–475
highway extension project, webcam view of, 416

highway rest areas with Wi-Fi hotspots, 311
Hilton hotels with Wi-Fi hotspots, 308
hiptop2, 300
home entertainment systems, 11. *See also* HDTV; IMfree instant messaging; media players; TiVo units
horoscope feature of SmartWatch, 328
hot-swappable, USB devices as, 98
hot zones in city centers (city clouds or Wi-Fi hotspots), 309–310
HotSpot Haven, The, hotspot Web site, 304
hotspots. *See* Wi-Fi hotspots
Hotsync, 276–279
HP (Hewlett Packard) portable printers, 258
Hyatt hotels with Wi-Fi hotspots, 308

I

icons used in this book, 5
ICS (Internet Connection Sharing) feature, 232
IEEE (Institute of Electronic and Electrical Engineers) standard, 28, 35, 151, 195
iGo Mobility Electronics, Inc., 257
images. *See also* photos
  through media servers, 410
IMfree instant messaging
  abbreviations and emoticons, 433–435
  AOL with, 419, 432
  avoiding interference, 431–433
  batteries and charging, 420
  configuring software options, 423–425
  connecting base station to PC, 422
  cost, capacity, and range, 419
  creating AIM screen name, 425–428
  installing AOL Instant Messenger software, 428–430
  installing software on PC, 420–422
  keyboard use, 430–431
  powering up and registering, 422–423
  running software, 422
  security considerations, 425
  sessions on PC, 431
  smileys, 433
  starting chat session, 431
IMs, instant messages. *See* IMfree instant messaging
in-network and out-of-network calling areas for cell phones, 342
  roaming charges, 342
  zip code, 342
Incoming Virtual Private Network (VPN) Connection dialog box, 321
infrastructure mode networks, 114, 147, 148, 156
instant messaging. *See also* IMfree instant messaging
  One-way Instant Messaging feature of SmartWatch, 329
integrated Ethernet switch ports, 42, 61–62
IntelliMouse Explorer, 365–366
interference. *See* obstacles and interference considerations
interlaced horizontal scan lines in HDTV, 462
Internet access
  AirCards, 13–14
  dial-up versus high-speed wireless connection, 9, 17, 38
  DSL (digital subscriber line), 17, 38, 39
  satellite service, 18–21
  3G (third-generation) networks, 17
Internet camera, D-Link Securicam DCS-5300G, 406
Internet Connection Sharing (ICS) feature, 232
Internet Protocol (TCP/IP) Properties window, 108–109
Internet radio, 260, 398, 402, 411

Internet relay chat (IRC), 432
Internet service providers (ISPs), 38
interoperability issues
  importance of compatible standards for equipment, 36
  between platforms with Bluetooth, 377
intranets (internal networks), 75
IP Address Pool. *See* DHCP (Dynamic Host Configuration Protocol)
IP addresses. *See also* DHCP servers
  assigning dynamic, 76–80
  assigning manually for wireless network adapters, 107–109
  assigning static, 81–83
  comparing static and dynamic, 74–75
  described, 74
  of gateways to broadband Internet connection, 75
  obtaining new with ipconfig /renew command, 242
  releasing with ipconfig /release command, 241
  of routers, factory-configured, 51
  troubleshooting incorrect, 236
  troubleshooting misconfigured on wireless network adapters, 121
  troubleshooting with tracert command, 244–245
iPAQ For Dummies (Wiley Publishing), 504
ipconfig command, 82, 239–242
IRC (Internet relay chat), 432
ISPs (Internet service providers), 38
iTune music store (Apple), 400

J

Jens of Sweden Excentrique, 410
JiWire hotspot Web site, 303, 305
joysticks, 370

K

Kenwood Entr_ Entertainment Hub, 411
keyboards, wireless, 368–369. *See also* peripherals, wireless
Kinko's print shops, 259
Kismet, 190

L

Labtec webcams, 417
LAN (local-area network), 236, 372
land-mobile radio service, 361
laptops for home use, 260
laptops for mobile computing
  caution against ignoring user's manual for wireless cards, 251
  caution against running up usage charges, 253
  activating card for use with cellular network, 252–253
  adapters for wireless networks, 31–32
  advantages of going wireless, 27, 249
  connecting to GPS with Bluetooth, 373
  extending battery life by turning off wireless card, 252
  finding Wi-Fi hotspots, 253, 255–256
  Hawking Technology Wi-Fi Locator as alternative to wireless network card, 255–256
  options for printing from, 258–260
  options for speed and cost, 250–251
  power considerations, 256–257
  security considerations, 253
  troubleshooting adapter card fit, 130
  wireless cellular data cards, 252–253
  wireless network cards, 253–254
latency on cordless game controllers, 369
lava lamp, Laserpod, 410

law enforcement use of LocatePlus database with Blackberry, 299
LCD flat panel HDTV sets, 463
LCD rear-projection HDTV sets, 463
lease time (DHCP setting on wireless router), 76
letterboxing, 522
limited account type, 206
line-of-sight considerations
  for LMDS (local multipoint distribution system), 22
  for satellite service Internet access, 18
Linksys devices
  webcam WVC54G Wireless-G Internet Video Camera, 417
  Wireless-B Internet Video Camera, 406
  Wireless-B Media Adapter, 405
  Wireless-B Music System, 402
  Wireless-G Game Adapter, 406
  Wireless-G PrintServer, 65
  wireless network adapter card, 94–96, 117–120, 123–124
  WMLS11B Wireless-B Music System, 411
Linux, 2. *See also* operating systems other than Windows XP
LMDS (local multipoint distribution system), 22
local-area network (LAN), 236, 372
local multipoint distribution system (LMDS), 22
LocatePlus database, 299
Logitech devices
  Bluetooth-enabled peripherals, 377
  diNovo Media Desktop, 376, 377
  webcams, 417
longitude, latitude, coordinates and geometry (GPS technology), 508–511
Los Angeles International airport hotspots, 307
lottery results feature of SmartWatch, 329

M

M3U music format, 399
MAC (Media Access Control) security with routers
  described, 43, 58–59
  displayed in NetStumbler, 177
  implementing, 188–189
  troubleshooting, 232–233, 236
Mac users
  AirPort Express, 404
  Bluetooth-enabled peripherals, 377
  Bluetooth-equipped computers, 373
  Bluetooth keyboard and mouse, 377
  iTune music store, 400, 404
  Mac OS X, 2
  moving files between PC and Mac with Bluetooth, 382–385
  StarBand satellite service Internet access unavailable, 18
Mailboxes, Etc. outlets with hotspots, 306, 311
management interface, resetting for wireless routers, 128, 234, 235, 236
manufacturer's mail-in rebates, 32
Map Network Drive Wizard, 442–443, 444–445
mapping, 442
Marriott hotels with Wi-Fi hotspots, 308
master/slave devices in Bluetooth, 375
McDonald's with Wi-Fi hotspots, 306, 311
media hubs, 397
media players. *See also* accessories; file sharing with Windows XP
  AlphaSmart Dana Wireless word processor, 406
  Apple AirPort Express, 404
  D-Link DVC-1100 Wireless Broadband Video Phone, 406
  D-Link MediaLounge Wireless Media Player, 403

media players *(continued)*
D-Link Securicam DCS-5300G Internet Camera, 406
described, 397
on Ethernet networks, 401
example of simple setup, 398
Gateway Connected DVD Player, 403
Jens of Sweden Excentrique, 410
Linksys Wireless-B Internet Video Camera, 406
Linksys Wireless-B Media Adapter, 405
Linksys Wireless-B Music System, 402
Linksys Wireless-G Game Adapter, 406
media servers, 410–412
movies and streaming video, 400–401
music, 398–399
Netgear Wireless Digital Music Player, 402
photo organizers, 399–400
Play@TV, 405
PRISMIQ MediaPlayer, 403–404, 411, 412–416
Rhapsody Digital Music Service, 402
Rockford Omnifi DMP1 mobile digital media player, 407
Rockford Omnifi DMS1 Digital Media Streamer, 405
Roku SoundBridge, 405
Sound Blaster Wireless Music, 403
user interface, TV, LED or LCD screen, and remote control, 401
media servers
definitions and types of services, 410–411
manufacturers, 411–412
MediaLounge DSM-320 Wireless Media Player (D-Link), 403, 411
MediaPlayer (PRISMIQ), 403–404, 411, 412–416
memory keys (USB), 259
messages, sending and receiving wirelessly, 14. *See also* IMfree instant messaging
messaging services with cell phones, 346–347
Mexico, Cabo San Lucas, webcam view, 417
mice. *See* peripherals, wireless
Microsoft ActiveSync, 274
Microsoft Bluetooth-enabled peripherals, 377
Microsoft SmartWatch. *See* SmartWatch
Microtel Inns & Suites with Wi-Fi hotspots, 308–309
microwave ovens, as source of interference with wireless network signals, 29, 456
microwaves, with LMDS (local multipoint distribution system), 22
Milner, Marius, 176
mini-PCI adapters, 31, 33, 130
MMS (Multimedia messaging service) for cell phones, 346
Mobile 2003 (Windows XP), 263
mobile computing. *See also* GPS (global positioning service) receivers; laptops for mobile computing
airports
with hotspot Internet services, 307–308
Sprint hotspot sites, 307
T-Mobile hotspot sites, 305
Wayport hotspot provider, 306
wireless networks in, 158
checking signal strength, 158
RVs
GPS-equipped laptops in, 503
StarBand satellite service Internet access for, 19
mobility, 27

modems
  broadband, 39–40
  cable modems for Internet access, 17, 38
  connecting to routers, 49–50
  internal versus USB port modems, 40
  troubleshooting, 236–238
motion sensors. *See* Motorola Home Monitoring and Control System
Motorola Home Monitoring and Control System
  caution on use as home security system substitute, 483
  archives, 491
  arming or disarming system, 491–492
  batteries, 486
  camera and sensor capacity, 484
  configuring software, 488–491
  door/window sensors, 483, 489
  download site for drivers, 485
  e-mail from, 490, 491
  editing sensor parameters, 489–490
  events/alerts settings, 490–491
  features, 483
  hardware setup, 485–486
  installing software, 486–488
  kit contents, 483
  motion sensors, 489
  other components, 483–484
  range, 484
  remote service, 485
  sound sensors, 489
  temperature sensors, 484, 489
  updating software, 488
  viewing alert log, 491
  water sensors, 484
Motorola IMfree instant messaging. *See* IMfree instant messaging
Mount St. Helens, Forest Service webcam view, 417
movie file transfers, size considerations, 438
movies and streaming video, 400–401
MP3 music format, 399
MPG video format, 400
MSN Direct Calendar Add-in for Outlook, 336–337
MSN Direct network, 325, 326
multi-standard devices, 37–38
multimedia servers, 397, 437. *See also* media players
music. *See also* media players
  formats, 399
  media players, 398–399, 402
  from Sirius and XM Radio satellite radio services, 467
  streaming devices, 397
  through media servers, 410
MX 700 Cordless Optical Mouse, 366–367
My Bluetooth Places icon, 381
My Network Places
  adding to or removing from Start menu, 146–147
  browsing shared folders, 446
  managing bridges, 160–164

N

navigation with GPS. *See* GPS (global positioning service) receivers
Netgear Wireless Digital Music Player, 402
NetStumbler
  described, 176
  downloading and installing, 176–177
  used as sniffer, 190
  using, 177–180
network adapters, 160. *See also* adapters
Network Connection Type dialog box, 321
Network Connections dialog box, 193, 316–318, 319, 320
Network Controller Properties dialog box, 225–226

Network and Internet Connections dialog box, 316–318
network keys, 151, 197
Networking Software dialog box, 322
networks. *See* wireless networks
Nevada Department of Transportation (NDOT) use of webcam, 416
New Connection Wizard, 318, 320–323
New York City's Wi-Fi hotspots, 309
news feature of SmartWatch, 328, 330
Nextel, 288, 343, 505
900 MHz cordless telephones, 354–355, 431
900 MHz digital unlicensed radio spectrum, for IMfree instant messaging, 431
NodeDB.com hotspot Web site, 304
Notebook Solar Laptop Computer Charger, 257–258

O

obstacles and interference considerations. *See also* troubleshooting wireless networks
  baby monitors, 357
  causing intermittent connection issues, 128–129
  cordless telephones, 29, 229, 352, 353, 354, 355, 357, 456
  IMfree instant messaging, 431–433
  line-of-sight considerations
    for LMDS (local multipoint distribution system), 22
    for satellite service Internet access, 18
  Logitech Cordless RumblePad, 370
  microwave ovens, 357, 456
  TiVo units, 456
  of wireless networks, 27–29, 125, 229
octets in IP addresses, 75
Omni hotels with Wi-Fi hotspots, 308
omnidirectional antennae, 45
Omnifi DMP1 mobile digital media player (Rockford), 407
Omnifi DMS1 Digital Media Streamer (Rockford), 405
One-way Instant Messaging feature of SmartWatch, 329
online auction sites, 32, 40
online stores, 32
operating systems other than Windows XP
  Bluetooth offering interoperability, 377
  timing of installing wireless network client software, 89, 94
  timing of wireless network hardware installation, 96
  upgrading to XP recommended, 146
  USB wireless network adapters, 101
Optical Mouse, 366
Optical Mouse for Notebooks, 367
Outlook e-mail client feature software, 336–338

P

packet data networks. *See* cellular-based packet data networks
packets, 242
pairing of Bluetooth devices, 379
Palm PDAs. *See also* Pocket PCs
  advantages, 261
  configuring, 267–268
  configuring for VPN, 270–271
  confirming settings, 269–270
  connecting to GPS with Bluetooth, 373
  connecting to VPN, 272
  making connection, 270
  synchronizing with desktop with HotSync, 276–279
  synchronizing information with Bluetooth, 388
Palm Tungsten C, 267
PANs (personal area networks), 372

paper distances, 375
passwords
for access points, 63–64
for routers, 51–52, 53–54
for Windows XP, 214–217
PC cards
for Bluetooth, 373
described, 31, 32, 33
PCI (peripheral component interconnect) adapters. *See also* wireless network adapters
compared to adapter-style cards, 86
described, 31, 33
installing, 86–89
installing adapter utilities, 94–96
installing client software *prior* to physically installing card, 94–96
installing drivers, 89–93
troubleshooting, 130
two styles of, 86, 87
PCs. *See also* Windows XP
moving outside without wires, 10
taking case off, 85, 87
Wi-Fi standard, 13
wireless peripherals for, 363–370
PDAs (personal digital assistants). *See also* Palm PDAs; Pocket PCs
advantages, 261–262
for sending and receiving text messages, 14
usefulness prediction, 22, 261
PDOP (Position Dilution Of Precision), 498
peer-to-peer (ad-hoc mode or computer-to-computer) networks, 114, 147–148, 156, 254
performance considerations
DirecWay satellite service Internet access, 21
eliminating PC bottlenecks by sharing printers, 65
LMDS (local multipoint distribution system), 22
StarBand satellite service Internet access, 18–19
WiMax, 21–22
peripheral component interconnect (PCI) adapters, 31, 33
peripherals, wireless. *See also* accessories
advantages, 11
base stations, USB ports and cables, 363
Bluetooth-enabled, 376–377
described, 363
game controllers and joysticks, 369–370
IntelliMouse Explorer, 365–366
keyboards, 368–369
Logitech's success, 364
MX 700 Cordless Optical Mouse, 366–367
Optical Mouse, 366
Optical Mouse for Notebooks, 367
Presenter (for remote control of presentations), 367
shared printers, 65, 165–170
Tilt Wheel Technology for optical mice, 366
trackballs, 368
personal area networks (PANs), 372
personal digital recorders (PVRs), 448
Peugeot Quark fuel cell-powered concept vehicle, 410
phones. *See also* cell phones; cordless telephones
advantages of conventional wired units in power outages, 12
photo organizers, 399–400
photos, through media servers, 410
photos, sending to PC with Bluetooth, 389–391
Photoshop Album (Adobe), 400

Picasa photo organizer software (Google), 400
piconets in Bluetooth, 375
pilots' use of GPS, 501
ping command, 242–243
plasma HDTV sets, 463
Play@TV, 405
PLS music format, 399
Pocket PC For Dummies (Wiley Publishing), 264, 504
Pocket PCs. *See also* Palm PDAs
  advantages, 10, 261–262
  connecting to GPS with Bluetooth, 373, 503
  connecting GPS units to, 504
  connecting to wireless network, 262–263
  Dell Axim 30 model, 262–266
  Dell Site Monitor, 266
  Dell WLAN utility, 265–266
  manually configuring settings, 263–264
  moving files and synchronizing information with Bluetooth, 385–388
  pocketWinc (Cirond utility), 267, 503–504
  synchronizing with desktop with Microsoft ActiveSync, 274–275
pocketWinc (Cirond utility), 267, 503–504
Point-to-Point Protocol over Ethernet (PPPoE), 55
Point-to-Point Tunneling Protocol (PPTP), 55, 237
police use of LocatePlus database with Blackberry, 299
portable printers, 258–259
power outages, 12
power supply for laptops for mobile computing, 257
PPPoE (Point-to-Point Protocol over Ethernet), 55
PPTP (Point-to-Point Tunneling Protocol), 55, 237
preferred networks, 111–113, 153–155
Presenter (for remote control of presentations), 367
price, versus performance standards, 12
prime meridian, 509
print servers, wireless
  advantages, 64–65
  advantages of static IP address, 81
  configuring changes through management interface, 72
  configuring drivers, 70–71
  configuring via web browser, 71–72
  connecting, 66–67
  in routers, 43
  running Setup Wizard, 67–71
printers, portable, 258–259
Printers and Faxes dialog box, 165–170
printers, sharing
  adding printers connected to other PCs on network, 167–169
  advantages, 65
  changing default printer, 169–170
  specifying printers for sharing, 165–166
  turning off sharing, 167
printing services, 259
PrintMe printing service, 259
PRISMIQ MediaPlayer, 403–404, 411, 412–416
problem solving. *See* troubleshooting wireless networks
progressive scan in HDTV, 462
public radio, from Sirius and XM Radio satellite radio services, 467
PVRs (personal digital recorders), 448
PY Software, Active WebCam, 417

Q

Quark fuel cell-powered concept car by Peugeot, 410
Quote of the Day feature of SmartWatch, 330

R

radio
broadcasts to MSN Direct subscribers, 326–327
Citizens Band Radio Services, 360, 362
Family Radio Service (FRS) two-way radios
advantages, 10, 359
channels for geocachers, 521
combining with GPS, 362
comparison to cell phones, 360–361
FCC's rules, 359, 360
GMRS (General Mobile Radio Service), 360, 361
range, 360
General Mobile Radio Service (GMRS), 360, 361
from Internet, 260, 398, 402, 411
satellite, 466–467
through media servers, 411
two-way Family Radio Service (FRS), 10, 359–362
wireless, 11
RADIUS servers, 199
range
antennae adjustment or replacement, 44
Bluetooth-connected peripherals, 365, 375, 388
capacity, 484
comparison of FRS and GMRS radio, 361
cordless mice and Bluetooth peripherals, 364–365
cordless telephones and frequencies, 352
for HDTV, 465
locating wireless networks, 44
Motorola Home Monitoring and Control System, 484
for Wi-Fi hotspots, 13
of wireless networks, 27–29
wireless networks range extenders, 27, 32, 44
rebates, manufacturer's mail-in rebates, 32
rechargeable batteries, 12
redundancy
ad-hoc mode (computer-to-computer or peer-to-peer) networks for, 148
cable plus wireless Internet access, 151
REMEMBER icon, 5
ReplayTV, 448
reverse SMA plugs, 43, 45
Rhapsody Digital Music Service, 402
Rino GPS (global positioning service) receivers, 362
Rio Rancho, New Mexico's Wi-Fi hotspots, 309
roaming charges with cell phones, 342, 360
Rockford Omnifi DMP1 mobile digital media player, 407
Rockford Omnifi DMS1 Digital Media Streamer, 405
Roku SoundBridge, 405
Rome, webcam view from Capitolium.org, 416
routers, wireless
caution against removing housing, 128
access points as alternative, 41–42
antennae considerations, 44–45
configuring, 50–53
configuring access points, 63–64
configuring WPA Security, 195–196
cost considerations, 30
date, time, and time zone information, 54–55
determining IP address assigned, 82
DHCP component, disabling or enabling, 109

routers, wireless *(continued)*
DHCP server feature, 73–74
DHCP settings, 76–78
factory default settings, resetting to, 128, 129, 234, 235, 236
features, 42–43
firmware upgrades, 133–138
firmware upgrades for WPA support, 195
going online, 55–57
locating, 44
MAC (Media Access Control) security or cloning, 43, 58–59
naming (resetting SSID), 59–60, 236
passwords, 51–52, 53–54
range considerations, 27–29
resetting management interface, 128, 234, 235, 236
security and upgrade support, 43
timeout value, 53
troubleshooting, 128–129, 235–236
troubleshooting with tracert command, 244–245
routers, wireless connecting, 47–50
RS-TX20 Digital Media Server (Toshiba), 411
Russia's global navigation system, 499
RVs
GPS-equipped laptops in, 503
StarBand satellite service Internet access for, 19

S

SanDisk MiniCruzer, 259
satellite radio, 466–467
satellite service Internet access, 18–21
bandwidth and fair use policies, 20
DirecWay (formerly DirecPC), 20–21
disadvantages, 18
StarBand, 18–20
WiMax, 21–22
satellite TV, 464, 465–466
scatternets in Bluetooth, 375
Seattle's Wi-Fi hotspots, 309
Securicam DCS-5300G Internet Camera (D-Link), 406
security considerations. *See also* Motorola Home Monitoring and Control System
caution on inherent insecurity of wireless technology, 393
access points' security settings, 64
administration and user accounts, 205–220
advantages of VPNs, 315, 316
alerts, diagnostics, and Buddy List, 425
Bluetooth risks, 392–393
configuring print server's IP address manually, 69
configuring wireless network adapters IP address manually, 109
cordless telephones with DSS (digital spread spectrum), 352
disabling automatic connection to non-preferred networks, 114–115
guest accounts, 206, 219–220
hackers and crackers, 184–185, 189–190
IMfree instant messaging, 425
laptops for mobile computing, 253
MAC (Media Access Control) with routers, 43, 188–189
making SSID invisible, 186–188
network keys, 151, 197
900 MHz cordless telephones, 354–355
overview, 184
passwords, 214–217
personalizing access point password, 63–64
personalizing router password, 51–52, 53–54
private webcams to monitor homes, 417
routers, 183

security updates to Windows XP, 200
static IP addressing, 81
staying current with patches and updates for hardware and software, 199–200
of updating drivers, 202
uselessness of firewalls, 183
user accounts, 205
war driving, 184–185
wireless home computer networks, 14–15
of wireless Internet access using public hotspots, 312–313
security systems. *See* Motorola Home Monitoring and Control System
Select Columns dialog box, 175–176
Selective Availability and Selective Deniability of GPS signals, 498
Service Set Identifier (SSID), 59–60, 63, 111
Setup Wizard, 67–71
780p resolution on HDTV, 462
Shared Documents folder, 438
sharing computer accessories and files. *See* file sharing with Windows XP; wireless networks
Shell HomeGenie service, 485, 488
Sheraton hotels with Wi-Fi hotspots, 308
shopping for wireless network hardware, 32
short messaging service (SMS), described, 14
sidebars, 3
Sidekick II from T-Mobile, 300–301
Sierra Solar Systems, 257
Sierra Wireless AirCard, 252
signal strength. *See also* obstacles and interference considerations
checking, 157–158, 172–173
checking status for wireless network adapters, 121, 125
degradation with distance, 125
monitoring of nearby access points with NetStumbler, 176–180
needed for video and audio files, 402
signal-to-noise ratio (SNR), 266
when to check, 171
Sirius satellite radio, 467
16:9 aspect ratio on HDTV, 462–463
SMA plugs, reverse, 43, 45
SmartWatch
caution on checking in when traveling, 327
choosing among models, 325–326
coverage considerations, 327
Glance mode, cycling through channels, 338
installing Outlook e-mail client feature software, 336–338
personalizing services, 333–336
recharging battery, 326
registering, 331–333
WristNet channels, 328–331
SMC
Barricade wireless router with built-in print server component, 66, 134–138
EZ-Stream wireless network adapter, 37–38
SMS (Short messaging service)
for cell phones, 346
described, 14
from PC with Bluetooth, 373
sniffing out of wireless networks by hackers and crackers, 184–185, 189–190
SNR (signal-to-noise ratio), 266
software. *See also* Windows XP
Active WebCam from PY Software, 417
described, 200
Trillian, 432
solar power unit, 257–258
Sony AIBO robotic dog, 410
Sound Blaster Wireless Music, 403
SoundBridge (Roku), 405

South Pole, live webcam view of the current conditions, 416
speakerphone feature on cordless telephones, 356
speakers, wireless, as sources of interference with wireless network signals, 29
speed. *See also* obstacles and interference considerations
  adjusting between router and wireless network adapters, 125
  Bluetooth, 375
  checking status for wireless network adapters, 121, 125
  considerations for laptops for mobile computing, 250–251
  degradation with distance, 125
speed. *See* performance considerations
Spokane's Wi-Fi hotspots, 309
sports broadcasts from Sirius satellite radio service, 467
sports feature of SmartWatch, 329
SPOT (Smart Personal Objects Technology), 326
Sprint
  airport hotspot sites, 307
  national cell phone service provider, 343
  PCS Network, 14
  wireless network, 250
SSID (Service Set Identifier)
  described, 59–60, 63, 111
  disabled, 229
  displayed in NetStumbler, 177
  making invisible as security precaution, 186–188
  troubleshooting, 236, 238
St. Cloud, Florida's Wi-Fi hotspots, 309
StarBand satellite service Internet access, 18–20
Starbucks as T-Mobile hotspot site, 305, 311
Start IP (DHCP setting on wireless router), 76
stateful firewalls, 42
static IP addresses, 75, 81–83
steel, as obstacle for wireless networks signals, 29
stock quotes feature of SmartWatch, 329
streaming video, 400–401
subnet masks, 75
Suuntro SmartWatches, 325, 326
switches (with commands from Command Prompt), 240

T

T-Mobile
  Blackberry carrier, 288
  hotspot finder utility, 306
  hotspot provider, 305
  national cell phone service provider, 343
  security cautions from, 312–313
Task Manager, 174–176
TCP/IP settings
  for access points, 64
  Internet Protocol (TCP/IP) Properties window, 108–109
  for TiVo units, 452–453
  troubleshooting, 229–232, 238
  troubleshooting with ping command, 242–243
Technical Stuff icon, 3, 5
telephones. *See also* cell phones; cordless telephones
  advantages of conventional wired units in power outages, 12
televisions. *See* TVs
temperature sensors. *See* Motorola Home Monitoring and Control System; weather forecasting
1080i resolution on HDTV, 462

tendency of air pressure (weather forecasts), 469
text messages, sending and receiving wirelessly, 14
Think Outside Bluetooth-enabled peripherals, 377
3G (third-generation) networks, 17
This Day in History feature of SmartWatch, 330
Tilt Wheel Technology for optical mice, 366
time, date, and time zone information, for routers, 54–55
timeout value for routers, 53
timepieces. *See* SmartWatch
TIP icon, 5
TiVo units
  advantages, 447, 449
  alternatives to, 448
  configuring, 450–452
  configuring TCP/IP settings, 452–453
  connecting to network, 449–450
  creating peer-to-peer network, 450, 457
  dial-up phone line connection, 453, 457
  obstacles and interference considerations, 456
  switching to broadband access, 453–454
  testing broadband connection, 454–455
  troubleshooting broadband connection, 455–456
  USB wireless adapters, restricted list of, 456
Toshiba RS-TX20 Digital Media Server, 411
tracert command, 244–245
trackballs, 368
traffic conditions, webcam view of, 416
travel with wireless networking. *See* GPS (global positioning service) receivers; mobile computing
Trillian, 432
troubleshooting wireless networks. *See also* obstacles and interference considerations
  access points, 129–130
  adapter cards, 130–133
  advantages of methodical and structured approach, 222–223
  connections and fully seated plug-ins, 227
  determining current status of network adapter card, 131–132, 224–227
  disabled DHCP server component, 229–231
  disabled network adapter (or wrong driver, or misconfigured), 225–227
  disabled SSID broadcast setting, 229
  enabled MAC address security, 232–233
  enabled WEP encryption, 233
  enabled WPA encryption, 233–234
  inability to connect to Internet, 234–235
  interference, 229
  with ipconfig command, 82, 239–242
  by looking in user manuals of wireless hardware devices, 239
  MAC address security, 232–233, 236
  mini-PCI adapters, 130
  missing driver, 227
  missing wireless network, 227–228
  modems, 236–238
  multiple DHCP servers, 231
  other devices/hardware, 238–239
  out-of-range condition, 228
  with ping command, 242–243
  returning to previous version of driver (driver rollback), 132, 226
  routers, 128–129, 235–236
  TCP/IP settings, 229–232
  with tracert command, 244–245
  typical problems, 221
  updating drivers, 138–141

troubleshooting wireless networks *(continued)*
updating utilities, 141–142
upgrading router or access point firmware, 134–138, 202
utilities/client software, 229
WEP encryption, 233, 236, 238
whether Windows XP "sees" wireless network adapter, 224–225, 227
truck stops, with Wi-Fi hotspots, 311
turntables, 12
TVs. *See also* HDTV (high-definition TV)
display of pictures and video on Play@TV, 405
PRISMIQ MediaPlayer, 403–404, 411, 412–416
program recording/playback with SnapStream Personal Video Station application, 412
programs or movies through media servers, 411
TiVo units, 447–460
transmitters, wireless as sources of interference with wireless network signals, 29
turning off with TV-B-Gone, 409
two-way Family Radio Service (FRS). *See* Family Radio Service (FRS) two-way radios
2.4 GHz frequency band
Bluetooth, 374
cordless telephones, 355

U

Underdahl, Brian, 504
UPS outlets with hotspots, 306, 311
USB hubs, 97, 98
USB memory keys, 259
USB overload, 98
USB port modems, 40
USB ports and cables for wireless peripherals, 363
USB wireless network adapters. *See also* wireless network adapters
advantages, 96
for Bluetooth, 373, 379–381
described, 32
disadvantages, 85
as hot-swappable, 98
installing, 96–98
installing driver, 99–101
installing utilities, 101–102
on non-Windows XP systems, 101
user accounts, managing, 207–219
User Permissions dialog box, 322
utilities with wireless networks adapter cards
for checking connection status, 123–124
configuring on operating systems other than Windows XP, 116–120
installing, 94–96, 101–102
troubleshooting, 229
upgrading, 141–142

V

vehicles, Peugeot Quark fuel cell-powered concept car, 410
vendors, importance of compatible standards for equipment, 36
Verizon Wireless
Blackberry carrier, 288
hotspot provider, 307
national cell phone service providers, 343
wireless network, 250
video cameras
Linksys Wireless-B Internet Video Camera, 406, 417
webcams, 416–417
video file transfers, size considerations, 438

video phone, D-Link DVC-1100 Wireless Broadband Video Phone, 406
video streaming, 400–401
virtual private network (VPN) connections, described, 270
virtual private networks (VPN). *See* VPNs (virtual private networks)
voice over IP (voIP) applications, not recommended for StarBand residential services, 20
Voom (satellite TV service), 466
VPNs (virtual private networks)
  configuring Palm for, 271
  connecting to, with Palm, 272
  connecting to remote computer, 319–320
  creating incoming connection, 320–323
  described, 270
  disconnecting from remote computer, 320
  security advantages, 315, 316
  setting up connection, 316–318
  unavailable over StarBand residential services, 20

W

WAN (wide-area network), 236
WARNING! icon, 5
Washington D.C.'s Wi-Fi hotspots, 309
watches. *See* SmartWatch
water sensors. *See* Motorola Home Monitoring and Control System; weather forecasting
WAV music format, 399
waypoints (GPS), creating and using, 515–517
Wayport hotspot provider, 306
weather considerations of satellite service Internet access, 18
weather feature of SmartWatch, 330
weather forecasting with Professional Weather Station 2310 (La Crosse Technology)
  batteries, 472
  cost, frequency, update rate, 469, 470
  hardware setup, 471–472
  installing and using Heavy Weather Publisher for sharing reports on Web site, 478–481
  installing and using Heavy Weather Review software for graphical representations, 475–478
  installing and using Heavy Weather software for real-time information display, 473–475
  rain, wind, and thermo-hygro (temperature and humidity) sensors, 470, 471
  settable alarms, 472
  solar powered and wired electrical, 471
  update interval for Web site updates, 480
Weather Underground, 480
Web-based e-mail, through media servers, 411
Web browsing, through media servers, 411
Web In-Flight hotspot Web site, 304
Web sites
  Adobe Photoshop Album, 400
  AIM (AOL Instant Messenger), 426
  ALK Technologies, 504
  AllAboutCabo.com, 417
  Anywhere Map (GPS mapping) from Control Vision, 501
  AvantGo, 280
  Blackberry, 288
  bluesnarfing-vulnerable phones, 393
  Bluetooth, 371
  Boingo Wireless hotspot provider, 305
  Cabo San Lucas, Mexico, webcam view, 417

Web sites *(continued)*
Caffeinated and Unstrung (Seattle), 310
Caltrans, 416
Cell-Block-R, 409
Cirond, 267
Climate Monitoring and Diagnostics Laboratory, 416
Cobra GPS units, 502
Consumer Electronics Association, 462
Control Vision, 501
D-Link, 403
D-Link webcams, 417
DeLorme GPS receivers, 497
designed for small web browsers like Blackberry, 299
downloadable free cell phone ringtones, 346
eFax (Internet-based fax service), 260
FCC site on cell phone number portability, 348–349
FCC wireless services sites, 360, 362
FDA site on safety of cell phones, 347
FedEx Kinko's print shops, 259
Forest Service webcam view of Mount St. Helens, 417
forums for users of SmartWatches, 326
Garmin GPS units, 496, 502
Gateway, 403
geocaching, 520
GeoGen Project, 523
Geographic Names Information System (GNIS) site, 525–526
GPS manufacturers, 504
GPS precision information, 498
GPS Waypoint Registry, 517
Hawking Technology webcams, 417
Hawking Technology Wi-Fi Locator, 255–256
HDTV, local antenna/range information, 465
Heavy Weather, 473, 474, 476
IEEE (Institute of Electronic and Electrical Engineers), 151
iGo Mobility Electronics, Inc., 257
Internet radio station, 398
Kenwood Entré Entertainment Hub, 411
letterboxing, 522
Linksys, 402
Linksys WMLS11B Wireless-B Music System, 411
Linksys WVC54G Wireless-G Internet Video Camera, 417
list of wireless networking utilities, 190
lists of Wi-Fi hotspots, 255
Logitech, 366
Logitech webcams, 417
Magellan GPS units, 502
Microsoft ActiveSync, 274
Microsoft Pocket PCs, 264
Mount St. Helens, Forest Service webcam view, 417
MSN Direct, 331
NetStumbler, 176
Nextel TeleNav GPS, 505
NOAA Climate Monitoring and Diagnostics Laboratory, 416
Omnifi Media, 405
online version of XP's Resource Kit, 132
Peugeot Quark fuel cell-powered concept vehicle, 410
Pharos GPS, 504
Picasa photo organizer software (Google), 400
PocketMapStore, 504
PrintMe printing service, 259
PRISMIQ, 403–404, 411
Rockford Corp., 405
Roku Labs, 405
Rome, webcam view from Capitolium.org, 416
SanDisk, 259
Shell HomeGenie service, 485, 488

Sierra Solar Systems, 257
Sierra Wireless, 252
Sony AIBO robotic dog, 410
South Pole, live webcam view of the current conditions, 416
Sprint, 307
Teletype, 504
Toshiba RS-TX20 Digital Media Server, 411
traffic conditions, webcam view of, 416
TV-B-Gone, 410
U.S. GeoGen Project, 523
Verizon Wireless, 307
war driving, 185
Wayport hotspot provider, 306
weather forecasts, 473
Weather Underground, 480
webcam view of progress of major highway extension project, 416
Wi-Fi-FreeSpot Directory, 13
Wi-Fi hotspots directories, 303–304
Windows Updates, 200, 201
webcams, 416–417
WEP (Wired Equivalent Privacy) encryption protocol support on routers
configuring Windows XP client systems, 193
described, 43, 122, 190
disadvantages, 190–191
enabling on routers, 191–193
reconnecting to network, 193–194
specifying, 153
troubleshooting, 233, 236, 238
Wi-Fi-FreeSpot Directory Web site, 13, 304
Wi-Fi hotspots
in city centers (city clouds or hot zones), 309–310
commercial providers, 305–307
described, 13
directories of, 303–304
finding with GPS-eqipped laptop, 503–504
finding for laptops for mobile computing, 255–256
in major airports, 307–308
in major hotel chains, 308–309
in retailers' premises, 311
in stadiums and arenas, 311
ubiquity, cost, and range considerations, 250–251
worldwide proliferation, 310
Wi-Fi Marine hotspot Web site, 304
Wi-Fi standard
described, 13
possible conflicts with some cordless telephones, 354
WiMax incompatibility, 22
Wi-Fi Zone Finder hotspot Web site, 304
Wi-FiHotSpotList.com hotspot Web site, 304
Wide-Area Augmentation System (WAAS) of GPS signals, 498
wide-area network (WAN), 236
WiFi Locator by Hawking Technology, 255–256
WiFiMaps.com hotspot Web site, 304
WiMax (world interoperability for microwave access), 21–22
Winc for configuring laptop security options, 253–254, 255
window/door sensors. *See* Motorola Home Monitoring and Control System
window glass, as obstacle for wireless networks signals, 29
Windows 2000. *See* operating systems other than Windows XP
Windows 98. *See* operating systems other than Windows XP

Windows XP. *See also* operating systems other than Windows XP; wireless networking with Windows XP
Add Bluetooth Device Wizard, 382–383
automatic private IP address default, 79–80
Automatic Updates, configuring for, 200–202
Bluetooth discovery setting, 378–379
Bluetooth File Transfer Wizard, 384–385, 389–391
Bluetooth support in Service Pack 2 (SP2), 379
Command Prompt, 240
Device Manager, 115–116, 131–133, 139–140, 224–227
drivers for hardware, 90
file sharing, 437, 438–446
"Found New Hardware" message, 90, 99
Found New Hardware Wizard, 91–92, 99–101, 487
Hardware Update Wizard, 140–141, 226
IMfree instant messaging icon, 422
Internet Connection Sharing (ICS) feature, 38, 232
ipconfig command, 82, 239–242
Map Network Drive Wizard, 442–443, 444–445
Mobile 2003, 263
My Bluetooth Places icon, 381
My Network Places, 146–147, 160–164, 446
Network Bridge, 62
New Connection Wizard, 318, 320–323
passwords for access, 214–217
ping command, 242–243
plug and play feature, 145, 146
Properties dialog box, 439, 440
recommended for wireless networks, 2
security updates, 200
service packs, 195, 202, 379
Setup Wizard, 67–71
Shared Documents folder, 438
Task Manager, 174–176
taskbar icon, Wireless Network Connection, 81–83
tracert command, 244–245
User Accounts, 207–220
"Wireless Network Detected" message, 92–93
Wireless Zero Configuration, 94, 103, 111
WPA support in Service Pack 2 (SP2), 195, 202
WINS server (DHCP setting on wireless router), 77
Wireless-B Internet Video Camera (Linksys), 406
Wireless-B Media Adapter (Linksys), 405
Wireless-B Music System (Linksys), 402, 411
Wireless Digital Music Player (Netgear), 402
Wireless-G Game Adapter (Linksys), 406
Wireless-G Internet Video Camera (Linksys), 417
wireless network adapters. *See also* PCI (peripheral component interconnect) adapters; USB wireless network adapters
adding, removing, or selecting preferred networks, 111–113
assigning IP addresses manually, 107–109
automatically connecting to non-preferred networks, 114–115
checking connection status, 109, 120–121
checking connection status with adapter's utilities, 123–124
configuring on operating systems other than Windows XP with adapter's utilities, 116–120

configuring on Windows XP manually with adapter's utilities, 146
configuring on Windows XP systems, 103–116
controlling types of wireless networks to attempt connecting to, 114–115
disabling, 105
estimating range, 124–125
repairing, restoring connectivity, 106
troubleshooting, 130–133
upgrading drivers for WPA support, 195
viewing available wireless networks, 105, 111, 122
viewing IP address and assignment mode, 105–106, 121
viewing name, connection speed, signal strength, and status, 104–105, 120–121, 131–132
Wireless Network Connection dialog box, 92–93, 228
Wireless Network Connection Properties dialog box, 107–109, 110–115, 152–153, 155–157
Wireless Network Connection Status dialog box, 105–106, 116, 120–121, 172–173, 229–231
"Wireless Network Detected" message, 92–93
wireless networking with Windows XP. *See also* file sharing with Windows XP; Windows XP
advantages, 145
checking signal strength, 157–158
configuring available networks, 152–153
creating infrastructure mode type, 114, 147, 148
preferred networks, adding, removing, viewing properties of, or reordering, 153–155
refreshing view of available wireless networks, 152
specifying type of networks to access (advanced options), 155–157
viewing available wireless networks, 150–151
wireless networks. *See also* obstacles and interference considerations; security considerations
ad-hoc mode (computer-to-computer or peer-to-peer) type, 114, 147–148, 156, 254
administration issues and users, 205–220
advantages, 10, 25, 26–27, 437
bridging multiple networks, 61–62
cost considerations, 29–32
importance of performance standards over price, 12
infrastructure mode type, 114, 147, 148, 156
monitoring activity, 173–175
print servers, 64–72
range, obstacles and interference considerations, 27–29
sharing Internet access, printers, files and games, 26
Wi-Fi standard, 13
wireless print servers, 64–72
wireless range extenders, 27, 32
wireless routers. *See* routers, wireless
wireless technology. *See also* accessories; Bluetooth; media players; security considerations
advantages, 1, 9
disadvantages, 14–15
need to understand security measures, 15
peripherals for computers, 363–370
Wireless Zero Configuration (Windows XP), 94, 103, 111
WMA music format, 399
WMLS11B Wireless-B Music System (Linksys), 411

WMV video format, 400
Word of the Day feature of SmartWatch, 330
word processor, AlphaSmart Dana Wireless, 406
WPA (Wi-Fi Protected Access) encryption protocol support on routers
  advantages, 195
  configuring routers or access points for, 195–197
  configuring wireless clients for, 197–198
  described, 43, 122, 190
  troubleshooting, 233–234, 236, 238
WPL music format, 399
WristNet, 326–327
WristNet channels, 328–331
WVC54G Wireless-G Internet Video Camera, 417

X

XM Radio satellite radio, 467
Xvid video format, 400

Z

zero-configuration networking, 94, 103, 111

Notes

Notes

Notes

Notes

Notes

Notes